For Pat

A
Finnegans Wake
Gazetteer

A
Finnegans Wake
Gazetteer

LOUIS O. MINK

INDIANA UNIVERSITY PRESS

BLOOMINGTON AND LONDON

Manufactured in the United States of America

Library of Congress Cataloging in Publication Data

Mink, Louis O.   1921–
   A Finnegans wake gazetteer.

   Bibliography
   1. Joyce, James, 1882–1941. Finnegans wake.
2. Joyce, James, 1882–1941—Knowledge—Geography.
3. Names, Geographical, in literature.   I. Title.
PR6019.09F593615   823'.9'12   77–74443
ISBN 0-253-32210-3   1 2 3 4 5 82 81 80 79 78 77

Contents

Maps

ACKNOWLEDGMENTS

The compilation and production of this Gazetteer have been possible only with the generous and indispensable collaboration of many people. This slight acknowledgment is much less than their due, but it is surely at least supplemented for them by the delight and fascination which *Finnegans Wake* engenders in its devotees.

STEPHEN B. WEISSMAN

— devoted three summers, and other time, to the building up of place-name files and the tracking down of sources, interrupting for this effort a career in chess, magic, and teaching. He is probably the only person in the world whose phone is listed under the name Felix Culpa.

ADALINE GLASHEEN
NATHAN HALPER
ROLAND MCHUGH
HUGH B. STAPLES

— walking encyclopedias of *Finnegans Wake* all, have made innumerable contributions to identification and explanation, many of them brilliantly original and gloriously apt; and have noted countless corrections and omissions. Nathan Halper has also, in correspondence, set standards for the identification of allusions in *Finnegans Wake* which have greatly improved, if not perfected, decisions about the inclusion or exclusion of proposed identifications.

JAMES S. ATHERTON
SEÁN V. GOLDEN
RUTH VON PHUL

— although they have not read the draft, have made numerous and original contributions to identifications. Seán Golden's *Bygmythster Finnegan: Etymology as Poetics in the Works of James Joyce* is a peerless extended study of Joyce's use of Irish place-names.

The list of rivers in the Linear Guide to Book I, Chapter 8 is based on the identifications in Fred H. Higginson's *James Joyce's Revisions of Finnegans Wake: A Study of the Published Versions.*

Uniquely useful information was provided in response to query-lists and otherwise by Ruth Bauerle, Bernard Benstock, Morris Beja, Edmund L. Epstein, Clive Hart, Mary Houston Pedrosa, and Fritz Senn.

Alexander Apfelbaum, Christopher Hughes, James Krantz, Steven Lobell, and Pantelis Nicolacopoulos assisted at various stages in the work of compilation. Betsy Nathanson, Nora Lumley, Amy Grimm, and Sandra Guyon did all of the draft typing, and Mss. Nathanson and Lumley managed the office.

David A. Harmin saw the project through to the end as designer and chief compositor of the text as it appears in this volume.

Joseph Mabel and Robert Strassfeld were chief copyeditors. Assisting in composition were Kate E. Carroll, Stephan M. Koplowitz, and Ellen L. Cohn; Elaine McDonough, Stephen D. Mink, Austin B. Sayre, and Barbara Spellman assisted as proofreaders and checkers. Kenneth Miller generously provided the facilities of the Sun-Up Press and the IBM Selectric Composer used in production.

Special thanks are due to Cathryn L. Lombardi for her skillful preparation of the maps of Chapelizod, Howth, Ireland, and Phoenix Park, which will be found under the respective headings in the Alphabetical Gazetteer.

Thanks also are due to the staff of Olin Library of Wesleyan University, and especially to William Dillon and Michael Durkan (now Librarian of Swarthmore College), wild geese from County Westmeath and County Mayo, respectively.

Virtually everything that has been written about *Finnegans Wake* has contributed directly or indirectly to the compilation of this Gazetteer. In particular, almost every issue of *A Wake Newslitter*, edited by Clive Hart and Fritz Senn, has contained articles or notes germane to the topography of *Finnegans Wake*. The books and a few of the articles which have been most useful or may be of interest to the reader are listed in the Bibliography. Unfortunately, to make appropriate citations of all sources in the body of the text would expand its size beyond all reason. But as *Finnegans Wake* is in many important ways unlike any other book, so the study of *Finnegans Wake* is to an unusual degree a collective enterprise, in which anyone must draw on the resources of all.

Finally, thanks are due to the American Council of Learned Societies, to the National Endowment for the Humanities, and to Wesleyan University, for grants supporting a substantial part of this project.

INTRODUCTION

—Impossible to remember persons in
improbable to forget places (617.08)

I

The word-world of *Finnegans Wake* has its own geography, and a very queer geography it is too, since it violates the geographical postulate of identification by fixed coordinates. Not only do the boundaries of Dublin expand to include the rest of the terrestrial globe and the indefinite loci of fiction and mythology, but the very dimensions of space itself become uncertainly elastic, and sometimes transform themselves into one or more dimensions of time. In this respect *Finnegans Wake* is unlike *Ulysses*, which is precisely mapped by exactly the same maps which represent the "real" Dublin. No one can tour the world of *Finnegans Wake* except in imagination. Nevertheless, as Alice's looking-glass world makes its effect by contrast with the everyday world on the hither side of the mirror, so the metamorphoses of *Finnegans Wake* can be understood only as a rearrangement of the elements of our matter-of-fact world. *Finnegans Wake* is thus full of matters of fact, almost all of them differently perceived and differently interrelated from the functional way in which they belong to compendia of human knowledge like encyclopedias and dictionaries. The *Wake*'s Dublin is very different from the real Dublin, but it is derived from it. Strictly speaking, it is largely derived from books *about* the real Dublin, since so many of its allusions are to a past Dublin reconstructed only in its histories. The Dublin of *Ulysses* is the city directly experienced and remembered by its citizens in 1904; its history appears only in their casual knowledge (and misinformation). In *Finnegans Wake*, on the other hand, layers of the city's history are superimposed on each other as on the site of the many Troys. Not even a Dubliner (except for local historians) can be expected to know that an eighteenth-century book attributed to Dublin an ancient Gaelic name which means "brow of a hazelwood," or that "William Inglis his house" refers to one of the boundary points of the late medieval practice of "riding the franchises," in which the Lord Mayor ceremonially traversed the boundaries of civic jurisdiction. But *Finnegans Wake* knows, although in such matters it tells the reader just enough to baffle him completely unless somehow he shares this arcane knowledge. It is no wonder that readers of *Finnegans Wake* find it difficult to see the trees for the forest.

For reading *Finnegans Wake*, the Age of Innocence is over. It ended, actually, in 1963, with the publication of Clive Hart's *Concordance*. Before this indispensable tool was available, the *Wake* could be read only impressionistically. A few driven pioneers, it is true, set out to develop their own cataloguing systems for identifying and cross-referencing allusions, but to *look for* something in the text was rather like trying to make a landfall without compass or sextant. For any reader with some familiarity with the text, a new experience could frequently (and delightfully) throw light on a remembered phrase or passage—which more often than not one could then find again in the text only by searching it through line by line. The *Concordance*, however, provided a new tool for systematic study, and transformed the focus of *Wake* exegesis from the analysis of particular pages and passages to the structure of the book as a whole. Only with a concordance, for example, can one explore the artful way in which the linguistic detail of Book I is echoed in Book III. And of course this has been done, and *Finnegans Wake* is now attended by an expanding shelf of reference works, which this Gazetteer extends by a little.

A new reader of *Finnegans Wake* can still choose to ignore what others have said about or pointed out in the *Wake*. But the Age of Innocence, in which one could bring to the *Wake* only one's own perception and experience because there was virtually nothing else available, is nevertheless only a memory. Alfred North Whitehead observed that education in any subject ideally goes through three stages: romance (the exciting sense of the distant and unknown horizons of the subject); precision (the mastery of the methods and principles of the subject); and generalization (in which the conceptual map of the subject is distinguished from its details, and seen in relation to other subjects and to human concerns). Romance which does not go on to the stage of precision is as inadequate as precision which does not eventuate in generalization; and generalization which has not graduated from precision is even worse, from a cognitive standpoint, than precision which has never experienced the lure of romance.

Like other topical and lexical studies of *Finnegans Wake*, this Gazetteer is the end-product of a process which began in the stage of romance and found itself increasingly trying to manage the minutiae of the stage of precision. At least, if we can be no more precise about the meanings of the *Wake* than it permits, we can seek to be exact about the matters of fact which in great number it disposes or presupposes. Brendan O Hehir's *Gaelic Lexicon of Finnegans Wake* demonstrated that Joyce's knowledge and use of Irish Gaelic was very much more extensive than had been commonly believed. Although the recognition of place-names has not been uncommon in *Wake* exegesis, this Gazetteer may convince many that Joyce was more prodigal, and perhaps more artful and systematic, in his allusions to places than has been generally assumed. As an aid in reading *Finnegans Wake*, this Gazetteer has at least three uses. First of all, it may succeed in bringing a topographical allusion to the consciousness of a reader preoccupied with other dimensions of meaning. Even veteran readers of the *Wake* know only too well the experience of noticing for the first time a relevant allusion in a familiar passage. Moreover, the significance of allusions is often explained by little-known facts which the entries in the Alphabetical Gazetteer attempt to note. Few readers of the phrase "like sixes and seventies as eversure as Halley's comet" (54.08) are likely to know offhand that the period of Halley's comet is seventy-six years.

As a second use, the Linear Guide brings into relief the many ways in which patterns of place-names are used by Joyce as allusive devices. Some of these, like the repeated litany of the provinces of Ireland in the order of Ulster, Munster, Leinster, and Connacht, are discussed below. But I am sure that there are place-name patterns which have not been explicitly identified in this Gazetteer but which other readers may discern with its aid. In the phrase "let naaman laugh at Jordan" (103.08), for example, everyone will recognize the River Jordan, and Adaline Glasheen's *Census* apparently completes the explication by noting from II *Kings* 5 that Naaman the Syrian general was cured of leprosy by bathing in the Jordan. However, this Gazetteer notes that there is also a Na'aman River in Palestine (better known as the Belus). Certainly the allusion to the river is secondary to the allusion to Naaman the Syrian, but it is marginally justified by the proximity of the two rivers. I suspect, however, that there is an as yet undemonstrable pattern of pairing river with river, and that each occurrence of river-pairs is intended to evoke either the Two Washerwomen of the Anna Livia Plurabelle "river" chapter, or Issy and her mirror-image *alter ego*, or both of these couples. But the discovered instances of this possible pattern are too few, and its analogy to the demonstrated coupling of mountain and river as HCE and ALP too tenuous, to canonize the connection.

In addition to these two uses, there is a third function of place-name identifications which has its place, although it is so to speak a negative utility. For all readers, veils of mystery seductively conceal (by partly revealing) the face of the *Wake*. No normally modest reader of the *Wake* (if indeed there are any such) is likely to advance *any* reading of any part of it as definitive. A simple reason for this is that a definitive reading must account for every letter of every word, and even a reading both illuminating and comprehensive is sure to leave some part of the *Wake*'s exotic orthography unexplained. As in other works of reference on the *Wake*, however, many place-name identifications and the accompanying explanatory information do bring to light why Joyce used a phrase or changed the spelling of a word. The period of Halley's comet does explain why "at sixes and sevens" becomes in that context "like sixes and seventies." To this extent the veil of mystery is lifted ever so slightly. The obscure always seems more portentous and metaphysical than the clear. In all riddles, the right answer even though satisfying never seems as deep as the unguessed riddle seemed to promise. But we must assume that Joyce never maliciously constructed a passage obscure even to himself in order to forestall forever the achievement of understanding by his readers. So the negative use of identifications is to reduce the areas of spurious "meaning" and to avoid the dead-ends into which arbitrary chains of association lead.

It is said that medical students studying pathology discover in themselves the symptoms of each new disease they learn. But they cannot be more prone to suggestibility than readers of the *Wake*. "Meanings" in the *Wake* are not uncommonly like the faces in clouds which one can see if one is determined to. By now it is notorious that anyone who approaches the text of the *Wake* with some specialized subject in mind will not fail to discover endless allusions to that subject. Of course this occurs in part because some of those allusions *are* there, by any standard of objectivity. But in part, as one learns when one has observed the results of monomaniac exegesis, the phenomenon reflects the fact that the language of the *Wake* will anchor one end of any chain of associative meanings. If one is bent on finding Midas, one can find him at the door of every house, because a house is sometimes a home, and Midas was an *homme d'or*. Since the language of the *Wake* is sounded as well as inscribed, one well-tuned ear may detect similarities of sound which escape another, so that the links of the chain of association can diverge at each step. And since allusions appear in different degrees of distortion, it is often a matter of intuitive judgment to decide whether a suggested allusion is only in the mind of the beholder or in that ideal text which oscillates between the printed word and the collective perception of the readers of the *Wake*.

Any specialized guide of the present sort inevitably encourages a narrow vision of its multidimensional object, and it is only fair to post a warning in advance that while this is a geographical dictionary of *Finnegans Wake*, the *Wake* itself is not a geographical dictionary. One might succumb to that illusion, at some level of consciousness below that of critical judgment, from the sheer mass of place-name identifications which follow. But the use of specialized guides is not to translate the *Wake* into their individual reference systems, but rather to enable the reader to go beyond every mode of single vision. Like logomania, topomania is one of the obsessions which the *Wake* maliciously encourages, but it can be benign as long as it is kept in check and used as a way of heightening perception. Allusions and patterns of allusions in the *Wake*, however, combine and confound classificatory schemes more often than they proceed on any single principle of construction, and until there is a single annotated version of the *Wake* which aggregates glosses of all types the reader must blink frequently to change the focus of the overburdened eye. Both the Linear Guide and the Alphabetical Gazetteer include from time to time, but incompletely and unsystematically, parenthetical mentions of non-topographical allusions, as a reminder that place-name references are often subordinate to more important and illuminating allusions.

II

TOPONYMIA

—nom de Lieu! (291.17)

Place-names in *Finnegans Wake* appear in varying concentrations. Often
we are treated to mere lists of names, variously distorted. The Seven Wonders of the Ancient World are slightly disguised as "chopes pyramidous and
mousselimes and beaconphires and colossets and pensilled turisses...of the
summiramies" (553.09—.12), and elsewhere as "cones...mured...pensils...
olymp...dianaphous...culosses...mosoleum" (261.09—.13)—both occurrences
associated with HCE as the builder of cities and monuments. The seven
birthplaces of Homer are also listed twice (129.33—.34, 481.21—.22), and
other lists of seven are the hills around Edinburgh (541.01—.04) and individual towers of the Tower of London (77.18—.20); the seven hills of Rome
and the seven churches of Glendalough are referred to but not listed. The
foxhunts on pages 97 and 622 can be traced on the map as they course
through named townlands in County Meath, in the vicinity of Ratoath and
The Naul, respectively. The mention of Fingal, a loosely-defined area just
north of Dublin, as the place where "the illassorted first couple first met"
evokes a shower of names of townlands in Fingal arranged as a commentary
on human coupling: "Littlepeace...Snugsborough...Slutsend with Stockins
of Winning's Folly Merryfalls," etc. (503.13—.17). And a mysterious line
such as "rialtos, annesleyg, binn and balls to say nothing atolk of New
Comyn" (130.20—.21) turns out to be merely a list of six Dublin bridges
(none over the Liffey). Since the *Wake* often presents itself as a game or
riddle, it generously offers clues: "rialtos" in the passage above, since everyone knows Venice's Rialto, while few know Dublin's Rialto, or the other
Dublin bridges. Sometimes a passage is artfully composed almost entirely
out of unrelated place-names to suggest a general meaning: "a babbel men
dub gulch of tears" (254.17) combines the Tower of Babel with Bab el
Mandeb ("Gate of Tears"), the strait separating Asia and Africa at the Gulf
of Aden, and Dublin Gulch in Idaho (named by or for what homesick Irishmen?). The theme is separation: separation of the races by the confusion of
language, separation of the continents in geological history, and separation
of the overseas Irish from their island home.

But for the most part such lists and combinations belong to the verbal
embroidery of the *Wake*. Other uses of place-names are more structural, and
amount to minor set-pieces. In Anna Livia's dying soliloquy at the end of
the book (623-24), she imagines an expedition with her husband to Howth—
as Molly's reverie ends *Ulysses* with her memory of saying yes to Bloom

among the Howth rhododendrons—and although Anna Livia's mind is wandering, the itinerary of the expedition is tied down to its local habitation
by the place-names of Howth: Howth Castle, Evora stream, Drumleck point,
The Summit, Sheilmartin hill, St. Fintan's church, and the point known as
the Nose of Howth. In a more compressed passage (264-65), Chapelizod is
described (exactly as in Thom's Dublin *Directories* of the late nineteenth
and early twentieth centuries) in terms of its population of 1280 ("four of
hundreds...[times] twenty six and six"), its area of 63 acres ("three and
threescore fylkers"), and its distance of three miles from the General Post
Office (265.25—.29; as Clive Hart calculated, 2,280,960 divided by 12
[months?] is 190,080, the number of inches in three miles); and the rest of
the passage is composed almost entirely of the names of Chapelizod houses
and other buildings. One final example of the minor topographical set-piece
is the list of Paris bridges which J. S. Atherton discovered scattered through
pages 7-17: a particularly puzzling case since these pages are not otherwise
Parisian or riverine. There may be an undisclosed pattern of relevance, but
then again Joyce may have been up to his old trick of adding graffiti to the
back side of a wall which normally would never be seen except from the
front. It is impossible to say how many such clusters of graffiti remain to
be discovered. A number have been explored without enough success to jus-
tify their inclusion in this Gazetteer: the list of Paris telephone exchanges
and of Metro stops, for example, as well as the cathedral cities of England
and France, the Wren churches of London (more London churches are named
in the *Wake* than has been generally realized), and the state capitals of the
United States and provincial capitals of Canada. I know of no study of allusions to islands in the *Wake*, but would not be surprised to learn that Joyce
was challenged by Canada's Thousand Islands to try to include a thousand—
or perhaps a thousand and one—allusions to islands, even without counting
Ireland itself. It is hard to think of a list which does not have some relevance to the *Wake*, and Joyce might have taken lists, or matrices, as Nathan
Halper calls them, from anywhere. Although the eleventh edition of the *En-
cyclopaedia Britannica* has long been the reader's guide to *Finnegans Wake*,
as it was one of Joyce's primary sources, it may yet prove to be hardly
tapped as the midden in which Joyce hunted for his treasures.

Beyond all other uses of place-names, the *Wake* contains three major topographical set-pieces. Two of these are already well-known to students of
the *Wake*; the third is explicated here for the first time. Not much need be
said about the Museyroom passage (pages 8-10), which in the context of the
confrontation of Wellington and Napoleon at Waterloo names most of Wellington's major engagements in India and in the Peninsular War, and adds
for good measure other historic battles, like Thermopylae, Agincourt, and
Bunker Hill. Most of the battles are common knowledge, though a few like
the Battle of the Golden Spurs are esoteric. One might regard the Musey-

room passage as Joyce's prentice piece for the Anna Livia Plurabelle or "river" chapter, in which the device of studding the text with names was refined and expanded into a wholly new literary dimension. In the Museyroom section the individual names are still important; it seems necessary that a reading of the text should recognize them, and recognize them all. In the river chapter, however, the river-names cluster so thickly and are so artfully disposed that they virtually cease to bear any meaning as individual names. In this new language, they are more like phonemes than like morphemes. In his drafts of this chapter, Joyce returned again and again to the task of adding river-names to the expanding text, which in its final version flows without any sign of effort, like the river it celebrates. About the middle of October 1927 he wrote to Valery Larbaud, "I have just finished revision of Anna Livia for transition no 8...Her fluvial maids of honour from all ends of the earth now number about 350 I think" (*Letters* III, 164). A few weeks later, on 9 November 1927, he wrote to Harriet Weaver, "Since [transition 8] came out I have woven into the printed text another 152 rivernames and it is now final as it will appear in the book" (*Letters* I, 261). But in fact he was not finished, and in late 1930 he wrote to Eugene Jolas asking him for the names of Austrian rivers (*A James Joyce Yearbook*, ed. Maria Jolas [Paris, 1949], 173).

How many of the 980 identifications of rivers given in the Linear Guide below are intentional is open to question, but I have thought it more useful to include marginal identifications, so that the reader can judge for himself. The list is based on Fred Higginson's *James Joyce's Revisions of Finnegans Wake*, which not only lists about 800 river-names but analyzes (pp. 172-74) the entry of names at four stages of revision of the text between 1925 and 1939. In Professor Higginson's view, the endless revisions and additions to this chapter very much *complicate* the text, but at the same time they sharpen its focus. In this respect the river-names were structurally effective in the process of composition, not merely ornamental as they have often been taken to be.

The third topographical set-piece is HCE's great *apologia pro vita sua* on pages 532-554, known as "Haveth Childers Everywhere." In eight speeches, separated by the comments of his interrogators (or judges), HCE begins haltingly. In his guilty stammer, he denies the unspecified charges against him, cries outrage against his accusers, appeals for pity, and (rather inconsistently) announces his repentance. But in a sudden metamorphosis (page 539) he is transformed from the pubkeeper and petty transgressor Earwicker into HCE, the archetypal builder of material civilization. I am the one, he says, who built the hospitals, the waterworks, the fountains, the parks, the museums, dancehalls, observatories, universities, and cathedrals; I built the roads and railroads; I bridged the rivers, paved the streets, and lit the city; I created cuisine and sports, introduced tea and wine, and brewed stout; I minted the money and gave the citizens laws and courts; I created both the seven wonders of the world and the seven statues that line the route from Dublin's Parnell Square to College Green. And I did it all to arouse and satisfy my wife's desire.

The city which HCE claims to be his creation is *prima facie* Dublin. Consistently enough, since the theme of the section is origins and the long view of history, references are for the most part to Dublin before its Georgian period of the late eighteenth century. The ancient cathedrals are mentioned, but not the Georgian Custom House or Four Courts; the medieval Tholsel but not the Georgian City Hall. Phoenix Park is given its seventeenth-century name, the "Queen's Garden," and the modern prisons of Mountjoy and Kilmainham are not mentioned but now-forgotten prisons such as Newgate, the Marshalsea, and the Provost are. And although at the first level this section is about Dublin, an observant reader will notice that a great many other cities are named; they include, in fact, all of the capitals of European countries, many in Africa and Asia, and some in the Western Hemisphere. Here too are the founders of cities: Radu Negru of Bucharest, Albert "the Bear" of Berlin, Pierre L'Enfant, the architect of Washington D. C., and of course Olaf (the White), the founder of Danish Dublin.

What has not been noted before, however, is the fact that often obscure local place-names of the cities of the world contribute almost as much to the texture of Haveth Childers Everywhere as do river-names to the Anna Livia Plurabelle chapter. Again, there is especial emphasis on the "old city" of each of the cities alluded to, or to ancient features such as Brussels' Porte de Hal, all that remains of its medieval walls, or New York City's Palisades —not the New Jersey cliffs across the Hudson, but rather the wooden wall which guarded the north side of the original New Amsterdam. London appears in this section as the disorderly city where public hangings took place at Tyburn, now the site of Marble Arch, and Bristol appears as the city to whose burghers Henry II gave Dublin as a colony and which later became the center of the English slave-trade. In some other cases the ancient name of the capital is given: Tokyo appears under its old name of Yedo as well as under its modern name, and Addis Ababa appears only as the old Ethiopian capital, Entotto. All this esoteric geography should not, however, overwhelm the reader with wonder at the vast learning of the *Wake*; except in the case of Dublin, it is taken directly and almost entirely from the articles on individual cities in the Eleventh *Britannica*. Joyce's friend C. P. Curran said that "Joyce was many things, but he was certainly the last forty volumes of *Thom's Directories* thinking aloud." Of *Ulysses* this is well said; of *Finnegans Wake* it might rather be said that it is often the Eleventh *Britannica* dreaming aloud. But toponymical arcana provide only the raw materials for what Haveth Childers Everywhere is finally about: the character HCE as a flawed Romulus, a touching mixture of guilty secrets, tipsy pride, and unmistakable nobility, the builder of a civilization measured both by its prisons and by its cathedrals.

III

PATTERNS

—Oh Kosmos! Ah Ireland! (456.07)

The Dublin of *Ulysses* has usually been regarded as both literal and symbolic, not only an exact description of the historical Dublin of 1904 but also an emblem of modern urban life anywhere. And no doubt it is, but nothing in the book *says* that Dublin is Everycity. That reading belongs, perhaps inescapably, to what readers of *Ulysses* bring to it. The Dublin and also the Ireland of *Finnegans Wake*, on the other hand, are symbolic throughout, and the book tells us so at every opportunity, by conflating the names of Dublin and other Irish places with place-names from the rest of the world. Its principle is that what happens in Ireland happens everywhere; and what happens anywhere happens in Ireland too. The motif is announced on the first page of the book—even before the Fall—by the invocation of the Dublin which is the county seat of Laurens County, Georgia. In continuously inventive variations, the motif provides one of the primary toponymical patterns of the *Wake*. There are of course general metamorphoses of place in the *Wake*, as well as of persons: Dublin's Phoenix Park is Eden, as the scene of Earwicker's "fall" in the incident involving the two girls and the three soldiers, but also thanks to its eponymous bird it is the site of the Resurrection; and it is very often also Valhalla and the battlefield of Waterloo. These identities belong to the imaginative structure of the *Wake*, but there are also many conflations which count rather as exploitations of linguistic accident. It is not so much, that is, that they are individually significant as that in aggregate they display and reinforce over and over the Here-and-Everywhere pattern. Sometimes the Irish allusion is primary and the non-Irish locus is secondary; sometimes it is the other way around.

It is linguistic coincidence that the name "Balaclava" so closely resembles Dublin's Irish name, Baile Átha Cliath (pronounced something like "ballya-cleeah"), but the *Wake* makes so much use of it that the Crimean War almost comes to seem an incident of Irish history (as for the Irish soldiers in the Crimea no doubt it was, whether they were aware of it or not). Less significant but among a surprisingly large number of Polish allusions is the conflation of Dublin with Lublin. Jokes, anagrams, charades keep proliferating. Dublin and Lublin trade only names initially; similar swaps have almost undetectable nuances. Poland is conflated in reverse with Dublin as "Poolland," a reminder that the name "Dublin" originally meant "black pool." Ireland itself combines as Erin with Iran, as the land of Finn MacCool with Finland, and as the New Ireland of the Free State with America's Irish nickname, the "New Island." Other conflations become increasingly esoteric. The Dublin district of Crumlin of course pairs with Moscow's Kremlin, the area of northeast Dublin once known as Goose Green with Scotland's Gretna Green ("Goosna Greene," 533.19), Dublin's undistinguished street called Appian Way with its Roman namesake, and the Old Bailey on Howth, former site of the Bailey lighthouse, with London's criminal court. In the confused memories of the Four Old Men (387.09—.10), four Dublin streets— Liffey, Aylesbury, Northumberland, and Anglesea—are indistinguishable from areas of Britain once ravaged by Vikings—who are named in the same sentence. Still other conflations sound like the amusing misperception of names by an ear attuned only to hearing Irish ones: Bulgaria is heard as Ballygarry, an otherwise not very important village, and the Balearic Islands as the Ballyhoura mountains, mixed up with the town Ballyhooly ("ballyhooric," 555.10). Even the famous name of London's Westminster is heard by this Irish ear as West Munster.

A second pervasive pattern identifies HCE with every mountain, as ALP is identified with any river ("Ainée Rivière," 289.25). This pattern appears most often in the pairing not of names but of common nouns ("Hill, rill" [23.17], "En elv, et fjaell," Norwegian for "river" and "mountain" [261.03], "Flowey and Mount" [197.14], and "Amnist anguished axes Collis," which not only parodies a Latin paradigm but begins and ends with the Latin words for "river" and "hill" [256.24; cf. 468.10]). But the pairing of mountain and river is also signalled by appropriate place-names. Thus "Ethna Prettyplume, Hooghly Spaight" (318.12) is Mt. Etna with its plume of smoke and India's Hooghly River in flood—rather distant from Howth and the Liffey and from each other, but avatars of HCE and ALP nonetheless. Sometimes the geography is very specific; "that Luxuumburgher avec cettehis Alzette" (578.35) refers not only to Luxembourg's capital city on the Alzette River but to the fact that the city is on a high bluff over the river. Not infrequently, the pattern of mountain and river clarifies or confirms an allusion. "A Hill of Allen, the Barrow for an People" (57.13) uses "barrow" in its sense of "burial-mound" but must also allude to the River Barrow (whose northern bend in fact is only ten miles or so from the Hill of Allen west of Dublin). Even in the phrase "steadied Jura or...raced Messafissi" (356.08), which is in part "studied law or read metaphysics," the mountain-river pattern confirms an allusion to the Jura mountains (as against the island of Jura in the Hebrides) and the Mississippi River.

For Ireland itself, the primary pattern is its (modern) division into the four provinces of Ulster, Munster, Leinster, and Connacht, almost invariably named in that order in the *Wake*, and usually associated with the Four Old Men, Matt Gregory, Mark Lyons, Luke Tarpey, and Johnny MacDougall. Sometimes, as in the fourth of the twelve questions in Book I, Chapter 6, the provinces are identified by their chief cities, Belfast, Cork, Dublin, and Galway (140.15–.36). Sometimes the allusions are more obscure, as in the series Armagh, Clonakilty, Deansgrange, and Barna (57.08), which in brief compass goes in canonical order from the well-known Ulster town to a little-known Connacht village; or in the series of four rivers, the Finn, the Nore, the Bray, and the Moy (203.09–.11). Sometimes the province-names are wildly deformed, as in "used her, mused her, licksed her and cuddled" (96.16). In addition to the Ulster-Munster-Leinster-Connacht pattern, there is an intersecting pattern of North-South-East-West references which is usually associated with the Four Old Men but not necessarily with the provinces. Because these two patterns overlap in uncertain ways, they are listed separately in the Alphabetical Gazetteer below.

It does not seem that the province-pattern is used primarily to characterize the Four Old Men individually or to invoke the differences of life and language among the four provinces which have been recognized for centuries—the Anglo-Irish character of Leinster, for instance, or the poverty and traditionalism of Connacht. But there are some exceptions to this. The unmistakable accents of Ulster and Munster can be heard in the passage on pages 140-141 and in the "Hymn to Iseult" on pages 398-399, and the Protestantism of Ulster is exhibited as interrogator Matt Gregory ("Northern Ire") bullies Roman Catholic Yawn on pages 519-522. But on the whole the provinces remain places rather than persons. Why they appear almost always in the N-S-E-W order, rather than by boxing the compass, is not clear. The order makes the sign of the cross from the standpoint of the land and the map, but this sign of piety is not otherwise confirmed in the contexts in which the pattern appears.

The province-pattern is firmly localized with respect to Ireland, and not generalized to other countries or to cities except as it generally represents the points of the compass. For Dublin, however, another pattern takes over as a primary organizing principle. From earliest times, Dublin has been divided into North and South by the River Liffey; Dubliners think and feel in terms of north and south, rather than in terms of east and west. The original Danish settlement was south of the river, and medieval Dublin occupied the same site, with the Danes consigned to Oxmantown ("town of the Eastmen") on the other side of the river, after the battle of Clontarf in 1014. In later centuries there were notorious faction fights between North and South Dublin, for example between the Ormonde Boys, butchers' apprentices from North Dublin, and the Liberty Boys, Huguenot weavers' apprentices from the Liberties south of the river. In modern times, south Dublin has been Anglo-Irish, middle-class, and the site of government and high culture; north Dublin has been Catholic, working-class, and the center of commerce and low culture. South of the Liffey are the two Protestant cathedrals, the Castle and the Bank of Ireland, the universities, the National

Library, Museum, and art Gallery, the Protestant cemetery of St. Jerome, the old and new buildings of Parliament, and until recently all the theaters but the Gate. North of the Liffey are the Roman Catholic Pro-Cathedral, the General Post Office (headquarters of the Rising of 1916), the Catholic schools such as Belvedere College, the prisons and poorhouses, the Catholic cemetery of Glasnevin, and almost all of the cinemas.

Joyce himself was born in the south Dublin suburb of Rathgar, and the Joyce family lived also in the southern suburbs of Bray and Blackrock until the elder Joyce's declining fortunes forced them to the already decaying vicinity of Mountjoy Square north of the river, and thereafter to frequent moves through increasingly worse lodgings in the northern suburbs of Drumcondra, Fairview, and Cabra. As Stanislaus Joyce said, "The slide to...poverty began when we left Blackrock for [North] Dublin." When James Joyce left his father's house to live alone, however, all his lodgings were in south Dublin, including his brief stay with Gogarty in the Martello Tower. North Dublin, it might be said, is particularly the quarter of postman-cleric Shaun-Stanislaus, while South Dublin is the quarter of cosmopolitan bohemian-artist Shem-James.

In the Dublin landscape, North and South are thus rich with associations and polarities, and these are implicitly invoked by the *Wake*'s habit of pairing a North Dublin name with a South Dublin one. These pairings always, I believe, instance a Shem-Shaun contrast, though often faintly. I list here only a few of the North-South pairings to indicate how ubiquitous the pattern is.

37.20	Grand [Canal] (S)...Royal [Canal] (N)
57.35	Marlborough Green (N)...Molesworth Fields (S)
73.30	coombe (S)...eolithostroton [Stoneybatter] (N)
106.18	*Stork* [Stock] *Exchange* (S)...*Customs* [Custom House] (N)
132.21	Raglan Road (S)...Marlborough Place (N)
147.26	Fibsburrow [Phibsborough] churchdome (N)...Saint Andrée's [St. Andrew's Church] (S)
248.33	Behind St (S)...Turnagain Lane (N)
252.07	everglass and even [Glasnevin] (N)...Harlot's Curse [Harold's Cross] (S)
294.20	Mary Owens [Merrion] (S)...Dolly Monks [Dollymount] (N)
354.17	*S. E. Morehampton* [Road] (S)...*E. N. Sheilmartin* [Road] (N)
354.18	*Meetinghouse Lanigan* [Lane] (N)...*Vergemont Hall* (S)
433.12	howth (N)...killiney (S)
497.06	scalpjaggers [The Scalp] (S)...houthhunters [Howth] (N)
497.11	Rountown [Terenure] (S)...Rush (N)
502.35	Foxrock (S)...Finglas (N)
533.19	Goosna Greene [Goose Green] (N)...cabinteeny [Cabinteely] (S)
543.16	villa of the Ostmanorum [Oxmantown] (N)...Thomars Sraid [Thomas St] (S)
549.02	Leonard's [Corner] (S)...Dunphy's [Corner] (N)
569.14	Agithetta [St. Agatha's Church] (N)...Tranquilla [Convent] (S)
576.27	Bobow [Bow Lane] (S)...cunnyngnest [Conyngham Road] (N)

585.28   Donnelly's orchard (N)...Fairbrother's field (S)
624.24   kolooney [Killiney] (S)...Houlth's [Howth] (N)

It might be added that in each of these pairings, the two places are just about the same distance north and south of the Liffey; and they match each other in other ways, such as street to street, district to district, church to church, cemetery to cemetery, and hill to hill; and as at 57.35, 248.33, 543.16, and 585.28, names no longer in use are matched as contemporary in their historical period. And there are many more such pairings. The North-South pattern extends beyond the limit of metropolitan Dublin to its environs, as in the pairing of the Vartry River (S) with the Boyne and Nannywater Rivers to the north (205.36, 126.21). In some cases there is a pattern behind the pattern, with a particular pleasure attending its discovery. At 183.05—.06, the Ondt's house ("Nixnixundnix") is identified with "your brass castle" and the Gracehoper's house ("Tingsomingenting") with "your tyled house in ballyfermont." In Le Fanu's *The House by the Church-yard*, which is laid in Chapelizod, central characters live in the Brass Castle, on the north bank of the Liffey, and in the Tiled House in Ballyfermot, across the river from Chapelizod; and these sides of the river belong respectively to the Ant-Shaun and to the Grasshopper-Shem. *Wake* geography plays fast and loose with latitude and longitude, and the dimensions of space expand, contract, and are otherwise transformed, but the compass points remain fixed forever by the left and right banks of the Liffey as it flows to the sea.

IV

THE DOODLES FAMILY IN DUBLIN

—Whose are the placewheres? (56.33)

Though mountains and rivers the world over incarnate HCE and ALP, uncivilized nature remains at a considerable distance from the *Wake*'s modes of thought and feeling. The things of nature are not real presences in the *Wake*, but enter it only by courtesy of the words by which they are denoted and described. Urban Joyce did not know the ways of untamed rivers as one who has lived with them in all their moods and seasons, and his knowledge of hills was less the intuitive knowledge of legs and lungs than that of the eye and of his language-saturated mind. As for Stephen Dedalus walking on Sandymount Strand, nature occasioned for Joyce a whirling spiral of words into which it then disappeared. Yet Joyce did understand and express in *Finnegans Wake* (although not in *Ulysses*) the ways in which a city in its growth domesticates and transforms its natural site without ever totally dominating it. There is for example a dialectical relation between cities and their rivers. The river first of all attracts the city and serves its purposes, but at the same time sunders it and threatens it with drought and flood. The city responds by subjecting the river with bridges, quays, and dams, which the river quietly tests and in an occasional fury destroys. Eventually, like an old married couple, city and river tacitly agree to replace excitement by dependability, though in the end the river always leaves the city and flows beyond its reach to the sea.

Finnegans Wake says all this much better. No doubt Dublin is more intimately related to its natural site than most cities. The vistas of most of its north-south streets are closed to the south by the Wicklow Mountains, apparently only a long walk away; Phoenix Park funnels the countryside into the heart of the city, and cows and deer graze there side by side; and ocean-going ships tie up by the cabman's shelter in front of the Custom House. River, sea, and mountains are at the end of the streets. A friend who grew up in London's East Side once told me that for years as a child he had thought that the grass and trees of the parks had been brought from somewhere else and put down on top of the natural pavement. Joyce was never so urban as to believe that the city's pavement and masonry go all the way down. Beneath the archaeological layers of modern, Georgian, medieval, and Danish Dublin, he knew, lies the landscape seen by the first Vikings to anchor in the Liffey and by the nameless Irish who had forded the river there from time immemorial. Thus the primal family of *Finnegans Wake* not only play all the roles of the world's history and fiction but double as the natural features of Dublin's site.

Anna Livia is of course the River Liffey which flows east through the city to Dublin Bay, rising and falling with the tide. On some older maps the river is actually called "Anna Liffey" (from Latin *amnis Livia*, or Irish *Abha na Life*). The twins Shaun and Shem, "two bredder [Norwegian, "riverbanks"] as doffered as nors in soun" (620.16), are her left and right banks. Most specifically they are the quays which canalize the river from Kingsbridge to the bay: "stout stays, the rivals [*rivae*, Latin "riverbanks"], lined her length" (208.14); but by extension they are also the streets and buildings of north and south Dublin. Since the repeated brother-battle in the *Wake* regularly ends with an exchange of identities, Shem and Shaun occasionally exchange sides of the river, as their comments exchange margins halfway through Book II, Chapter 2. In the fable of the Mookse and the Gripes the Mookse-Shaun begins on the "yonder bank" (153.09) and winds up on the "hither bank" (158.11, .32), which is apparently the right bank, since the Mookse "had reason" (158.31), i.e., was *right*. So the Mookse moves from the north bank of the river to the south, and the Gripes the other way. Here, as elsewhere, "Reeve Gootch [*Gauche*] was right and Reeve Drughad [*Droite*; also *droichead*, Irish "bridge"] was sinistrous" (197.01). The last quotation in context is actually a reference to HCE, who as the city itself combines the often opposite characteristics of his twin sons.

Daughter Issy is both figuratively and literally the young or upstream Anna Liffey, who retains her youth until she reaches Chapelizod, where she enters greater Dublin and shortly becomes tidal at Islandbridge. Exactly at Chapelizod the river divides into two channels, forming the only island in its length: "her arms encircling Isolabella, then running with reconciled Romas and Reims," i.e., Shem and Shaun as the riverbanks, again face to face after being separated by beautiful Issy, their sister as island (209.24).

Although HCE (for whom Joyce's working siglum was ⋔) is the whole city—always at greater or less remove from the family intimacy of river, island, and riverbanks—he is also, as Ш (*Letters* I, 254), a sleeping giant interred in the landscape, his head the Hill of Howth, his torso the gentle ridge running east and west through north Dublin, and his upturned feet the two hills or knocks of Castleknock Hill and Windmill Hill, just west of Phoenix Park (about 12 miles from Howth). Sometimes his feet are located as the hill of the Magazine Fort within Phoenix Park (7.30–.32; 12.35–.36); St. Thomas's Hill is separated only by a gully from its neighboring Whitebridge Hill. Most readers of *Finnegans Wake* have seen the Wellington Monument in Phoenix Park as the erect penis of this sleeping giant; but in geographical fact this would make him remarkably, and ridiculously, short in the leg.

This is the merest outline of the *Wake*'s identification of the features of Dublin's natural site with the members of its primal and theatrical family. For anyone familiar with the repetitions and details of this pattern of allusions, the very appearance of present-day Dublin is imaginatively changed. Howth comes to look more and more like the head of a supine giant; the river looks more and more feminine. Joyce has marvelously resurrected in the twentieth century the ancient Irish propensity to personify the landscape—as in the two hills in County Kerry called the "Paps of Dana," in other hills called "Finn's Seat" or "Finn's Table," or in the innumerable "beds of Dermot and Grania." He even identified the sleeping giant HCE with Finn MacCool, although there is no legend or tradition which sees Finn in the north Dublin landscape. But the *Wake* is more specific than mythology, and it carries its personification of places into the most playful detail. The geometrical diagram on page 293, for example, is constructed by prematurely knowledgeable Shem ostensibly to instruct Shaun in geometry, actually to reveal to him the secrets of their mother's sexual geography. Clive Hart (in *Structure and Motif in Finnegans Wake*, 248-249) has ingeniously interpreted the diagram as constructed by circles centered on Uisneach (traditionally the geographical center of Ireland) and Lambay Island, just north of Howth; and this is clearly one denotation of the diagram. But as Roland McHugh (in *The Sigla of Finnegans Wake*, 68-69) has pointed out, the "doubling bicirculars" are also Dublin's encircling Grand and Royal Canals (paralleled by the South and North Circular Roads), with the "straight line" of the diagram joining the village elm ("Great Ulm," 293.14) of Chapelizod and the mearing-stone (293.14) noted by the historian J. T. Gilbert in central Dublin. The diagram thus corresponds to the map of Dublin, if one can imagine the map revolving through 90°.

But the diagram can be seen as a view of Dublin (293.12) as well as a map. Since Anna Liffey reaches the sea feet first, her hair trailing behind her, the view of her vulva in the diagram is from Dublin Bay. And if "capital Pee...on the batom" and "modest mock Pie [π]...up your end"—the "tew tricklesome poinds" (295.30)—mean what I think they do, Anna Liffey is lying prone, her head upstream and her feet toward "my salt troublin bay and the race of the saywint up me ambushure" (201.19). Beside her on the north, supine HCE lies head to foot—exactly as Leopold Bloom lies head to foot next to Molly, prone in her bed, at the end of *Ulysses*. The unchanging natural features of Dublin's landscape re-enact forever in *Finnegans Wake* the secret idiosyncrasies of Leopold and Molly, cosmologized almost but not quite beyond recognition.

V

PRINCIPLES

> —a ground plan of the placehunter
> (585.23)

What *counts* as a place-name allusion in *Finnegans Wake*? The Linear Guide of this Gazetteer contains more than 7800 identifications; is this too many, or too few? To answer such questions is to take a position on general issues of interpretation which have not been settled and no doubt, for the health of literary interpretation and the pleasures of reading, should not be. For the literary theorist, a text has a wholly anomalous mode of being, hovering somewhere between the inaccessible universe of the author's intentions and the pluralistic universe of readers' interpretations. Some critics seem to believe in the integrity of "the text," independent of either of these universes of discourse; others in their approach to the text lean more or less to "intentions," others more or less to "readings." Whatever the uncertainties of these positions, a reader's guide like the present one must, I believe, lean strongly toward the concept of the author's intention as a regulative principle. (In Kant's sense, a regulative principle is one which functions as a necessary hypothesis for pursuing inquiry, although it is not literally true or cannot be known to be true—like the hypothesis that the organs of the body have "purposes.") The supposition that everything in *Finnegans Wake* is intentional is peculiarly appropriate because of the unusual method of its composition. Joyce never explained the meaning of the *Wake* as a whole to anyone, and we have no reason to think that he even thought this possible. But he did gloss particular passages, in a way which shows not only that he intended a rich detail of allusiveness, but also that he *didn't* intend an even larger list of allusions which *some* reader's ingenuity might impose on the text. And although we shall never know very much more than we do now about Joyce's intentions from evidence other than the text itself, I think that the working hypothesis of interpretation must be that everything in the text has its reasons, and that those reasons are Joyce's own.

Thus there can be no authoritative criteria for the identification of allusions. Yet, clearly, some are indisputable, some are better than others, and some are, in the absence of confirmation, quite arbitrary—coincidences, that is, which may strike a reader but which there is no reason to believe were noticed or intended by Joyce. An important feature of this Gazetteer is the hundreds of place-names which have *not* been included. Many of these are separated by a very thin line indeed from others which are, with some hesitation, included. In both cases, the identifications seem arbitrary in context. But in the case of marginal inclusions, there is some suspicion that they may belong to an evident or as yet undiscerned pattern, while in the case of exclusions, sheer coincidence seems uppermost. For example, on page 537 of the *Wake* there is a reference to "Hodder's and Cocker's erithmatic." As Glasheen's *Census* explains, Hodder and Cocker were authors of (separate) seventeenth-century arithmetic texts. But these are also the names of two rivers in Lancashire and Cumberland, and Erith is a town in Kent, on the south bank of the Thames. If they were in the Anna Livia Plurabelle chapter, Hodder and Cocker would unquestionably be river-names. But nothing in their actual context—HCE's *apologia*, dominated by cities and urban landmarks—is riverine, and they are therefore excluded here, although someone may discern a pattern which would tend to confirm them. If one were a river and the other a mountain, they *would* be included, since HCE's discourse is always mindful of his wife in relation to himself.

Similarly, not every wheelbarrow in the *Wake* is regarded here as the River Barrow in disguise, nor is "rushgreen epaulettes" (208.18) treated as an allusion to the town of Rush in North County Dublin. Neither the phrase itself nor any pattern involving Rush or County Dublin names supports such an identification. The Lapac who "walks backwords" at 478.31 is so obviously Irish *capall*, "horse," that we can ignore the island of Lapac in the Philippines; and at 110.36, "Tipperaw" (associated with potatoes) is clearly part of "Tipperary" and not the town of Tippera in India, though in spelling and even in sound it is somewhat closer to the latter.

Many identifications are quite certain even though (as in the Linear Guide) they may seem impossibly remote from the look and sound of the text. The justification is nearly always a matter of contextual confirmation. And there are at least three quite different kinds of "contexts." One, of course, is the surrounding passage, which may be anything from a paragraph to many pages in length, in which the putative allusion occurs. Not infrequently such a contextual confirmation depends on some matter of fact which a reader would know only by happy accident. "Undermined lung-achers" (579.33) quite certainly refers to the fact that the Piccadilly Line tube of the London Underground was bored directly underneath the entire length of Long Acre street. (And the naming of four other London places in the surrounding three lines confirms the identification of Long Acre, although it would not otherwise explain "undermining.") "Juno Moneta" (538.01) is not primarily the goddess but her temple on Rome's Capitoline Hill which the Romans used as a mint. It is followed by a paragraph of commercial terms and venereal terms conflated with old names for coins, ending with the name of the old Edinburgh mint, the Cunzie House. Simpson's Hospital in Dublin may seem to have little to do with "symposium's syrup for decayed and blind and gouty Gough"; but in fact the hospital was founded for the relief of "decayed, blind and gouty men." A major purpose of this Gazetteer is to collect confirmatory facts of this sort. Would that all identifications were so directly confirmable as these examples.

The second kind of "context" is equally significant but more difficult to perceive. Topographical motifs, like other kinds of motifs, are often repeated in the *Wake* with different degrees of distortion. Thus an allusion distorted beyond *prima facie* recognition may be confirmable by comparison with other occurrences of the allusion scattered throughout the book. Borneo seems an impossibly strained guess for "Barleyholme" (382.26), and even the whole phrase "our wineman from Barleyholme" would hardly make the song-title "The Wild Man From Borneo" leap off the page; but the intentionality of the allusion becomes perfectly evident if one compares (see the Alphabetical Gazetteer) all five allusions to this title. Yet a third kind of context consists of the lists of names which Joyce kept in his notebooks and in his mind, for the purpose of feeding them into the revisions of the text more or less independently of the immediate context. In some cases, like the list of Paris bridges, such lists are concentrated in successive pages, often beginning with a scattered name or two, building up to a cluster of names, and then tailing off with more dispersed occurrences—like the normal-distribution curve of statistical frequency. In other cases, like the names of London churches, they may be scattered throughout the book without particular concentrations. In either case, however, I take it that the presence of an identifiable list increases the likelihood that a marginally identifiable member of the list is intentional.

The two sections of this Gazetteer are designed to bring into relief as far as possible the first two kinds of context, and to make it easier to discover the items constituting the third. The Linear Guide shows the relation of a topographical allusion to others in its immediate context—for example, the conflation of Dublin districts with the "seven birthplaces of Homer" on pages 129 and 481. The Alphabetical Gazetteer shows the pattern of repetition-with-variation of individual names in widely separated sections. In the case of the Dublin districts and the birthplaces of Homer, for example, it instances the way—significant far beyond topographical allusions—in which the allusions and verbal patterns of Book I are mirrored and parodied in Book III.

Nevertheless, a great many identifications remain more or less intuitive guesses at the riddle. I have made liberal use of question-marks (and in the Alphabetical Gazetteer of the first person singular) in order to diminish as much as possible the spurious authority of the printed page. Question-marks mean either that I think there may be a topographical allusion but don't know to what, or that there is an apparent allusion to a specific place or places which is nevertheless doubtful for lack of adequate confirmation. But the binary classification of questionable-unquestionable is misleading, too. Where identifications are concerned, probabilities are continuously variable, displeasing as this may be to those whose tolerance of ambiguity is low. (Yet *Finnegans Wake* is in greater danger from those whose tolerance of ambiguity knows no bounds.) Nevertheless, there are certain principles for the choice of identifications. Independently of contextual confirmation (which *also* is continuously variable in degree), an identification can be regarded as more probable (1) if it is an allusion to a Dublin place (allusions to the rest of Ireland have somewhat lower antecedent probability, allusions to the rest of the world a yet lower probability); (2) if there are at least two other allusions to the same place (and the probability is very roughly a function of the total number of allusions; thus a questionable allusion to the Tower of Babel has *ceteris paribus* greater merit than a questionable allusion to Rabelais's Abbey of Thélème); (3) if it belongs to a specifiable list, for example the capitals of European countries, nearly all of whose members are clearly identifiable elsewhere in the *Wake*; (4) or if it belongs to a domain of allusions otherwise ubiquitous in the *Wake*, for example the Crimea, or the field of Waterloo, or Zurich (which is rich in allusions)—but not Trieste (to which allusions are surprisingly few). But this category re-introduces the notion of context, with all the uncertainties of judgment which accompany interpretation. And as far as possible, this Gazetteer eschews interpretation and concentrates on the background of fact to which any interpretation must be responsible.

All of these considerations of what counts as an identification reflect the problems of separating the intentions of the text from coincidental associations of ideas. Another class of decisions has to do not with Joyce's intentions but with the definition of "place." This Gazetteer construes "place" rather broadly. Included are fictional places, like Proust's Balbec and Mark Twain's Jackson Island; places which belong only to the *Wake*'s own topography, like Nixnixundnix and Tingsomingenting, the homes of the Ondt and the Gracehoper; places named in the titles of songs and books—for which see further Hodgart and Worthington's *Song in the Works of James Joyce* and J. S. Atherton's *The Books at the Wake*; names of languages derived from relevant place-names, e.g., Greek, but not Latin; nicknames and other identifying descriptions, such as "this albutisle" for Howth and "overgrown milestone" for Dublin's Wellington Monument; adjectival uses of place-names; ships (on the authority of Bea Lillie, who on the maiden voyage of the *Queen Mary* asked the captain, "When does this place get to New York?"); astronomical bodies and constellations—but not sun, moon, or earth; Hell— but not Heaven; Dublin organizations and societies, and a few others; and periodical publications which bear some interesting relation to Joyce's life, or have an Irish connection, or occur in a pattern in which other members are identified. Not included are trade-names, companies, organizations and societies whose locations are not significant (for example, GBD pipes, Lips's locks, or Nestle, Maggi, and Pears, manufacturers of chocolate, soup, and soap); and place-names which have become common nouns (for example, "champagne" and "cologne"). A list of the latter is given separately in the Appendix.

Citations of *Finnegans Wake* are given in the form of Clive Hart's *Concordance*; for example, 349.06 means the sixth printed line on page 349. The marginal comments and footnotes of Book II, Chapter 2 are indicated by "L," "R," and "F." City place-names are listed separately in the Alphabetical Gazetteer for Dublin, London, and Paris, collected under the city names for all other cases. In Dublin, local place-names in Chapelizod, Howth, and Phoenix Park are collected under those entries. Because so many of the entries are for Dublin places, reference to Dublin has for the most part been omitted and is to be understood if no other place is specified; also, dates have for the most part been omitted for Dublin shops and the like which flourished "around the turn of the century," that is, between 1890 and 1910. For Dublin places of any period, map coordinates are given according to the system of the Irish Ordnance Survey; the numbers indicate the western and southern coordinates of the appropriate grid-square—thus "17/34" refers to the lower left-hand corner of the indicated square as one sees it on the map. Ordnance Survey maps are readily available in shops in Dublin and elsewhere, or from the Ordnance Survey offices in Phoenix Park, Dublin. The 1:18,000 map (3.52 inches to the mile), with index, is the most useful.

BIBLIOGRAPHY

I

BOOKS ON DUBLIN AND IRELAND

Works used, or probably used, by Joyce are indicated by an asterisk.

Anonymous. *The Compleat Irish Traveller.* 2 vols. London, 1788.

------------------. *Dublin Delineated.* Dublin, 1837. Reprinted 1971 by S.R. Publishers, East Ardsley, Yorks.

------------------. *The Story of Dublin City and County.* Dublin: Fred Hanna Ltd., n.d.

*Ball, F. Elrington. *History of the County of Dublin.* 4 vols. Dublin: Alex. Thom & Co., 1903-06.

-------------------------. *Howth and its Owners.* Dublin: University Press, 1917.

-------------------------. *Southern Fingal.* Dublin: University Press, 1920.

*Bartholomew's *Handy Reference Atlas of the World.* Edinburgh, 1923.

Boate, Gerard. *A Natural History of Ireland.* Dublin, 1755; original edition 1675.

Brewer's Dictionary of Phrase and Fable. New York: Harper & Bros., n.d.

Brewer's Historic Notebook. Philadelphia: J. B. Lippincott Co., n.d.

Burton, Nathanael. *Oxmantown and its Environs.* Dublin, 1845.

Bush, John. *Hibernia Curiosa.* Dublin, 1769.

Carey, F. P. *Catholic Dublin; A Guide to All the Principal Churches and Places of Interest.* Dublin: Trinity Press, n.d.

*Census of Ireland. *General Alphabetical Index to the Townlands and Towns of Ireland*, 1861, 1901.

*Chart, D. A. *The Story of Dublin.* London: J. M. Dent & Co., 1907.

Collins, James. *Life in Old Dublin.* Dublin: James Duffy & Co., 1913.

*Cosgrave, Dillon. *North Dublin, City and Environs.* Dublin: Catholic Truth Society, 1909; 2nd ed. M. H. Gill and Son, 1932.

Cosgrave, E[phraim] MacDowel. *Dublin and County Dublin in the Twentieth Century.* Brighton: W. T. Pike & Co., 1908.

Cosgrave, E. MacDowel, and Strangways, Leonard R. *The Dictionary of Dublin.* Dublin: Sealy, Bryers & Walker, 1907.

Craig, Maurice. *Dublin 1660-1860*. London: Cresset Press, 1952.

D'Alton, John. *The History of the County of Dublin*. Dublin: Hodges and Smith, 1838.

Dublin Penny Journal, 2 vols., 1832-34. Vol. I, No. 1 contains John O'Donovan's "Annals of Dublin."

*Falkiner, C. Litton. *Illustrations of Irish History and Topography*. London and New York: Longmans, Green and Co., 1904.

*Fitzpatrick, Samuel A. Ossory. *Dublin. A Historical and Topographical Account of the City*. London: Methuen & Co., 1907.

Gerard, Frances A. *Picturesque Dublin, Old and New*. London: Hutchinson, 1891. Many illustrations.

*Gilbert, J. T. *A History of the City of Dublin*. 3 vols. Dublin: McGlashan and Gill, 1854. Reprinted by Irish University Press with added Index, 1972.

Gillespie, Elgy, ed. *The Liberties of Dublin*. Dublin: E. & T. O'Brien, 1973.

*Haliday, Charles. *The Scandinavian Kingdom of Dublin*. Dublin, 1881. Reprinted by Irish University Press, 1969.

Hansbrow, G. *An Improved Topographical and Historical Hibernian Gazetteer*. Dublin, 1835.

Harris, Walter. *The History and Antiquities of the City of Dublin*. Dublin, 1766.

Harrison, Wilmot. *Memorable Dublin Houses*. Dublin, 1890. Reprinted 1971 by S.R. Publishers, East Ardsley, Yorks.

Harvey, John. *Dublin*. London: B. T. Batsford, 1949.

Irwin, George. *Irwin's Dublin Guide*. Dublin, 1853. Printed "For the Great Industrial Exhibition of 1853."

*Joyce, Patrick Weston. *Irish Names of Places*. 3 vols. London: Longmans Green & Co.; Dublin: M. H. Gill and Son, 1910-13. Vol. I reprinted 1972 by EP Publishing, Yorks. James Joyce owned the 1922 edition.

Joyce, P. W. and Sullivan, A. M. *Atlas and Cyclopedia of Ireland*. New York: Murphy & MacCarthy, 1900.

*Joyce, Weston St. John. *The Neighbourhood of Dublin*. Dublin: M. H. Gill & Son, 1921. 1939 edition reprinted 1971 by S.R. Publishers, East Ardsley, Yorks.

-----------------------------------. *Rambles Around Dublin*. Dublin: Evening Telegraph Reprints, 1887.

Keating, Geoffrey. *The History of Ireland*. Trans. by D. Comyn and P. S. Dinneen. 4 vols. Dublin: Irish Texts Society, Vols. IV, VIII, IX, XV. Index of persons and places in Vol. XV.

Lewis, Samuel. *A Topographical Dictionary of Ireland*. 2 vols. London:

S. Lewis & Co., 1837. Reprinted in 3 vols. by Kennikat Press, Port Washington, N.Y., 1970.

Little, George A. *Dublin Before the Vikings.* Dublin: M. H. Gill & Son, 1957.

Longford, Christine. *A Biography of Dublin.* London: Methuen and Co., 1936.

McCall, P. J. *In the Shadow of St. Patrick's.* Dublin: Sealy, Bryers and Walker, 1894.

*M'Cready, C. T. *Dublin Street Names Dated and Explained.* Dublin, 1892. Reprinted by Carraig Books, Blackrock, Ire., 1975.

MacGowan, Kenneth. *The Phoenix Park.* Dublin: Kamac Publications, 1966.

Malton, James. *A Picturesque and Descriptive View of the City of Dublin.* London, 1792-99. 25 plates.

O'Donovan, John. *Annals of the Kingdom of Ireland, by the Four Masters.* 7 vols. Dublin: Hodges, Smith and Co., 1856.

Ordnance Survey of Ireland. *Books of Reference to the Plans of Parishes, Co. Dublin.* Dublin, 1868-72.

*Peter, A[da]. *Dublin Fragments, Social and Historic.* Dublin: Hodges Figgis and Co., 1925.

*------------------. *Sketches of Old Dublin.* Dublin: Sealy, Bryers & Walker, 1907.

Price, Liam. *The Place-Names of County Wicklow.* Dublin: Dublin Institute for Advanced Studies, 1945-67 (7 parts).

*Thom's *Official Directory of the United Kingdom of Great Britain and Ireland.* Dublin, published annually.

Todd, J. H., ed. *War of the Gaedhil with the Gaul.* London, 1867.

Wakeman, W. F. *Old Dublin.* First and Second Series. Dublin, 1887. (Reprinted from the *Evening Telegraph.*)

Walsh, John Edward. *Ireland 120 Years Ago.* Dublin: M. H. Gill and Son, 1911. Revised edition by Dillon Cosgrave of Walsh's *Ireland Sixty Years Ago*, Dublin, 1847.

*Warburton, J[ohn], Whitelaw, J., and Walsh, Robert. *History of the City of Dublin.* 2 vols. London: T. Cadell and W. Davies, 1818.

Ward, Lock's *Guide to Dublin and its Environs.* 21st edition. London, n.d. [1928].

Wheeler, H. A. and Craig, M. J. *The Dublin City Churches of the Church of Ireland.* Dublin, 1948.

Wright, G. N. *An Historical Guide to Ancient and Modern Dublin.* London: Baldwin, Cradock and Joy, 1821.

II
MAPS

DUBLIN:

John Speed, 1610

T. Philipps, 1685

Charles Brooking, 1728

John Rocque, 1765 (reprinted by Ordnance Survey, 1966)

Allen and Son, 1816

Baldwin, Cradock and Joy, 1821

6" Ordnance Survey, revised 1935-36, 1943-44

2.5" Ordnance Survey, revised 1962

3.52" Ordnance Survey, revised 1972

1" Dublin District, Ordnance Survey, revised 1973

1" Wicklow District, Ordnance Survey, revised 1970

IRELAND:

Sir William Petty's *Hiberniae Delineatio, Atlas of Ireland.* (The "Down Survey.") First published 1685; reprinted 1968 by Frank Graham, Newcastle-upon-Tyne.

Beaufort, Daniel Augustus. *Memoir of a Map of Ireland.* London, 1792. With Index.

½" Ordnance Survey sheets for Ireland.

III
WORKS ON *FINNEGANS WAKE*

Atherton, James S. *The Books at the Wake: A Study of Literary Allusions in James Joyce's Finnegans Wake.* London: Faber & Faber, 1959. Reprinted by Southern Illinois University Press, Carbondale, Ill., 1974 (Arcturus Books).

Begnal, Michael H. and Senn, Fritz, eds. *A Conceptual Guide to Finnegans Wake.* University Park, Pa.: Pennsylvania State University Press, 1974.

Benco, Silvio. "James Joyce in Trieste," *The Bookman* LXXII (1930), 375-380.

Benstock, Bernard. *Joyceagain's Wake.* Seattle: University of Washington Press, 1965.

Cerny, James W. "Joyce's Mental Map," *James Joyce Quarterly* IX (1971), 218-224.

Christiani, Dounia Bunis. *Scandinavian Elements of Finnegans Wake.* Evanston, Ill.: Northwestern University Press, 1965.

Crise, Stelio. *Epiphanies & Phadographs, Joyce e Trieste; con un album Joyciano.* Milan: All'insegna del pesce d'oro, 1967.

Dalton, Jack P. and Hart, Clive, eds. *Twelve and a Tilly. Essays on the Occasion of the 25th Anniversary of Finnegans Wake.* Evanston, Ill.: Northwestern University Press, 1965.

Daly, Leo. *James Joyce and the Mullingar Connection.* Dublin: The Dolmen Press, 1975.

Ellmann, Richard. *James Joyce.* New York: Oxford University Press, 1959.

-----------------------, ed. *Letters of James Joyce.* 3 vols. New York: Viking Press, 1966. (Vol. I edited by Stuart Gilbert, 1957.) Vol. II contains a chronological list of Joyce's addresses.

Garvin, John. *James Joyce's Disunited Kingdom and the Irish Dimension.* Dublin: Gill & Macmillan; New York: Barnes and Noble, 1976.

Glasheen, Adaline. *Third Census of Finnegans Wake.* Berkeley: University of California Press, 1977.

Golden, Seán Valentine. *Bygmythster Finnegan: Etymology as Poetics in the Works of James Joyce.* Ph.D. dissertation, University of Connecticut, 1976.

Gorman, Herbert. *James Joyce.* New York: Farrar and Rinehart, 1939.

Graham, Philip L., Sullivan, Philip B., and Richter, G. F. "Mind Your Hats Goan In!" *The Analyst* XXI (1962) and XXII (1962).

Halper, Nathan. "Four Old Men," *A Wake Newslitter* XII (1975), 3-5.

----------------------. "Paris," *A Wake Newslitter* XII (1975), 81-82.

Hart, Clive. *A Concordance to Finnegans Wake.* Minneapolis: University of Minnesota Press, 1963. Reprinted by Paul P. Appel, Mamaroneck, N.Y., 1974.

----------------. *Structure and Motif in Finnegans Wake.* London: Faber and Faber, 1962.

----------------, and Senn, Fritz. *A Wake Digest.* Sydney: Sydney University Press, 1968.

Hayman, David. *A First-Draft Version of Finnegans Wake.* Austin: University of Texas Press, 1963.

Higginson, Fred H. *James Joyce's Revisions of Finnegans Wake: A Study of the Published Versions.* Ph.D. dissertation, University of Minnesota, 1953.

Hodgart, Matthew J. C., and Worthington, Mabel. *Song in the Works of James Joyce.* New York: Columbia University Press, 1959.

Hutchins, Patricia. *James Joyce's Dublin.* London: Grey Walls Press, 1950.

--------------------------. *James Joyce's World.* London: Methuen and Co., 1957.

Kelleher, John V. "Notes on *Finnegans Wake* and *Ulysses*," *The Analyst* X (1956).

Lyons, F. S. L. "James Joyce's Dublin," *20th Century Studies*, No. 4 (1970), 6-25.

McHugh, Roland. *The Sigla of Finnegans Wake*. London: Edward Arnold, 1976.

O'Connor, Ulick, ed. *The Joyce We Knew*. Cork: Mercier Press, 1967.

O Hehir, Brendan. *A Gaelic Lexicon for Finnegans Wake*. Berkeley: University of California Press, 1967.

Rocco-Bergera, Niny. "James Joyce and Trieste," *James Joyce Quarterly* IX (1972), 342-349.

Senn, Fritz. "Some Zurich Allusions in *Finnegans Wake*," *The Analyst* XIX (1960).

----------------. "Ossianic Echoes," *A Wake Newslitter* III (1966), 25-36.

Skrabanek, Petr. "Imaginable Itinerary Through the Particular Universal (260.R3)," *A Wake Newslitter* X (1973), 22-23.

Tindall, William York. *A Reader's Guide to Finnegans Wake*. New York: Farrar, Strauss and Giroux, 1969.

Troy, Mark L. *Mummeries of Resurrection: The Cycle of Osiris in Finnegans Wake*. Uppsala: University of Uppsala, 1976.

Tysdahl, Bjørn J. *Joyce and Ibsen*. Oslo: Norwegian Universities Press; New York: Humanities Press, 1968.

Weir, Lorraine. "Phoenix Park in *Finnegans Wake*," *Irish University Review* V (1975), 230-249.

Worthington, Mabel P. "The World as Christ Church, Dublin," *A Wake Newslitter* II (1965), 3-7.

ABBREVIATIONS

acc	according	cf	compare
AD	Anno Domini	ch	church, chapter
Adm	Administrative	chap	chapter
Afr	Africa	*Chr*	*Chronicles*
aka	also known as	CI	Church of Ireland
Ala	Alabama	co	company, county
AM	Ante Meridian	coll	college
Amer	America(n)	colloq	colloquial
anc	ancient	cor	corner
angl	anglicized	corp	corporation
Apr	April	C-word	100-lettered word (in *FW*)
Arab	Arabic	Czech	Czechoslovakia(n)
Arr	Arrondissement		
assn	association	d	died
asst	assistant	Dan	Danish
Aug	August	*Dan*	*Daniel*
ave	avenue	Dec	December
AWN	*A Wake Newslitter*	Del	Delaware
		Den	Denmark
b	born	dept	department, département
bar	barony	Devon	Devonshire, England
BBC	British Broadcasting Corporation	dist	district
BC	Before Christ, British Columbia	DMP	Dublin Metropolitan Police
Belg	Belgium	Dub	Dublin
Berks	Berkshire, England	Dut	Dutch
Bibl	Biblical		
bldg	building	E	East(ern)
blvd	boulevard	*EB*	*Encyclopaedia Britannica* (11th edition)
bor	borough		
br	bridge	ed	edition
Brit	Britain, British	eg	for example
btwn	between	emp	empire
Bucks	Buckinghamshire, England	Eng	England, English
BVM	Blessed Virgin Mary	esp	especially
		est	established
ca	*circa*	*et al*	and others
Cal, Calif	California(n)	Eur	Europe, European
Cambs	Cambridgeshire, England	*Exod*	*Exodus*
Can	Canada	*Ezek*	*Ezekiel*
cap	capital		
cas	castle	Feb	February
cath	cathedral	fig	figure
cem	cemetery	Fin	Finland, Finnish
cen	center, central	Fla	Florida
cent	century	fn	footnote

form	former(ly)	L	Lake, left
Fr	Father, France, French	lang	language
Fri	Friday	Lat	Latin
ft	feet, foot, fort	Leics	Leicestershire, England
FW	*Finnegans Wake*	Lith	Lithuania(n)
		Lt	Lieutenant
Ga	Georgia	Lwr	Lower
Gael	Gaelic		
Gen	General	Mar	March
Gen	*Genesis*	Mass	Massachusetts
Ger	German(y)	*Matt*	*Matthew*
Gk	Greek	med	medieval
Glocs	Gloucestershire, England	Medit	Mediterranean
gov	governor	mem	memorial
govt	government	Mex	Mexico
GPO	General Post Office (Dublin)	mi	mile(s)
Gr	Greece	mid	middle
Gt	Great	Min	Minor
		misc	miscellaneous
harb	harbor	mod	modern
Hants	Hampshire, Eng	Mon	Monday, monument
Heb	Hebrew	mt	mount, mountain
Herts	Hertfordshire, England	mus	museum
hist	history, historical	myth	mythology
HM	Her (His) Majesty's		
ho	house	N	North(ern)
hosp	hospital	Nat	National
hqs	headquarters	NCR	North Circular Road
Hung	Hungary, Hungarian	Neth	Netherlands
		NH	New Hampshire
I	Island	No(s)	Number(s)
ie	that is	Nor	Norway, Norwegian
Ill	Illinois	Northants	Northamptonshire, England
imp	imperial	Notts	Nottinghamshire, England
incl	including	Nov	November
Ind	India(n)	NPN	not a place-name
inst	institution	NS	Nova Scotia
Ir	Irish	NSW	New South Wales
IRA	Irish Republican Army	*NT*	*New Testament*
Ire	Ireland	*Num*	*Numbers*
Isa	*Isaiah*	NY	New York
isl	island	NYC	New York City
It	Italy, Italian	NZ	New Zealand
Ital	Italian		
		O	Ocean
Jan	January	obs	observatory
Jap	Japan, Japanese	Oct	October
Jer	*Jeremiah*	OE	Old English
JJ	James Joyce	*OED*	*Oxford English Dictionary*
Josh	*Joshua*	opp	opposite
Judg	*Judges*	orig	origin(al)(ly)

OS	Ordnance Survey (Irish)	SCR	South Circular Road
OT	*Old Testament*	sep	separate(d)
		Sept	September
p, pp	page, pages	Soc	Society
Pal	Palestine	Soms	Somersetshire, England
par	paragraph, parish	Sp	Spain, Spanish
parl	parliament	Sq	Square
penin	peninsula	SS	Saints
Penn	Pennsylvania	SSR	Soviet Socialist Republic
Pers	Persia(n)	St	Saint, Street
Pl	Place	sta	station
PM	Post Meridian	Staffs	Staffordshire, England
Pol	Poland, Polish	stat	statue
pop	popular(ly)	Sun	Sunday
Port	Portugal, Portuguese	Sw	Swiss
pris	prison	Swed	Sweden, Swedish
prob	probably	Switz	Switzerland
Prof	Professor		
pron	pronounced, pronunciation	tav	tavern
prop	proprietor	TCD	Trinity College, Dublin
Prot	Protestant	Terr	Terrace, territory
prov	province	Thur	Thursday
Pruss	Prussia(n)	tnld	townland
Ps	*Psalms*	trad	tradition(al)(ly)
Pt	Point	trans	translated, translation
pub	public	trib	tributary
publ	published, publication	Tue	Tuesday
		Turk	Turkey, Turkish
Que	Quebec		
quot	quoted, quotation	U	University
qv, qqv	see	*U*	*Ulysses*
		UK	United Kingdom
R	River, right	Univ	University
RC	Roman Catholic	Upr	Upper
rd	road	US	United States of America
ref	reference, refers	USSR	Union of Soviet Socialist Re-
regt	regiment		publics
rel	religion, religious		
rep	republic	vall	valley
res	residence, residential	vill	village
Rev	Reverend	vol	volume
Rev	*Revelations*		
riv	river	W	West(ern)
rlwy	railway	Wed	Wednesday
Russ	Russia(n)	WI	West Indies
		Wilts	Wiltshire, England
S	South(ern)	Wm	William
Sans	Sanskrit	Worcs	Worcestershire, England
Sat	Saturday	WW I, II	World War I, II
Scand	Scandinavia(n)		
sch	school	Yorks	Yorkshire, England
Scot	Scotland, Scottish	Yugo	Yugoslav(ia)

PART I
Linear Guide

3.01	riverrun		.22	knock out in the park (*Cont.*)
	Liffey			Phoenix Park
.01	Eve and Adam's		.23	devlinsfirst
	Adam and Eve's			?Devlin R
.02	bay			Dublin
	Dublin Bay		.24	livvy
.02	vicus			Liffey
	Vico Rd		4.04	Verdons
.03	Howth Castle and Environs			Verdun: Épée de Verdun
	Howth: Howth Castle		.05	Hoodie Head
.05	North Armorica			Howth (Head)
	America		.07	Killykillkilly
	Armorica			Dublin: Drom Cuill-Choille
.06	isthmus			?Kilkelly
	Sutton, Isthmus of			?Kilkenny
.06	Europe Minor		.08	a toll, a toll
	Europe			?Turnpike: Tollgates
	Ireland: Misc Allusions		.08	cashels
.06	penisolate war			Cashel
	Iberian Peninsula			Castle, The
.07	Oconee		.11	how hoth sprowled
	Oconee R (Georgia)			?Howth
.08	Laurens County's		.17	phoenish
	Laurens Co (Georgia)			Phoenix Park
.08	gorgios		.18	Stuttering Hand
	Georgia			?
.08	doublin		.21	Helviticus
	Dublin			?Switzerland: Helvetia
	Dublin, Georgia		.27	Toper's Thorp
.13	Jhem or Shen			?
	?Jameson, John, and Son		.28	Soangso
.15	bababadal— [in C-word]			Hwang Ho R
	?Babel, Tower of		.30	balbulous
.17	wallstrait			?Babel, Tower of
	NYC: Wall St		.35	waalworth of a skyerscape
.18	life			NYC: Woolworth Bldg
	Liffey		.36	eyeful hoyth entowerly
.20	erse			Eiffel Tower
	Ireland: Erse			Howth
.20	humptyhillhead		.36	erigenating
	Howth			Ireland
.22	upturnpikepointandplace		5.01	the himals and all
	Turnpike			Himalaya Mts
.22	knock out in the park		.02	baubletop
	Castleknock (Hill)			Babel, Tower of
	Knockmaroon (Hill)			

.06 Riesengeborg
    Riesengebirge
.14 Our cubehouse
    Mecca: Kaaba
.15 arafatas
    Arafat
.17 blackguardise...whitestone...
    heaven
    Mecca: Black Stone
.23 jebel
    Nile R: Bahr-el-Jebel
.23 the jpysian sea
    Egypt
.27 collupsus
    Colossus of Rhodes
.30 wallhall's horrors
    ?Phoenix Park: Hole in the
    Wall
    Valhalla
.30 rollsrights
    Rollright Stones
.31 carhacks
    Carhaix
.31 stonengens
    Stonehenge
.32 streetfleets
    Fleet St
.32 tournintaxes
    Thurn and Taxis
.33 aeropagods
    Athens: Areopagus
.34 hoyse
    ?Hoey's Court
.35 mecklenburk bitch
    Mecklenburgh St
.35 merlinburrow burrocks
    Marlborough Barracks
.36 fore old porecourts
    Four Courts
.36 bore the more
    Bohermore
6.01 blightblack workingstacks
    Blue Stack Mts
.01 twelvepins
    Twelve Bens (Mts)
.02 Safetyfirst Street
    ?
.02 derryjellybies
    ?Derry
.03 Tell-No-Tailors' Corner
    ?

.04 ville's indigenous romekeepers
    London: "Romeville"
    Rome
    Sick and Indigent Roomkeepers
    Society
.07 butt under his bridge
    Butt Br
.19 Agog and magog
    Gog and Magog
.21 kinkin corass
    Kincora
.24 pillowscone
    Lia Fáil
.27 finisky
    Phoenix Park
.31 overgrown babeling
    Babel, Tower of
    Wellington Monument

*6.33–.35: the first of each pair is in
the area of Chapelizod–Castleknock, the
second in Howth & Environs.*

.33 Shopalist
    Chapelizod
.33 Bailywick
    Bailey Lighthouse (Howth)
.33 ashtun
    Ashtown
.33 baronoath
    Howth
.34 Buythebanks
    Chapelizod: The Bank
.34 Roundthehead
    Howth (Head)
.34 the foot of the bill
    ?Chapelizod: Martin's Row
.35 ireglint's eye
    Ireland's Eye
7.01 livvylong
    Liffey
.05 telling a toll
    ?Turnpike: Tollgates
.05 teary turty Taubling
    Dublin Allusion: "Dear Dirty
    Dublin"
.07 pool the begg
    Poolbeg (Lighthouse)
.08 pass the kish
    Kish Lightship
.10 baken head
    ?Bailey Lighthouse (Howth)

.11 Kennedy bread
Kennedy, Peter (bakery)

.12 U'Dunnell's...ayle
Phoenix Brewery

.12 Dobbelin
?Dobbin
Dublin
Paris Bridges

.27 nannygoes
?Nannywater

.28 Benn Heather
Howth: Ben Edar

.28 Seeple Isout
Chapelizod

.30 Whooth
Howth

.31 magazine wall...maggy seen all
Magazine Fort

.33 belles' alliance
Waterloo: La Belle Alliance

.33 Ill Sixty
Hill 60

.34 tarabom, tarabom
Tara

.35 lyffing-in-wait
Liffey

.36 clouds
Paris Bridges

8.01 Wallinstone national museum
Wellington Museum
Williamstown

.01 national
Paris Bridges

.02 waterloose
Waterloo

.03 two quitewhite villagettes
Waterloo: Hougomont and
La Haye Sainte

.06 invalids
Invalides, Hôtel des
Paris Bridges

.09 goan
?Goa

.10 Willingdone Museyroom
Wellington Museum

.10−.11 Prooshious...Prooshious
Prussia

.13−.14 flag of the Prooshious...
Prooshious
Prussia

.14 Saloos
Loos (Battle)

.14 Saloos (*Cont.*)
Salo (Battle)

.14 Crossgunn
Corsica
?Cross Guns

.15 triplewon
?Tripoli

.17 white harse
White Horse

.17 Cokenhape
Copenhagen

.18 magentic
Magenta (Battle)

.18 goldtin spurs
Golden Spurs, Battle of the

.19 quarterbrass
Waterloo: Quatre Bras

.20 bangkok's
‥ Bangkok

.20 goliar's
?Goliad (Battle)
Gwalior (Battle)

.20 pulluponeasyan
Peloponnese (War)

.21 wide harse
White Horse

.22 boyne
Boyne R (Battle)

.23 inimyskilling
Enniskillen: "the Inniskillings"

.25 Gallawghurs
Gawilghur (Battle)

.25 argaumunt
Argaum (Battle)

.25 petty
Paris Bridges

.26 Assaye
Assaye (Battle)

.27 Hairy
Ireland

.28 Delian alps
Alps
Delium
?Delos

.28 Mont Tivel
?

.29 Mont Tipsey
?Ipsus (Battle)

.29 Grand Mons Injun
Mons
Waterloo: Mont St Jean

.30   crimealine
         Crimea
.30   alps
         Alps
.31   legahorns
         Leghorn
.35   Willingdone mormorial
         Wellington Monument
9.01 me Belchum
         Belgium
.01   phillippy
         Paris Bridges
         Philippi (Battle)
.01   Awful Grimmest Sunshat Crom-
         welly. Looted
         Guinness's Brewery
.02   hastings
         Hastings (Battle)
.04   me Belchum
         Belgium
.06   fontannoy
         Fontenoy (Battle)
.07   agincourting
         Agincourt (Battle)
.08   boycottoncrezy
         Crécy (Battle)
.10   Belchum
         Belgium
.13   me Belchum
         Belgium
.13   Salamangra
         Salamanca (Battle)
.15   me Belchum
         Belgium
.16   stampforth
         Stamford Bridge (Battle)
.21   Tarra's widdars
         Tara
         Torres Vedras (Battle)
.23   Cork
         Cork
.23   Tonnerre
         ?Tonnerre
.24   camelry
         Camel, Battle of the
.24   floodens
         Flodden (Battle)
.25   solphereens
         Paris Bridges
         Solferino (Battle)
.25   their mobbily
         Thermopylae (Battle)

.25   panickburns
         Bannockburn (Battle)
.26   Almeidagad
         Almeida (Battle)
.26   Arthiz
         Orthez (Battle)
.26   too loose
         Toulouse (Battle)
.28   Finnlambs
         England
         Finland
         Ireland: Misc Allusions
.28   ousterlists
         Austerlitz (Battle)
         Paris Bridges
.29   bunkersheels
         Bunker Hill (Battle)
.30   trip so airy
         Tipperary
.30   me Belchum's
         Belgium
.32   cool of his canister
         ?Canister, The
.33   marathon
         Marathon (Battle)
.34   marmorial
         Wellington Monument
.35   royal
         Paris Bridges
.36   Delaveras
         Talavera de la Reina (Battle)
.36   fimmieras
         Ireland
         Vimeiro (Battle)
.36   pettiest
         Paris Bridges
10.02 Capeinhope
         Copenhagen (Battle)
         Good Hope, Cape of
.04   hiena
         Jena (Battle)
         Paris Bridges
.05   lipsyg
         Leipzig (Battle)
.06   Shimar Shin
         ?Shinar
.08   fromoud
         Oudh
.09   ranjymad
         ?Runnymede
.13   Culpenhelp
         Copenhagen

.16 madrashattaras
    ?Hatteras, Cape
    Madras
    Mahratta War
    ?Tara
.17 Ap Pukkaru
    Aboukir (Battle)
.17 Pukka Yurap
    ?Europe
.17 bornstable
    Barnstaple
.18 ghentleman
    Ghent
.18 cursigan
    Corsica
.18 Shimar Shin
    ?Shinar
.19 Basucker
    Busaco (Battle)
.21 Copenhagen
    Copenhagen
.22 goan
    ?Goa
.27 houthse
    Howth
.29 wagrant
    Wagram (Battle)
.30 piltdowns
    Piltdown Common
.31 spy
    Spy
11.03 niver
    Nive R (Battle)
.05 No nubo no! Neblas
    ?Nebo, Mt
.05 liv
    Liffey
.16 nebo
    Nebo, Mt
.19 rattlin buttins
    Butt Br
.21 keys and woodpiles
    Wood Quay
.21 haypennies
    Wellington Br ("Ha'penny")
.22 bloodstaned breeks
    Barrack Br ("Bloody")
.22 boaston...masses of shoesets
    Boston
.23 allmicheal
    Paris Bridges

.32 livving...laffing
    Liffey
.35 solly
    Paris Bridges
.35 Gricks
    Greece
.36 Troysirs
    Troy
12.05 Luntum
    London
.06 marriedann
    ?France: "Marianne"
    Paris Bridges
.09 Herrschuft Whatarwelter
    ?
.19 review of the two mounds
    Revue des Deux Mondes
.20 two mounds
    Castleknock: Castleknock Hill
    and Windmill Hill
.23 Wharton's Folly
    Phoenix Park: Starfort
.24 purk
    Phoenix Park

*The following five "Hills" are all
sts in cen Dub. Olaf Rd and Sitric Rd
are just N of Arbour Hill, and Ivar St is
two blocks further N.*

.27 Corkhill
    Cork Hill
.27 Arbourhill
    Arbour Hill
.28 Summerhill
    Summerhill
.28 Miseryhill
    Misery Hill
.29 Constitutionhill
    Constitution Hill
.30 several
    Paris Bridges
.31 Olaf's on the rise
    Olaf Rd
.31 Ivor's
    Ivar St
.32 Sitric's place's
    Sitric Rd
.35 macroborg of Holdhard
    Howth: Howth Castle
.36 microbirg of Pied de Poudre
    Magazine Fort
    Piepowder Court

13.01	Irish		14.01	Kish...Kish
	Ireland			?Kish Lightship
.01	English		.02	blay of her Kish
	England			Dublin: Baile Átha Cliath
.02	Royally		.03	sawl
	Paris Bridges			?Saul (Co Down)
.04	Dyoublong		.03	sackvulle
	Dublin			O'Connell St
.05	Echoland		.04	so rich
	?			?Zurich
.09	Mitchel		.05	Hurdlesford
	Paris Bridges			Dublin: Baile Átha Cliath
.14	old butte new		.09	Ballyaughacleeaghbally
	Butt Br			Dublin: Baile Átha Cliath
	Leixlip (Br)		.13	santryman
	O'Connell Br			Santry
	Paris Bridges		.14	Winehouse
	Whitworth Br			Paris
.14	Dbln		.15	Blotty words for Dublin
	Dublin			Dublin Allusion: "Rocky Rd
.14	mausolime wall			to Dublin"
	Magazine Fort		.16	ginnandgo gap
	?Mausoleum at Halicarnassus			Ginnunga Gap
.21	Boriorum		.18	billy
	Boreum			Paris Bridges
.22	Dyfflinarsky		.29	*Liber Lividus*
	Dublin: Dyfflinarsky			Liffey
.23	Eire's ile		.30	eirenical
	Ireland			Ireland
.24	bulbenboss		.31	our fredeland's plain
	Benbulben			Friedland (Battle)
.25	puir old wobban		.36	Ballymun
	Ireland: Shan van Vocht			Ballymun (N of Dublin)
.26	auburn mayde		15.01	duskrose
	Auburn			?Ireland: Little Black Rose
.27	desarted. Adear, adear		.01	Goatstown's
	Adare			Goatstown (S of Dublin)
	Dysart O'Dea		.02	Rush
	Paris Bridges			Rush (NE of Dublin)
.28	polepost		.03	mayvalleys
	?Wellington Monument			Moyvalley (NW of Dublin)
.30	leaves of the living		.04	Knockmaroon
	Liffey			Knockmaroon (W of Dublin)
.32	events grand and national		.06	tooath of the Danes
	Fairyhouse Racecourse			Denmark (+ Tuatha Dé
	Grand National, The			Danaan)
.32	national		.08	Little on the Green
	Paris Bridges			Little Green
.32	pass how		.11	Killallwho
	?Passau			Killala
.34	Ublanium			Killaloe
	Dublin: Eblana			

.12 babbelers
    Babel, Tower of
.14 pollyfool fiansees
    France
.16 Kerry
    Kerry
.18 aspace of dumbillsilly
    ?Dublin: Misc Allusions
.24 old as the howitts
    ?Howitt Mts
    Howth
.24 whillbarrow
    ?Barrow R
.33 mousterious
    Moustier, Le
.35 Comestipple Sacksoun
    Saxony
16.03 marrogbones
    ?Marrowbone Lane
    Paris Bridges
.04 Hirculos pillar
    Pillars of Hercules
.06 donsk
    Denmark
.06 tolkatiff
    Tolka
.06 scowegian
    Norway
.06 anglease
    England
.07 saxo
    Saxony
.07 Jute
    Jutland
.10 Yutah
    ?Utah
.21 poddle
    Poddle R
.21 Wherein
    Ireland
.22 Inns of Dungtarf
    Clontarf
.27 rath in mine mines
    Rathmines
.31 Ghinees
    Guinness's Brewery
.33 Louee, louee
    Paris Bridges
.35 dabblin
    Dublin
17.01 liveries
    ?Liberties, The

.01 missers moony
    Mooney's
.02 Minnikin passe
    Brussels: Manneken-Pis
.06 brookcells
    Brussels
.07 riverpool
    Liverpool
.08 Load Allmarshy
    Paris Bridges
.09 bull
    Bulls, North and South
.09 clompturf
    Clontarf
.11 neck I am sutton
    Sutton
.12 Brian d' of Linn
    Dublin
    ?Howth: Black Linn
.13 Boildoyle
    Baldoyle
.13 rawhoney
    Raheny
.13 beuraly
    England (*beurla*, Ir "English")
.14 sturk
    Turkey
.14 finnic
    Finland
    Phoenix Park
.15 rutterdamrotter
    Rotterdam
.18 this albutisle
    Howth
.18 olde ye plaine of my Elters
    Moyelta
.22 his Inn the Byggning
    ?
.23 Finishthere Punct
    Finisterre
    Phoenix Park
.23 erehim
    Ireland
.33 olso
    ?Oslo
.33 babylone
    Babylon
.34 alp
    Alps
    Liffey
.35 this sound seemetery
    ?

18.06   O'c'stle
        Oldcastle
        Royal Manors of Dublin
  .06   n'wc'stle
        Newcastle
        Royal Manors of Dublin
  .06   tr'c'stle
        Dublin Coat of Arms
        Royal Manors of Dublin
        ?Three Castles
  .07   crumbling
        Crumlin
        Royal Manors of Dublin
  .07   Humblin
        Dublin
  .07   Humblady Fair
        ?
  .12   Howe
        Thing Mote
  .13   viceking's graab
        NPN: Ibsen, *The Viking's Barrow*
  .16   thing mud
        Thing Mote
  .22   Meades
        Media
  .22   Porsons
        Persia
  .22   meandertale
        Meander R
        Neanderthal
  .23   Heidenburgh
        Eden
        Edinburgh
        Heidelberg
  .29   Ramasbatham
        ?
19.12   durlbin
        Dublin
  .14   triangular Toucheaterre
        England (Angleterre)
  .25   meanderthalltale
        Meander R
        Neanderthal
  .29   dugters of Nan
        Dana, Paps of
  .32   mightmountain Penn
        ?
20.03   charmian
        Germany
  .07   cromagnom
        Les Eyzies: Cromagnon Cave

  .16   Doublends
        Dublin
  .19   Nondum
        London
  .23   torytale
        ?Tory Island
  .24   lettice leap
        Leixlip
  .25   strubbely beds
        Strawberry Beds
21.01   norewhig
        ?Nore R
        ?Norway
  .06   delvin
        Delvin R
  .07   mountynotty
        Montenotte
  .13   homerigh, castle and earthen-
        house
        ?Castle, The
        Howth: Howth Castle
  .16   fireland
        Ireland
  .17   perusienne
        Paris
  .20   nossow
        Nassau
  .23   dovesgall
        Dubh-Gall
  .24   my earin
        Ireland
  .26   Erio
        Ireland
  .27   Tourlemonde
        Tir na mBan
  .34   bristolry
        Tavern, The: Bridge Inn
22.03   a paly one
        Pale, The
  .08   lilipath
        Lilliput
  .08   Woeman's Land
        Tir na mBan
  .10   finegale
        Fingal
  .10   earring
        Ireland
  .13   Erio
        Ireland
  .14   Turnlemeem
        Tir na mBan

.14 cromcruwell
?Crom Cruach

.21 mansionhome
?Mansion House

.28 arkway of trihump
Arch of Triumph

.34 three shuttoned castles
Dublin Coat of Arms
Howth: Howth Castle
?Sutton
Three Castles

.35 allabuff hemmed
?

.35 bullbraggin soxangloves
Balbriggan
?Saxony

.36 ladbroke breeks
Ladbroke

.36 cattegut bandolair
Cattegat

23.01 panuncular cumbottes
Iberian Peninsula

.03 rude hand
?Ulster: Red Hand

.04 spck
?Society for the Propagation of
Christian Knowledge

.11 Narwhealian captol
Norway
Oslo

.14 hearsomeness of the burger...
Dublin Motto

.19 Norronesen
Norway (norrøn, Nor "Norse")

.19 Irenean
Ireland: Irena
(irene, Nor "the Irish")

.19 Quarry silex
NPN: Quare silex?, Lat "Why are
you silent?"

.20 Homfrie Noanswa
Albert Nyanza

.20 Livia Noanswa
Liffey
Victoria Nyanza

.27 wave of roary
Four Waves of Erin

.27 wave of hooshed
Four Waves of Erin

.28 wave of hawhawhawrd
Four Waves of Erin

.28 wave of neverheedthemhorse-
luggarsandlistletomine
Four Waves of Erin

.29 Landloughed by his neaghboor-
mistress
Neagh, Lough

.31 louthly
?Louth

24.01 Novo Nilbud
Dublin
?Nile R

.04 auspice for the living
Hospice for the Dying

.05 dragon volant
Dragon Volant

.18 Healiopolis
Heliopolis

.19 Kapelavaster
Kapilavastu

.19 North Umbrian
Northumberland (Rd)

.20 Fivs Barrow
Phibsborough (Rd)

.20 Waddlings Raid
Watling St

.21 Bower Moore
Bohermore

.22 Cottericks'
?Catterick

.25 Devlin
Devlin R
Dublin

.31 sycamore
?Sycamore St

.31 Tory's clay
Tory Island

25.11 Bothnians
Bothnia

.14 Salmon House
Chapelizod: Salmon House

.15 supershillelagh
Shillelagh
Wellington Monument

.16 manument...battery block
Wellington Monument:
Salute Battery

.17 Eirenesians
Ireland

.26 Tuskar
Tuskar Lighthouse

.27 Moylean Main
?Lena

.27   Moylean Main (*Cont.*)
      Moyle, Sea of
.27   Great Erinnes
      Ireland
.28   Brettland
      Bretland
.28   Pike County
      Pike Co (Missouri)
.29   hung king
      ?Hong Kong
.31   the stone that Liam failed
      Lia Fáil
26.02   Hopkins and Hopkins
      Hopkins and Hopkins
.02   the pale
      ?Pale, The
.04   Jerusalemfaring
      Jerusalem
.04   Arssia Manor
      Asia (Minor)
.07   Papa Vestray
      Papa Westray Island
.08   Liffey
      Liffey
.11   system of the Shewolf
      ?
.12   tropic of Copricapron
      Capricorn
.13   cloister of Virgo
      Virgo
.14   region of sahuls
      ?
.15   texas
      Texas
.16   roam to Laffayette
      Lafayette
      Liffey
.17   chempel of Isid
      Chapelizod
.22   Christpatrick's
      Christchurch Cath
      St Patrick's Cath
.23   Howe of the shipmen
      Thing Mote
.29   Diet of Man
      Man, Isle of
.30   Jacob's lettercrackers
      Jacob, W and R, Co
.34   nessans
      St Nessan's Church
27.01   Glassarse
      ?Glasshouse

.06   bag of knicks
      ?Nixnixundnix
.09   tarandtan
      Tara
.15   Luna's Convent
      ?
.16   redminers
      ?Rathmines
.17   Williamswoodsmenufactors
      Williams and Woods, Ltd
.19   Lanner's
      NPN? (See *Census* for Katty
      Lanner)
.26   Portobello
      Portobello
.26   Pomeroy
      Pomeroy
.27   Be nayther
      Howth: Ben Edar
28.01   queenoveire
      Ireland
.12   Findrinny Fair
      NPN: *Findrina*, an alloy used
      in ancient Ireland for jewelry
.20   Evening World
      Evening World
.22   Fez
      Fez
.22   Stormount
      Stormont
.24   China
      China
.26   *Selskar*
      ?Selskar
.27   *Pervenche*...bluebells blowing
      ?Bluebell
.27   *Novvergin's Viv*
      Norway
.28   salty sepulchres
      ?St Sepulchre's
.32   Adams and Sons, the wouldpay
      actioneers
      Adam, James (auctioneer)
29.01   haunt of the hungred bordles
      Dublin: Baile Átha Cliath
.01   Shop Illicit
      Chapelizod
.03   yardalong
      Ardilaun
.04   ivoeh
      Iveagh

.04 Brewster's chimpney
     Guinness's Brewery
.21 hull
     Hell
     Hull
.22 *The Bey for Dybbling*
     Dublin Bay
.23 wicklowpattern
     Wicklow
.24 deadsea
     Dead Sea
.35 Edenborough
     Eden
     Edinburgh

     BOOK I
     Chapter 2

30.07 Sidlesham
       Sidlesham
.08 Hundred of Manhood
     Manhood, Hundred of
.11 Hofed-ben-Edar
     Howth: Ben Edar
.14 Chivychas
     Chevy Chase
·16 ye olde marine hotel
     Royal Marine Hotel
.22 hasting
     Hastings
.23 forecourts
     Four Courts
31.01 turnpike keys
       Turnpike
.18 Leix
     Laois
.18 Offaly
     Offaly
.18 Drogheda
     Drogheda
.20 Waterford
     Waterford
.20 Italian
     Italy
.21 Canmakenoise
     Clonmacnoise
.25 Pouringrainia
     ?Pomerania
.27 bailiwick
     Bailey Lighthouse
.27 turnpiker
     Turnpike

.31 Holmpatrick
     ?Holmpatrick
     ?Skerries
.33 Bourn
     ?
32.15 Dook Umphrey
       Duke Humphrey's Walk
.16 Lucalizod
     Chapelizod
     Lucan
.26 king's treat house
     ?Chapelizod: King's House
     Gaiety Theatre
     King St, S
.35 *The Bo' Girl*
     Bohemia
.35 *The Lily*
     Killarney
.35 all horserie show
     Dublin Horse Show
33.03 cecelticocommediant
       Cecilia St
.16 Mohorat
     NPN: *maharath*, Heb "mor-
     row"
.26 Welsh fusiliers
     Wales
.27 people's park
     Phoenix Park: People's Park
.36 stambuling
     Constantinople: Stamboul
34.01 Dumbaling
       Dublin
       ?Umballa
.01 tarrk
     Turkey
.03 Mallon's
     NPN? See *Census* for John
     Mallon
.08 alicubi...old house
     Mecca: Kaaba
.08 old house for the chargehard
     Chapelizod: House by the
     Churchyard
.09 Roche Haddocks off Hawkins
     Street
     Hawkins St
     ?Leinster Market
.12 meal
     Meles R
.20 rushy hollow
     Phoenix Park: The Hollow

.29	Rosasharon		.08	gildthegap Gaper
	Sharon			Gaping Ghyl
35.05	confusioning of human races		.18	Druidia
	Babel, Tower of			Ireland: Misc Allusions
.08	our greatest park		.18	Deepsleep Sea
	Phoenix Park			?
.09	great belt		.19	Charlatan Mall
	Great Belt (Denmark)			Charlemont Mall
.10	Bhagafat gaiters		.20	Grand
	NPN: *Bhagavad-Gita*			Grand Canal
.16	ouzel		.20	Royal
	Ouzel Galley Society			Royal Canal
.16	Poolblack		.22	castelles...blowne
	?Blackpool (England)			Castle Browne
	Dublin: Dubh-linn		.25	Irish
.30	Fox Goodman			Ireland
	?Goodman's Lane		.26	Iro-European ascendances
.32	speckled church			Europe
	Kilbarrack			Ireland (play on "Anglo-
	Speckled Church			Irish Ascendancy")
36.05	Morganspost		.32	Peach Bombay
	Morning Post			Bombay
.14	drumdrum		.32	Lukanpukan
	Dundrum			Lucan
.15	Berlin gauntlet		.33	senaffed and pibered
	Berlin			?Rome: SPQR
.18	*duc de Fer's* overgrown milestone		38.03	erebusqued
	Wellington Monument			Erebus
.22	hotel and creamery establishments		.04	Phenice-Bruerie '98
	?			Phœnix Brewery
.24	monument		.09	Bareniece Maxwelton
	Wellington Monument			Maxwelltown
.26	hoath		.11	persicks
	Howth			Persia
.29	Bishop and Mrs Michan		.11	armelians
	St Michan's Church			Armenia
.29	High Church of England		.11	Pomeranzia
	England			Pomerania
.30	sohole		.22	Esnekerry
	Soho			Enniskerry
.32	British		.24	Irish
	England			Ireland
.35	Gaping Gill		.30	Hippo
	Gaping Ghyl			Hippo
37.01	Heidelberg mannleich		39.02	hippic runfields of breezy
	Heidelberg			Baldoyle
.02	bad Sweatagore			Baldoyle (Racecourse)
	?		.04	events national
.03	dublnotch			Fairyhouse Racecourse:
	Dublin			Ir Grand National
.08	Tyskminister		.04	Dublin
	Germany: Tyskland			Dublin

.07 Bold Boy Cromwell
    British Broadcasting Corp
.09 Saint Dalough
    St Doolagh
.17 Kehoe, Donnelly and Packenham's
    Kehoe, Donnelly and Pakenham
.17 Finnish pork
    Finland
    Phoenix Park
.22 Seaforths
    Seaforth Highlanders
.29 land of counties capalleens
    Ireland: Cathleen ni Houlihan
.34 Eglandine's
    Eglantine
.35 the Duck and Doggies
    Dog and Duck Tavern
.35 the Galopping Primrose
    ?
.36 Brigid Brewster's
    ?
.36 the Cock
    Cock, The
.36 the Postboy's Horn
    ?
40.01 the Little Old Man's
    ?
.01 All Swell That Aimswell
    ?
.01 the Cup and the Stirrup
    ?
.02 a housingroom Abide With One-
    another
    ?
.03 Block W.W.
    ?
.04 Pump Court, The Liberties
    Liberties, The
    Pump Court
.05 voltapuke
    ?Volta Cinema
.07 rusinurbean
    ?Rus in Urbe
.19 bunk of iceland
    Bank of Ireland
    Iceland
.19 stone of destiny
    Lia Fáil
.21 illstarred
    Ulster

.29–.30 Dullkey Downlairy and Bleak-
    rooky tramaline
    Dalkey, Kingstown, and
      Blackrock Tram
    Blackrock
    Dalkey
    Dun Laoghaire
.34 Madame Gristle
    Steevens' Hospital
.35 Sir Patrick Dun's
    Sir Patrick Dun's Hospital
.35 Sir Humphrey Jervis's
    Jervis Street Hospital
.36 Saint Kevin's bed
    Glendalough: St Kevin's Bed
    St Kevin's Hospital
.36 Adelaide's hosspittles
    Adelaide Hospital
41.01 incurable welleslays
    Hospital for Incurables
.02 Sant Iago...Lazar
    Lazy Hill
.10 meed of anthems
    Athens
.17 hogshome...The Barrel
    Barrel, The
.18 Ebblinn's chilled hamlet
    Dublin: Eblana
    Dublin Allusion: "Dublin's
      Fair City"
.20 tubenny
    Underground (London)
.20 metro
    Métropolitain (Paris)
.22 cremoaning
    Cremona
.22 levey
    Liffey
.25 fraiseberry beds
    Strawberry Beds
.26 foyneboyne
    Boyne R
.32 Cujas Place
    Cujas, Rue de (Paris)
.32 Old Sots' Hole
    Old Sot's Hole
.32 parish of Saint Cecily
    Cecilia St
    ?Sainte-Cécile (Paris)
.33 the liberty of Ceolmore
    ?

.35   statue of Primewer Glasstone
        ?Gladstone, Statue of
        ?Parnell Monument
42.05   gee and gees
        Jameson, John, and Son
.15   bogeyer
        Ireland (*ey*, old Dan "island")
.18   col de Houdo
        Howth
.19   monument of the shouldhavebeen
        legislator
        ?
.21   Lenster
        Leinster
.25   liffeyside
        Liffey
.26   Watling
        Watling St (England)
.26   Ernin
        Erning St
.26   Icknild
        Icknield St
.27   Stane
        Foss Way
        Stoneybatter
.28   northern tory...southern whig
        Belfast: *The Northern Whig*
        ?Tory Island
.28   eastanglian chronicler
        (no such newspaper)
.29   landwester guardian
        Manchester: *The Manchester
        Guardian*
.30   dublinos
        Dublin
.30   Cutpurse Row
        Cut-Purse Row
.34   palesmen
        Pale, The
.35   Daly's
        Daly's Club
.36   Rutland heath
        Rutland Square
43.01   Hume Street
        Hume St
.03   Mosse's Gardens
        Rotunda
.03   Skinner's Alley
        Skinners Alley
.04   a fleming
        ?Belgium

.05   hammersmith
        Hammersmith (London)
.06   bluecoat scholars
        King's Hospital
.07   Simpson's on the Rocks
        Simpson's-on-the-Strand
        (London)
        Simpson's Hospital
.08   Turkey Coffee
        Turkey
.09   tickeyes door
        Hickey's

*The following four names are
listed as tabinet (poplin) manufacturers, the only four so listed, in Thom's
Directories of the 1920's and 1930's.*

.09   Peter Pim
        Pim, Brothers & Co
.09   Paul Fry
        Fry and Co
.09   Elliot
        Elliott, Thomas
.09   O, Atkinson
        Atkinson, Richard, and Co
.12   roman easter
        Rome
.13   greek uniates
        Greece
.13   lace lappet
        Lace Lappet, The
.16   the uncle's place
        NPN? (pawnshop)
.18   weaver's almshouse
        Weavers' Almshouse
.26   Delville
        Delville
.29   five pussyfours green
        Ireland: The Five Fifths
.29   united states of Scotia Picta
        America
        Ireland: Scotia
        Scotland
.32   Piggott's
        Pigott and Co
.36   Gaul
        Gaul
44.02   fezzy fuzz
        Fez
.04   our maypole
        Maypole
        ?Wellington Monument

.06   old tollgate
        Turnpike
.06   Saint Annona's Street and Church
        ?St. Anne's Church
.11   dub him Llyn
        Dublin
.27   *Mag-a-zine Wall...Mag-a-zine Wall*
        Magazine Fort
45.04 Magazine Wall
        Magazine Fort
.07   the Castle
        Castle, The
.09   Green street
        Green St Courthouse
.10   jail of Mountjoy
        Mountjoy (Prison)
.20   dairyman darling
        ?Derry
.21   bull of the Cassidys
        ?Ballycassidy
46.01 E'erawan
        ?Erewhon
.04   Bargainweg, Lower
        ?Baggot St, Lower
.13   hammerfast
        Hammerfest (Norway)
.14   Eblana bay
        Dublin: Eblana
        Dublin Bay
.18   Poolbeg
        Poolbeg
.18   Cookingha'pence
        Copenhagen
.21—.23 Norveegickers...Norveegickers...
        Norwegian
        Norway
.33   maidenloo
        ?Waterloo
47.07 Wellinton's monument
        Wellington Monument
.21   Scandiknavery
        Scandinavia
.22   Oxmanstown
        Oxmantown
.23   Danes...Danes
        Denmark
.28   Connacht
        Connacht

BOOK I
Chapter 3

48.03 Shanvocht
        Ireland: Shan van Vocht
.03   Blackfriars
        Blackfriars
.05   Humidia
        Ireland: Misc Allusions
        ?Numidia
.10   Inkermann
        Inkerman
.11   St Just
        St Just (Cornwall)
.12   Ste Austelle
        St Austell (Cornwall)
.12   Lucan
        Lucan
.14   *Loch Neach*
        Neagh, Lough
.16   merrymen all
        Magazine Fort
.16   persins
        ?Persia
.16   Eyrawyggla
        Ireland
49.04 Zassnoch!
        England
        ?Uisneach
.05   Crimean war
        Crimea
.07   Tyrone's horse
        ?Tyrone
.07   Irish
        Ireland
.10   Pump Court Columbarium
        Pump Court
.13   field of Vasileff's Cornix
        ?Cornwall
.15   mouther-in-louth
        Louth
        Meath
.18   Dublin Intelligence
        Dublin Intelligencer
.18   Ridley's
        Ridley's
.21   dour decent deblancer
        Dublin: Eblana
        Dublin Allusion: "Dear Dirty
        Dublin"
.24   upsomdowns
        Epsom Downs

.28   Northwegian
         Norway
.29   last...glimt his baring
         Ireland ("Last Glimpse of Erin")
50.03 cockspurt start
         ?Cockspur St (London)
.06   druriodrama
         Drury Lane (London)
.09   French leaves
         France
.17   funster's...finsterest
         Finisterre
.20   Iar-Spain
         Spain
.30   dunhill
         Dun Hill
.34   mix Hotel
         Mick's Hotel
51.08 Slypatrick
         Patrick St
.08   llad in the llane
         Lad Lane
.14   edventyres
         ?Tyre
.19   shrine of Mount Mu
         ?
.22   Battlecock Shettledore-Juxta-Mare
         ?
.24   Loo of Pat
         St Patrick's Cath
.25   sisterisle
         Ireland: Misc Allusions
.25   Meathman
         Meath
.25   Meccan
         Mecca
.26   lucal
         Lucan
.27   clownturkish
         Clonturk
.27   capelist's
         ?Capel St
         Chapelizod
.29   Silurian
         Siluria
.29   Ordovices
         Ordovices
.30   pats' and pigs' older inselt
         Ireland: Pig Island
.30   the stranger stepshore
         Ireland: Misc Allusions

.34   duldrum
         Howth: Doldrum Bay
52.01 Anny Oakley
         ?New Freewoman: Oakley
         House
.03   cork
         ?Cork
.09   Tolkaheim
         Dublin: Misc Allusions
         Tolka
.09   English
         England
.10   Whiddington Wild
         ?
.16   ushere
         ?Usher's Island, Usher's Quay
.25   Kang the Toll
         ?Turnpike: Tollgates
.25   elbaroom
         Elba
53.03 seventyseventh kusin of krist-
         ansen
         Dublin Allusion: Seventh
         City of Christendom
.04   kristansen
         Oslo (Christiania)
.04   os
         ?Os (Norway)
.04   Ere...eerie
         Ireland
.06   tingmount
         Thing Mote
.07   Irish
         Ireland
.08   Christianier
         Oslo (Christiania)
.12   how on the owther
         Howth
.13   eren
         Ireland
.14   Thurston's
         ?
.15   the monolith
         ?Wellington Monument (cf
         54.28)
.17   rowdinoisy
         Rhodes
         Rhone R
.24   lekan
         Lecan
.24   lukan
         Lucan

.28 Eagle Cock Hostel
?Eagle Tavern
.29 Lorenzo Tooley street
Tooley St

The following four names are "God, Mary, Bridget, and Patrick," but also Irish places, out of the usual Ulster-Munster-Leinster-Connacht order.

.30 Gort
Gort (Connacht)
?Gorteen: Gortin (Ulster)
.30 Morya
Moyra (Ulster)
.30 Bri Head
Bray (Head) (Co Wicklow, Leinster, or Co Kerry, Munster)
.30 Puddyrick
Croagh Patrick (Connacht)
Downpatrick (Co Down, Ulster, or Co Mayo, Connacht)
.31 St Tomach's
?St Thomas, Ch of
?Thomas St
54.01 Downaboo
Down (Ulster)
.04 Poolaulwoman...Ann van Vogt
Ireland: Shan van Vocht
.08 Halley's comet
Halley's Comet
.08 ulemamen
Ulema (Moslem "parliament" of scholars)
.08 sobranjewomen
Bulgaria: Sobranje (parliament)
.09 storthingboys
Oslo: Storthing (parliament)
.09 dumagirls
Russia: Duma (parliament)
.10 Casaconcordia
?Hague, The: Palace of Peace
.16 portocallie
?Portugal
.24 moyliffey
Moyliffey
.25 yorehunderts of mamooth
Manhood, Hundred of
.26 British
England
.28 that neighbouring monument's
Wellington Monument

55.03 Ilyam, Ilyum
Troy
.03 Maeromor
Miramar
.04 Mournomates
?Mourne
.04 mundibanks of Fennyana
?
.05 Life
Liffey
.13 custom huts
Custom House
.20 transhibernian
Ireland: Hibernia
Siberia (Transsiberian Railway)
.24 airish chaunting car
Ireland
.26 cladagain
?Claddagh
.28 phoenix in our woodlessness
Phoenix Park
.31 *Irish Field*
Irish Field
.32 Castlebar
Castlebar
.36 orerotundity
?Rotunda
56.04 cockshyshooter's
?Cocytus
.07 Thounawahallya Reef
NPN: *Toun a' mhathsháile*, Ir "Wave of the good salt sea" (O Hehir)
.09 fez
Fez
.12 overgrown leadpencil
Glasnevin: O'Connell Monument
.13 Molyvdokondylon...mausoleum
Glasnevin: O'Connell Monument
.14 tillsteyne
?Steyne
.15 Roland
Ghent: "Roland"
.21 van Demon's Land
Tasmania: Van Dieman's Land
.26 Angel...herberged
Angel

.28   presquesm'ile
       Presque Ile
.35   cudgelplayers' country
       ? (England?)
.35   orfishfellows' town
       ? (Scotland?)
.36   leeklickers' land
       ?Cockaigne
       Wales
.36   panbpanungopovengreskey
       Hungary
57.08 Armagh
       Armagh (Ulster)
.09   Clonakilty
       Clonakilty (Munster)
.09   Deansgrange
       Deansgrange (Leinster)
.10   Barna
       Barna (Connacht)
.11   alplapping streamlet
       Liffey
.13   Hill of Allen
       Allen, Hill of
.13   the Barrow for an People
       Barrow R
.14   Jotnursfjaell
       Jotunfjell
.20   Madam's Toshowus
       Madame Tussaud's Exhibition
       (London)
.21   notional gullery
       National Gallery (London)
.24   Tom Quad
       Oxford U: Christ Church College
.27   maugdleness
       Oxford U: Magdalen College
.31   Ceadurbar-atta-Cleath
       Dublin: Baile Átha Cliath
.32   Dablena Tertia
       Dublin: Eblana
.35   Marlborough Green
       Marlborough Green
.35   Molesworth Fields
       Molesworth Fields
.36   Jedburgh justice
       Jedburgh
58.01 Thing Mod...madthing
       Thing Mote
.08   annuhulation
       Annu
.10   Mannequins pause
       Brussels: Manneken-Pis

.10   Longtong's breach
       London (Br)
.13   ring and sing wohl
       Magazine Fort
.24   saxonlootie
       Saxony (= English)
.25   cockaleak
       Wales
.25   Coldstream. Guards
       Coldstream (Scotland)
.26   Montgomery Street
       Montgomery St
.28   Finner Camps
       NPN? ("Finnegans"?)
.31   ruth redd
       Redruth (Cornwall)
.33   Vauxhall
       Vauxhall (London)
.35   waistend
       West End (London)
.36   cherryderry
       ?Derry
59.01 padouasoys
       Padua

*The following four names are
of shops noted in Peter's Dublin Fragments, 154-55.*

.01   Halfmoon and Seven Stars
       Halfmoon and Seven Stars,
       The
.02   Blackamoor's Head
       Blackamoor's Head, The
.03   Eagle and Child
       Eagle and Child, The
.04   Black and All Black
       Black and All Black
.09   feeatre of the Innocident
       ?
.16   Sevenchurches
       Glendalough: Seven Church-
       es
.17   Achburn...Ashreborn
       ?Ashbourne
.18   Glintalook
       Glendalough
.23   O'Dea's
       ?
60.01 Spilltears Rue
       ?
.01   Dole Line, Death Avenue
       Dole Line

.01 Dole Line, Death Avenue (*Cont.*)
   NYC: Eleventh Ave
.08 done, Drumcollakill
   Dundrum
.08 Drumcollakill
   Dublin: Drom Cuill-Choille
.12 Bawlonabraggat
   Ballynabragget
.14 sahara
   Sahara
.16 sanit Asitas
   Sanità, Via (Trieste)
.22 Cuxhaven
   Cuxhaven
.25 park
   Phoenix Park
.27 Eastrailian
   Australia
.27 Sydney Parade
   Sydney (Australia)
   Sydney Parade
.32 S.S. Smack and Olley's
   Smock Alley Theatre
.35 dirty dubs
   Dublin Allusion: "Dear Dirty
   Dublin"
61.01 una mona
   ?Mona
.02 Doveland
   Dublin
.04 John a'Dream's mews
   ?
.12 Jelsey
   Chelsea
.14 fishshambles
   Fishamble St
.23 Horniman's Hill
   Horniman Museum (London)
.26 blarneys
   Blarney
.27 Keysars Lane
   Keysar's Lane
.36 seventh city
   Dublin Allusion: "Seventh City
   of Christendom"
.36 Urovivla
   Uruvela
62.02 gales of Atreeatic
   Adriatic Sea
.05 Rahoulas
   NPN: Rahula, son of Buddha

.05 ostmen's dirtby on the old vic
   Old Vic
   Oxmantown
.11 Emerald-iliuim
   Ireland: Misc Allusions
   Troy
.16 agora
   Athens: Agora
.19 ere-in-garden
   Ireland
   Wicklow ("Garden of Erin")
.25 Errorland
   Ireland
.26 Amenti
   Amenta
.28 Wednesbury
   Wednesbury
.30 Boore and Burgess Christy Men-
   estrels
   British Broadcasting Corp
.31 Roy's Corner
   Roy's Corner
.35 Lucalizod
   Chapelizod
   Lucan
.35 Glendalough see
   Glendalough
.36 Little Britain
   Britain, Little
63.14 ann...liv
   Liffey
.14 hir newbridge is her old
   Leixlip (Br)
   O'Connell Br
   Whitworth Br
.18 Haveyou-caught-emerod's tem-
   perance gateway
   ?
.21 Irish
   Ireland
.22 hanguest or hoshoe
   ?Hwang Ho R

The following 6 names are of
18th-cent taverns noted in Peter's
Dublin Fragments, *93-96.*
.23 House of Blazes
   House of Blazes, The
.23 Parrot in Hell
   "Hell"
   Parrot, The

.23	Orange Tree		.18	Dubblenn
	Orange Tree, The			Dublin
.24	Glibt		.18	lappish
	Glibb, The			Lapland
.24	the Sun		.19	Maggyer
	Sun, The			Hungary
.24	Holy Lamb		.20	siamixed
	Holy Lamb, The			Siam
.25	Ramitdown's ship hotel		.24	Owen K.
	Ship Hotel and Tavern			Owenkeagh R
.35	the swan		.31	Oetzmann and Nephew
	Swan, The: "The Boots at the			Oetzmann and Co
	Swan"		67.09	gasbag
64.02	norse			Gasometer
	Norway		.09	warderworks
.03	Delandy is cartager			Waterworks
	Carthage		.13	choorch round the coroner
.03	the raglar rock to Dulyn			NYC: Little Church Around
	Dublin Allusion: "Rocky Road			the Corner
	to Dublin"		.13	Norewheezian
.05	land of byelo			?Nore R
	Beulah, Land of			Norway
.09	Mullingcan Inn		.15	querrshnorrt
	Tavern, The: Mullingar House			*Querschnitt, Der*
.09	battering babel		.18	Eastman...Victuallers
	?Babel, Tower of			Eastmans Ltd
.11	belzey babble		.18	Limericked
	?Babel, Tower of			Limerick
.13	martiallawsey marses		.25	meatman's
	Marseilles			Meath
.15	Pompery		.31	hollow heroines
	Pompeii			Phoenix Park: The Hollow
.17	liffopotamus		.33	Lupita Lorette
	Liffey			?Loreto
.19	Rejaneyjailey		.36	Luperca
	Rome: Regina Coeli (Prison)			?Rome: Lupercal
.23	Astrelea...astrollajerries		68.08	coal or an
	Australia			?Coleraine
.24	Keavens pike		.11	coast of emerald
	?Kevin St			?
.25	Pamintul			(just the Irish coast?)
	?Armentières		.13	leinster's
65.15	Peter Robinson			Leinster
	Peter Robinson (London)		.14	Forty Steps
.32	tiptoptippy canoodle			Forty Steps
	Tippecanoe R		.15	Cromwell's Quarters
66.11	Letters Scotch, Limited			Cromwell's Quarters
	Scotland		.29	Phenicia
.17	Edenberry			Phoenicia
	Eden			Phoenix Park
	Edinburgh		.29	Little Asia
				Asia

.30 pobalclock
  ?(Ir, *pobal*, "people," *cloch*,
  "stone")
.30 folksstone
  ?Folkestone
.31 Tomar's Wood
  Clontarf
  Tomar's Wood
69.05 whole of the wall
  Phoenix Park: Hole in the Wall
.06 Gyant Blyant
  ?
.06 Peannlueamoore
  Glasnevin: O'Connell Monument
  ?Wellington Monument
.07 wallhole...Odin
  Phoenix Park: Hole in the Wall
  Valhalla
.08 Aaarlund
  Ireland
.08 Dair's Hair
  ?
.09 Diggin Mosses
  ?
.10 garthen of Odin
  Eden
.10 eddams ended with aves
  ?Adam and Eve's
  Eden
.11 Armen
  ?Armenia
.15 Sorestost Areas, Diseased
  Irish Free State
.15 stonehinged gate
  Stonehenge
.24 iron gape
  ?Iron Gate
.33 Rum and Puncheon
  ?
.34 Dirty Dick's free house
  Dirty Dick's
.34 Laxlip
  Leixlip
.36 Zentral Oylrubber
  Europe
70.01 Osterich
  Austria
.01 U.S.E.
  ?Europe (+ "U.S.A.")
.01 Gaul
  Gaul

.02 wholly romads
  Rome
.04 swobbing
  Swabia
.04 broguen eeriesh
  Ireland
.04 brockendootsch
  Brocken, The (+ "broken
  German")
.05 Frankofurto Siding
  Frankfurt: *Frankfurter Zeitung*
.06 Fastland
  NPN: Dan, *Fastland*, Ger,
  Festland, "continent"
.08 zurichschicken
  Zurich
.12 roebucks
  Roebuck
.15 Bullfoost Mountains
  Belfast
.17 Cloudy Green
  ?
.17 deposend
  ?Posen
.19 houseking's keyhole
  ?Chapelizod: King's House
.23 lankyduckling
  Languedoc
.29 o'connell
  ?Phoenix Brewery: O'Connell's Ale
.30 irsk irskusky
  Ireland: Irsk
.36 ear...Dionysius
  Dionysius's Ear
71.04 wild guineese
  Guinness's Brewery
.07 Milltown
  Milltown
.08 Inkermann
  Inkerman
.09 loo water
  Waterloo
.10 clean turv
  Clontarf
.12 *York's Porker*
  York: Richard III
.12 *Baggotty's Bend*
  Baggot St

.14 *Ireland's Eighth Wonderful Wonder*
     Bank of Ireland

.16 *Hebdromadary Publocation*
     Revue Hebdomadaire

.17 *Blau Clay*
     Dublin: Baile Átha Cliath

.19 *Dook of Ourguile*
     Argyle

.19 *Gibbering Bayamouth of Dublin*
     Dublin Bay

.21 *Burnham and Bailey*
     Bailey Lighthouse
     Burnham Lighthouse

.22 *Waterfood*
     Waterford

.26 *Magogagog*
     Gog and Magog

.29 *Hellena*
     St Helena
     Hell

.29 *Connies*
     Connacht

.30 *Burke's*
     NPN? (not a pub, but Burke's
     Peerage?)

.33 *Clandorf*
     Clontarf

.34 *Lord's Holy Ground*
     Marylebone Cricket Club (Lon-
     don)

.34 *Stodge Arschmann*
     Ireland ("stage Irishman")

72.02 *Bombard Street*
     Lombard St

.02 *Sublime Porter*
     Constantinople: Sublime Porte

.03 *Burgaans*
     ?Belgium

.04 *Ruttledges*
     Russia

.05 *Castlecostello*
     Castlemore

.07 *Fingal*
     Fingal

.07 *in his Falling*
     Ireland: Inisfail

.11 *Armenian Atrocity*
     Armenia

.11 *Edomite*
     Edom

.12 *Irish*
     Ireland

.12 *Bad Humborg*
     Bad Homburg

.14 *Woolworth's Worst*
     NYC: Woolworth Bldg

.14 *Easyathic*
     Asia

.20 Kimmage Outer 17.67
     Kimmage

.24 rowmish devowtion
     Rome

.34 diablen lionndub
     Dublin

73.02 Hyland
     ?Ireland (+ *Heiland*, Ger
     "Saviour")

.05 Mockerloo
     Waterloo

.06 Crumlin
     Crumlin

.06 Gog's
     Gog and Magog

.14 manjester's
     Manchester

.18 falladelfian
     Philadelphia

.18 Hubbleforth
     Dublin: Baile Átha Cliath

.20 duff and demb institutions
     Deaf and Dumb Institution

.21 Patself on the Bach
     NPN?

.23 rochelly
     Rochelle, La
     Rochelle Lane

.23 Bully Acre
     Acre
     Bully's Acre
     Clontarf

.24 our archicitadel
     Castle, The

.26 Bar-le-Duc and Dog-an-Doras
     Bar-le-Duc
     Dog and Duck Tavern

.26 Bangen-op-Zoom
     Bergen-op-Zoom

.28 Oxmanswold
     Oxmantown

.30 coombe
     Coombe, The

.30 eolithostroton
     Stoneybatter

.31 Howth
    Howth
.31 Coolock
    Coolock
.31 Enniskerry
    Enniskerry
.34 stone
    Steyne
74.02 haught
    Thing Mote
.02 valle of briers
    ?
.02 Greenman's Rise
    Green Man
.05 roll, orland, roll
    Ghent: "Roland"
    Jordan R
.09 Truiga
    NPN: "The Green Woods of
    Truiga" is the air of Moore's
    "Silence Is In Our Festal Halls"
.11 Comestowntonobble
    Constantinople
.13 Liverpoor
    Dublin ("Riverpool")
    Liverpool
.15 Fengless
    Finglas (NW Dublin)
.15 Pawmbroke
    Pembroke (SE Dublin)
.15 Chilblaimend
    Kilmainham (SW Dublin)
.16 Baldowl
    Baldoyle (NE Dublin)
.17 Rethfernhim
    Rathfarnham (S Dublin)

BOOK I
Chapter 4

75.01 our teargarten
    Phoenix Park: Zoo
.02 Nile
    Nile R
.02 Arioun
    ?
.03 Marmeniere
    Armentières
.04 sigilposted
    Sihl R
    Zurich: Sihlpost

.14 broadsteyne 'bove citie
    British Broadcasting Corp
    Broadstone Station
    ?Steyne
.15 kingbilly whitehorsed
    White Horse
    William III, Statue of
.16 Finglas
    Finglas
.20 Girahash
    ?
76.01 connemaras
    Connemara
.04 Meadow of Honey
    Clonmel
.04 Mountain of Joy
    Mountjoy
.09 obedience of the citizens...
    Dublin Motto
.11 Pughglasspanelfitted
    Pugh's Glass Factory
.14 thinghowe
    Thing Mote
.21 Moyelta
    Moy
    Moyelta
.21 Lough Neagh...misonesans
    Neagh, Lough
.23 Isle of Man...limniphobes
    Man, Isle of
.24 fairly fishy...handful
    Neagh, Lough
.24 kettlekerry
    Kerry
.25 dear dutchy deeplinns
    Dublin Allusion: "Dear Dir-
    ty Dublin"
.26 troutbeck
    Troutbeck (R)
.32 Donawhu
    Danube R
.34 phallopharos
    ?Pharos at Alexandria
.36 Peurelachasse
    Père Lachaise Cemetery
    (Paris)
77.03 Castlevillainous
    NPN: Cassivellaunus, Brit
    chieftain defeated by Julius
    Caesar.

.14   the Ryan vogt
         Ireland: Shan van Vocht
         Rhine R (*Rhine Vogt*, Dan
           "Watch on Rhine")
.14   Dane to pfife
         Denmark
         Fife
.18   heptarchy of his towerettes
         Tower of London, with the fol-
           lowing 7 individual towers:
         .19 beauchamp
              Beauchamp
         .19 byward
              Byward
         .19 bull
              Bell
         .19 lion
              Lion
         .19 white
              White
         .20 wardrobe
              Wardrobe
         .20 bloodied
              Bloody
.21   hoofd
         ?Howth
.25   Mac Pelah
         Machpelah, Cave of
78.03 whole of the while
         ?Phoenix Park: Hole in the Wall
.04   lethelulled
         Lethe R
.05   Donnaurwatteur
         Danube R
.09   Gehinnon
         Gehenna
.10   Unterwealth
         Unterwelt
.10   sheol om sheol
         Sheol
.11   Uppercrust Sideria of Utilitarios
         Uppercross
.15   heights of Abraham
         Abraham, Plains of
.18   Finntown
         Dublin Allusion: "Finn's Town"
.19   three monads
         Man, Isle of: **"Mona"**
.21   dreyfussed
         Man, Isle of: "Three Legs of
         Man"

.25   both Celtiberian camps
         Ireland: Iberiu
         Spain
.26   New South Ireland
         Ireland
         New Ireland
.27   Vetera Uladh
         Ulster: Ulidia
.27   bluemin
         Blaaland
.27   pillfaces
         Pale, The
.28   letts
         Latvia
79.04 bully on the hill
         Dublin: Misc Allusions
.11   ladderleap
         Leixlip
.15   Danadune
         Dana, Paps of
.28   dreariodreama
         Drury Lane
.29   dumplan
         Dublin
.29   elvanstone
         ?Elphin
.30   moggies' duggies
         Moggy's Alley
.35   gulden dayne
         Denmark
80.02 Bryant's Causeway
         Giant's Causeway
.06   Serpentine
         Serpentine (Phoenix Park)
.06   Phornix Park
         Phoenix Park
.07   Finewell's Keepsacre
         Phoenix Park
.07   Pat's Purge
         St Patrick's Purgatory
.08   butcherswood
         Phoenix Park: Butcher's
           Wood
.09   castlemallards
         NPN: Lord Castlemallard, in
           Le Fanu's *The House by the
           Churchyard*
.20   sprack
         Society for the Propagation
           of Christian Knowledge
.33   Hatchettsbury Road
         Heytesbury St

.36 Issy-la-Chapelle
      ?Aix-la-Chapelle
      Chapelizod
.36 lucans
      Lucan
81.01 viability of vicinals if invisible is
      invincible
      Dublin Motto
.03 Fluminian
      Flaminia, Via
.03 Hannibal's walk
      Alps
.05 mausoleum
      Glasnevin: O'Connell Monu-
      ment
.09 rhedarhoad
      Rhaetia
.09 more boher O'Connell
      Bohermore
      O'Connell St
.11 fane of Saint Fiacre
      St Fiacre (Paris)
.12 howe's
      ?Howth
      ?Thing Mote
.14 saddle of the Brennan's...pass
      ?Brandon Mt
      ?Brenner Pass
.15 Malpasplace
      Malpas
.16 traums halt (Beneathere! Bena-
      there!)
      Howth: Ben Edar
.17 livland
      Livland
.18 cropatkin
      Croagh Patrick
.28 patrecknocksters
      Knockpatrick
.31 oblong bar
      ?Dublin Bar
.33 Nippoluono
      Japan (+ Napoleon)
.34 Wei-Ling-Taou
      (pseudo-Chinese "Wellington")
82.03 tipperuhry
      Ruhr
      Tipperary
.03 Swede
      Sweden
.19 christchurch
      Christchurch Cathedral

.22 knobkerries
      Kerry
83.03 J. J. and S.
      Jameson, John, and Son
.08 sheol
      Sheol
.09 lux apointlex
      NPN: "Lux upon Lux," see
      Louth.
.17 Dun Bank pearlmothers
      Red Bank
.19 Ruadh Cow
      Red Cow
.19 Tallaght
      Tallaght
.19 Good Woman
      Good Woman, The
.20 Ringsend
      Ringsend
.20 Conway's Inn
      Conway's Tavern
.20 Blackrock
      Blackrock
.22 Adam and Eve's
      Adam and Eve's
.22 Quantity Street
      NPN? J M Barrie's *Quality*
      Street
.23 gamy queen Tailte
      Teltown: Tailteann Games
.28 German grit
      Germany
.30 friend's
      France
.31 French
      France
.34 hillelulia...allenalaw
      Allen, Hill of
.34 killelulia
      Killala
      Killaloe
.35 schmallkalled...treatyng
      Schmalkalden (Treaty)
.36 cognac
      Cognac (Treaty)
.36 fez
      Fez
.36 menialstrait
      Menai Strait
84.01 Moscas
      Mecca
      Moscow

.02   levanted
         Levant
.02   tubular
         Menai Strait: Tubular Br
.02   bull's run
         Bull Run
         Bulls, North and South
.03   assback bridge
         Menai Strait: Suspension Br
.04   danegeld
         Denmark
.07   rialtos
         Rialto (Bridge)
.07   Pearidge
         Pea Ridge
.08   Littlehorn
         Little Big Horn
.09   ballsbluffed
         Ball's Bluff
.15   nobiloroman
         Rome
.15   conclusium
         Clusium
.18   watchhouse in Vicar Lane
         Vicar St
.27   a whit the whorse
         White Horse
         ?Whitworth Bridge
.31   bank
         ?Bank of Ireland
.31   Dublin stone
         Dublin
         Steyne
.31   olympiading
         Olympia
85.07   pacific
         Pacific O
.08   British
         England
.09   semitary thrufahrts
         ?
.10   Wellington Park road
         Wellington Rd
.11   auxter...redhand
         Ulster
.11   alpenstuck
         Alps
.15   Butt's...bridges
         Butt Br
.15   blackpool
         ?Blackpool (England)
         Dublin: Dubh-linn

.20   atlantic
         Atlantic O
.20   Phenitia Proper
         Phoenicia
         Phoenix Park
.23   Maam
         Maam (Co Mayo)
.25   Mayo of the Saxons
         Mayo of the Saxons
         Saxony
.26   Old Bailey
         ?Bailey Lighthouse
         Old Bailey (London)
.35   corkscrew
         ?Cork
.36   cymtrymanx bespokes
         Man, Isle of
         Wales
.36   mamertime
         Rome: Carcer (Mamertine)
         Prison
86.01   royal Irish vocabulary
         Ireland (Royal Irish Constab-
         ulary)
.04   Alum on Even
         Adam and Eve's
.06   coold raine
         Coleraine
.09   any luvial
         Liffey
.10   clanetourf
         Clane
         Clontarf
.11   Mudford
         Dublin: Baile Átha Cliath
.15   sea by the plain of Ir
         Ireland: (+ Ir, son of Miled)
         Moyle, Sea of
.20   Irish Angricultural and Prepos-
         toral Ouraganisations
         Irish Agricultural Organisa-
         tion Society
.21   Irish muck
         Ireland: Pig Island
.22   brother dane
         Denmark
.24   scattery kind
         Scattery Island
.24   ballybricken
         ?Balbriggan
         Waterford: Ballybricken

.29   struggle Street
       ?

.29   *Troia*
       Troy

.29   hiss or lick
       Troy: Hissarlik

.34   Nullnull
       NPN? "OO" is Ger symbol for
       a public toilet.

.34   Medical Square
       NPN? "Square," colloq for a
       latrine or toilet.

87.08   Tournay
       Tournay

.08   Yetstoslay
       ?

.08   Temorah
       Temora

.14   Gaeltact
       NPN, but any area where Ir is
       spoken as the common lan-
       guage

.15   bullycassidy...friedhoffer
       Ballycassidy
       Bully's Acre

.18   unlucalised
       Chapelizod
       Lucan

.19   wallops
       Wallop Fields

.20   Mise of Lewes
       Lewes

.21   boer's...bull
       Clontarf
       Clonturk
       (+ Boer War, John Bull)

.24   meace...meathe
       Meath

.25   congsmen
       Cong

.25   arans
       Aran Islands

.25   dalkeys
       Dalkey (Island)

.26   mud
       Mud Island

.26   tory
       Tory Island

.26   Killorglin
       Killorglin

.28   Carrothagenuine
       Carthage

.29   Isod's towertop
       Chapelizod
       Isod's Tower

.30   macdublins
       Dublin

.31   bohernabreen
       Bohernabreena

.31   Banagher
       Banagher

.33   Deadman's Dark Scenery Court
       NPN: London street game,
       "Dead Man's Dark Scene-
       ry"

88.01   Waterhose's Meddle Europeic
       Time
       Europe
       Waterhouse and Co

.01   Stop and Think
       ?

.05   basel to boot
       Basle

.22   Saxon
       Saxony

.23   Yggdrasselmann
       Yggdrasil

.24   Eiffel...phoenix
       Eiffel Tower
       Phoenix Park: Wellington
       Monument

.26   auza de Vologue
       ?

.27   Vuncouverers Forests
       Vancouver Foresters

.30   aleland
       Ireland

.31   Long's gourgling barral...gargling
       bubbles
       Gougane Barra

.33   five lamps
       Five Lamps

.33   Portterand's praise
       Portland Row (?Place)

.34   laving...leaftime
       Liffey

.34   Blackpool
       ?Blackpool (England)
       Dublin: Dubh-linn

.35   Tem...time...anytom
       Tib and Tom

89.07   Rooskayman
       ?Roosky
       Roscommon

.07　Gallwegian
　　　Galway
.10　ajaciulations
　　　Corsica: Ajaccio
.10　Crosscann Lorne
　　　Corsica
　　　?Cross Guns
.11　corso...cursu...coarser again
　　　Corsica
.12　yellowatty on the forx
　　　Yellow Ford
.17　dtheir gcourts marsheyls
　　　Marshalsea

*.18　Riddle: "Londonderry, Cork and
Kerry, spell me that without an 'R'."
　　　Answer: "T–H–A–T."*

.18　Lindendelly
　　　Derry (Ulster)
.18　coke
　　　Cork (Munster)
.19　skilllies
　　　Kerry
　　　Skerries (Leinster)
.19　gart
　　　Gort (Connacht)
.24　maundarin tongue
　　　China
　　　Tuscany
.25　pounderin jowl
　　　Ireland
　　　Rome
.27　No answer
　　　Albert Nyanza
.27　No ah
　　　Victoria Nyanza
.28　danzzling
　　　?Danzig
.35　ital
　　　Italy
.36　hankowchaff
　　　Hankow
90.05　king's head
　　　King's Head
.05　republican's arms
　　　?
.10　bettygallaghers
　　　Katty Gollogher
.10　soords
　　　?Swords
.13　Angel's
　　　Angel

.13　Guinney's Gap
　　　?Ginnunga Gap
　　　Guinness's Brewery
.17　Saturn's mountain fort
　　　Saturn (+ "Slattery's Mount-
　　　ed Foot")
.21　whole in the wall
　　　Phoenix Park: Hole in the
　　　Wall
.24　Multifarnham
　　　Monte Carlo
　　　Multyfarnham
.26　Roebuckdom
　　　Roebuck
.27　yappanoise
　　　Japan
.31　–moecklenburgwh–[in C-word]
　　　Mecklenburgh St
.34　Oincuish!
　　　Ireland: Oinciu
.36　punic
　　　Carthage
91.07　king's commons
　　　Four Courts
.08　Dundalgan
　　　Dundalk
.19　pleas bench
　　　Four Courts
.20　Jury's
　　　Jury's Hotel (+ "juries")
.20　Masterers
　　　NPN: "Master," a court offi-
　　　cer
.22　Dublin
　　　Dublin
.22　coddling
　　　?Codling Lightship
.22　Inishman
　　　Aran Islands: Inishmaan
　　　?Ireland
　　　Man, Isle of
.23　cantonnatal
　　　?Canton
　　　?Natal
　　　(+ "continental")
.25　Tyre-nan-Og
　　　Tir na nOg
　　　?Tyre
.30　Warhorror
　　　Valhalla
.30　exchequered
　　　Four Courts

.31   chancery
      Four Courts
.34   castleknocker's
      Castle, The
      Castleknock
92.01 Castilian
      Castle, The
      Spain
.06   Pegger's Windup
      ?
.07   Wet Pinter's
      ?West Point
.11   antipathies
      Antipodes
.18   Oirisher Rose
      Ireland: Little Dark Rose
.26   Makegiddyculling Reeks
      McGillycuddy's Reeks
.35   four justicers
      Four Courts
93.02 English
      England
.03   scotfree
      Scotland
.05   britgits
      Ireland
.06   Switz bobbyguard's
      Switzerland
      Vatican
.07   firewaterloover
      Waterloo
.08   rawdownhams
      ?Rathdown
      Rhodes
      Rhone R
.14   Parish Poser
      ?Paris
.16   Drinkbattle's Dingy Dwellings
      ?Inkbottle House
.18   Bottome...dun
      Woovil Doon Botham
.27   dark Rosa Lane
      Ireland: Little Black Rose
.28   Coogan Barry
      Gougane Barra
.30   Suffering Dufferin
      Ireland
.33   Op. 2 Phil Adolphos
      Philadelphia
94.01 greene...gretnass
      Gretna Greene

.03   Moate
      Moate
.14   Danaides
      Greece
.24   judges' chambers
      Four Courts
.25   muniment room
      City Hall: Muniment Room
.25   marshalsea
      Marshalsea
.28   Accourting...king's evelyns
      King's Inns
.31   four...court
      Four Courts
95.02 Minster York
      York: York Minster
.02   Ballybock manure works
      Ballybough
.03   O'Moyly
      Moyle, Sea of
.04   O'Briny rossies
      Brie
.08   gasometer
      Gasometer
.10   dear divorcee darling
      Dublin Allusion: "Dear Dir-
      ty Dublin"
.11   our isle's cork float
      Cork
.14   Kay Wall
      North Wall Quay
.15   Whiteside
      ?
.18   Lankyshied
      Lancaster
.21   Sycomore Lane
      Sycamore St
.36   Nunsbelly Square
      ?
96.01 rose...darik
      Ireland: Little Black Rose
.03   rhyme
      Rome
.07   the old house by the churpelizod
      Chapelizod: The House by
      the Churchyard
.10   Milton's Park
      Milltown (Park)
.14   meeting waters
      Meeting of the Waters
.16   used her
      Ulster

.16   mused her
       Munster
.17   licksed her
       Leinster
.17   cuddled
       Connacht

The fox hunt (with HCE [= Parnell] as the fox) described in 97.02 ff takes place in Co Meath near Ratoath, beginning in the parish of Ratoath and moving through the parishes of Kilbride and Dunshaughlin. The names are those of townlands.

97.02   holt outratted
        Ratoath
.03   Juletide's genial corsslands
        ?
.03   Humfries Chase
        ?
.03   Mullinahob
        Mullinahob
.04   Peacockstown
        Peacockstown
.04   Tankardstown
        Tankardstown
.07   Raystown
        Raystown
.07   Horlockstown
        Harlockstown
.08   Tankardstown
        Tankardstown
.08   for doubling
        Dublin
.09   Cheeverstown
        Cheeverstown
.10   Loughlinstown
        Loughlinstown
.10   Nutstown
        Nuttstown
.10   Boolies
        Boolies
.11   Ye Hill of Rut
        ?Rath Hill
        Rutland Square
.33   Saturnalia
        Saturn
.34   Forum
        Rome: The Forum
.35   Yardstated
        Scotland Yard

98.01   hundred of manhood
        Manhood, Hundred of
.05   sidleshomed
        Sidlesham
.07   Arsa
        ?
.07   S.S. Finlandia
        Finland
.10   Asia Major
        Asia
.10   Turk
        Turkey
.11   theater...king
        Gaiety Theatre
.16   saggarth
        ?Saggart
.19   vicious circle
        Vico Rd
.22   buoyant waters
        Boyne R
.24   Umbrella Street
        ?
.28   Dub's
        Dublin
.30   Cope
        Cope St
.31   Bull
        Bull Alley
.31   Bull...Cassidy
        ?Ballycassidy
.31   rome and reme
        Rome
99.03   Guinnesses
        Guinness's Brewery
.12   bloody antichill cloak
        ?Dublin: Baile Átha Cliath
.13   V.P.H.
        ?Victoria Palace Hotel
.13   Scaldbrothar's Hole
        Scaldbrother's Hole
.26   Breffnian empire
        Breffny
.26   hill of Tullymongan
        Tullymongan
.27   rayheallach royghal
        Breffny
        Reilig na Riogh
.29   fidd of Verdor
        ?
.30   dexter handcoup...bloody proper
        Ulster: Red Hand

.32 clontarfminded
    Clontarf
.33 O'Roarke
    Breffny
.34 D. Blayncy's
    Dublin: Eblana
100.01 Transocean
    transition
.03 lack of lamentation
    Leman, Lac
.04 Bartholoman's Deep
    Bartholomew Deep
.06 Paisdinernes
    Ireland
.06 Lochlanner
    Lochlann
.07 Fiounnisgehaven
    Dublin Allusion: "Finn's
    Town"
    Phoenix Park (Ir, *fionn-*
    uisce)
.07 Bannalanna
    ?Bann R
    (+ *Bean na leanna*, Ir "ale-
    woman")
.07 Ballyhooly
    Ballyhooly
.08 Bullavogue
    Boleyvogue
.13 Parteen-a-lax Limestone. Road
    Parteen
.15 infallible...smoke's
    Vatican
.16 seventh gable
    House of the Seven Gables,
    The
.17 porphyroid buttertower
    Tours de Beurre
.23 fineglass
    Finglas
.30 dode canal
    Dodecanese
101.06 ards and downs
    Down: Baronies of the Ards
.11 Lucalizod
    Chapelizod
    Lucan
.18 Dublin Wall
    Dublin
.23 three castles
    Castle, The
    Dublin Coat of Arms

.24 queen's head
    ?Queen's Head (+ postage
    stamp)
.27 holenpolendom
    ?Poland
.29 upper reaches of her mouthless
    face
    Niger R
.35 hungray
    Hungary
102.07 Pearlfar sea
    ?
.13 Parisienne's
    Paris
.16 Esquoro
    Basque: Eskuara
.17 biskbask
    Basque
.18 *Notre Dame de la Ville*
    ?
103.01 *Island Bridge*
    Island Bridge
    Trinity Church (song)
.08 naaman
    Na'aman R
.08 Jordan
    Jordan R
.11 waters of babalong
    Babylon

BOOK I

Chapter 5

104.01 Annah the Allmaziful
    ?Amazon R
.06 *Augusta...Seabeastius'*
    ?Sevastopol
.06 *Rockabill Booby*
    Rockabill Lighthouse
.12 *to Morra*
    ?Temora
.13 *Flee Chinx*
    China
.14 *Hibernicis*
    Ireland: Hibernia
.14 *Britoness*
    England
.18 *Porthergill*
    Portugal
.20 *Cleopater's Nedlework*
    Cleopatra's Needle

.20 *Aldborougham on the Sahara*
    ?Aldborough House
    Sahara
.21 *Coombing*
    Coombe
.22 *Aegypt*
    Egypt
105.01 *Venice*
    Venice
.02 *Chiltern*
    ?Chiltern (Hundreds)
.02 *Oremunds Queue*
    Ormond Quay
.02 *Amen Mart*
    ?Amen Close
.05 *House with the Golden Stairs*
    ?
.06 *O'Jerusalem*
    Jerusalem
.07 *Po*
    Po R
.07 *Stream of Zemzem*
    Mecca: Well of Zemzem
.07 *Zigzag Hill*
    ?
.08 *the Marlborry Train*
    ?(there was never a tram on
    Marlborough St)
.10 *Dantsigirls*
    ?Danzig
.11 *Extorreor Monolothe*
    ?
.14 *Victrolia Nuancee*
    Victoria Nyanza
.14 *Allbart Noahnsy*
    Albert Nyanza
.18 *Hear Hubty Hublin*
    Dublin Allusion: "Dear Dir-
    ty Dublin"
.18 *My Old Dansh*
    Denmark
    Netherlands
.20 *Dual of Ayessha*
    Asia
.21 *Lapps*
    Lapland
.21 *Finns*
    Finland
.22 *Rush*
    ?Rush
.23 *Dudge Pupublick*
    Netherlands

.23 *Fall of the Potstille*
    Bastille
.25 *The Tortor of Tory Island*
    Tory Island
.26 *Abbeygate*
    Abbey Theatre
    Gate Theatre
.27 *Crowalley...Smocks*
    Crow St Theatre
    Smock Alley Theatre
.29 *Waherlow*
    Aherlow, Glen of
    Waterloo
.32 *Gage Street*
    ?
.35 *Twelve Acre Terriss*
    ?
.36 *Unique Estates of Amessican*
    America
106.01 *Wide Torsos*
    White Horse
.02 *White Donogh*
    White Horse: O'Donohue
.04 *Norsker Torsker*
    Norway
.05 *Poddle*
    Poddle R
.08 *Inglo-Andean Medoleys*
    Andes Mts
    England
    India (+ Moore's "Irish Melo-
    dies")
.08 *Tommany Moohr*
    ?NYC: Tammany Hall
    ?Tommen-y-mur
.09 *Polynesional*
    Polynesia
.12 *Stitchioner's Hall*
    Stationers Hall
    ?Tailors' Hall
.16 *La Belle Sauvage*
    Belle Sauvage, La
.17 *Douchka*
    ?Douce, Mt
.17 *Marianne*
    ?France: "Marianne"
.17 *Fingallians*
    ?Fingal
.18 *Stork Exchange*
    Stock Exchange
.19 *His Customs*
    Custom House

.19   *China*
    China
.20   *Pimpimp Pimpimp*
    ?Jameson, Pim and Co
.22   *Spreadeagles*
    Spread Eagle
.24   *Seen Aples*
    Naples
.26   *Delvin*
    Delvin R
.26   *Life*
    Liffey
.30   *Allfor Guineas,...Libidous*
    Guinness's Brewery
.33   *Manorlord Hoved*
    Howth
.35   *the Colleagues on the Green*
    College Green
107.05   *Lucalizod*
    Chapelizod
    Lucan
.14   Oriolopos
    ?Orion
.36   hallhagal
    Hell
108.15   Scotch spider
    Scotland
.15   Elberfeld's
    Elberfeld
.19   Carrageehouse
    ?Carrigeen
.26   Siam
    Siam
.26   Hell
    Hell
.26   Tophet
    Tophet
.27   Aludin's Cove
    Aladdin's Cave
109.06   Fung Yang
    Fengyang
110.04   the clovery kingdom
    China ("Flowery Kingdom")
    Ireland: Misc Allusions
.05   middlesins people
    China ("Middle Kingdom")
.06   Sainge
    ?
.08   Isitachapel-Asitalukin
    Chapelizod
    Lucan

.09   madh vaal of tares
    ?Maida Vale
    ?Moyvalley
.11   tamelised
    ?Tamil
.11   Drainophilias
    NPN: *Drainafilia*, Albanian
     "rose"
.11   where the possible was the improb-
    able...
    Dublin: Misc Allusions
.23   kischabrigies
    Dublin ("wickerbridge"; *cis*, Ir
     "wicker")
.26   dump for short
    Dublin: Misc Allusions
.27   orangery
    ?Orangerie
.33   a strate that was called strete
    Straight St
.35   Ardagh chalice
    Ardagh
.36   Tipperaw raw
    Tipperary
111.01   Now Sealand
    New Zealand
    Zealand (Sealand)
.06   Cheepalizzy's
    Chapelizod
.09   Boston (Mass.)
    Boston
.17   twoinns
    Tavern, The: Mullingar House
     and Bridge Inn
.18   whollyisland
    Ireland: Misc Allusions
.23   Irish
    Ireland
112.07   Zingari shoolerim
    Zingari Cricket Club
.30   teasy dear
    Trinity College, Dublin (TCD)
.32   *Notre Dame du Bon Marché*
    Bon Marché (Paris)
.33   heart of Arin
    Ireland
    (+ *ari*, Albanian "gold")
113.02   postmantuam
    Mantua
    Tuam
.02   lapins...grigs
    Greece

.02 lapins...grigs (*Cont.*)
    Rome
.03 almeanium
    Armenia
.05 dmzn!
    ?Amazon R
.08 outerrand
    ?Witwatersrand
.12 schwrites
    ?Switzerland
.18 dapple inn
    Dublin
    Tavern, The: Mullingar
    House and Bridge Inn
.19 Mons held by tentpegs
    Mons
    Waterloo: Mont St Jean
    (+ Gulliver)
.20 whatholoosed
    Waterloo
.21 Genoaman
    Genoa
.21 Venis
    Venice
.26 straight turkey
    Turkey
114.04 Nemzes
    Germany
.04 Bukarahast
    Bucharest
.05 Maliziies
    Asia Minor
.05 Bulgarad
    Belgrade
    Bulgaria
.12 shillelagh
    Shillelagh
.25 Dalbania
    Albania
    Dublin
    ?Scotland ("Albania")
.25 portogal
    Portugal
.36 battle of the Boyne
    Boyne R
115.11 Tiberias
    Tiberias
116.11 corknered
    ?Cork
.13 Dumbil's fair city
    Dublin Allusion: "Dublin's
    Fair City"

.15 down swords
    Swords
.15 oldowth guns
    Howth
.17 parks...fornix
    Phoenix Park
.18 makeussin wall
    Magazine Fort
.23 hell's hate
    Hell
.26 basically English
    England
117.04 iordenwater
    Jordan R
.06 hell's well
    Hell
.15 strassarab
    Arabia
.15 ereperse
    Ireland: Erse
.19 talkatalka
    ?Tolka
.24 Nieuw Amsteldam
    Amsterdam
    New York City
.24 Paoli's where the poules go
    ?Hamburg: Sankt Pauli
.25 sooth american
    South America
.31 dutchy hovel
    Netherlands
.34 wee free state
    Irish Free State
118.02 Irish daily independence
    Irish Independent
.13 Coccolanius or Gallotaurus
    Cock Lane
.18 Soferim Bebel
    Babel, Tower of (+ *sopherim*,
    Heb "scribes")
.32 rest thankful
    ?Edinburgh: "Rest and Be
    Thankful"
119.16 tiberiously
    Tiberias
.23 Cathay
    China
.24 siangchang
    Siang-chang-kiang
.25 hongkong
    Hong Kong

.27 village inn
?

.28 upsidown bridge
?

.30 bucker's field
?

.31 allblind alley
?

.32 Irish plot
?
Ireland

.32 Champ de Mors
Champ de Mars

120.19 Greek ees
Greece

.20 Athens
Athens

.23 Etruscan
Etruria

.29 muddy terranean
Mediterranean Sea

121.05 basque of bayleaves
Basque Provinces
?Biscay, Bay of

.12 *Aranman*
Aran Islands

.14 Aran man
Aran Islands

.20 serpentine
?Serpentine

.23 corkhorse
?Cork

122.08 redhandedly
?Ulster: Red Hand

.12 Roe's Distillery
Roe's Distillery

.23 Book of Kells
Kells

123.10 meandering
?Meander R

.14 Chromophilomos, Limited
?

.25 Punic admiralty report
Phoenicia

.27 dodecanesian baedeker
Dodecanese

.30 Tiberiast duplex
Tiberias

124.07 singleminded men's asylum
?St Patrick's Hospital

.08 Yard inquiries
Scotland Yard

.14 ire
Ireland

.17 Cockspur Common
?Cockspur St (London)

.19 plain English
England

.24 Pratiland
Ireland: Misc Allusions

.30 Kvinnes country
Laois (Queen's County)

.33 fox and geese
Fox and Geese

.34 *L'Auberge du Père Adam*
Eden

.35 Jeromesolem
Jerusalem

.35 Huffsnuff
?Ephesus

.36 Andycox
Antioch

.36 Olecasandrum
Alexandria

125.01 R.Q.
?

.03 oceanic
Oceania (+ "Ossianic")

.04 Tulko MacHooley
?Tolka

.15 cheeks
Greece

.17 Essex bridge
Essex Br

.20 Bruisanose
Oxford U: Brasenose College

BOOK I
Chapter 6

126.05 Jhon Jhamieson and Song
Jameson, John, and Son

.12 Wellingtonia Sequoia
?Wellington Monument

.13 liffeyette
Liffey

.15 esker
Esker

.15 hooth
Howth

.16 hullender's
Netherlands

.21 wartrey
Vartry R

.22	boyne		.03	Megalopolis
	Boyne R			Megalopolis
.22	hungery		.09	underground
	?Hungary			Underground (London)
.24	Hirish		.12	pinkun's
	Ireland			*Sporting Times*
.24	Cornish		.13	Pale
	Cornwall			Pale, The
127.06	billbailey		.14	Anna Livia
	Bailey Lighthouse			Liffey
.10	F.E.R.T.		.16	notion of shopkeepers
	Rhodes			England
.11	outharrods		.17	three caskles
	Harrods Ltd (London)			Dublin Coat of Arms
.11	barkers			Three Castles
	Barker, John, and Co (London)		.18	strombolist
				Stromboli
.11	shoolbred		.22	metro for the polis
	Shoolbred's Dept Store (London)			Métropolitain (Paris)
			.23	hoved by
.12	whiteley			Howth
	Whiteley's Dept Store (London)		.32	all khalassal
				?St Patrick's Cathedral
.13	germhuns		.35	phoenix
	Germany			Phoenix Park
.15	eddistoon		.35	pelium
	Eddystone Lighthouse			Pelion, Mt
.18	booseworthies		.36	ossas
	Bosworth Field			Ossa, Mt
.26	Sahara		.36	pilluls of hirculeads
	Sahara			Pillars of Hercules
.26	oxhide on Iren		129.01	wurstmeats
	Ireland (+ "oxide of iron")			Westmeath
.28	banck of Indgangd		.01	cowcarlows
	Bank of England			Carlow
.29	chapel exit		.04	Cattermole Hill
	Chapelizod			?Cahermohill
.29	franks			"Cattermole" Hill
	France		.09	canyouseehim
.31	Morgen's			Rome: Coliseum
	Morgan, Mrs Joseph (Hatter)		.09	hatched at Cellbridge
.33	the Head			Celbridge
	?			Hazelhatch
.33	Rump		.10	beguinnengs
	?			?Big Gun (+ Guinness)
.33	Early English		.12	Danes
	England			Denmark
.35	wellworthseeing		.16	emillian via
	NYC: Woolworth Bldg			Aemilia, Via
128.01	Benn of all bells		.16	no street hausmann
	Big Ben			Haussmann, Boulevard (Paris)

.17 allphannd
Alphand, Rue (Paris)
.17 andies
Andes Mts
.17 alleghant
Allegheny Mts
.20 dub...limn
Dublin
.23 pigeonheim
?Pigeonhouse, The

The following 7 names conflate
Dublin suburbs (the first 4 are S of the
Liffey, the last 3 N of the Liffey) with
the 7 cities each of which in anc times
was claimed as the birthplace of Homer.
Cf 481.21–.22.

.23 Smerrnion
Merrion
Smyrna
.23 Rhoebok
Roebuck
Rhodes
.24 Kolonsreagh
Clonskeagh
Colophon
.24 Seapoint
Seapoint
Salamis
.24 Quayhowth
Howth
Chios
.24 Ashtown
Ashtown
Argos
.24 Ratheny
Raheny
Athens
.26 Rome
Rome
.27 Illbelpaese
Italy
.27 Iceland's ear
Iceland
Ireland's Eye
.32 Africa
Africa
.34 Aryania
Iran: Airyana
Ireland
.34 Suiss family Collesons
Switzerland

.34 *les nouvelles roches*
Alps
130.03 yeladst glimse of Even
?Eden
Ireland ("Last Glimpse of
Erin")
.04 Lug
?Lugnaquilla, Mt
.04 Luk
?Luke's Mt
.07 Advent Lodge
?
.08 New Yealand
New Zealand
.11 phoenished a borgiess
Phoenix Park
.13 buttle of the bawn
Boyne R
.19 earish
Ireland

The following two lines name 6
Dublin bridges (none of them over the
Liffey):

.20 rialtos
Rialto (Br)
.21 annesleyg
Annesley (Br)
.21 binn
Binns's Br
.21 balls
Ballsbridge
.21 atolk
Tolka (Br)
.21 New Comyn
Newcomen Br
.24 Barnehulme
Borneo
Bornholm
.27 twenty four or so cousins
Dublin, Georgia
.28 cousins germinating
Germany
.28 United States of America
America
.29 namesake...Poland
Lublin (Poland)
Poland
.30 French-Egyptian
Egypt
France
Nile R (Fr, *Nil*)

.31   whole...Christie's
     Christie's
     Dublin ("young rose":
      "bud"; "French-Egyptian":
      "Nil")

.33   buyshop of Glintylook
     Glendalough

.33   eorl of Hoed
     Howth

.34   you and I...bldns
     Dublin (dUblIns)

.34   Elin's flee polt
     Ireland (Dublin)

.35   Hwang Chang
     Peking: Hwang Cheng

131.01   Mount of Mish
     Slieve Mish

.01   Mell of Moy
     Mell of Moy
     Moy R

.04   T.C.H.
     ?Toc H

.05   topperairy
     Tipperary

.06   dirty...dear
     Dublin Allusion: "Dear Dir-
     ty Dublin"

.07   hoveth
     ?Howth

.08   two mmany
     NYC: Tammany Hall

.09   parisites
     Paris

.09   Tiara
     Tara

.10   scones...Liam Fail
     Lia Fáil: Stone of Scone

.10   Westmunster
     Munster
     Westminster

.12   demask us
     Damascus

.13   Buddapest
     Budapest

.13   aspenstalk
     Alps (alpenstock)

.14   living a fire
     Liffey

.23   Mora and Lora...hill
     Lora
     Mora

.26   lakemist of Lego
     Lego (Lake)

.28   morvenlight
     Morven

.34   Chinchin
     China

.35   Taishantyland
     ?Ashanti
     T'ai Shan (Mt)

132.01   Raggiant Circos
     Regent Circus
     Regent's Park

.02   amirican
     America

.04   Baddersdown
     Batterstown
     ?Booterstown

.06   Camlenstrete
     Camden St
     Camlan

.12   whitehorse hill
     White Horse

.21   Raglan Road
     Raglan Rd

.22   Marlborough Place
     Marlborough Place

.22   Cromlechheight and Crommalhill
     Lubar R: Cromleach and
     Crommal

.23   lurch as lout
     ?Louth

.24   Lubar
     Lubar R

.24   mareschalled
     ?Marshalsea

.24   wardmotes
     Wardmote

.26   Banba
     Ireland: Banba

.27   Beurla
     England (Ir, "English")

.27   Colossus
     ?Colossus of Rhodes

.29   Gran Turco
     Grand Turk Island

.29   lachsembulger, leperlean
     ?Leixlip
     Luxembourg

.30   the sparkle...benevolence
     Crampton's Monument

.32   our tribal tarnpike
     Turnpike

.33   partitioned Irskaholm
        Ireland

.34   united Irishmen
        Ireland

133.02   you rope
        Europe

.02   Amrique
        America

.06   Riesengebirger
        Riesengebirge

.28   boys of wetford
        Wexford

.28   indanified
        Denmark

.29   brigstoll
        ?Bristol
        Tavern, The: Bridge Inn

.35   Allthing
        Iceland: Althing

.36   Dee mouth
        Dee R

134.01   Baulacleeva
        Balaclava
        Dublin: Baile Átha Cliath

.01   eldorado
        El Dorado

.01   ultimate thole
        Thule

.15   stars of the plough
        Ursa Major: the Plough

.15   province of the pike
        ?

.16   Eelwick
        ?

.16   vicous cicles
        ?Vico Rd

.18   Portobello
        Portobello

.19   softclad shellborn
        ?Shelbourne Hotel

.20   earned in
        Erne St
        Erning St

.20   Watling Street
        Watling St

.21   land of younkers
        Tír na nOg
        Yonkers

.22   Apostolopolos
        ?

.22   gale of his gall
        ?Gaul

.26   frankeyed
        ?France

.35   Theban
        Thebes (Egypt)

135.01   cornerwall
        Cornwall

.02   furry...hawthorns
        Phoenix Park: Furry Glen

.06   annacrwatter
        ?Anna Carter Br

.08   Pimploco
        Pimlico

.08   Dutchlord, Dutchlord
        Germany

.09   Headmound, king and martyr
        St Edmund, King and Martyr
        (London)

.09   dunstung in the Yeast
        St Dunstan-in-the-East (London)

.10   Pitre-le-Pore-in Petrin
        Prague: Petrin Hill
        St Peter-le-Poer (London)

.10   Barth-the-Grete-by-the-Exchange
        St Bartholomew-by-the-Exchange (London)
        St Bartholomew the Great (London)

.11   dames troth
        Dame St

.12   prince of Orange and Nassau
        Nassau St
        Orange
        William III, Statue of

.12   trinity
        Trinity College, Dublin

.13   brow of a hazelwood
        Dublin: Drom Cuill-Choille

.14   pool in the dark
        Dublin: Dubh-linn

.14   blowicks into bullocks
        Bullock Castle

.15   well of Artesia...bird of Arabia
        Arabia
        Phoenix Park ("foinn-uisce" into "Phoenix")

.16   exprussians
        Persia
        Prussia

.17   herospont
        Hellespont
        O'Connell Br

.18   pleasant little field
          Glasnevin (Cemetery)
.18   yldist kiosk on the pleninsula
          Constantinople: Yildiz
          Kiosk
          ?Howth (Castle)
.19   unguest hostel in Saint Scholar-
          land
          ?Howth (Castle)
          Ireland: Misc Allusions
.21   fifteen acres
          Phoenix Park: Fifteen Acres
.22   little white horse
          White Horse
.23   Mairie Quai
          America
.25   Ostenton
          Oxmantown
.27   upright one
          ?Wooden Man
.28   ebblanes
          Dublin: Eblana
.29   Hewitt Castello...Rhoda Dun-
          drums
          Howth (Castle, and rhodo-
          dendrons)
.31   Dundrums
          Dundrum
.36   saggarts
          ?Saggart
136.01 sonogog
          Gog and Magog
.01   Dilmun
          Dilmun
.02   Mudlin
          Dublin
.08   Ostrov
          Ostrov (Russ, "island")
.08   Inferus
          Mare Inferus
.08   Mabbul
          NPN: Heb, "flood"
.09   Moyle
          Moyle, Sea of
.11   a house, Uru
          ?
.15   Osterich
          ?Austria
.20   dire dreary darkness
          Dublin Allusion: "Dear Dir-
          ty Dublin"

.21   Tortur
          ?
.22   puffing...doffing
          Guinness's Brewery: Liffey
          barges
.22   king's brugh
          ?Boyne: Brugh of the Boyne
          ?Chapelizod: King's House
          King's Br
.23   new customs
          Custom House
.24   breach of all size
          Venice: Bridge of Sighs
.30   Baslesbridge
          Ballsbridge
          Basle
.31   Koenigstein's Arbour
          Dun Laoghaire (Kingstown)
.33   bally clay
          ?Balaclava
          Dublin: Baile Átha Cliath
.34   the hollow of the park
          Phoenix Park: The Hollow
.35   phoenix
          Phoenix Park
.35   moultain boultter
          ?Boulter's Hill
.36   pale
          Pale, The
137.01 boinyn water
          Boyne R
.05   Florence
          ?
.05   Wynn's Hotel
          Wynn's Hotel
.06   bequiet hearse
          White Horse
.07   Swed Albiony
          Albion
          Auburn
          ?Sweden
.07   Canterel—Cockran
          Cantrell and Cochrane's
.09   sadurn's mounted foot
          Saturn (+ "Slattery's Mounted
          Foot")
.09   Lund's kirk
          Lund (Sweden)
.13   bann
          ?Bann R
.17   Megacene
          ?Magazine Fort

.17   Searingsand
      ?Ringsend
.21   Charterhouse's
      Charterhouse
.24   lymphyamphyre
      Liffey
.32   holpenstake
      Alps (alpenstock)
.32   new yoke
      New York City
.33   jugoslaves
      Yugoslavia
.34   selfridgeousness
      Selfridge's (London)
.36   La Belle
      Waterloo: La Belle Alliance
.36   Grand Mount
      Waterloo: Mont St Jean
138.05 towns of X, Y and Z
      ?
.07   Europe
      Europe
.10   ath...cleah
      Dublin: Baile Átha Cliath
.11   fingallian
      Fingal
.11   hiberniad
      Ireland: Hibernia
.11   hodge
      England
.12   frenchy
      France
.12   brabanson
      Belgium
      Brabant
.13   fritz
      Germany
      Siemens Schuckert
.14   Jacob's arroroots
      Jacob, W and R, Co (bakers)
.19   Mullingar Inn
      Tavern, The: Mullingar
      House
.21   coast of Iron
      Ireland
.23   see in Ebblannah
      Dublin: Eblana
      Four Sees of Ireland
.24   Dampsterdamp
      Amsterdam
.25   Hoily Olives
      St Olave's

.26   Scent Otooles
      Christchurch Cathedral
      St Lawrence's Church
139.02 three gaols
      Prisons
.06   father Nakedbucker
      NYC: "Father Knickerbocker"
.10   Timb...Tomb
      ?Tib and Tom
.12   Babylon
      Babylon
.13   wan wubblin wall
      Dublin
      Magazine Fort
.19   Ann alive
      Liffey
.20   the bergs of Iceland
      Iceland
      Ireland
.21   Rageous Ossean
      NPN: Oisin, son of Fionn
.22   Dann's dane
      Denmark
.23   auburnt streams
      ?Auburn
.24   dabblin drolleries
      Dublin
.29   motto-in-lieu
      Dublin Motto
.33   Whichcroft Whorort
      ?
.33   Ousterholm Dreyschluss
      ?
      Dublin Coat of Arms
.34   Vatandcan
      Vatican
.36   Ebblawn Downes
      Dublin: Eblana
      Epsom Downs
140.01 Benjamin's Lea
      Guinness's Brewery
.01   Tholomew's Whaddingtun
      ?
.02   Antwarp
      Antwerp
.02   Musca
      Moscow
.02   Corry's
      Corry's Pub
.02   Weir's
      Weir's Pub

.02 the Arch
     Arch, The (pub)

.03 The Smug
     (any pub's "snug"?)

.03 The Dotch House
     Scotch House, The (pub)

.03 The Uval
     Oval, The (pub)

.06 Thine obesity...orb
     Dublin Motto

.08 Irish
     Ireland

.10 most extensive public park
     Phoenix Park

.11 most expensive brewing industry
     Guinness's Brewery

.12 most expansive peopling tho-
     roughfare
     O'Connell St

.15 Delfas
     Belfast

.19 orange garland
     Belfast: Harland and Wolff

.21 Dorhqk
     Cork

.22 chimes
     Shandon

.22 Mash
     Cork: The Marsh

.27 soapstone of silvry speech
     Blarney (Castle)

.27 Nublid
     Dublin

.30 Georgian mansion's lawn
     Leinster House: Duke of
     Leinster's Lawn
     ?Mansion House

.31 Irish in my east hand
     Power's Distillery (John's
     Lane)

.32 James's Gate in my west
     Guinness's Brewery (James's
     Gate)

.35 Atlanta
     Atlanta (Georgia)

.35 Oconee
     Oconee (R) (Georgia)

.36 Dalway
     Galway

141.01 Spanish Place
     Galway: Spanish Place

.01 Mayo
     Mayo

.02 Tuam
     Tuam

.02 Sligo's
     Sligo

.02 Galway's
     Galway

.05 Shalldoll Steepbell...Shand...gon
     Shandon

.08 loughladd
     Lochlann

.12 sweeds
     ?Sweden

.13 malafides
     Malahide

.14 buggelawrs
     Luggela

.14 three barnets
     ?Barnet

.18 X.W.C.A. on Z.W.C.U.
     YWCA

.21 irers' langurge
     Ireland

.22 jublander
     Jutland

.22 northquain
     North Wall Quay

.25 pershoon
     ?Persia

.35 blackcullen jam...pickneck
     Cullenswood

.35 Tomorrha's
     ?Temora

.36 Climate of all Ireland
     Ireland

142.04 kilkenny
     Kilkenny (cat)

*The list of suburbs at .12–.15 en-
circles Dub from SE to SW to NW to NE;
the first 5 are S of the Liffey, the last 6
N of the Liffey.*

.12 prés salés
     (S coast of Dublin Bay, for-
     merly marshy)

.12 Donnybrook
     Donnybrook

.12 Roebuck's
     Roebuck

.13 Arountown
     Terenure (Roundtown)

.13 Crumglen's
    Crumlin
.13 Kimmage's
    Kimmage
.14 Ashtown
    Ashtown
.14 Cabra
    Cabra
.14 Finglas
    Finglas
.15 Santry
    Santry
.15 Raheny
    Raheny
.15 Baldoygle
    Baldoyle
.19 vaticination
    ?Vatican
143.03 on anew
    ?Annu
    ?Heliopolis
.03 panaroma
    Rome
.05 sooty
    ?London: the City
.07 camelot
    Camelot
.07 dinmurk
    Denmark
.10 old hopeinhaven
    Copenhagen
.12 his tory
    Tory Island
.15 such a none
    Nonesuch
.17 lucan's
    Lucan
.24 pales
    ?Pale, The
.27 seem seeming
    ?Mecca: Well of Zemzem
.35 pigaleen
    Pigalle (Paris)
.36 Perisian
    Paris
144.10 ovally
    Oval, The
.10 provencial
    Provence
.10 Balldole
    Baldoyle

.10 Eilish
    Ireland
.12 belle alliance
    Waterloo: La Belle Alliance
.13 Spanish
    Spain
.14 turkish
    Turkey
.18 Iran
    Iran
    Ireland
145.23 the Post
    ?Swan, The
.29 New Free Woman
    New Freewoman
146.20 French college
    France
    French College (Blackrock)
.23 leapy
    Liffey
.34 bigtree
    ?Big Tree
147.03 four courtships
    Four Courts
.05 Old Sot's Hole
    Old Sot's Hole
.10 Saint Yves
    St Ives
.22 Chaperon Mall
    ?Charlemont Mall
.26 Fibsburrow churchdome
    Phibsborough: All Saints
    Church
.26 Sainte Andrée's Undershift
    ?St Andrew's Church (St Andrew St)
    ?St Andrew's Church (Westland Row)
    St Andrew Undershaft (London)
.32 Smock Alley
    Smock Alley Theatre
148.08 Rutland blue's
    ?Rutland Square
.10 sheeps' lane
    ?Ship St
.13 twinkly way
    Milky Way
.22 Uian
    ?
.22 alpin
    Alps

.33   acheseyeld from Ailing
       Ireland ("The Exile of
       Erin")
149.04 quhimper
       ?Quimper
.06   larn
       Larne (R)
.07   lech
       Lech R
.25   D.B.C.
       Dublin Bread Co
.32   harrogate and arrogate
       ?Harrogate
150.02 irish
       Ireland
.04   the Craterium
       Criterion Theatre (London)
.06   his duly mile
       Daily Mail
.08   The Ague
       Hague, The
.11   Stoutgirth
       Stuttgart
.20   Jericho
       Jericho (+ Jerry)
.21   Cavantry
       Cavan
       Coventry (+ Kevin)
.27   Judapest
       Budapest
.31   endswell of Man
       ?Man, Isle of
151.08 neoitalian
       Italy
.09   paleoparisien
       Paris
.10   romanitis
       Rome
.11   Sexe-Weiman-Eitelnaky
       Saxe-Weimar-Eisenach
.13   Nuremberg eggs
       Nuremberg
.19   accornish
       Cornwall
.20   taradition
       Tara
.22   retaliessian
       Taliesin
.29   royal gorge
       Dun Laoghaire: Royal
         George Yacht Club
       "Royal George"

152.05 lattlebrattons
       Britain, Little
.12   javanese
       Java
.18   ere wohned
       Erewhon
.23   vacticanated
       Vatican
.26   *De Rure Albo*
       Alba
.27   borgeously letout gardens
       Rome: Villa Borghese
.28   currycombs
       Rome: Catacombs
.28   Ludstown
       London
       Vatican

       Beginning with "azylium," pre-
       historic cultures (named after the places
       of discovery) are named from 152.36 to
       154.09.

.36   his azylium
       Mas d'Azil
.36   Shinshone Lanteran
       Rome: St John Lateran
153.01 Saint Bowery's-without-his-Walls
       ?NYC: The Bowery
       Rome: St Paul's-without-the-
         Walls
.02   *Amnis Limina Permanent*
       Liffey
.18   Dubville
       Dublin
.21   aurignacian
       Aurignac
.22   Moodend
       ?
.23   roaming...Room
       Rome
.30   wallat's collectium
       Wallace Collection (London)
.36   maudelenian
       Madeleine, La
154.03 mouster
       Moustier, Le
.04   aulne and lithial
       Liffey (+ elm and stone)
.05   awn and liseias? Ney?
       Les Eyzies
.08   robenhauses
       Robenhausen

.09   tardeynois
       Tardenois
.19   nase serene
       Nazareth
.23   Pauline
       ?
.23   Irene
       Ireland: Irena
.24   Beeton
       ?
.24   Los Angeles
       England
       Los Angeles
.27   *Como? Fuert it?*
       ?Como, Lake
.31   cannos
       Canossa
155.01 my corked father
       Cork
.05   Tugurios-in-Newrobe
       Europe
       Turkey (in Europe)
.05   Tukurias-in-Ashies
       Asia
       Turkey (in Asia)
.05   Novarome
       Constantinople: New Rome
.06   lyonine city
       Vatican
.09   constantinently
       Constantinople
.12   newwhere
       Erewhon
.16   Parysis...parises
       Paris
.19   Cospol's not our star
       Constantinople
.25   Maples
       Maples's Hotel
.26   Teresa street
       ?
.26   Sophy Barratt's
       ?Barrett's Hotel
.27   gresk
       Greece (Orthodox Ch)
.27   letton
       (Rome)
.28   russicruxian
       Russia (Orthodox Ch)
156.03 the penic walls
       Carthage

.03   the ind
       ?India
.06   Sick Bokes' Juncroom
       ?Croom
.25   Vale Hollow
       Valhalla
.28   The Pills
       ?
.28   Nasal Wash
       Naze, The
       Wash, The
.29   british
       England
.29   bondstrict
       Bond St
.30   Nuzuland
       New Zealand
.32   Veiled Horror
       Valhalla
157.01 viterberated
       Viterbo
.08   sisteen shimmers
       Vatican: Sistine Chapel
.15   Fuerst quarter...Number 28
       NPN? (First quarter of lunar
       month)
.16   Norwood's sokaparlour
       Norway
       ?Norwood
.26   curiasity...buchstubs
       Vatican
.33   *Petite Bretagne*
       Britain, Little
.34   Cornwallis-West
       Cornwall (+ Ireland as "West
       Cornwall")
.36   Irelande
       Ireland
158.02 daisy's worth
       ?Daisy Market
.02   Florida
       Florida
.04   dubliboused
       Dublin
.10   Metamnisia
       ?Melanesia
.11   citherior spiane
       Spain
.11   eaulande
       ?
.19   Vallee Maraia to Grasyaplaina
       NPN: "Ave Maria, gratia plena"

.29   *Aquila Rapax*
    NPN: Motto of Pope Pius
    VII ("fierce eagle")

159.01   *De Rore Coeli*
    NPN: Motto of Pope Urban
    VII ("of heavenly manna")

.12   Missisliffi
    Mississippi R
    Liffey

.15   hopeharrods
    Harrods Ltd
    Hope Brothers

.19   romescot
    NPN: Name of "Peter's
    Pence" in Anglo-Saxon
    times

.28   Horoseshoew
    Dublin Horse Show

.30   baileycliaver
    Balaclava
    Dublin: Baile Átha Cliath

.32   Tristan da Cunha
    Tristan da Cunha

.32   isle of manoverboard
    Man, Isle of

.33   Inaccessible
    Tristan da Cunha: Inaccessi-
    ble Island

.34   meeting...waves
    ?Meeting of the Waters

160.06   Curraghchasa
    Curragh, The
    Curragh Chase

.07   pinetacotta of Verney Rubeus
    ?

.11   olivetion
    Olivet

.12   East Conna Hillock
    Conna

.22   unenglish
    England

.27   billfaust
    Belfast (Ulster)

.27   Wilsh
    ?

.27   curks
    Cork (Munster)

.27   deblinite
    Dublin (Leinster)

.28   Mr Wist
    Galway (Connacht)

.28   Wilsh...wist...faust...deblinite
    ?Munster
    Connacht
    Ulster
    Leinster

.31   Kiel
    ?Kiel

161.27   Slatbowel at Commons
    ?

162.08   sandhurst
    Sandhurst

.11   *champ de bouteilles*
    ?NPN: field of battles-bottles
    = pub

.12   Persic-Uraliens
    Persia
    Ural Mts

.14   Coucousien
    Caucasus

.15   Tobolosk
    Tobolsk

.15   *Ostiak...Vogul*
    Ostiak Vogul

.17   weste point
    West Point

.30   Poutresbourg
    St Petersburg
    (?Rome)

.32   augstritch
    ?Austria

.32   Ireland's Eye
    Ireland's Eye

163.08   brutherscutch
    Scotland

.12   ambusheers, beggar
    Beggarsbush

.27   the Bure
    ?Bure R (+ *beurre*, Fr "but-
    ter")

.28   the Brie
    Brie (+ Brie cheese)

.30   Silkebjorg
    Silkeborg

164.05   *Skotia*
    Ireland: Scotia

165.09   tonehall
    Zurich: Tonhalle

.16   national cruetstand
    National Gallery (London)

.21   congorool
    Congo (+ "kangaroo")

.22   lady Trabezond
          Trebizond
.28   Philadespoinis (Ill)
          Philadespoinis (NPN)
.36   slade
          Slade School
166.32   eastasian
          Asia
167.13   acropoll
          Athens: Acropolis
.14   blasphorus blesphorous
          ?Bosporus
.16   cong
          Cong
.18   Tarpeia
          Rome: Tarpeian Rock
.18   Mister Abby
          ?Abbey Theatre
.22   Olymp
          Olympus, Mt
168.05   *Noisdanger*
          ?

BOOK I

Chapter 7

169.14   megageg
          ?Gog and Magog
.23   Griefotrofio
          NPN? *Brefotrofio*, It "or-
          phanage"
.23   Phig Streat 111
          ?
.23   Shuvlin, Old Hoeland
          Dublin
          Ireland: Misc Allusions
          ?New Holland
170.10   Bohemeand
          Bohemia
.29   Leixlip
          Leixlip
.29   Island Bridge
          Island Bridge
.32   Findlater
          Findlater, Alexander, and
          Co
          ?Findlater's Church
.32   Corner House
          Lyons Corner Houses (Lon-
          don)
.32   Englend
          England

.33   Balaclava
          Balaclava
          Dublin: Baile Átha Cliath
.34   Grex's
          Greece
171.01   greekenhearted
          Greece
.02   Old Zealand
          England
          ?New Zealand
          Zealand
.06   Europe
          Europe
.06   Irrland's
          Ireland
.11   kcedron
          Kedron
.12   Lebanon
          Lebanon (Mountains)
.25   magyansty
          Hungary
.26   she has a feherbour
          Székesfehérvár (Hungary)
.28   Fanny Urinia
          ?Urania Wineshop
          ?Uranus
.34   Caer Fere
          ?Fear, Cape
.35   Soak Amerigas
          South America
.35   *Pridewin*
          NPN: King Arthur's ship was
          called "Prydwen"
172.01   Patatapapaveri's
          ?
.03   bridewell
          Bridewell ·
.11   moravar
          Moravia
.15   Eden Quay
          Eden Quay
.19   Liffey
          Liffey
.22   Guardacosta
          ?
.23   Nearapoblican asylum
          Naples
173.13   Albiogenselman
          Albion (+ Albigensian heresy)
.20   cornaille
          Corneille, Grand Hôtel de

.21 tarabooming
   Tara
.25 cruaching
   Crom Cruach
   ?Cruachan
174.25 deserted village
   Auburn
.26 Tumblin-on-the-Leafy
   Dublin
   Liffey
.26 Mr Vanhomrigh's house at 81
   bis Mabbot's Mall
   Mabbot's Mill
   Vanhomrigh's House
.27 Green Patch
   Green Patch
.27 brickfields
   Brickfields, The
.28 Salmon Pool
   Salmon Pool
.31 Auborne-to-Auborne
   Auburn
175.03 Quicklow
   Wicklow
.05 All Saints
   Oxford U: All Souls College
.05 Belial
   Oxford U: Balliol College
.11 *Corpsica*
   Corsica
.11 *Engleterre*
   England
.12 *Sachsen and Judder*
   Jutland
   Saxony
.15 *Hoath*
   Howth
.23 *Rillstrill liffs*
   Liffey
.25 *Tory Island*
   Tory Island
.25 *Eirewhiggs*
   Ireland
.31 gaasy pure...games
   Gaelic Athletic Assn
176.04 *Adam and Ell*
   Adam and Eve's
.04 *Moggie's on the Wall*
   Magazine Fort
.05 *American Jump*
   America

.10 *Dreamcolohour*
   Drumcolliher
   Dublin: Drom Cuill-Choille
.10 *Waterloo*
   Waterloo
.20 germogall
   Gaul
   Germany
.22 marshalaisy
   Marseilles
.22 Irish eyes
   Ireland
.27 Talviland
   ?
.30 kuskykorked
   ?Cork
   ?Corsica
.31 inkbattle house
   Inkbottle House
.35 Schwitzer's
   Switzer's
   Switzerland
177.02 monkmarian
   ?Merrion, Mount
.04 pawdry's purgatory
   St Patrick's Purgatory
.05 *Daily Maily*
   Daily Mail
.09 Kairokorran
   Cairo
   Karakorum
.10 Sheols
   Sheol
.22 Bethgelert
   Beddgelert
.23 gipsy's bar
   Gipsy Bar
.24 old Belly
   Bailey Lighthouse
   Old Bailey (London)
.25 nexmouth
   Exmouth
.28 dubbed
   Dublin
.28 *Waterclocks*
   ?Waterhouse and Co
.36 teashop lionses
   Lyons Corner Houses (London)
178.01 Lumdrum
   London
.06 english spooker
   England

.07   erse
            Ireland: Erse
.09   Lucalizod
            Chapelizod
            Lucan
.16   Monster Book
            ?Munster
.17   Paltryattic Puetrie
            NPN: *Oxford Book of*
                Greek Verse
.22   Lady Smythe
            Ladysmith (S Africa)
.22   MacJobber
            Majuba Hill (S Africa)
.29   Nassaustrass
            Nassau (St)
.33   Kroukaparka
            Croke Park
.33   Kalatavala
            ?
179.12 Lorencao Otulass
            Christchurch Cathedral
.13   Calumnious Column of Cloaxity
            ?
.14   Bengalese Beacon of Biloxity
            ?Bailey Lighthouse
            Bengal
            ?Biloxi (Miss)
.14   Annamite Aper of Atroxity
            Annam
.19   the *Popapreta*
            ?
.27   Blue Book of Eccles
            Eccles St (+ *Ulysses*, the
                cover of whose early edi-
                tions was blue)
.32   roseschelle
            Rochelle, La
.33   liberty
            ?Liberty and Co (London)
.35   operahouse
            Opera House
180.04 gaiety pantheomime
            Gaiety Theatre
.06   *Yellin*
            Ireland (Song: "Dear Little
                Shamrock of Ireland")
.09   trinity plumes
            ?Trinity College, Dublin
.11   sponiard's digger
            Spain

.13   Cardinal Lindundarri
            Derry
            Ulster
.14   Cardinal Carchingarri
            Cork
            Kerry
            Munster
.14   Cardinal Loriotuli
            Leinster
.15   Cardinal Occidentaccia
            Connacht
.15   dearby darby doubled
            Derby
            Dublin Allusion: "Dear Dirty
                Dublin"
.16   first over the hurdles
            Dublin: Baile Átha Cliath
181.01 stage Englesemen
            England
.04   klondykers
            Klondike
.04   Pioupioureich
            ?
.05   Swabspays
            ?Netherlands (Les Pays Bas)
            Swabia
.05   land of Nod
            ?Netherlands
            Nod, Land of
.05   Shruggers' Country
            ?
.05   Pension Danubierhome
            Danube R
.06   Barbaropolis
            ?
.13   Nigerian
            Nigeria
.17   Dustbin's
            Dublin
.22   Turk
            Turkey
.22   ungreekable
            Greece
.23   armenable
            Armenia
.25   Sniffey
            ?Liffey
.35   Drumcondriac
            Drumcondra
182.07 beerlitz
            Berlitz Language Schools

.09 zinnzabar
Zanzibar

.15 idlish tarriers'
Ireland
"Irish Harriers" as well as
Irish terriers, but I know
of no hunt by that name

.24 Broken Hill stranded estate
Broken Hill (Australia)

.24 Camebreech
Cambridge

.25 brandnew two guinea
New Guinea

.26 hogsford
Oxford

.27 Italian
Italy

.30 *Quivapieno*
NPN: The Italian proverb,
"Chi va piano va sano e
lontano."

.31 Haunted Inkbottle
Inkbottle House

.31 Brimstone Walk
?

.31 Asia in Ireland
Asia
Ireland

183.01 Queasisanos
Qui si Sana

.05 brass castle
Chapelizod: Brass Castle

.05 tyled house
Chapelizod: Tiled House

.05 ballyfermont
Ballyfermot

.05 Niggs, niggs and niggs
Nixnixundnix

.06 stinksome inkenstink
Tingsomingenting

.07 Angles
England

.08 Edam reeked more rare
Edam
Eden
Edinburgh: "Auld Reekie"

.10 persianly literatured
Persia

.22 goblins
?Gobelins

.23 limerick damns
Limerick

.30 Swiss condensed bilk
Switzerland

.31 antipodes
Antipodes

.35 Hades
Hades

184.12 ˙stourbridge
Stourbridge

.21 Carrageen
?Carrigeen

.21 blaster of Barry's
Paris

.27 Gabrielle de l'Eglise
Saint-Gabriel, Église de

.31 Mère Puard
Poulard, Mère

185.01 Robber and Mumsell
Maunsell and Co

.05 romeruled
Rome

.06 kathartic ocean
Arctic

.09 sporting times
Sporting Times

.10 Anglican ordinal
England

.11 dunsky tunga
Denmark
?Dún-na-sciath

.12 Babylon
Babylon

.12 pink one
Sporting Times

.24 *Orionis*...O'Ryan's
Orion

.29 nichthemerically
?America

.31 United Stars of Ourania
America
Uranus: *Ouranos*, "Heaven"

.33 gallic
Gaul

.33 iron
Ireland

186.25 Knockmaree, Comty Mea
Knock (Co Mayo)
?Knocknarea (Co Sligo)
?Meath

.30 bethels
Bethel

187.02 balltossic
Baltic Sea (+ *baltas*, Lith
"white")
.07 caledosian
Caledonia (+ *Kaledos*, Lith
"Christmas")
.08 Lieutuvisky
Lithuania: Lieutuva
.11 arrahbejibbers
Arabia
.19 Winterwater's
?
.19 Silder Seas
NPN: *silde*, Dan "herring"
.28 Noland
?
188.10 two easter island
Ireland: Misc Allusions
.16 disunited kingdom
England
.23 pool of Sodom
Cities of the Plain
Dead Sea
189.06 ppenmark
Penmark
.11 cantreds of countless catchaleens
Ireland: Cathleen ni Houlihan
.14 Chalwador
?

*189.34–.36 refers to the de-
struction of Dublin public buildings
in 1916 and 1921-22.*

.34 auguries of rooks in parlament
Parliament House
.35 dynamitisation of colleagues
College of Surgeons, Royal
.35 reducing of records to ashes
Four Courts
.36 levelling of all customs by
blazes
Custom House
190.02 hell
Hell
.09 Irish stew
Ireland
.17 Guinness's
Guinness's Brewery
.19 boskop
Boskop

.19 Yorek
York
.25 armenial
Armenia
.29 Galway
Galway
.30 song of alibi
Arabia
.30 cuthone
Cuthone
.31 greybounding
?Graubünden
.36 Irish emigrant
Ireland
191.01 quackfriar
Blackfriars
.03 serendipitist
Serendip
.04 Europasianised
Asia
Europe
.04 Afferyank
Africa
America
.05 drowner...liege...refreshment
?Tristan da Cunha
.10 Novena Lodge
?
.10 Novara Avenue
Novara (Ave)
.10 Patripodium-am-Bummell
? (just "father's foot on
bum"?)
.17 celebesty
Celebes
.21 Tindertarten
?
.27 daybroken donning
?Donnybrook
192.08 Parish funds
Paris: "Paris Funds"
.11 crown of Thorne's
? (just "crown of thorns"?)
.12 coat off Trevi's
Trèves
.15 French
France
.21 Paraskivee
NPN: *Parasceve*, "eve of the
sabbath," ie, Friday, esp
Good Friday.

.21   Danmark
        Denmark
.26   Airish
        Ireland
.27   hornmade ivory
        Gates of Horn and Ivory
.29   flushpots of Euston
        Egypt
        Euston (London)
.29   hanging garments of Marylebone
        Gardens of Semiramis
        Marylebone (London)
.35   Templetombmount joyntstone
        ?Mountjoy
        Zion, Mt
.35   pleasegoodjesusalem
        Jerusalem
193.02 dulpeners
        Dublin
.19   Bluecoat schooler
        King's Hospital
194.05 athands
        Atha
.14   Thundery
        ?
.14   Ulerin's dogstar
        Sirius
        Ulerin
.18   coalhole
        ?Coal Hole (London)

.25   Punchestime...racecourseful
        Punchestown

The course of turfbrown mummy
Liffey, described in 194.33–195.01, is a
little mixed up. Neither Tallaght nor Sal-
lynoggin is near the valley of the Liffey.
However, if Tallaght's green hills are the
Dublin mountains and Sallynoggin is Sal-
ly Gap at the head of the Liffey valley,
then the course of the Liffey is described
in reverse, from the point at Ringsend,
past the Dublin bridges and the salmon
weirs between Island Bridge and Leixlip,
through the Poulaphuca waterfall and
past Blessington to the source of the Lif-
fey below Sally Gap.

.35   Tallaght's green hills
        Greenhills
        Tallaght
.36   pools of the phooka
        Poulaphuca
.36   Blessington
        Blessington
195.01 Sallynoggin
        Sally Gap
        Sallynoggin
.04   Anna Livia
        Liffey

BOOK I
Chapter 8

For this chapter only, quotations are given in the left-hand column, and references to the alphabetical gazetteer in the right-hand column. The indented columns, left and right, list all allusions to rivers and to their identifications respectively. Rivers named only in this chapter appear only in the indented columns and are not listed in the alphabetical gazetteer; rivers named elsewhere in *FW* as well are listed in both the indented and unindented columns and are cited in the alphabetical gazetteer.

196.02		tell	Tel, Ind
.03−.05	Anna Livia...Anna Livia		Liffey
.06		cheb	Cheb, Czech
		futt	Futa, S Amer
.08	dabbling		Dublin
.09	butt		Butt Br
.11	Fiendish park		Phoenix Park
.12	water black		Blackwater R; Dublin: Dubh-linn
		water black	Blackwater, Ire
.13		steeping	Steeping, Eng
		stuping	Stupia, Pol
.15		saale	Saale, Ger
.15	duddurty devil		Dublin Allusion: "Dear Dirty Dublin"
		duddurty devil	Duddon, Eng; Dirty Devil, US
		devil	Devil's, passim
.16	Wallop		Wallop Fields
.17		battle	Battle, Can
		mouldaw	Moldau, Czech
.18		dneepers	Dnieper, USSR
		gangres	Ganges, Ind
.19	Animal Sendai		Sendai (+ *Anima Mundi*)
		Animal	Annamoe, Ire
		Sendai	Sendai, Jap
.20	loch and neagh		Neagh, Lough
.21		nicies	Neisse, Ger; Nisi, Afr
		fierceas	Fier, Fr
		illysus	Ilissus, Gr
.22		toms	Tom, USSR
		till	Till, Eng
.24		roughty	Roughty, Ire
		loof	Loo, Eng
197.01	Reeve Gootch...Reeve Drughad		Drogheda (St); Left and Right Bank (Paris)
.03	howeth		Howth
		eld	Elde, Ger
.04		wiesel	Wiesel, Ger
		rat	Rat, Can
.04	derry's		Derry (Ulster)
		derry's	Derry, Ire
.05	corksown		Cork (Munster)

197.05	doubling		Dublin (Leinster)
.06	gullaway		Galway (Connacht)
.07		elster	Elster, Ger
.08		Qu'appelle	Qu'appelle, Can
.09	Urgothland		Sweden
		Urgothland	Ur, USSR; Gotha, Swed (Canal)
.09	Tvistown		?
.10	Kattekat		Cattegat (strait)
.10	New Hunshire		New Hampshire
.10	Concord on the Merrimake		Concord
		Concord	Concord, US
		Merrimake	Merrimack, US
.12	banns		Bann R
		banns	Bann, Ire
.12	Adam and Eve's		Adam and Eve's
.13		duck	Duck, US
		drake	Drake Creek, US
.17		may	May, Australia
		passmore	Passmore, Australia
		oxus	Oxus, USSR & Afghanistan
.17	Don		Don R
		Don	Don, passim
.18	Dombdomb		Dublin
.19	Stork and Pelican		?Eagle Life and Annuity Insurance Co; Pelican Insurance Co
		Pelican	Pelican, US
.20	delvan		?Delvin R
		delvan	Delvin, Ire
.20	duvlin		?Devlin R; Dublin
		duvlin	Devlin, Ire
.21		Sabrine	Sabrainn, Ire; Sabrina (Severn), Eng
		asthore	Astor, Ind
.23		shadda	Adda, It
.24	auld min's manse		Old Men's Home; Royal Hospital (Kilmainham)
		auld	Aude, Fr
		min's	Min, China
.24	Maisons Allfou		St Patrick's Hospital
.25	rest of incurables		Hospital for Incurables
.26	quaggy waag for stumbling		Dublin Allusion: "Rocky Road to Dublin"
		waag	Waag, Czech
.27		grasshoop	Grass, Can, US
.28		barqued	Arques, Fr
.29	Ivernikan Okean		Irish Sea
.30		tilt	Tilt, Scot
.31		gran	Gran, Hung
.31	Phenician		Phoenicia
		Phenician	Pheni, Ind
.32	pigeonhouse		Pigeonhouse
.33		marchantman	March, Czech; Marchan, Sp
		suivied	Sui, Afr, China

197.35		runagate	Runa, USSR
		bowmpriss	Bomu, Afr; Bow, Australia; Riss, Ger
.35	Pilcomayo		?Mayo
		Pilcomayo	Pilcomayo, S Amer
.36		Suchcaughtawan	Saskatchewan, Can
		whale's	Whale, Can
198.01	ijypt		Egypt
.03		swift	Swift, US
		sheba	Seba, Pal
.04		salomon	Solomon, US
.04	her bulls		Bulls, North and South
		ruhring	Ruhr, Ger
.05		spree	Spree, Ger
		Boyarka	Boyarka, USSR
		buah	Bua, Afr
		Boyana	Boyana, Albania
		bueh	Buëch, Fr
.05	erned		Erne (R)
		erned	Erne, Ire
		lille	Lille, Den
.05	Bunbath		Bath; Ireland: Banba
		Bunbath	Batha, Afr
.06		trader	Trader Creek, US
.08		Wasserbourne	Winterbourne, Eng
.09		Shyr	Syr Darya, USSR
.10	Anna Livia...Anna Livia		Liffey
.11		sals	Salso, It
		chamba	Chambal, Ind
		choo	Chu, China, USSR
.12	erring		Ireland
		cheef	Chef, Can
		aisy-oisy	Oise, Fr
.13	Gota		Gota R
		Gota	Gota, Swed
		Yssel	Ysel, Neth
.13	limmat		Limmat R
		limmat	Limmat, Switz
		El Negro	Negro, Argentina
.14		La Plate	Plate, Argentina
.15		laddery	Ladder Burn, Scot
		coneywink	Conewango, US; Coney, Fr
.16		sina	Sina, Bolivia, Ind
		absantee	Santee, US
.17		passession	Asse, Fr
.18		Emme	Emme, Switz
		reussischer	Reuss, Switz
		Honddu	Honddu, Wales
.18	franca langua		France
.19		sharee	Shari, Afr
		ebro	Ebro, Sp
.20		skol	Skollis, Gr

198.20	antiabecedarian	Abecedarian Society
.22	coxyt	Cocytus R
	coxyt	Cocytus, Hades; Cox, Australia
	Botlettle	Botletle, Afr
.23	loa	Loa, Chile
	windaug	Windau, USSR
.24	wubbling	Wu, China
	meusic	Meuse, Fr
.25	ribble	Ribble, Eng
	reedy	Reedy, US
	derg	Derg, Ire
.26	bogans	Bogan, Australia
	a band on...abandon	Bandon, Ire
	Sure...Sure	Sure, Ind
	fiddan	Fiddown, Ire
.26	dee	Dee R
	dee	Dee, passim
.27	bow or...moher	Bohermore
	bow	Bow, Australia
	Tista	Tista, Ind
	suck	Suck, Ire
.29	Humber	Humber R
	Humber	Humber, Eng
	glommen	Glommen, Nor
	tares	Tar, Ire, US
.30	buboes	Bubi, Afr; Bubu, Afr
	bowman	Bowman, US
.31	bales	Bale, Afr
	allbrant	Alle, Eur; Brantas, Java
.31	crests of rockies	Rocky Mts
	nera	Nera, It, Sp
.32	giant's holes in Grafton's cause-way	Giant's Causeway; Grafton St
.33	Funglus grave	Fingal's Cave; Finglas; Glasnevin (Cemetery)
.33	the great tribune's barrow	Barrow R; Glasnevin Cemetery: O'Connell's Grave
	barrow	Barrow, Ire
.34	sittang	Sittang, Burma
	sambre	Sambre, Belg & Fr
	sett	Sette, Brazil
	drammen	Drammen, Nor
.35	drommen	Drome, Fr
	usking	Usk, Eng
	ruful	Rufu, Afr
199.01	mormon's	Mormon, US
.01	thames	Thames R; *Times, The*
	thames	Thames, Eng
.02	toiling moil	*Daily Mail*; Moyle, Sea of
	moil	Moi, Afr; Moyle, Ire
.03	pecking	Peck, Afghanistan
.04	crocs	Crow, US

199.05		hunselv	Hunse, Neth
.06		droming	Drome, Fr
.07		zwarthy	Zwarte, Neth
		kowse	Kowsha, USSR
.07		weedy broeks	Brussels: Willibroek Canal
		weedy broeks	Willibroek Canal, Belg
.08		buddy...pest	Budapest
.08	Parish		Paris
		thette	Tete, Afr; Thet, Eng
.09		dodo	Dodo, Afr
		durmed	Durme, Belg
.10		adranse	Adra, Sp; Adranos, Turk; Dranse, Switz
		durance	Durance, Fr
		vaal	Vaal, Afr
		severn	Severn, Eng
.11	Anna Livia		Liffey
		darent	Darent, Eng
.12		Wendawanda	Wandle, Eng; Wando, US
.13	damazon		Amazon R
		damazon	Amazon, S Amer
		ishim	Ishim, USSR
.14	dear dubber Dan		Dublin Allusion: "Dear Dirty Dublin"
		Dan	Dan, US
		neuphraties	Euphrates, Asia Min
.15		maggias	Maggia, Switz
		blooms	Bloem, Afr
.17	staynish beacons		Arklow; Denmark; Wicklow
		staynish	Stenness, Scot
.17	cupenhave		Copenhagen
.18	Greenland's		Greenland
		tay	Tay, Scot
		dzoupgan	Dzubgan, USSR; Oup, Afr
		Kaffue	Kafue, Afr
		mokau	Mokau, New Zealand
		an sabie	Au Sable, US
.19		Sikiang	Sikiang, China
		sukry	Sukri, Ind
		ale	Ale, Scot
		shinkobread	Shinko, Afr
.20		bana	Bana, Arabia
.21		stomicker	Tomi, USSR
.21	pyrraknees		Pyrenees
.22		goyt	Goyt, Eng
		russ	Russ, Ger
.23		vivers	Vivero, Sp
		sieve	Sieve, It
		metauwero	Metauro, It
		swales	Swale, Eng
.24		rieses	Reese, US
		hardey	Hardey, Australia
		frome	Frome, Eng

199.24		stour	Stour, Eng
.25		sow	Sow, Eng
		sozh	Sozh, USSR
.26		platteau	Platte, US
		tawe	Tawe, Wales
.27		esk	Esk, Eng, Scot
		vistule	Vistula, Pol & USSR
.28	*Mallow*		Mallow
.29		Sucho	Sucio, S Amer
.30		hen	Heng, China
.31	turrace of Babbel		Babel, Tower of
.31	cockle her mouth		Cock (Cockle) Lake
.34	roya romanche		Rhaetia
		roya	Roya, It
		romanche	Romanche, Fr
.34	Annona		?St Anne's Church
		gebroren	Ebro, Sp
		aroostokrat	Aroostook, US
		Nivia	Navia, Sp; Nive, Fr
.35		Sense	Sense, Switz
		Art	Arta, Gr
		pirryphlickathims	Pyriphlegethon, Hades (river of fire)
.36	anner		Anner R
		anner	Anner, Ire
		dasht	Dasht, Pakistan
		virevlies	Vire, Fr; Vlie, Neth (strait)
200.01		nith	Nith, Scot
.02		jade	Jade, Ger
		robe	Robe, Australia
.02	wood		?Wood Quay
		wood	Wood, Can, US
.04		brahming	Brahmani, Ind
.06	*Vuggybarney*		Vouga, Port
.11		var	Var, Fr
.12		sangs	Sanga, Afr
		holmen	Holme, Den, Eng
	lilyhung		Lulanga, Afr
.13	*pigger*		Pig Creek, US
.13	soay		Hebrides: Soay Island
		soan	Soan, Ind (+ Soan Island, Korea)
.13	firth...forth		Forth, Firth of
		forth	Forth, Scot
.14		sonora	Sonora, Mex
		Bheri-Bheri	Bheri, Ind
.15		umvolosy	Umvolosi, Afr
		yawn	Yaw, Burma
.16		deef	Dee, passim
.16	Yare		Yare R
		Yare	Yare, Eng
		teasing	Tees, Eng
.16	Anna Liv		Liffey

200.16		chalk	Chalk, Can
.17		sorgues	Sorgues, Fr
		doon	Doon, Scot
.18		douro	Douro, Port & Sp
		dudheen	Dudhi, Ind
		shirvant	Shirvan, Iran
.19		siligirl	Siligir, USSR
		wensum	Wensum, Eng
.19	pilend roads		?Mile End Rd; ?Pile Ends
.20		Daery	Daer Water, Scot; Derry, Ire
.22	the sillypost		Sihl R; Zurich: Sihlpost
		sillypost	Sihl, Switz
.23		Shoebenacaddie	Shubenacadie, Can
.24	sihl		Sihl R
		sihl	Sihl, Switz
.28		silliver	Siller, Ind; Silver, Can, Ire
.29		neiss	Neisse, Ger
.30		inny	Inny, Eng, Ire
.31		pleissful	Pleisse, Ger
		adda	Adda, It
		tammar	Tamar, Eng
		lizzy	Liz, Port
		lossie	Lossie, Scot
.32		hab	Hab, Pakistan
.33	wyerye		Rye R
		wyerye	Wye, Eng; Rye, Eng, Ire
		Odet	Odet, Fr
.34	trent		Trent R
		trent	Trent, passim
.35		pian piena	Pian Creek, Australia; Piana, USSR; Pienaars, Afr
.36		lerryn	Lerryn, Eng
.36	Anna Livia's		Liffey
		cushingloo	Cushina, Ire; Cushing Creek, US; Loo, Eng
201.01		rede	Rede, Eng
.02		tummel	Tummel, Scot
.03		Tarn	Tarn, Fr
.04		ore	Ore, passim
		ouse	Ouse, Eng
		Essonne	Essonne, Fr
		inne	Inn, Eur; Inny, Eng, Ire
.08	*my old Dane*		Denmark
		Dane	Dane, Eng
		hodder	Hodder, Eng
.08	*dodderer*		Dodder R
		dodderer	Dodder, Ire
.10		*maymoon's*	May, Australia
		honey	Honey Creek, US
		Decemberer	Embira, S Amer
.13		*irwell*	Irwell, Eng
		shire	Shira, Eng; Shire, Afr

201.17	*Brittas*	Brittas
.18	*slobs della Tolka*	Tolka R
	Tolka	Tolka, Ire
.18	*plage au Clontarf*	Clontarf
.19	*feale*	Feale, Ire
	gay aire	Gaya, Sp; Aire, Eng, Fr
.19	*troublin bay*	Dublin Bay
.21	Onon! Onon!	Onon, USSR
	teign	Teign, Eng
.22	ingul	Ingul, USSR
	potters	Potters, Ire
.23	jagsthole	Jagst, Ger
	vesles	Vesle, Fr
	vet	Vet, Afr
	fever's	Fever, US
.24	mahun	Mahon, Ire; Mahu, S Amer
	hard	Arda, Bulg & Turk
.25	hazelhatchery	Hazelhatch
	hazelhatchery	Hazel Creek, US
.26	Clondalkin	Clondalkin
.26	Kings's Inns	King's Inns Quay
	Inns	Inn, Eur
.27	aleveens	Leven, Eng
	tool	Tule, US
.28	rede	Rede, Eng
.30	meanacuminamoyas	Moy R
	meanacuminamoyas	Mina, N Afr; Minchumina (lake), Alaska; Cumina, S Amer; Moy, Ire
	Olaph	Ola, USSR
.34	Yakov Yea	Yea, Australia
.36	loddon	Loddon, Eng
202.01	nordsihkes	Nord, Australia
.02	sudsevers	Suda, USSR
.03	Messamisery	Missouri, US
.05	Shoal	Shoal Creek, US
.06	owen	Owen, passim
.06	toss	Töss R
	toss	Töss, Switz
	nare	Nare, S Amer
.07	cam	Cam, Eng
	camlin	Camlin, Ire
.08	neckar	Neckar, Ger
.08	the diveline	Dublin
	diveline	Dive, Fr
.09	Fonte-in-Monte	?
.09	Tidingtown...Tidingtown	?Teddington
.10	Linking	Link, US
.11	tapting	Tapti, Ind
	jutty	Jutaí, S Amer
	pietaring	Pietar, Sp
.12	clyding	Clyde, Scot

202.12		Waiwhou	Waihou, New Zealand
		thurever	Thur, Switz; Ure, Eng
.13		whuebra	Huebra, Sp
.14		tilar	Tilar, Iran
		souldrer	Sauldre, Fr
		salor	Salor, Sp
		Pieman	Pieman, Australia
		Peace	Peace, Can, US
.15		Polistaman	Polista, USSR
		elwys	Elwy, Wales
		esk	Esk, Eng, Scot
.16		vardar	Vardar, Yugo & Gr
.17	waterlows		Waterloo
.17	Grattan		?Essex Br
.18		Arc	Arc, Fr
		Fidaris	Fidaris, Gr
.19		Doubt	Doubs, Fr
		Nieman	Niemen, USSR
.19	Nirgends		NPN? (Ger, "nowhere")
.19	Nihil		Nile R
		Nihil	Nile, Egypt
.20	Albern, O Anser		Albert Nyanza
.21	Qvic and Nuancee		Victoria Nyanza
		Nuancee	Nuanetsi, Afr
.22		Tez	Tez, USSR
		thelon	Thelon, Can
		langlo	Langlo, Australia
.22	walking weary		?Tipperary
		loon	Loon, Can
.22	waybashwards		Wabash R
		waybashwards	Wabash, US
.23		sid	Sid, Eng
		whuon	Huon, Australia
		annals	Annalee, Ire
.24		graveller	Gravelly, US
.24	Leinster		Leinster
		wolf	Wolf, US
.25		blyth	Blyth, Eng
.26		offon	Ofin, Afr
		jumpnad	Jumna, Ind; Jump, US
.28		silvamoonlake	Silva, S Amer
.29	Curraghman		Curragh, The
		hay	Hay, Can, US
.30		sun	Sun, US
		shine on	Shinano, Jap
.31	Kildare		Kildare
.32		forstfellfoss	Foss, Eng
		sankh	Sankh, Ind
.33		neathe	Neath, Wales
.34		tigris	Tigris, Asia Min
.35		corribly	Corrib, Ire
		anacheronistic	Acheron, Hades

202.36	nullahs	Nula, S Amer
203.01	Wickenlow	Wicklow
.01	garden of Erin	Eden; Ireland
.02	Kilbride	Kilbride
	Kilbride	Bride, Ire
.02	Horsepass bridge	Horsepass Br
.02	great southerwestern	Great Southern and Western Railway
.03	traces	Tresa, It & Switz
.03	midland's grainwaster	Midland Great Western Railway
.04	robecca	Robe, Ire; Robec, mentioned by Rabelais
.06	lifey	Liffey
.06	barleyfields	Barley Fields; Rotunda
.06	pennylotts	Lotts
.07	fordofhurdlestown	Dublin: Baile Átha Cliath
.07	wellingtonorseher	Norway; ?Wellington Br; ?Wellington Quay
.08	Alesse	Lesse, Belg
.08	lagos	Saint-Lazare (Paris)
	lagos	Lagos, Afr, Port
	dove	Dove, Eng
.08	dunas	Danube R
	dunas	Duna (Danube), Hung; Duna, USSR
.09	sarthin	Sarthe, Fr
.09	suir	Suir R
	suir	Suir, Ire
.09	Finn	Finn R (Ulster)
	Finn	Finn, Ire
.10	Mourne	Mourne R (Ulster)
	Mourne	Mourne, Ire
.10	Nore	Nore R (Munster)
	Nore	Nore, Ire
.10	takes lieve of Bloem	Slieve Bloom (Munster)
	Bloom	Bloem, Afr
.11	Braye	Bray R (Leinster)
	Braye	Bray, Ire; Braye, Fr
	divarts	Divatte, Fr
.11	Farer	?
.11	Moy	Moy R (Connacht)
	Moy	Moy, Ire
.12	Cullin...Collin	Cullin, Lough (Connacht)
.12	Conn...Cunn	Conn, Lough (Connacht)
.12	Neptune	?Neptune; Neptune Boat Club
.13	Tritonville	?Neptune: Triton; Tritonville Rd
.13	leandros	Leander Boat Club
.14	Neya	Neya, USSR
	narev	Narev, Pol
	nen	Nen, Eng
	nonni	Nonni, China
	nos	Nos, It

Perhaps because Anna Livia renews herself by falling as rain throughout the Wicklow mountains, on page 203 she doubles as the Annamoe R, which rises on the other side of Sally Gap from the sources of the Liffey, flows through Lough Tay in the valley of Luggela, then as the Cloghoge R through Lough Dan to become the Avonmore R, which joins the Avonbeg R at Avoca (The Meeting of the Waters), and finally as the Avoca R flows through the Vale of Arklow to reach the Irish Sea at Arklow, the river's end (203.18).

203.14	Ow		Ow R	
		Ow		Ow, Ire
.15	Ovoca		Avoca;	Meeting of the Waters
		yst with		Ystwith, Wales
.15	Lucan		Lucan	
		Yokan		Yo, Afr; Yukon, US; Yokanka, USSR
.16		Dell		Dell Creek, US
		fairy		Fairy Water, Ire
		ferse		Ferse, Ger
.17		dinkel		Dinkel, Neth
		dale		Dale, Ire
.17	Luggelaw		Luggela	
		Luggelaw		Lugela, Afr; Lugg, Wales & Eng
.18	Michael Arklow		Arklow	
.19		lavabibs		Lava, Pol & USSR
.20	venersderg		Derg, Lough	
		venersderg		Derg, Ire
		junojuly		Juna, Ind; Juny, Ire
		oso		Oso, Afr
.21		Nance the Nixie		Nance Creek, US
		Nanon L'Escaut		Nan, China; Scheldt (Escaût), Belg
		sycomores		Sycamore Creek, US
.24		singimari		Singimari, Ind
.24	strumans		Strumon	
		strumans		Struma, Bulg; Strumen, USSR
.26	Vale Vowclose's lucydlac		Valeclusa; Vaucluse	
		lucydlac		Lucy Creek, Australia
.27		arronged		Arrone, It
		orranged		Orange, Afr
.29		Mavro		Mavri, Gr
.30		teasesong		Tees, Eng
.31		Maass		Maas, Eur
		meshes		Mesha, USSR
.32		Simba		Simba Uranga, Afr
		Oga		Ogi, Jap
.33		thurso		Thurso, Scot
.35		lippes		Lippe, Ger
		akiss		Acis, Sicily
		kisokushk		Kiso, Jap; Kushk, USSR
.36	niver		Nive R	
		niver		Nièvre, Fr; Nive, Fr
		nevar		Neva, USSR

204.01	she hielt her souff'	Liffey
.02	ruz	Val de Ruz (not a riv), Switz
	aisne	Aisne, Fr
.03	bantur	Tura, USSR
.05	Livvy	Liffey
.05	Naama's	Na'aman R
	Naama's	Na'aman, Pal
.05	navn	?Navan
.06	scoutsch...pickts	Scotland
.06	Barefoot Burn	?
.07	Wallowme Wade	?
.07	Lugnaquillia's	Lugnaquilla, Mt
.09	canoedler	Canoe, Can, US
.09	porterhouse barge	Guinness's Brewery
.10	leada	Lea, Eng; Leda, Ger
	unraidy	Raidak, Bhutan & Ind
.12	Chirripa	Chirripo, Costa Rica
	poing	Po, It
.13	old Kippure	Kippure, Mt
.14	livvly	Liffey
.15	gap...Sally	Sally Gap
.15	Devil's glen	Devil's Glen
.18	black pools	Dublin: Dubh-linn
	rainy	Rainy, Can & US
.19	innocefree	Inisfree
	drove	Drowes, Ire
.21	findhorn's	Findhorn, Scot
.22	flenders	Belgium
	flenders	Flinders, Australia
.25	florry	Fleury, Ire
	aback	Back, Can, US
.26	loth	Loth, Scot
.28	Rother	Rother, Eng
.30	jub on	Juba, Afr
	wipers	Wieprz, Pol; Wipper, Ger
	rancing	Rance, Fr
.31	Arran	?Aran Islands; Arran Quay; ?Queen's Br
.32	vesdre	Vesdre, Belg
.33	*Colo*	Colo, Australia
.34	oder	Oder R
	oder	Oder, Eur
	Magrath's	Magra, It
.35	aird	Aird, Indonesia
.36	crampton lawn	?Crampton Quay; ?Crampton's Monument
	lawn	Laune, Ire
	Baptiste	Baptiste, Can
205.03	old the plain	Moyelta
	old	Old, US
	Welland	Welland, Can, Eng
.05	Belvedarean	Belvedere College
.06	oarsclub	Oarus, USSR
	hoo	Hou, Laos

205.07		hoa	Ho, Australia
		nubilee	Nuble, Chile
.07	Ellis on quay		Ellis Quay
		Ellis	Ellis, US
.09		Annan	Annan, Scot
		exe	Exe, Eng
.10		twisk	Wiske, Eng
.12		drawars	Drava, Eur
.13	aston		Aston Quay
.15	amstel		Amstel R
		amstel	Amstel, Neth
		Garonne, garonne	Garonne, Fr
.16	Mericy Cordial		Maritza R (Meriç); ?Mater Misericordiae Hospital
		Mericy	Meriç, Turk
		Cordial	Corda, Brazil
.17		Zindeh	Zindeh, Iran
		Munaday	Mun, Thailand; Una, Yugo
.19		beggin	Egg, Can
.21	snowdon		Snowdon, Mt
		skunner	Kunna, Ind
.22		Thaw, thaw	Thaya, Czech
		sava	Sava, Yugo
		savuto	Savuto, It
.23		erriff	Erriff, Ire
		arver	Arve, Fr

The following 4 inns were all meeting places of the Ouzel Galley Society (qv).

.24	Rose and Bottle		Rose and Bottle (Inn)
.25	Phoenix Tavern		Phoenix Tavern
.25	Power's Inn		Power's Inn
.25	Jude's Hotel		Jude's Hotel
.26	Nannywater		Nannywater R (N Co Dublin)
		Nannywater	Nannywater, Ire
.26	Vartryville		Vartry R (S Co Dublin)
		Vartryville	Vartry, Ire
.27	Porta Lateen		Rome: Porta Latina
.27	lootin quarter		Latin Quarter (Paris)
		ikom	Ikom, Afr
		etsched	Etsch, It
.28	cammocking		Cammock R
		cammocking	Cammock, Ire
.29		royss	Reuss, Switz; Ross, Can
		turgos	Turco, Bolivia; Turgai, USSR
.29	Evropeahahn cheic house		Europe; Maritza R (Evros); Zurich: Pfauen Restaurant
		Evropeahahn	Evre, Fr; Evros, Gr
.30		sooit	Soo Canals, Can & US
.30	hamman		?Hammam
.32		peihos	Pei-ho, China
		ubanjees	Ubangi, Afr
.33		tiara	Tiaret, Algeria

205.33	rotundarinking	Rotunda
.34	Pate-by-the-Neva	St Petersburg (USSR)
	Neva	Neva, USSR
.34	Pete-over-Meer	?St Petersburg (Missouri)
.35	Hausman all paven	Haussmann, Blvd (Paris)
	Cabin	Cabin Creek, US
.36	hennad	Enna, It
	Egg	Egg, Can
206.01	mauldrin	Mauldre, Fr
.01	areopage	Athens: Areopagus
.02	bingkan	Kan, China
	cagnan	Caguán, S Amer
.03	Ma	Ma, Burma
	Hong	Hong, China
.04	a law	Alaw, Wales
.04	croststyx	Styx
	croststyx	Styx, Hades
.05	wyndabouts	Wynd Brook, Eng
.06	Mary del Dame	St Mary del Dam
.08	niever	Nièvre R
	niever	Nièvre, Fr
	dongu	Dongu, Afr
.09	meurther	Meurthe, Fr
	mague	Mague, Ire
	zakbag	Zak, Afr
.12	chapboucqs	Boucq, Belg
.14	gigguels	Giguela, Sp
.15	rabbit	Rabbit, US
.16	minneho	Minho, Port
.17	dusky dirgle dargle	Dargle R; Dublin Allusion: "Dear Dirty Dublin"
.18	dargle	Dargle, Ire
.18	holy well of Mulhuddart	Mulhuddart
.19	chanza	Chanza, Sp & Port
.19	Tirry and Killy's	Kelly, Terence (pawnbroker)
	Tirry	Tirry, Scot
.19	mount of impiety	Monte de Pietà
.20	aviary	Avre, Fr
.24	overthepoise	Oise, Fr
	slaney	Slaney, Ire
	Deel	Deel, Ire
	longsome	Longa, Afr, S Amer
.25	Tongue	Tongue, US
	thet	Thet, Eng
	Thouat's	Thouet, Fr
.26	scheldt	Scheldt, Belg
	Lynd	Lynd, Australia
.27	ashes	Ash, Eng, US
	canons	Cannon, US
.27	Ower more	Avoca
	Ower more	Owenmore, Ire
.29	fal	Fal, Eng

206.30	teviots	Teviot, Scot
	sampood	Sampú, Panama
.31	galawater	Gala Water, Scot
	fraguant	Fragua, S Amer
	wupper	**Wupper**, Ger
	lauar	Laua, Ind
.32	greesed	Greese, Ire
.33	warthes	Warthe, Pol
	wears	Wear, Eng
	mole	Mole, Eng
	itcher	Itchen, Eng
.33	butterscatch	Scotland
.34	serpenthyme	?Serpentine
	serpenthyme	Serpentine, Can
.35	ushered...isles	Usher's Island, Usher's Quay
	ushered	Ushkh, USSR
	prunella	Prunelli, Fr
	eslats	Esla, Sp
	allover	Allow, Ire
.36	Peeld	Peel, Australia, Can
	jellybelly	Jelei, Borneo; Belly, Can
207.06	richmond	Richmond; Richmond Br
	richmond	Richmond, Australia
.07	rehr	Rehr, Ind
.07	Irish	Ireland
.07	rhunerhinerstones	Rhone R; Rhine R
	rhunerhinerstones	Rhone, Eur; Rhine, Eur
.08	dawk of	Daugava, USSR
.08	her airy ey	Ireland: Eire (*ey*, Dan "island")
	ey	Ey Burn, Scot
.08	Lutetiavitch	Paris: "Lutetia"
.09	lippeleens	Lippe, Ger
.10	strawbirry reds	Birr; Strawberry Beds
	strawbirry	Birrie, Australia
.11	sendred	Indre, Fr
.11	boudeloire	Loire R
	boudeloire	Loire, Fr
.11	His Affluence	Kippure, Mt
.12	Ciliegia Grande	Grand Canal
	Grande	Grande, passim
.12	Kirschie Real	Royal Canal
	Real	Real, S Amer
	chirsines	Chirin, China
.13	missus, seepy	Mississippi R
	missus, seepy	Mississippi, US
	missus...sewery	Missouri, US
.14	passe...minnikin	Brussels: Manneken-Pis
.15	Brie-on-Arrosa	Brie
	Arrosa	Arros, Fr
.16	mine	Mine, Ire
	stalls	Tall, Ire
	bridely	Bride, Eng, Ire

207.16	sign	Sig, Afr
	Zambosy	Zambesi, Afr
.17	half her length away	Liffey (the Liffey in Dublin is less than half its length from its source as the crow flies)
.18	slang	Langa, Iceland
.19	Anna Livia	Liffey
	oysterface	Oyster, US
	forth	Forth, Scot
	bassein	Bassein, Burma
.21	Spitz	Spiti, Ind
.21	iern	?Ireland: Iernia
.22	irthing	Irthing, Eng
	nerthe	Nethe, Belg
.23	lomba strait	Lombard Street
	lomba	Lomba, Afr
.23	Oceans of Gaud	?
	mosel	Mosel, Eur
.24	Ogowe	Ogowe, Afr
	Julia	Julia, Switz
	Ishekarry	Ishikari, Jap
	washemeskad	Washimeska, Can
.25	carishy	Arish, Syria
	caratimaney	Caratimani, S Amer
.26	Bon a ventura	Bonaventure, Can
.26	Malagassy	Madagascar
	liddel	Liddel, Scot
	oud	Oudon, Fr
.28	Amnisty Ann	Liffey (*amnis*, Lat "river")
.30	test	Test, Eng
.31	peace	Peace, Can, US
.33	hoogly	Hooghly R
	hoogly	Hooghly, Ind
	igloo	Iglau, Czech
.34	toetippit	Oti, Afr; Iput, USSR
	moma	Moma, USSR
.35	ems	Ems, Ger
	embarras	Embarras, US
.36	aues	Aue, Ger
	awe	Awe, Scot
	judyqueen	Judy Creek, US
208.01	elb	Elbe, Eur
	saise	Saisi, Afr
.02	Save	Save, Fr
	tagus	Tagus, Sp
	Werra	Werra, Ger
.03	ourthe	Ourthe, Belg
.03	Lambay	Lambay Island
	Lambay	Liambai, Afr
.04	epte	Epte, Fr
.05	Liviam	Liffey
	Liddle	Liddel, Scot
	Loveme	Eme, Afr

208.05		Long	Longa, Afr, S Amer
.05	linth		Limmat (Linth) R
		linth	Linth, Switz
.07	sugarloaf		Sugarloaf
		guadyquiviry	Guadalquivir, Sp
.08		arnoment	Arno, It
.09		guildered	Guil, Fr
.10		fishnetzeveil	Fish, passim; Netze, Pol
.11		hydeaspects	Hydaspes, Ind
		laubes	Aube, Fr
.12	cuba		Cuba
.13		galligo	Gallegos, Argentina
		shimmy	Simme, Switz
		hazevaipar	Vaipar, Ind
		tinto	Tinto, Sp
.15		bloodorange	Blood, Afr; Orange, Afr
.16	nigger		Niger R
		nigger	Niger, Afr
		blackstripe tan	Black, passim; Tana, passim
.17		joseph	Joseph, US
.17	sequansewn		Seine R
		sequansewn	Seine, Fr (Lat, *Sequana*)
.18		leadown	Lea, Eng
.19		swansruff	Swan, passim
		gaspers	Gaspereau, Can
		hayrope	Hay, passim; Roper, Australia
.20		codroy	Codroy, Can
.20	alpheubett buttons		Alpheus R; ?Butt Br
		alpheubett	Alph, Xanadu; Alpheus, Gr
.21		twobar	Tubarão, S Amer
.22		windrush	Windrush, Eng
.23		kep on	Chepo, Cen Amer
.24		sommething	Somme, Fr
.24	fiumy		Fiume
.25		siouler's	Sioule, Fr
.26	ffiffty odd Irish miles		Ireland; Liffey (length)
.26	lungarhodes		?Rhodes
		lungarhodes	Lunga, Afr; Rhodanus, Fr
.27	Hellsbells		Hell
		gumptyum	Gumti, Ind
.28	naze		?Naze, The
		naze	Nazas, Mex
.29	dowce		Douce, Mt
.29	delia		?Delos
		delia	Deli, Turk
.30		Lotsy	Lotsani, Afr
		trotsy	Trothy, Eng
.30	poddle		Poddle R
		poddle	Poddle, Ire
.31		Fenny	Fenny, Ind
		hex	Hex, Afr
		charred	Charr, Scot

208.32		mush	Musha, USSR
.32	mullet's eyes		Mullet Penin
		mullet's	Mullet, US
.32	boys dobelon		Dublin Bay
.33		chariton	Chariton, US
.34		may	May, Australia
.35		recknitz	Regnitz, Ger
		wharfore	Wharfe, Eng
		darling	Darling, Australia
		murrayed	Murray, Australia
.36		Mersey	Mersey, Eng
		koros	Körös, Hung
209.03	North Lazers' Waal		Lazy (Lazar's) Hill; North Wall Quay
		Waal	Waal, Neth
.04		eelfare	Eel, US
.04	Jukar Yoick's		?
		Jukar	Jucar, Sp
		Yoick's	Oich, Scot
.05	meander		Meander R
		meander	Meander, Asia Min
.06		bonnet	Bonnet, Ire
.06	Avondale's		Avondale
		Avondale's	Avon, passim
.07		Clarence's	Clarence, Australia, NZ
		an	An, Burma
		aneber	Anabar, USSR
.08		Crutches	Crouch, Eng
		Bates	Bates Creek, US
		southsates	South, passim
.09		*granite*	Granite Creek, US
.09	*Alp*		?Dublin: Alp Uí Laoghaire
.10		baggyrhatty	Bhagirathi, Ind
.11		tembo	Tambo, Australia; Tembe, Afr
		pilipili	Pili, China
.12		thunder	Thunder, US
.13		battle	Battle, Can
.14		soorce	Soo Canals, Can & US
		aubette	Aube, Fr
		bearb	Bearba, Ire
.15		son	Son, Ind
.16		worth	Worth, Eng
.17		Spey	Spey, Scot
		pruth	Pruth, Romania & USSR
.18		arundgirond	Arun, Eng; Gironde, Fr
		waveny	Waveney, Eng
		lyne	Lyne, Eng
		aringarouma	Garumna, Fr
.19		boulder	Boulder Creek, US
		narrowa	Narova, USSR
.21		curara	Curaray, S Amer
.21	medway		Medway R
		medway	Medway, Eng

209.22		weser	Weser, Ger
		edereider	Eder, Ger; Eider, Ger
.22	chattahoochee		Chattahoochee R
		chattahoochee	Chattahoochee, US
.23		ain	Ain, Fr
		chichiu	Chichui, China
		cree	Cree, Scot
.23	the pale		Pale, The
.24		nistling	Nisling, Can
.24	Isolabella		Chapelizod; Liffey
.25	Romas and Reims		Reims; Rome
		Romas	Rom, Eng
		Reims	Rima, Afr
.26	lech		Lech R
		lech	Lech, Ger
		dart	Dart, Eng
.26	Dirty Hans' spatters		?
.27		aisch	Aisch, Ger
		iveryone	Ivari, S Amer
.29		fleetly	Fleet, Eng, Scot
		pourch	Ource, Fr; Ourcq, Fr
.30	glashaboys		Glashaboy
		glashaboys	Glashaboy, Ire
.31	pollynooties		?Pollanalty
		pollynooties	Polimounty, Ire; Polly, Scot
.31	paunschaup		?Punjab
		paunschaup	Gave de Pau, Fr
.33	Smyly boys		Birds' Nest Institution
.34	vicereine's levee		?Phoenix Park: Viceregal Lodge
		Vivi	Vivi, USSR
.34	vienne...Annchen		Vienna
		vienne	Vienne, Fr
.35		sula	Sulak, USSR
		susuria	Usuri, China & USSR; Susurlu, Turk
.35	Ausone sidulcis		?Ausonia
		Ausone	Sone, Ind
.36		tambre	Tambre, Sp
		chir	Chir, USSR
210.01		jary	Jary, S Amer
		dive	Dive, Ire
		neb	Neb, Isle of Man
		sacco	Sacco, It
.01	wabbash		Wabash R
		wabbash	Wabash, US
.02		raabed	Raab, Austria & Hung
		maundy	Maun, Eng
.03		aringarung	Arigna, Ire
.04	dribblederry		Derry
		dribblederry	Ribble, Eng; Derry, Ire
.05		wickerpotluck	Luch, USSR
.07	tinker's bann		Bann R

210.07	bann	Bann, Ire
.07	barrow to boil	Barrow R
	barrow	Barrow, Ire
.07	Gipsy Lee	Lee R
	Lee	Lee, Ire
.12	brazen nose	Oxford U: Brasenose College
.15	Techertim	Tech, Fr
	Tombigby	Tombigbee, US
.16	Hayes	Hayes, Can
.18	Clonliffe	Clonliffe; Liffey
	Val	Val, Nor
.19	Skibereen	Skibbereen
.19	Doolin	Dublin
.19	Ballyclee	Dublin: Baile Átha Cliath
.21	Jerry Coyle	Jericho
	Mackenzie	Mackenzie, Can
.24	Blanchisse's	Blanche, Fr; Ise, Ger
.27	scotched	Scotland
.27	vaticanned	Vatican
.28	reiz	Reisa, Nor
.28	Standfast Dick	Standfast Dick
.30	appletweed	Tweed, Scot
	Mobbely	Mobile, US
	Saara	Saar, Ger
.30	jordan	Jordan R
	jordan	Jordan, passim
.31	tearorne	Orne, Fr
	Aruna	Arun, Eng
.32	Arhone	Rhone R
	Arhone	Rhone, Switz & Fr
.33	Coleraine	Coleraine
.33	Butterman's Lane	?Butter Lane
.35	niester	Dniester, USSR
	egg	Egg, Can
211.01	collera	Coll, Scot
.01	starr and girton	Cambridge: Girton College; Star and Garter
	starr and	Tarrant, Eng
.02	Deane	Dean, Can, Eng
.03	noble...sweeden	Sweden: Nobel Prize
	Oliver	Olivera, S Amer
.04	in his frey	Inisfree
.05	tibertine's	Tiber, It
.05	Congoswood cross	Clongowes Wood College; Cong (Cross of); Congo R
	Congoswood	Congo, Afr; Wood, Can, US
	cross	Cross, passim
.07	lubilashings	Lubilash, Afr
	Olona	Olona, It
.08	Lena	Lena, USSR
.08	Magdalena	Magdalen
	Magdalena	Magdalena, S Amer
	Camilla	Cam, Eng, Ire

211.08		Dromilla	Drome, Fr
.09	Nancy Shannon		Shannon R
		Shannon	Shannon, Ire
.10	Tuami		Tuam
		Dora Riparia	Dora Riparia, It
		Hopeandwater	Hope, Scot
.11	Blarney		Blarney
.12		toby	Tobique, Can
.13	volgar		Volga R
		volgar	Volga, USSR
.14		Bellezza	Bell, Australia; Belle, US
		Missa	Misa, It
.15		Taff de Taff	Taff, Wales
.16	Rogerson Crusoe's		?Rogerson's Quay, Sir John
		Rubiconstein	Rubicon, It
.17		tyne	Tyne, Eng
.19	varians		Varian and Co
.21	daulphins born		Dolphin's Barn
.22		Maggi	Maggia, Switz
.23	Lusk		Lusk
.23	Livienbad		Dublin: Misc Allusions; ?Evian-les-Bains
.24	symposium's syrup		Simpson's Hospital
.25	gouty Gough		?Phoenix Park: Gough Statue
.25	change of naves		Christchurch Cathedral
		ills	Ill, Austria, Fr
.26	Armoricus		Armorica
		Amoor	Amur, China & USSR
		Saint Lawrence	St Lawrence, Can
.27		suspendeats	Dease, Can; Pende, Afr
.28	oakanknee		Oconee R
		oakanknee	Oconee, US
		musquodoboits	Musquodoboit, Can
.30	map of the month		Mappa Mundi
.32	Browne but Nolan		Browne and Nolan
.33	lock		Westmoreland Lock Hospital
.34	Billy Dunboyne		Boyne R; Dunboyne
		Dunboyne	Boyne, Ire
.35		Ida Ida	Ida, USSR
.36	swilly		Swilly, Lough
		swilly	Swilly, Ire
.36	swash		Wash, The
212.01		Yuinness	Yün, China; Huisne, Fr (+ Guinness)
		Yennessy	Yenesei, USSR (+ Hennessy cognac)
		Laagen	Laagen, Nor
.01	Niger		Niger R
		Niger	Niger, Afr
.03		Magrath	Magra, It
.04		O'Delawarr	Delaware, US
		Rossa	Rossaa, Nor
.06		Selina	Selinus, Asia Min

212.06	Susquehanna		Susquehanna R
	Susquehanna		Susquehanna, US
.07	Ward		Ward, Ire
.07	Peggy Quilty		?Quilty
.07	Briery Brosna		Brosna R
	Brosna		Brosna, Ire
.08	Maassy		Maas, Eur
	Zusan		Zusam, Ger
.08	Camac		Cammock R
	Camac		Cammock, Ire
.09	Bradogue		Bradogue R
	Bradogue		Bradogue, Ire
.09	Flora Ferns		Fern, Lough
.10	Grettna Greaney		Gretna Green
	Grettna Greaney		Greta, Eng; Greaney, Ire
	Lezba		Lezba, USSR
.11	Licking		Licking, US
	Leytha		Leytha, Hung
	Liane		Liane, Fr
	Rohan		Rohan, Ind
.12	Sohan		Sohan, Ind
	Una		Una, Yugo
	Bina		Bina, Ind
	Laterza		Laterza, It
.13	Irmak Elly		Kelkit Irmak, Turk
	Josephine		Joseph, US
	Foyle		Foyle, Ire
.13	Snakeshead		Snake, passim
.14	Fountainoy Laura		?Fontenoy; Vaucluse
	Fountainoy		Fountain Creek, US; Noya, Sp
	Laura		Laura, Afr
	Marie		Marie, S Amer
.15	Macleay		Macleay, Australia
	ilcka		Ilek, USSR
	madre's		Madre, S Amer
.16	bloodvein		Bloodvein, Can
.17	devide		Devi, Ind
.20	wardha		Wardha, Ind
	bakereen's		Baker, US
	dusind		Sind, Ind
.21	Hibernonian market		Ireland: Hibernia
.24	pison		Pison, Paradise
	hudson		Hudson, US
.25	Clane		Clane; ?Slane
	raft		Raft, US
.26	marne		Marne, Fr
	Merced		Merced, US
	mulde		Mulde, Ger
.27	lohaned		Lohan, China
.31	dvine		Dvina R
	dvine		Dvina, USSR
.31	marsh narcissus		Marsh's Library

212.35	*Omo...omo*	Omo, Afr
.36	*Windermere*	Windermere
213.01	old *House by the Coachyard*	Chapelizod: The House by the Churchyard
.02	*Ditto on the Floss...flossies*	(*The Mill on the Floss*)
	Altmuehler	Altmuehl, Ger
.04	isker	Isker (Siberian town)
	isker	Isker, Bulgaria
	suda	Suda, USSR
.05	chayney	China
	chayney	Chay, SE Asia
.06	Hoangho, my sorrow	Hwang Ho R ("China's Sorrow")
	Hoangho	Hwang Ho, China
.07	Aimihi	Aimihi, Iran
.08	gihon	Gihon, Paradise
	lovat	Lovat, USSR
	maure	Maur, Malacca; Aure, Fr
.09	moravar	Morava, Eur
	Regn	Regen, Ger
.11	kennet	Kennet, Eng
.12	taling	Ta-ling, China
.13	root	Root, US
.14	cher's	Cher, Fr
	ashley	Ashley, US
	Fieluhr	Fie, Afr
.15	saon	Saône, Fr
.15	senne	Seine R
	senne	Seine, Fr; Senne, Belg
.15	erewone	Erewhon
.16	Waterhouse's clogh	Waterhouse and Co
	clogh	Clogh, Ire
.18	Aches-les-Pains	Aix-les-Bains
	Aches-les-Pains	Ache, Austria
	Pingpong	Ping, Thailand; Pongo, Afr
	Belle	Belle, US
.19	Pang	Pang, passim
.20	Godavari	Godavari, Ind
	vert	Verte, Can
	showers	Shur, Iran
.21	thaya	Thaya, Czech
	Aman	Amana, Syria; Amman, Pal
.23	churning	Churn, Eng; Churni, Ind
	Der went	Derwent, Eng
.29	Jossiph	Joss, Ger; Joseph, US
.30	Mutter	Mutt, Switz
	Wharnow	Warnow, Ger
	alle	Alle, Ger, Switz
.32	Allalivial, allalluvial	Liffey
.34	Shannons	Shannon R
	Shannons	Shannon, Ire
.34	Spain	Spain
.35	Markland's	Markland
.35	Vineland	Vinland

213.35	Brendan's herring pool	Atlantic O
.36	yangsee's	America; Yangtsze R
	yangsee's	Yangtsze, China
	hats	Hat Creek, US
214.01	lost	Lost, US
.01	histereve	Danube R
	histereve	Ister (Danube), Eur
.02	a main drain	Main Drain
	main	Main, Ger
.03	manzinahurries	Manzanares, Sp
.03	Bachelor's Walk	Bachelor's Walk
	Bachelor's Walk	Bachelor's Run, US
.04	loup	Loup, US
.06	Orara	Orara, Australia
	Orbe	Orbe, Fr
	Las Animas	Las Animas, US
.07	Ussa	Ussa, USSR
	Ulla	Ulla, USSR, Sp
	umbas	Umba, USSR, Afr
	Mezha	Mezha, USSR
.08	ufer...ufer	Ufa, USSR
	deed...deed	Dee, passim
.09	irrawaddyng	Irrawaddy, Burma
	stoke	Stoke, Eng
	aars	Aar, Switz & Ger
.10	lethest	Lethe R
	lethest	Lethe, Hades
	Oronoko	Orinoco, S Amer
.11	Finnleader	Finn, Ire
.12	Father of Otters	Mississippi R
	Father of Otters	Otter, passim
.13	Yonne	Yonne, Fr
.13	Fallareen Common	Fallarees Commons
.14	Astley's Amphitheayter	Astley's Amphitheatre; Molyneux Asylum for Blind Females
.15	ghostwhite horse	White Horse
.18	Ireland...Ireland	Ireland (Father Mathew: "Ireland sober is Ireland free")
	grease	Greese, Ire
.19	I sonht zo	Isonzo, It
	Madammangut	Madame, W Indies; Amman, Pal
.20	Conway's Carrigacurra canteen	Carrigacurra; ?Conway's Pub; Conway's Tavern
	Conway's	Conway, Wales
.22	rere	Rer, Ind
.22	creakorheuman	Greece; Rome
.27	son	Son, Ind
.28	limpopo	Limpopo, Afr
.30	Carlow	Carlow
.30	Scamander	Xanthos (Scamander) R
	Scamander	Scamander, Asia Min
	I sar	Isar, Ger

214.31	golden falls		Golden Falls
.31	Icis		Thames R
		Icis	Isis (upper Thames), Eng
		Seints	Seint, Wales
		Zezere	Zezere, Port
.32		hamble	Hamble, Eng
.33	dwyergray ass		Man, Isle of
.34		meanam	Me Nam, Thailand
		Lyons	Lyons, Australia
		Gregory	Gregory, Australia
		meyne	Meyne, Fr
.35		draves	Drave, Yugo & Hung
215.01	Poolbeg flasher		Poolbeg
.01	pharphar		Pharos at Alexandria
		pharphar	Pharphar, Syria (2 *Kings* 5:12)
.02		nyar	Nyar, Ind
.02	Kishtna		Kish Lightship
		Kishtna	Kistna, Ind
.03		Garry	Garry, Scot
.03	Indes		India
		Indes	Indus, Ind & Pakistan
.04		lune	Lune, Eng
.06	blue milk's		Milky Way
.07		milk's	Milk, US & passim
		Bubye	Bubye, Afr
.08		evenlode	Evenlode, Eng
		save	Save, Fr
.09		jurna's	Jurua, S Amer
.10		sow	Sow, Eng
.10	moyvalley		Moy R; Moyvalley
		moyvalley	Moy, Ire; Valley, US
.11		Towy	Towy, Wales
.11	rathmine		Rathmines
.12	Anna Livia		Liffey
.13		quare	Quarai, S Amer
.13	**Dear Dirty Dumpling**		Dublin Allusion: "Dear Dirty Dublin"
.14	fingalls		?**Fingal**
		fingalls	Fingal, Australia
.15	seven dams		(JJ said of this chapter [*Letters* I, 373] that "the splitting up towards the end [seven dams] is the city abuilding.")
.17	Sudds		Nile R: The Sudd
.19		Bifur	Biferno, It
.20	Etrurian		Etruria
		limony	Lim, Yugo
.21	turkiss		Turkey
.21	indienne		India
		indienne	Indian, US
		milkidmass	Milk, US & passim
.22		Tys Elvenland	Tys Elv ("river"), Nor
		Teems	Teme, Eng
.23		seim	Seim, USSR

215.23	Ordovico		Ordovices	
.24	Anna...Livia		Liffey	
.24	Northmen's thing		Thing Mote	
.25	southfolk's place		Suffolk St	
.26	trinity scholard		Trinity College, Dublin	
		eure	Eure, Fr	
.27		oure	Our, Ger & Lux; Ure, Eng	
.27	eryan		Ireland	
.27	*Eblanensis*		Dublin: Eblana	
.33	liffeying		Liffey	
.34		foos	Oos, Ger	
		moos	Moose, Can, US	
.35		elm	Elm, US	
.35	Livia's		Liffey	
.36		halls	Hall, US	
216.01 –.03		Tell...tell	Tel, Ind	
.03		elm	Elm, US	

BOOK II
Chapter 1

219.02	Feenichts Playhouse ?	.01	St. Patricius' Academy for Grown- up Gentlemen (*Cont.*) St Patrick's Training College
.03	Diddlem Club NPN: Brit slang (pre-WW II) for a lottery	.08	Glen of the Downs Glen of the Downs
.08	daily dubbing Dublin Allusion: "Dear Dir- ty Dublin"	.09	his geyswerks Gasometer
.11	Findrias, Murias, Gorias and Falias Finias, Murias, Failias, Gorias	.09	his earsequack Ireland: Erse
		.12	Miss Rachel Lea Varian Varian and Co
		.15	whouse be the churchyard Chapelizod: The House by the Churchyard
.11	Falias...Pierre Dusort Lia Fáil		
.14	Adelphi Adelphi Theatre	.15	aasgaars ?Asgard
.14	Bratislavoff Bratislava	.27	R.I.C. Ireland (Royal Irish Constabu- lary)
.15	King's Hoarsers ?Chapelizod: King's House Gaiety Theatre	.28	Crooker and Toll Kreuger and Toll
.16	Queen's Mum Adelphi Theatre	.29	Kappa Pedersen Kapp and Peterson
.19	Ballymooney Ballaghmoon Ballyhooly: "Ballyhooly Blue Ribbon Army"	.30	Morgen Morgan, Joseph, Mrs
		.32	Phenecian Phoenicia Venice
220.03	St. Bride's Finishing Establish- ment St Brigid's	.32	Sourdanian Sardinia
.19	Grischun Greece	.35	Cork Cork
.25	Schweden Sweden	222.07	Annapolis Annapolis Dublin: Annapolis
.34	The Rockery, Poopinheavin Copenhagen Vatican	.12	*The Bearded Mountain* ?
.35	pilgrimst customhouse Custom House	.12	Baretherootsch ?Bayreuth
.35	Caherlehome-upon-Eskur Caerleon-on-Usk Esker	.13	Maidykins ?Belfast: Cave Hill (Ben Madi- gain)
221.01	St. Patricius' Academy for Grownup Gentlemen ?St Patrick's Hospital	.14	thugogmagog Gog and Magog

.25 duvlin
 Dublin

.31 athletes longfoot
 ?Athlone
 ?Longford

223.03 airish
 Ireland

.05 Mutther Masons
 Mason's Restaurant

.06 Sevilla
 Seville

.16 Copenhague-Marengo
 Copenhagen
 ?Hague, The
 Marengo

.17 Glenasmole of Smiling Thrushes
 Glenasmole

.19 scaldbrother
 Scaldbrother's Hole

.20 Saint Joan's Wood
 St John's Road (Kilmain-
 ham)

.20 kill or maim him
 Kilmainham

.28 Ethiaop lore
 Abyssinia
 (+ anagram of "heliotrope")

.29 hoothed
 ?Howth

224.02 goodda purssia
 ?Persia
 ?Prussia

.03 injine ruber
 India

.06 fourd...hurtled stones
 Dublin: Baile Átha Cliath

.12 towerable...baublelight
 Babel, Tower of

.17 limbopool
 Limbo
 ?Liverpool

.21 Cicely, awe
 Cecilia St (medical school)

.29 Madama Lifay
 Liffey

225.02 ringsoundinly
 Ringsend

.04 troy
 Troy

.05 ulstramarines
 Ulster

.15 Rigagnolina
 ?

.15 Mountagnone
 ?

.24 Hellfeuersteyn
 Hell

.26 Van Diemen's
 Tasmania: Van Dieman's Land

226.02 Carolinas
 Carolina, N and S

.06 Hey, lass
 Greece

.09 France's
 France (+ St Francis)

.10 Clare
 Clare (+ Poor Clares, Franciscan nuns)

.15 Dee
 Dee R

.24 libertyed garters
 ?Liberty and Co

.31 greeneriN
 Ireland

.34 th'avignue
 Avignon

.35 Luvium
 ?Lee R: Luvius

227.01 Eirae
 Ireland

.02 Winsure
 Windsor

.18 ancelles' garden
 ?

.20 anger arbour
 ?

.20 treerack monatan
 Three Rock Mt

.22 divlun...punchpoll
 Devil's Punchbowl
 Dublin

.27 unconnouth
 ?Connacht

.35 tarrascone
 Lia Fáil: Stone of Scone
 Tara
 Tarascon (France)

228.01 Machonochie Middle
 ?

.02 MacSiccaries of the Breeks
 McGillycuddy's Reeks

.06 hells where
 Hell

.07 yank islanders
    America

.13 conansdream
    Cona

.13 lodascircles
    Loda

.15 Aram
    Aram

.15 Era
    Ireland

.16 Dora
    Dora

.17 sheolmastress
    Sheol

.18 carberry
    ?Carberry Hill

.19 Pencylmania
    Pennsylvania

.19 Bretish Armerica
    America
    Armorica
    Bretland (Wales)

.20 Bunkers' Trust, recorporated
    ?

.21 laracor
    Laracor

.22 Paname-Turricum
    Paris: "Paname"
    Zurich: "Turicum"

.22 tarry easty...città immediata
    Trieste

.26 Euro pra nobis
    Europe

.26 cashel
    Cashel
    ?Mt Cashel

.28 Fuisfinister
    ?Finisterre

.30 the raging canal
    Regent's (Canal)

.31 Jorden
    Jordan R
    (+ *jorden*, Nor "the earth")

.32 knockonacow
    Knocknagow

.33 gheol ghiornal
    Sheol (+ John Mitchell's
    Jail Journal)

.34 Toumaria
    Samaria
    Tara
    Temora

.35 Anteach
    Antioch
    (*an teach*, Ir "the house")

229.03 Fenlanns
    England
    Finland

.03 Mary Inklenders
    England

.07 S.P.Q.R.ish
    Ireland
    Rome: SPQR

.08 nation of sheepcopers
    England
    ?Ireland: Misc Allusions

.10 lyonesses
    ?Lyonesse
    Lyons

The names at 229.13–.16 are the
Homeric names of the chapters of Ulysses, *in order, minus the first three and*
last three.

.13 Had Days
    Hades (Glasnevin Cemetery)

.14 Skilly and Carubdish
    Scylla and Charybdis (National
    Library)

.15 Mermaids' Tavern
    Mermaid Tavern (Ormond Ho-
    tel)

.15 Mother of Misery
    Mater Misericordiae Hospital
    (but in *U*, the maternity hos-
    pital in Holles St)

.17 Leimuncononnulstria
    Leinster
    Munster
    Connacht
    Ulster

.23 malters...jemassons
    Jameson, John, and Son

.24 gap as down low
    Dunloe, Gap of

.33 the suchess of sceaunonsceau
    ?Chenonceaux
    ?Sceaux

.34 Boyrut season
    Bayreuth

230.05 provencials
    Provence

.05 narrowedknee domum
    Czechoslovakia: Narodni Dum

.06	osco de basco	.32	Atlangthis
	Basque Provinces		Atlantis
.13	Parisise	.36	Rio Grande
	Paris		Rio Grande
.15	Casanuova	233.09	frenge
	?Newcastle		France
.15	Armentières	.09	such as touch...show and show
	Armentières		?Chenonceaux
.16	Occitantitempoli		?Sceaux
	?	.14	ingle end
.25	liffe		England
	Liffey	.27	Gau on!
.27	grand carriero		Goa
	?	.27	Micaco
.33	germane faces		Macao
	Germany	.31	segur
.35	castle throwen		Ségur
	Castle Tirowen	.33	a skarp snakk
.35	propsperups treed		?Slieve Snacht
	?Prosperous	.33	engelsk
.36	stohong baroque		England
	?	.35	baskly
231.02	tingtumtingling		Basque Provinces
	Tingsomingenting	.35	spanich
.02	next, next and next		Spain
	Nixnixundnix	.35	Makoto
.09	Shina		Japan
	China	234.03	tristiest
.10	Timor Sea		?Trieste
	Timor Sea	.04	Hal
.12	shellies		Hell
	?Shelly Banks	.09	breiches...goldenest
.12	googling Lovvey		Goldenbridge
	Liffey		?Whitworth ("Old") Br
.21	Holihowlsballs	.31	arrahbeejee
	Hell		Arabia
.21	bloody acres	235.06	Osman glory
	Bloody Acre		?Turkey
.24	birdsplace	.08	turquewashed
	Rathgar: Brighton Square		Turkey
.28	Malthos Moramor	.09	Xanthos
	Mora		Xanthos
232.03	mostly Carbo	.11	bank midland mansioner
	Monte Carlo		Midland Bank
.11	venicey	.13	La Roseraie
	?Venice		?
.13	forecotes	.13	Ailesbury Road
	Four Courts		Ailesbury Road
.16	errind	.16	nebohood
	Ireland		Nebo, Mt
.21	Tintangle	.16	Oncaill's plot
	Tintagel		?(on-caill, Ir "great damage")

.16 Luccombe oaks
   Luccombe
.17 Turkish hazels
   Turkey
.17 Greek firs
   Greece
.17 hypsometers of Mount Anville
   Mt Anville
.19 Larix U'Thule
   Thule
.19 Manelagh
   Ranelagh
'.21 Fortune
   ?Wheel of Fortune
.29 cousin gourmand
   Germany: "cousin-German"
.30 Seemyease
   Siam
.36 Bootiestown
   Booterstown
236.07 Cork
   Cork
.08 Niomon
   NPN: *Nionon*, Bog Lat
   "heaven"
.10 Dublin's
   Dublin
.17 Anneliuia
   Liffey
.19 Roamaloose
   Rome
.20 Chapelldiseut
   Chapelizod
.21 purly ooze of Ballybough
   Ballybough
.22 hercourt strayed reelway
   Harcourt St Railway
.24 Grangegorman
   Grangegorman
237.05 Mullabury
   ?
.15 barnaboy
   ?Barnaboy House
   (+ *barna*, Swahili "letter")
.18 Daneygaul
   Denmark
   Donegal
   Gaul
.22 Leperstower
   Leopardstown
.22 the karman's loki
   ?Carman

.22 the karman's loki (*Cont.*)
   Carmanhall
.26 Amanti
   Amenta
.30 Demani...masikal...Baraza
   NPN: *demani*, Swahili "spring-
   time" (dry season); *masika*,
   "fall" (rainy season); *baraza*,
   "veranda"
.33 Labbeycliath
   ?Abbey Theatre
   Dublin: Baile Átha Cliath
.36 magdalenes
   Magdalen
238.01 pinmarks
   ?Penmark
.24 finnishfurst
   ?Finland
.32 iris riflers
   Ireland
.36 Gizzygazelle Tark's bimboowood
   ?
239.07 Monkmesserag
   ?Misery Hill
.24 Connie Curley
   ?Carlow
.24 Carminia
   ?Carman
.30 wherebus
   Erebus
.31 a place...viands
   Dublin: Misc Allusions
.31 miry hill
   ?Drumsallagh
.32 belge end
   Belgium
.33 hellabelow
   Hell
.34 Helldsdend, whelldselse
   Hell
.34 Lonedom's breach
   London (Bridge)
240.10 Trinitatis kink
   Trinity Church
.17 swuith Aftreck
   Africa
.18 Zundas
   ?
.18 nudgemeroughgorude
   Nizhniy-Novgorod
.20 tirnitys
   Trinity College, Dublin

.27 Anaks Andrum
?Alexandria
.28 Erserum spoking
?Erzerum
Ireland: Erse
.29 Drugmallt storehuse
?
241.03 Spinshesses Walk
?
.08 Collosul rhodomantic
Colossus of Rhodes
.16 mish...mountain
Slieve Mish
.19 dolomite
Alps: Dolomites
.22 benighted queendom
England (United Kingdom)
.24 lochkneeghed
Neagh, Lough
.25 rhomatism
Rome
.29 Sea of Deceit
?
.30 Sands of Calumdonia
Caledonia
.34 lick their lenses
Jupiter: Lick Observatory
.34 jom petter...sodalites
Jupiter
242.01 sorestate hearing, diseased
Irish Free State
.02 laxtleap
Leixlip
.05 howthold of nummer seven
Eccles St
Howth
.10 at 81
?Mabbot's Mill
.11 ecrazyaztecs
?Asia
.13 glycorawman
Greece
Rome
.15 from one 18 to one 18 biss
? (cf Mabbot's Mill)
.20 samhar
Samhair
.20 some make one noise
?Clonmacnoise
.21 Gigantic
"Titanic"

.23 stoney badder
Stoneybatter
.23 Thing
Thing Mote
.24 Suffrogate Strate
Suffolk St
.28 the Mem, Avenlith
Liffey
(*mem, ebhen*, Heb "water,"
"stone"; *abhainn*, Ir "river";
lithos, Gk "stone")
.28 couple of lizards
Chapelizod
.31 allaph foriverever
Alpheus R
.33 her eckcot hjem
?
.33 Howarden's Castle
?Castle Howard
Hawarden
.33 Englandwales
England
Wales
.34 iern
?Ireland: Iernia
243.02 fiuming
Fiume
.11 antient consort ruhm
Antient Concert Rooms
.19 blowick
Bullock Castle
.22 devlins
?Devlin R
Dublin
.23 honeycoombe
Coombe, The
.26 Ostmannstown
Oxmantown
.27 Saint Megan's
St Michan's Church
.28 shookerloft hat
Sugarloaf Mts
.29 Alpoleary
Dublin: Alp Uí Laoghaire
.31 Vatucum
Vatican
.33 Hrom
Rome
244.02 Daintytrees, go dutch
British Broadcasting Corp:
Daventry
Netherlands

.05 tents of Ceder
  NPN: Kedar, son of Ishmael
.06 Inisfail
  Ireland: Inisfail
.07 Ondslosby
  London: Ondlosbu
.20 Nancy Hands
  Phoenix Park: Hole in the
  Wall
.24 craggy road for rambling
  Dublin Allusion: "Rocky
  Road to Dublin"
.29 deerhaven
  Deer Park
.34 leabarrow
  ?Barrow R
.34 While loevdom shleeps
  London
245.01 tusker toils
  Tuskar Lighthouse
.01 Rhinohorn
  ?Rhine R
.07 coast of amethyst
  ?
.08 arcglow's
  Arklow
.08 siemens
  Siemens Schuckert
.08 wextward
  Wexford
.08 warnerforth's
  Waterford
.08 hookercrookers
  Crook
  Hook Head
.11 Liffeyetta's
  Liffey
.16 Finnyland
  ?Finland
  Ireland: Tír na bhFionn
.17 Darkpark's
  ?
.18 Rosimund's...well
  ?Rosamond's Bower
.21 elbownunsense
  Dublin: Eblana
.22 waltzers of. Stright!
  Walker St
.23 Hesperons
  Venus: "Hesperus"
.23 Livmouth
  Liffey

.24 Jacqueson's Island
  Jackson's Island
.25 hellpelhullpulthebell
  Hell
  Hull
.28 quean of Scuts
  Scotland
.30 troublebedded rooms...Mr Knight,
  tuntapster
  Euston Hotel
.35 A's...one's
  Findlater, Alexander and Co:
  A.1 whiskey
.35 Chavvyout Chacer
  Chevy Chase
.36 De oud huis bij de kerkegaard
  Chapelizod: The House by the
  Churchyard
246.02 Jug and Chambers
  ?
.04 the felled of Gorey
  Gorey
.04 starfort
  Phoenix Park: Starfort
.04 brass castle
  Chapelizod: Brass Castle
.05 Gadolmagtog
  ?Gog and Magog
.06 Brandenborgenthor
  Berlin: Brandenburg Gate
.18 lily of Bohemey
  Bohemia
  Killarney
.23 horseshow
  Dublin Horse Show
.24 Sorrento
  Sorrento (Rd)
.25 Vico's road
  Vico Rd
.26 old orangeray, Dolly Brae
  ?Orangerie
  (+ "Dolly Brae," an Orange
  song)
.27 baffle of Whatalose
  Waterloo
.32 French
  France
247.03 arubyat knychts
  Arabia
.04 Elmstree to Stene
  ?Chapelizod: Village Elm
  ?Mearingstone

.04   Elmstree to Stene (*Cont.*)
       Steyne
       (ie, from Chapelizod to cen-
       tral Dublin; cf 293.14)
.14   kerry
       Kerry
.18   momourning
       Mourne
.27   moramor maenneritsch
       ?Miramar
       Mora
.28   Tarara
       Tara
.30   forebanned
       ?Bann R
.34   dandymount
       ?Sandymount
248.07 Doubtlynn
       Dublin
.08   Land-under-Wave
       Atlantis
       Neagh, Lough
       Tír Fa Thuinn
.11   Achill's low
       Achill Island
.20   Turkey's delighter
       Turkey
.23   thicketloch
       St Patrick's Cathedral
.23   swanwater
       Swan Water, The
.25   cope of heaven
       ?Copenhagen
.30   Glendalough
       Glendalough
.31   Long Entry
       Long Entry
.32   Blanche de Blanche's
       ?
.33   3 Behind Street
       Behind St
.33   2 Turnagain Lane
       Turnagain Lane
.33   Awabeg
       Awabeg
.35   Seven Sisters
       Seven Sisters
249.07 elfinbone
       ?Elphin
.08   Tyrian
       Tyre

.26   maypole
       Maypole
250.03 rossy
       Russia
.04   rumpffkorpff
       ?Ruhmkorff, Rue de
.07   Sheidam
       ?
.16   burning would...dance inane...
       Glamours...Coldours
       Dunsinane (Birnam Wood,
       Glamis, Cawdor)
.20   Libnius
       Libnius R
.22   loop to lee
       ?Lee R
.24   the rand
       Witwatersrand ("The Rand")
.36   dabble on the bay
       Dublin Bay
251.11 totter of Blackarss
       ?
.36   songdom...gemurrmal
       Cities of the Plain
252.04 Dvoinabrathran
       Dvina R
.05   manchind's parlements
       Man, Isle of
.07   Saint Mowy of the Pleasant Grin
       Glasnevin: St Mobhi
.07   everglass and even prospect
       Glasnevin: Prospect Cemetery
.11   Saint Jerome
       Mt Jerome (Cemetery)
.11   Harlots' Curse
       Harold's Cross
253.01 Peruvian
       Peru
.01   ersebest idiom
       Ireland: Erse
.03   Russky...slove
       Russia
.05   mappamund
       Mappa Mundi
.08   no thing making newthing
       Tingsomingenting
.10   London's...regionals
       British Broadcasting Corp
       London
.11   pigmyland
       ?

.28 Myama's
    ?
.31 Barnado's bearskin...childergar-
    ten
    Barnardo, J M and Son
.32 Lucanhof
    ?Howth
    Lucan
.34 tomestone of Barnstaple
    Barnstaple
254.02 Rurie, Thoath and Cleaver
    Four Waves of Erin
.03 Orion
    ?Orion
.08 sulpicious
    ?St Sulpice
.10 Irenews eye-to-eye
    ?Ireland's Eye
.11 livvying
    Liffey
.12 Sara's drawhead
    Island Br (Sarah Br)
.13 Isaac's, the lauphed butt one
    Butt Br
.14 moanolothe
    Wellington Monument
.16 abu abiad
    Nile R: Bahr-el-Abiad
.17 babbel men dub gulch
    Bab el Mandeb
    ?Babel, Tower of
    Dublin Gulch
.18 mar of murmury mermers
    Marmora, Sea of
.22 Potollomuck
    ?Potomac R
.23 Lollapaloosa
    NPN: Amer slang "some-
    thing extraordinary"
.25 Java Jane
    Java
.30 hissarlik
    Troy: Hissarlik
.31 selm ashaker
    Selma
.33 berrathon
    Berrathon
.33 aisles of Skaldignavia
    Scandinavia
.35 Bunnicombe
    Buncombe

255.01 Capellisato
    Chapelizod
.04 Tamor
    NPN: Bog Lat "Earth"
.10 Aquileyria
    ?Aquileia
.12 Jehosophat
    Jehoshaphat
.13 Moykill
    ?
.13 Bulljon
    ?Belgium
    England: John Bull
.14 Calavera
    NPN: Sp "daredevil"
.15 Bearara Tolearis
    Polaris
.15 Danamaraca
    Denmark
.21 Buke of Lukan
    Lecan
    Lucan
.21 Dublin's capital
    Dublin
.22 Coombe
    Coombe, The
256.19 French
    France
.23 Eire
    Ireland
.23 limbo
    Limbo
.26 rancoon
    ?Rangoon
.28 the doil
    Dáil Éireann
.29 old provaunce
    Provence
.29 G.P.O.
    General Post Office
.30 D.U.T.C.
    Dublin United Tramways Co
.32 N.C.R.
    North Circular Rd
.32 S.C.R.
    South Circular Rd
.34 alps
    Alps
257.01 angelland
    England
.09 Boorman's clock
    ?

.12   Trinity
       Trinity College, Dublin

.23   jurys
       Jury's Hotel

.27   −fermoy− [in C-word]
       Fermoy

.36   Fionia
       ?Finland
       ?Ireland: Tír na bhFionn

.36   Fidge Fudgesons
       ?Jameson, John, and Son

.36   Sealand
       Zealand (Sealand)

258.01   Rendningrocks
       Matt 27:51: "temple was
         rent...rocks were rent"
         (+ Ragnarok)

.02   Hlls vlls
       Hell
       Valhalla

.04   rowdownan
       Rhodes
       Rhone R

.05   Kidoosh
       Kadesh

.08   jambses, in his gaits
       Guinness's Brewery (James's
       Gate)

.08   Mezouzalem
       Jerusalem

.11   Babel...Lebab
       Babel, Tower of

.34   kerrybommers
       Kerry

BOOK II
Chapter 2

260.L1   *Ireland*
       Ireland

.L2   *Menly about peebles*
       Mainly About People
       ?Peebles, Scot

*Conflating representatives of the
arts and sciences with Dublin, 260.09−
.13 suggests a tour which circles N and
W from O'Connell St, and back again
along the Liffey.*

.09   Livius Lane
       Liffey St
       ?Love Lane

.09   Mezzofanti Mall
       ?Gardiner's Mall (O'Connell St)

.10   Lavatery Square
       ?Rutland Square

.10   Tycho Brache Crescent
       Berkeley Rd: Royal Circus

.11   Berkeley Alley
       Berkeley Rd

.12   Gainsborough Carfax
       ?Phibsborough

.12   Guido D'Arezzo's Gadeway
       ?Royal Hospital

.13   New Livius Lane
       Liffey St
       ?Love Lane

.15   Vico Roundpoint
       Vico Rd

.F2   Mater Mary Mercerycordial
       Mater Misericordiae Hosp
       Mercer's Hosp
       St Mary's Hosp

261.L3   *Cronwall*
       ?Cornwall

*The Seven Wonders of the Ancient
World (qv) are reviewed one by one in
261.09−.13.*

.09   cones
       Pyramids

.10   mured
       Babylon: Walls of Babylon

.10   pensils
       Gardens of Semiramis

.11   dianaphous
       Temple of Artemis (Diana) at
       Ephesus

.11   olymp
       Olympia: Statue of Zeus

.12   culosses
       Colossus of Rhodes

.13   mosoleum
       Mausoleum at Halicarnassus

.15   Cave of Kids
       ?

.15   Hymanian Glattstoneburg
       Hy Many

.16   denary, danery
       Denmark

.23   this upright one
       ?Wooden Man

Mr. Tumulty's (261.19) address (261.F2) is given in the old form of schoolboys locating themselves in the world. Stephen Dedalus wrote on the flyleaf of his geography book (A Portrait, 15): "Stephen Dedalus/Class of Elements/Clongowes Wood College/ Sallins/County Kildare/Ireland/Europe /The World/The Universe."

.F2 Kellywick
    ?
.F2 Longfellow's Lodgings
    ?
.F2 House of Comments III
    House of Commons
.F2 Cake Walk
    ?
.F2 Amusing Avenue
    ?
.F2 Salt Hill
    Salt Hill
.F2 Co. Mahogany
    Monaghan
.F2 Izalond
    Ireland
.F2 Terra Firma
    (the Earth)
262.L4 *Terrierpuppy*
    ?Tipperary
.03 upper. Cross.
    Uppercross (Barony)
.05 castle. Knock.
    Castleknock (Barony)
.15 Erdnacrusha
    Ardnacrusha
.21 the Boote's at Pickardstown
    ?Boötes
    Pickardstown: Boot Inn
.25 ballyhouraised
    Ballyhooly
    Ballyhoura
.26 Bacchus e'en call
    Magazine Fort
.26 Inn inn! Inn inn!
    Tavern, The
.F1 Gotahelv!
    Gota R, Sweden
.F3 tynwalled
    Man, Isle of: Tynwald Court
263.05 a father theobalder brake
    Whitworth Br (Father Theobald Br)

.06 Egyptus
    Egypt (= Africa)
.07 Major A. Shaw
    Asia (Major)
.07 A. Shaw...miner
    Asia (Minor)
.08 old Whiteman
    Europe
.10 ottomanic
    Ottoman Empire
.11 Pandemia's
    NPN (*pan-demos*, Gk "all the people")
.13 Hispano-Cathayan-Euxine
    Spain
    China (Cathay)
    Black Sea (Euxine)
.13 Castillian-Emeratic-Hebridian
    Spain (Castile)
    ?Ireland
    Hebrides
.14 Espanol-Cymric-Helleniky
    Spain
    Wales (Cymry)
    Greece (Hellas)
.20 garden of Idem
    Eden
.24 inkbottle authority
    ?Inkbottle House
.F2 meditarenias
    Mediterranean Sea
.F2 isle we love in spice
    Spice Islands
.F2 Punt
    Punt
264.03 Allsap's ale
    Allsop and Sons
.05 saturnine settings
    Saturn
.05 Horn of Heatthen
    Howth
.06 Brook of Life
    Liffey
.09 Canaan
    Canaan
.15 Eblinn water
    Dublin: Eblana
.20 hundreds of manhood
    Manhood, Hundred of
.21 three and threescore fylkers
    Chapelizod (area 63 acres)

.22 twenty six and six
      Ireland: Misc Allusions

.23 riverside
      Chapelizod: Riverside House

.23 sunnybank
      Chapelizod: Sunnybank

.24 buona the vista
      Chapelizod: Buena Vista

.24 Santa Rosa
      Chapelizod: Santa Rosa

.24 field of May
      Chapelizod: Mayfield House

.25 vale of Spring
      Chapelizod: Spring Vale

.25 Orchards...lodged
      Chapelizod: Orchard Lodge

.26 sainted lawrels
      Chapelizod: Saint Laurence
      House and Lodge

.27 hoig view ashwald
      Chapelizod: Ashview
      Chapelizod: Hill View

.27 glen of marrons
      Chapelizod: Glenmaroon

.27 glen...thorns
      Chapelizod: Glen Thorn

.28 Gleannaulinn
      Chapelizod: Glenaulin

.28 Ardeevin
      Chapelizod: Ardeevin

.29 Norman court
      Chapelizod: Norman Court

.30 boundary of the ville
      Chapelizod: Boundary Villa

.31 church of Ereland
      Chapelizod: Chapelizod
      Church (CI)

.32 king's house
      Chapelizod: King's House

.32 house of stone
      Chapelizod: Stone House

.F2 marble arch
      Marble Arch

.F2 pool beg
      Poolbeg

.F3 Olbion
      Albion (England)

265.01 belgroved
      Chapelizod: Belgrove

.01 mulbrey
      Chapelizod: Mulberry Hill
      House

.01 the still that was mill
      Chapelizod: Phoenix Park Dis-
      tillery

.02 Kloster that was Yeomansland
      Chapelizod: Mt Sackville (Con-
      vent)

.03 ghastcold tombshape
      ?

.04 elm Lefanunian
      Chapelizod: Village Elm

.06 Sweetsome auburn
      Auburn
      Chapelizod: Auburn

.08 fraisey beds
      Strawberry Beds

.08 phoenix, his pyre
      Chapelizod: Phoenix Tavern
      Tavern, The: Mullingar House

.10 wren his nest
      Wren's Nest (Tavern)

.11 turrises of the sabines
      Chapelizod: Sabine Terrace

.12 the cottage
      Chapelizod: The Cottage

.12 the bungalow
      Chapelizod: The Bungalow

.13 brandnewburgher
      ?Berlin: Brandenburg Gate

.13 Izolde, her chaplet gardens
      Chapelizod: Isolde Gardens

.14 liefest
      Liffey

.20 two barreny
      Chapelizod (in two baronies:
      Castleknock and Uppercross)

.23 wine tap and warm tavern
      Chapelizod: Carlisle Tavern
      and The Tap

.24 contact bridge
      ?Butt Br

.25 lease lapse
      Leixlip

.28 Finntown's
      Dublin Allusion: "Finn's
      Town"

.28 generous poet's office
      General Post Office

.28 Distorted mirage
      Auburn ("The Deserted Vil-
      lage")

.29 wherein
      Ireland

.F2 Summerhill
Summerhill

266.01 boxomeness...hole
Dublin Motto

.02 store and charter
Star and Garter

.03 Treetown Castle
Dublin Coat of Arms
Three Castles

.03 Lynne
?Dublin: Dubh-linn

.03 Rivapool
Liverpool
Liffey

.05 its toll but a till
?Turnpike

.06 D'Oblong's by his by
Dublin
?Dublin Bay

.18 doldorboys
?Zurich: Dolder

.24 catalaunic
Catalaunian Plains

.F1 Dublin
Dublin

.F1 Turkey
Turkey

.F2 Glens of Antrim
Antrim

.F2 Swords
Swords

267.L2 *Big Bear*
Ursa Major

.L2 *Sailor's Only*
Polaris

.L3 *Forening Unge Kristlike Kvinne*
YWCA

.02 Maidadate
?Maida Vale

.04 greeces
Greece

.07 gall
?Gaul

.12 Belisha beacon
NPN: in Gt Brit, the flashing
signals at pedestrian cros-
sings are called "Belisha
beacons"

.13 earong
Ireland (+ anagram of "orange")

.18 Adamman, Emhe
?Adam and Eve's

.22 Vetus
Venus

.F1 Rose Point
?Rosses Point

.F1 Inishmacsaint
Innishmacsaint

.F2 Mannequins' Pose
Brussels: Mannekin-Pis

.F6 Tarararat
Ararat, Mt
Tara

268.L1 *annaryllies*
Liffey

.L4 *erse*
Ireland: Erse

.08 Browne and Nolan's
Browne and Nolan

.15 bodikin a boss
?Brussels: Manneken-Pis

.15 Thimble Theatre
? (US comic strip)

.F6 Mrs Lappy
Liffey
?Mississippi R

.F6 Locklaun
Lochlann

269.08 pale
?Pale, The

270.L4 *Ulstria*
Austria
Ulster

.11 Irish
Ireland

.13 Humphreystown
Dublin Allusion: "Humphreys-
town"
?Humphreystown

.20 Wonderlawn's
Wonderland

.27 Nebob
?Nebo, Mt

.30 Hireling's
Ireland

.30 puny wars
Carthage

271.L1 *Monastir*
Monastir (Turkey)
Munster

.L1 *Leninstar*
Leinster (+ Russia)

.L1	*Connecticut*		.07	Madderhorn
	Connacht			Matterhorn
	Connecticut (US)		.12	Saint Barmabrac's
.29	the garden Gough gave			NPN? (*barmbrack*, Ir bread
	Phoenix Park: Gough Statue			made with currants)
.F3	cumpohlstery English		.12	Number Thirty two West Eleventh
	England			streak
272.L4	*atthems*			NYC: Eleventh St (+ 1132 **AD**)
	Athens		.29	Clane's clean hometown
.11	actiums			Clane
	Actium			Slane
.20	errings		.F2	Genuas
	Ireland			Genoa
.23	Lough Murph		.F3	Texas
	?			Texas
.31	Staffs		275.L3	*Buffalo Times*
	(Staffordshire, Eng)			Buffalo: *Buffalo Times*
.31	herds		.01	Erin's
	(Hertfordshire, Eng)			Ireland
.31	bucks		.04	Pacata Auburnia
	(Buckinghamshire, Eng)			Auburn
.31	barks			Ireland: Hibernia
	(Berkshire, Eng)		.05	Eire
.F3	lethemuse			Ireland
	Lethe R		.10	bastille
273.L1	*Curragh*			Bastille
	Curragh, The		.12	lavy
.L1	*bosthoon*			Liffey
	Boston		.14	Airyanna
.L3	*Cowdung Forks*			?Iran: Airyana
	Caudine Forks			Ireland
.L3	*Kine's*		.14	Blowyhart
	?Cannae			?
.L4	*bombambum*		.15	palace of quicken boughs
	?Ireland: Banba			Palace of the Quicken Trees
.01	Grumbledum's walls		.16	The Goat and Compasses
	Magazine Fort			Goat and Compasses, The
.05	peace! Live, league		.F2	Arabia
	?Slieve League			Arabia
.11	Hanah Levy		.F6	jinglish janglage
	Liffey			England
.12	nievre		.F6	dolphins born
	Nièvre R			Dolphin's Barn
.12	anore		276.L5	*Porterstown*
	Nore R			Porterstown
.18	bracelonettes...barcelonas		.05	dove without gall
	Barcelona			?Dubh-Gall
.28	hoerse		.07	lettereens
	Ireland: Erse			?Lettreen
274.02	Monte Sinjon		.08	monster man
	Monte Carlo			Munster
	Waterloo: Mont St Jean			

.15	Nippon	.F3	pohlmann's piano	
	Japan		Pohlman and Son	
.16	Eldorado	.F7	Eddems and Clay's	
	El Dorado		?Eden Quay	
.26	hoodie hearsemen	279.03	Erigureen	
	Howth		?Ireland	
.F1	Castlecowards	.07	athclete...bally	
	?Castle Howard		Dublin: Baile Átha Cliath	
.F7	hunterland	.08	Towntoquest, fortorest...hurley	
	Wonderland		Dublin: Baile Átha Cliath	
277.L1	*Fluminian Road*	.F3	cecilies	
	Flaminia, Via		?Cecilia St	
	Liffey	.F5	erringnesses	
.L3	*throne...umbrella*		Ireland	
	?	.F12	pettigo	
.01	Ochone		?Pettigo	
	Oconee R	.F20	old nourse Asa	
.02	Ochonal [with 277.F2]		Norway	
	O'Connell Statue	.F24	Trestrine von Terrefin	
.07	mountain mourning		?Land's End	
	Mourne (Mts)		?Trieste	
.08	obedient...felicity	.F27	Skokholme	
	Dublin Motto		Stockholm	
.10	poll and Peter's burgess	.F27	Drewitt's Altar	
	St Petersburg: Peter and		?Phoenix Park: Druid's Altar	
	Paul Fortress	280.L2	*A shieling in coppingers*	
.15	Drommhiem		Coppinger	
	?	.01	dreamoneire	
.16	Westwicklow		Ireland	
	Wicklow	.07	lex leap	
.16	little black rose		Leixlip	
	Ireland: Little Black Rose	.15	pershan...cates	
.18	Sein annews		Persia	
	?St Andrew's Church	.27	Auburn chenlemagne	
	?Seine R		?Auburn	
	?Xanadu	.32	fount Bandusian	
.21	Blath		Bandusia	
	Dublin: Baile Átha Cliath	281.L4	*saxum shillum*	
.21	city self of legionds		Saxony (+ "the king's shilling")	
	Caerleon-on-Usk	.05	*Gaules*	
.F2	lucreasious togery [with 277.02]		Gaul	
	O'Connell Statue	.06	*Illyrie*	
.F4	ancient homes		Illyria	
	Rome	.07	*Numance*	
.F7	redbanked...bakset of yosters		Numantia	
	Red Bank	.20	Sickamoor's...sally	
278.L4	*babel*		Sycamore St	
	Babel, Tower of	.23	Ruhm	
.L5	*Gent*		Rome	
	Ghent	.24	oxyggent	
.10	grey nuns' pond		(Occident)	
	?			

.F1   arks day triump
  Arch of Triumph
.F2   turfish
  Turkey
.F2   poliss
  Poland
282.18   Eden
  Eden
.F4   Pigott's
  Pigott and Co
283.L1   *ulstra*
  Four Sees of Ireland: Ar-
  magh
  Ulster
.L1   *Elba*
  ?Elba
  Four Sees of Ireland: Dub-
  lin (Eblana)
  (Leinster)
.L1   *cashellum*
  Cashel
  Four Sees of Ireland: Cashel
  (Munster)
.L1   *tuum*
  Four Sees of Ireland: Tuam
  Tuam
  (Connacht)
.L2   *Dondderwedder*
  ?Dodder R
.01   Enoch Thortig
  ?Enoch
.14   weys in Nuffolk
  ?Norfolk
  Suffolk
.14   tods of Yorek
  York
.17   Irish
  Ireland
.17   alliving stone allaughing
  Liffey
.F2   road to Rouen
  Rouen
.F3   Phoenix
  Phoenix Park
284.L1   *stodge Angleshman*
  England
.01   median
  ?Meath
.05   Tullagrove pole
  ? (just "telegraph"?)
.05   Height of County Fearmanagh
  Fermanagh

.07   Lower County Monachan
  Monaghan
.09   involted
  ?Volta Cinema
.24   Aysha Lalipat
  ?Asia (Minor)
  Lilliput
.26   NCR
  North Circular Rd
.27   ottomantic
  Ottoman Empire
.28   turquo-indaco
  Turkey
.F3   richview press
  Richview Press
.F4   V...P...H
  ?Victoria Palace Hotel
.F5   jaunts cowsway
  Giants' Causeway
  North Circular Rd
285.L1   *Cincinnati*
  Cincinnati
.L2   *Arthurgink's hussies and Ever-*
  guin's men
  Gaiety Theatre
  ?Guinness's Brewery
.01   habby
  ?Abbey Theatre
.11   ersed
  Ireland: Erse
.12   erroroots
  ?Ararat, Mt
.15   MPM
  ?
.15   a rainborne pamtomomiom
  Gaiety Theatre
.18–.21   volts...volts...
  ?Volta Cinema
.22   finish
  Finland
.25   bullyclavers
  Balaclava
  Dublin: Baile Átha Cliath
.27   Iris
  Ireland: Iris
.27   Evenine's World
  Evening World
.F2   Barneycorrall
  ?
.F4   Myriom square
  Merrion (Square)

.F5 Asia
    Asia

.F6 Indiana Blues
    Indiana

286.L3 *Mullingar*
    Tavern, The: Mullingar
    House

.04 bagdad
    Bagdad

.06 begath
    Gath

.06 arab
    Arabia

.07 nor anymeade or persan
    Media
    Persia
    ?Runnymede

.10 Hickey's
    Hickey's

.11 Wellington's Iron Bridge
    Wellington Br

.14 rossecullinans
    Cullinan (Diamond)

.F1 rhomes
    Rome

.F3 disorded visage
    Auburn ("The Deserted
    Village")

287.05 royol road to Puddlin
    Dublin Allusion: "Rocky
    Road to Dublin"

.07 liffle
    Liffey

.09 alp
    Liffey

.09 howlth on her bayrings
    Dublin Bay
    Howth

.12 nod
    Nod, Land of

.15 isle of Mun, ah!
    Man, Isle of
    Mona

.18 spires...dean of idlers
    St Patrick's Cathedral

.21 *lingua romana*
    Rome

.21 *liviana*
    Liffey

.22 *letitiae...situm lutetiae*
    Paris: "Lutetia"

.24 *Jordani*
    Jordan R (+ Giordano Bruno)

.30 Backlane Univarsity
    Back Lane

.F3 Canorian words
    ?

.F4 Basqueesh
    Basque Provinces (language)

.F4 Finnican
    Finland (language)

.F4 Hungulash
    Hungary (language)

.F4 Teangtaggle
    Tintagel (Cornish language)

288.11 Oxatown
    Oxmantown

.13 ourland's
    Ireland

.14 leinster
    Leinster

.15 Lipton's strongbowed launch, the
    Lady Eva
    "Shamrock"

.18 barcelonas
    Barcelona

.19 Mr Dane
    Denmark (+ Swift, "Mr Dean")

.21 that other familiar temple
    St Patrick's Cathedral

.22 humdrum dumb
    ?Dundrum

.23 Hymbuktu
    Timbuktu

.24 galloroman
    Gaul
    Rome

.25 land of nods
    Nod, Land of

.28 Wickerworks...ford
    Dublin: Baile Átha Cliath

.F6 Ireland...erring
    Ireland

.F6 erring under Ryan
    Ehren on the Rhine
    Rhine R

289.02 Swanny
    Swanee R
    ?Swan Water

.06 Indus
    India
    Indus R

.08	old Pales time		.24	Arklow Vikloe (*Cont.*)
	Pale, The			Wicklow
	Palestine		.24	Louth super Luck
.10	Benjermine			Louth
	Germany			Lucan
.10	Empyre		.28	unirish title
	Empire Theatre			Ireland
.13	Byrne's		.28	Nash
	?			?
.13	Flamming's		.F1	Muckross Abbey
	?Belgium			Muckross (Abbey)
.13	Furniss's		.F5	Pomeroy Roche
	?			Pomeroy
.14	Bill Hayses's		.F5	Portobello
	Hades			Portobello
.14	Ellishly Haught's		.F7	rusin's hat
	Hell			Russia
	?Thing Mote		291.01	Saint Yves
.16	ostrovgods			St Ives (Cornwall)
	Ostrov		.01	Landsend
.18	gigglehouse...manias			Land's End (Cornwall)
	?St Patrick's Hospital		.01	cornwer
.20	murty magdies			Cornwall
	Magdalen		.05	lonely peggy
.20	medeoturanian			"Lovely Peggy"
	Mediterranean Sea		.05	Crampton's peartree
.25	Ainée Rivière			Crampton's Pear Tree
	?Riviera		.09	ives of Man
.26	Hotel des Ruines			?Man, Isle of
	?Rouen		.10	Lochlaunstown
.28	Idleness, Floods Area			Dublin Allusion: "Lochlauns-
	?			town"
.28	Liv's			Lochlann
	Liffey			Loughlinstown
.29	Prima Vista, Abroad		.11	Staneybatter
	?			Stoneybatter
290.02	La Chapelle		.18	Rectory
	Chapelizod			?
.16	doubling back...bymby		.18	Vicarage Road
	Dublin			?
	?Dublin Bay		.19	Bishop's Folly
.18	iselands			?
	?Iceland		.19	Papesthorpe
	Ireland			?
.18	mount miss		.23	gaulish
	Slieve Mish			Gaul
.18	wooeds of Fogloot		.26	Sexsex
	Foclut			Essex
.19	vartryproof		.26	Somehow-at-Sea
	Vartry R			Southend-on-Sea (Essex)
.24	Arklow Vikloe		.F6	freeman's
	Arklow			?*Freeman's Journal*

292.06 *Westend Woman*
       West End (London)
   .07 indiapepper
       India
   .10 Huggin Green
       Hoggen Green
   .17 laggin...search lighting
       Lagan R
   .19 pharahead
       ?
   .23 launer's lightsome
       ?
   .27 landsmaul
       Norway: landsmaal
   .F1 Glass and Bellows
       ?
   .F2 Matter of Brettaine
       Britain, Little
   .F3 Bussmullah
       Bushmills
293.12 DVbLIn
       Dublin
   .13 Turnpike
       Turnpike
   .14 Great Ulm
       Chapelizod: Village Elm
       ?Ulm
   .14 Mearingstone
       Mearingstone
   .15 ann linch
       ?Lynch, Anne, and Co
   .15 enn all
       ?Ennell, Lough
   .19 liv...annalive
       Liffey
   .F1 Draumcondra's Dreamcountry
       Drumcondra
294.04 Lambday
       Lambay Island
       ?Lamb Island
   .04 Modder ilond
       ?Ireland
       ?Mud Island
   .13 Makefearsome's Ocean
       NPN: MacPherson's *Ossian*
   .16 Swift's...galehus
       St Patrick's Hospital
   .17 Bigdud
       Bagdad
   .19 turvku
       Turkey
       ?Turku (Finland)

   .20 lydias
       Lydia

       The following five names are of
       seaside suburbs along S Dublin Bay:

   .20 Mary Owens
       Merrion
   .21 Dolly Monks
       Dollymount
       Monkstown
   .22 Blake-Roche
       Blackrock
   .22 Kingston
       Dun Laoghaire
   .23 Dockrell
       Dalkey
.22–.23 Blake-Roche...Dockrell
       Dalkey, Kingstown, and Black-
       rock Tram Line
   .24 papacocopotl
       Popocatepetl
   .25 magmasine fall
       Magazine Fort
   .27 Byzantium
       Constantinople
   .29 Gaudyanna
       Guadiana R
   .F1 Ex jup pep off
       ?General Post Office
   .F1 Carpenger Strate
       Coppinger
   .F1 The kids' and dolls' home
       ?
   .F4 Bagnabun
       Baginbun
   .F4 Banbasday
       Ireland: Banba
295.01 istherdie forivor
       Danube R: Ister
   .07 Sundaclouths
       ?Malaysia: Sunda Islands
   .12 comeallyoum saunds
       ?
   .13 Dairy
       Derry
   .19 mudland Loosh
       Louth
   .20 Luccan
       Lucan
   .24 gyrotundo
       ?Rotunda

.31	doubling
	Dublin
.31	bicirculars
	North Circular Rd
	South Circular Rd
.F1	Kelleiney
	Killiney
296.04	Araxes
	Araxes R (Armenia)
.06	Hoddum and Heave
	Adam and Eve's
.08	Airmienious
	Armenia
.F3	swimford
	Swinford
.F3	Suksumkale
	Sukhum-Kaleh (Armenia)
297.05	Sibernia
	Ireland: Hibernia
	Siberia
.11	Ocone! Ocone!
	Oconee R
.20	Hurdlebury Fenn
	Dublin: Baile Átha Cliath
.25	appia lippia
	Appian Way
	Liffey
.32	Afrantic
	Atlantic O
.F1	the Nacion
	Nation, The
.F5	Whangpoos
	Hwang-p'u R
.F5	paddle
	?Poddle R
298.33	Rome
	Rome
299.L1	*Canine Venus*
	Venus
.L1	*Aulidic Aphrodite*
	Aulis
.06	Lourde...Lourde
	Lourdes
.16	loiternan's lamp
	?Rome: St John Lateran
.25	yangsheepslang
	Yangtsze R
.30	Guinness's
	Guinness's Brewery
.31	Parson Rome's
	Rome

.F1	Hen's bens
	Hell
300.07	invernal
	Inferno
.09	Wherapool
	?
.12	jacob's
	?Jacob, W and R, Co
.F2	youreups
	Europe
.F4	men-in-the straits
	?Menai Strait
301.02	Dr Brassenaarse
	Oxford U: Brasenose College
.05	bosthoon, late for Mass
	Boston
.09	Christ's Church
	Oxford U: Christ Church College
.10	Bellial
	Oxford U: Balliol College
.16	trieste...trieste
	Trieste
.25	Cartesian spring
	Pierian Spring
.27	goblin castle
	Castle, The
.30	croakpartridge
	Croagh Patrick
	Croke Park
.F2	irish
	Ireland
.F5	Penmark
	?Denmark
	Penmark
302.R1	LEMAN
	?Leman, Lac
.01	Bhagavat
	NPN: "Bhagavad," a Hindu name for the Supreme Being
.13	Skibbering's eagles
	Skibbereen: *Skibbereen Eagle*
.14	Whiteknees Archway
	?
.25	Romain
	Rome
303.R2	PIG AND WHISTLE
	Pig and Whistle
.07	Doubbllinnbbayyates
	Dublin Bay (+ W B Yeats)
.14	Eregobragh
	Ireland

.16 Jacoby...puppadums
　　Jacob, W and R, Co

.23 pergaman
　　Pergamum

.F3 Brownes...Castlehacknolan
　　Castle, The
　　Castle Browne

304.21 Endsland's
　　England
　　Land's End

.F2 Childaman
　　China

.F5 Alls Sings
　　?All Saints Church

305.R1 LUG IN A LAW
　　Luggela

.R1 OHIO OHIO IOIOMISS
　　?Mississippi R
　　Ohio

.07 deep dartry dullard
　　Dartry Rd
　　Dublin Allusion: "Dear Dirty Dublin"

.08 celebridging
　　Celbridge

.17 curse again
　　Corsica

.17 Jamesons
　　Jameson, John, and Son
　　?Jameson, Pim and Co

.28 Vale. Ovocation
　　Avoca

.28 maiding waters
　　Meeting of the Waters

.29 auld lang salvy steyne
　　Steyne

.33 whaboggeryin
　　Ireland

306.04 Noblett's surprize
　　Noblett, Leonard, and Co
　　Sweden: Nobel Prize

.06 hung cong
　　Cong
　　Hong Kong

.07 mizpah
　　Mizpah

.16 South City Markets
　　South City Market

.24 Dublin Metropolitan Police
　　Dublin Metropolitan Police

.25 Ballsbridge
　　Ballsbridge

.26 Anglian
　　England

.27 Hesperus
　　Norman's Woe: "Hesperus"

307.L1 *Cincinnatus*
　　Cincinnati

.01 Guinness' Brewery
　　Guinness's Brewery

.05 Clontarf
　　Clontarf

.05 Brother Johnathan
　　America

.08 Hengler's Circus Entertainment
　　Hengler's Circus

.11 American Lake Poetry
　　America

.17 Slumdom
　　Cities of the Plain
　　London

.17 Roman Pontiffs
　　Rome

.25 India
　　India

.26 Eu
　　Eu

.F2 spookeerie
　　?

.F3 Paris
　　Paris

.F8 Eu
　　Eu

308.01 Gobble Anne
　　Gobelins (Paris telephone exchange)

.20 livvey
　　Liffey

.22 new yonks
　　New York City

BOOK II

Chapter 3

309.01 concern of the Guinnesses
　　Guinness's Brewery

.05 wades a lymph
　　Liffey

.09 Etheria Deserta
　　Arabia ("Arabia Deserta")
　　Howth: Edri Deserta

.09 Grander Suburbia
　　?

.11 Hiberio-Miletians
Ireland: Iberio

.11 Argloe-Noremen
Arklow
Norway
(+ "Anglo-Norman")

.13 Ibdullin
Dublin

.14 Himana
Hy Many

.14 daildialler
Dáil Éireann

.16 duchy of Wollinstown
Wolin
(+ Duke of Wellington)

.21 vaticum cleaners
Vatican

.24 allirish earths
Ireland

310.02 magazine battery
Magazine Fort

.03 Jomsborg, Selverbergen
Jomsborg

.05 lackslipping
Leixlip

.05 liffing
Liffey

.06 howdrocephalous
Howth (Head)

.07 circumcentric megacycles
North Circular Rd
South Circular Rd

.07 antidulibnium
Dublin
Libnius
(+ antediluvian)

.08 serostaatarean
Irish Free State

.12 Eustache Straight
Eustace St
O'Reilly and Co

.12 Bauliaughacleeagh
Dublin: Baile Átha Cliath

.13 Naul
Naul, The

.13 Santry
Santry

.13 forty routs of Corthy
Enniscorthy

.16 O'Keef-Rosses and Rhosso-
Keevers
Kiev

.17 Zastwoking
?

.20 Iren
Iran
Ireland

.24 Nur
Nur (Iran)

.28 o'connell's
Phoenix Brewery: O'Connell's
Ale

.29 canterberry
Canterbury

.31 ale of man
Man, Isle of

.32 Patagoreyan
?Gorey
Patagonia

.34 turfeycork
?Cork
Man, Isle of

.34 Lougk Neagk
Neagh, Lough

311.01 lift-ye-landsmen
Liffey

.05 lealand
?

.12 Anow...Thenanow
Annu
Heliopolis

.16 dubble in
Dublin
Tavern, The

.18 O Connibell
Phoenix Brewery: O'Connell's
Ale

.21 translatentic
Atlantic O

.33 fringe sleeve
France

312.01 Moy Eireann
Ireland

.05 Norgean
Norway

.07 fram
"Fram"

.07 Franz José Land
Franz Josef Land

.08 Cabo Thormendoso
Good Hope, Cape of

.08 evenstarde
Venus

.09 Rivor Tanneiry
?

.09 Golfe Desombres
?

.19 whol niet godthaab
Godthaab (Greenland)
Good Hope, Cape of

.19 Cape of Good Howthe
Good Hope, Cape of
Howth

.20 loretta lady
Loreto

.25 wohl yeas sputsbargain
Spitsbergen

.26 Muggleton
Muggleton

.30 wanderlook
Waterloo

.30 shaunty irish
Ireland

313.17 hairing
Ireland

.19 duff point
?

.19 dorkland
?

.23 lewdbrogue
Ladbroke

.27 frameshape
"Fram"

.31 brayvoh
Bray

.31 little bratton
Britain, Little

.34 Meade-Reid
?Madrid
?Meath
(+ mead)

.34 Lynn-Duff
Dublin (+ *lionn dubh*, Ir
"black ale")

314.01 deiffel
Eiffel Tower

.02 babeling
Babel, Tower of

.05 dyfflun's kiddy
Dublin

.08 —drumstrum— [in C-word]
?Dundrum

.09 —waultopoofooloo— [in C-word]
Waterloo

.13 muddies scrimm ball...maidies
scream all
Magazine Fort

.17 luck's leap
Leixlip

.21 Ballaclay
?Balaclava
Dublin: Baile Átha Cliath

.22 dutchuncler
Netherlands

.27 noirse-made-earsy
Ireland: Erse
Norway

315.01 Cullege Trainity
Trinity College, Dublin

.12 Moyle herring
Ireland (Moy Éireann)
Moyle, Sea of

.22 bierhiven
Berehaven

.22 nogeysokey
Nagasaki

.23 oerasound
Øresund

.23 snarsty weg for Publin
Dublin Allusion: "Rocky Road
to Dublin"

.24 lug in the lee
?Lee R
Luggela

.28 mone...Kidballacks
Kilbarrack: Chapel of Mone
Speckled Church

.29 suttonly
Sutton

.30 strandweys
North Strand Rd

.30 penincular
Howth

.31 talka
Tolka

.31 clown toff
Clontarf

.32 Clifftop
?Clifden

.34 Skibbereen
Skibbereen

.34 pokeway paw
"Pourquoi Pas"

.36 frankish...gallic
France
Gaul

316.02 ulstravoliance
        Ulster
   .04 aerian
        Ireland
   .05 tysk
        Germany ("Tyskland")
   .06 Kish met
        Kish Lightship
   .12 skerries
        Skerries
   .13 Kinkincaraborg
        Kincora
   .14 Montybunkum
        Buncombe
   .15 Mitropolitos
        ?
   .15 hiberniating
        Ireland: Hibernia
   .18 Erinly
        Ireland
   .19 boelgein
        ?Belgium
   .22 eeriebleak
        Ireland
   .28 Blasil the Brast
        Brazil
   .28 portocall
        Portugal
   .28 furt on the turn of the hurdies
        Dublin: Baile Átha Cliath
   .32 iceslant
        Iceland
        ?Ireland
   .36 dobblins
        Dublin
317.01 kennedy's
        Kennedy, Peter (bakery)
   .05 dallkey
        Dalkey
   .06 north star
        Polaris
   .07 tolk
        ?Tolka
   .09 Afram
        ?"Fram"
   .15 Shackleton
        Shackleton, George, and
            Sons (bakery)
   .16 Osler
        Oslo
   .30 big bailey bill
        Bailey Lighthouse

   .31 promonitory...headth of hosth
        Howth
   .32 obliffious
        Liffey
   .33 zembliance
        Novaya Zemlya
   .34 mansk
        Murmansk
   .34 dun darting dullemitter
        Alps: Dolomites
        Dublin Allusion: "Dear Dirty
            Dublin"
318.04 live
        Liffey
   .09 youngfree yoke
        Jungfrau: Jungfraujoch
   .11 Annexandreian
        Alexandria
   .12 Ethna Prettyplume
        Etna, Mt
   .12 Hooghly Spaight
        Hooghly R
   .15 amilikan honey
        America
   .18 Mina
        ?Mina (Arabia)
   .21 backonham
        Buckingham
   .24 Annapolis
        Annapolis
        Dublin Allusion: Annapolis
   .25 Mussabotomia
        Mesopotamia
   .27 slope
        ?Howth: Species Slope
   .28 Join Andersoon
        Anderson, John
   .32 Alpyssinia
        Abyssinia
        Alps
   .32 Memoland
        ?
   .33 ulvertones
        ?Ulverton Rd
   .34 irised sea
        Ireland: Iris
        Irish Sea
319.01 Hillyhollow
        Phoenix Park: The Hollow
   .04 ersewild
        Ireland: Erse

.04 Bembracken
  ?Pseudo-placename: *Beinn*
    Breacain, Ir "little speck-
    led hill" (O Hehir)
.05 Demetrius
  ?Demetrias
.06 suirsite's
  ?Suir R
.11 three swallows
  Power's Distillery
.16 Ampsterdampster
  Amsterdam
.17 netherlumbs
  Netherlands
.24 double dyode dealered
  Dublin Allusion: "Dear Dir-
    ty Dublin"
.25 Tarra water
  Tara (+ Berkeley's tar-water)
.26 trombsathletic
  Atlantic O
.27 gulpstroom
  Gulf Stream
320.03 tarrapoulling
  Tara
.03 shinar
  ?Shinar, Plain of
.07 civille row faction
  Savile Row (London)
.08 bag...bun
  Baginbun
.13 mundering eeriesk
  Ireland
.15 unitred stables
  America
.17 wastended
  West End (London)
.20 Fellagulphia
  Philadelphia
.21 dhruimadhreamdhrue
  ?Pseudo-placename: *druim*
    a' dhreama dhruadha, Ir
    "ridge of the druidical ad-
    herents" (O Hehir)
.21 Brighten-pon-the-Baltic
  Baltic
  Brighton
  Ireland: Misc Allusions
.21 our lund's rund turs
  Ireland
  Lund (Sweden)

.24 May Aileen
  Ireland (Moy Éireann)
.26 ire
  Ireland
.28 Afferik Arena
  Africa
.28 Blawland Bearring
  ?Bering Sea
  Blaaland (Africa)
.29 brazen sun...snows
  Oxford U: Brasenose College
.33 Infernal machinery
  ?Inferno
.33 Bullysacre
  Bully's Acre
  Clontarf
321.01 powers
  Power's Distillery
.07 kipsie point
  ?
.07 Dublin bar
  Dublin Bar
.08 Glasthule Bourne
  Glasthule
  Thule
.08 Boehernapark Nolagh
  Glasthule: Park Road
  ?Nolagh
.09 astraylians
  Australia
.09 island
  ?Ireland
.12 Wazwollenzee Haven
  Walensee
  Wolin
  (+ "Was wollen Sie haben?")
.13 beerings
  Bering Sea
.13 east circular route
  North Circular Rd
  South Circular Rd
.13 elegant central highway
  ?
.14 Lifeboat Alloe
  ?
.14 Noeman's Woe
  Norman's Woe
.16 Phoenix
  Phoenix Tavern
.17 old lotts
  Lotts

.17	Irinwakes
	Ireland
.20	Copeman helpen
	Copenhagen
.23	gaul
	Gaul
.23	ourmenial
	Armenia
.31	spring alice...down under
	Alice Springs
	Australia
.33	mulligar scrub
	?Tavern, The: Mullingar
	House
322.02	Boildawl stuumplecheats
	Baldoyle (racecourse)
.02	rushirishis Irush-Irish
	Ireland
	?Rush
.06	hwen ching hwan chang
	Peking: Hwang Cheng
.08	welsher
	Wales
.11	old bridge's
	?Whitworth Br
.12	hung hoang tseu
	Hung-Tse Hu
	Hwang Ho R
.16	doyle
	Dáil Éireann
.19	raze acurraghed
	Curragh, The (racecourse)
.20	spark to phoenish
	Phoenix Park (racecourse)

The following 3 Dublin monuments are (or were) the main symbols of British rule.

.32	pillary of the Nilsens
	Nelson's Pillar
.33	statutes of the Kongbullies
	William III, Statue of
.33	millestones of Ovlergroamlius
	Milestones
	Wellington Monument
323.02	shandymound
	Sandymount
.04	Ship Alouset
	Chapelizod
.04	baltxebec
	Baltic Sea

.06	lumbsmall
	Norway: landsmaal
.09	Donnerbruch fire
	Donnybrook (Fair)
.12	Bar Bartley
	?
.13	Gaascooker
	Gaelic Athletic Assn
.20	Iseland
	Ireland: The Five Fifths
	Iceland
.20	Skunkinabory
	Scandinavia
.21	Drumadunderry
	Derry
	Dundrum
.21	rumnants of Mecckrass
	Mecca
	Muckross
.23	hell of a hull
	Hell
.23	camelump
	?Camelot
.26	Riland's
	Ireland (+ Roland)
.30	palers
	Pale, The
.34	sham cram bokk
	Ireland: Shan van Vocht
.35	steerage way for stabling
	Dublin Allusion: "Rocky Road to Dublin"
.36	dane
	Denmark
324.03	erning his breadth
	?Erne
.04	emberose
	Ambrose (Lightship)
.04	the lizod lights
	Lizard, The (Lighthouse)
.07	sphinxish pairc
	Phoenix Park
.07	Ede was a guardin
	Eden
.09	Thallasee
	NPN? *Thalassa*, Gk "sea"
.10	Tullafilmagh
	?Tullow
.18	Rowdiose wodhalooing
	?Radio Éireann
	Waterloo

.20	Hoved	.04	Trinity judge	
	Howth		Trinity Church	
.20	Clontarf	.07	Erievikkingr	
	Clontarf		?Erie, Lake	
.27	Schiumdinebbia		Ireland	
	Scandinavia	.08	gielgaulgalls	
.29	kokkenhovens		Gaul	
	Copenhagen	.12	hellsinky	
.30	middelhav		Hell	
	Mediterranean Sea		Helsinki	
.31	same gorgers' kennel	.13	howtheners	
	St George's Channel		Howth	
.32	lucal	.13	be danned	
	Lucan		Denmark	
.36	Aden	.14	Tera	
	Aden		Tara	
	Eden	.16	athems	
325.04	Art thou...Limited		?Athens	
	Guinness's Brewery	.18	fairioes	
.04	Anna Lynchya		Faeroe Islands	
	Lynch, Anne, and Co	.18	Edar	
.12	finnisch		Howth: Ben Edar	
	Finland	.19	the loyd	
.14	Capel Ysnod		?Lloyd's of London	
	Chapelizod	.25	Diaeblen-Balkley	
.17	jonjemsums		Dublin: Baile Átha Cliath	
	Jameson, John, and Son	.25	Domnkirk Saint Petricksburg	
.24	Banba		St Patrick's Cathedral	
	Dana, Paps of		St Petersburg: Cathedral of	
	Ireland: Banba		St Isaac	
.25	Idyall	.27	sutor	
	NPN? *Judges* 6:36: "If thou		?Sutor St	
	wilt save Israel...as thou	.31	americle	
	hast spoken..."		America	
.31	our quadrupede island	.34	Dybblin water	
	Ireland: Misc Allusions		Dublin	
.32	madhugh	.34	Ballscodden	
	(Ulster)		Howth: Balscadden Bay	
.32	mardyk	.35	Thyrston's Lickslip	
	Cork: The Mardyke		Leixlip	
	(Munster)	327.01	juteyfrieze	
.32	luusk		Frisia	
	Lusk (Leinster)		Jutland	
.32	cong	.06	anny livving	
	Cong (Connacht)		Liffey	
.33	bray	.07	Totty go, Newschool	
	?Bray		?	
326.01	Horrocks	.08	tramity trimming	
	Horrocks		?Trinity College, Dublin	
.01	Toler	.09	trent of the thimes	
	?		Thames R	
			Trent R	

.10 dee in flooing
  Dee R
.10 Hyderow
  ?
.11 rheadoromanscing
  Rhaetia
.17 Dinny dingle
  ?Dingle
.18 Dargul dale
  Dargle
.21 Combria
  Wales: Cambria
.22 Wiltsh muntons
  Wales
.23 flyend...touchman
  Netherlands
.23 English Strand
  England
.24 Kilbarrack
  Kilbarrack
  Speckled Church
.25 dollimonde
  ?Dollymount
.30 Norgeyborgey
  Norway
.31 airish timers
  Irish Times
.32 Eriweddyng
  Ireland
328.03 wattling way for cubblin
  Dublin Allusion: "Rocky
  Road to Dublin"
  Watling St
.16 Elding, my elding
  Ireland
.17 Lif, my lif
  Liffey
.19 Hullespond
  Hellespont
.22 Coxenhagen
  Copenhagen (battle)
.22 Nile
  Nile R (battle)
.23 Kitty Cole
  Coleraine
.24 Sing Mattins in the Fields
  St Martin's in the Fields
  (London)
.25 ringsengd ringsengd
  Ringsend
.26 Referinn
  Ireland

.27 Thingavalley
  Thingvellir
.35 help of me cope
  Copenhagen
329.02 suomease
  Finland: Suomi
  Siam
.03 divlin's
  Dublin
.04 mimmykin puss
  Brussels: Manneken-Pis
.06 *Ulivengrene*
  ?(*Olivengrene*, Dan "olive
  branches")
.06 Onslought
  Oslo
.07 norse norse east
  Norway
.09 hulldread pursunk manowhood
  Manhood, Hundred of
.10 chenchen
  China
.10 bonzeye nappin
  Japan
.11 an olewidgeon
  Norway
.14 Dub
  Dublin
.14 Fingal of victories
  Fingal
.14 Cannmatha
  Can-Mathon (star)
.15 Cathlin
  Cathlin (star)
.17 bolgaboyo
  Bolga
  ?Volga R
.20 Holyryssia
  Russia
.21 Sandgate
  ?Sandgate
.22 ryce
  Rye R
.23 Demidoff's tomb
  ?
.25 Ghoststown Gate
  ?Ashtown (Gate)
  ?Goatstown
.25 Pompei
  Pompeii
.28 owfally
  ?Offaly

.29 Granjook Meckl
    Mecklenburg (Germany)
    ?Mecklenburgh St
.30 Route de l'Epée
    Rue de l'Abbé de l'Epée
    Rue de la Paix
.31 Freestouters and publicranks
    Irish Free State
.32 Cymylaya Mountains
    Himalaya Mts
    Wales
.33 louthmouthing
    Louth
.35 Tarar
    Tara
.36 bethehailey
    ?Bethel
330.06 Dane
    Denmark
.09 Tyrrhanees
    Pyrenees
    Tyrrhenian Sea
.09 Laxembraghs
    Luxembourg
.10 Our Lader's
    ?
.21 banbax
    ?Ireland: Banba
.24 Finn's Hotel Fiord
    Dublin: Baile Átha Cliath
    ("Hurdle Ford")
    Finn's Hotel
    ?Ford of Fine
.25 Nova Norening
    ?Nore R
.30 The Twwinns
    Tavern, The
.34 barneydansked
    Denmark
.35 kathareen
    Ireland: Cathleen ni
    Houlihan
331.02 phaymix cupplerts
    Phoenix Park
.04 liamstone
    Lia Fáil
.06 mourning
    ?Mourne Mts
.08 The threelegged man
    Man, Isle of
.09 Lludd hillmythey
    London

.09 Lludd hillmythey (*cont.*)
    (Lud's Town, Ludgate Hill)
.12 barents
    ?Barents
.18 mounden of Delude
    Gibeon (Jerusalem)
.19 Haraharem
    Jerusalem: Haram
.19 diublin's owld mounden...haughs
    Dublin
    Thing Mote
.23 eira area
    Ireland
.29 yare
    Yare R
.30 imageascene all
    Magazine Fort
.32 kristianiasation
    Oslo (Christiania)
.36 Borneholm
    Borneo
    Bornholm
332.02 big treeskooner
    Big Tree
    Yggdrasil
.05 —uaragheallach— [in C-word]
    Breffny
.05 —tullaghmongan— [in C-word]
    Tullymongan (E Breffny)
.06 —debblen—dubblan— [in C-word]
    Dublin
.08 frankfurters on the odor
    Frankfurt-an-der-Oder
    Oder R
.10 tolk of
    ?Tolka
.10 Doolin
    Dublin: Dinas-Doolin
.11 pale
    Pale, The
.14 gaauspices
    Gaelic Athletic Assn
.14 roammerin
    Ireland
.17 lifflebed
    Liffey
.26 gaames
    Gaelic Athletic Assn
.27 bridge of the piers
    ?Butt Br
.28 Inverleffy
    Liffey (*inbhear*, Ir "mouth")

.29	nilly...first cataraction...assuan	.11	mahonagyan
	damm		?Monaghan
	Nile R	.13	Danelagh
.31	phoenix his calipers		Danelagh
	Phoenix Park		Ranelagh
.33	Dinny Oozle	.18	goff stature
	?Ouzel Galley Society		Phoenix Park: Gough Statue
.34	suburbiaurealis in his rure	.24	mizzatint wall
	?Rus in urbe		Magazine Fort
.36	Check or slowback	.25	crimm crimms
	Czechoslovakia		Crimea
333.04	anni slavey	.33	Finndlader's Yule
	Liffey (*amnis Livia*)		Findlater, Alexander, and Co
.08	darsey dobrey...pimpim	.33	Hey Tallaght Hoe
	D'Arcy's Anchor Brewery		Tallaght
.08	danzing corridor	.35	Donnicoombe Fairing
	Danzig (Corridor)		Coombe, The
.09	pimpim		Donnybrook (Fair)
	Jameson, Pim, and Co,	.35	Millikin's Pass
	Brewers		Brussels: Manneken-Pis
.10	cavarnan men	.36	Izd-la-Chapelle
	?Cavan		Aix-la-Chapelle
.11	corkedagains upstored		Chapelizod
	?Cork	.36	Carlowman's Cup
	Corsica		Carlow (+ Charlemagne)
.15	behomeans	335.03	izba
	Bohemia		Poland: Izba
.16	jammesons	.07	Holispolis
	Jameson, John, and Son		?
.17	juinnesses	.07	Parkland
	Guinness's Brewery		?
.28	prayhasd	.10	chivvychace
	?Prague: Praha		Chevy Chase
.33	dour dorty dompling	.13	neuziel and oltrigger
	Dublin Allusion: "Dear		New Zealand
	Dirty Dublin"	.13	Bullyclubber
.33	dompling obayre		Balaclava
	Dublin Bay		Dublin: Baile Átha Cliath
.35	dauberg den	.16	Niutirenis...Niutirenis
	Dubber (foxhunting)		New Zealand
.36	Naul	.17	Wullingthund...Wellingthund
	Naul (foxhunting)		Wellington (New Zealand)
.36	toplots	.24	roosky
	Teplitz (spa)		?Roosky
.36	morrienbaths		Russia
	Marienbad (spa)	.26	hibernian knights underthaner
	Merrion (Strand)		Ireland: Hibernia ("Hibernian
334.07	toll hut		Nights Entertainment")
	?Turnpike	.27	sint barbaras
.08	Delgany		St Barbara's
	Delgany	.28	tublin
			Dublin

.29 Nowhare's yarcht
 (Noah's Ark)
.33 obelisk
 ?Wellington Monument
.36 aramny
 ?Aram
336.03 Danis
 Denmark
.06 louthly meathers
 Louth
 Meath
.15 awebrume
 ?Auburn (+ Abraham)
.15 Sahara
 Sahara (+ Sarah)
.27 atalantic's
 Atlantic O (+ Atalanta)
.29 peckadillies
 Piccadilly (London)
.29 wristsends
 West End (London)
.33 Calabashes
 ?
337.08 annapal livibel
 Liffey
.11 bleakhusen
 ?Bleak House
.26 Budlim
 Dublin
.26 do, dainty daulimbs
 Dublin Allusion: "Dear Dirty Dublin"
.29 hahititahiti
 Society Islands: Tahiti
.33 Borrisalooner
 Borris
.34 Gereland
 ?
338.03 Germanon
 Germany
.03 Ehren...gobrawl
 Ehren on the Rhine
 Ireland
.04 public plouse
 Tavern, The
.07 *paraguastical*
 ?Paraguay
 (+ *paraguas*, Sp "umbrella")
.14 Sea vaast a pool
 Sevastopol
.16 *yurrup*
 ?Europe

.17 unt
 Unt
.17 jubalant
 Jubaland (+ Jubal-Cain)
.19 laut-lievtonant
 Lithuania
 Livland
.19 Baltiskeeamore
 Baltic Sea
 ?Baltimore
.20 leporty hole
 ?Liberty Hall
.22 Malorazzias
 Ukraine
.26 man d'airain
 Aran Islands
 Ireland
.32 hear in
 Ireland
.36 *grain oils of Aerin*
 Aran Islands
 Ireland
.36 *laugh neighs*
 Neagh, Lough
339.01 *lipponease*
 Japan: Nippon
.02 Ullahbluh
 Ulster
.09 Chromean
 Crimea
.11 malakoiffed
 Malakhof, The (Crimean War)
.11 varnashed
 Varna (Crimean War)
.11 roscians
 Russia
.13 perikopendolous
 Perekop
.14 Karrs and Polikoff's
 ?Carr, Henry L (confectioner)
 Kars
.18 *Perssiasterssias*
 Ireland: Erse
 Persia
.18 *waggonhorchers...stargapers*
 Ursa Major: the Wagon
.19 *bulgeglarying*
 Bulgaria
.21 Grozarktic
 Arctic
.24−.25 *farused...allasundery*
 Pharos at Alexandria

.26 Wymmingtown
     ?
.27 the calves of Man
     Man, Isle of: Calf of Man
.29 Erminia's
     ?Armenia
.31 *lusky*
     Lusk
     Lutsk
.31 *Lubliner*
     Dublin
     Lublin
.33 *El Monte de Zuma*
     NPN: Montezuma, Aztec
     king
.33 *wilnaynilnay*
     Vilna
.34 *minkst*
     Minsk
.34 *Krumlin*
     Crumlin
     Moscow: Kremlin
.35 *vatercan*
     Vatican
340.05 *rutene...Lissnaluhy*
     Ruthenia
.06 *Djublian Alps*
     Alps
     Dublin: Alp Uí Laoghaire
.06 *Hoofd Ribeiro*
     Howth
.07 *trulock*
     Trulock, Harriss and Rich-
     ardson
.08 karhags
     ?Carhaix
.09 lomondations of Oghrem
     Aughrim
     Lomond, Loch
.09 Warful doon's bothem
     ?Denmark
     Woovil Doon Botham
.09 furry glunn
     Phoenix Park: Furry Glen
.13 *blackseer*
     Black Sea
.13 *regulect*
     Zurich: St Regula
.15 *relix*
     Zurich: St Felix
.16 rath!...mines!
     Rathmines

.16 moy
     ?Moy R
.17 Osro
     Oslo
.18 prolettas
     Loreto
.21 Meideveide
     Maida Vale
     Meath
.22 annal livves
     Liffey
.24 Finnland
     England
     Finland
     Ireland: Tír na bhFionn
.27 *roshashanaral*
     ?Sharon
.33 Piping Pubwirth
     Pebworth
.34 Haunted Hillborough
     Hillborough
.35 Russers
     Russia
341.06 boyne
     Boyne R
.09 balacleivka
     Balaclava
     Dublin: Baile Átha Cliath
.17 mlachy way for gambling
     Dublin Allusion: "Rocky Road
     to Dublin"
     Milky Way
.18 *curkscraw bind*
     Cork: St Patrick's St
     ?Corkscrew
.19 *Caerholme Event*
     ?Caerleon-on-Usk
.20 Irish Race and World
     Irish Race and World
.23 *winsor places*
     ?Windsor Palace
     Windsor Place
.27 *Saint Dhorough's*
     St Doolagh
342.05 *Boozer's Gloom*
     NPN? See *Census*, for the horse
     of that name
.06 *Baldawl the curse, baledale the day*
     Baldoyle (racecourse)
.09 *Casabianca*
     ?Casablanca

.13 *Gabbarnaur-Jaggarnath*
    Juggernaut

.14 *Pamjab!*
    Punjab

.15 *Thousand to One Guinea-Goose-*
    berry's
        Curragh, The ("1000 Guin-
        eas")

.16 *Lipperfull Slipver Cup*
    Liverpool ("Summer Cup")

.18 *the fourth of the hurdles*
    Dublin: Baile Átha Cliath

.19 *Bumchub!*
    Punjab

.20 *Creman*
    ?Crimea

.23 *Bailey Beacon*
    Bailey Lighthouse

.24 *Ratatuohy*
    ?Pseudo-placename: *Rath an*
    Tuathaigh, Ir "Fort of the
    Territorial-Lord" (O Hehir)

.25 *Leavybrink*
    Liffey

.30 *eeridreme*
    Ireland

.32 Irish Race and World
    Irish Race and World

.33 *Loundin Reginald*
    British Broadcasting Corp
    London

.35 *dipperend*
    Ursa Major: the Dipper

.35 *tiomor of malaise*
    Malaysia
    Timor (Malaysia)

343.01 *orangultonia*
    Ulster
    (*orang*, Malay "man")

.01 *Sagittarius*
    Sagittarius

.02 *Draco on the Lour*
    Draco

.03 Boyle, Burke and Campbell
    British Broadcasting Corp

.04 strangbones tomb
    Christchurch Cathedral:
    Strongbow's Tomb

.05 Saint Sepulchre's
    St Sepulchre's

.06 scattering
    ?Scattery Island

.06 giant's hail over the curseway
    Giant's Causeway

.09 Perfedes Albionias
    Albion (England)

.09 Think some ingain think
    Tingsomingenting

.10 Galwegian caftan
    Galway
    (+ Norwegian Captain)

.10 Orops
    Europe

.10 Aasas
    Asia

.15 *scoopchina's*
    China
    Yugoslavia: Skupshtina

.16 *awstooloo*
    Austerlitz
    Waterloo

.16 *valdesombre...hero*
    NPN?
    (*Valet de chambre*; "No man is
    a hero to his valet")

.17 *greak*
    Greece

.20 Ichts nichts on nichts
    Nixnixundnix

.28 allafranka
    France

.31 lewdbrogue
    Ladbroke

.32 santry
    Santry

.33 haftara
    Tara

344.03 *croak*...[.07] partridge's
    ?Croagh Patrick

.08 *scimmianised twinge*
    Siam

.14 nitshnykopfgoknob
    Nizhniy-Novgorod

.15 rudeman cathargic
    Carthage
    Rome

.16 Mebbuck at Messar
    NPN: Nebucchadnezzar

.18 cowruads...airish pleasantry
    ?Red Cow (Tallaght)

.18 airish
    Ireland

.20 carcasses
    Caucasus

.26 aurals
      Ural Mts
.28 babbeing...bibbelboy
      Babel, Tower of
.29 gnaas
      ?Naas
.30 solongopatom
      ?Seringapatam
.31 Arram
      ?Aram
.31 Eirzerum
      Erzerum
      Ireland
.33 Saur of all the Haurousians
      Russia
345.01 Irmenial hairmaierians
      Armenia
      Ireland
.05 *Burnias*
      Borneo
.15 to bagot
      ?Baggot St
.19 *lagan on lighthouse*
      Lagan R
.19 *silent power*
      Power's Distillery
.22 *guidness*
      Guinness's Brewery
.25 To bug at
      ?Baggot St
.30 Theres scares...so svend
      Meeting of the Waters
.34 *Mullingaria*
      Tavern, The: Mullingar
      House
346.01 *Fruzian Creamtartery*
      Crimea
      ?Frisia
.02 *neatschknee Novgolosh*
      Nizhniy-Novgorod
.03 *spinach ruddocks*
      Spain
.04 *Aromal*
      Rome
.06 *Arumbian Knives*
      Arabia
.07 *Nunsturk*
      Turkey
.07 *Old Yales boys*
      Yale U

.15 *Colliguchuna*
      ?Pseudo-placename: *Colg a'*
      tiuine, Ir "fury of the tune"
      (O Hehir)
.15 *dubrin*
      Dublin
.18 *pollyvoulley foncey*
      France
.18 *pitchin ingles*
      England
.19 Buccleuch
      Buccleuch
.21 az ov
      Azov, Sea of
.23 Vaersegood
      Ireland: Erse
.23 Sayyessik, Ballygarry
      Ballygarry
      Bulgaria
.26 howed
      ?Howth
      ?Thing Mote
.31 *cushlows*
      Cush (near Howth)
.31 *hoarth*
      Howth
.32 *pimple spurk*
      Phoenix Park: People's Park
.33 *baggutstract upper*
      Baggot St
347.01 white horsday
      White Horse
.01 bulg
      ?Bulgaria
.03 plain of Khorason
      Khorasan
.03 mount of Bekel
      ?Bethel
.04 Steep Nemorn
      NPN? ("Macbeth shall sleep no
      more")
.09 Krzerszonese
      Crimea (Gk, *Chersonesus*)
.09 asundurst
      Sandhurst
.09 Woolwichleagues
      Woolwich
.10 Crimealian wall
      Crimea
.11 Ayerland
      Ireland

.11   weeping stillstumms
      Wapping (+ *Waffenstillstand*,
      Ger "truce")

.11   the freshprosts of Eastchept
      Eastcheap (London)
      Egypt

.12   the dangling garters of Marrow-
      bone
      Gardens of Semiramis (Bab-
      ylon)
      ?Marrowbone Lane
      Marylebone

.13   wapping stiltstunts
      Wapping (cf 347.11)

.13   Bostion Moss
      Boston

.15   moskats
      ?Moscow

.19   Hajizfijjiz
      Hodges Figgis and Co

.20   Bok of Alam
      Allen, Bog of

.21   Erin gone brugk
      Ireland

.31   roaming cartridges
      Carthage
      Rome

.31   orussheying
      Russia

.32   Crummwiliam wall
      Crimea

.35   *durblinly*
      Dublin

.35   *obasiant to...the skivis*
      Dublin Motto

.36   *turfkish*
      Turkey

348.01   *laddios*
      Lydia

.10   waulholler
      Valhalla

.11   alma
      Alma R

.16   Neuilands
      ?Ireland
      ?New Island

.21   Kong Gores Wood
      Clongowes Wood College

.21   thurkmen
      Turkey

.22   toileries
      ?Tuileries Gardens (Paris)

.23   Vjenaskayas
      Vienna

.28   Lancesters
      Lancaster

.30   *Espionia*
      Spain

.31   *the bustle Bakerloo*
      Underground (London): Baker-
      loo Line

349.26   *Hll*
      Hell

350.02   *garerden*
      Eden

.03   *Hillel*
      ?

.03   *Dalem*
      ?

.04   *the place of the stones*
      ?

.05   *pontofert*
      Rhodes

.08   *field of Hanar*
      ?

.12   *Oldbally Court*
      Old Bailey

.20   basquibezigues
      Basque Provinces

.21   aprican
      Africa

.21   eskermillas
      ?Esker

.22   duckish delights
      Turkey

.24   sassenacher
      England

.25   th'osirian
      Assyria

.27   Parishmoslattary
      ?

.28   crimsend
      Crimea

.29   Slobabogue
      ?
      (*slava bogu*, Russ "glory to
      God")

.33   Sunda schoon
      Malaysia: Sunda Islands

351.04   chipping nortons
      Chipping Norton

.06   loyal leibsters
      Leinster (regiment)

.07 prettish...engrish
England

.08 waynward islands
Windward Islands

.09 durck rosolun
Ireland: Little Black Rose

.14 S. Pivorandbowl
St Petersburg: Peter and Paul
Fortress

.22 Tanah Kornalls
? (*Tanah*, Malay "land")

.24 sunpictorsbosk
St Petersburg

.27 reptrograd leanins
St Petersburg: Petrograd

.29 Lyndhurst Terrace
?Lyndhurst Terrace (London)

.30 belle the troth...alliance
Waterloo: La Belle Alliance

.32 Mellay Street
?Malaysia

.35 Jova
Java (Malaysia)

352.01 scutt's
Scotland

.09 oreland
Ireland

.09 the splunthers of colt
Cork

.11 Almagnian Gothabobus
Germany

.12 meath
Meath

.12 dulwich
Dulwich

.17 *volkar boastsung*
Volga R

.17 *sea vermelhion*
California, Gulf of
?Red Sea

.22 Oholy rasher
Russia

.23 bullyclaver
Balaclava
Dublin: Baile Átha Cliath

.24 Umsturdum
Amsterdam

.25 race of fiercemarchands
France

.26 counterination oho of shorpshoopers
England

.32 dead men's hills
Mort Homme, Le

.33 frustate
?Irish Free State

.33 Russkakruscam
Russia

.36 *pungataries of sin praktice*
St Patrick's Purgatory

353.03 souber civiles
Savile Row (London)

.04 all of man
?Man, Isle of

.09 sobre saviles
Savile Row (London)

.11 Killtork
?Clonturk
Killtork

.13 arctic
Arctic

.13 a bull in a meadows
Clontarf

.15 rolland
Ghent: "Roland"

.16 ourloud's lande
Ireland

.18 culothone
?Cuthone

.18 erseroyal
Ireland: Erse

.19 Igorladns
Ireland
Russia

.19 dobblenotch
Dublin

.23 *Hurtreford*
Dublin: Baile Átha Cliath

.24 *Parsuralia*
?Persia
Ural Mts

.26 *coventry*
Coventry

.27 *Landaunelegants*
London

.28 *Pinkadindy*
Piccadilly

.28 *Hullulullu*
Honolulu

.29 *Bawlawayo*
Bulawayo

.29 *empyreal Raum*
Rome

.29 *mordern Atems*
Athens
Edinburgh: "The Modern
Athens"

.31 *Oldanelang's Konguerrig*
Danelagh
Denmark

.31 *dawnybreak*
Donnybrook

.32 *Aira*
Ireland

.33 *cromlin*
Crumlin

.34 *birstol boys*
Borstal
?Bristol
Tavern, The: Bridge Inn

.34 *artheynes*
Artane

.34 *is it her tour*
Isod's Tower

.35 *fullfour fivefirearms*
Ireland: The Five Fifths

354.10 *Old Erssia's*
Ireland: Erse

.12 *too foul for hell*
Hell (*Teufel*, Ger "devil")

.14 *Cicilian*
Sicily

.16 *S. E. Morehampton*
Morehampton Rd (SE Dub-
lin)

.16 *E. N. Sheilmartin*
Shelmartin (Ave) (NE Dub-
lin)

.17 *Meetinghouse Lanigan*
Meeting House Lane

.17 *Vergemout Hall*
Vergemount Hall

.22 gadden
Eden

.23 wanderloot
?Waterloo

.24 samuraised twimbs
Siam

.25 mouldhering iries
Ireland

.27 babble towers
Babel, Tower of

355.11 alldconfusalem
Jerusalem

.13 Beauty's bath
Bath

.15 Hersy Hunt
?

.16 harrow the hill
Harrow-on-the-Hill
Hell

.16 rollicking rogues from...rockery
rides from. Rambling
Dublin Allusion: "Rocky Road
to Dublin"

.21 Solidan's Island
NPN: Saladin's Islam. 1st
Draft: "Islamd"

.22 Moltern Giaourmany
Germany (+ *giaour*, Turk "infi-
del," ie, "Christian")

.22 Amelakins
America (+ Amalekites)

.23 engined Egypsians
Egypt

.24 oxmanstongue
Oxmantown

.26 sat...ring
Saturn

.30 Teewiley
?Tivoli

.31 Khummer-Phett
?

.32 An-Lyph
Liffey

356.02 ilkermann
Inkerman

.08 Jura
Jura (Mts) (+ law)

.09 Messafissi
Mississippi R (+ metaphysics)

357.02 English
England

.03 wellwillworth
?NYC: Woolworth Bldg

.04 Bismillafoulties
Bushmills

.09 perssian
Persia

.29 gobelimned
?Gobelins

.30 Eonochs
?Enoch

.30   Cunstuntonopolies
           Constantinople
.31   general golf stature
           Phoenix Park: Gough Statue
.32   thems elves
           ?Thames R
.32   howthern folleys
           Howth
           Phoenix Park: Furry (Haw-
           thorn) Glen
358.08 happy...homesweetstown...my
           mottu propprior
           Dublin Motto
.08   burgages
           Burgage
.14   Magellanic clouds
           Magellanic Clouds
.20   Perseoroyal
           Persia (Iran)
.21   Ere
           Ireland
.21   Iran
           Iran
           Ireland
.22   gryffygryffygryffs...Wildemanns
           Basle
.24   jonahs
           ?Iona
.25   baillybeacons
           Bailey Lighthouse
.34   maypole
           Maypole
359.03 taratoryism
           Tara
.03   orenore
           ?Nore R (+ iron ore)
.04   chiltern
           Chiltern
.14   Danelope
           Denmark
.14   laurettas
           Loreto
.16   camelottery
           Camelot
.16   lyonesslooting
           Lyonesse
.19   the oldcant rogue
           Old Kent Road
.25   hoovthing
           ?Howth
.26   Oreland
           Ireland

.26   Goes Tory
           ?Tory Island
.28   Lucan
           Lucan
.34   waldalure
           Waterloo
.34   Mount Saint John's, Jinnyland
           Waterloo: Mont St Jean
.35   Mooreparque
           Moor Park
.36   Sunsink gang
           Dunsink Observatory
360.02 sweetishsad lightandgayle
           Sweden (Jenny Lind)
.16   Secret Hookup
           Sekhet Hetep
.30   yellowhorse
           ?Yellow House
.32   eeriewhigg airywhugger
           Ireland
361.02 nought...nil...nix...nothing
           ?Nixnixundnix
.05   guineases
           Guinness's Brewery
.07   tongue irish
           Ireland
.16   Killykelly
           ?Dublin: Drom Cuill-Choille
           ?Kilkelly
.18   o'liefing
           Liffey
.20   County Shillelagh
           Shillelagh
.22   bridge of primerose
           ?Primrose St
.22   blueybells
           Bluebell
.23   Dandeliond
           ?
.25   bester of the boyne
           Boyne R
.26   leavely of leaftimes
           Liffey
.32   gestare romanoverum
           Rome: *Gesta Romanorum*
.35   Droughty
           ?
362.01 druid circle
           ?
.02   Clandibblon
           Dublin

.07	islands empire	365.07	cerpaintime
	England		Serpentine
.10	soldr of a britsh	.09	sebaiscopal
	England		Sevastopol
.12	finn	.09	virginial water
	Finland		?Acqua Vergine
.13	lap		Virginia Water
	Lapland	.16	wholenosing...whallhoarding
.22	yearin out yearin		?Phoenix Park: Hole in the
	Ireland		Wall
.28	equitable...societies	.16	Don
	Equitable Insurance Cos		?Don R
.31	Amodicum cloth	.17	kuschkars
	?America		Kars
.34	prospect	.17	tarafs
	?Glasnevin: Prospect Ceme-		?Tara
	tery	.18	double densed
.36	Dulby		?Dublin
	Dublin	.29	marly...salthorse
363.04	princer street		Champs Elysées: Marly Horses
	Prince's St	.33	Taylor's Spring
.08	Almayne Rogers		?
	?Germany	366.15	Saturnay Eve
.19	friends' leave		Saturn
	France	.17	increaminated
.31	board of wumps and pumps		Crimea
	?	.19	turk
	(+ "I renounce the devil and		Turkey
	all his works and pomps")	.20	barrakraval
.35	angelsexonism		Balaclava
	Saxony	.20	Jambuwel's
364.06	post puzzles deparkment		England (John Bull)
	General Post Office (Parcels	.21	Terry Shimmyrag's
	Office)		Ireland: Tír na Simearóig
.14	Ears to hears	.21	upperturnity
	Ireland: Erse		Eupatoria
.18	apoclogypst	.24	dire daffy damedeaconesses
	Egypt		Dublin Allusion: "Dear Dirty
.19	Kinahaun		Dublin"
	Canaan	.27	Houtes...scotchem
.20	water of Elin		?Hades
	Ireland		Scotland
	Nile R	.34	Weald
.22	city of Analbe		Weald, The
	Dublin: Eblana	.34	bays of Bawshaw
.25	duvlin		?
	Dublin	367.04	chinchinatibus
.31	Cutey Strict		China
	NPN? "Strict Q. T."		?Cincinnati
.35	boastonmess	.05	haygue
	Boston		Hague, The

.12   Dan Leary
           Dun Laoghaire
.12   the corner house
           Lyons Corner Houses
.32   kingcorrier
           Kincora (+ Mark's lion)
.33   eyriewinging
           Ireland (+ John's eagle)
368.09 jerumsalemdo
           Jerusalem
.22   Zumschloss
           NPN? (Ger, "in conclusion")
.32   lousiany
           ?Louisiana
369.08 S. Bruno's Toboggan Drive
           ?
.08   Bellchimbers, Carolan Crescent
           ?
.09   Hilly Gape, Poplar Park
           ?
.10   The View, Gazey Peer
           ?Ghazipur
.11   Multiple Lodge, Jiff Exby Rode
           ?
.12   Fert Fort
           Rhodes
.12   Woovil Doon Botham
           ?Denmark
           Woovil Doon Botham
.18   inn court
           King's Inns
.26   Paullabucca
           ?Poolbeg
           ?Poulaphuca
.28   Senders
           ?Saunders' News Letter
.29   Poulebec
           Poolbeg
           ?Poulaphuca
.34   goumeral's postoppage
           General Post Office
370.07 Cobra Park
           Cabra
           Eden
.08   howe
           Thing Mote
.09   Dix Dearthy Dungbin
           Dublin Allusion: "Dear Dir-
           ty Dublin"
.19   drooplin
           Dublin

.19   dunlearies
           Dun Laoghaire (+ dundreary
           [NPN] whiskers)
.23   bluebleeding boarhorse
           Bleeding Horse (Tavern)
           Blue Boar Alley
.24   soresen's head
           ? (imaginary tavern?)
.24   rumpumplikun oak
           ? (imaginary tavern?)
.27   marringaar
           Tavern, The: Mullingar House
.28   Lochlunn
           Lochlann
.28   feof...foef...forfummed
           Ireland: The Five Fifths
.29   Ship-le-Zoyd
           Chapelizod
.34   maynoother
           Maynooth (+ *fire minutter
           endnu*, Dan "four minutes
           to go")
.35   clandoilskins
           ?Clondalkin
.36   Capolic Gizzards
           Chapelizod
371.03 sunkentrunk
           ?Sunken Road (Switz)
.09   Ostia...Ostia
           Ostia (Rome's seaport)
.11   reromembered
           Rome
.16   grooves of blarneying
           Blarney
.25   hostillery With his chargehand
           Chapelizod: The House by the
           Churchyard
.26   almaynoother
           Maynooth
.30   Dancingtree
           ?Dunsink
.30   Suttonstone
           Sutton
.33   Awaindhoo's
           ? (*abhainn dubh*, Ir "black riv-
           er")
.33   selverbourne
           ? (cf 549.29)
.33   Rochelle Lane
           Rochelle Lane
.34   liberties
           Liberties, The

.34 Mullinguard
     Tavern, The: Mullingar
     House
.35 tunepiped road
     Turnpike
.35 perked on hollowy hill
     Phoenix Park: The Hollow
.36 poor man of Lyones
     Lyons
.36 errindwards
     Ireland
372.01 belles bows
     St Mary-le-Bow (London)
.02 Dublin
     Dublin
     Dublin, Georgia
.07 barttler of the beauyne
     Boyne R
.08 frankling
     France
.12 Café Béranger
     Béranger, Café
.13 sheep was looset
     Chapelizod
.14 Wobbleton Whiteleg Welshers
     NPN: *History of the City of
     Dublin* by Warburton,
     Whitelaw, and Walsh
.14 kaillykailly...Brownhazelwood
     Dublin: Drom Cuill-Choille
.16 dinnasdoolins
     Dublin: Dinas-Doolin
.16 labious banks
     Liffey
.17 Danesbury Common
     Danesbury
     Denmark
.20 rockers on the roads
     Dublin Allusion: "Rocky
     Road to Dublin"
.25 His bludgeon's bruk
     Barrack ("Bloody") Bridge
.28 Free rogue Mountone
     Three Rock Mt
.28 Dew Mild Well
     ?
.28 corry awen and glowry
     Garryowen
.30 lyncheon...burgherbooh
     Galway (City)
.30 Shanavan Wacht...O'Ryne
     Ireland: Shan van Vogt

.30 Shanavan Wacht...O'Ryne (*Cont.*)
     Rhine R ("Die Wacht am
     Rhein")
     ?Shanavon
.34 the mailing waters
     ?Moyle, Sea of
.36 Bothersby North
     ?Battersby and Co (+ North)
373.01 Poors Coort, Soother
     Powerscourt (+ South)
.03 The Eats
     ? (+ East)
.04 sailalloyd
     ?Lloyds of London
.05 Moherboher to the Washte
     Bohermore
     Moher, Cliffs of
     ?Wash, The
     (+ West)
.08 Waves
     Four Waves of Erin
.12 ebblynuncies
     Dublin: Eblana
.19 Alddaublin
     Dublin
.20 Deblinity
     Dublin
.20 the pairk
     Phoenix Park
.25 distillery
     Power's Distillery
.25 Broree
     Guinness's Brewery
.25 johnsgate...jameseslane
     Guinness's Brewery (James's
     Gate)
     Power's Distillery (John's
     Lane)
.28 the mall
     Mall, The (London)
.30 Rorke relly
     Breffny
.34 allalilty
     Liffey
374.03 wonderland's
     Wonderland
.03 trancedone boyscript
     Boston (*Transcript*)
.06 Torkenwhite
     York
.06 Radlumps, Lencs
     Lancaster

.12 the Murdrus dueluct
     NPN: J C Mardrus translated
     the *Koran* into French;
     "mudras" are Indian finger
     signs
.16 Boy of Biskop
     Biscay, Bay of
     ?Bishop's Bay
.18 deep dorfy doubtlings
     Dublin Allusion: "Dear Dir-
     ty Dublin"
.18 bunk of basky
     Biscay, Bay of
.19 Our island...
     Ireland
     (+ "For England, home, and
     beauty")
.19 Rome
     Rome
.19 Batt in, boot!...breach
     Butt Br
.21 Finnish Make Goal
     Finland (+ Finn MacCool)
.25 yard
     Scotland Yard
.28 Finsbury Follies
     Finsbury (London)
.29 batter see
     Battersea (London)
.29 regent
     Regent's (Park) (London)
.31 Estchapel
     Eastcheap (London)
.32 King's Avenance
     King's Ave
.34 Hung Chung
     ?Hong Kong
     ?Peking: Hwang Cheng
375.05 Hunphydunphyville'll
     Dublin Allusion
     ?Dunphy's Corner
.08 Brittas
     Britain, Little
     Brittas
.09 hundreds of manhoods
     Manhood, Hundred of
.12 Misses Mountsackvilles
     Chapelizod: Mt Sackville
     (Convent)
.19 earse
     Ireland: Erse

.21 Richmond Rover
     Richmond
.23 Dalymount's
     Dalymount
.23 Don
     ?Don R
.24 Tara Tribune
     Tara
.28 Berkness cirrchus
     ?
.32 Furr-y-Benn
     ?Phoenix Park: Furry Glen
     (+ *beann*, Ir "mountain")
.32 Ferr-y-Bree
     ?
     (*bri*, Ir "hill")
.33 Vikloe
     Wicklow
376.01 Lima
     ?Lima
.04 Mudquirt accent
     ?
     (*Midgaard*, Nor "The Earth")
.04 bulgen horesies
     Belgium
.05 wollan indulgencies
     Belgium (Walloon)
.05 flemsh
     Belgium (Flanders)
.06 *chemins de la croixes*
     ?
.08 Clontarf
     Clontarf
.08 voterloost
     Waterloo
.09 Norris
     Norway
.11 Delphin
     Dolphin Hotel
.11 Grusham
     Gresham Hotel
.12 Real Hymernians
     Royal Hibernian Hotel
.17 Neffin
     ?Nephin
.18 Gormagareen
     ?
.18 Gunting Munting Hunting Punting
     ?
.32 Blennercassel
     Blennercassel

.32	Clanruckard	.19	Walsall
	Clanrickard		Walsall (football team)
.34	Croonacreena	.31	dunsker's brogue
	?Crona		Denmark
377.05	gull	.36	foul a delfian
	Gaul		Philadelphia
.07	Shallburn Shock	379.01	Knockcastle
	Shelbourne Rd (football		Castleknock
	team)	.04	Bugle and the Bitch
.13	oldboy Welsey Wandrer		*Horn and Hound*
	Irish Rugby Union (Old	.10	Carlow
	Wesley; Wanderers)		Carlow
.16	*Ivy Eve in the Hall of Alum*	.11	Aerian's Wall
	?Adam and Eve's		Ireland (+ "Wallerian degener-
	Allen, Hill of		ation" of nerve fiber?)
.22	Dovlen	.12	Fall of Toss
	Dublin (+ "dove")		?Töss
.22	Rathfinn	.12	volleyholleydoodlem
	? (*Rath fionn*, Ir "Finn's		Valhalla
	Castle") (+ "raven")	.13	liverpooser
.27	Poshtapengha		Liverpool
	? (just "penny post"?)	.17	delysiums
.33	aaskart		Elysian Fields
	?Asgard	.20	pappappoppopcuddle
.33	Allsup, allsop		Popocatepetl
	Allsop and Sons	.28	Gorteen
378.06	Arrahland		Gorteen
	Ireland	.31	Megantic
.09	rollorrish rattillary		"Titanic"
	Ireland (Royal Irish Artil-	.34	Timmotty Hall
	lery)		NYC: Tammany Hall
.10	—allucktruckalltraum—	.36	Keyhoe, Danelly and Pykemhyme
	?Killdroughalt		Kehoe, Donnelly and Paken-
.11	nonirishblooder		ham
	Ireland	380.01	Variants' Katey...Variants' Katey
.11	Greenislender		Varian and Co
	Greenland	.03	Aquasancta Liffey Patrol
	Ireland: Misc Allusions		Liffey
.14	Magtmorken	.05	Malincurred Mansion
	?		Malin Head
.14	Kovenhow		Tavern, The: Mullingar House
	Copenhagen	.07	hoose uncommons
.15	causcaus		House of Commons
	?Caucasus	.09	Glenfinnisk-en-la-Valle
.18	Partick Thistle		Phoenix Park (+ song "Glen-
	Partick: Partick Thistle		finishk")
	(football team)	.13	Ireland
.19	S. Megan's		Ireland
	?St Michan's Church	.15	house of the hundred bottles
.19	Brystal Palace		?
	Bristol		(+ Conn of the Hundred Bat-
	Crystal Palace (football team)		tles)

.18 Ireland
     Ireland
.20 Ireland...Ireland
     Ireland
.21 Taharan
     Tara
     Teheran
.34 Ireland
     Ireland
381.04 Hauburnea's
     Auburn
     Ireland: Hibernia
.06 ramblers from Clane
     Clane
     Clare
.13 Ghenter's gaunts
     Ghent
.14 Macclefield's swash
     ?Macclesfield
.16 heart of Midleinster
     Leinster
     Midlothian
.17 black...water
     ?Blackwater R
.22 blurney Cashelmagh crooner
     Blarney (Castle)
     Cashel
.22 lerking Clare air
     Clare
.25 but, arrah
     Tara
.29 Irish
     Ireland
.30 sliggymaglooral
     ?
     (*slighe*, Ir "road")
.31 Trojan
     Troy
382.03 Guiness's
     Guinness's Brewery
.04 Phoenix brewery...O'Connell's
     ...ale
     Phoenix Brewery
.04 John Jameson and Sons
     Jameson, John, and Son
.05 Roob Coccola
     ?
.06 Dublin
     Dublin
.13 Litvian Newestlatter
     Latvia
     Liffey

.22 Faugh MacHugh O'Bawlar
     ?Carlow
.26 Barleyhome
     Borneo
.27 *Nansy Hans*
     Phoenix Park: Hole in the Wall
.27 Liff
     Liffey
.28 Nattenlaender
     NPN? (Nor, "lands of night")
.28 Farvel
     Farewell, Cape (Greenland)
.28 Farvel, farerne
     ?Erne
     Faeroe Isls
.30 Starloe
     Carlow

BOOK II

Chapter 4

383.06 *Palmerstown Park*
     Palmerston Park
.15 Overhoved
     ?Howth
.23 Dubbeldorp
     Dublin
     ?Düsseldorf
384.05 Moykle ahoykling
     ?Moyle, Sea of
.06 four maaster waves of Erin...four
     waves
     Four Waves of Erin
.10 Miracle Squeer
     ? (cf 86.34 Medical Square)
.16 the interims of Augusburgh
     Augsburg
385.01 Cullen's barn
     Cullen's Barn
     ?Cullenswood
.04 Two-tongue Common
     NPN: Tutankhamen
.07 O'Clery
     ?Clery and Co
.09 Nodderlands Nurskery
     Netherlands
     Nod, Land of
     Norway
.13 Queen's Ultonian colleges
     Belfast
     Queen's Colleges
     Ulster

.15   Clumpthump
        Clontarf
.16   dane
        Denmark
.18   mercias
        ?Mercia
.25   Luvillicit
        Chapelizod
.33   crusted hoed
        Howth
.34   Arctic Newses Dagsdogs
        Arctic
.35   darblun
        Dublin
386.18 Merquus of Pawerschoof
        Powerscourt
.20   O'Clery's
        ?Clery and Co
.20   darkumound numbur wan
        Thing Mote
.21   Dame street
        Dame St
.22   statue of Mrs Dana O'Connell
        O'Connell Statue
.22   Trinity College
        Trinity College, Dublin
.24   Bootersbay Sisters...Battersby
        Sisters
        Battersby and Co
.26   Hoggin Green
        Hoggen Green
.27   tailturn horseshow
        Teltown: Tailteann Games
.28   angler nomads
        England ("Anglo-Normans")
.30   cappunchers
        ?Capuchin Friary
        Coppinger
.35   hopolopocattls
        Popocatepetl
387.01 Curragh
        Curragh, The
.02   Noord Amrikaans...Suid Aferi-
        can
        Africa
        America
        South America
.03   tiara dullfuoco
        Tierra del Fuego
.05   scotobrit
        England
        Scotland

.07   Mr Dame James
        Dame St

        *The two lines at 387.09–.10 com-
        bine Dublin streets with territories on the
        British mainland ravaged by Vikings in
        the 9th and 10th centuries.*
.09   Strathlyffe
        Liffey
        Liffey St
        Strathclyde (Scot)
.09   Aylesburg
        Ailesbury Rd
        Aylesbury (Eng)
.09   Northumberland
        Northumberland (Rd)
        Northumberland (Eng)
.10   Anglesey
        Anglesea (Rd)
        Anglesey (Wales)
.11   hayastdanars
        Armenia: Hayasdan
        Denmark
.12   our seaborn isle
        Ireland: Misc Allusions
.13   andesiters
        Andes Mts
.13   pantellarias
        Pantelleria
.14   Marcus of Lyons
        Lyons
.18   Momonian
        Munster
.19   Swede Villem
        Sweden
.21   Wormans' Noe
        Norman's Woe
.24   Baltersby...Buzzersbee
        Battersby and Co
.25   the whate shape
        White Ship, The
.27   the red sea
        Red Sea
.28   Merkin Cornyngwham
        Cornwall (+ Martin Cunning-
        ham)
.29   the castle
        Castle, The
.29   Erin Isles
        ?Aran Islands
        Ireland

.30   suir
       Suir R
.30   the red sea
       Red Sea
.34   Grocery Trader's Manthly
       ?
388.02 Llawnroc
       Cornwall
.06   is Elsker woed
       Selskar
.10   Flemish armada
       Belgium
.13   coast of Cominghome
       NPN? (Martin Cunningham)
.15   Porterscout
       Powerscourt
.16   whuite hourse of Hunover
       White Horse: House of Han-
       over
.17   Clunkthurf
       Clontarf
       ?Clonturk
.17   Cabinhogan
       Copenhagen
.18   Frankish floot
       Belgium: Flanders ("Flem-
       ish fleet")
       France
.19   Hedalgoland
       Helgoland
       Spain
.26   Queen's Colleges
       Queen's Colleges
.26   1132 Brian or Bride street
       Bride St
.30   Hibernia
       Ireland: Hibernia
.32   Latimer Roman history
       Rome
.35   collegians green
       College Green
.36   trinitarian senate
       Trinity College, Dublin
389.01 Plymouth brethren
       Plymouth
.04   four trinity colleges
       Queen's Colleges
       Trinity College, Dublin
.04   Eringrowback
       Ireland
.05   Ulcer
       Ulster

.05   Moonster
       Munster
.05   Leanstare
       Leinster
.05   Cannought
       Connacht
.06   four grandest colleges
       Queen's Colleges
.06   Erryn
       Ireland
.06   Killorcure...Killthemall...Killeach-
       other and Killkelly-on-the-Flure
       (In context, the medical
       schools of the Queen's Col-
       leges of Belfast, Cork, Gal-
       way, and the National Uni-
       versity, Dublin)
.07   Killkelly-on-the-Flure
       ?Dublin: Drom Cuill-Choille
       ?Kilkelly (Connacht)
.10   Janesdanes Lady Andersdaughter
       Universary
       ?Dame St (cf 387.07)
       ?Denmark
.12   Bambam's
       Ireland: Banba
.13   No. 1132 or No. 1169, bis, Fitz-
       mary Round
       ?
.19   romano
       Rome
.24   troad
       Troy: Troad
.36   Senders Newslaters
       Saunders' News Letter
390.01 Saint Brices
       St Bricin's Hospital
.03   ballest master
       Ballast Office
.03   Gosterstown
       ?Goatstown
.04   the Lagener
       Lagan R
.04   Locklane Lighthouse
       Lochlann
.09   Artsichekes Road
       Artichoke Rd
.10   Oran mosque
       Oran (+ "iron mask")
.12   cabbangers
       ?Capuchin Friary
       Coppinger

.12 cabbangers (*Cont.*)
St Thomas à Becket, Abbey of

.13 Welshman
Wales

.14 nangles, sangles, angles and wangles
North, South, East, West

.15 four of the Welsh waves
Four Waves of Erin
Wales

·16 Lumbag Walk
?Lambay Island
?Lambeg
Lambeth (London)

.16 Battleshore and Deaddleconche
?

.17 Roman hat
Rome

.18 Greek gloss
Greece

.18 Chichester College
Chichester (House)

.25 the wettest indies
India, West Indies

.25 *Burrymecarott*
Belfast: Ballymacarret

.26 *Peebles*
Peebles (Scot)

.29 Dalkymont nember to
Dalkey
?Dalymount
Dollymount

.30 Ivel
?

.31 Kunut
?Connacht
Kent

.32 Koombe
Coombe, The

.35 Poolland
Poland

391.01 Erminia Reginia
?Armenia

.01 aring
Ireland

.02 Y.W.C.A.
Y.W.C.A.

.03 Married Male Familyman's Auctioneer's court
?

.03 Arrahnacuddle
?

.04 Scuitsman
Scotland

.09 borstel
?Bristol
?Borstal

.12 the middle of the temple
Temple (London)

.14 Marcus Bowandcoat
Powerscourt

.14 brownesberrow
?Barrow R

.16 Herrinsilde
Ireland

.18 Neptune's...sculling
Neptune Rowing Club

.18 giamond's courseway
Giant's Causeway

.27 Wedmore
Wedmore

.28 Ire
Ireland (+ "lyre")

.29 Manx
Man, Isle of

.30 Rosse is
Russia

.31 rom
Rome

.32 marrowbones
?Marrowbone Lane

392.04 the Connachy
Connacht (= Johnny MacDougall)

.06 the rude ocean
Red Sea

.06 dead seasickabed
Dead Sea

.07 housepays for the daying
Hospice for the Dying

.08 Martyr Mrs MacCawley's
Mater Misericordiae Hospital

.14 Abbotabishop
?

.15 ffrench
France

.15 gherman
Germany

.17 Aran crown
Aran Islands

.23 Caucuses
Caucasus

.24 multilingual tombstone
?

.25 Navellicky Kamen
NPN? *Na velikiy kamen,*
Russ "toward (or on) the
great stone"

.27 oxsight of Iren
Ireland

.31 Newhigherland
Ireland
?New Ireland
?New Island

.31 Bristolhut
Bristol
Tavern, The: Bridge Inn

.32 Anne Lynch
Lynch, Anne, and Co

.33 Shackleton's
Shackleton, George, and
Sons

393.01 Shakeletin
Shackleton, George, and
Sons

.09 Hungerford-on-Mudway
Dublin: Baile Átha Cliath
Hungerford
Medway R

.24 alum and oves
?Adam and Eve's

.27 Shandon bellbox
Shandon

.28 hell
Hell

.29 knockneeghs
Neagh, Lough

.30 (ys! ys!)
Ys

.31 Transton Postscript
Boston (*Transcript*)

394.12 Oldpatrick
? (cf 393.10)

.16 tyred
Tyre

.17 five fourmasters
Ireland: the Five Fifths

.27 parkside...queens
Phoenix Park: "Queen's Garden"

.28 Earl Hoovedsoon's
Howth

.29 orhowwhen
?Erewhon

.34 Errin
Ireland

395.01 murky whey
Milky Way

.06 foreretyred
Tyre

.08 lakes of Coma
Como, Lake

.14 a lass spring
Alice Springs

.35 Amoricas
Armorica

396.01 Eburnea's
Ireland: Hibernia

.08 Irish
Ireland

.26 four...fiveful...poor [four]
Ireland: The Five Fifths

.31 chapellledeosy
Chapelizod

397.02 owneirist
Ireland

.14 Old Man's House
Old Men's Home
Royal Hospital

.14 Millenium Road
?

.17 shackle
Shackleton, George, and Sons

.24 phlegmish
Belgium: Flanders

398.03 scullogues
?Scullogue Gap

.05 Eren
Ireland

.05 braceoelanders
?Barcelona

.14 temple an eslaap
?

.16 Fionnachan sea
Ireland: Tír na bhFionn

.18 Ladyseyes
?Lady's Island

.23 wellworth
?NYC: Woolworth Bldg

.27 kohinor
Kohinor

.28 shanghai
Shanghai

.29 Lambeg drum
Lambeg

.30 Lombog...Lumbag...Limibig
?Lambay Island

.30 brazenaze
?Oxford U: Brasenose College

The 4 stanzas of the "Hymn to Iseult" on 398–399 are sung in turn by Matt, Mark, Luke, and Johnny, who are identified by place-names of their provinces.

.33 *Ulster*
Ulster

399.03 *Dingle beach*
Dingle (Munster)

.04 *Sybil*
Sybil Head (Munster)

.05 *curragh*
?Curragh, The (Leinster)

.14 *Balbriggan*
Balbriggan (Leinster)

.25 *cross of Cong*
Cong (Connacht)

.28 *barony of Bohermore*
Bohermore (Connacht)

BOOK III
Chapter 1

403.08   gorsecone...Gascon
             Gascony
    .09   Tegmine – sub – Fagi
             NPN: 1st line of Virgil's 1st
             Eclogue: "Sub tegmine
             fagi"
    .12   blautoothdmand
             Blaaland (Africa)
    .13   wild hindigan
             India, West Indies
    .16   voult
             ?Volta Cinema
    .21   cute old speckled church
             Speckled Church
    .23   greatbritish
             England
    .23   Irish
             Ireland
404.01   affluvial
             Liffey
    .18   indigo braw
             Ireland
    .19   Irish
             Ireland
    .21   scotsmost
             Scotland
    .22   providence
             Providence Woollen Mills
    .26   loud boheem
             Bohemia
    .27   damasker's
             Damascus
    .27   starspangled...crinklydoodle
             America
    .30   R.M.D.
             Dublin: Misc Allusions
405.13   Beaus' Walk
             Beaux' Walk
             ?Phoenix Park: Beau-Belle
             Walk
    .18   Duke Humphrey
             Duke Humphrey's Walk
    .19   err in
             Ireland

    .20   lees of Traroe
             Tralee
    .23   porterhouse
             ?
    .24   Saint Lawzenge of Toole's
             ?
    .24   Wheel of Fortune
             Wheel of Fortune
    .26   the house...admired
             (See U 251/255: "On North-
             umberland and Landsdowne
             roads...the house said to have
             been admired by the late
             queen when visiting the Irish
             capital...in 1849...")
    .27   Bristol
             Bristol
             Tavern, The: Bridge Inn
    .27   Balrothery
             Balrothery
    .28   Dacent Street
             ?Dawson St
406.02   Portarlington's Butchery
             Portarlington
    .03   Corkshire
             Cork
    .06   gaulusch gravy
             ?Gaul
    .09   Appelredt's
             ?
    .09   Kitzy Braten's
             NPN? *Gitzibraten*, Sw Ger
             "roast goat"
    .10   phoenix portar
             Phoenix Brewery
    .11   Irish
             Ireland
    .13   Boland's
             Boland's Ltd
    .19   green free state
             Irish Free State
    .20   rheingenever
             ?Rhine R

.20 rheingenever (*Cont.*)
("fingerhut of rheingenever," Ger and Dut, "thim-
bleful of neat gin")

.21 typureely jam
Tipperary

.24 St Jilian's of Berry
Berry

.26 custard house quay
Custom House: Custom
House Quay

.27 Anne Lynch
Lynch, Anne, and Co

.30 sign of Mesthress Vanhungrig
Hungary
Vanhomrigh's House

.32 jaffas
Jaffa (+ Japheth)

407.04 ardilaun
Ardilaun
Guinness's Brewery

.14 Irish, voise
Foclut
Ireland

.14 palestrine
?Palestine (+ Palestrina)

.17 Italicuss
Italy

.18 Yverzone
Ireland: Iwerddon

.18 brozaozaozing sea
?

.18 Inchigeela
Inchigeelagh

.19 morepork! morepork!
Moor Park

.20 Clifden
Clifden

.21 mauveport! mauveport!
Moor Park

.21 Nova Scotia's
Nova Scotia

.35 briefs
Brie (cheese)

.35 billpasses
Italy: Il Bel Paese (also a
cheese)

408.08 Erin
Ireland

.11 Candia
Candia

.22 Sam Dizzier's feedst
St Dizier

.26 musichall pair
Music Hall

.27 swimmyease
Siam

.27 Guinness
Guinness's Brewery

.28 Badeniveagh
Iveagh (Baths)

.33 John's Lane
Power's Distillery (John's
Lane)

.36 Piscisvendolor
Pisces

409.01 Wouldndom
London

.01 Gemini
Gemini

.02 pantry bay
Bantry Bay

.19 Greeks
Greece

.19 Roman
Rome

.21 Thinker's Dam
NPN? "Tinker's damn"

.22 glasshouse
Glasshouse

.23 Headfire Clump
Hell Fire Club

.24 beliek
Belleek

410.08 new hikler's highways
Germany: Autobahnen

.09 bleak forest
Black Forest

.11 Dublin river
Dublin
Liffey

.13 Lumbage Island
Lambay Island

.14 wineupon ponteen
Richmond ("Winetavern St")
Br

.21 limricked
Limerick

.23 Emailia
?Emania

.33 eilish mires
Ireland

.36   thieves' rescension
    Thebes

411.08   dearies
    ?Derry

.11   Amen, ptah
    Amenta

.12   Eironesia
    Ireland

.13   so I am
    Siam

.15   Geity's Pantokreator
    Gaiety Theatre

.18   Hek domov muy
    Czechoslovakia (National
    Anthem)

.22   tarabred
    Tara

.30   Saozon ruze
    Saxony

412.03   scotographically
    Scotland

.04   whofoundland
    Newfoundland

.08   *Emenia*
    ?Emania

.10   Pontoffbellek
    Belleek
    ?Portobello (Br)

.10   Kisslemerched
    Castle Market

.19   French pastry
    France

.22   past purcell's office
    General Post Office

.24   Scotic Poor Men's Thousand
    Gallon Cow Society
    Ireland: Scotia

.25   her in
    Ireland

.33   capri
    ?Capri

.34   Welsfusel
    Wales

.36   Nolaner and Browno
    Browne and Nolan

413.05   the Loyd insure her
    Lloyd's of London

.25   doubling
    Dublin

414.01   rhine...rhine
    ?Rhine R

.04   van Howten of Tredcastles
    ?Howth (Castle)

.04   Tredcastles
    ?Dublin Coat of Arms
    Tredcastles

.04   Clowntalkin
    Clondalkin

.06   Bois in the Boscoor
    ?Bay of Biscay
    (+ *bassecour*, Fr "poultry
    yard," "inner court")

.12   Goonness's
    Guinness's Brewery

.20   —cashl— [in C-word]
    ?Cashel

.32   Spinner's housery
    NPN: Spinoza (+ spider)

.34   Tingsomingenting
    Tingsomingenting

415.01   elytrical
    ?Illyria

.05   fussfor
    Venus: "Phosphorus"

.08   Bourneum
    Borneo

.09   soturning...retrophoebia
    Saturn: Phoebe (satellite)

.10   dance McCaper
    Capricorn

.14   *Satyr's*
    Saturn

.25   bagateller
    Tingsomingenting

.29   Nixnixundnix
    Nixnixundnix

.33   Nefersenless
    Nefer-sent

.34   Seekit Hatup...Suckit Hotup
    Sekhet Hetep

.36   Beppy's realm
    Egypt: Pepi II

416.01   Heppy's hevn
    Hapi

.02   Hummum
    ?Hammam

.05   chairmanlooking...wisechairman-
    looking
    Germany

.07   muravyingly
    Moravia

.11   durrydunglecks
    Derry

.11 durrydunglecks (*Cont.*)
   ?Dunleckny

.17 Nichtsnichtsundnichts
   Nixnixundnix

.17 muscowmoney
   Moscow

.27 Tingsomingenting
   Tingsomingenting

.30 Tossmania
   Tasmania

.30 sees of the deed
   Dead Sea

.31 hevre
   Havre, Le (+ "heaven")

.32 hull
   Hell
   Hull

.34 Boraborayellers
   Society Islands: Bora Bora
   (+ Aurora Borealis)

417.12 Papylonian
   Babylon

.17 Libido
   Lido

.26 thingsumanything
   Tingsomingenting

.31 Dorsan from Dunshanagan
   NPN: *Dun Seangáin*, Ir
   "Ant's Fort" (*Dorsán*, Ir
   "grasshopper") (O Hehir)

418.01 Artalone
   Ardilaun

.01 parisites
   Paris

.02 Highfee
   Iveagh

.06 sekketh rede
   Sekhet Hetep

.06 Amongded
   Amenta

.17 *Moyhammlet*
   ?Moy R (+ Mohammed)

.17 *Mount*
   ?

.22 *pulladeftkiss*
   Philadelphia

.26–.30 *nort...syf...farrest...Accident*
   [Occident]...heartseast...ori-
   ence...Wastenot
   North, South, East, West

419.12 fokloire
   ?Loire R

.14 earopen
   ?Europe

.15 tingtingtaggle
   Tintagel (Cornwall)

.16 blarneyest
   Blarney

.16 Corneywall
   Cornwall

.20 Greek
   Greece

.22 Roman
   Rome

.24 Persse
   Persia

.25 Otherman
   Ottoman Empire

.27 hellas
   Greece

.35 Charley Lucan's
   Lucan
   see *Census*, "Charley Lucan"

420.09 Francie
   France

.09 Fritzie
   Germany

.12 stayne
   Steyne

.13 Dutches
   Germany
   Netherlands

.14 his pon
   Spain

The addresses of the Letter, on pp 420.19–421.11, contain many of the addresses of the Joyce family between 1894 and 1904; in several cases the numbers are incorrect. Streets in which the Joyces lived are marked with an asterisk.

.19 29 Hardware Saint
   *Hardwicke St

.20 Laonum
   ?

.20 Baile-Atha-Cliath
   Dublin: Baile Átha Cliath

.21 13 Fitzgibbets
   *Fitzgibbon St

.22 B.L. Guineys, esqueer
   Guinness's Brewery

.23 12 Norse Richmound
   *Richmond St, North

.24   92 Windsewer. Ave.
        *Windsor Ave (Fairview)
.25   Finn's Hot
        Finn's Hotel
.26   Fearview
        Fairview
.28   8 Royal Terrors
        *Royal Terrace (Fairview)
.29   Danes
        Denmark
.29   Philip's Burke
        Philipsburgh Ave (Fairview)
.30   Clontalk
        Clonturk
.31   3 Castlewoos
        *Castlewood Ave (Rathgar)
.32   Bank of Ireland's
        Bank of Ireland
.33   City Arms
        City Arms Hotel
.33   2 Milchbroke
        *Millbourne Lane (Drum-
        condra)
.33   Traumcondraws
        Drumcondra
.34   Bunk of England's
        Bank of England
.34   Laffey
        Liffey
.35   Foundlitter
        Findlater's Church
.35   7 Streetpetres
        *St Peter's Terrace (Cabra)
.36   Cabranke
        Cabra
421.01 Patersen's Matches
        Paterson and Co
.02   Orchid Lodge
        NPN? (Orange lodge?)
.04   60 Shellburn
        *Shelbourne Rd
.06   Park...Hollow*
        Phoenix Park: The Hollow
.10   Boston (Mass)
        Boston
.13   Bloody Big Bristol
        Barrack ("Bloody") Bridge
        Bristol
        Tavern, The: Bridge Inn
.14   Auld Aireen
        Ireland

.18   penmarks
        Penmark
.27   irelitz
        Berlitz Language Schools
        Ireland
.29   Denmark
        Denmark
.32   Gilligan's maypoles
        ?
        Maypole
422.01 drapery institution
        ?St Patrick's Hospital
.02   antipopees
        Antipodes
.04   four divorce courts
        Four Courts
.05   the King's paunches
        Four Courts: King's Bench
.06   Scotch snakes
        Scotland
.07   dalickey
        ?Dalkey
.16   two worlds
        Two Worlds
.29   Baden
        Baden
.29   commonpleas
        Four Courts: Common Pleas
.30   bunkum
        ?Buncombe
.30   Nelson his trifulgurayous pillar
        Nelson's Pillar
        Trafalgar
423.03 Balt
        Baltic Sea
.04   Alemaney
        Germany
.13   thank the Bench
        Four Courts: King's Bench
.14   chancery
        Four Courts: Chancery
.19   eggschicker
        Four Courts: Exchequer
.25   coombe
        Coombe, The
.25   lock
        Westmoreland Lock Hospital
.34   Thingamuddy's school
        ?
.35   europicolas
        Europe

.36	Fran Czeschs		.25	Charley's Wain
	Czechoslovakia			Ursa Major: Charles's Wain
	France		.26	lacteal
424.01	Bruda Pszths			Milky Way
	Budapest		.35	Rattigan's corner
.01	Brat Slavos			?
	Bratislava		427.01	Killesther's lapes and falls
.03	*Ikish Tames*			Killarney
	Irish Times			Killester
.04	Hooley Fermers		.02	corks
	Farm St (London)			Cork
.07	Cecilia's treat		.04	Mac Auliffe's, the crucethouse
	Cecilia St (medical school)			Christchurch Cathedral
.09	Tiberia			Delgany
	Siberia		.06	ere in
	?Tiberias			Ireland
.10	Gattabuia and Gabbiano's		.22	the inds of Tuskland
	NPN: *Gattabuia*, It "jail";			Africa
	gabbiano, It "seagull"			?Germany (Nor, *Tyskland*)
.11	TCD			India
	Trinity College, Dublin		.22	the ousts of Amiracles
	(medical school)			America
.20	–mudgaard– [in C-word]		.27	Sean Moy
	Midgaard			Moyelta: "*Sean Magh*"
	Utgard		.34	Cockpit
.27	Sweeney's			Kildare
	? (just "swine"?)		.36	Biddyhouse
.27	Jon Jacobsen			St Brigid's (Kildare)
	Jameson, John, and Son		428.02	Samoanesia
.29	four waves			Samoa
	Four Waves of Erin		.07	Sireland
.34	threestar monothong			Ireland
	?Three Rock Mt		.08	Gladshouse Lodge
425.06	Shamous Shamonous, Limited			?Glasshouse
	Jameson, John, and Son		.10	yougander
.16	Siamanish			Uganda (+ *Jugend*, Ger
	Siam			"youth")
.18	arrah go braz		.11	prosperousness
	Ireland			?Prosperous
.20	Book of Lief		.16	Votre Dame
	?Liffey			NPN?
.22	soamheis		.18	Don Leary
	Siam			Dun Laoghaire
426.04	soho		.20	Jonnyjoys
	?Soho			"John Joyce" (ship)
.08	mooherhead		.20	waterloogged
	?Moher, Cliffs of			Waterloo
.21	joepeter's		.20	Erin's king
	Jupiter			"Erin's King" (ship)
.24	sirious		.21	Moylendsea
	Sirius			Moyle, Sea of

BOOK III

Chapter 2

429.06	Lazar's Walk	
	Lazy (Lazar's) Hill	
.17	Ireland	
	Ireland	
430.02	Benent Saint Berched's national	
	nightschool	
	St Brigid's	
.06	yellowstone landmark	
	Yellowstone Park	
.14	Dutchener's	
	Netherlands	
.31	chapplie of sixtine	
	Vatican: Sistine Chapel	
.36	tubberbunnies	
	?Toberbunny	
431.04	Irish legginds	
	Ireland	
.35	erigenal house	
	Ireland	
432.05	galaxy girls	
	Milky Way	
.15	hell	
	Hell	
.20	Dubloonik	
	Dublin	
.21	Dellabelliney	
	Dublin: Eblana	
.29	lisieuse	
	Lisieux	
433.05	dietcess of Gay O'Toole and	
	Gloamy Gwenn du Lake	
	Glendalough	
.06	Danish spoken	
	Denmark	
.07	in china dominos	
	China	
.09	inkerman	
	Inkerman	
.11	mere pork	
	Moor Park	
.12	howth	
	Howth	
.13	Killiney	
	Killarney	
	Killiney	
.14	Lord's	
	?Marylebone Cricket Club	
.16	Dar Bey Coll Cafeteria	
	Dublin Bread Co	

.19	*Manxmaid...Man*	
	Man, Isle of	
.20	bun...bag	
	?Baginbun	
.20	bisbuiting His Esaus and Cos	
	Jacob, W and R, Co	
.31	ern	
	Erne	
.32	gate...golden	
	?Golden Gate	
434.07	Rhidarhoda	
	Rhaetia	
.09	coalhole	
	Coal Hole (London)	
.10	big gun's	
	Big Gun	
.12	Hayes, Conyngham, and Erobin-	
	son	
	Hayes, Conyngham, Robinson	
.15	Harlotte Quai	
	Charlotte Quay	
.15	Britain Court	
	Britain Court	
.16	Marie Maudlin	
	Magdalen	
.18	get to henna	
	Gehenna	
.21	limenick's disgrace	
	Limerick	
.27	Dolphin's Barncar	
	Dolphin's Barn	
.30	old cupiosity shape	
	Old Curiosity Shop	
.34	Gravesend	
	Gravesend	
435.01	ciudad of Buellas Arias	
	Buenos Aires	
.02	*Smirching of Venus*	
	Venice (*Merchant of Venice*)	
.12	icepolled globetopper	
	North Pole	
.15	Blue Danuboyes	
	Danube R	
.18	oval	
	Oval, The (cricket ground)	
.27	chine	
	China	
.27	jupan	
	Japan	
.34	Mr Tunnelly's hallways	
	?	

436.12	nursemagd	.03	castle bar
	Norway		?Castle, The
.23	Cat and Coney		Castlebar
	? (cf 577.09)	.05	nazional labronry
.23	Spotted Dog		National Library
	?	.09	Carnival Cullen
.24	Lot's Road		?Cullenswood
	Lotts	.09	*Percy Wynns*
.26	Dublin		?Wynn's Hotel
	Dublin	.10	S. J. Finn's
.28	meeth		?Finn's Hotel
	Meath	.10	Curer of Wars
.29	Navan		Ars
	Navan (+ heaven)	.12	Linzen and Petitbois
.29	Kellsfrieclub		NPN? *Linsen*, Ger "lentils";
	Hell Fire Club		*petits pois*, Fr "peas"
	Kells	.12	Hibernites
.30	Hull		Ireland: Hibernia
	Hull	.14	Gill the father...Gill the son
.30	Hague		Gill, M H, and Son
	Hague, The	.20	*Send Fanciesland*
.31	Kildare		?
	Kildare	441.05	Mikealy's whey
.32	Mades of ashens		Milky Way
	Athens	.07	walked...Jook Humprey
.36	rouse commotion		Duke Humphrey's Walk
	?Roscommon	.11	Comtesse Cantilene
437.05	Rutland Rise		Ireland: Cathleen ni Houlihan
	Rutland Square	442.03	tammany
.06	Dunlob		NYC: Tammany Hall
	Dublin	.03	hang who
.10	abdominal wall		Hwang Ho R
	Magazine Fort	.05	constantineal
.11	liver asprewl		?Constantinople
	Liverpool	.05	namesuch
.17	Punt's Perfume's		?Nonesuch
	Punt	.06	enoch
.30	olt Pannonia		Enoch
	Pannonia	.07	Spooksbury
438.15	Bush and Rangers		?
	?	.08	Baas of Eboracum
.30	dammymonde of Lucalamplight		York
	?Dublin by Lamplight Insti-	.08	Old Father...Knickerbocker
	tution		NYC: "Father Knickerbocker"
	Lucan	.09	Ulissabon
439.34	allassundrian bompyre		Lisbon
	Alexandria	.09	lanky sire
.36	*Weekly Standerd*		Lancaster
	Standard, The	.09	Wolverhampton
440.01	five wits...four		Wolverhampton
	Ireland: The Five Fifths	.10	bristelings
			Bristol

.11   Twoways Peterborough...news-
      ky prospect
         Peterborough
         St Petersburg: Prospekt
         Nevskiy
.13   land of breach of promise
         America
.14   Kerribrasilian sea
         Atlantic O
         Brazil
         Kerry
.24   balm of Gaylad
         Gilead
.25   songs of Arupee
         Arabia
.30   Leinsterface
         Leinster
.33   turkest
         Turkey
.35   coomb
         Coombe, The
.36   libs
         Liberties, The
         ?Marsh's Library
.36   Close Saint Patrice
         St Patrick's Close
443.09   meadow of heppiness
         ? (cf 191.06)
.10   clonmellian
         Clonmel ("meadow of hon-
         ey")
.15   pensamientos...peace
         Amiens
.16   Dumnlimn
         Dublin
.22   Arnolff's
         Arnott's Dept Store
.24   Toc H
         Toc H
.28   Father Mathew's bridge pin
         Whitworth Br
.29   Rhoss's
         Ross's
.32   Buinness's
         Guinness's Brewery
.33   Normandy
         Normandy
.34   Mothrapurl skrene
         ?
.35   Michan
         St Michan's Church

.35   corkyshows
         ?Cork
444.24   pigeonhouse
         Pigeonhouse, The
.29   Rosemiry Lean
         Rosemary Lane
.29   Potanasty Rod
         Paternoster Row
.33   chapel...isod
         Chapelizod
.36   Luperca...palatine
         Rome: Lupercal
.36   palatine in Limerick
         Limerick
         Palatinate, The (Co Limerick)
445.13   *Roma*
         Rome (+ *amor*)
.32   Ostelinda
         ?
.34   Liffalidebankum
         Liffey
446.01   sands on Amberhann
         NPN? (Abraham)
.06   man of Armor
         ?Armorica
.08   U.M.I. hearts
         ?
.11   hong, kong
         Hong Kong
.14   meeting waters
         Meeting of the Waters
.17   united I.R.U. stade
         Irish Rugby Union
.19   greengeese
         ?Fox and Geese
         ?Goose Green Ave
.20   cuckoo derby
         ?Derby
.21   Ealing
         Ealing
         Ireland
.24   Coppal Poor
         ?
.25   suirland
         Suir R (+ South)
.25   noreland
         Nore R (+ North)
.25   kings country
         Offaly
.25   queens
         Laois

.30 Euphonia
NPN? see *Census* for "Eu-
phemia," Jacqueline Pas-
cal's (447.01) religious
name
.31 Warchester Warders
?Barchester: *The Warden*
Manchester (Martyrs)
.35 Dublin country
Dublin (Co)
447.04 Irish
Ireland
.06 Anglia's
England
.06 Armourican's
?America
Armorica
.08 Henrietta's sake
Henrietta St
.13 drawadust
Drogheda (St)
.13 Henry, Moore, Earl and Talbot
Streets
Drogheda (St)
Talbot St
.15 Castleknock Road
Castleknock
.16 first glimpse of Wales
?Howth: Black Linn
Wales
.17 Ballses Breach Harshoe
Ballsbridge
Dublin Horse Show
.17 Dumping's Corner
Dunphy's Corner
.18 Mirist fathers' brothers eleven
Marist Fathers
.18 White Friars
Carmelite (Calced) Church
.19 caponchin trowlers
Capuchin Friary
.20 Bridge of Belches in Fairview
Ballybough (Br)
Fairview
.20 noreast Dublin's
Dublin
.21 souwest wateringplatz
Fairview
.23 liffe
Liffey
.23 Dufblin
Dublin

.24 Baughkley
Dublin: Baile Atha Cliath
.25 Asea
Asia
.27 greenest island
Ireland: Misc Allusions
.27 black coats of Spaign
Spain
.30 town of the Fords in a huddle
Dublin: Baile Átha Cliath
.32 Drumgondola
Drumcondra
.33 midlimb and vestee
Midland Great Western Railway
.35 Aston's...quaith
Aston Quay
448.02 hoyth
?Howth
.03 Kane
Kane and Co (11 Aston Quay)
.03 Keogh's
Keogh, Ambrose (12 Aston
Quay)
.09 Capels and then fly
Capel St
Naples
.10 Cowtends Kateclean
Ireland: Cathleen ni Houlihan
.11 d'lin
Dublin
.11 Troia of towns
Troy (+ *troia*, It "sow")
.12 Carmen of cities
?
.13 l'pool
Liverpool
.14 m'chester
Manchester
.14 grandnational
Liverpool: the Grand National
.14 goldcapped
Ascot: the Gold Cup
.14 dupsydurby
Derby
.17 Pope's Avegnue
Avignon
.18 Opian Way
Appian Way
.18 brighton
Brighton
.18 Brayhowth
Bray

.18 Brayhowth (*Cont.*)
    Howth
.19 Bull Bailey
    Bailey Lighthouse
    Bulls, North and South
    ?Old Bailey (London)
.19 Lorcansby
    Dublin Allusion: "Lorcans-
    by"
.30 bourse
    Bourse
.30 bon Somewind
    ?
.31 Badanuweir
    Baden
449.02 onsaturncast...stellar
    Saturn
.08 deerdrive
    ?
.08 conconey's run
    ?
.08 wilfrid's walk
    ?
.11 lady of Lyons
    Lyons
    Lyons Corner Houses
.26 Drumsally
    Drumsallagh
.27 heoll's
    Hell
    Sheol
.30 Aerial
    Ireland
.31 moor park! moor park!
    Moor Park
.33 belleeks
    Belleek
.35 rugaby
    Rugby
450.01 down under
    Australia
.05 swansway
    Swan Water
.14 griffeen
    Griffeen R
.15 king's royal college of sturgeone
    College of Surgeons, Royal
.16 L'Alouette's Tower
    ?Lalouette, Henry (funeral
    establishment)
.17 Adelaide's naughtingerls
    Adelaide

.19 musicall airs
    Music Hall
.28 athlone
    Athlone
.29 lillabilling of killarnies
    Killarney
.33 Birdsnests...birdsnests
    Bird's Nest Institution
.36 Latouche's
    La Touche's Bank
451.04 cold strafe illglands
    England
.10 the Bective's
    Bective
.13 Ulster Rifles
    Ulster
.13 Cork Milice
    Cork (Munster)
.13 Dublin Fusees
    Dublin (Leinster)
.14 Connacht Rangers
    Connacht
.14 channon
    Shannon R
.15 leip a liffey
    Leixlip
    Liffey
.15 annyblack water
    Blackwater R
    Liffey
.17 Varian's balaying
    Varian and Co
.30 ottoman
    Ottoman Empire
452.02 perish the Dane
    Denmark
.11 Hothelizod
    Chapelizod
    Howth
.18 annals of...livy
    Liffey
.21 Vico road
    Vico Rd
.27 Hither-on-Thither Erin
    Ireland
.29 Ireland
    Ireland
.29 Lucan
    Lucan
.36 Norawain
    Norway

453.06	clambake to hering	.25	Gaieties
	Ireland		Gaiety Theatre
.06	braggart of blarney	.26	Royal Revolver...regally
	Blarney		?Theatre Royal
.15	Clo goes...wood	.26	globoes
	Clongowes Wood College		Globe Theatre
.22	Po	.28	SPQueaRking
	?Po R		Rome: SPQR
.25	Paris	456.07	Ah Ireland
	Paris		Ireland
.32	fieldnights eliceam	.08	Cincinnatis
	Elysian Fields		?Cincinnati
.33	Johannisburg's	.08	Italian
	Johannesburg		Italy
454.03	swisstart	.20	spice isles
	Switzerland		Spice Islands
.04	Haugh! Haugh!	.26	Terminus Lower
	?Thing Mote		?
.09	westminstrel	.26	Killadown
	?Munster		Killadoon
	?Westminster	.26	Letternoosh
.16	geepy, O		Letternoosh
	General Post Office	.26	Letterspeak
.20	mercury		Letterpeak
	?Mercury	.27	Lettermuck
.30	suburrs		Lettermuck
	Rome: Suburra	.27	Littorananima
.32	Derby and June		Letterananima
	Derby	.27	the roomiest house
.33	the scorchhouse		Castletown House
	Hell	.28	Ireland
	Scotch House, The		Ireland
.34	felixed...parked	.32	marshalsea
	Phoenix Park		Marshalsea
.35	seanad and pobbel queue's re-	.34	calendar, window
	mainder		Castletown House (365 win-
	Rome: SPQR		dows)
.35	Seekit headup	457.01	old Con Connolly's residence
	Sekhet Hetep		Castletown House
455.01	Cohortyard		?Hell Fire Club
	? (just "courtyard"?)	.07	Hungkung...Hangkang
.05	Toussaint's wakeswalks exper-		Hong Kong
	dition	458.02	linenhall valentino
	Madame Tussaud's Exhibi-		Linen Hall
	tion	.09	galways
.08	Iereny...irelands		Galway
	Ireland: Iernia	459.05	poor old dutch
.17	atoms and ifs		Netherlands
	Adam and Eve's	.08	cleryng's
.18	Moy Kain		Clery and Co
	St Michan's Church	.18	Erne street Lower
			Erne St

460.08	Ships...beside the Ship		462.02	brindising
	Ship Hotel and Tavern			Brindisi
.09	lovemountjoy square		.04	Erin go Dry
	Mountjoy (Sq)			Ireland
.10	caroline		.05	Staffetta
	Carolina, N and S			Fingal's Cave: Staffa Island
.11	louther			Hebrides
	?Louth		.05	mullified
.15	Dargle			Hebrides: Mull Island
	Dargle R		.08	in his fail
.20	Jungfraud's Messongebook			Ireland: Inisfail
	?Jungfrau		.09	douce
.22	libans			Douce, Mt
	Lebanon		.15	Isley
.23	sickamours			Hebrides: Islay Island
	Morocco		.16	innerman monophone
.23	cyprissis			Man, Isle of
	Cyprus			?Mona
.23	babilonias		.19	doubling
	Babylon			Dublin
.26	Margrate von Hungaria		.24	Leperstown
	Hungary			Leopardstown
.26	Quaidy ways		.28	Jaunstown
	?			?
.27	boysforus		.29	Ousterrike
	Bosporus			Austria
.29	lex leap		.32	mourn mountains
	Leixlip			Mourne (Mts)
.32	Thingavalla		.34	French evolution
	Thingvellir			France
.32	do be careful teacakes		463.04	Paddyouare
	Dublin Bread Co			Padua
461.01	wagon...star		.07	Auxonian
	Ursa Major: the Wagon			?Auxonne
.03	way for spilling cream			Oxford U
	Milky Way		.10	anny living
.05	rainproof of...elephant's			Liffey
	Elvery's Elephant House		.13	cantanberous
.07	Hope Bros.			Cambridge (U)
	?Hope Brothers		.19	portugal's nose
.07	Faith Street			Portugal
	?		.24	Rossya
.07	Charity Corner			Russia
	?		.24	Alba
.09	the dusess of yore			Alba
	York			?Scotland: Alba
.10	Finest Park		.25	Ourishman...Yourishman
	Phoenix Park			Ireland
.14	russians		.31	Columbsisle Jonas
	Russia			Iona
.24	chineknees		.31	wrocked...belly
	China			Rockabill Lighthouse

.35	spanish breans		.36	french
	Spain			France
464.06	Canwyll y Cymry		465.09	bothsforus
	Wales			Bosporus
.07	Brazel		.11	almeans
	?Brazil			Germany
.08	diamond skull		.12	frank
	Henley: Diamond Sculls			France
.10	khyber schinker		.15	lyonised mails
	Khyber Pass			Lyons: "The Lyons Mail"
.17	Paris addresse		.16	corks again
	Paris			Corsica
.21	Moulsaybaysse		.16	hungry and angry
	France			?Hungry Hill
	Marseilles (+ bouillabaisse)		.21	county de Loona

.21   yunker doodler
       America

.24   Claddagh clasp
       Claddagh

Lines .26–.32 (?36) tour, if not the map of the world, at least most of Europe, by name or kenning.

.26   the moppamound
       Mappa Mundi

.27   cock and the bullfight
       Spain

.27   Auster and Hungrig
       Austria
       Hungary

.28   Beer and Belly
       Germany

.28   Boot and Ball
       Italy
       Sicily

.29   oils of greas
       Greece (Isles of)

.29   turkey in julep
       Turkey (in Europe)

.29   Father Freeshots Feilbogen...
       costard
       Switzerland (William Tell)

.31   Peadhar the Grab
       Russia (Peter the Great)

.32   Tower Geesyhus
       Scandinavia (Turgesius)

.32   Mona
       Man, Isle of
       Mona

.35   Lambay
       Lambay Island

.21   county de Loona
       NPN: Conte de Luna, villain of
         Verdi's *Il Trovatore*

.27   earring
       Ireland

.31   irish
       Ireland

.32   offalia
       ?Offaly

.32   Yorick
       York

.33   Lankystare
       Lancaster

.35   rome
       Rome

466.02   Curlew
       Carlow

.04   fuchu
       Foochow

.13   europe
       Europe

.23   dockandoilish
       Dáil Éireann

.25   Rochelle
       Rochelle, La

.31   *Taurus periculosus*
       ?

.35   Ireland's eye
       Ireland's Eye

.35   ovocal
       Avoca R
       Meeting of the Waters

467.03   heaven's reflexes
       Killarney

.14   japlatin
       Japan

.15   stomebathred
       ?Stoneybatter (+ "stone deaf")

.16   Tower of Balbus
        Babel, Tower of

.22   the river airy
        Riviera

.24   the churchyard in the cloister
        of the depths
        ?

.25   beurlads scoel
        Berlitz Language Schools
        England
        (*beurla,* Ir "English")

.27   allemanden huskers
        Germany

.29   Illstarred
        Ulster

.29   punster
        Munster

.29   lipstering
        Leinster

.30   cowknucks
        Connacht

.30   Trinity
        Trinity College, Dublin

.31   cantab
        Cambridge (U)

.31   oxon
        Oxford U

.32   Erin's ear
        Ireland (cf Ireland's Eye)

.34   read the road roman
        Rhaetia
        Rome

.34   ad Pernicious
        Parnassus

468.03 Fukien mission
        Fukien

.31   corthage
        ?Carthage

.34   azores
        Azores

.36   Bansheeba
        Ireland: Banba (+ Bathshe-
        ba, banshee)

.36   Orcotron
        ?

.36   hoaring ho
        Hwang Ho R

469.01 twinn her ttittshe
        Dana, Paps of

.04   Seven oldy oldy hills
        Rome

.05   the one blue beamer
        ?

.06   Banbashore
        Ireland: Banba

.09   Jehusalem's wall
        Jerusalem

.10   Cheerup street
        ?

.11   Winland
        Vinland

.11   moyne
        ?Moyne

.14   olty mutther
        ?Altamaha R
        Olt R (tributary of Danube)

.14   Sereth
        Sereth R (tributary of Danube)

.14   Maritza
        Maritza R

.16   Groenmund's Circus
        ?Greenland
        Green Man

.18   Hazelridge
        Dublin: Drom Cuill-Choille

.18   Kew
        Kew

.21   Linduff
        Dublin

.21   Lood Erynnana
        Ireland

.25   panromain apological
        Rome

.26   kerrycoys
        ?Kerry

.34   rheda rodeo
        Rhaetia

*The threnody at 470.15−.20 is
the litany of the B.V.M. (A Portrait, 105).
According to JJ (Letters I, 263), it also
represents the Maronite ritual (470.14)
"as used on Mt. Lebanon."*

470.15 Leafboughnoon
        Lebanon

.16   onmountof Sighing
        Zion, Mt

.17   Gladdays
        Kadesh

.18   anjerichol
        Jericho

.33   Irish frisky
        Ireland

.33 Juan Jaimesan
     Jameson, John, and Son
471.09 star and gartergazer
     Star and Garter
.12 southern cross
     Southern Cross
.14 meccamaniac
     Mecca

Through the rest of p 471, Jaun is a "barrel of beer rolling down the Liffey" from King's Br past Butt Br eastward to the sea.

.15 kingscouriered...bridge
     Kincora
     King's Br
.16 Ladycastle
     ?Castle, The
.17 fouling her buttress...but
     Butt Br
.18 acqueducked
     ?
.26 highroad of the nation, Trai-
     tor's Track
     Irish Sea
.36 sweet wail of evoker
     Avoca
     Meeting of the Waters
472.01 Shamrogueshire
     Ireland: Tír na Simearóig
.06 disdoon blarmey...groves
     Blarney
     Lisdoonvarna
.07 sweet rockelose
     ?Rochelle, La
.17 antipodes
     Antipodes
.22 lampaddyfair
     NPN: *Lampadephoros*, Gk
     "torch-bearer"
.23 light lucerne
     Lucerne, Lake
.24 four cantons
     Four Cantons
.35 Ireland
     Ireland
473.09 darby's
     Derby
.16 Erebia
     Arabia
.18 sphoenix spark
     Phoenix Park

.20 sphanished
     Spain

BOOK III

Chapter 3

474.02 mead
     Meath
.07 lucan
     Lucan
.20 Brosna's furzy
     Brosna R
475.06 Conn's half
     Conn's Half
.07 Owenmore's five quarters
     Ireland: The Five Fifths
     Mogh's Half
     Munster
.12 Aran chiefs
     Aran Islands
.15 phosphor
     ?Venus: "Phosphorus"
.22 esker ridge
     Esker (Rd)
.22 Mallinger parish
     Mullingar
.23 mead
     Meath
476.06 the knoll Asnoch
     Uisneach, Hill of
.11 the watchers of Prospect
     ?Glasnevin: Prospect Cemetery
     ?Tara ("Prospect Hill")
.13 in his fallen
     Ireland: Inisfail
477.26 spanishing gold
     Spain
.30 mellifond
     Mellifont Abbey
.34 land of lions' odor
     ?
.36 the orangery...orangery
     ?Orangerie
478.10 alpman
     ?Dublin: Alp Uí Laoghaire
.12 vallums of tartallaght
     Tallaght
.13 rheda rhoda
     Rhaetia
.13 torpentine path
     ?

.13   hallucinian via
       ?

.14   aurellian gape
       Aurelia, Via

.14   sunkin rut
       Sunken Road (Switzerland)

.14   grossgrown trek
       ?

.15   crimeslaved cruxway
       Crimea

.15   moorhens cry
       ?

.15   mooner's plankgang
       ?

.16   hopenhaven
       Copenhagen

.19   perfrances
       France

.20   boche
       Germany

.20   provenciale
       Provence

.21   *Moy jay trouvay*
       ?Moy R

.30   sohohold
       ?Soho

.34   woods of fogloot
       Foclut

.34   mis
       Slieve Mish

479.02 Tear-nan-Ogre
       Tír na nOg

.03   Mayo
       Mayo

.05   Burb! Burb! Burb!
       Benburb

.06   Tucurlugh
       Carlow

.06   claire
       Clare

.06   Polldoody
       Polldoody

.07   County Conway
       ?

.09   Meads
       ?Meath (as 5th province)

.11   Anchor on the Mountain
       ?

.13   wolves of Fochlut
       Foclut

.18   Dunlin
       Dublin

.24   plague-burrow
       ?Tallaght

.28   *Pourquoi Pas*
       "Pourquoi Pas"

.29   Weissduwasland
       NPN? Ger, "Do-you-know-
       what-land"; Goethe's
       "Kennst du das Land" is
       about Italy (479.36–480.01
       "Connais-tu le pays")

.30   Frenchman
       France

.32   Danemork
       Denmark

.35   Allmaun away
       ?Germany

480.01 Norsker
       Norway

.02   jordan's scaper
       NPN: *jordens skaber*, Dan
       "creator of the earth"

.03   pigeons three
       Three Jolly Pigeons

.04   Folchu! Folchu!
       NPN: Ir, "wolf"

.08   green hills
       ?Green Hills

.10   levantine
       Levant

.10   Daneland
       Denmark

.12   welsher
       Wales

.18   old Bailey
       ?Bailey Lighthouse
       Old Bailey (London)

.21   Emania
       Emania
       "Titanic"

.27   lyceum
       Athens: Lyceum

.30   dobbling
       ?Dublin

.34   fingall harriers
       Fingal

481.05 *Eirae*
       Ireland

.06   Skiffstrait
       ?Ship St

.14   Mr Tupling Toun
       Dublin

.14 Morning de Heights
    NYC: Morningside Heights

.15 undergroands
    Underground (London)

.16 Romeo
    ?Rome

.21 humeplace
    ?Hume St

.21 Chivitats Ei
    NPN? *Civitas Dei*, Lat "City of God"

The following 7 names refer to the 7 cities each of which in anc times was claimed as the birthplace of Homer; cf 129.23–.24.

.21 Smithwick
    Smethwick (= England)
    Smyrna

.21 Rhonnda
    Rhondda (= Wales)
    Rhodes

.21 Kaledon
    Caledonia (= Scotland)
    Colophon

.22 Salem (Mass)
    Salem (= USA)
    Salamis

.22 Childers
    Chios

.22 Argos
    Argos

.22 Duthless
    Athens

.28 Huddlestown
    Dublin: Baile Átha Cliath

.35 Ranelagh
    Ranelagh

.36 Tam Tower
    Oxford U: Christ Church College

.36 jagger
    Oxford U: Jesus College

.36 pemmer
    Oxford U: Pembroke College

.36 the house...Eddy's Christy
    Oxford U: Christ Church College

482.07 Lucas
    Lucan (+ Luke, = Leinster)

.07 Dublinn
    Dublin

.09 Atlantic City
    ?Atlantic City
    ?Galway (City) (Connacht)

.09 chuam
    Tuam (Connacht)

.10 coughan
    Cavan (Connacht)

.11 Maho
    Mayo (Connacht)

.11 yokohahat
    Yokohama

.13 Ireland
    Ireland

.15 spreadeagle
    Connacht: Arms
    ?Spread Eagle

.16 gander of Hayden
    Eden

.19 Posthorn in the High Street
    Post-House (High St)

.27 Matty Armagh
    Armagh (Ulster)

.29 You're up-in-Leal-Ulster
    Europe
    Ulster ("loyal Ulster")

.29 I'm-free-Down-in-Easia
    Asia
    Down
    Irish Free State

.33 book of kills
    Kells

483.06 bells of scandal
    Shandon

.08 two turkies
    Turkey (in Europe and in Asia)

.08 dindians
    India (+ *dindin*, Fr "turkey")

.08 master the abbey
    ?Abbey Theatre

.16 blarneying
    Blarney

.29 ayr
    Ayr (+ air)

.29 plage
    ? (+ earth; Fr, "strand")

.30 watford
    ?Waterford
    Watford (+ water)

.33 palegrim
    Pale, The

.36	humble down	.29	angly
	?Hambledon		England
484.03	Audeon's	.29	Yellman's lingas
	St Audoen's Church		China
.09	ersed	.36	chinchin chat
	Ireland: Erse		China
.14	twosides uppish	.36	nipponnippers
	Ireland		Japan
.15	meer hyber irish	486.11	chink
	?Hyperborean O		China
	Ireland: Hibernia	.12	jape
.16	chink...avtokinatown		Japan
	China	.13	psychosinology
.21	Aud Dub		China
	Dublin	.14	Tuttu
.22	P.Q.R.S. of legatine powers		Tattu
	Rome: SPQR	.17	blackfrinch
.25	loups of Lazary		France
	?Lazy Hill	.24	isisglass
.33	Kelly Terry		Thames R: Isis
	Kelly, Terence (pawnbroker)	487.01	iberborealic
.33	Derry		Hyperborean O
	Derry	.09	odinburgh
.35	Pumpusmugnus		Eden
	?Portsmouth		Edinburgh
.36	Anglicey	.15	Scotch and pottage
	England (*anglaise*)		Scotland
485.07	in alleman	.16	Bewley in the baste
	Germany		Bewley
.07	Suck at!	.22	Roma...Amor
	Siemens Schuckert		Rome (+ Patrick, Tristan)
.12	Rose Lankester	.31	Leelander
	Lancaster		?Lee R (addressed to Mark of
.12	Blanche Yorke		Munster)
	York	.32	Capalisoot
.12	d'anglas landadge		Chapelizod
	England	488.04	Bruno and Nola
.13	Djoytsch		Browne and Nolan
	Germany	.05	orangey
.16	Bullydamestough		Orange
	Ballyjamesduff	.05	Saint Nessau Street
.21	Jenkins' Area		Nassau (St)
	NPN: War of Jenkins' Ear	.14	zoohoohoom
.24	shanghaied		Phoenix Park: Zoo
	Shanghai	.16	unegoistically
.24	Wanstable		*New Freewoman* (*The Egoist*)
	NPN? "One stable"	.20	ostralian
.28	Ho ha hi he hung! Tsing tsing!		Australia
	Hwang Ho R	.21	Negoist
.28	Tsing tsing!		*New Freewoman* (*The Egoist*)
	Sing Sing	.24	High Brazil
			Brazil: Hy Brasil

.25 midden Erse
    Ireland: Erse
.25 clare
    Clare
.25 Noughtnoughtnought
    Nixnixundnix
.26 Dublire
    Dublin (cable address "Dub-
    lin, Ireland"?)
    ?Dun Laoghaire
.26 Neuropaths
    Europe
.30 switlersland
    Switzerland
.33 Capeler
    ?Capel St
.33 united Irishmen
    Ireland
489.03 *V.V.C.*
    ?British Broadcasting Corp
    (+ Victoria Cross)
.10 antipathies
    Antipodes
.10 austrasia
    Asia
    Australia
    Austrasia
.13 The Workings, N.S.W.
    New South Wales
.16 roamin
    Rome
.20 Amharican
    Abyssinia: Amhara
    America
.21 Doubly Telewisher
    Dublin
.27 africot lupps
    Africa
.31 benighted irismaimed
    Ireland: Iris
.31 Sydney
    Sydney (Australia)
.32 Alibany
    Albany (Australia)
490.01 bostoons
    Boston
.17 doblinganger
    Dublin
.18 erstwort
    Ireland: Erse
.20 Holy Baggot Street
    Baggot St

.23 Noel's Arch
    NPN? "Noah's Arch," rainbow
.23 foster's place
    Foster Place
.28 Tuwarceathay
    ?China: Cathay
491.06 Baggut's...straat
    Baggot St
.09 straat that is called corkscrewed
    Baggot St
    Cork: St Patrick's St
    Corkscrew Rd
    Straight St
.10 boulevard billy
    ?
.11 Lismore
    Lismore
.11 Cape Brendan
    Brandon Mt
.11 Patrick's
    Cork: Patrick St
.14 raabraabs
    Arabia
.15 Mallowlane
    ?
.15 Demaasch
    ?
.18 *Mansianhase parak*
    Mansion House
.19 *arkbashap of Yarak*
    York
.21 Braudribnob's
    Brobdingnag
.22 lillypets
    Lilliput
.26 O Tara's thrush
    Tara
.30 drary lane
    Drury Lane
.32 horrockses' sheets
    Horrocks, Ltd
.32 welshtbreton
    Ireland: Misc Allusions
    Wales
.35 Baltic Bygrad
    Baltic Sea
    ?Belgrade
.36 Iran
    Iran
    Ireland
492.09 rusish
    Russia

.10   Crasnian Sea
       Red Sea

.15   back haul of Coalcutter
       Calcutta

.17   hindustand
       Hindustan

.23   1001 Ombrilla Street
       ?

.23   Syringa padham
       Seringapatam (India)

.23   Alleypulley
       Allapalli (India)

.30   trinidads
       Trinidad
       ?Trinity College, Dublin

.34   crossing the singorgeous
       St George's Channel

493.02   Foraignghistan
       ?

.13   gulughurutty
       ?Gawilghur
       ?Gujarat

.13   Yran
       Iran
       Ireland

.19   Ota...bumpsed her dumpsydid-
       dle
       Clonmacnoise

.20   woolsark
       Woolsack

.27   Eivin
       Ireland

.27   Gates of Gold
       ?Golden Gate

494.06   etnat
       Etna, Mt (volcano)

.06   athos
       Athos, Mt (not a volcano)

.07   lava of Moltens
       NPN ("molten lava")

.08   erupting, hecklar
       Hekla, Mt (volcano)

.09   Ophiuchus
       Ophiucus

.09   muliercula
       NPN? Lat, "weak little
       woman"

.10   Satarn's serpent ring system
       Saturn

.10   pisciolinnies
       Pisces

.10   Nova Ardonis
       ?

.11   Prisca Parthenopea
       ?Naples (*prisca*, Lat "old")

.12   Ers
       (The Earth)

.12   Mores
       Mars

.12   Merkery
       Mercury

The following line combines towers of Rabelais's Abbey of Thélème with the cardinal points of the terrestrial and celestial spheres, and with night, dawn, twilight, and noonday.

.13   Arctura
       Arcturus (North, night)
       Thélème

.13   Anatolia
       Anatolia (East, dawn)
       Thélème

.13   Hesper
       Venus: "Hesperus" (West,
       evening)
       Thélème

.13   Mesembria
       NPN: *mesembria*, Gk "noon"
       (South)
       Thélème

.14   Noth, Haste, Soot and Waste
       North, South, East, West

.16   Ural Mount
       Ural Mts

.17   strombolo
       Stromboli (volcano)

.19   bullsrusshius
       ?Russia

.21   Obeisance...Orp
       Dublin Motto

.29   giant sun...his seventh
       Uranus

.32   fleshambles
       ?Fishamble St

.32   canalles
       Grand Canal
       Royal Canal

.34   Nile Lodge
       Nile R

.35   Mrs Hamazum's
       Amazon R

495.03	Parsee Franch
	France (+ Percy French)
.04	Power's spirits
	Power's Distillery
.10	black patata...church
	?St Mary's Chapel of Ease
.11	Lynch Brother
	Galway
.12	Warden of Galway
	Galway
.18	Granny-stream-Auborne
	Auburn
.21	lifing
	Liffey
.24	Shadow La Rose
	?
	("Chateau la Rose"?)
.27	Saxontannery
	Saxony (+ 6/10 or 6/6)
.27	ffrenchllatin
	France
496.08	Dane's Island
	Dane's Island
	Denmark
.08	minx...Isle of Woman
	Man, Isle of
	Tír na mBan
.09	four cantins
	Four Cantons
.11	ingen meid
	India, West Indies
.15	old Eire
	Ireland
.18	my fingall's ends
	Fingal
.27	Abha na Lifé
	Liffey
497.06	panhibernskers
	Ireland: Hibernia
.06	scalpjaggers
	Scalp, The (+ *Jaeger*, Ger "hunter")
.07	houthhunters
	Howth
.11	Rathgar
	Rathgar
.11	Rathanga
	Rathangan
.11	Rountown
	Terenure
.11	Rush
	Rush

.11	America Avenue
	America
.12	Asia Place
	Asia
.12	Affrian Way
	Africa
	Appian Way
.12	Europa Parade
	Europe
.13	Noo Soch Wilds
	New South Wales

The following 4 roads are all in SE Dublin; Vico and Sorrento Rds intersect (in Dalkey), but otherwise they do not describe a route or a direction.

.13	Vico
	Vico Rd
.13	Mespil
	Mespil (Rd)
.14	Rock
	Rock Rd
.14	Sorrento
	Sorrento (Rd)
.16	Mount Maximagnetic
	?

The following 12 names are (primarily) names of Dublin suburbs.

.17	Merrionites
	Merrion
.17	Dumstdumbdrummers
	Dundrum
.18	Luccanicans
	Lucan
.18	Ashtoumers
	Ashtown
.18	Batterysby Parkes
	Battersby and Co
	Battersea (Park) (London)
	NYC: Battery Park
.19	Krumlin Boyards
	Crumlin
	Moscow: Kremlin
.19	Phillipsburgs
	Philipsburgh Ave
.19	Cabraists
	Cabra
.19	Finglossies
	Finglas
.20	Ballymunites
	Ballymun

.20   Raheniacs
       Raheny
.20   bettlers of Clontarf
       Clontarf
.23   *ad Inferos*
       Inferno
.24   delhightful bazar
       Delhi
.25   magazine wall
       Magazine Fort
.29   indiarubber
       India
.31   jordan almonders
       Jordan R
.33   claddagh ringleaders
       Claddagh
.35   German selver geyser
       Germany
.36   silfrich
       ?Selfridge's
498.01 ourish times
       Irish Times
.01   French
       France
.02   Cesarevitch
       Curragh, The
.03   Sant Legerleger
       Curragh, The
.03   the oakses
       Curragh, The
.07   Oldloafs Buttery
       ?
.08   houses of Orange and Betters
       M.P.
       Orange

In Irish heraldry, the King of
Arms was Ulster, with Cork and Dublin
as Heralds, and Athlone as Poursuivant.

.11   Ulster Kong
       Ulster
.11   Munster's Herald
       Cork
       Munster
.12   Athclee Ensigning
       Dublin: Baile Átha Cliath
       (Leinster)
.12   Athlone Poursuivant
       Athlone (Connacht)
.14   epheud
       Iveagh

.14   ordilawn
       Ardilaun
.14   diamondskulled
       Henley: Diamond Sculls
.15   Irish
       Ireland
.16   paunchjab
       Punjab
.16   dogril
       Dogra
.17   pammel
       Tamil
.17   gougerotty
       Gujarat
.18   oels a'mona
       ?Mona
.19   his pani's
       ?Spain
.19   Kennedy's kiln
       Kennedy, Peter (bakery)
       Trinity Church (song)
.30   italian warehouse
       Italy
499.08 Woh Hillill! Woe Hallall!
       Valhalla
.23   this altknoll
       Uisneach, Hill of
.29   Dingle bagpipes
       Dingle
.33   Rawth of Gar
       Rathgar
.33   Donnerbruck Fire
       Donnybrook (Fair)
.34   babel
       Babel, Tower of
500.04 Dovegall and finshark
       Dubh-Gall
       Fingal
.11   Up Lancs!
       Lancaster
.14   irish times
       Irish Times
.14   airs independence
       Irish Independent
.15   freedman's chareman
       Freeman's Journal
.15   dully expressed
       Daily Express
.24   Bayroyt
       Bayreuth (+ "by the right")
501.04 Ballymacarett
       Belfast: Ballymacarret

.08 Cigar shank and Wheat
    Ségur ("cinquante huit")

.09 Gobble Ann's Carrot Cans
    Gobelins ("quarante
    quinze")

.11 Challenger's Deep
    Challenger Deep

.12 swish channels
    ?

.13 Sybil...Sybil Head
    Sybil Head

.19 isles is Thymes
    Irish Times

.19 ales is Penzance
    Irish Independent
    Penzance

.19 Vehement Genral
    Freeman's Journal

.20 Delhi expulsed
    Daily Express
    Delhi

.23 Ireland
    Ireland

.32 andeanupper
    Andes Mts

.33 balkan
    Balkans (Mts)

502.04 snaachtha
    Slieve Snacht (Mt)

.05 zimalayars
    Himalaya Mts

.11 Pacific
    Pacific O

.12 Muna
    ?Mona

.20 hellstohns
    Hell

.27 Maidanvale
    Calcutta: Maidan
    Maida Vale

.35 Foxrock
    Foxrock

.35 Finglas
    Finglas

.36 lambskip
    ?Lambay Island

503.01 joints caused ways
    Giant's Causeway

.07 An evernasty ashtray
    Yggdrasil

.13 Fingal
    Fingal

Except for "Yellow House," the names (503.13–.17) from "Littlepeace" to "tolkar" all refer to townlands or other places in Fingal, N Co Dublin.

.13 Littlepeace
    Littlepace

.14 Yellowhouse
    ?Yellow House

.14 Snugsborough
    Snugborough

.14 Westreeve-Astagob
    Astagob
    Westereave

.14 Slutsend
    Slutsend

.15 Stockins
    Stockens

.15 Winning's
    Winnings

.15 Folly
    Folly

.15 Merryfalls
    Merryfalls

.16 skidoo
    Skidoo

.16 skephumble
    Skephubble

.17 Godamedy
    Goddamendy

.17 delville
    Delville

.17 tolkar
    Tolka

.21 stow on the wolds
    Stow on the Wold

.21 Woful Dane Bottom
    ?Denmark
    Woovil Doon Botham

.23 Eireann
    Ireland

.30 overlisting eshtree
    Yggdrasil

.31 Annar
    Anner R

.31 ford of Slivenamond
    Slievenamond

.33 maypole
    Maypole

.34 Wilds
    ?Wales

.34 Browne's...Nolan's
    Browne and Nolan

.35   Prittlewell Press
       ?
504.06 Summerian
       Shinar (Sumer)
.07   Cimmerian
       Cimmeria
.18   italiote
       Italy (in context, the Roman
       papacy)
.19   Tonans Tomazeus
       ?Jupiter Tonans, Temple of
.22   Idahore
       ?
.24   Orania epples
       Emania of the Apples
       Uranus
.24   Tyburn fenians
       Tyburn
.26   Erasmus Smith's burstall boys
       Borstal
.27   underhand leadpencils
       ?Glasnevin: O'Connell Mon-
       ument
.30   anatolies
       Anatolia (= East)
.31   killmaimthem pensioners
       Kilmainham
       Royal Hospital (Kilmainham)
.32   overthrown milestones
       Wellington Monument
.35   eggdrazzles
       Yggdrasil
505.04 infernal shins
       Inferno
.04   triliteral roots
       Yggdrasil
.21   shrub of libertine
       ?
.21   steyne of law
       Steyne
.24   Dr Melamanessy
       ?Zurich: Manessestrasse
.30   weeping of the daughters
       ?Meeting of the Waters
506.03 midhill of the park
       Phoenix Park
.12   the coombe
       Coombe, The
.19   capocapo promontory
       Howth
.24   Lansdowne Road
       Lansdowne (Rd)

.26   this socried isle
       Ireland: Misc Allusions
.29   Finoglam
       ?
.34   Anna Lynsha's Pekoe
       Lynch, Anne, and Co
507.02 Kimmage
       Kimmage
.04   the Green Man
       Green Man
.09   greats
       Oxford U
.09   littlegets
       Cambridge (U)
.10   cattegut belts
       Cattegat
.15   basque of his beret
       Basque Provinces
.22   ur sprogue
       Ireland: Erse
.26   Lower O'Connell Street
       O'Connell St
.28   Pekin packet
       Peking
.29   Laura Connor's treat
       O'Connell St
.35   Boaterstown
       Booterstown
.36   Big Elm
       ?Chapelizod: Village Elm
508.01 the Arch
       Arch, The
.02   none Eryen
       Ireland (+ "non-Aryan")
.23   Clopatrick's
       ?Croagh Patrick
509.05 Tomsky
       Tomsk
.07   rooshian
       Russia
.13   rooshiamarodnimad
       Russia
.19   Greek
       Greece
.19   Cairo
       Cairo
.20   Gaul
       Gaul
.21   sunflower state
       Kansas
.24   Putawayo
       ?Putamayo

.24 Kansas
　　Kansas
.24 Liburnum
　　Liburnia
.24 New Aimstirdames
　　Amsterdam
　　New York City
.36 Cleaned
　　Clane
　　Slane
510.13 Gunner Shotland
　　Scotland
　　?Shetland Isles
.13 Guinness Scenography
　　Guinness's Brewery
.14 Tailors' Hall
　　Tailors' Hall
.15 Mailers' Mall
　　?
.15 Gaelers' Gall
　　?
.17 old house of the Leaking Barrel
　　?Tavern, The
.19 brandywine
　　?Brandywine
.20 trou Normend fashion
　　Normandy
.21 bank...nasty blunt clubs
　　Nast, Kolb and Schumacher
　　　(bank)
.24 ehren of Fyn's Insul
　　Ireland: Tír na bhFionn
.25 wapping
　　?Wapping
.25 Heaven and Covenant
　　?
.27 e'er a one
　　Erewhon
　　Ireland
.28 Scandalknivery
　　Scandinavia
.30 innwhite horse
　　White Horse
.33 Inishfeel
　　Ireland: Inisfail
511.02 Northwhiggern cupteam
　　Belfast: *Northern Whig* (+
　　　Norwegian Captain)
.15 she laylylaw
　　Shillelagh
512.05 brustall
　　Tavern, The: Bridge Inn

.05 the bear
　　?Ursa Major
.05 Megalomagellan
　　Magellan, Strait of
　　?Magellanic Clouds
.06 liffey
　　Liffey
.07 zodisfaction
　　Sirius (Sotis)
.08 kished
　　Kish Lightship
.10 Annabella
　　?Annabella
.11 Titentung Tollertone
　　?
.11 S. Sabina's
　　?
.12 lee
　　?Lee R
.15 stricker the strait
　　Magellan, Strait of (512.05)
　　Straight St
.16 antelithual
　　Liffey
.18 puttagonnianne
　　Patagonia
.23 Anglys...ingles
　　England
.26 Dublin bar
　　Dublin Bar
.28 shekleton's
　　?Shackleton, George, and Sons,
　　　Ltd
.30 artained
　　?Artane
.31 Flatter O'Ford...hurdley
　　Dublin: Baile Átha Cliath
.34 Toot and Come-Inn
　　NPN: Tutankhamen
.34 bridge called Tiltass
　　NPN: *tiltas*, Lith "bridge"
.36 canicular
　　Sirius: Canicula
513.01 Siriusly
　　Sirius
.05 Amnis Dominae
　　Liffey
.05 Marcus of Corrig
　　?Cork (+ *carraig*, Ir "crag")
.09 Delphin's Bourne
　　Dolphin's Barn

.10   Tophat
       Tophet
.12   Taranta
       ?Tara
       Taranto
.20   Prisky Poppagenua
       Genoa
.21   *Oropos*
       Oropus (theatre)
.21   *Roxy*
       NYC: Roxy Theater
.22   the Gaiety
       Gaiety Theatre
.33   Kerry quadrilles
       Kerry
.33   Listowel lancers
       Listowel
.34   fifth...four
       Ireland: The Five Fifths
514.02 Normand
       Ulster
.02   Desmond
       Munster (*deas*, Ir "south-
       ern")
.02   Osmund
       Leinster
.02   Kenneth
       Connacht
.05   ranky roars assumbling
       Dublin Allusion: "Rocky
       Road to Dublin"
.06   Annie's courting
       Enniscorthy
.08   hoy's house
       Phoenix Tavern (Werburgh
       St)
.09   a hellfire club
       Hell Fire Club
.14   Ecclesiastes...Eccles's hostel
       Eccles St
.15   hay
       ?Hay Hotel
.18   .i..'. .o..l
       Finn's Hotel
.22   A Little Bit Of Heaven
       ?
.23   Howth
       Howth
.24   Sackville-Lawry
       O'Connell St: Lower Sack-
       ville St

.24   Morland-West
       Westmoreland St
.25   Auspice for the Living
       Hospice For The Dying
.25   Bonnybrook
       Bonnybrook
       Donnybrook
.26   A. Briggs Carlisle
       O'Connell Bridge
.32   Flood's
       ?
.33   Gaa...Fox
       ?Fox and Geese
       Gaelic Athletic Assn
.36   eirest race...ourest...airest...eresta-
       tioned
       Ireland
515.04 Richman's periwhelker
       ?Richmond
.09   *rhodammum*
       Rhodes
       Rhone R
.21   Capel Court
       Capel Court (London)
.24   homer's kerryer pidgeons
       ?Kerry
.29   mincethrill...christie
       ?Christie's
       See *Census* for Christy Min-
       strels
.29   Dublin own
       Dublin
.30   bebattersbid
       Battersby and Co
.35   Haywarden
       Hawarden
516.04 badgeler's rake
       ?Bachelor's Walk
.05   Cattelaxes...Kildare
       Kildare
.11   naas
       Naas (Co Kildare)
.13   coocoomb
       Coombe, The
.15   Ump pyre
       Empire Theatre
.20   John Dunn's field
       ?
.25   bog of the depths
       NPN: *The Book of the Dead*
.27   Turbot Street...paumpshop
       ?Talbot St

.29   compuss memphis
     Memphis (+ "compos men-
     tis")
.32   annusual
     Annu
.35   finister
     ?Finisterre
517.05   Swede
     Sweden
.09   bawling green
     Bowling Green
.15   Black Pig's Dyke
     Black Pig's Dyke
.25   Grinwicker time
     Greenwich (Observatory)
518.01   Dunsink
     Dunsink Observatory
.01   rugby
     Rugby (Observatory)
.01   ballast and ball
     Ballast Office
.06   the Ruins, Drogheda Street
     Drogheda (now O'Connell)
     St
.09   wreek me Ghyllygully
     McGillycuddy's Reeks
.10   headlong stone of kismet
     Lia Fáil ("Stone of Desti-
     ny")
     Mecca: Black Stone
     Steyne (Long Stone)
.13   vegateareans
     Vega
.16   Hostages and Co, Engineers
     ?
.18   ersatz lottheringcan
     Alsace-Lorraine
.21   Picturshirts and Scutticules
     Scotland
.22   Irish Ruman
     Ireland
     Rome
.23   Danos
     Denmark
     Greece
.24   upright man
     ?Wooden Man
.24   Limba romena
     Rome
.25   Bucclis tucsada
     Tuscany

.26   in finnish...in Feeny's
     Finland
.29   Co Canniley...Da Donnuley
     ?
.35   houlish like Hull
     Hell
     Hull
519.01   hellish
     Hell
.01   neuropeans
     Europe
.19   thathens of tharctic
     Arctic
     Athens
     Belfast: "Athens of the North"
.24   Corth examiner
     Cork: *Cork Examiner*
.33   Aunt Tarty Villa
     ?Arctic (Antarctic)
520.01   feelmick's park
     Phoenix Park
.02   tarrable Turk
     Tara
     Turkey
.09   borrowsaloaner
     ?Barcelona
.15   paraguais
     Paraguay
.16   saints withins
     St Swithin's Church
.17   African man
     Africa
.19   N.D. de l'Ecluse
     St Mary del Dam
.20   hell's flutes
     Hell
.22   Angly as arrows
     England
.22   Nils
     Leinster
.23   Mugn
     Munster
.23   Cannut
     Connacht
.25   wabblin
     Dublin (+ "in Scotland before
     you")
.27   lamelookond
     Lomond, Loch
.33   boolyhooly
     Ballyhooly

.34   rubricated annuals
      Ulster: Arms (Red Hand)
.34   saint ulstar
      Ulster
521.04 Essexelcy
      Essex Br
.05   Golden Bridge's
      Goldenbridge
      ?Whitworth Br ("Old Br")
.06   Lucan
      Lucan
.07   three crowns
      Munster: Arms (three
      crowns)
.10' *Pro tanto quid retribuamus*
      Belfast: city motto
.11   scotty pictail
      Scotland
.13   Raven and Sugarloaf
      Raven and Sugar Loaf, The
      ?Sugarloaf Mt
.13   Jones's lame
      Power's Distillery (John's
      Lane)
.14   Jamesy's gait
      Guinness's Brewery (James's
      Gate)
.15   Bushmillah
      Bushmills (whiskey)
.17   Dove and Raven tavern
      NPN? Noah's birds
.24   illconditioned ulcers
      Ulster
.28   leinconnmuns
      Leinster
      Connacht
      Munster
.30   hulstler
      Ulster
.32   Emania Raffaroo
      Emania
.35   Queen's road
      Queen's Road (Belfast)
522.04 Northern Ire
      Ireland
      Ulster
.04   red hand
      Ulster: Red Hand
.08   Crimeans
      Crimea
.28   tonedeafs
      Tonduff

.30   bray
      Bray
523.08 Saint Yves
      St Ives
.16   S. Samson and son
      Jameson, John, and Son
.17   Bay (Dublin)
      Dublin Bay
.18   Miss or Mrs's MacMannigan's Yard
      ?
.25   West Pauper Bosquet
      ?
.26   Doddercan Easehouse
      Dodder R
      Dodecanese
      Tavern, The
.28   middlesex party
      Anglo-Saxon Kingdoms: Mid-
      dlesex
.32   tour of bibel
      Babel, Tower of
.34   norsect's divisional
      Anglo-Saxon Kingdoms
524.01 exess
      Anglo-Saxon Kingdoms
      Essex
.02   metropolitan
      Dublin Metropolitan Police
.06   our beloved naturpark
      Phoenix Park
.14   England
      England
.15   Soussex Bluffs
      Anglo-Saxon Kingdoms: Sus-
      sex
.19   windwarrd eye
      ?Windward Islands (*ey*, Dan
      "island")
.20   school of herring
      Ireland
.21   Bloater Naze
      Anglo-Saxon Kingdoms
      Naze, The (Essex)
.26   errings
      Ireland
.26   Wissixy kippers
      Anglo-Saxon Kingdoms: Wes-
      sex
525.06 Tallhell
      Hell
.06   Barbados
      Barbados

.06 Errian coprulation
    Ireland
.07 Montgomeryite
    ?Montgomery St
.10 leixlep
    Leixlip
.13 ruttymaid fishery
    Runnymede
.17 seven parish churches
    Glendalough: Seven Church-
    es
.19 runnymede landing
    Runnymede
.21 *Herrin*
    Ireland
.24 *Howth*
    Howth
.25 *Humbermouth*
    Humber R
.29 Longeal of Malin
    Malin Head
.30 newisland
    Ireland
    New Island
.31 Three threeth...Manu ware
    ?Man, Isle of
.33 Dee
    Dee R
.33 Romunculus Remus
    Rome (+ Uncle Remus)
.35 pool her leg
    Poolbeg
.35 butt
    Butt Br
526.01 liffeybank
    Liffey
.06 Rush
    Rush
.09 bubblye...babblyebubblye wa-
    ters of
    Babylon
.16 three slots and no burners
    Dublin Coat of Arms
.18 patmost
    Patmos Island
.20 Cruachan
    ?Crom Cruach
    Cruachan
.22 furry glans
    Phoenix Park: Furry Glen

.28 Corrack-on-Sharon, County Rose-
    carmon
    Carrick-on-Shannon
    Roscommon
    Sharon
.30 Tarpeyan
    ?Rome: Tarpeian Rock
.33 Lough Shieling's love
    Sheelin, Lough
527.01 Iscappellas
    Chapelizod
.11 lickle wiffey
    Liffey
.13 Boileau's
    Boileau and Boyd
528.01 convent loretos
    Loreto Convents
.06 St Audiens...chapelry
    St Audoen's Church
.13 Tolka
    Tolka
.18 alas in jumboland
    Wonderland
.22 Cluse her, voil her
    Valeclusa
    Vaucluse
.23 aglo iris
    England
    Ireland: Iris
.28 Moonster
    Munster
.28 2 R.N.
    Radio Éireann
.28 Longhorns Connacht
    Clifden: Marconi station
    Connacht
.29 capital
    Dublin: Misc Allusions
.30 lion's shire since 1542
    Ireland: Misc Allusions
.31 Ireland...borderation
    Ireland
.32 leinstrel boy
    Leinster
.32 moreen
    ?Moreen
.33 Monn
    Munster
.33 Conn
    Connacht
.37 skullabogue
    Scullabogue House

529.07 six disqualifications
    Ulster: Northern Ireland

.08 Committalman Number Underfifteen
    Committee Room No Fif-
teen

.13 J. H. North and Company
    North, J H and Co

.15 anterim
    ?Antrim

.15 three tailors on Tooley Street
    Tooley St (London)

.17 Butt and Hocksett's
    (just "butt and hogsheads"?)

.19 the coombe
    Coombe, The

.20 Manofisle
    Man, Isle of

.21 Fredborg
    Friedrichshafen

.22 bullgine
    Belgium

.23 Glassthure cabman
    Glasthule (Rd, Dun Laogh-
aire)

.24 cavehill
    Belfast: Cave Hill

.26 glenagearries
    Glenageary (Rd, Dun Laogh-
aire)

.27 R.U.C's
    Ulster (Royal Ulster Con-
stabulary)

.27 trench ulcers
    Ulster (overcoat)

.30 Paterson and Hellicott's
    ?Kapp and Peterson
    Paterson and Co
    (Hellicott's, "Holy Ghost's")

.34 Bar Ptolomei
    ?

.34 hengster's circus
    Hengler's Circus

.35 North Great Denmark Street
    Denmark St, Great

530.02 two worlds
    Two Worlds

.10 Saint Patrick's Lavatory
    St Patrick's Cathedral
    ?St Patrick's Purgatory

.11 Roman
    Rome (Roman Catholic)

.12 balbriggans
    Balbriggan (stockings)

.13 Morgue and Cruses
    NPN? J P Morgan, Croesus?

.15 lagenloves
    ?Lagan R

.16 Heliopolitan
    Heliopolis

.18 arianautic
    Ireland

.19 morse-erse wordybook
    Ireland: Erse
    Norway

.21 lizzyboy...magnon
    Les Eyzies

.21 Errick
    ?Errick
    Ireland

.22 Sackerson! Hookup!
    Sekhet Hetep

.27 frullatullepleats
    Philadelphia

.31 Norganson
    Norway

.33 Tipknock Castle
    ?Castleknock
    ?Tiknock

.34 cookinghagar
    ?Copenhagen

.36 tuckish
    Turkey

.36 armenities
    Armenia

531.03 Councillors-om-Trent
    Trent (Council of)

.04 half dreads Log Laughty
    ?Luggela (*halvtreds*, Nor "fif-
ty")

.15 Wexford-Atelier
    Wexford

.18 toulong
    Toulon

.18 touloosies
    Toulouse (+ Toulouse-Lautrec)

.21 Romiolo Frullini's flea pantamine
    ?

.33 Coole
    Coole

.33 primapatriock of the archsee
    Armagh

.34 Trancenania
    ?

.34 Terreterry's Hole
?Coal Hole: Terry's Theatre
?Tartarus

.35 Stutterers' Corner
?

.36 Kovnor-Journal
Kovno

532.01 eirenarch's
Ireland

.02 persians
Persia (slippers)

.06 Amtsadam
Amsterdam

.06 Eternest cittas
Rome

.10 Allenglisches Angleslachsen
England
Saxony

.11 –.12 Augustanus...Ergastulus
NPN? *Augustanus*, Lat
"imperial"; *ergastulum*,
Lat "debtors' prison"

.12 Farnum's rath
Rathfarnham

.12 Condra's ridge
Drumcondra

.13 meadows of Dalkin
Clondalkin

.13 Monkish tunshep
Monkstown

.14 a cleanliving man...cleanliving
?Clonliffe

.19 crim crig
Crimea

.22 Kissilov's Slutsgartern
Berlin: Lustgarten
Bucharest: Kisilev Park

.22 Gigglotte's Hill
Giglotte's Hill

.24 anniece...nieceless
?Annecy
?Nice

.24 bahad
?Bagdad

.25 Babbyl Malket
?Babel, Tower of

.28 toombs and deempeys
Dublin Metropolitan Police
(DMP)
NYC: Tombs

.32 haram's
Mecca: Haram

.32 haram's (*Cont.*)
Jerusalem: Haram

.32 Skinner's circusalley
Skinner's Alley

.33 Mannequins Passe
Brussels: Manneken-Pis

533.02 heliotrope ayelips
?Tripoli

.05 Evans's eye
Ireland ("Erin's Isle")

.06 chinatins
China
?San Francisco: Chinatown

.06 spekin
Peking

.08 Lambeyth
Lambay Island
Lambeth

.08 Dolekey
Dalkey

.11 olso
Oslo

.12 Upper Room
NPN? Jesus celebrated the
Last Supper with his disciples
in the "upper room."

.15 Frankfurters
Frankfurt

.16 tunies
Tunis

.17 whapping oldsteirs
Wapping (Old Stairs)

.18 cagehaused duckyheim
?
(Ibsen's *A Doll's House*, "Et
Dukkyeheim")

.19 Goosna Greene
Goose Green Ave (N Dublin)
Gretna Green

.19 cabinteeny
Cabinteely (S Dublin)

.22 Nowhergs
Norway

.23 Kerk Findlater's
Findlater's Church

.23 ye litel chuch rond ye coner
NYC: The Little Church
Around the Corner

.26 hedjeskool
Hejaz (+ "hedgeschool")

.28 Caulofat's bed
?

.30   Sutton
         ?Sutton (+ "Satan")
.33   Hiemlancollin
         Oslo: Holmenkollen
.33   Pimpim's Ornery
         Jameson, Pim and Co
         Pim Brothers
.35   Holmstock
         Stockholm
.35   Livpoomark
         Liverpool
.36   Big Butter Boost
         ?Butter Lane
534.02 anew York
         New York City
         York
.02   Kyow! Tak
         Kyoto
         ?Tokyo
.07   Big big Calm
         British Broadcasting Corp
.12   Pynix Park
         Phoenix Park
.13   provost
         Provost, The
.13   gramercy
         NYC: Gramercy Park
.15   Misrs
         Cairo: Misr
.18   Keisserse Lean
         Ireland: Erse
         Keysar's Lane
.18   waring
         Belfast: Waring St
.19   knockbrecky
         Belfast: Knockbreckan res-
         ervoir
.19   bullfist
         Belfast
.20   fallse roude axehand
         Belfast: Falls Road
         Ulster: Red Hand
.20   Saunter's Nocelettres
         ?Belfast: *Newsletter*
         Saunders' News Letter (Dub-
         lin)
.22   Belgradia
         Belgrade
         Belgravia
.23   nonesuch
         Nonesuch

.27   North Strand
         North Strand Rd
         Strand, The (London)
.28   soffiacated
         Sofia
.29   double inns
         Dublin
         Tavern, The
.31   béltspanners
         Gothenburg: Bältespännere
.33   atkinscum's
         Atkinson, Richard, and Co
.34   Hanging Tower
         Hanging Tower
.35   Instaunton!
         ?Staunton (Eng)
535.01 waddphez
         Fez: Wad Fez
.02   von Hunarig
         ?Hungary
.04   Sexsex...Sexencentaurnary
         Essex St
.05   Gate of Hal
         Brussels: Porte de Hal
         "Hell"
.05   Wodin Man
         Wooden Man (Essex St)
.07   city's leasekuays
         City Quay
.08   Nova Tara
         Dublin: Misc Allusions
         Tara
.09   yeddonot
         Tokyo
.10   Noreway
         ?Nore R
         Norway
.12   ecclesency
         Eccles St
.15   spiking Duyvil
         NYC: Spuyten Devil
.15   Londsend
         Land's End
         London
.15   scargore
         Stockholm: *skärgård*
.16   skeepsbrow
         Stockholm: Skeppsbro
.19   Noksagt
         ?Nagasaki (+ *Nok sagt*, Dan
         "Enough said")

.21 Enouch!
　　 Enoch
.22 Whitehed
　　 Whitehead
.24 mespilt
　　 Mespil
.26 Whitehowth...whiteoath
　　 Howth
　　 Whitehead
.28 hells
　　 Hell
536.01 Rivera in Januero
　　 Rio de Janeiro
.04 Everscepistic
　　 ?Everest, Mt
.08 tonguer of baubble
　　 Babel, Tower of
.09 ye staples, (bonze!)
　　 ?Barnstaple
.09 ould reekeries'
　　 Edinburgh: "Auld Reekie"
.10 krumlin
　　 Crumlin
　　 Moscow: Kremlin
.10 aroundisements
　　 Paris
.11 stremmis
　　 ?
.12 nobelities
　　 Sweden: Nobel Prize
.13 bronxitic
　　 NYC: Bronx
.13 achershous
　　 Oslo: Akershus
.14 haute white toff's
　　 ?Howth
　　 ?Whitehead
.14 stock of eisen
　　 Vienna: Stock im Eisen
.15 Royal Leg
　　 Royal Leg, The
.16 puertos mugnum
　　 ?Portsmouth
.21 Oscarshal's
　　 Oslo: Oscarshall
.21 winetavern
　　 Winetavern St
.21 *Buen retiro*
　　 Madrid: Buen Retiro Park
.27 Kanes nought
　　 Connacht

.28 yeamen
　　 ?Yemen (+ *yamen*, Chinese ad-
　　 ministrative offices)
.31 Thing of all Things
　　 Iceland: Althing
　　 Thing Mote
.31 court of Skivinis
　　 Skivini, Court of (London)
.31 marchants grey
　　 ?Merchant's Quay
.35 Homelan
　　 ?
.35 Harrod's
　　 Harrods Ltd (London)
537.01 gladshouses
　　 Glasshouse
.01 elephant's house is his castle
　　 Elephant and Castle (London)
　　 Elvery's Elephant House
.06 filthered Ovocnas
　　 Avoca
　　 Meeting of the Waters
　　 Prague: Ovocna
.06 Christina Anya
　　 Oslo: Christiania
.07 Irishers
　　 Ireland
.10 *Ehren*
　　 Ireland
.11 outbreighten
　　 Brighton
.12 land's eng
　　 Land's End
.13 peebles
　　 Peebles (Scotland)
.16 entyrely
　　 ?Tyre
.17 *in toto*
　　 Addis Ababa: Entotto
.23 mouthless niggeress
　　 Niger R
.24 Cherna Djamja
　　 Niger R
　　 Sofia: Tcherna Djamia
.24 Blawlawnd-via-Brigstow
　　 Blaaland
　　 Bristol
.29 two punt scotch
　　 Scotland
.34 Mons Meg's Monthly
　　 Edinburgh: Mons Meg

.34	Fanagan's Weck	.28	contey Carlow's
	?Fanagan, Wm, funeral estab-		Carlow
	lishment		Monte Carlo
.34	bray	.32	Schottenhof
	Bray		Vienna: Schottenhof
.35	clownsillies	.33	Gothamm
	Clonsilla		Gotham
.35	Donkeybrook Fair	.34	oathhead
	Donnybrook (Fair)		Howth
.36	unpurdonable	539.01	our mostmonolith
	Purdon St		Wellington Monument
538.01	Juno Moneta	.02	minhatton
	Rome: Capitoline Hill (mint)		NYC: Manhattan
.01	irished	.03	longstone erectheion
	Ireland		Athens: Erechtheium
.01	Marryonn Teheresiann		Steyne (Long Stone)
	Loreto (Convent)		Wellington Monument
	Merrion: Sisters of Charity	.05	wordworth's
	St Teresa, Monastery of		NYC: Woolworth Bldg
	Teheran	.06	Shopkeeper, A. G.
.07	ochtroyed		England (*A.G.*, Ger "Ltd")
	Octroi	.11	cramkrieged
	Troy		Crimea
.09	Brixton	.12	prudentials
	Brixton		Prudential Assurance Co
.10	Auction's Bridge	.14	sooth of Spainien
	NPN?		Spain
.12	roohms of encient cartage	.17	Athacleeath
	?Antient Concert Rooms		Dublin: Baile Átha Cliath
	Carthage	.18	Irrlanding
	Rome		Ireland
.16	cunziehowffse	.20	platzed mine residenze
	Edinburgh: Cunzie House		?Berlin: Residenzstadt
	(mint)	.20	bourd and burgage
.18	herrings		?Burgage
	Ireland	.21	starrymisty
.21	boyne		Prague: Staré město
	Boyne R	.21	brixtol
.22	Street Fleshshambles		Bristol
	Fishamble St		Tavern, The: Bridge Inn
.23	hespermun	.22	thollstall
	Venus: "Hesperus"		Tholsel
.24	covin guardient	.22	mean straits male
	Covent Garden (London)		Menai Strait
.25	Haddem	.22	evorage fimmel
	?Amsterdam (A'dam)		?Howth: Evora
	?Edam	.24	Poplinstown
.25	suistersees		Dublin Allusion: "Poplins-
	Zuider Zee		town"
.26	theirn	.24	Fort Dunlip
	Ireland		Dublin

.25   Serbonian bog
      Serbonian Bog

.25   city of magnificent distances
      Madras

.26   walldabout
      NYC: Wallabout Bay and
      Market

.26   pale
      Pale, The

.26   palisades
      NYC: Palisades

.27   martiell siegewin
      ?Marshalsea

.28   cleantarriffs
      Clontarf

.30   prusshing
      Prussia

.30   Allbrecht the Bearn
      Berlin: Albert the Bear

.31   kingsinnturns
      King's Inns

.33   tenenure
      Terenure

.36   Englisch sweat
      England

The description of Dublin at 540.03–.08 is quoted as the motto of Chart's Dublin *from Stanihurst's "Description of Irelande" in Holinshed's* Chronicle.

540.07   called of Ptolemy the Libnia
      Labia
      Libnius R
      Liffey R

.09   *Drumcollogher...Drumcollogher*
      Drumcolliher
      Dublin: Drom Cuill-Choille

.11   *so ersed*
      Ireland: Erse

.12   *Vedi Drumcollogher...*
      Naples

.12   *Moonis*
      Mooney's

.15   Tyeburn
      Tyburn

.15   murmars march
      Marble Arch

.17   hold of my capt
      Howth

.18   the mortification that's my fate
      Magazine Fort

.21   Redu Negru
      Bucharest: Radu Negru

.25   rothmere's homes
      NPN: Ibsen's *Rosmersholm*

.25   Obeyance...toun
      Dublin Motto

.26   bourse
      Bourse (Paris)

.31   lepers lack
      Leixlip

.33   mallsight
      Mall, The (London)

.34   Me ludd in her hide park
      Hyde Park (London)
      London ("Lud's town")

.35   Blownose aerios
      Buenos Aires

541.01   Seven ills
      Edinburgh
      ?Rome

.02   hill prospect
      ?Galway: Prospect Hill
      Peking: Prospect Hill
      Tara: Prospect Hill

.02   Braid Blackfordrock
      ?Blackrock
      Edinburgh: Braid Hills, Blackford Hill

.03   Calton
      Edinburgh: Calton Hill

.03   Liberton
      Edinburgh: Liberton Hill

.03   Craig and Lockhart's
      Edinburgh: Craiglockhart Hills

.03   A. Costofino
      Edinburgh: Corstorphine Hill
      (+ *Écosse*, Fr "Scotland")

.04   R. Thursitt
      Edinburgh: Arthur's Seat

.04   chort of Nicholas Within
      St Nicholas Within, Church of

.05   dome...Michan
      St Michan's Church

.06   awful tors
      Eiffel Tower

.06   wellworth building
      NYC: Woolworth Bldg

.09   mains...drains
      Main Drain

.13   Sirrherr of Gambleden
      ? (just "gambling den"?)

.13   Madame of Pitymount
    Monte de Pietà (pawnshop)
.14   Paybads floriners
    Netherlands (Les Pays Bas)
.15   barthelemew
    ?Thélème, Abbey of
.16   Daniel in Leonden
    London
.16   Bulafests
    Belfast
    Budapest
.17   Corkcuttas
    Calcutta
    Cork
.17   Atabey
    Cairo: Place Atabeh
.18   Loughlins
    Lochlann
.18   tolkies
    ?Tolka
.19   Lusqu'au bout
    Lusk
.19   ire
    Ireland
.22   Walhalloo...Walhalloo
    Valhalla
    Waterloo
.23   law's marshall
    Warsaw: Marszalkowska
.23   warschouw
    Warsaw
.23   I thole till
    ?Tholsel
.24   praharfeast
    Prague
.25   acorpolous
    Athens: Acropolis
.25   Neederthorpe
    Zurich: Niederdorf
.25   faireviews
    Fairview
.26   slobodens
    Fairview (the sloblands)
    (+ *sloboda*, Russ "suburb")
.26   rothgardes
    Rathgar
.26   wrathmindsers
    Rathmines
.27   bathandbaddend
    Baden
    Bath

.27   mendicity
    Mendicity Institution
.27   the unoculated
    Vaccine or Cow Pock Institu-
    tion
.28   plain of Soulsbury
    Salisbury (Plain)
.31   musky
    Moscow
.33   westinders
    India, West Indies
    West End (London)
.34   gorges in the east
    St George's-in-the-East (Lon-
    don)
.34   ourangoontangues
    Rangoon
.35   Escuterre ofen
    Budapest: Eskü-Ter, Ofen
.35   meckling of my burgh
    ?Burgh Quay
    Mecklenburg (Ger)
    Mecklenburgh St
.36   Belvaros
    Budapest: Belváros
542.02   Irish shou
    Ireland
.02   libertilands
    Liberties, The
.03   curraghcoombs
    Coombe, The
    Curragh
    Rome: Catacombs
.04   hurusalaming...Wailingtone's Wall
    Jerusalem: Wailing Wall
.04   richmounded
    Richmond Basin
    ?Richmond·Br
.05   rainelag
    Ranelagh
.05   bathtub of roundwood
    Roundwood (reservoir)
.08   Putzemdown cars
    Rangoon: Pazundaung
.08   Kommeandine hotels
    Rangoon: Kemmendine
.09   fontaneously...Philuppe
    ?Crampton's Monument (foun-
    tain)
.13   meckamockame
    ?Mecca

.14 caabman's sheltar
Cabman's Shelter
.16 Janus's straight
?
.16 Christmas steps
Bristol: Christmas Steps
.18 Forum Foster
Foster Place
.21 auntieparthenopes
Naples
.25 hillsaide...bunkers'
Bunker Hill
.28 bethel of Solyman's...rotunda-
ties
Bethel
Rotunda (Hospital)
.28 turnkeyed most insultantly
Turkey
.29 lutetias
?Paris:Lutetia
.29 lock
Westmoreland Lock Hospital
.29 bax of biscums to the jacobeat-
ers
?Biscay, Bay of
Jacob, W and R, Co, Bakers
.31 dehlivered
Delhi
.33 chandner's chauk
Delhi: Chandni Chauk
.35 beggered about the amnibushes
Beggarsbush
543.01 ballwearied
?Balwearie (Scotland)
.01 doubling megalopolitan poleet-
ness
Dublin Metropolitan Police
.04 Botany Bay
Botany Bay
Trinity College, Dublin: Bot-
any Bay
.11 my vonderbilt hutch
?
.13 Rest and bethinkful
Edinburgh: Rest and Be
Thankful
.16 villa of the Ostmanorum
Oxmantown
.16 Thorstan's, recte Thomars Sraid
?Clontarf
Thomas St

.17 Huggin Pleaze
Hoggen Green
.17 William Inglis his house...Loundres
Castle, The: Henry de Londres
Englysh, William, House of
.18 barony of Saltus
Salt, Barony of
.19 foeburghers...oges...macks...darsy
Galway (City)
.20 darsy jeamses
?D'Arcy's Anchor Brewery
.20 drury joneses
Drury Lane
.21 bleucotts
King's Hospital
.25 German
Germany
.28 Mountgomery
?Montgomery St
.33 Roe's distillery
Roe's Distillery
544.01 Zetland
Shetland Islands
.03 Baltic
Baltic Sea
.21 ottawark
Ottawa
545.09 Uganda chief
Uganda
.10 Goodmen's Field
?
.20 Tolbris...Tolbris
Bristol
.24 livramentoed
Rio de Janeiro: Livramento
Hill
.29 superb
Genoa: "La Superba"
.30 dustyfeets
Piepowder Court
.32 loy for a lynch
Galway (City)
.33 revolucanized
Lucan
.34 graben
Vienna: The Graben
.35 Sheridan's Circle
NYC: Sheridan Square
.35 black pitts
Blackpitts
.35 pestered Lenfant
Washington, D C

.36	Hearts of Oak	.19	embankment
	Hearts of Oak (insurance co)		Embankment, The (London)
546.01	Rechabites obstain	.20	Ringsend Flott and Ferry
	Rechabite and Total Absti-		Ringsend
	nence Loan and Investment	.26	norsemanship
	Society		Norway
.02	Sigh lento, Morgh!	.27	done abate
	Moyle, Sea of		Donabate
.06	etoiled	.27	maidan race
	?L'Etoile, Place de (Paris)		Calcutta: Maidan (racecourse)
.14	ouzel galley	.29	Heydays
	Ouzel Galley Society		Hades
.17	dubildin	.30	blissforhers
	Dublin		Bosporus
.18	Feejeean	.30	tenspan joys
	Fiji Islands		Bridges, Dublin
.20	freeman's journeymanright	.31	echobank
	?Freeman's Journal		Edinburgh: Echobank Cemetery
.31	wiening	.32	Galata! Galata!
	Vienna		Constantinople: Galata
.33	Earalend	.32	malestream
	Ireland		Maelstrom
.33	Chief North Paw	.33	shegulf
	Ulster		Gulf Stream
.33	Chief Goes in Black Water	.33	ringstresse
	Blackwater (Co Cork)		N Circular Rd
	Munster		S Circular Rd
.34	Chief Brown Pool		?Vienna: Ringstrasse
	Dublin: Dubh-linn	.33	iern of Erin
	Leinster		Ireland: Iernis
.34	Chief Night Cloud by the Deeps	.34	lieflang
	Connacht		Liffey
547.01	Moabit	.35	imorgans
	Berlin: Moabit		Hebrides: I-Mor
	?Moab	548.01	Livland...Lettland
.01	foxrogues		Latvia
	Foxrock		Lithuania
.02	pellmell		Livland
	Pall Mall (London)	.02	Impress of Asias
.17	lacksleap...liffsloup		Asia
	Leixlip		Canada: "Empress" ships
	Liffey	.02	Columbia
.17	tiding down		"Columbia"
	?Teddington (London)	.03	singing sands
.18	Kevin's creek		Hebrides: Isle of Eigg
	Kevin St: Kevin's Port	.03	herbrides' music
.18	Hurdlesford		Hebrides
	Dublin: Baile Átha Cliath	.06	Appia Lippia Pluviabilla
.19	Gardener's Mall		Appian Way
	Gardiner's Mall		Liffey
.19	rivierside drive	.07	amstell
	NYC: Riverside Drive		Amstel R

.08 fiuming
  Fiume

.08 spunish furiosos
  Spain

.09 everest
  Everest, Mt

.12 trinity huts
  Trinity Church
  Trinity College, Dublin

.13 dame
  Dame St

.15 cattagut
  Cattegat

.16 constantonoble's
  Constantinople

.19 liberties
  Liberties, The

.24 waterroses
  ?Waterhouse and Co

.26 Pim's
  Pim Brothers and Co

.27 Slyne's
  Slyne, W, and Co

.27 Sparrow's
  Sparrow and Co

.27 luxories on looks
  Luxor (+ "Lux upon Lux";
  see Louth)

.32 cupandnaggin
  Copenhagen

.33 swanchen's neckplace
  Swan Water, The

.33 school of shells of moyles marine
  ?Marine School
  Moyle, Sea of

.35 king's count
  Offaly

549.01 Danabrog
  Denmark

.02 Leonard's
  Leonard's Corner (S Dublin)

.02 Dunphy's
  Dunphy's Corner (N Dublin)

.05 blackholes
  Calcutta

.07 Blackheathen
  ?Blackheath

.15 Wastewindy tarred strate
  ?

.15 Wasterwindy tarred strate (*Cont.*)
  (W 23rd St, NYC?)

.15 Elgin's marble halles
  British Museum (London)

.16 Livania's volted ampire
  Liffey
  ?Livland
  ?Volta Cinema

.17 topazolites of Mourne
  Mourne

.18 Wykinloeflare
  Wicklow

.18 Arklow's...lure
  Arklow

.18 siomen's
  Siemens Schuckert

.18 Wexterford's hook and crook
  lights
  Crooke
  Hook Head
  Waterford
  Wexford

.19 Hy Kinsella
  Hy Kinselagh

.20 avenyue ceen
  NYC: Avenue C

.22 bellomport
  ?Portobello

.24 sankt piotersbarq
  St Petersburg

.26 island of Breasil
  Brazil

.28 O'Connee
  Oconee R (Georgia)

.28 Alta Mahar
  Altamaha R (Georgia)

.28 the tawny ["the town"]
  Dublin, Georgia

.31 amiens pease
  Amiens

.33 Conn
  Conn's Half
  Conn, Lough

.34 Owel
  Mogh's Half
  Owel, Lough

.34 Guinnass...bargeness
  Guinness's Brewery

550.06 Steving's grain
  St Stephen's Green

.06 greet collegtium
  College Green

.07   S. S. Paudraic's
        ?
.08   barelean
        Berlin
.08   linsteer
        Leinster
.10   marrolebone
        ?Marrowbone Lane
        Marylebone (London)
.11   gothakrauts
        Germany
.13   Saint Pancreas
        St Pancras (London)
.14   store dampkookin
        Oslo: Dampkjökken
.15   Kafa
        NPN? (Kava, a Polynesian
        shrub whose root is used
        to make an intoxicating
        drink)
.16   Ascalon
        Ascalon
.18   Biorwik's powlver
        Oslo: Björvik
.23   doveling...civicised
        Dublin
.24   saloons esquirial
        Escorial (Palace)
.24   fineglas bowbays
        Finglas
.25   telltale sports
        Teltown: Tailteann Games
.27   bray
        ?Bray
.28   kiotowing
        Kyoto
.34   dabblingtime
        Dublin
.35   aljambras
        Alhambra (Palace)
.35   duncingk
        Dunsink Observatory
.35   bloodanoobs
        Danube
.35   vauxhalls
        Vauxhall
551.01   interloopings
        ?Loop Line Br
.01   fell clocksure off my ballast
        Ballast Office
.01   windtor palast
        St Petersburg: Winter Palace

.01   windtor palast (*Cont.*)
        Windsor (Palace)
        Winter Garden Palace
.03   Wigan's jewels
        Wigan
.04   mermeries
        Constantinople: Alti Mermer
        (Palace)
.04   paycook's thronsaale
        Delhi: Peacock Throne
.06   Rideau Row
        ?Ottawa: Rideau
        Rhaetia
.07   pantocreator
        Constantinople: Church of
        Pantocreator
.10   champdamors
        Champ de Mars (Paris)
.15   prater
        Vienna: Prater
.23   canal grand
        Grand Canal
        Venice: Canale Grande
.24   Regalia Water
        Royal Canal
.24   *Urbs in Rure*
        ?Aldborough House
        Rus in Urbe
.25   upservatory
        Dunsink Observatory
.28   unniversiries...rational
        National University of Ireland
.30   rosetted
        Rosetta
.30   little egypt
        Egypt
.31   triscastellated
        Dublin Coat of Arms
        Three Castles
.32   sevendialled
        Seven Dials (London)
.32   Hibernska Ulitzas
        Ireland: Hibernia
        Prague: Hibernská Ulice
.33   twelve Threadneedles
        Threadneedle St (London)
        ?Twelve Bens ("Pins")
.34   Newgade
        Newgate Gaol
.34   Vicus Veneris
        Love Lane

.34 camels' walk
      ?
.35 kolossa kolossa!
      Colossus of Rhodes
.35 porte sublimer
      Constantinople: Sublime
      Port
.35 benared my ghates
      Benares
552.01 old Sarum
      Old Sarum
.02 Geenar
      Great Northern Railway
.02 Greasouwea
      Great Southern and Western
      Railway
.02 Debwickweck
      Dublin, Wicklow, and Wex-
      ford Railway
.02 Mifgreawis
      Midland Great Western Rail-
      way
.03 twinminsters, the pro and con
      Christchurch Cathedral
      Pro-Cathedral
.04 norcely
      Norway
.04 attachatouchy floodmud
      ?Chattahoochee R
.07 Hagiasofia
      Constantinople: St Sophia
.07 Astralia
      Australia
.13 gobelins
      Gobelins (Paris)
.14 tect my tileries
      Tuileries (Paris)
.15 four great ways
      (the railways at 552.02)
.15 infernals
      Inferno
.16 Sweatenburgs Welhell
      ?Helsinki: Sveaborg
      Valhalla
.19 Neeblow's garding
      NYC: Niblo's Garden
.22 sweet...auburn
      Auburn
.22 coolocked
      Coolock
.23 paddypalace on the crossknoll
      Petit Palais (Paris)

.23 paddypalace on the crossknoll
      (Cont.)
      St Patrick's Cathedral
.26 tellforth's
      Telford and Telford (organ
      builders)
.26 slub...hellfire
      Hell Fire Club
.28 babazounded
      Algiers: Bab Azoun
.29 tararulled
      Tara
.29 she sass her nach...altarstane
      Clonmacnoise
      England
.35 snaeffell
      Snaefell Mt
553.03 dundrum
      Dundrum
.04 Livvy
      Liffey
.05 Lord street
      ?
.05 Cammomile Pass
      Camomile St (London)
.06 Primrose Rise
      Primrose St (London)
.06 Coney Bend...Mulbreys Island
      NYC: Coney Island, Mulberry
      Bend Park
.08 blighty acre
      Acre
      Bloody Acre
.09 lecheworked
      Garden City: Letchworth
.09 Guerdon City
      Garden City
.10 chopes pyramidous
      Pyramids (Cheops)
.10 mousselimes
      Mausoleum at Halicarnassus
.10 beaconphires
      Pharos at Alexandria
.10 colossets
      Colossus of Rhodes
.11 pensilled turisses...summiramies
      Gardens of Semiramis
.12 esplanadas
      ?Esplanade
.12 statuesques
      Olympia: Statue of Zeus

.12   templeogues
           Temple of Artemis at Ephe-
           sus
           Templeogue

The following is a list of the
statues in exact order from the N end
of O'Connell St, S to College Green.
Smith O'Brien's statue is listed at its
former site at the S end of O'Connell
Br.

.12   Pardonell of Maynooth
           Maynooth: "Pardon of *M*"
           Parnell Monument
.13   Fra Teobaldo
           Mathew, Father Theobald,
           Statue
.13   Nielsen, rare admirable
           Nelson's Pillar
.13   Jean de Porteleau
           Gray, Sir John, Statue
.14   Conall Gretecloke
           O'Connell Statue
.14   Guglielmus Caulis
           O'Brien, William Smith,
           Statue
.14   eiligh ediculous Passivucant
           Moore, Thomas, Statue
           ?Pass-if-you-can
.18   lisbing
           Lisbon
.19   Chesterfield elms
           Phoenix Park: Chesterfield
           Rd
.19   Kentish
           Kent
.20   rigs of barlow
           Mallow
.20   bowery nooks
           NYC: The Bowery
.20   greenwished villas
           NYC: Greenwich Village
.21   pampos animos
           ?
.21   necessitades iglesias
           Lisbon: Paço das Necessi-
           dades
.22   hawthorndene
           Edinburgh: Hawthornden
           Phoenix Park: Furry (Haw-
           thorn) Glen

.22   feyrieglenn
           Phoenix Park: Furry Glen
.22   hallaw vall
           Phoenix Park: The Hollow
           Valhalla
.23   dyrchace
           ?Deer Park
.23   Finmark's Howe
           ?Thing Mote
.24   magicscene wall
           Magazine Fort
.24   Queen's garden of her phoenix
           Phoenix Park: "Queen's Gar-
           den"
.24   alpine
           Alps
.27   Dublin lindub
           Dublin (*linn dubh*, Ir "black
           ale")
.29   eblanite
           Dublin: Eblana
.29   stony battered
           Stoneybatter
.30   nordsoud circulums
           N Circular Rd
           S Circular Rd
.30   eastmoreland
           Eastmoreland Lane
.30   westlandmore
           Westmoreland St
.31   running boullowards
           ?
.31   syddenly parading
           ?Sydney (Australia)
           Sydney Parade Ave
.32   opslo
           Oslo
.32   storting
           Oslo: Storthing
.33   dutc
           Dublin United Tramway Co
.35   arabinstreeds
           Arabia
.35   Roamer Reich's
           Rome
.36   Hispain's
           Spain
.36   madridden
           Madrid
554.01 buckarestive
           Bucharest

.01 turnintaxis
    Thurn und Taxis
.03 priccoping
    Prague: Prikopy
.06 shjelties
    Shetland Islands (ponies)
.06 awknees
    Orkney Islands (ponies)

    BOOK III
    Chapter 4

555.09 majorchy
    Balearic Islands: Majorca
.09 minorchy
    Balearic Islands: Minorca
.09 everso
    Balearic Islands: Iviza
.09 fermentarian
    Balearic Islands: Formentera
.10 ballyhooric
    Balearic Islands
    Ballyhooly
    Ballyhoura
.13–.15 esker...esker
    Esker
    Royal Manors of Dublin
.13–.15 newcsle...newcsle
    Newcastle
    Royal Manors of Dublin
.13–.15 saggard...saggard
    Saggart
    Royal Manors of Dublin
.13–.15 crumlin...crumlin
    Crumlin
    Royal Manors of Dublin
.14 the way to wumblin...bumblin
    Dublin
.18 auspices
    Hospice for the Dying
.18 irishsmiled
    Ireland
.18 milky way
    Milky Way
.21 night refuge
    St Joseph's Night Refuge
556.06 Samaritan
    Samaria
.23 nowth
    ?Howth
.25 curserbog
    ?

.25 grassgross bumpinstrass
    ?Zurich: Bahnhofstrasse
.33 basquing
    Basque Provinces
557.01 Esquara
    Basque Provinces: Eskuara
.02 Norreys, Soothbys, Yates and
    Welks
    North, South, East, West
.06 hapspurus
    Norman's Woe: "Hesperus"
.11 ivileagh
    Iveagh
.14 fox and geese
    Fox and Geese
.28 sweeds
    ?Sweden (Fr, *Suede*)
.36 Sammon's in King Street
    King St, N
    Sammon's (King St, N)
558.10 Adam Findlater
    Findlater, Alexander, and Co
.19 seven honeymeads
    Clonmel
.22 Leixlip
    Leixlip
.27 Albatrus Nyanzer
    Albert Nyanza
.28 Victa Nyanza
    Victoria Nyanza
.35 House of the cederbalm of mead
    Teach Miodhchuarta
.35 Garth of Fyon
    ?
559.02 Irish grate
    Ireland
.04 Argentine in casement
    Argentina
.06 strawberry bedspread
    Strawberry Beds
.07 millikinstool
    ?Brussels: Manneken-Pis
.13 Yverdown
    ?Ireland: Iwerddon
    ?Yverdon
.24 ghazometron
    Gasometer
.25 Armenian bole
    Armenia
.28 Welshrabbit teint
    Wales (+ "yellow tint")

.28	Nubian		.08	park...Finn his park
	Nubia			Phoenix Park
.35	Mesopotomac		.09	grekish
	Mesopotamia			Greece
	Potomac R		.09	romanos
560.07	humburgh...head			Rome
	Bad Homburg		.10	straight road down the centre
	?Hamburg			Phoenix Park: Chesterfield Rd
.09	castle arkwright		.13	vinesregent's lodge
	?Castle, The			Phoenix Park: Viceregal Lodge
.15	maggies in all		.15	chief sacristary's residence
	Magazine Fort			Phoenix Park: Chief Secretar-
.18	beneadher			y's Lodge
	Howth: Ben Edar		.22	liveside
.27	iszoppy chepelure			Liffey
	Chapelizod		.23	in norlandes
561.06	Corsicos			?
	Corsica		.24	weald
.18	Grecian language			?Weald
	Greece		.28	pities of the plain
562.07	Allaliefest			Cities of the Plain
	Liffey		.30	fionghalian
.10	Mount of Whoam			Fingal
	?		.32	Saint Lucan's
.13	brigidschool			Lucan
	St Brigid's		.35	royal park
.21	two maggots			Phoenix Park (belonged to Brit
	Deux Magots, Les			sovereign)
.29	gorgeous...Amorica		.35	shyasian gardeenen...public
	?Georgia			?Asia
.30	dane's pledges			Phoenix Park: People's Gar-
	Denmark			dens
.30	our ingletears		565.02	Holl Hollow
	England			Phoenix Park: The Hollow
.31	Amorica			Valhalla
	America		.04	pentapolitan poleetsfurcers
	?Armorica			Dublin Metropolitan Police
563.11	the pale			Pentapolis
	Pale, The		.09	Amsterdam
.14	bulgar			Amsterdam
	Bulgaria		.10	guineeser...beutel of staub
.19	the Cat and Cage			Guinness's Brewery
	Cat and Cage		.12	Gortigern
.21	the elm			Babel, Tower of: Gortighern
	Chapelizod: Village Elm		.12	Mercia
.26	Donnybrook Fair			Mercia
	Donnybrook (Fair)		.15	Putshameyu
.27	Hoy's Court			Putamayo
	Hoey's Court		.17	eire
564.06	our zoopark			Ireland
	Phoenix Park: Zoo		.21	Gothgorod
				?Novgorod

.22 lucky load to Lublin
    Dublin Allusion: "Rocky
    Road to Dublin"
    Lublin
    Lutsk

.29 little brittle
    Britain, Little

.33 Lucalised...the sulphur spa
    Chapelizod
    Lucan (spa)

.34 his inn
    Tavern, The

.35 pickts
    Scotland

.35 saxums
    Saxony

.36 snugger to burrow
    Snugborough

.36 ballet on broadway
    NYC: Broadway

566.11 duntalking
    Dundalk (Co Louth)

.11 droghedars
    Drogheda (Co Louth)

.14 runameat
    Runnymede

.16 maidbrides...joybells
    ?Malahide

.20 the tower royal
    Tower of London

.20 daulphin
    Delvin R

.20 deevlin
    Devlin R
    Tower of London: Develin
    Tower

.25 Herein
    Ireland

.32 finister
    Finisterre

.36 the dunleary obelisk
    Dun Laoghaire

567.01 the rock
    Rock Rd

.02 general's postoffice
    General Post Office

.02 Wellington memorial
    Wellington Monument

.03 Sara's bridge
    Island Br

.04 the point
    Ringsend

.11 Courtmilits' Fortress
    Magazine Fort
    (+ *Cead Mile Failte*, Ir
    "100,000 welcomes")

.17 all the king's aussies
    ?Chapelizod: King's House
    ?Gaiety Theatre

.22 aryan
    Ireland

.24 littlego
    Cambridge (U): "Little Go"

.27 Me Eccls
    Eccles St

.34 troykakyls
    ?Troy (+ "troikas")

.35 Polo north
    North Pole

.35 Sibernian
    Ircland: Hibernia
    Siberia

.35 Plein Pelouta
    ?
    (the Spanish game jai alai)

.36 yerking
    York

.36 lawncastrum
    Lancaster

568.04 livliness
    Liffey

.12 meise
    Meise

.16 *Instopressible*
    Insuppressible, The

    *The following 7 names are old
names of Dublin streets.*

.22 pinchgut
    Pinchgut Lane

.22 hoghill
    Hog Hill

.22 darklane
    Dark Lane

.22 gibbetmeade
    Gibbet Meadow

.22 beaux
    Beaux Lane

.23 laddes
    Lad Lane

.23 bumbellye
    Bumbailiff's (Fumbally's) Lane

.23 broadstone barrow
    ?Barrow R

.23 broadstone barrow (*Cont.*)
    Broadstone Station

.27 horse elder yet cherchant
    ?St Sepulchre's

.27 graveleek in cabbuchin garden
    Cabbage Garden Graveyard
    ?Capuchin Friary

.28 Caubeenhauben
    Copenhagen

.33 lomdom
    ?London (+ "lambda")

569.02 crimosing
    Crimea

.02 balkonladies
    Balkans

The following are all Dublin churches, CI, RC, and non-conformist. John Kelleher identified the churches in the Analyst *X, 4 f. This list differs only for "S. Gardener" and "S. Nicholas Myre." The first 4 churches also represent the 4 provinces, and they are located in N, S, E, and W Dublin.*

.05 S. Presbutt-in-the-North
    Findlater's Church
    (+ Ulster)

.05 S. Mark Underloop
    St Mark's Church
    Loop Line Br
    (+ Munster)

.06 S. Lorenz-by-the-Toolechest
    St Lawrence O'Toole's
    Church
    (+ Leinster)

.06 S. Nicholas Myre
    St Nicholas of Myra's
    Church
    (+ Connacht)

.07 S. Gardener
    St Francis Xavier's Church
    (Gardiner St)

.07 S. George-le-Greek
    St George's Church

.07 S. Barclay Moitered
    St Joseph's Church (Berkeley St)

.08 S. Phibb
    All Saints Church (Phibsborough Rd)
    St Peter's Church (Phibsborough)

.08 S. Phibb (*Cont.*)
    Phibsborough

.08 Iona-in-the-Fields
    St Columba's Church (Iona Rd)
    ?Iona

.08 Paull-the-Aposteln
    St Paul's Church (King St, N)
    St Paul's Church (Arran Quay)

.09 S. Jude-at-Gate
    St Jude's Church (Kilmainham)

.09 Bruno Friars
    St Mary of the Angels Church ("Brown Friars")

.09 S. Weslen-on-the-Row
    St Andrew's Church (Westland Row)

.10 S. Molyneux Without
    Old Molyneux Church

.10 S. Mary Stillamaries
    Stella Maris Church

.11 Bride-and-Audeons-behind-Wardborg
    Castle, The: Wardrobe Tower
    St Audoen's Church
    St Bride's Church
    St Werburgh's Church

.14 Agithetta
    St Agatha's Church

.14 Tranquilla
    Tranquilla Convent

.14 Marlborough-the-Less
    Pro-Cathedral (Marlborough St)

.15 Greatchrist
    Christchurch Cathedral

.15 Holy Protector
    St Patrick's Cathedral

.17 Cantaberra
    Canberra
    Canterbury (archdiocese)

.18 Neweryork
    New York City
    York (archdiocese)

.20 Deublan
    Dublin

.25 fellhellows
    ?Valhalla

.29 Ithalians
    Italy

.30 gate
    Gate Theatre

.31	Veruno	573.30	Canicula
	Verona ("Two Gentlemen		?Sirius: Canicula
	of Verona")	574.09	Judge Doyle
.36	Granby in hills...Grandbeyond		Dáil Éireann
	Mountains	.15	Wieldhelm, Hurls Cross
	Grampian Hills		Harold's Cross
570.03	Deep Dalchi Dolando	.18	bank...national misery
	Dalkey		Bank of Ireland
	Dublin Allusion: "Dear Dir-	.32	doyles
	ty Dublin"		Dáil Éireann
.04	piketurns	575.06	Ann Doyle
	Turnpike		Dáil Éireann
.05	crosshurdles	.06	2 Coppinger's Cottages
	?Dublin: Baile Átha Cliath		Coppinger
	?Harold's Cross	.07	Doyle's country. Doyle (Ann)
.05	viceuvious		Dáil Éireann
	Vesuvius, Mt	.09	doylish
.06	pyrolyphics		Dáil Éireann
	Liffey	.24	Mack Erse's Dar
.12	Ys		Ireland: Erse
	?Ys	.26	little green courtinghousie
.21	Hurtleforth		Green St Courthouse
	Dublin: Baile Átha Cliath		Little Green
.29	sairey's place	.32	JeremyDoyler
	Sarah Place		Dáil Éireann
.31	our national first rout	576.01	Liffey
	?Esker (Rd)		Liffey
.32	ford...hurdley	.03	Calif of Man
	Dublin: Baile Átha Cliath		Man, Isle of: Calf of Man
.36	everthrown...sillarsalt	.03	Eaudelusk Company
	Wellington Monument		Lusk
571.02	clear springwell...park	.06	Hal Kilbride
	Phoenix Park		Kilbride (+ Henry VIII)
.08	cull dare	.06	Una Bellina
	Kildare (+ Gaelic "tree-let-		Ballina (+ Anne Boleyn)
	ters" C and D)	.15	my wee mee mannikin
.10	hedjes		Brussels: Manneken-Pis
	?Hejaz	.18	giant...causeways
.11	chapelofeases...Ziod		Giant's Causeway
	Chapelizod	.19	hopping offpoint
	Zion, Mt		?
.18	littleeasechapel	.20	straxstraightcuts
	Chapelizod		?Straight St
.19	Ireland	.20	corkscrewn perambulaups
	Ireland		?Cork: St Patrick's St
.22	limmenings lemantitions		Corkscrew (Rd)
	Leman, Lac (+ *limnos*, Gk	.21	wonderlust
	"lake")		?Wonderland
.24	saarasplace	.22	York
	Sarah Place		York
572.25	philadelphians	.22	Leeds
	?Philadelphia		Leeds

.26	hungerford	.21	Enos
	Dublin: Baile Átha Cliath		NPN: Enos salts, once favored
	Hungerford		for hangovers
.27	Bogy Bobow	.22	Goerz
	Bow Lane		Goerz (Austria)
.28	cunnyngnest	.22	Harleem
	Conyngham Rd		Harlem (Netherlands)
.28	Phenicia Parkes	.22	Hearths of Oak
	Phoenix Park		Hearts of Oak (Life Assurance
.36	neoliffic		Co)
	Liffey (+ "neolithic")	.22	Skittish Widdas
.36	magdalenian		Scottish Widows' Fund
	Madeleine, La	.23	via mala
577.01	wiffeyducky		Via Mala
	Liffey	.23	hyber pass
.01	Morionmale		Khyber Pass
	?	.23	heckhisway
.01	Thrydacianmad		?
	?	.23	alptrack
.05	peccadilly		Alps
	Piccadilly	.24	mandelays
.06	dipper douce		Mandalay (Road to)
	Douce, Mt	.25	cozenkerries
.07	norsebloodheartened and lands-		Kerry
	moolwashable	.28	sizzleroads
	Norway		NPN? (Cecil Rhodes?)
.09	cod and coney	.28	arthruseat
	? (cf 436.23)		?Edinburgh: Arthur's Seat
.11	constant lymph	.28	the derby
	Liffey		Derby
.11	nazil hose	.29	unterlinnen
	Howth: Nose of Howth		Berlin: Unter den Linden
.12	river mouth	.30	rue to lose
	Liffey		Toulouse: Rue de Toulouse
.12	big smoke	.30	ca canny
	London (= Dublin?)		?
.13	lickley roesthy	.30	shipside
	?		Cheapside (London)
.14	Urloughmoor	.30	convent garden
	Tullamore (Co Offaly)		Covent Garden (London)
.14	Miryburrow	.33	strangfort planters
	Maryborough (Co Laois)		Strangford (Ulster)
.15	leaks	.34	karkery felons
	Laois		Cork (Munster)
.15	awfully		Rome: Carcer
	Offaly	.34	leperties' laddos
.15	basal curse		Liberties, The (Leinster)
	?Basle	.35	slogo slee
.15	grace abunda		Sligo (Connacht)
	?Graubünden	578.04	greyed brunzewig
.21	Bushmills		Great Brunswick St
	Bushmills (whiskey)		

.05   caspian asthma
     Caspian Sea
.11   Misthra Norkmann
     (North)
.11   Mr O'Sorgmann
     (South)
.14   doublin
     Dublin
.16   voulzievalsshie
     Voulzie R
.19   Donauwatter
     Danube R
.20   Ardechious me!
     Ardèche R
.21   allabalmy
     Alabama R
.21   troutbeck
     Troutbeck (R)
.23   rhaincold draughts
     Rhine R: Rheingold
.25   Pont Delisle
     Island Br
.25   Brounemouth
     ?Bournemouth
.26   Hatesbury's Hatch
     Heytesbury St
.27   old Love Lane
     Love Lane
.29   Angell sitter
     Angel (London)
.29   Amen Corner
     Amen Close (London)
.30   Norwood's
     Norwood (London) (+
     North)
.30   Southwalk
     Southwark (London) (+
     South)
.30   Euston
     Euston (London) (+ East)
.30   Waste
     (West)
.35   Luxuumburgher
     Luxembourg
.36   Alzette
     Luxembourg: Alzette R
.36   konyglik shire
     Offaly (King's Co)
.36   queensh countess
     Laois (Queen's Co)
.36   Stepney's shipchild
     Stepney (London)

579.01   Dunmow's flitcher
     Dunmow
.04   Elder Arbor
     ?
.05   La Puirée
     ?
.21   english
     England
.23   Gomorrha...Lots
     Cities of the Plain
.28   Thawland
     ? (just "Thor's land"?)
.28   Har danger
     Hardanger Fjord
.32   cripples gait
     Cripplegate (London)
.33   lungachers
     Long Acre (London)
.33   seven sisters
     Seven Sisters (London)
.33   warmwooed woman scrubbs
     ?Wormwood Gate
     Wormwood Scrubs (London)
580.01   arenotts
     ?Arnott's Dept Store
.01   ponted vodavalls
     ?Vauxhall (London)
.03   congested districts
     Congested Districts
.04   Peter's sawyery...Paoli's wharf
     St Peter's, Paul's (Wood)
     Wharf (London)
.05   Rachel's lea
     ?
.05   Dominic's gap
     ?
.12   battle of Multaferry
     Mullafarry
     Multyfarnham
.17   Pervinca calling
     ?Bluebell
.18   Soloscar hears
     ?Selskar
.22   dollymount
     Dollymount
.22   tumbling
     Dublin
.25   his hydrocomic establishment
     Lucan: Hydropathic Spa and
     Hotel
     Tavern, The

.25   ambling limfy
         Liffey
.28   fenian's bark
         Phoenix Park
.31   O'Connell
         O'Connell Br
.32   butted
         Butt Br
.32   grattaned
         Essex Br
.34   Eryan's isles
         Ireland
.34   Malin
         Malin Head (N-most point
         of Ire; in Ulster)
.34   Clear
         Clear Island (S-most point
         of Ire; in Munster)
.34   Carnsore Point
         Carnsore Point (SE-most
         point of Ire; in Leinster)
.34   Slynagollow
         Slyne Head (W-most point
         of mainland Connacht)
581.06 swanee
         Swanee R
.09   cornerwall fark
         Cornwall
.10   tark
         Turkey
.12   nagginneck pass
         ?
.14   dipper
         Ursa Major: the Dipper
.14   martian's
         Mars
.19   maidavale
         Maida Vale
.20   illian...willyum
         ?Troy
.24   monomyth
         Wellington Monument
.27   hebdromadary
         Revue Hebdomadaire
.31   grippes
         Greece
.31   rumblions
         Rome
582.06 devil's punchbowl
         Devil's Punchbowl
.07   angleseaboard
         Anglesey

.21   Dyfflinsborg
         Castle, The
         Dublin (Dyflin)
.25   Iarland
         Ireland
.26   Maizenhead
         Mizen Head (W Co Cork)
.26   Youghal
         Youghal (E Co Cork)
.28   Derg
         Derg, Lough
.29   patrick's purge
         St Patrick's Purgatory
.31   Redspot
         Jupiter: Red Spot
.32   dullakeykongsbyogblagroggers-
         wagginline
         Blackrock
         Dalkey
         Dalkey, Kingstown, and Black-
         rock Tram Line
         Dun Laoghaire
.33   Lootherstown
         Booterstown
.33   Onlyromans
         Rome
.35   Leary, leary...kings down
         Dun Laoghaire (Kingstown)
583.02 juniper arx
         Jupiter
         Rome: Capitoline Hill
.03   tartanelle...strait's
         Hellespont (Dardanelles)
.09   Bigrob dignagging
         Brobdingnag
.09   lylyputtana
         Lilliput
.10   io, io
         Jupiter: Io (satellite)
.11   ganymede
         Jupiter: Ganymede (satellite)
.12   Bossford
         Bosporus
.13   phospherine
         Venus: "Phosphorus"
.14   Persia's blind
         Persia
.16   Urania
         Uranus
.17   titaning
         Saturn: Titan (satellite)

.17 rhean
    Saturn: Rhea (satellite)

.18 china's dragon
    China

.18 japets
    Japan
    Saturn: Japetus (satellite)

.19 Satyrdaysboost
    Saturn

.19 Phoebe's nearest
    Saturn: Phoebe (satellite)

.20 Irryland
    Ireland

.21 malahide
    Malahide

.21 Liv
    Liffey

.22 jettyblack rosebuds
    Ireland: Little Black Rose

.22 nonpaps of nan
    Dana, Paps of

.24 park's police
    Phoenix Park

.25 county bubblin
    Dublin County

.36 yorkers
    York

584.06 old kent road
    Old Kent Road (London)

.09 empsyseas
    Marylebone Cricket Club

.16 norsery pinafore
    Marylebone Cricket Club:
      "The Nursery"

.18 hambledown
    Hambledon

.19 ovalled
    Oval, The (London)

.21 laugh...neigh
    ?Neagh, Lough

.29 belle to the beau
    ?Phoenix Park: Beau-Belle
      Walk
    St Mary-le-Bow: Bow Bells

.31 tipherairy
    Tipperary

585.02 Neptune's Centinel
    Neptune
    Neptune Rowing Club
      (Ringsend)

.02 Tritonville Lightowler
    Neptune: Triton

.02 Tritonville Lightowler (*Cont.*)
    Tritonville Rd (Ringsend)

.09 ringasend
    Ringsend

.21 Dublin
    Dublin

.28 Donnelly's orchard
    Donnelly's Orchard

.29 Fairbrother's field
    Fairbrother's Fields

586.09 Madeleine
    Magdalen

.11 humbledown
    Hambledon

.12 maudlin river
    Magdalen

.15 Mag Dillon
    Magdalen

.15 Dupling
    Dublin

.18 homelet...hothel
    ?Home's Hotel

.25 roamer's numbers
    Rome

.27 cornish token
    Cornwall

.27 appullcelery
    Appenzell

.29 crumlin
    Crumlin

.30 turkling
    ?Turkey

587.04 Jimmy d'Arcy
    ?D'Arcy's Anchor Brewery

.06 Mountjoys
    Mountjoy

.08 Theoatre Regal's
    Theatre Royal

.08 Cambridge Arms
    ?Cambridge

.11 his Whitby hat
    Whitby

.15 wall...afore the hole
    ?Phoenix Park: Hole in the
      Wall

.21 Melmoth
    Melmoth

.21 Natal
    Natal

.23 sutton
    Sutton

.25	Phoenix Rangers'...parkies		.08	three golden balls
	Phoenix Park			?Golden Ball
.25	meeting of the waitresses		.09	the bourse
	Meeting of the Waters			Bourse
.26	Elsies from Chelsies		.20	seven...parishlife
	Chelsea			?Glendalough: Seven Churches
588.02	beggar's bush		.22	fenland
	Beggarsbush			?Finland
.02	Carryone			Ireland: Misc Allusions
	Garryowen		.27	fives' court
.04	old face's			Four Courts
	Iveagh			?Ireland: The Five Fifths
.05	hardalone		.30	plateglass housewalls
	Ardilaun			?Glasshouse
.09	musichall visit		.36	explosium of his distilleries
	Music Hall			?Roe's Distillery
.11	corkiness		590.05	Phoenis
	?Cork			Phoenix Fire Insurance Co
.13	brown freer		.05	Lloyd's
	?St Mary of the Angels			Lloyd's of London
	Church ("Brown Friars")		.09	grand tryomphal arch
.14	dolour, O so			Arch of Triumph (+ rainbow)
	?Our Lady of Dolours		.13	Wu Welsher
	Church			Wales
.15	seepoint		.17	Nebob
	Seapoint			?Nebo, Mt
.15	kingmount shadow		.17	Nephilim
	?			?Niflheim
.16	hofd a-hooded			(+ Nephilim, Biblical giants)
	Howth		.20	sweetish mand
.24	Mizpah			Sweden
	Mizpah		.21	bagdad
.29	Killdoughall fair			Bagdad
	Killdroughalt		.22	easteredman
.32	windy arbour			Norway (Ostmen)
	Windy Arbour		.25	oldbrawn
589.01	maypoleriding			Oldbawn (SW Dublin)
	Maypole		.26	scalp
.02	chiltren's hundred			Scalp, The (SE Dublin)
	Chiltern		.26	drummed all he dun
.04	rushroads			Dundrum (S Dublin)
	Rush		.27	inch of his core
.07	mayom			Inchicore (W Dublin)
	Mayo		.29	Rumbling
.07	tuam			Dublin
	Tuam			

BOOK IV

593.02   downs to dayne
         Denmark
   .03   Eireweeker
         Ireland
   .05   Osseania
         Ireland: Misc Allusions
         Oceania
   .11   daynes...daynes to dawn
         Denmark
   .13   albas Temoram
            Scotland: Alba
            Temora
   .17   **genghis**
         Guinness's Brewery
   .21   domnatory of Defmut
         ?Deaf and Dumb Institution
   .24   Ntamplin
         Dublin
594.02   Arcthuris
            Arcturus (+ King Arthur)
   .04   Tirtangel
         Tintagel
   .05   Durbalanars
         Dublin
         ?Durban
   .08   semitary of Somnionia
         Iona
         ?Ionia
   .08   Heliotropolis
         Heliopolis
         (+ Dublin)
   .09   castellated
         Dublin Coat of Arms
   .12   warful dune's battam
         ?Denmark
         Woovil Doon Botham
   .15   annew
            Annu: Heliopolis
   .18   Ahlen Hill's
            Allen, Hill of
   .23   Fangaluvu Bight
            ?Fingal
            ?Galway (Bay)
   .27   Dane the Great
         Denmark

   .28   Edar's
            Howth: Ben Edar
   .29   duan Gallus
            ?Donegal
   .30   Sassqueehenna
            Susquehanna R
   .34   Alliman
            ?Germany
   .34   turnkeyed trot
            Turkey
   .34   Seapoint
            Seapoint
   .35   Noel's Bar and Julepunsch
            ?
   .36   Henge Ceolleges
            ?
            (just "hedge schools"? *Ceol*,
               Ir "music")
595.01   Exmooth
            ?Exmouth
   .01   Ostbys
            ?Oxmantown
   .03   Hill of Hafid
            Howth
   .03   knock and knock
            Castleknock: Castleknock Hill,
               Windmill Hill
   .03   nachasach
            England: Sasanach
   .04   gazelle channel
            ?Gazelle Peninsula
   .06   evar for a damse
            Adam and Eve's
   .10   Newirgland's premier
            Ireland
            New Ireland
            New Island

         Page 595 contains the names of
         27 Irish counties. Missing: Cos Derry,
         Down, Dublin, Mayo, and Tyrone.
   .10   korps
            Cork
   .12   limericks
            Limerick

.12 waterfowls
    Waterford
.12 wagsfools
    Wexford
.12 louts
    Louth
.13 cold airs
    Kildare
.13 late trams
    Leitrim
.13 curries
    Kerry
.13 curlews
    Carlow
.13 leekses
    Laois (Leix)
.14 orphalines
    Offaly
.14 tunnygulls
    Donegal
.14 clear goldways
    ?Claregalway (town)
    Clare
    Galway
.14 lungfortes
    Longford
.15 moonyhaunts
    Monaghan
.15 fairmoneys
    Fermanagh
.15 coffins
    Cavan
.15 tantrums
    Antrim
.16 armaurs
    Armagh
.16 waglugs
    Wicklow
.16 rogues comings
    Roscommon
.16 sly goings
    Sligo
.17 larksmathes...homdsmeethes...
    quailsmeathes
    Meath
    Westmeath
.17 kilalooly
    ?Kilkenny
    ?Killala
    ?Killaloe
.19 alpsulumply
    Alps

.19 alpsulumply (*Cont.*)
    ?Dublin: Alp Uí Laoghaire
.20 youpoorapps
    ?Europe
.22 vellumtomes muniment
    ?City Hall: Muniment Room
    Wellington Monument
.22 Arans Duhkha
    Aran Islands (+ "Iron Duke")
.23 hoseshoes
    ?Dublin Horse Show
.26 Mankaylands
    ?Man, Isle of
.28 Deepereras
    Tipperary
.33 Syd
    ?Nova Scotia: Sydney
    Sydney (Australia)
596.01 milchgoat fairmesse
    ?Killorglin
    Zurich: Milchbuck
.02 hundering...manhood
    Manhood, Hundred of
.05 ersekind
    Ireland: Erse
.07 fram
    ?"Fram"
.08 Banba
    Ireland: Banba
.11 Tumbarumba mountain
    Tumbarumba
.12 rassias
    Russia
.12 leery subs of dub
    Dublin
    Dun Laoghaire
.12 the Diggins ·
    ?
.13 Woodenhenge
    Woodhenge
.13 spawnish oel
    Spain
.14 the sousenugh
    England: Sasanach
.15 fert in fort
    ?Forth, Firth of
    Rhodes
.16 forefivest
    Ireland: The Five Fifths
.21 maybole gards
    Maypole

.22   Elga
           Ireland: Inis Ealga
.24   atman as evars
           Adam and Eve's
.25   palatin
           ?Palatinate, The
.29   Jambudvispa Vipra
           Jambu
.31   sorensplit and paddypatched
           ?Irish Free State
.36   Fingal
           Fingal
.36   Loughlin's Salts
           Lochlann
597.06 oddes bokes
           Oddi (Iceland)
.07   livesliving
           Liffey
.13   the sourdsite...Moskiosk
           Djinpalast
           Mecca
           Moscow
.14   the bathouse and the bazaar
           Turkish Baths (and Fred
             Barrett's Bazaar)
.14   the sponthesite...the alcovan
           and the rosegarden
           NPN? Al-Koran, and "The
             Rosegarden" by 13th-
             century poet, Sadi
.20   lucksloop
           Leixlip
.35   eaden fruit
           Eden
598.06 the Nil
           Nile R
.06   Victorias neanzas
           Victoria Nyanza
.06   Alberths neantas
           Albert Nyanza
.15   earopean .
           Europe
.16   Ind
           India
.19   Tamal
           Tamil
.28   Ysat Loka
           Chapelizod
           Lucan
.28   Hearing
           Ireland

599.09 tolkan
           Tolka
.20   Angar
           ?
.20   Anker
           ?
600.02 this drury world
           Drury Lane
.04   lad..lane
           ?Lad Lane
.05   pool of Innalavia
           Liffey
.05   Saras the saft as
           ?Island Bridge
.06   Deltas Piscium
           Pisces
.06   Sagittariastrion
           Sagittarius
.08   poddlebridges
           Poddle R
.08   river of lives
           Liffey
.10   Cleethabala
           Dublin: Baile Átha Cliath
.10   the kongdomain of the Alieni
           ?
           (just "foreigners"?)
.11   Libnud Ocean
           Dublin
           Irish Sea
.11   Moylamore
           Moyle, Sea of
.12   Allbroggt Neandser
           Albert Nyanza
.12   Viggynette Neeinsee
           Victoria Nyanza
.13   Linfian Fall
           Lia Fáil
           Liffey
.15   Gage's Fane
           NPN: "Gage Fane," the air
             of Moore's " 'Tis Believed
             That This Harp"
.22   Vitalba
           ?Scotland: Alba
           (vit, Swed "white"; alba, Lat
             "white")
.24   Saxenslyke
           Saxony
.25   Anglesen
           Anglesey

.25   juties
    Jutland
.28   Barindens
    ?
28   white alfred
    White Horse (of Wanstead)
.29   *Elochlannensis*
    Lochlann
.30   Leeambye
    ?Lambay Island
    ?Williamstown
.33   goodbroomirish
    Ireland
.35   Mainylands
    ?Hy Many
.36   by that look...sure
    Glendalough: "By That Lake
      Whose Gloomy Shore"
.36   glaum is
    ?Dunsinane: Glamis
601.04   lake lemanted
    Leman, Lac
.05   citye of Is
    Ys
.05   atlanst
    Atlantis
.06   wasseres of Erie
    Erie, Lake
    Ireland
.11   the samphire coast
    ?Ireland's Eye
    ?Samphire Island
.17   Botany Bay
    Botany Bay (prison colony)
    Trinity College, Dublin
.18   singsing
    Sing Sing (prison)

The churches in 601.21−.28 are
all in Dublin and environs, and all RC.
Identifications for the most part follow
John Kelleher's in The Analyst *X, 5f.*

.21   S. Wilhelmina's
    St Agatha's Church (William
      St)
.21   S. Gardenia's
    St Francis Xavier's Church
      (Gardiner St)
.21   S. Phibia's
    St Peter's Church (Phibsbor-
      ough)
    Phibsborough

.21   S. Veslandrua's
    St Andrew's Church (Westland
      Row)
.22   S. Clarinda's
    Carmelite (Discalced) Church
      (Clarendon St)
.22   S. Immecula's
    Immaculate Heart of **Mary**
      Church
.22   S. Dolores Delphin's
    Our Lady of Dolours Church
      (Dolphin's Barn)
    Dolphin's Barn
.22   S. Perlanthroa's
    St Joseph's Church (Portland
      Row)
.23   S. Errands Gay's
    St Paul's Church (Arran Quay)
    Arran Quay
.23   S. Eddaminiva's
    Adam and Eve's (Church)
.23   S. Rhodamena's
    Our Lady of Refuge Church
      (Rathmines)
    Rathmines
.23   S. Ruadagara's
    Three Patrons, Church of the
      (Rathgar)
    Rathgar
.24   S. Drimicumtra's
    Corpus Christi Church (Drum-
      condra)
    Drumcondra
.24   S. Una Vestity's
    St Kevin's (University) Chapel
.24   S. Mintargisia's
    St Paul's College (Mt Argus)
.25   S. Misha-La-Valse's
    St Michan's Church
.25   S. Churstry's
    St Mary of the Angels Church
      (Church St)
.25   S. Clouonaskieym's
    Milltown Park Chapel (Clons-
      keagh)
    Clonskeagh
.25   S. Bellavistura's
    Visitation, Church of the (Fair-
      view)
    Fairview

.26   S. Santamonta's
    Stella Maris Church (Sandy-
    mount)
    Sandymount
.26   S. Ringsingsund's
    St Patrick's Church (Rings-
    end)
    Ringsend
.26   S. Heddadin Drade's
    St Mary's Church (Hadding-
    ton Rd)
.27   S. Glacianivia's
    Our Lady of Dolours Church
    (Glasnevin)
    Glasnevin
.27   S. Waidafrira's
    Carmelite (Calced) Church
    ("White Friars")
.27   S. Thomassabbess's
    St Thomas à Becket, Abbey
    of
.28   S. Loellisotoelles
    St Lawrence O'Toole's
    Church
.30   Euh...seu
    Eu
.32   bed, cavern...shrine
    Glendalough: St Kevin's Bed
.32   Kathlins...kitchin
    Glendalough: St Kevin's
    Kitchen
.34   austrologer
    Australia
.35   Newer Aland
    New Ireland
.36   Milenesia
    Melanesia
.36   Be smark
    Bismarck Archipelago
602.02−.05 leeward...windward
    Society Islands
.11   Rowlin's tun
    ? (just "rolling stone"?)
.13   Jarama
    Jarama R
.13   Roga's stream
    ?
.14   Croona
    Crona R
.15   Greyglens
    NPN: Song, "John O'Dwyer
    of the Glen"

.15   Potterton's forecoroners
    Four Courts
    ?Porterstown
.17   independant reporter
    Irish Independent
.17   Portlund...burrow
    ?Portland Row
.18   the latterman's Resterant
    ?
.19   Durban Gazette
    Dublin Gazette
    Durban
.20   Upper and Lower Byggotstrade
    Baggot St
.21   Ciwareke
    NPN? Anagram of "Earwicker"
.22   Valleytemple
    ?
.28   Londan
    London
.30   polar bearing
    Bering Sea
    Polaris
.30   touthena
    Ton-thena (star)
.35   Grimstad galleon
    ?Grimstad
.36   geese and peeas and oats
    General Post Office (GPO)
603.17 pursueded
    ?Sweden
.19   samoans
    ?Samoa
.22   Greet Chorsles street
    Charles St, Great
.27   Debbling
    Dublin
.29   dubbledecoys
    Dublin
.34   tora
    Tora R
604.04 Bregia's plane
    Bregia, Plain of
.04   Teffia
    Teffia
.06   mess...close. Withun
    St Swithin's Church
.08   theirinn
    Ireland
.12   greek Sideral Reulthway
    ?Great Southern and Western
    Railway

.12   greek Sideral Reulthway (*Cont.*)
        Greece

.14   vialact...milk train...gallaxion
        Milky Way

.17   Strubry Bess
        Strawberry Beds

.17   waggonwobblers
        Ursa Major: the Wagon

.22   Gaulls
        Gaul

.23   free state on the air
        Irish Free State

.24   Eyrlands Eyot
        Ireland's Eye

.25   Meganesia
        ?Melanesia

.25   Habitant
        Canada: "Les Habitants"

.25   onebut thousand insels
        Thousand Islands (Canada)

In the St Kevin passage, on
605.04–606.12, St Kevin is concen-
trically located in his bath/altar, on
an islet in a pond on an island in one
of the Glendalough lakes, which is
on the island of Ireland surrounded
by the ocean: seven circles.

605.04 ysland of Yreland
        Ireland

.05   yrish archipelago
        Ireland

.11   Glendalough-le-vert
        Glendalough

.12   meeting waters
        Meeting of the Waters

.12   river Yssia...Essia river
        ?

.15   orders hibernian
        Ireland: Hibernia

.17   lake Ysle
        ?Innisfree

.19   Yshgafiena...Yshgafiuna
        Phoenix Park (*fionn uisge*)

606.14 the three Benns
        ?

.17   Bristol
        Bristol

.20   franklings
        France

.25   monster trial
        ?Munster

.26   penmark
        ?Penmark

.32   claddaghs
        Claddagh

607.01 Marino
        Marino

.08   Jakob van der Bethel
        Bethel

.08   Essav of Messagepostumia
        Mesopotamia

.12   Heroes' Highway
        ?

.14   Champelysied...Chappielassies
        Champs Elysées
        Chapelizod
        Elysian Fields

.20   Sveasmeas
        Sweden

.26   departamenty
        Amenta

.27   hothehill
        Howth

.27   the hollow
        Phoenix Park: The Hollow

.30   Tumplen Bar
        Dublin Bar
        Temple: Temple Bar

.34   Blanchardstown
        Blanchardstown

608.04 bunkum
        Buncombe

.08   Niece
        Nice

.08   Ballyhooly
        Ballyhooly

.10   bledprusshers
        Prussia

.14   Mister Ireland
        Ireland

.14   And a live
        Liffey

.20   beckerbrose
        Becker, Brothers (tea)

.21   foochoor
        Foochow (tea)

.24   ohahnthenth
        ?Waterloo: Sunken Road of
        Ohain

.25   royalirish uppershoes
        Ireland

.29 the blackshape, *Nattenden Sorte*
?
(quotes Ibsen's poem
"Borte," "før natten den
sorte," "With the night
coming on")

.29 hindled firth and hundled furth
Dublin: Baile Átha Cliath
Forth, Firth of

.31 Ashias
Asia

.32 Phoenician wakes
Phoenicia

609.15 inplayn unglish
England

.15 Wynn's Hotel
Wynn's Hotel

.16 Bullbeck
Balbec
Heliopolis: Baalbek

.16 Oldboof, Sassondale, Jorsey
Uppygard, Mundelonde, Ab-
beytotte, Bracqueytuitte with
Hockeyvilla, Fockeyvilla
Balbec

.18 Hillewille
Hell

.18 Wallhall
Valhalla

.25 Old Head of Kettle
?Kinsale, Old Head of

.34 cabrattlefield
Cabra

.34 slaine
Slane

610.04 the memorialorum
?Wellington Monument

.06 Rhedonum
Rhodes
Rhone R

.07 ubideintia...fenicitas
Dublin Motto

.08 fenicitas
Zurich: St Felix

.10 rugular
Zurich: St Regula

.12 Eurasian Generalissimo
Asia
Europe
(+ "Russian General")

.32 Erinmonker
Ireland

.35 Grand Natural
Fairyhouse Racecourse: the
Grand National

611.05 islish
Ireland

.05 chinchinjoss
China

.30 hunghoranghoangoly tsinglontseng
Hwang Ho R

.35 essixcoloured
?Essex St

612.08 Indian gem
India

.15 Ebblybally
Dublin: Eblana

.20 Iro's Irismans
Ireland: Iris

.35 His Ards
Down: Baronies of The Ards

613.01 Good safe firelamp...Goldselfor-
elump!
England
Ireland

.05 Taawhaar
?Tara

.09 Taborneccles
?Eccles St

.15 laud of laurens
Christchurch Cathedral: Chapel
of St Laud
?Laurens Co

.18 Amenta
Amenta

.28 olympically
Olympia
Olympus, Mt

614.02 Annone Wishwashwhose
?

.03 Ormepierre Lodge
NPN: *orme, pierre*, Fr "elm,"
"stone"

.03 Doone of the Drumes
Dundrum
Dundrum Bay

.08 mournenslaund
Mourne (Mts)

.13 mannormillor
Manor Mill Steam Laundry
(Dundrum)

.24 plainplanned liffeyism
Liffey

.25   Eblania's
            Dublin: Eblana
.25   dim delty Deva
            Deva
            Dublin Allusion: "Dear Dir-
            ty Dublin"
.27   vicociclometer
            ?Vico Rd
615.04 all-too-ghoulish
            Gaul
.04   illyrical
            Illyria
.04   innumantic
            Numantia
.04   our mutter nation
            Ireland: Misc Allusions
.12   Dear...Dirtdump
            Dublin Allusion: "Dear Dir-
            ty Dublin"
.20   Williamstown
            Williamstown
.20   Mairrion Ailesbury
            Ailesbury (Rd)
            Merrion (Rd)
            (These roads intersect N of
            Williamstown)
.26   brinks of the wobblish
            Wabash R
.31   margarseen oil
            Magazine Fort
616.02 Coolock
            Coolock
.03   Eirinishmhan
            ?Aran Islands: Inishmaan
            Ireland
.04   Oldhame
            Oldham
.05   Hibernia metal
            Ireland: Hibernia
.11   three Sulvans of Dulkey
            Dalkey
            ?Turkey
.11   two Peris of Monacheena
            ?
.21   Cloon's
            ?
.30   giantstand of manunknown
            ?Man, Isle of: Manannan
.33   Ruggers' Rush
            Beggarsbush
            Irish Rugby Union (Beggars-
            bush)

617.06 old Fintona
            Dublin Allusion: "Finn's
            Town"
            Fintona
.06   thank Danis
            Denmark
.12   pork martyrs
            Phoenix Park: Phoenix Park
            Murders
.21   Allso brewbeer
            Allsop and Sons (ale)
.22   Manchem House Horsegardens
            Mansion House
.22   Morning post
            Morning Post
.23   Boston transcripped
            Boston: *Boston Transcript*
.36   Swees Auburn
            Auburn
.36   straith fitting
            ?
618.02 virgils...Armsworks, Limited
            NPN: 1st line of *Aeneid*, "Arma
            virumque cano"
.08   Bully's Acre
            Bully's Acre
            Clontarf
.08   Boot lane
            Boot Lane
.11   the Sweeps hospital
            St Patrick's Hospital
.15   sympowdhericks purge
            St Patrick's Purgatory
.22   Wanterlond Road
            Waterloo (Rd)
            Wonderland
.22   cubarola
            Cuba
.23   beaux to my alce
            ?Beaux' Walk
.23   Hillary Allen
            Allen, Hill of
.24   opennine knighters
            Apennine Mts
.34   Nollwelshian
            Norway
            Wales
619.03 Finnlatter...grocerest churcher
            Findlater, Alexander, and Co
            Findlater's Church
.06   Rathgarries
            Rathgar

.11   pigs and scuts
      Scotland

.11   two worlds
      Two Worlds

.12   himp of holth
      Howth

.16   Alma Luvia
      ?Alma R
      ?Lee R
      Liffey

.20   I am leafy
      Liffey

.25   man of the hooths
      Howth

.29   I am leafy...life
      Liffey

.32   offly
      ?Offaly

.36   everthelest
      ?Everest, Mt

620.03   nill, Budd
      Dublin
      Nile R

.04   Rosensharonals
      Sharon

.05   Proudpurse Alby
      Albion (England)

.05   pooraroon Eireen
      Ireland

.08   Lucan
      Lucan

.09   erse
      Ireland: Erse

.09   the Dark Countries
      ?

.11   Rathgreany way
      ?Athgreany

.15   twinngling
      ?Tavern, The

.21   Laundersdale Minssions
      Lauderdale Mansions (London)

.30   gricks
      Greece

.34   cove and haven
      Copenhagen

621.01   Phoenix
      Phoenix Park

.06   Gustsofairy
      Ireland

.08   Send Arctur guiddus
      Arcturus (+ King Arthur,
        Arthur Guinness, and "St
        Anthony Guide")

.11   Finvara
      Finvarra
      Kinvara

.13   Blugpuddels
      ?Blackpool
      ?Dublin

.14   Oaxmealturn
      ?Oxmantown

.18   Market Norwall
      ?North Wall Quay

.19   Isaacsen's
      ?

.21   Mineninecyhandsy
      Phoenix Park: Hole in the Wall

.34   church by the hearseyard
      Chapelizod: House by the
        Churchyard, The

622.01   Coole
      ?Coole

.06   lodge of Fjorn na Galla
      ?Fingal

.07   Uncle Tim's Caubeen...Viker Eagle
      Phoenix Park: Viceregal Lodge

.20   Les go dutc
      Dublin United Tramways Co
      Netherlands

.20   Danegreven
      Denmark
      Howth: Duncriffan

.24   moskors
      ?Moscow

The foxhunt described at 622.24–623.03 is the Ward Union Staghounds and takes place near the Naul, Co Meath, mainly in the parish of Clonalvy, barony of Duleek Upper. The names in lines .34–.35 are (except for Snowton) all of townlands.

.25   Wald Unicorns
      Ward Union Staghounds

.25   the Naul
      Naul, The

.27   Tallyhaugh
      NPN? "Tally-ho"

.27   Ballyhuntus
      NPN? "Town of the hunt"

.34   Heathtown
         Heathtown
.34   Harbourstown
         Harbourstown
.34   Snowtown
         Snowton Castle
.34   Four Knocks
         Fourknocks
.34   Flemingtown
         Flemingstown
.35   Bodingtown
         Bodingtown
.35   Ford of Fyne on Delvin
         Delvin R
         Ford of Fyne
.36   the Platonic garlens
         Botanic Gardens (N Dublin)

   On pp 623–625 Anna Livia im-
agines an excursion (by tram, 622.20)
to Howth with her husband – one they
will never take.

623.06   promnentory
         Howth
.10   hoothoothoo
         Howth
.10   ithmuthisthy
         Sutton
.15   Armor
         Armorica
.16   magyerstrape...Hungerig
         Hungary
.19   castles air
         ?Castle, The
         Howth: Howth Castle
.24   rollcky road adondering
         Dublin Allusion: "Rocky
         Road to Dublin"
.25   heathery benn
         Howth: Ben Edar
.26   Drumleek
         Howth: Drumleck Point
.27   Evora
         Howth: Evora
.27   moon of mourning
         ?Mourne
.28   Glinaduna
         Glen of the Downs
.31   mains of me draims
         Main Drain
.36   traumscrapt from Maston, Boss
         Boston: *Boston Transcript*

624.09   bubel runtoer
         Babel, Tower of
.11   Scale the summit
         Howth: The Summit
.15   limpidy marge
         Trinity Church
.16   Donachie's yeards
         ?
.18   sinfintins
         Howth: St Fintan's
.19   bailby
         ?Bailey Lighthouse (Howth)
.21   shield Martin
         Howth: Sheilmartin
.22   Leafiest
         Liffey
.24   oiled of kolooney
         ?Collooney
         ?Killiney
.25   Alpine Smile
         Alps
.26   Houlth's nose
         Howth: Nose of Howth
.32   Bray
         Bray
.33   Brostal
         ?Bristol
         Borstal
         Tavern, The: Bridge Inn
625.01   Marienne Sherry
         France: "Marianne"
.02   Jermyn cousin
         Germany
.03   Pharaops
         ?Pharos at Alexandria
.04   king of Aeships
         Egypt

   From 625.05 to the end, the Lif-
fey is flowing through Dublin, meeting
the tide at Island Bridge (626.07), to the
sea.

.11   barsalooner
         Barcelona
.13   *Finglas since the Flood*
         Finglas
.17   Clane turf
         Clane
         Clontarf
.20   Dom on dam
         Christchurch Cathedral

.21 olympics...Steadyon
　　Olympia: Stadion

.22 Cooloosus
　　Colossus of Rhodes

.25 Neighboulotts
　　Lotts

.26 Eblanamagna
　　Dublin: Eblana

.27 dumblynass
　　Dublin

.28 I lose my breath...I'll begin again
　　Liffey

.33 jiffey
　　Liffey

.34 vagurin
　　?

.36 Londub
　　Dublin
　　London

626.01 Annamores leep
　　Annamoe

.02 if you le, bowldstrong
　　?St Mary-le-Bow (+ Strong-
　　bow)

.03 adamant evar
　　Adam and Eve's

.04 norewere
　　Norway

.06 **Lashlanns**
　　Lochlann (Norway)

.07 island, bridge
　　Island Bridge

.11 Shackvulle Strutt
　　O'Connell St

.18 Vikloefells
　　Wicklow (Hills)

.19 blubles
　　Bluebell

.19 sealskers
　　Selskar

.25 I'd frozen up...Three times
　　Liffey

.28 Indelond
　　Ireland

.33 duv...div. Inn this linn
　　Dublin
　　Howth: Black Linn

627.03 Imlamaya
　　?Himalaya Mts

.27 allaniuvia
　　Liffey

.28 Amazia
　　Amazon R

.30 Niluna
　　Nile R

.31 Ho hang! Hang ho!
　　Hwang Ho R

628.03 moyles and moyles
　　Moyle, Sea of

.03 moananoaning
　　?Mona
　　(+ Manannan)

.05 therrble prongs
　　(N and S Walls, extending into
　　Dublin Bay)

.06 moremens
　　Irish Sea: *Muir Meann*

.06 Avelaval
　　Liffey

.07 Lff
　　Liffey

.09 bearing
　　?Bering Sea

.10 Arkangels
　　Archangel

PART II
Alphabetical Gazetteer

A

ABBEY THEATRE (16/34). Cor of Lwr Abbey St and Marlborough St. Sponsored by Lady Gregory and W B Yeats, among others, to produce Ir plays by Ir authors, it opened 27 Dec 1904, burned 1951; the new *A* was completed in 1966.

    105.26   *From Abbeygate to Crowalley*
    ?167.18   This thing, Mister Abby, is nefand
    ?237.33   Labbeycliath longs
    ?285.01   habby cyclic erdor
    ?483.08   this master the abbey

ABECEDARIAN SOCIETY. Instituted 1789 in Dub, it became in 1797 the Literary Teacher's Soc; it was a "friendly society" for the protection and relief of its members.

    198.20   at skol, you antiabecedarian

ABOUKIR (ABUKIR). Bay and vill, 13 mi NE of Alexandria, Egypt; site of anc Canopus. In *A* Bay was fought the "Battle of the Nile" (1798) in which Nelson defeated the Fr fleet. Later, Napoleon defeated Turks (1799) and Sir Ralph Abercromby defeated Fr (1801) there.

    10.17   Ap Pukkaru

ABRAHAM, PLAINS OF (HEIGHTS OF ABRAHAM). SW of the upr town of Quebec City, Can, above steep cliffs to the St Lawrence R. Gen Wolfe's army scaled the heights and took Quebec in Sept 1759 in a battle in which both Wolfe and Montcalm were killed.

    78.15   The other spring offensive on the heights of Abraham

ABYSSINIA. Now Ethiopia, kingdom, E Afr; cap, Addis Ababa (qv). It contains the Blue Nile (see *Nile*). Main lang is Amharic, after the cen prov, Amhara.

    223.28   O theoperil! Ethiaop lore, the poor lie [anagrams of "heliotrope"]
    318.32   wefting stinks from Alpyssinia
    489.20   as we sayed it in our Amharican

ACHILL ("EAGLE") ISLAND. Largest isl off Ire, in Co Mayo, just off Curraun penin.

    248.11   My top it was brought Achill's low [with Achilles: the answer to the
                 riddle is "heel-eye-trope," heliotrope]

ACQUA VERGINE. Roman aqueduct built by Agrippa in 19 BC. By legend, a young girl (some say her name was Trivia) first showed its source near Salone, 14 mi from Rome, to some thirsty Roman soldiers. It feeds the Trevi fountain and is considered by Romans the best of local waters.

    ?365.09   these mispeschyites of the first virginial water

ACRE. Seaport city, N Pal; anc 'Akka, later Ptolemaïs. Its hist since bibl times has been a succession of sieges and captures. Contested for cents by Israelites and Syrians. Chief Pal port for Crusaders from 1110, recaptured by Saladin 1187, by

Crusaders 1191, by Muslims 1291, by Turks 1517. Napoleon besieged it unsuccessfully in 1799. The Brit captured it in 1840 and restored it to the Ottoman Emp.

> 73.23   Bully Acre...last stage in the siegings round our archicitadel
> 553.08   the whole blighty acre was bladey well pessovered

ACTIUM.   Promontory and anc town, NW Gr; site of the naval victory, 31 BC, in
which Octavius defeated Marc Antony (and Cleopatra) and became emperor of Rome.

> 272.11   hot off Minnowaurs and naval actiums

ADAM AND EVE'S CHURCH (RC)   (15/34).   The 1st place name in *FW* (3.01).
Since the mid-18th cent it has been the pop name for the Franciscan ch, officially
the Church of St Francis of Assisi, on Merchant's Quay, Skipper's Alley (form Adam
and Eve's Lane, and Rosemary Lane, qv), and Cook St. *Ca* 1618, the back house of
Adam and Eve's Tav on Cook St was rented by the Franciscans as a secret chapel. In
1629 on St Stephen's Day, the chapel and Franciscan convent were demolished and
the friars arrested, on orders of the Prot Archbishop Bulkeley. A Franciscan ch was
built in 1715 off Rosemary Lane, which took its name from the tav and form chapel,
so that by 1731 "two Popish Mass Houses," "Adam and Eve's" and SS Michael and
John's, were mentioned in a survey. The ch was demolished in 1832, and the present
ch built in 1834. A plaque on the par house on Merchant's Quay identifies it as Adam
and Eve's. Presumably not every mention of "Adam and Eve" in *FW* is an allusion to
the ch, but any might be.

> 3.01   riverrun, past Eve and Adam's
> ?69.10   eddams...aves
> 83.22   Adam and Eve's in Quantity Street
> 86.04   chrystalisations of Alum on Even
> 176.04   *Adam and Ell*
> 197.12   Was her banns never loosened in Adam and Eve's
> ?267.18   Adamman,[5] Emhe
> 296.06   Hoddum and Heave, our monsterbilker
> ?377.16   *Ivy Eve in the Hall of Alum*
> 393.24   from alum and oves
> 455.17   from atoms and ifs
> 595.06   evar for a damse
> 596.24   atman as evars
> 601.23   S. Eddaminiva's
> 626.03   adamant evar

ADAM, JAMES   (16/33).   James Adam, auctioneer, had offices at 17 Merrion
Row and 19 Stephen's Green. (The only auctioneer on Wood Quay in the early 20th
cent was John Bentley.)

> 28.32   Adams and Sons, the wouldpay actionneers

ADDIS ABABA.   Cap of Abyssinia, now Ethiopia; it was founded only in 1892
by Menelek II to replace the old cap of Entotto, a few miles N.

> 537.17   I deny wholeswiping *in toto* at my own request

ADELAIDE.   (1) *A* Rd, part of S Circular Rd btwn Harcourt and Leeson Sts. It
contains the Royal Victoria Eye and Ear Hosp (15–16/32).   (2) *A* Hosp, in Peter
St; founded 1839 "for Protestants only" (15/33).   (3) City, cap of S Australia.
(4) *A* Isl, Antarctica. Penguins nest there, but no nightingale jug-jugs.

> 40.36   the Adelaide's hosspittles
> 450.17   all Adelaide's naughtingerls

ADELPHI THEATRE   (16/34).   The old name (before 1871) for the late Queen's
(Royal) Theatre, btwn 209 and 210 Gt Brunswick St. The orig Adelphi in London
was an 18th-cent version of Diocletian's palace at Split. *Adelphi*, Gk "brothers."
    219.14   As played to the Adelphi by the Brothers Bratislavoff...all the
            Queen's Mum

ADEN.   Seaport city, penin, and dist, Saudi Arabia, the "Arabia Felix" of the Romans.
    324.36   Giant crash in Aden

ADRIATIC SEA.   Arm of Medit Sea E of It. Venice is the "Queen of the *A*," but
the allusion is to Trieste, also an *A* city, where JJ fled when he left Dub in 1904.
    62.02   his citadear of refuge...beyond the outraved gales of Atreeatic

AEMILIA, VIA.   Roman rd, late 2nd cent AD, from Ariminum (Rimini) on the
Adriatic to Placentia (Piacenza). A 2nd rd of the same name was constructed in the
early 2nd cent along the NW coast of It through Genoa across the mts to join the
Via Postumia.
    129.16   half emillian via bogus census

AFRICA.   The 2nd largest continent. The Norse sagas call Afr "Blueland" (Nor,
Blaaland, qv) and its inhabitants "blue-men."
    129.32   Africa for the fullblacks
    191.04   Europasianised Afferyank
    240.17   the stem of swuith Aftreck
    320.28   he fared from Afferik Arena...Blawland
    350.21   No more basquibezigues for this pole aprican!
    387.02   Noord Amrikaans and Suid Afferican
    427.22   the inds of Tuskland where the oliphants scrum
    489.27   man who has africot lupps
    497.12   Affrian Way
    520.17   midnight mask...for African man

AGINCOURT.   Vill, N Fr, where the Eng under Henry V defeated the Fr, 25 Oct
1415.
    9.07   The jinnies is jillous agincourting

AHERLOW, GLEN OF.   Trad refuge of hunted men (in caves in the Galtee Mts)
Co Tipperary. Important as pass btwn the Golden Vale and Cork. Song: "In the Glen
of Aherlow."
    105.29   *Inn the Gleam of Waherlow*

AILESBURY   (18/31).   Rd (also Drive, Gardens, Grove and Park) in SE Dub. It
forms the bottom of a triangle whose sides are Anglesea and Merrion Rds, which
converge at Ballsbridge to become Northumberland Rd. There was a tram stop at the
intersection of Ailesbury and Merrion Rds. The Fr embassy is on the S side of *A* Rd.
See *Aylesbury*.
    235.13   among Burke's mobility at La Roseraie, Ailesbury Road
    387.09   from Strathlyffe and Aylesburg and Northumberland Anglesey
    615.20   between Williamstown and the Mairrion Ailesbury

AIX-LA-CHAPELLE.   Ger, Aachen; in NW Ger. Charlemagne's N cap and favorite
res.
    ?80.36   Issy-la-Chapelle
    334.36   Izd-la-Chapelle...Carlowman's Cup

AIX-LES-BAINS.   Thermal spa in Savoy, Fr, 8 mi N of Chambéry. Its waters were recommended for rheumatism and gout.
>   213.18   I'd want to go to Aches-les-Pains

ALABAMA RIVER.   From cen *A* State, US it flows W and then S to join the Tombigbee Riv N of Mobile, *A*. Dialect pron to rhyme with "mammy," as in "I'm Alabammy Bound."
>   578.21   her halfbend as proud as a peahen, allabalmy

ALADDIN'S CAVE.   Wyndham Lewis in *Time and Western Man* speaks of the "Aladdin's Cave" where JJ manufactured *Ulysses*.
>   108.27   this Aludin's Cove of our cagacity

ALBA.   Anc name for area in Latium, It, incl the Alban Hills. Castel Gandolfo, the papal villa and summer res, is in the Alban country and may be on the site of *A* Longa, a city imp before Rome. The motto of Pope Adrian IV was "De Rure Albo," "of the Alban country."
>   152.26   Mookse...his immobile *De Rure Albo*
>   463.24   red in Rossya, white in Alba

ALBANIA.   Mountainous country btwn Gr and Yugo on E coast of Adriatic. Cap Tirane (form Scutari). For the Albanian words on *FW* 114 see *AWN* 14 (1963), 6.
>   114.25   a darka disheen of voos from Dalbania

ALBANY.   Seaport town, SW Australia, on King George Sound. Michael Davitt, the Fenian who founded the Land League and was elected to Parliament, after spending years in Eng jails, spent 8 months in Australia in 1895, lecturing to Ir communities.
>   489.32   S. H. Devitt, that benighted irismaimed, who is tearly belaboured by
>   Sydney and Alibany

ALBERT NYANZA.   Lake (*nyanza*) in cen Afr; receives the Victoria Nile from L Victoria (Victoria Nyanza, qv) and is the source of the Albert Nile. *Quare silex*, Lat "Why are you silent?"
>   23.20   soorcelossness. Quarry silex, Homfrie Noanswa!
>   89.27   *Quare hircum?* No answer.
>   105.14   *Allbart Noahnsy*
>   202.20   found the Nihil. Worry you sighin foh, Albern, O Anser?
>   558.27   Albatrus Nyanzer
>   598.06   Nil...Alberths neantas
>   600.12   Allbroggt Neandser...Linfian Fall...Caughterect

ALBION.   Oldest name of Brit, reatined as poetical name of Eng. Many explanations for name; most prob it is derived from *albus*, Lat "white," from white cliffs that face Gaul, or perhaps from Celtic *alp*. Albion, the son of Neptune, is said to have discovered Brit and ruled for 44 years. It was Napoleon who called Eng "perfide Albion." See *Alba*.
>   137.07   Swed Albiony
>   173.13   Albiogenselman
>   264.F3   Porphyrious Olbion, redcoatliar
>   343.09   Perfedes Albionias!
>   620.05   Proudpurse Alby

ALDBOROUGH HOUSE (16/35).   At Portland Row and Killarney (form Gloucester) St. Built in the last decade of the 18th cent by the eccentric Lord Aldborough, whose wife refused to live in it. Built in the then outskirts of Dub, it bears the carved motto *Rus in Urbe*. Rechristened "Luxembourg" by Professor von Feinagle, who operated a successful sch in it from 1813. Often empty, it has been used at various times as a barracks and as a warehouse.

?104.20   *Aldborougham on the Sahara*
?551.24   I built in *Urbs in Rure*...an erdcloset

ALEXANDRIA.   Egyptian seaport city, on narrow strip of land btwn Medit Sea and L Mareotis, just W of Aboukir Bay (qv) and Rosetta mouth of the Nile (qv). On T-shaped penin; the stem was orig a mole leading to Pharos, which formed the crosspiece. Site of Pharos lighthouse (qv) and of famous library, burned by the caliph Omar in the 7th cent. Many sieges and captures; 318.11 prob refers to Cleopatra's capture of Caesar and Antony.

124.36   Jeromesolem...Huffsnuff...Andycox...Olecasandrum
?240.27   this remarklable moliman, Anaks Andrum
318.11   The Annexandreian captive conquest
439.34   burn the books...an allassundrian bompyre

ALGIERS.   Largest city and cap of Algeria. The Bab Azoun ("Gate of Grief") gave its name to one of the principal sts and to the now demolished Ft Bab Azoun.
552.28   zackbutts babazounded

ALHAMBRA.   The Moorish fortress in Granada, Sp; but in *FW* primarily the *A* Music Hall, Paris, frequented by Joyce in the 1920's, or the *A* Palace music hall in Leicester Square, London. There was also an *A* in Belfast, but none in Dub.
550.35   exhibiting her grace of aljambras...duncingk...vauxhalls

ALICE SPRINGS.   The main town in the cen Australian desert.
321.31   spring alice...down under...desert roses
395.14   a lass spring as you fancy

ALLAPALLI.   Seaport city, Kerala, SW Ind; now usually Allepey, aka Aulapalay. No known connection with Seringapatam (qv).
492.23   Syringa padham, Alleypulley

ALLEGHENY MOUNTAINS.   E US; a range of the Appalachian system.
129.17   andies [Andes] and a most alleghant spot

ALLEN, BOG OF.   Series of peat bogs, cen Ire, from about 17 mi W of Dub almost to Shannon R, in Cos Kildare, Offaly, Laois, and Westmeath; source of the Brosna, Boyne, and Barrow Rivs; traversed by Grand and Royal canals. *Móin Almhain*, Ir "Bog of Almha."
347.20   that's told in the Bok of Alam

ALLEN, HILL OF.   Hill (676 ft), 8 mi NE of Kildare, Co Kildare; famous in legend as the Otherworld seat of Finn MacCool. Seefin, a mound on its summit, is known as Finn's Chair. *Alma* or *Almhain*, Ir "whitened."
57.13   Our antheap we sensed as a Hill of Allen
83.34   hillelulia...allenalaw
377.16   *Hall of Alum*
594.18   with the rosinost top Ahlen Hill's, clubpubber
618.23   Hillary Allen sang to the opennine knighters

ALL SAINTS CHURCH (CI)   (15/35).   In Phibsborough Rd. There is no All Souls Ch in Dub.
?304.F5   Alls Sings and Alls Howls

569.08   S. Phibb

ALLSOP AND SONS   (15/34).   Ale Stores, 30 Bachelor's Walk, around the turn
of the cent. Allsop's was a Brit ale.
264.03   this ernst of Allsap's ale halliday of roaring month
377.33   Allsup, allsop!
617.21   Allso brewbeer

ALMA RIVER.   Small riv, SW Crimea, S USSR; enters Black Sea 17 mi N of Sevastopol. The Brit-Fr-Turk allies won their first battle of Crimea campaign on field of
A, 20 Sept 1854. The Charge of the Light Brigade was at Balaclava (qv).
348.11   boyars...me alma marthyrs...[.25] charme of their lyse brocade
?619.16   Alma Luvia, Pollabella

ALMEIDA.   Town, NE Port, form fortress guarding N approach from Sp. Wellington captured it from the Fr, 10 May 1811.
9.26   Almeidagad!

ALPHAND.   Rue, 13th Arr, and Ave, 16th Arr, Paris. Jean Alphand was an asst to
Baron Haussmann (see *Haussmann, Blvd*) in the 19th-cent rebuilding of Paris.
129.17   a no street hausmann when allphannd

ALPHEUS (ALPHEIOS) RIVER.   Riv in W Peloponnese, S Gr. Hercules diverted it
to clean the Augean stables. A is also a Gk riv god. The sacred riv Alph of Coleridge's
"Kubla Khan" may have derived from the A.
208.20   alpheubett buttons
242.31   His cheekmole of allaph foriverever

ALPS.   The name of the great mt system of S Eur is uncertainly derived from
either Celtic *alp*, "height," or Lat *albus*, "white," and its associations in *FW* are cor-
respondingly equivocal, even androgynous: (1) as *Anna Livia Plurabelle*, it is an oxy-
moron for the Liffey (qv); (2) as generic for "mountain," it alludes to HCE; (3) via
Alp Uī Laoghaire, mason's jargon for Dub (qv), it evokes both HCE as the city and
ALP as its river. In this entry, only more or less specific allusions to the mt chain
are listed.
The Julian Alps (?8.28, 340.06) are in NW Yugo. The Dolomite Alps (241.19,
317.34) are in NE It. Dolomite is a kind of crystalline rock, white or colored.
The pass which Hannibal crossed (81.03) with his elephants from Gaul to Italy
in 218 BC (2nd Punic War) has not been certainly identified; the passes of Mt Gen-
èvre and Mt Cenis and the Col d'Argentère have all been suggested.
8.28−.30   This is Delian alps...crimealine of the alps
17.34   alp on earwig, drukn on ild
81.03   this was Hannibal's walk
85.11   his alpenstuck in his redhand
129.34   looks down on the Suiss family Collesons whom he calls *les nouvelle*
            roches
131.13   a matchhead on an aspenstalk
137.32   he holds the holpenstake
148.22   by this alpin armlet
241.19   complexion of blushing dolomite
256.34   an alps on his druckhouse
317.34   dun darting dullemitter...moultain
318.32   wefting stinks from Alpyssinia
340.06   *the Djublian Alps and the Hoofd Ribeiro*

553.25   my alpine plurabelle
577.23   heckhisway per alptrack
595.19   You are alpsulumply wroght!
624.25   me parafume...Alpine Smile from Yesthers

ALSACE-LORRAINE.   Historically disputed region between Fr and Ger, E of the
Rhine R. Ger, *Elsass-Lothringen*.
518.18   changed feet several times...ersatz lottheringcan

ALTAMAHA RIVER.   Riv, Georgia, US; formed by confluence of the Oconee (qv)
and Ocmulgee Rivs.
469.14   my olty mutther, Sereth Maritza
549.28   where bold O'Connee weds on Alta Mahar

AMAZON RIVER.   Called the "King of Waters," but feminine in *FW*; largest riv in
the world (but Nile is longer); flows from Peruvian Andes through Brazil to Atlantic O.
?104.01   Annah the Allmaziful
113.05   dmzn!
199.13   damazon cheeks
494.35   Mrs Hamazum's
627.28   the wild Amazia...Niluna

AMBROSE.   Channel and lightship in NY harb, S of NYC.
324.04   picking up the emberose of the lizod lights

AMEN CLOSE (COURT).   London st, continues Paternoster Row, N of St Paul's
Cath. Amen Corner is the W end of Paternoster Row, so named because the monks
finished the Paternoster there as they turned down Ave Maria Lane toward St Paul's,
on Corpus Christi.
?105.02   *Oremunds Queue Visits Amen Mart*
578.29   Angell sitter or Amen Corner

AMENTA (AMENTI, AMENTET).   Egyptian Underworld (*Book of the Dead*), the
abode of spirits of the dead not yet purified. Used by Christian Egyptians to translate the Gk word *Hades*.
62.26   to be reading our Amenti...going forth by black
237.26   into the house of Amanti
411.11   Amen, ptah!
418.06   lord of loaves in Amongded
607.26   regn of durknass...dimbelowstard departamenty
613.18   glume involucrumines the perinanthean Amenta

AMERICA.   The continent or the US. Trad the "westernmost parish of Ireland,"
A is in *FW* seen, as it were, through Ir eyes, and there is little sense of its hist, its
political events, or its geographical extent. "Brother Jonathan" was an 18th cent personification of the US, giving way after the Civil War to "Uncle Sam."
3.05   rearrived from North Armorica
43.29   united states of Scotia Picta
105.36   *Unique Estates of Amessican*
130.28   United States of America
132.02   amirican
133.02   though you rope Amrique your home ruler is Dan
135.23   Mairie Quai!
176.05   *American Jump* [London st game]

?185.29	nichthemerically [*Nuchthemeron* is the Gr name for the whole period of a natural day and night]
185.31	United Stars of Ourania
191.04	Europasianised Afferyank
213.36	Brendan's herring pool...yangsee's hats
228.07	Seek hells where from yank islanders
228.19	Bretish Armerica
307.05	Brother Johnathan Signed the Pledge [Prohibition]
307.11	American Lake Poetry
318.15	aten of amilikan honey
320.15	an innvalet in the unitred stables
326.31	lief eurekason and his undishcovery of americle
355.22	Amelakins
?362.31	with Amodicum cloth
387.02	Noord Amrikaans and Suid Aferican
404.27	starspangled...crinklydoodle
427.22	the ousts of Amiracles...toll stories
442.13	land of breach of promise
?447.06	Armourican's iron core
489.20	Amharican
497.11	America Avenue
562.31	wend him to Amorica

AMIENS.   City, N Fr, on Somme R 72 mi N of Paris, site of Notre Dame Cath. The Treaty of *A*, 27 Mar 1802, was a diplomatic victory for Napoleon, but the "Peace of *A*" lasted only until 1803. *A* St and *A* (now Connolly) Rlwy Sta in Dub are rather surprisingly missing in *FW*.

443.15	pensamientos, howling for peace
549.31	potatums for amiens pease in plenty

AMSTEL RIVER.   Riv, Netherlands, now canalized, on which Amsterdam is built and after which it is named.

205.15	I amstel waiting
548.07	whiles I herr lifer amstell and been

AMSTERDAM.   City, cap, W Netherlands. Name from Amstel R; citizens abbreviate it "A'dam" (?538.25). The song runs "In Amsterdam there lived a maid,/ Now mark well what I say...." New York City (qv) was originally New *A*.

117.24	Pieter's in Nieuw Amsteldam
138.24	to find a dubbeltye in Dampsterdamp
319.16	Ampsterdampster...in his netherlumbs
352.24	Umsturdum Vonn
509.24	New Aimstirdames
532.06	Amtsadam, sir, to you
?538.25	Haddem
565.09	In Amsterdam there lived a...But how? [ellipsis in *FW*]

ANATOLIA.   Part of Turkey-in-Asia, the penin of Asia Min. Name from Gk *anatole*, "sunrise" (= east).

494.13	Arctura, Anatolia
504.30	proferring praydews to their anatolies

ANDERSON, JOHN (16/35).   Stained glass window manufacturer, at 107 Lwr Gloucester St around the turn of the cent.

318.28   Join Andersoon and Co

ANDES MOUNTAINS.   The great mt system of S Amer. Andesite is a type of lava
first investigated in the *A* by C P Buch (387.13).
    106.08   *Inglo-Andean Medoleys*
    129.17   handiest of all andies...alleghant
    387.13   explutor...three andesiters...pantellarias
    501.34   like an andeanupper balkan

ANGEL.   (1) St in the City, London, 1 block NE of Paternoster Sq and Amen Cor.
(2) The Tube stop and civic cen in Islington, London; named after the *A* tav, long
since gone.   (3) Hotel, 10-12 King's Inns Quay (15/34). There seems to have been
no *A* inn or tav in Dub's 17th-19th cent hist.
    56.26   at the Angel were herberged for him poteen
    90.13   On the site of the Angel's, you said?
    578.29   Angell sitter or Amen Corner

ANGLESEA.   (1) St, from Dame St to Aston Quay (15/34).   (2) Rd, SE Dub,
btwn Ballsbridge (Northumberland Rd) and Donnybrook (intersects Ailesbury Rd)
(17/31−32).
    387.10   from...Aylesburg and Northumberland Anglesey

ANGLESEY.   Co, NW Wales; site of Holyhead, terminus of main Brit-Ire rail-sea
route. Edwin, King of Northumberland, briefly annexed Anglesey and Isle of Man, in
early 7th cent. Among the many Viking raiders in the 9th and 10th cents was Sweyn
Forkbeard (d 1014). See *Mona.*
    387.10   forkbearded...Northumberland Anglesey
    582.07   devil's punchbowl and the deep angleseaboard
    600.25   Saxenslyke...going soever to Anglesen, free of juties

ANGLO-SAXON KINGDOMS.   The mod Eng cos of Essex, Middlesex, and Sussex
are more or less coextensive with the Saxon kingdoms of the same names which
warred agaisnt each other from the 5th to the 9th cent, when they came under the
dominion of the West Saxons of Wessex. There never was a "North Saxon" kingdom.
In *FW* they figure mainly as compass points; the Naze is a promontory on the Essex
coast, and thus the NSEW order is preserved in "norsect's...Soussex...Naze...Wissixy."
See *Saxony.*
    523.28   old middlesex party
    523.34   the norsect's divisional
    524.01   public exess females
    524.15   fronting on to the Soussex Bluffs
    524.21   by the Bloater Naze
    524.26   Wissixy kippers

ANNABELLA.   Vill, Co Cork, near Mallow. *Eanach-bile*, Ir "marsh of the old tree."
    ?512.10   Annabella, Lovabella

ANNA CARTER BRIDGE.   On rd from Sally Gap SE to Roundwood, Co Wicklow,
just W of Roundwood (Vartry) Reservoir.
    ?135.06   washes his fleet in annacrwatter

ANNAM.   Form name of cen Vietnam; cap Hue.
    179.14   Annamite Aper of Atroxity

ANNAMOE.   Vill (form *A* Br), 2 mi SW of Roundwood, Co Wicklow. Laurence

Sterne fell into the mill race here when he was 11. *A* Riv rises S of Sally Gap, flows through Luggela, Lough Tay, Lough Dan. There is an Annamore Ho on Ballyfermot Hill (Rd), just S of Chapelizod.

 626.01 Into the deeps. Annamores leep

ANNAPOLIS. (1) "Anna's City" (*polis*), and thus Dub. (2) Seaport, Maryland, US, site of US Naval Academy.

 222.07 the ambiamphions [Amphion, son of Zeus, legendary singer] of An-
      napolis, Joan MockComic
 318.24 Annapolis, my youthrib city

ANNECY. Fr city and resort, Dept of Haute-Savoïe, at end of L Annecy.

 ?532.24 anniece and far too bahad, nieceless to say

ANNER RIVER. Riv, Co Cork. Charles J Kickham's poem about the peasant girl who "lived beside the Anner, at the foot of Slievenamon," describes her as "a snow-drift 'neath the beechen bough,/ Her neck and nutbrown hair."

 199.36 anner frostivying tresses
 503.31 Beside the Annar...Slivenamond...snoodrift...beerchen bough

ANNESLEY. Br (also Rd) over Tolka R, W of Fairview Park (17/35).

 130.21 annesleyg [with other bridges]

ANNU. (1) Anc Egyptian city, aka Heliopolis (qv). (2) In Egyptian mythology, the abode of the gods; it had no geographical location.

  58.08 muertification and uxpiration and dumnation and annuhulation
 ?143.03 to be on anew
 311.12 comer forth from Anow...from Thenanow
 516.32 the annusual curse of things
 594.15 Heliotropolis...We annew

ANTARCTIC. See *Arctic.*

ANTIENT CONCERT ROOMS (16/34). 42½ Gt Brunswick (now Pearse) St. Orig Dub Oil Gas Co, by 1928 Eason's bookstore, now a cinema. The first produc-tion of Nat Theatre Soc (later Abbey Theatre) given here in 1902.

 243.11 antient consort ruhm
 ?538.12 mightyevil roohms of encient cartage

ANTIOCH. Anc city on the Orontes R, now Antakya in Turk; a very early cen for Christian missionary activity (*Acts* 14, 15, 16). There were 15 other *A*s founded by Hellenistic monarchs.

 124.36 Jeromesolem...Andycox
 228.35 to the clutch in Anteach [*an teach*, Ir "the house"]

ANTIPODES. Any 2 points at opposite ends of a diameter passing through the center of the earth, but generally used for Australia and New Zealand. *A* Isls, 458 mi SE of NZ, are almost the exact antipodes of London.

  92.11 polarised...by the symphysis of their antipathies
 183.31 kisses from the antipodes
 422.02 off the antipopees
 472.17 pilgrimage to your antipodes in the past
 489.10 antipathies of austrasia

ANTRIM. Co, NE Ulster, and a town in the Co; Belfast is cap of *A. Aontruim*, Ir "one-elder [tree]." The Glens of *A* are a series of 9 coastal valls running down to the N Channel of Lough Larne.

Baronies: Upr and Lwr Antrim, Upr and Lwr Belfast, Carrickfergus, Cary, Upr and Lwr Dunluce, Upr and Lwr Glenarm, Kilconway, Upr and Lwr Massereene, Upr and Lwr Toome.

    266.F2   an old gardener from the Glens of Antrim
    ?529.15   tell the board in the anterim
    595.15   tantrums

ANTWERP.   Prov and city, 23 mi N of Brussels, N Belg. JJ visited it in 1926 and called it "Gnantwerp" because of the mosquitoes (*Letters* I, 245).

    140.02   gnot Antwarp gnat Musca

APENNINE MOUNTAINS.   Mt range, cen Ital, from the Ligurian Alps in the N to Reggio di Calabria in the S; source of most It rivs.

    618.24   as Hillary Allen sang to the opennine knighters

APPENZELL.   E canton of Switz, first a dominion of the prince abbot of St Gall, the monastery founded by the Ir exile St Gall. Fritz Senn has recorded this song, in Appenzeller dialect:

    Min Vatter ischt en Appenzeller
    Er frisst de Chäs mit samt em Teller.
    ("My father is from Appenzell
    He eats up the cheese and the plate as well.")

    586.27   mean fawthery eastend appullcelery

APPIAN WAY.   Lat *Via Appia*, the 1st paved Roman rd, built 312 BC, SE from Rome. Dub's *AW* (16/32) extends SW from Upr Leeson St in Ranelagh.

    297.25   appia lippia pluvaville
    448.18   who'll uproose the Opian Way?
    497.12   Asia Place and the Affrian Way
    548.06   Appia Lippia Pluviabilla

AQUILEIA.   Town, It, N end of Gulf of Trieste. Aquila is a town and prov of cen It, 54 mi NE of Rome.

    ?255.10   for whose it was the storks were quitting Aquileyria

ARABIA.   The great penin of SW Asia, now Saudi *A*. Ptolemy divided it into *A* Petraea, *A* Felix, and *A* Deserta. Song, "I'll Sing Thee Songs of Araby." *Dubliners* story, "Araby." The "Arabian Bird" is the phoenix. C M Doughty wrote *Travels in Arabia Deserta*, 1888.

    117.15   strassarab
    135.15   well of Artesia into a bird of Arabia
    187.11   arrahbejibbers
    190.30   sing us a song of alibi
    234.31   arrahbeejee
    247.03   velos ambos and arubyat knychts
    275.F2   looking for my shoe all through Arabia
    286.06   the arab in the ghetto
    309.09   Etheria Deserta
    346.06   *Arumbian Knives Riders*
    442.25   singthee songs of Arupee
    473.16   The phaynix...Erebia sank his smother!
    491.14   alcove, turturs or raabraabs
    553.35   claudesdales with arabinstreeds

ARAFAT.   Granite hill 15 mi SE of Mecca, Saudi Arabia; for Muslims, the "Greater Pilgrimage" must include a ceremony on *A*.
　　　5.15   thunder of his arafatas

ARAM.   Heb name for anc Syria, the area extending from the Lebanon Mts to beyond the Euphrates R.
　　228.15   all the sems of Aram
　?335.36   there aramny maeud
　?344.31   meac Coolp, Arram of Eirzerum

ARAN ISLANDS.   (1) Isls off Galway Bay: Inishmor, Inishmaan, Inisheer. Robert Flaherty's classic film *Man of Aran* (1934) made the isls famous. JJ saw the film in Feb 1935 and thought it boring (*Letters* I, 358).   (2) *A* Isl, Co Donegal, off NW coast of Ire.
　　87.25   kings of the arans and the dalkeys
　　91.22   an Inishman was as good as any cantonnatal
　121.12   *Aranman*
　121.14   Aran man
　?204.31   Arran, where's your nose?
　338.26   man d'airain
　338.36   *fed up the grain oils of Aerin*
　387.29   drowned off Erin Isles
　392.17   poorboir Matt in his saltwater hat, with the Aran crown
　475.12   Aran chiefs
　595.22   Arans Duhkha
　?616.03   A nought in nought Eirinishmhan

ARARAT, MT.   Isolated mt in E extremity of Turk near Iranian border; it has 2 peaks, Great *A* and Little *A*. Legendary landing place of Noah's Ark.
　267.F6   All abunk for Tarararat!
　?285.12   the losed farce on erroroots

ARAXES RIVER.   Anc name of Araks (Turk, *Aras*) R, which rises in Turk Armenia and flows 600 mi to the Caspian Sea.
　296.04   I'd likelong, by Araxes...Airmienious

ARBOUR HILL   (14/34).   Dub st, runs N of Marlborough (now Collins) Barracks to Stoneybatter.
　　12.27   Arbourhill

ARCH, THE   (15/34).   Pub, 32 Henry St.
　140.02   not the Arch not The Smug
　508.01   always with him at the Big Elm and the Arch

ARCHANGEL (ARCHANGELSK).   N prov and city at head of the delta of Dvina R, USSR. Named after monastery of the Archangel Michael. As early as 10th cent, Norsemen frequented this territory, calling it Bjarmeland. *A* was for long the only Russ seaport.
　628.10   under whitespread wings like he'd come from Arkangels

ARCH OF TRIUMPH.   Fr *Arc de Triomphe*, Place de l'Étoile, Paris. The Arc in Paris was modeled after Roman triumphal arches. In Dub it was common practice to erect a triumphal arch for visiting monarchs. One was erected for Queen Victoria in Aug 1849, at Baggot St, and another in Apr 1900 at Leeson St Br.
　　22.28   she made her wittest in front of the arkway of trihump

281.F1   Valsinggiddyrex and his grand arks day triump
590.09   through the grand tryomphal arch...reignbolt's

ARCTIC, ANTARCTIC.   Arctic O, N of *A* Circle, N Polar region; Antarctic Regions, Antarctica, and S waters of Pacific, Atlantic, and Indian Oceans, S Polar region. The barnacle goose breeds only in the arctic seas (185.06).

185.06   wildgoup's chase...kathartic ocean
339.21   Grozarktic! Toadlebens!
353.13   all the rattles in his arctic
385.34   Arctic Newses Dagsdogs
519.19   thathens of tharctic [see *Belfast*]
?519.33   Aunt Tarty Villa

ARCTURUS.   The brightest star in the N hemisphere, in the constellation Boötes. At 494.13 it represents North and night.

494.13   Arctura, Anatolia, Hesper and Mesembria
594.02   reneweller of the sky...Arcthuris comeing!
621.08   Send Arctur guiddus!

ARDAGH.   Vill, Co Limerick, 4 mi N of Newcastle West. The *A* Chalice is a jeweled gold and silver chalice from the 8th or 9th cent, discovered in 1868 by a child and now in the Nat Museum, Dub.

110.35   the finding of the Ardagh chalice by another heily innocent

ARDÈCHE RIVER.   Trib of the lwr Rhone R; and *A* Dept, SE Fr.

578.20   Ardechious me!

ARDILAUN.   Isl at N end of Lough Corrib, Co Galway, near the Guinness family estates at Cong. Arthur Guinness was Lord *A*; his brother was Lord Iveagh.

29.03   yardalong (ivoeh!)...Brewster's
407.04   a bottle of ardilaun
418.01   Artalone the Weeps...Highfee [Iveagh]
498.14   gemmynosed sanctsons in epheud and ordilawn
588.05   his old face's hardalone

ARDNACRUSHA.   Vill on Shannon R, Co Clare, W of Limerick. Ir "Height of the Cross." Site of the main power sta of the Shannon Hydro-Electric Scheme (completed 1929).

262.15   Erdnacrusha, requiestress, wake em!

ARGAUM.   Vill in N Ind, N of Purma R (trib of Tapti R). Wellington defeated a Mahratta army there 29 Nov 1803, shortly before the attack on Gawilghur fortress.

8.25   A Gallawghurs argaumunt

ARGENTINA.   Rep, S Amer. Roger Casement held Brit consulates in Brazil, 1907-1911, never in *A*.

559.04   Argentine in casement

ARGOS.   Anc city, E Peloponnese, Gr; burnt to the ground in 1825 by the Turks. It was one of the 7 cities claimed in anc times as the birthplace of Homer.

129.24   pigeonheim to this homer...Ashtown
481.22   humeplace...Argos

ARGYLE (ARGYLL).   Co, W Scot. Scot highlanders once said "God Bless the Duke of Argyle" when they scratched themselves. The Duke erected scratching-posts for his cattle, and the herdsmen used them, too.

71.19   *Thinks He's Gobblasst the Good Dook of Ourguile*

ARKLOW.   Seaside town, 16 mi S of Wicklow, Co Wicklow. The lighthouse at *A* was fitted out by Ger firm of Siemens Schuckert (245.08, 549.18). *Loe*, Dan "fire"; the Danes had navigational beacons at Wicklow and *A*. The Avoca R flows through the Vale of *A* from the "Meeting of the Waters," the confluence of the Avonbeg and Avonmore; the latter's source is very near the source of the Liffey (203.18). In the decisive battle of the 1798 Insurrection, Fr Michael Murphy led the Wexford Insurgents in a hopeless attack on *A* and was killed.

     199.17   staynish beacons on toasc
     203.18   Michael Arklow was his riverend name
     245.08   arcglow's seafire siemens lure
     290.24   from Arklow Vikloe to Louth super Luck
     309.11   Hiberio-Miletians and Argloe-Noremen
     549.18   Wykinloeflare, by Arklow's sapphire siomen's lure

ARMAGH.   Co, S Ulster; *A* Town was the chief Christian cen of Ire from the time of St Patrick, became seat of the RC Primate of Ire and the CI Archbishop. Of the 2 Caths of St Patrick, the Prot is anc, the RC is 19th cent.

     Baronies: Armagh, Upr and Lwr Fews, E and W Oneilland, Upr and Lwr Orior, Tiranny.

     George, 5th duke of Gordon (1770-1836) was called "Cock of the North" – no connection with *A*.

     57.08   I, says Armagh...Clonakilty...Deansgrange...Barna
     482.27   a cock of the north there, Matty Armagh
     531.33   primapatriock of the archsee
     595.16   armaurs

ARMENIA.   Bibl *Minni*, Armenian *Hayasdan*, anc country in W Asia, now divided btwn USSR, Turk, and Iran. The NE part of Turk-in-Asia is Turk *A*; the Russ part is the Armenian SSR. Under Turk rule, there was a series of massacres of Armenians in almost every town of importance in 1895; over 200,000 Armenians were killed (72.11). The classical Armenian lang is "Grabar" (113.03).

     38.11   armelians
     ?69.11   Armen?
     72.11   *Armenian Atrocity*
     113.03   Grabar...almeanium adamologists
     181.23   ungreekable...armenable
     190.25   as popular as an armenial with the faithful
     296.08   Airmienious
     321.23   ourmenial servent
     ?339.29   Erminia's capecloaked hoodoodman
     345.01   Irmenial hairmaierians
     387.11   hayastdanars
     391.01   Erminia Reginia!
     530.36   tuckish armenities
     559.25   Armenian bole

ARMENTIÈRES.   Town, N Fr, 8 mi NW of Lille. WW I song: "Mademoiselle from *A*"; all the refs in *FW* are to the song.

     ?64.25   puddywhackback to Pamintul
     75.03   Marmarazalles from Marmeniere
     230.15   Mademoisselle from Armentières

ARMORICA.   Anc name for region in NW Fr comprising the coast of Gaul btwn
Seine and Loire Rivs. Inhabited by Cymric Celts, later a Roman prov; extreme NW
part invaded in 5th cent AD by Britons and thereafter called Brittany; E part became
Normandy. *Letters*, I, 247: "Amory Tristam [first Lord of Howth] b. in Brittany
(North Armorica)." See *Britain, Little.*

3.05	North Armorica
211.26	Armoricus Tristram Amoor Saint Lawrence
228.19	Bretish Armerica [Bretland = Wales]
395.35	Amoricas Champius
?446.06	I'm a man of Armor
447.06	Anglia's and touch Armourican's iron core
?562.31	to wend him to Amorica
623.15	the Old Lord [of Howth]...might knight you an Armor

ARNOTT'S DEPARTMENT STORE   (15/34).   Arnott and Co, owned a block of
bldgs (near GPO) from Henry St to Prince's St; it was destroyed by fire 4 May 1894.
Arnott St (15/32–33) in S Dub borders the Meath Hosp.

443.22	son of a wants a flurewaltzer to Arnolff's
?580.01	wayleft the arenotts

ARRAN QUAY   (14/34).   N side of Liffey btwn Queen St and Church St. *A* Br
across Liffey was later Queen's Br. St Paul's Ch on *AQ* is often called "the *AQ* ch."

204.31	Arran, where's your nose?
601.23	S. Errands Gay's

ARS.   Town, N Fr, about 3 mi SW of Metz. The Curé d'Ars was St Jean-Marie
Vianney (1786-1859), patron of par priests.

440.10	*Pease in Plenty* by the Curer of Wars

ARTANE   (19/38).   Dist, NE Dub; site of *A* industrial sch for boys. Goal of Fr Conmee's trip in "Wandering Rocks," *U.*

353.34	*cromlin...birstol boys artheynes*
?512.30	Eversought of being artained?

ARTICHOKE ROAD.   The old rd to Merrion via St Patrick's Well Lane (now Nassau St), Denzil St (now Denzille Lane) and Grand Canal St.

390.09	in the bohereen, off Artsichekes Road

ASCALON (ASHKELON).   Seaport vill on coast of Pal, now ruins near El Majdaly.
In Bibl times a city of the Philistine confederation (*Joshua* 13:2).

550.16	the drugs of Kafa and Jelupa and shallots out of Ascalon

ASCOT.   Vill, Berks, Eng. There has been a race track on *A* Heath since 1711, since
1807 the site of the Gold Cup race (which figures so largely in *U*).

448.14	grandnational goldcapped dupsydurby

ASGARD (ASGAARD).   (1) The realm of the Aesir or Scand gods; situated in cen
of universe, accessible only by the rainbow br (*Bifrost*); among regions contained are
Gladsheim and Valhalla. Believed by some to lie E of Tanakvisl (Don R in Russ); aka
Asaland.   (2) The yacht in which Erskine Childers delivered rifles to the Ir Volunteers at Howth in July 1914.

?221.15	whouse be the churchyard or whorts up the aasgaars
?377.33	And the aaskart, see, behind!

ASHANTI.   Kingdom, E Afr, which throughout the 19th cent waged war with the

Brit forces on the Gold Coast; annexed to Brit Gold Coast Colony 1901, and since 1957 a part of Ghana.

    ?131.35   a footsey kungoloo around Taishantyland

ASHBOURNE.   Vill, Co Meath, on Dub-Slane rd; kennels of the Ward Union Staghounds.

    ?59.17   Messrs Achburn, Soulpetre and Ashreborn

ASHTOWN (11/37).   Res dist N of Phoenix Park. Phoenix Park racecourse is just outside the park at *A* Gate. *A* Cas in *PP* became the Under Secretary's Res, now the Papal Nunciature.

    6.33   from ashtun to baronoath
    129.24   Quayhowth, Ashtown, Ratheny
    142.14   Ashtown fields and Cabra fields
    ?329.25   legged in by Ghoststown Gate
    497.18   Luccanicans, Ashtoumers, Batterysby Parkes

ASIA, ASIA MINOR.   Asia is trad regarded by Europeans as beginning at the Bosporus and Hellespont. *A* Minor is the Anatolian Penin, which forms the greater part of Turk. Song: "The Jewel of Asia" (105.20).

    26.04   Arssia Manor
    68.29   from Phenicia or Little Asia
    72.14   *Easyathic Phallusaphist*
    98.10   in Asia Major, where as Turk of the theater
    105.20   *He Calls Me his Dual of Ayessha*
    114.05   Maliziies [Russ, "Asia Minor"]
    155.05   Tukurias-in-Ashies
    166.32   chee...eastasian
    182.31   Haunted Inkbottle...Asia in Ireland
    191.04   Europasianised Afferyank
    ?242.11   ecrazyaztecs and the crime ministers
    263.07   Major A. Shaw...miner
    ?284.24   Aysha Lalipat
    285.F5   Try Asia for the assphalt body
    343.10   Orops and Aasas
    447.25   orders of religion in Asea
    482.30   I'm-free-Down-in-Easia
    489.10   antipathies of austrasia
    497.12   America Avenue and Asia Place
    548.02   Impress of Asias and Queen Columbia [for "Empress of Asia" see
            Canada]
    ?564.35   tvigate shyasian gardeenen
    608.31   from ennemberable Ashias...the Phoenican wakes
    610.12   Eurasian Generalissimo

ASSAYE.   Vill, S India, 260 mi NW of Hyderabad. Wellington defeated far superior Mahratta forces there, 23 Sept 1803.

    8.26   Assaye, assaye!

ASSYRIA.   The great anc emp of W Asia. "The Assyrian came down like the wolf on the fold": Byron, "Destruction of Sennacherib."

    350.25   th'osirian cumb dumb like the whalf on the fiord

ASTAGOB.   (1) Tnld, par of Castleknock, bar of Castleknock, Co Dub.   (2) Tnld,

par of Clonsilla, bar of Castleknock, Co Dub.
>   503.14   Westreeve-Astagob

ASTLEY'S AMPHITHEATRE (15/33).   Equestrian circuses, originating in London
in late 18th cent, and est at many different locations. The Dublin *AA* was erected
1787 at the NW cor of Darby Sq, W of Werburgh St. An *AA* for horsemanship opened
in Peter St in 1789; in 1815, the Molyneux Asylum for Blind Females took over its
bldgs.
>   214.14   You're thinking of Astley's Amphitheayter...horse...Throw the cob-
>   webs from your eyes, woman

ASTON (ASTON'S) QUAY   (15/34).   S side of Liffey W of O'Connell Br. On
Rocque's map, 1765, it extended on both sides of the present br, from Anglesea St
to Hawkins St.
>   205.13   Rinse them out and aston along with you!
>   447.35   stand on, say, Aston's...along quaith

ATHA.   The seat of Cairbar, in Macpherson's *Temora*. Macpherson locates it in Connacht, Hugh Campbell (1822) on banks of Lough Neagh, near its tributary the Main-
water. Lough Neagh was called by the bards Lake Ardha or Atha (Macpherson).
>   194.05   Cathmon-Carbery...being alone athands itself

ATHENS.   Anc city-state and mod Gk cap, on the plain of Attica. Earliest settlement was on the Acropolis (Gk, "high city"), the precipitous hill which later became
the site of temples, including the Parthenon and the Erechtheium; latter named for
Erechtheus, mythical king of *A* (and subject of a poem by Swinburne); its N porch
is supported by caryatids, one of which was taken to London by Lord Elgin.
    Near the Acropolis is the Agora, the marketplace and site of the Assembly of anc
A, and the Areopagus (Gk, "hill of Ares"), seat of the highest judicial tribunal and
the spot where St Paul preached. (The literary group around Sidney at Leinster Ho
was called the Areopagites by Spenser). The gymnasium where Aristotle taught was
named the Lyceum after the nearby temple of Apollo Lyceus; the Greeks themselves
were uncertain whether the epithet meant "of Lycia," "god of light," or "wolf-like,"
and they punned on these meanings, as Joyce does (480.27). The emblem of *A* was
the owl (of Athena); "sending owls to Athens" has the same meaning as "sending
coals to Newcastle" (120.20). In anc times, *A* was one of the 7 cities claimed to be
the birthplace of Homer (129.24, 481.22).
    Byron's "Maid of Athens" begins, "Maid of Athens, ere we part," (41.10, 436.32).
    "The modern Athens" is Edinburgh (353.20); the "Athens of the North" is Bel-
fast (519.19).
>   5.33   aeropagods
>   41.10   meed of anthems here we pant!
>   62.16   astea as agora, helotsphilots
>   120.20   like sick owls hawked back to Athens
>   129.24   pigeonheim to this homer...Ratheny
>   167.13   strongholes of my acropoll
>   206.01   mauldrin rabble around him in areopage
>   272.L4   Hoploits and atthems
>   ?326.16   like expect chrisan athems
>   353.29   *mordern Atems*
>   436.32   Mades of ashens when you flirt
>   480.27   as milky at their lyceum...volp...wolfwise
>   481.22   humeplace...Duthless [with other birthplaces of Homer]

519.19   grand jurors of thathens of tharctic
539.03   longstone erectheion
541.25   praharfeast upon acorpolous

ATHGREANY.   Tnld, par of Hollywood, bar of Talbotstown Lwr, Co Wicklow. *Achadh gréine*, Ir "field of the sun."
?620.11   And go abroad. Rathgreany way perhaps.

ATHLONE.   Town, W Co Westmeath, on Shannon R. The main transmitting sta of Radio Éireann (qv) is 2 mi E. John MacCormack (450.25) was born in *A*. The pursuivant of the Ir Office of Arms is called *A*.
?222.31   athletes longfoot
450.28   whatyoumacormack...I'm athlone in the lillabilling of killarnies
498.12   Athlone Poursuivant and his Imperial

ATHOS, MT.   Mt, NE Gr; the "Holy Mountain" of the Gk ch; an autonomous rep since 1927. The mt is not volcanic.
494.06   etnat athos...vulcanology

ATKINSON, RICHARD, AND CO (15/39).   31 College Green; tabinet and poplin manufacturers.
43.09   Elliot and, O, Atkinson
?534.33   atkinscum's

ATLANTA.   City, cap of Georgia, US. There is no *A* Riv.
140.35   from Atlanta to Oconee

ATLANTIC CITY.   City and resort, SE New Jersey, US, on Atlantic O. Johnny MacDougall represents Connacht, and "Atlantic City" may thus be Galway (qv).
?482.09   Macdougal, Atlantic City, or his onagrass

ATLANTIC OCEAN.   In *FW*, the *A* is not primarily the highway from Cobh to N Amer, but the sea of legend, St Brendan's sea. See *Atlantis, Brazil, Tír na nOg, Tír na mBan*.
85.20   to return to the atlantic and Phenitia Proper
213.35   Brendan's herring pool
297.32   tidled boare rutches up from the Afrantic
311.21   translatentic norjankeltian
319.26   down his gargantast trombsathletic...gulpstroom
336.27   like an atalantic's breastswells
442.14   Brendan's mantle whitening the Kerribrasilian sea

ATLANTIS.   The legendary isl which sank beneath the Atlantic O. *Letters* III, 348: "This melody is about Lough Neagh under which there is said to be buried a King of Atlantis..."
232.32   a glaciator to submerger in Atlangthis
248.08   Arise, Land-Under-Wave
601.05   (atlanst!)...under wasseres of Erie

AUBURN.   Oliver Goldsmith's poem, "The Deserted Village" ("Sweet Auburn! loveliest village of the plain"), is about *A*, an idealized vill set in Eng but based on memories from the poet's Ir childhood, generally associated with Lissoy, 5 mi SW of Ballymahon, Co Longford, where Goldsmith lived.
13.26   auburn mayde...desarted
137.07   Swed Albiony, likeliest villain of the place

?139.23   with her auburnt streams
174.25 –.31   deserted village...Auborne-to-Auborne
265.06   Sweetsome auburn
265.28   Distorted mirage, aloofliest of the plain
275.05   Pacata Auburnia
?280.27   From Auburn chenlemagne
286.F3   the disordered visage
?336.15   his awebrume hour...Sahara
381.04   Hauburnea's liveliest vinnage on the brain
495.18   Granny-stream-Auborne
552.22   sweet coolocked, my auburn coyquailing one
617.36   the Swees Aubumn vogue is hanging down

AUGHRIM.   Par and town, Co Galway, 30 mi E of Galway. Scene of decisive victory of Wm III over James II, 12 July 1691, which, with Battle of Boyne, is commemorated in N Ire on Orange Day (July 12). "The Lamentations of Aughrim" is the tune of T Moore's "Forget not the field..."
340.09   Forget not the felled! For the lomondations of Oghrem!

AUGSBURG.   City in Swabia, Bavaria. The "Augsburg Interim" was a confession of faith drawn up in 1548 at the command of Charles V as a temporary compromise between Prot and RC doctrines, after the A Diet of 1547.
384.17   after the interims of Augusburgh for auld lang syne

AULIS (AULIDIS).   Anc city and port, in Boeotia, Gr, where Agamemnon sacrificed his daughter Iphigenia to Artemis to insure the success of the Gk expedition to Troy; Aphrodite was not esp connected with A.
299.L1   *Canine Venus sublimated to Aulidic Aphrodite*

AURELIA, VIA.   Roman highroad which left Rome to the W through the Aurelian Gate. There were 14 gates in the Aurelian walls, built 271-280. Porta A is now Porta San Pancrazio.
478.14   aurellian gape

AURIGNAC.   Cave, Dept of Haute Garonne, 37 mi SW of Toulouse, S Fr. Caves in the region contain significant paleolithic remains, hence the "Aurignacian period."
153.21   aurignacian

AUSONIA.   Poetic name for Italy (from Ausones, old name of primitive inhabitants of Cen It).
?209.35   Ausone sidulcis!

AUSTERLITZ.   Town, Czech, 12 mi SE of Brno, scene of battle 12 Dec 1805, in which Napoleon defeated Russians and Austrians.
9.28   to their ousterlists
343.16   *awstooloo was valdesombre* [valet de chambre]

AUSTRALIA.   Australia (specifically, Tasmania and New South Wales, qqv) was known in the 19th cent primarily as the place to which the Brit transported convicts and other undesirables. Prof Hart (*Structure and Motif in Finnegans Wake*) has pointed out that A or the antipodes (qv) is Shem's land, an appropriately hellish place from which Shem is forever cabling for money. Often it is identified by its slang (321.32 fossickers and swagglers), or by its unique animals (165.21 wallopy...congorool). "Eastralia" (60.27) was proposed by the Sydney *Bulletin* as a name for a name for a section of A.

60.27   Eastrailian poorusers of the Sydney Parade Ballotin
64.23   leave Astrelea for the astrollajerries
321.09   astraylians in island
321.31   spring alice...down under
450.01   down under in the shy orient
488.20   in ostralian someplace
489.10   antipathies of austrasia...The Workings, N.S.W.
552.07   Hagiasofia of Astralia
601.34   austrologer Wallaby

AUSTRASIA.   Name for the E Frankish kingdom; its cap was Metz. There was great rivalry btwn Austrasia and Neustria within the Frankish kingdom. Under Charlemagne, the now Franconia-Frankish territory beyond the Rhine was called Austrasia.
489.10   the antipathies of austrasia

AUSTRIA.   Form (Austro-Hungarian) emp and later rep, cen Eur, orig inhabited by Celtic tribes, conquered by Rome (14 BC) and later ruled by various sovereignties. Trieste and Pola were Austro-Hungarian when JJ lived there. Ger, *Österreich*; Fr, *Autriche*.
70.01   a Kommerzial...from Osterich
?136.15   Osterich
?162.32   he could still make out with his augstritch
270.L4   *Ulstria, Monastir*
462.29   Jaunstown, Ousterrike
464.27   old Auster and Hungrig

AUXONNE.   Town, 18 mi SE of Dijon, E Fr. Manufactures cloth and plaster of paris.
?463.07   every Auxonian aimer's ace

AVIGNON.   City, SE Fr, near confluence of Rhône and Durance Rivs. Res of Popes, 1309-77; Petrach lived there and saw Laura in the Ch of St Clara. Children dance to the song "Sur le pont d'Avignon."
226.34   I' th' view o' th'avignue dancing goes entrancing roundly
448.17   who'll disasperaguss Pope's Avegnue

AVOCA (OVOCA).   Riv and vall, Co Wicklow; formed by confluence of Avonmore and Avonbeg Rivs at the "Meeting of the Waters" (qv), celebrated as T Moore's "Sweet Vale of Avoca." "Avoca" is a mod name given the Avonmore (or Owenmore) by mod pedantry, which mistakenly identified it with Ptolemy's *Oboca*.
203.15   whereabouts in Ow and Ovoca?
206.27   Ower more
305.28   Vale. Ovocation of maiding waters...steyne
466.35   Sweet fellow ovocal, he stones out of stune
471.36   sweet wail of evoker
537.06   by virchow of those filthered Ovocnas

AVONDALE.   Town, 1 mi NW of Castle Howard, Co Wicklow. Prince Albert Victor (nicknamed "Collars and Cuffs"), Duke of Clarence and Avondale, elder son of the Prince of Wales, later Edward VII, was stationed in Dub as a Hussar. Parnell's estate in Co Wicklow was also called "*A*."
?209.06   Avondale's fish and Clarence's poison

AWABEG.   (1) Awbeg R, Co Cork.   (2) Avonbeg R, Co Wicklow.   (3) Owenbeg, town, Co Tipperary; also name of rivs in Cos Donegal, Laois and Derry.

Abha Beig, Ir "little river."
 248.33 Awabeg is my callby

AYLESBURY. Town, and Vale of *A* (known in archaeology for Viking relics), Bucks, Eng. It was ravaged by (among others) the Viking King of Den, Sweyn Forkbeard (d 1014).
 387.09 forkbearded...Aylesburg

AYR. Co and town, SW Scot, on Firth of Clyde. Robert Burns was born in the suburb of Alloway.
 483.29 ayr, plage and watford [air, earth, water]

AZORES. Group of 9 isls and several islets belonging to Port in the N Atlantic O, about 800 mi off coast of Port.
 468.34 I'm dreaming of ye, azores

AZOV, SEA OF. Shallow sea, NE arm of the Black Sea E of the Crimea, connected with the Black Sea by the strait of Kertch. In May 1855, an allied force captured Kertch and opened the sea to Brit gunboats.
 346.21 A hov and az ov

B

BABEL, TOWER OF. *Gen* 11:1–9: After the flood, the men who migrated to the east built in the plain of Shinar (qv) a city "and a tower with its top in the heavens." But God confused their language (35.05); therefore the city was called Babel (*babal*, Heb "confound"). Acc to the Ir *Book of Invasions*, the universal lang spoken before the confusion of tongues was "Gortighern" (565.12).
 ?3.15 bababadal– [in C-word]
 ?4.30 balbulous
 5.02 a burning bush abob off its baubletop
 6.31 overgrown babeling
 15.12 babbelers...confusium hold them
 35.05 confusioning of human races
 ?64.09 battering babel
 ?64.11 belzey babble
 118.18 Soferim Bebel
 199.31 turrace of Babbel
 224.12 towerable...baublelight
 ?254.17 babbel men dub gulch of tears
 258.11 And shall not Babel be with Lebab?
 278.L4 *Rockaby, babel, flatten a wall*
 314.02 scaffolding...babeling
 344.28 babbeing...bibbelboy
 354.27 babble towers
 467.16 Tower of Balbus
 499.34 what static babel
 523.32 tour of bibel
 ?532.25 Babbyl Malket

536.08   confused by his tonguer of baubble
565.12   Gortigern
624.09   bubel runtoer

BAB EL MANDEB.   The strait btwn the S end of the Red Sea and the Gulf of
Aden; Arab, "gate of tears." Acc to legend, named from the deaths in the earthquake
which separated Asia and Afr.
254.17   A babbel men dub gulch of tears

BABYLON.   Anc city on left bank of Euphrates R; mod Hillak. "Whore of Babylon" was the Puritan name for RC Ch (*Rev* 17:19) (185.12). 2 of the 7 Wonders of
the Anc World (qv) were in *B*: the Walls of *B* (261.10), and the Gardens of Semiramis (qv). Arnold Bennett wrote *The Grand Babylon Hotel*, 1902 (17.33). *Psalms* 137:
"By the waters of Babylon we sat down and wept: when we remembered thee, O Sion" (103.11, 526.09).
17.33   babylone the greatgrandhotelled
103.11   by the waters of babalong
139.12   best bunbaked bricks in bould Babylon...wan wubblin wall
185.12   brow of her of Babylon
261.10   meditated the mured
417.12   in his Papylonian babooshkees
460.23   the cyprissis and the babilonias
526.09   Besides the bubblye waters of, babblyebubblye waters of?

BACHELOR'S WALK   (15/34).   Quay, N side of Liffey, W of O'Connell St. Named
for Batchelor, an early property owner in area, although it is pop believed to come
from its supposed former use as a promenade for bachelors.
214.03   a manzinahurries off Bachelor's Walk
?516.04   badgeler's rake to the town's major from the wesz

BACK LANE   (15/33).   Btwn Cornmarket and St Nicholas Sts. A RC chapel and
"University" was est in *BL* early in reign of Charles I, seized by govt in 1630 and
transferred to Univ of Dub (Trinity Coll). Form Rochelle Lane (qv).
287.30   Backlane Univarsity

BADEN.   (1) Spa in Lwr Austria, 14 mi SW of Vienna; known as spa since Roman
times.   (2) Baden-Baden, 18 mi SW of Karlsruhe, Ger; known as spa since Roman
times.   (3) Badenweiler, vill in SW Ger, 28 mi NE of Basel, Switz; spa and Roman
baths.
422.29   Baden bees of Saint Dominoc's
448.31   for a cure at Badanuweir
541.27   I bathandbaddend on mendicity...corocured

BAD HOMBURG.   Aka Homburg, or Homburg vor der Hohe; city in Hesse state,
Ger; resort and spa. Homburg hats were first made here.
72.12   *Bad Humborg*
560.07   The old humburgh...head

BAGDAD (BAGHDAD).   City, cap of Iraq, on Tigris R, and an anc caliphate of
Turkey-in-Asia in the Tigris-Euphrates region, W of the present city.
286.04   So, bagdad,...begath...arab...anymeade or persan
294.17   like your Bigdud dadder in the boudeville song
532.24   far too bahad
590.21   Jumbluffer, bagdad, sir

BAGGOT ST   (16/33).   Runs SE from Stephen's Green, "Lwr" N of the Grand
Canal, "Upr" S of the canal. Form called Baggotrath (Battle of Baggotrath, 1649)
Lane. Both Lwr and Upr *B* St curve slightly in the middle of their lengths. Straight-
ened by Wide Sts Commission in 18th cent (491.06). Baggotrath Ch (CI) is in Upr *B*
St (346.33). Also, "Mr Baggot's Tavern" is mentioned on Cook St in 1635.

> ?46.04   his bucketshop store/Down Bargainweg, Lower
> 71.12   *At Baggotty's Bend He Bumped*
> ?345.15–.25   when you smugs to bagot...To bug at?
> 346.33   *the babybell in his baggutstract upper*
> 490.20   Treble Stauter of Holy Baggot Street
> 491.06   Tugbag is Baggut's...straat that is called corkscrewed
> 602.20   Upper and Lower Byggotstrade, Ciwareke

BAGINBUN.   Headland, S Co Wexford, btwn Bannow Bay and The Hook. An old
jingle about the defeat in 1169 of the Norse-Ir army by Anglo-Norman Raymond le
Gros runs: "At the creek of Baginbun, Ireland was lost and won." Acc to Hansbrow's
Hibernian Gazetteer (which is unreliable), the Normans landed in two ships called Bag
and Bun, and "two rocks in that place retain these names."

> 294.F4   At the foot of Bagnabun Banbasday was lost on one [Banba = Ire]
> 320.08   the big bag of my hamd...his pudny bun brofkost
> ?433.20   by the bun...bisbuiting...throws them bag

BAILE ÁTHA CLIATH.   See *Dublin*.

BAILEY LIGHTHOUSE   (29/36).   Lighthouse, SE tip (Duncriffan promontory) of
Howth. The mod lighthouse, erected 1814, replaced the old Bailey, dating from the
time of Charles II, of which only the base remains, adjoining a cottage known as the
"old Bailey." It was placed so high that it was often obscured by fog when it was
clear at sea-level, and the Kish lightship (qv) served the traffic for Dub Bay.

   Allusions to the *BL* are most often conflated with either the Old Bailey (qv) in
London or to HCE as the Bill Bailey of the song, "Bill Bailey, won't you please come
home?"

> 6.33   Bailywick
> ?7.10   pool...begg...kish...baken head
> 31.27   bailiwick a turnpiker
> 71.21   *Burnham and Bailey* [see *Burnham Lighthouse*]
> ?85.26   Old Bailey
> 127.06   billbailey
> 177.24   old Belly
> ?179.14   Bengalese Beacon of Biloxity
> 317.30   big bailey bill
> 342.23   *Bailey Beacon*
> 358.25   baillybeacons
> 448.19   Who'll brighton Brayhowth and bait the Bull Bailey
> ?480.18   Bill of old Bailey!
> ?624.19   the bailby pleasemarm

BAKERLOO.   London Underground line, joining Baker St and Waterloo Rlwy Sta.
> 348.31   *in thatthack of the bustle Bakerloo,* (11.32)

BALACLAVA (BALAKLAVA).   Seaport vill, Crimean penin, USSR, 8 mi SE of
Sevastopol; site, 25 Oct 1854, of indecisive battle of Crimean War memorable for the
Charge of the Light Brigade. A chromo of the Charge of the Light Brigade hangs on

the wall of HCE's tav (334.24 – .27). *Balyklava*, Osmanli "fish pond." *B* may not be where Buckley shot the Russ Gen, but no other Crimean War site is so closely associated with that story in *FW*. *B* is regularly conflated in *FW* with Baile Átha Cliath, the Ir name of Dub.

134.01	stood into Dee mouth, then backed broadside on Baulacleeva
?136.33	if his feet are bally clay
159.30	halfaloafonwashed...baileycliaver
170.33	blueblooded Balaclava fried-at-belief-stakes
285.25	twos twos fives fives of bullyclavers
?314.21	here in a present booth of Ballaclay
335.13	Bullyclubber burgherly shut the rush in general
341.09	Buckily...Rumjar Journaral...balacleivka
352.23	bullyclaver of ye, bragadore-gunneral
366.20	a barrakraval of grakeshoots

BALBEC.   The imaginary seaside resort in Normandy which figures largely in Proust's *Á la Recherche du Temps Perdus*; the Narrator's sojourns there are at the Grand Hôtel de la Plage. Proust took the name from Bolbec (a town on the Seine NE of Le Havre), the ambience from Cabourg, and other place-names from the areas around Cabourg and Cherbourg. In *Sodome et Gomorrhe*, the Academician Brichot etymologizes endlessly on place-names. Refs for the following names are to the Pléiade edition, Vol II:

Oldboof: Elbeuf, town on the Seine above Rouen (1098)
Sassondale: springs of Sissonne, named for the Saxons (1099)
Jorsey: the packetboat to Jersey (998)
Uppygard: ?Heudicourt, location not given (487)
Mundelonde: ?
Abbeytotte: ? (Abbeville, in Somme Dept, not mentioned by Proust)
Bracqueytuitte: Braquetuit, location not given (890)
Hockeyvilla: Orgeville, or Octeville (near Cherbourg) (1100)
Fockeyvilla: Forcheville (after Swann's death, Odette marries the Comte de Forcheville)

609.16	Wynn's Hotel. Brancherds at: Bullbeck, Oldboof, Sassondale, Jorsey Uppygard, Mundelonde, Abbeytotte, Bracqueytuitte with Hockeyvilla, Fockeyvilla, Hillewille and Wallhall

BALBRIGGAN.   Seaport and manufacturing town 19 mi NE of Dub. Famous for hosiery (textile mills). *Baile Breacan*, Ir "Town of [St] Brecan."

22.35	his bullbraggin soxangloves
?86.24	scattery...the ballybricken he could get no good of
399.14	*Balbriggan surtout*
530.12	balbriggans

BALDOYLE   (24/40).   Vill, N of Sutton and Howth; site of race course.

17.13	Boildoyle and rawhoney
39.02	hippic runfields of breezy Baldoyle
74.16	Baldowl
142.15	Santry...Raheny...and Baldoygle
144.10	so ovally provencial at Balldole
322.02	Boildawl stuumplecheats
342.06	*Baldawl the curse, baledale the day*

BALEARIC ISLANDS.   Isl group and Sp prov, in Medit off E coast of Sp. The 4 largest isls are Majorca, Minorca, Iviza, and Formentera (latter said to derive name from production of wheat); there are 11 smaller isls. The isls have been Sp since 1349, but were occupied several times in the 18th cent by the Brit or Fr.

 555.09 all four of them...the majorchy, the minorchy, the everso and the fermentarian with their ballyhooric blowreaper

BALKANS. *B* Penin, SE Eur btwn Adriatic and Ionian Seas on the W, Medit Sea on the S, and Aegean and Black Seas on the E. The *B* Mts extend E and W across Bulg from the Yugo border to the Black Sea.

 501.33 like an andeanupper balkan
 569.02 crimosing balkonladies

BALLAGHMOON. Vill, Co Kildare, 3½ mi NE of Carlow town; site of battle of Bealach Mughna, 908 AD, in which Mac Máel Sechnaill, King of Tara, defeated Cormac mac Cuilenáin, king-bishop of Munster, who was slain and decapitated.

 219.19 Ballymooney Bloodriddon Murther

BALLAST OFFICE (15/34). The office of Ballast Master was created in the 17th cent to carry out the extension of the embankment of the Liffey by walls and fill, or "ballast." It evolved into the authority supervising all Dub harb operations, with hqs in the *BO* on Westmoreland Row at O'Connell Br. The timeball on a staff on its roof fell daily at 1:00 PM true Dub time; "worked by a wire from Dunsink [Obs]," Bloom reflected (*U* 152/154).

 390.03 Lally, the ballest master of Gosterstown
 518.01 Dunsink, rugby, ballast and ball
 551.01 duncingk...fell clocksure off my ballast

BALLINA. (1) Town, Co Mayo, on Moy R at head of Killala Bay. (2) Town, Co Tipperary, across Shannon R from Killaloe, Co Clare. *Béal an Átha*, Ir "mouth of the ford." (3) *B* Ho, near Moyvalley, Co Meath. Like Kilbride (qv), it is near but not quite on the Liffey.

 576.06 Hal Kilbride *v* Una Bellina

BALL'S BLUFF. Locality near Leesburg, NE Virg, US. Site of minor Civil War battle 21 Oct 1861, in which Union forces were defeated by the Confederates.

 84.09 confederate...who albeit ballsbluffed

BALLSBRIDGE (17/32). Dist, SE Dub; site of Royal Dub Soc grounds, site of the Aug Horse Show and of athletic meetings. The locality is named after the br which carries the anc highway from Dub to Blackrock over the Dodder R.

 130.21 rialtos, annesleyg, binn and balls [all bridges]
 136.30 Baslesbridge
 306.25 The Dublin Metropolitan Police Sports at Ballsbridge
 447.17 Ballses Breach Harshoe

BALLYBOUGH (16/35). Rd, br over Tolka R, NE Dub, and name of surrounding area btwn Summerhill and Fairview. Vitriol works at *B* Br were operated by the Dub and Wicklow Manure Co, Ltd. *Baile bocht*, Ir "poortown."

 95.02 Ballybock manure works
 236.21 the purly ooze of Ballybough
 447.20 Bridge of Belches in Fairview

BALLYCASSIDY. Town, Co Fermanagh.

 ?45.21 bumping bull of the Cassidys
 87.15 bullycassidy
 ?98.31 Cope and Bull go cup and ball. And the Cassidy – Craddock

BALLYFERMOT (10/33).   Vill, S of Chapelizod. The Tiled Ho of Le Fanu's *House By the Churchyard* is in *B*; see *Chapelizod: Tiled House.*
    183.05   your brass castle or your tyled house in ballyfermont

BALLYGARRY.   Town, Co Mayo. Ballingarry, Co Tipperary, was the scene of Wm Smith O'Brien's 1848 "cabbage garden" rising (553.14).
    346.24   Sayyessik, Ballygarry

BALLYHOOLY.   Town, Co Cork, on Blackwater R. Robert Martin of Ross, nicknamed "Ballyhooly," wrote *Bits of Blarney,* containing the song "The Ballyhooly Blue Ribbon Army," about a temperance movement in a notoriously intemperate town. The town was known for its faction fights. "Ballyhooly" is proverbial for "a tongue-lashing."
    100.07   Bannalanna Bangs Ballyhooly
    219.19   Ballymooney Bloodriddon Murther
    262.25   Burials be ballyhouraised!
    520.33   rooly and cooly boolyhooly
    555.10   with their ballyhooric blowreaper
    608.08   Billyhealy, Ballyhooly and Bullyhowley

BALLYHOURA MOUNTAINS.   In Co Cork, on Cork-Limerick border.
    262.25   Burials be ballyhouraised!
    555.10   the fermentarian with their ballyhooric blowreaper [the ass]

BALLYJAMESDUFF.   Town, Co Cavan. Percy French wrote "Come Back, Paddy Reilly, to Ballyjamesduff," in response to a challenge that he work the name into a song.
    485.16   Come back, baddy wrily, to Bullydamestough!

BALLYMUN (15/40).   Vill, N Dub suburb on road to Naul.
    14.36   the cornflowers have been staying at Ballymun
    497.20   Ballymunites

BALLYNABRAGGET.   Tnld, par of Donaghcloney, bar of Iveagh Lwr, Co Down. *Baile na Bragoide,* Ir "Town of the Pot-Ale." "Bragget" was the product of professional brewers.
    60.12   Brian Lynsky...at his shouting box, Bawlonabraggat

BALROTHERY.   (1) Vill, N Co Dub, SW of Balbriggan, and name of 2 baronies (E, W Balrothery), N Co Dub. *Baile an Ridire,* Ir "Town of the Knight."   (2) Form vill SW of Dub, E of Tallaght, and form tramstop on the Terenure-Tallaght tram line. *Balrudery* is an Ir "country dance."
    405.27   the once queen of Bristol and Balrothery

BALTIC SEA.   An arm of the Atlantic O connected with the North Sea by the Skagerrak and Cattegat. Ger, *Ostsee*; Russ, *Baltiskoye More* (338.19). The *B* States are the former Estonia, Latvia, and Lith, sometimes also Fin and Pol.
    The "long ships" of the Vikings (such as Eric Bloodaxe and Harold Bluetooth, 323.04) were developed by *B* tribes as early as the time of Tacitus.
    187.02   pulpably of balltossic stummung
    320.21   Brighten-pon-the-Baltic
    323.04   the bloedaxe bloodooth baltxebec ["xebec," a type of 3-masted
              Medit ship]
    338.19   laut-lievtonant of Baltiskeeamore
    423.03   about the Balt with the markshaire parawag

491.35   riding apron in Baltic Bygrad
544.03   hallway pungent of Baltic dishes

BALTIMORE.   (1) Vill, 8 mi SW of Skibbereen, W Co Cork, at tip of penin.
(2) City, Maryland, US.
?338.19   Baltiskeeamore

BALWEARIE.   Ruined fort, 2 mi W of Kirkcaldy, Fifeshire, Scot; res of Sir Michael
Scot (1210-1291), whose tomb figures in Scott's *Lay of the Last Minstrel*.
?543.01   heyweywomen to refresh the ballwearied

BANAGHER.   Vill, Co Offaly, on Shannon R. To anything unusual, people say,
"Well, that bangs Banagher" (P W Joyce).
87.31   Mind the bank from Banagher

BANBA.   See *Ireland*.

BANDUSIA.   A fountain celebrated by Horace (*Odes* III, xiii), prob on his Sabine
farm. JJ translated this Ode while at Belvedere Coll: his earliest writing which survives.
280.32   fount Bandusian

BANGKOK.   City, cap of Siam (now Thailand) on the Chao Phaya R 25 mi above
its mouth.
8.20   bangkok's best

BANK OF ENGLAND.   Located on Threadneedle St in the City of London, the *B*
of *E* has a venerable trad and is pop known as the "Old Lady of Threadneedle St"
(qv).
127.28   catches his check at banck of Indgangd [*Indgang*, Dan "entrance";
            bank, Dan "knock"]
420.34   Now Bunk of England's

BANK OF IRELAND (15/34).   Located on College Green, the *B* of *I* occupies
the bldgs which were once Parl House (qv). Beginning in March 1804, the old Parl
was modified considerably. Swift called the Bank "The Wonderful Wonder of Wonders" in a satire in 1720. The "stone of destiny" in 40.19 is the Lia Fáil (qv) but
possibly also the cornerstone of Parl House, laid 3 Feb 1729.
See *Chichester (House)*.
40.19   under the blankets of homelessness on the bunk of iceland...stone
            of destiny
71.14   *Ireland's Eighth Wonderful Wonder*
?84.31   savings...so many miles from bank and Dublin stone
420.32   Once Bank of Ireland's
574.18   bank particularised, the national misery

BANN RIVER.   The Upr *B* Riv, 25 mi long, rises in Co Down and flows NW into
Lough Neagh; the Lwr *B*, 33 mi long, flows N out of Lough Neagh into the Atlantic.
At its mouth is Tonn Tuaithe, "The Wave of the North"; see *Four Waves of Erin*.
?100.07   Bannalanna
?137.13   bann if buckshotbackshattered
197.12   Was her banns never loosened in Adam and Eve's
210.07   A tinker's bann and a barrow
?247.30   forebanned and betweenly

BANNOCKBURN.   Town, cen Scot, 2½ mi SE of Stirling; site of battle 23 June 1314 in which Robert Bruce routed the Eng under Edward II and took Stirling Cas.
    9.25   this is panickburns

BANTRY BAY.   Ocean inlet, SW Co Cork, site of unsuccessful Fr attempts at landing in 1689 and 1796 to help Ir insurrections.
    409.02   I heard the man Shee shinging in the pantry bay

BARBADOS.   Isl in the Lesser Antilles, WI. When Cromwell dispatched the "mere Irish" "to hell or Connaught" after 1652, thousands were also deported into virtual slavery in *B.*
    525.06   Tallhell and Barbados wi ye and your Errian coprulation!

BARCELONA.   City and port in E Sp, form cap of Catalonia. Barceloneta is a suburb to the E. A "barcelona" is a neck-cloth, pop in Brit Isles in 18th and early 19th cents, which *FW* doesn't always distinguish from "Borsalino," an It make of hat.
    273.18   muchas bracelonettes gracies barcelonas
    288.18   to put off the barcelonas[5] from their peccaminous corpulums
    ?398.05   heroest champion of Eren and his braceoelanders
    ?520.09   to push on his borrowsaloaner
    625.11   always snugging in your barsalooner

BARCHESTER.   The imaginary shire of Trollope's Barchester novels, the first of which is *The Warden.* See *Manchester.*
    ?446.31   Up Murphy, Henson and O'Dwyer, the Warchester Warders!

BARENTS.   Wm Barents, 16th cent explorer, discovered Spitsbergen (qv), an Arctic archipelago including *B* Isl and surrounded by the *B* Sea.
    ?331.12   I'll tittle your barents

BARKER, JOHN, AND CO.   Dept store in Kensington High St, London.
    127.11   if he outharrods against barkers

BAR-LE-DUC.   Town, NE Fr, cap of Meuse Dept, S of Verdun. In the siege of the fortress of Verdun, 1916, it was the railhead for the fortifications.
    73.26   siegings round our archicitadel...as Bar-le-Duc

BARLEY FIELDS (15/34–35).   The old name for the area on which the Rotunda (qv) Hosp now stands; purchased by Dr Mosse as *BF* in 1748, renamed "New Gardens" by 1756; later Rutland (now Parnell) Sq (qv).
    203.06   barleyfields and pennylotts of Humphrey's fordofhurdlestown

BARNA.   Vill and resort, Co Galway, SW of Galway City. The allusion is to Johnny MacDougall as the prov of Connacht.
    57.10   Hear the four of them...Armagh...Clonakilty...Deansgrange...I, says
        Barna, and whatabout it?

BARNABOY HOUSE.   Demesne, 1 mi NW of Kilcormac (aka Frankford), Co Offaly. See also *Barna.*
    ?237.15   our barnaboy, our chepachap

BARNARDO, J M AND SON (15/33).   Barnardo's the furriers has long been a landmark at 108 Grafton St. The related Thomas John Barnardo, b 1845 in Dub, established more than 100 homes for waifs and strays throughout the UK; still known as "Dr Barnardo's Homes." See *Stepney.*
    253.31   Barnado's bearskin...this village childergarten

BARNET.   Town, Herts, SE Eng, 12 mi N of London, scene of decisive Yorkist victory in War of Roses, 14 Apr 1471, in which Earl of Warwick, "The Kingmaker," was killed. The three divisions are High *B* (aka Chipping *B*), East *B*, and New *B*.
    ?141.14   might underhold three barnets

BARNSTAPLE.   Market town and seaport, N Devon, SW Eng; one of the most anc royal boroughs. The allusion is also to Thackeray, *Lectures on the English Humorists*, "If Swift was Irish, then a man born in a stable is a horse." Wellington (whose birthplace in Ire is still a matter of dispute) is also supposed to have denied his Irishness on the grounds that "a man is not a horse because he was born in a stable."
    10.17   Willingdone, bornstable ghentleman
    253.34   tomestone of Barnstaple
    ?536.09   Ring his mind, ye staples, (bonze!)

BARRACK BRIDGE   (14/34).   Br over the Liffey, pop called "Bloody Bridge" after the battle btwn apprentices and soldiers at opening of orig wooden br in 1671. Present br built 1863, called Victoria Br, now Rory O'More Br.
    11.22   bloodstaned breeks
    372.25   His bludgeon's bruk
    ?421.13   Bloody Big Bristol [*bristol*, OE "bridge"]

BARRETT'S HOTEL   (16/33).   Around the turn of the cent, Jane Barrett ran a restaurant and hotel at 15 Lincoln Pl, attached to the Lincoln Pl Turkish Baths, a short distance from Maple's Hotel in Kildare St. (See *Census* for St Madeleine, Sophie Barat.)
    ?155.26   Maples...a stopsign before Sophy Barratt's

BARREL, THE   (14/33).   The area behind a stone archway (recently a shop) on the W side of Meath St, where the Friends' Meeting House stood; thus called in the Liberties because the Quakers gave out soup to the hungry.
    41.17   the hogshome they lovenaned The Barrel

BARROW RIVER.   Riv, 112 mi long, SE Ire, flows S from Co Offaly to Waterford Harb. Connected to Liffey by canal.
    ?15.24   Lave a whale...in a whillbarrow
    57.13   Hill of Allen, the Barrow for an People
    198.33   the great tribune's barrow [+ O'Connell's grave]
    210.07   A tinker's bann and a barrow to boil
    ?244.34   Send leabarrow loads
    ?391.14   from the brownesberrow in nolandsland
    ?568.24   Dom King at broadstone barrow

BARTHOLOMEW DEEP.   One of 5 deeps in Pacific O close to coast of S Amer.
    100.04   in deep Bartholoman's Deep

BASLE (BASEL, BÂLE).   Sw canton and city on both sides of Rhine R, where in an annual ceremony 2 legendary figures, *der wilde Mann* and the bird *Vogel Gryff* arrive on a float on the Rhine. Site of 1st br (1225 AD) over Rhine btwn Lake Constance and North Sea. Btwn the mod Rhine brs there are 3 passenger ferries called "Wilde Mann," "Vogel Gryff," and "Leu" (Sw-Ger "lion").
    88.05   bluntly broached, and in the best basel to boot
    136.30   Baslesbridge
    358.22   Qith the tou loulous and the gryffygryffygryffs, at Fenegans Wick, the Wildemanns
    ?577.15   basal curse yet grace abunda [?Graubünden]

BASQUE PROVINCES.   Region, N Sp. Basque, *Euskadi* or *Eskualkerria*; the Basque lang is *Euskerra* or *Eskuara*. See *AWN* I.2 (4/64). The beret (507.15) originated with the Basques.

102.16	Handiman the Chomp, Esquoro, biskbask
121.05	its basque of bayleaves all aflutter
230.06	domum (osco de basco de pesco de bisco!)
233.35	as baskly as your cheesechalk cow cudd spanich
287.F4	Basqueesh, Finnican, Hungulash and Old Teangtaggle
350.20	No more basquibezigues for this pole aprican!
507.15	the basque of his beret
556.33	was basquing to her pillasleep
557.01	for Hemself and Co, Esquara

BASTILLE.   The great prison-fortress of Paris, whose fall signalled the beginning of the Fr Revolution.

105.23	*the Fall of the Potstille*
275.10	signs is on the bellyguds bastille back

BATH.   City and spa (Ger, *Bad*) in Somerset, Eng, on the Avon R. "*B* buns" are more edible than they sound. The "Beauty of *B*" is an apple.

198.05	He erned his lille Bunbath hard
355.13	Beauty's bath she's bound to bind beholders
541.27	bathandbaddend

BATTERSBY AND CO (15/34).   Estate agents and auctioneers in Dub for more than a cent, long (but no longer) at 6 Westmoreland St.

?372.36	number one lived at Bothersby North
386.24	Bootersbay Sisters...auctioneer Battersby Sisters
387.24	Queen Baltersby, the Fourth Buzzersbee
497.18	Batterysby Parkes
515.30	me bebattersbid hat

BATTERSEA.   Dist and Park, on S bank of the Thames, London.

374.29	Finsbury...you batter see...regent
497.18	Batterysby Parkes

BATTERSTOWN.   Town, Co Meath, 15 mi NW of Dub. *Baile an Bóthair*, Ir "town of the road."

132.04	at Baddersdown in his hunt for the boar trwth

BAYREUTH.   Town, Upr Franconia, Ger. Wagner festivals have been held there since 1876 in the Festspielhaus, designed by Wagner.

?222.12	Songs betune the acts...Polymop Baretherootsch
229.34	on block at Boyrut season
500.24	Fort! Fort! Bayroyt! March!

BEAUX LANE (15/33).   Mid-18th cent name for Digges Lane, near Stephen St, just S of Mercer St Hosp (not Digges St, several blocks S).

568.22	beaux and laddes

BEAUX' WALK (16/33).   18th-cent name for N side of Stephen's Green.

405.13	the Bel of Beaus' Walk
?618.23	make their beaux to my alce

BECKER, BROTHERS.   Tea merchants; at 7 Gt George's St, S (15/33), and 17 Earl

St, N (15/34), around the turn of the cent.
   608.20   milkee muchee bringing beckerbrose, the brew with the foochoor in it

BECTIVE.   Vill, Co Meath, with *B* Abbey (ruins), founded 12th cent. The allusion
is mainly to the *B* Rangers, a Dub rugby club.
   451.10   the Bective's wouldn't hold me

BEDDGELERT.   "Gelert's Grave"; vill in Carnarvonshire (now Gwynedd), N Wales,
named after the legend of the hound Gelert, who was left by his master King Llewelyn
to guard his infant son. Returning to find Gelert covered with blood, his master slew
him before he discovered the body of the wolf Gelert had killed in protecting the baby.
   "Beth-Gelert" is a doggerel poem on the subject by Wm Robert Spencer (1769-
1834).
   177.22   dogpoet...hangname he gave himself of Bethgelert

BEGGARSBUSH   (17/32).   The area of Dub in the vicinity of the present Ballsbridge, on the Dub-Blackrock Rd. Near the present Haddington Rd was once a large
bush where beggars congregated and often ambushed travelers. Dub's rugby grounds
are in Lansdowne Rd (qv), *B*.
   163.12   ambusheers, beggar
   542.35   beggered about the amnibushes like belly in a bowle
   588.02   behind the beggar's bush
   616.33   Order now before we reach Ruggers' Rush!

BEHIND ST   (15/33).   A passage from Werburgh St to Nicholas St, so-called from
its position *behind* Skinners Row. Form Sutor or Sutter St or Lane; aka Hind St.
The Phoenix Tav was located here in mid-18th cent.
   248.33   3 Behind Street

BELFAST.   City, Co Antrim (Ulster), cap N Ireland; since the 17th cent the center
of Ir Protestantism. The shipbuilding yards and shipways of Harland and Wolff
(140.19) (which preferred Prot employees, 140.19) were at one time the world's largest. Queens Coll, *B*, founded 1849, now Queens Univ under Ir Univ Act of 1908
(385.13). The *Northern Whig* began publication in 1824 (42.28, 511.02). Letterpress
printing was introduced in *B* in 1693 by James Blow (534.18), and the *Belfast Newsletter* (not Saunder's), main Prot daily newspaper (534.20), was founded in 1737 by
Henry and Francis Joy (534.15). The city motto is *Pro tanto quid retribuamus*
(521.10). As a cen of culture in the late 18th and early 19th cents, *B* was called the
"Athens of the North" (519.19).
   Other place-names are Falls Road (534.20) in the Prot working class dist; Knock-
breckan Reservoir (534.19), the *B* water supply; Waring St (534.18) in cen *B*; Ballymacarret (390.24, 501.04), an industrial dist on *B* Lough, which, with MacArt's Fort
(*Baile Mhic Airt*) on Cave Hill (529.24), NW of *B*, is named for Brian MacArt O'Neill,
slain 1601 by Lord Deputy Mountjoy. On Cave Hill, aka Ben Madighan (?222.13),
Wolfe Tone and others pledged themselves to Ir independence, 1795.
   42.28   a northern tory, a southern whig
   70.15   Bullfoost Mountains
   140.15   Delfas
   140.19   orange garland
   160.27   I am underheerd by old billfaust
   ?222.13   *Mountain*...Maidykins in Undiform
   385.13   Queen's Ultonian colleges
   390.25   *As I was going to Burrymecarott*
   501.04   Hellohello! Ballymacarett!

511.02	Northwhiggern cupteam...papers before us carry
519.19	thathens of tharctic
521.10	[Matt speaking] *Pro tanto quid retribuamus?*
529.24	cavehill exers or hearts of steel
534.18	waring lowbelt suit
534.19	with knockbrecky kenees and bullfist rings
534.20	fallse roude axehand
?534.20	Saunter's Nocelettres
541.16	Bulafests

BELGIUM.   Constitutional monarchy since 1831; form part of Neth, briefly of Fr. The two langs and cultures of *B* are Walloon (Fr) and Flemish. The nat anthem is "La Brabançonne" by Campenhout (138.12). Waterloo is of course in *B*, and for some reason Napoleon appears in the Museyroom passage (*FW* 9) as "me Belchum." See *Brabant.*

9.01	This is me Belchum
9.04	me Belchum
9.10	bode Belchum
9.13	me Belchum
9.15	me Belchum
9.30	me Belchum's
?72.03	*Le King of the Burgaans*
138.12	a brabanson for his beeter
239.32	belge end sore footh
?255.13	Bulljon Bossbrute
?316.19	into the boelgein
376.04	a bulgen horesies
376.05	wollan indulgencies, this is a flemsh
529.22	made in Fredborg into the bullgine

Flanders.   The NW portion of *B*, now divided into 2 of *B*'s 9 provinces, E Flanders and W Flanders. The landing of the Normans at Baginbun (qv) in 1169 is described in the Ir annals as "The fleet of the Flemings came to Erin" (388.10,18). Flemish crossbowmen in the invading army were the first the Ir had ever seen.

?43.04	a fleming
204.22	why in the flenders was she frickled
?289.13	Byrne's and Flamming's
376.05	this is a flemsh
388.10	Flemish armada
388.18	Frankish floot of Noahsdobahs
397.24	since the phlegmish hoopicough

BELGRADE (BEOGRAD).   Cap of Serbia, of Yugo only since 1945.

114.05	from Maliziies with Bulgarad
?491.35	Baltic Bygrad
534.22	Belgradia

BELGRAVIA.   Once-fashionable London dist. It reaches *FW* by way of the limerick: "There was a young man from Belgravia/Who didn't believe in our Saviour./He walked down the Strand/With his balls in his hand/And was fined for indecent behaviour."

534.22–31	Belgradia...paviour...North Strand...Thom's towel in hand...behaviour

BELLE ALLIANCE, LA.   See *Waterloo.*

BELLEEK.   Town, Co Fermanagh; known for its china, and for salmon and trout fishing on the Lwr Erne R.
>   409.24   beliek
>   412.10   Pontoffbellek
>   449.33   tealeaves for the trout and belleeks for the wary

BELLE SAUVAGE, LA.   Famous London coaching inn off Ludgate Hill. Pocahontas stayed there 1616-17 when she came to London with her husband John Rolfe, but the name antedates her visit.
>   Brougham's burlesque "La Belle Sauvage" (about Pocahontas) was performed on the opening night of the Gaiety Theatre (Dub), 27 Nov 1871.
>   106.16   *La Belle Sauvage Pocahonteuse*

BELVEDERE COLLEGE   (15/35).   In Gt Denmark St; a Jesuit preparatory sch since 1841. JJ attended it, 1893-1898, and was an "exhibitioner" throughout, winning cash prizes in all-Ire competitive exhibitions, or exams, in 1894, 1895, 1897, and 1898 (didn't compete in 1896).
>   205.05   Belvedarean exhibitioners

BENARES.   Ind city and state on the Ganges R, 400 mi NW of Calcutta; the holy city of the Hindus. The Ganges is lined with "ghats," or landing-places where pilgrims bathe in the sacred riv.
>   551.35   benared my ghates

BENBULBEN.   Mt, Co Sligo, W peak of Dartry Mts; aka "Table Mt." The legendary hero Diarmuid died there, and Yeats is buried at Drumcliffe, "Under Ben Bulben."
>   ?13.24   a bulbenboss surmounted upon an alderman

BENBURB.   Vill, Co Tyrone, a former O'Neill stronghold. On 4 June 1646 a Scot and Eng army was defeated by Owen Roe O'Neill, last of the Ir chiefs, who died shortly after.
>   ?479.05   Burb! Burb! Burb!

BENGAL.   NE Ind prov; cap Calcutta; form E Bengal is now Bangladesh.
>   179.14   Bengalese Beacon of Biloxity

BÉRANGER, CAFÉ.   Paris café where Hugo, Sainte-Beuve, Gautier, *et al*, met as "La Cénacle litteraire." For Pierre Jean de Béranger, author of *Le Sénateur*, see *Census*.
>   372.12   the snug saloon seanad of our Café Béranger. The scenictutors

BEREHAVEN.   A strait btwn Bere Isl and N shore of Bantry Bay, Co Cork.
>   315.22   he put into bierhiven

BERGEN-OP-ZOOM.   Town, N Brabant prov, S Neth, at mouth of Zoom R, on the Scheldt estuary. Form a strongly fortified town, besieged in 1588, 1622, 1747, 1795, and 1814-15.
>   73.26   siegings round our archicitadel...as...Bangen-op-Zoom

BERING SEA.   Sea, N Pacific O, btwn Alaska, US, and E Siberia, USSR; *B* Strait connects *B* Sea with Arctic O.
>   ?320.28   Afferik Arena...till Blawland Bearring
>   321.13   to give them their beerings
>   602.30   wave his polar bearing
>   ?628.09   If I seen him bearing down on me

BERKELEY ROAD (15/35).   Runs N from Blessington St past the W end of Eccles St to the NCR; the S section is called *B* St, the N, *B* Rd.

An elliptical (double crescent) "Royal Circus" was planned by Luke Gardiner, Vis-
count Mountjoy, before his death in 1798, to encircle the area at the W end of Eccles
St; a map of 1821 still shows it by anticipation. It was never built, and *B* Rd and the
Mater Misericordiae Hosp now occupy the E portion of the site.

    260.11   Tycho Brache Crescent,[2] shouldering Berkeley Alley [260.F2: Mater
            Mary Mercerycordial]

BERLIN.   Ger city and former cap, on Spree R. According to doubtful trad, it was
founded by Margrave Albert the Bear (d 1170) (539.30). It was the Residenzstadt of
the Hohenzollerns from the 15th cent (539.20). The Brandenburg Gate (Brandenbur-
ger Tor), the only remaining gate of the *B* walls (246.06, ?265.13), is the entrance
to Unter den Linden (577.29). The Lustgarten (Ger, "Pleasure Garden") is a park surrounded by the former royal palace, the cath, and museums (532.22). Moabit is a
B dist, incl Moabit pris (547.01). "*B* gloves" (36.15) are of knitted wool.

    36.15   one Berlin gauntlet
    246.06   From Brandenborgenthor
    ?265.13   brandnewburgher
    532.22   Kissilov's Slutsgartern
    ?539.20   platzed mine residenze
    539.30   Allbrecht the Bearn
    547.01   from Moabit
    550.08   my barelean linsteer
    577.29   in the grounds or unterlinnen

BERLITZ LANGUAGE SCHOOLS.   JJ taught at the *B* schs in Trieste and Pola.
    182.07   to ensign the colours by the beerlitz in his mathness
    421.27   impulsory irelitz
    467.25   out of beurlads scoel

BERRATHON.   In Macpherson's poem of that name, an isl of Scand where Ossian
rescues the king, Larthmor, after he has been imprisoned by his own son.
    254.33   the best berrathon sanger in all the aisles of Skaldignavia

BERRY.   Form duchy and prov, cen Fr. For St Julien of *B*, see *Census*. St Julien
wine is a claret from Bordeaux.
    406.24   All St Jilian's of Berry

BETHEL.   Anc city of Pal, 11 mi N of Jerusalem; a holy place. Orig called Luz
[?528.13]; Jacob renamed it *B*, Heb "House of God," after his dream, later set up
an altar (*Gen* 12:8, 28:19, 35:1-7). As a generic term, a chapel or place of worship.
Acc to one legend, the Lia Fáil (qv) is the stone Jacob slept on. Dr Bethel Solomon
(542.28) was a president of the Rotunda (qv) (Lying-In) Hosp.
    186.30   the rival doors of warm bethels of worship
    ?329.36   The grandest bethehailey seen or heard
    ?347.03   from the mount of Bekel, Steep Nemorn
    542.28   in my bethel of Solyman's
    607.08   Jakob van der Bethel

BEULAH, LAND OF.   *Isa* 62:4: "You shall be called my delight is in her, and your
land Married" (Heb, *Beulah*). In Bunyan's *Pilgrim's Progress*, the land of joy where pilgrims wait until called to the Celestial City. *Byelo*, Russ "white," as in Byelorussia.
    64.05   a fourth loud snore out of his land of byelo

BEWLEY. *B*'s Oriental Cafes (coffee, tea, pastry) are Dub institutions, but I don't know what they have to do with bouillabaisse or Beauty and the Beast. Bewley and Draper, general merchants, manufacturers of mineral waters, and wholesale druggists, were at 23 and 27 Mary St (15/34) (cf *U* 616/632).
    487.16   Bewley in the baste

BIG BEN. Properly the bell, not the clock, on the Tower of Westminster, London.
    128.01   a horologe unstoppable and the Benn of all bells

BIG GUN (17/36). St in Fairview, named for former tav; renamed Merville Ave at the beginning of the cent.
    ?129.10   in the biguinnengs...battle of Boss
    434.10   in the coalhole trying to boil the big gun's dinner

BIG TREE (15/35). A big tree, so known to local citizenry, once grew in Drumcondra Lane (now Dorset St), just N of the NCR.
    ?146.34   You know bigtree are all against gravstone
    ?332.02   a lil trip trap and a big treeskooner

BILOXI. Seaport on Gulf of Mexico, Mississippi, US.
    ?179.14   Bengalese Beacon of Biloxity

BINNS'S BRIDGE (15/35). Br carrying Drumcondra Rd across the Royal Canal.
    130.21   rialtos, annesleyg, binn and balls [all bridges]

BIRD'S NEST INSTITUTION. Now in Blackrock, it was formerly in Kingstown (Dun Laoghaire). A Prot boys' home for the care and conversion of destitute Roman Catholics, its name, like "soupers," became a pejorative nickname for Prot proselytizing. Its inmates also known as "Smyly boys."
    209.33   like the Smyly boys at their vicereine's levee
    450.33   Birdsnests is birdsnests

BIRNAM WOOD. See *Dunsinane.*

BIRR. Town, W Co Offaly, noted for its astronomical obs. Sir Wm Petty called it "Umbilicus Hiberniae." Form Parsonstown.
    ?207.10   strawbirry reds

BISCAY, BAY OF. Inlet of Atlantic O off N coast of Sp. Song: "The Bay of Biscay."
    ?121.05   basque of bayleaves
    374.16   Boy of Biskop
    374.18   bunk of basky
    ?414.06   Bois in the Boscoor
    ?542.29   bax of biscums...jacobeaters

BISHOP'S BAY. SW coast of Lambay Isl (qv).
    ?374.16   Boy of Biskop

BISMARCK ARCHIPELAGO. Chain of isls E of New Guinea, containing New Ireland and New Britain, separated by St George's Channel. Part of Melanesia.
    601.36   arkypelicans...Newer Aland...Milenesia...Be smark

BLAALAND. Old Norse name ("Blueland") for Afr (qv). In the Sagas, Africans (usually Moors) are called "bluemen."
    78.27   Celtiberian...bluemin and pillfaces...moors or letts

320.28   from Afferik Arena...till Blawland Bearring
403.12   blautoothdmand...wild hindigan
537.24   Cherna Djamja, Blawlawnd-via-Brigstow

BLACKAMOOR'S HEAD, THE   (14/33, later 15/34).   18th-cent shop in Francis
St, later in Dame St. Acc to Peter's *Dublin Fragments* (156), paduasoys and "russets
for petticoats" could be seen there.
59.02   padouasoys...russets from the Blackamoor's Head

BLACK AND ALL BLACK.   18th-cent Dub farrier's shop and stables. Acc to Peter's
Dublin Fragments (157), "corn and hay were sold there."
59.04   the corn and hay emptors at their Black and All Black

BLACK FOREST.   Mountainous region, SW Ger, along E bank of upr Rhine from
the Neckar R to the Sw border. Ger, *Schwarzwald*.
410.09   in this bleak forest

BLACKFRIARS.   Lane, br, form theatre in London. *B* Lane occupies part of the
site of Dominican monastery of the Black Friars (1276-1538), where Henry VIII held
his Black Parl and was granted a divorce from Catherine of Aragon. James Burbage
founded *B* Theatre (*ca* 1596, demolished 1655), where Shakespeare frequently acted.
B Br, built 1769, spans the Thames just S of the old monastery site.
48.03   The Blackfriars treacle plaster outrage be liddled!
191.01   an unfrillfrocked quackfriar...Scheekspair

BLACKHEATH.   SE London pleasure resort, mainly in Lewisham, S of Thames,
where golf was first introduced into Eng in 1608. Hqs of Kentish rebels in 1381 and
again in 1450. The area was notorious for highwaymen.
?549.07   our folk had rest from Blackheathen

BLACK PIG'S DYKE.   Aka Dane's Cast, Worm Ditch, Black Pig's Race. A great
wall and fortification built by Ulstermen in 3rd cent AD as a boundary btwn Ulaidh
and Oriel. Remnants of the wall are still discernible, esp near Granard, Co Longford,
where portions extend btwn Lough Kinale and Lough Gowna; btwn Dowra on the
Leitrim-Cavan border and Lough Allen; and in Co Down, 1 mi E of Poyntzpass. The
Dyke ran across the whole of Ire, roughly from Carlingford Lough to Donegal Abbey.
517.15   they rolled togutter into the ditch together? Black Pig's Dyke?

BLACKPITTS   (14/32).   St in the Coombe, W of Clanbrassil St.
545.35   in black pitts of the pestered Lenfant

BLACKPOOL.   City and resort, Lancs, Eng, on Ir Sea 30 mi N of Liverpool. "Blackpool" in *FW* refers primarily to Dub, since it translates the Norse "Dubh-linn"; but
it just may carry a hint of the rich associations of the Brit nation noisily, sadly, and
often damply at play in its greatest seaside resort. Black (blood) pudding is a Lancs
specialty.
?35.16   a nice how-do-you-do in Poolblack
?85.15   Butt's, most easterly (but all goes west!) of blackpool bridges
?88.34   laving his leaftime in Blackpool
?621.13   roly polony from Blugpuddels

BLACKROCK.   Town on Dub Bay btwn Dub and Dun Laoghaire; the old name
was Newtown. Since the 18th cent a place of resort for Dubliners, reached by the
"Rock Road" (qv) (now Merrion Rd), later by the Dalkey, Kingstown, and *B* tram
(qv). Conway's Tav and Vauxhall Gardens (qqv) were two of its attractions.

40.30	somewhere off the Dullkey Downlairy and Bleakrooky tramaline
83.20	Conway's Inn at Blackrock
294.22	Blake-Roche, Kingston and Dockrell
?541.02	Braid Blackfordrock
582.32	dullakeykongsbyogblagroggerswagginline

BLACK SEA.   Aka Euxine, anc Pontus Euxinus, the sea btwn Europe and Asia.

| 263.13 | Hispano-Cathayan-Euxine |
| 340.13 | TAFF...*a blackseer* |

BLACKWATER.   There are *B* Rivs, and vills, in half the cos of Ire. Best known: (1) rises from Lough Ramor in Co Cavan, flows through Co Meath to join Boyne R at Navan;   (2) rises in mts of Slievelogher, Kerry-Cork border, flows E through Co Cork past Lismore, then S to sea at Youghal. Spenser: "Swift Awniduffe, which by the Englishman/is callde Blackewater."

196.12	He has all my water black on me
?381.17	with black ruin like a sponge out of water
451.15	drink annyblack water that rann onme way
546.33	Chief Goes in Black Water [the Co Cork, ie Munster, riv]

BLANCHARDSTOWN   (8/38).   Vill NW of Dub on Navan Rd. Never has had a newspaper, never will.

| 607.34 | Blanchardstown mewspeppers pleads coppyl |

BLARNEY.   Town, Co Cork, 4 mi NW of Cork City. In the 15th-cent cas is the *B* Stone, believed (but by whom?) to make anyone who kisses it proficient in blarney (smooth-talk). Songs, "The Groves of Blarney"; "O Blarney Castle, My Darling" (air: "The Blackbird").

61.26	you bet your boughtem blarneys
140.27	sinking ofter the soapstone of silvry speech
211.11	a pair of Blarney braggs
371.16	their grooves of blarneying
381.22	like a blurney Cashelmagh crooner...blackberd's ballad
419.16	blarneyest blather in all Corneywall
453.06	braggart of blarney
472.06	disdoon blarmey...groves
483.16	blarneying Marcantonio [Mark = Munster]

BLEAK HOUSE.   The Dickens novel about the Court of Chancery; name is sometimes used as a symbol for Eng. Stanislaus Joyce: "I called 7, St Peter's Terrace, Cabra, [a Joyce res] 'Bleak House'." There was a *BH* in Dub in Marino Ave. *Blaekhuse*, Dan "inkwell."

| ?337.11 | maleybags, things and bleakhusen |

BLEEDING HORSE TAVERN   (15/32).   Anc tav which stood into 19th cent at junction of Charlotte and Camden Sts. It figures prominently in J S LeFanu's *The Cock and Anchor.*

| 370.23 | Stunner of oddstodds on bluebleeding boarhorse! |

BLENNERCASSEL.   (1) Ballyseedy Ho, 3 mi E of Tralee, Co Kerry; built 1760 for the Blennerhasset family. Blennerville, SW of Tralee, also named after this family. (2) Blennerhasset, a palatial house on an isl in the Ohio R, US, built by Herman Blennerhasset, the Irishman mixed up in Aaron Burr's conspiracy.   (3) Castle Caldwell (ruins), 6 mi NE of Belleek, Co Fermanagh, was built 1612 by the Blennerhassets

but passed to the Caldwell family in late 17th cent.
>   376.32   Slick of the trick and Blennercassel of the brogue. Clanruckard for
>   ever!

BLESSINGTON.   Town, Co Wicklow, 15 mi SW of Dub. The Liffey R and King's
R join at *B*; since 1938 they flow into the N arm of the *B* (hydroelectric) Reservoir,
also called Poulaphuca (qv) after the Liffey waterfall farther S, downstream. *FW* remembers the Liffey before it was dammed. Until 1683, *B* was called Burgage (qv).
>   194.36   the pools of the phooka and a place they call it Blessington

BLOODY ACRE   (14/37).   A field now incorporated into Glasnevin (qv) Cem; acc
to Cosgrave's *North Dublin*, 30, it prob commemorates the Battle of the Wood of
Tolka, btwn 2 Ir armies before the Norman invasion.
>   231.21   bloody acres
>   553.08   blighty acre

BLUEBELL (BLUE BELL)   (10/32).   Ave and Rd, Kilmainham area: btwn Grand
Canal and Naas Rd. Also a tnld in par of Drimnagh, and the stream supplying moat
of Drimnagh Cas, just S of *B*.
>   *Jacinthe des prés* is Fr "bluebell." Allusions are to the immortal flowers of the
Quinet sentence (*pervenche*, Fr "periwinkle"), but the associations with *B* in Dub
and Selskar (St Sepulchre) (qv) in Wexford are unexplained.
>   ?28.27   *Les Loves of Selskar et Pervenche*...bluebells blowing in salty sepul-
>   chres
>   361.22   bridge of primerose...blueybells near Dandeliond
>   ?580.17   Pervinca calling, Soloscar hears
>   ?626.19   while blubles blows there'll still be sealskers

BLUE BOAR ALLEY   (15/33).   Aka Blue Coat Alley; S of St Werburgh's Ch,
Werburgh St, now obliterated by a mod sch.
>   370.23   Stunner of oddstodds on bluebleeding boarhorse!

BLUE STACK MOUNTAINS.   Mts, Co Donegal, N of Donegal Town.
>   6.01   blightblack workingstacks...twelvepins

BODINGTOWN.   Tnld, par of Clonalvy, bar of Duleek Upr, Co Meath.
>   622.35   Bodingtown

BOHEMIA.   Prov, W Czech, subject of Balfe's opera, "The Bohemian Girl." Because
the first gypsies came to Fr by way of *B*, it was believed to be the home of the gypsies and thence "bohemian" became a term for artists of unconventional habits. The *B*
Brethren were a 15th-cent religious sect in Prague (170.10).
>   32.35   *The Bo' Girl* and *The Lily*
>   170.10   quakers...when Bohemeand lips...a gnawstick
>   246.18   lily of Bohemey
>   333.15   farabroads and behomeans
>   404.26   his loud boheem toy...damasker's

BOHERMORE.   The name is from *Bóthar Mór*, Ir "Great Road." There were 5
"great roads" built in Ire in the 2nd cent, but none was uniquely called the Bóthar
Mór. There is no "Barony of *B*"; there are tnlds named *B* in Cos Carlow, Kilkenny,
and Longford.
>   24.21, 373.05, and 399.28 refer to the home of Johnny MacDougall. Since he
represents West and the prov of Connacht, the allusion may be to the anc Esker (qv)
Rd from Dub to Galway. *B* Rd in Galway City, now the main rd to Tuam, was once

the rd to Dub; it is the site of *B* Cem.

 5.36 the bore the more
 24.21 and Waddlings Raid and the Bower Moore
 81.09 So more boher O'Connell!
 198.27 with bow or abandon!...Tell me moher
 373.05 he was berthed on the Moherboher to the Washte
 399.28 *from the barony of Bohermore*

BOHERNABREENA. *Bóthar-na-Bruighne*, "Road of the mansion." Tnld, rd, and reservoir, 2 mi S of Tallaght in Glenasmole (qv); named for the famous "Hostel of Da Derga," destroyed by pirates *ca* 1st cent AD. It was the site of a famous murder and execution in 1816: one Kearney and his 2 sons were hanged for the hatchet slaying of a gamekeeper.
 87.31 thicksets in court and from the macdublins on the bohernabreen

BOILEAU AND BOYD. Wholesale druggists, chemists, and colour merchants, 88-93 Bride St, 46 Mary St, and 6 Merrion Row.
 527.13 coldcream...from Boileau's

BOLAND'S, LTD (15/33). Boland's City of Dublin Bakery has been at 9A Lwr Grand Canal St; also on Grand Canal Quay. De Valera commanded a detachment at Boland's Mills during the Rising of 1916.
 406.13 and Boland's broth broken into the bargain...green free state

BOLEYVOGUE (BOOLAVOGUE). Town, 8 mi NE of Enniscorthy, Co Wexford. Eng troops burned RC chapel and other buildings, 26 May 1798, setting off the Wexford insurrection. "Boulavogue" is a song about the rising and Fr Murphy.
 "Bullavogue" in Ir-Eng means a rough bully of a fellow.
 100.08 Of A Bullavogue

BOLGA. Acc to MacPherson's notes, the S parts of Ire were known by the name of Bolga, from the Firbolg, or Belgae; *bolga*, "quiver"; *Fir-bolg*, "bowmen."
 329.17 Roscranna's bolgaboyo

BOMBAY. Ind state and city, W Ind. But in *FW*, only a pun on "peach *bombé.*"
 37.32 Peach Bombay

BOND ST. In London's West End; synonymous with expensive fashion. Dub's Bond St (14/33) is undistinguished.
 156.29 as british as bondstrict

BON MARCHÉ, MAGASIN DU. Paris dept store, 7th Arr; *bon marché*, Fr "bargain."
 112.32 watermark: *Notre Dame du Bon Marché*

BONNYBROOK. Tnld, and *B* House, W of Coolock, N Dub. There are no hosps in the vicinity; the Hospice for the Dying (qv) is in S Dub. See *Donnybrook.*
 514.25 the Auspice for the Living, Bonnybrook, by the river

BOOLIES. Tnld, par of Kilbride, bar of Ratoath, Co Meath. (Other tnlds of this common name, which means "milking places," are excluded by the context.)
 97.10 by the Boolies

BOOTERSTOWN (20/30). Dist, SE Dub, on shore rd to Blackrock. It was on the Dalkey, Kingstown, and Blackrock tram line (qv). The earliest name was "Ballybothyr," "town of the road," Ir *bóthar*, angl "booter," "batter," or "boher."

    ?132.04   sticklered rights and lefts at Baddersdown
    235.36   the briskly best from Bootiestown
    507.35   this salt son of a century from Boaterstown, Shivering William
    582.33   change here for Lootherstown

BOÖTES.   Constellation, whose brightest star is Arcturus. *Boötes*, Gk "ploughman";
it was seen as "driving" Ursa Major (qv) seen as the Plough or Wagon.
    ?262.21   the Boote's at Pickardstown

BOOT LANE   (15/34).   Now Arran St E; named for an inn with "the sign of a
boot." Btwn the site of *BL* and Capel St was the anc Abbey of St Mary.
    618.08   The Boot lane brigade

BOREUM.   Ptolemy's name for NW Ire (Donegal). Hyperborean Sea: the Atlantic
N of Ire. The Annals of the Four Masters were written in a monastery in Donegal.
    13.21   his grand old historiorum, wrote near Boriorum

BORNEO.   Isl in the Malay Archipelago. All *FW* references are to the song "The
Wild Man From Borneo Has Just Come to Town."
    130.24   the viled ville of Barnehulme
    331.36   the wild main from Borneholm
    345.05   *such waldmanns from Burnias*
    382.26   our wineman from Barleyhome
    415.08   the Boubou from Bourneum

BORNHOLM.   Isl, a co of Den, in Baltic Sea W of Den and S of Swed. It was an-
ciently a haven for pirates, Vikings, and "wild Danes."
    130.24   the viled ville of Barnehulme
    331.36   the wild main from Borneholm

BORRIS.   Vill, Co Carlow. The song "Eileen Aroon" has its origin in the elopement
of Eileen Kavanagh from *B* Cas in the 14th cent.
    337.33   Bud...There he is in his Borrisalooner [+ bar-saloon and Borsalino
            hat]

BORSTAL.   Vill near Rochester, Kent, SE Eng; site of orig *B* Reformatory for Juvenile Delinquents (known as "*B* boys"). The Brit scheme for correctional insts for
adolescents was adopted in 1902.
    Erasmus Smith was a 17th-cent London merchant who gave his Ir land-holdings to
endow Prot schs throughout Ire.
    353.34   *birstol boys*
    391.09   to borstel her schoon
    504.26   Erasmus Smith's burstall boys
    624.33   bragged up by Brostal

BOSCO'S CASTLE.   Part of Cromwell's Barrack, 17th-cent starfort (ruins) at harb
entrance to Inishbofin, Co Galway. Bosco was a pirate allied with Grace O'Malley.
    The allusion is questionable, but may echo faintly in this and other allusions to
Tabasco and the Basque Provs (qv).
    ?230.06   osco de basco de pesco de bisco

BOSKOP.   Locality in the Transvaal, S Afr; known as site of discovery of fossil prehistoric human skull in 1913.
    190.19   taken the scales off boilers like any boskop of Yorek

BOSPORUS (BOSPHORUS).   Strait joining Black Sea and Sea of Marmara, with
Istanbul at outlet to the latter, on the Eur side.

    ?167.14   blasphorus blesphorous idiot
    460.27   beyond the boysforus
    465.09   plenty of woom in the smallclothes for the bothsforus
    547.30   Heydays, he flung blissforhers...Galata [see *Istanbul*]
    583.12   tartanelle...strait's...Bossford

BOSTON.   Seaport city, cap of Mass, US, home of the former *B Evening Transcript*
and in *FW* the origin of the Letter, or "transhipt from *B*." The earlier *B Newsletter*
(11.22, 489.35) was founded 1704. *Bastún* (angl "bosthoon"), Ir "blockhead." T S
Eliot is associated with some, perhaps all, allusions to *B*. Despite the waves of Ir emigration to *B*, there are notably no allusions in *FW* to local sites or events in *B*, except for Bunker Hill (qv).

    11.22   boaston nightgarters and masses of shoesets
    111.09   by transhipt from Boston (Mass.)
    273.L1   *me bosthoon fiend*
    301.05   Ask for bosthoon, late for Mass
    347.13   Bostion Moss
    364.35   well shoving off a boastonmess like lots wives
    374.03   A trancedone boyscript
    393.31   Transton Postscript
    421.10   Boston (Mass)
    490.01   allnights newseryreel...bostoons
    617.23   shown in Morning post as from Boston transcripped
    623.36   traumscrapt from Maston, Boss

BOSWORTH FIELD.   Area in Leics, Eng, site of the last battle (1485) of the War
of the Roses; Richard III ("Crookback") was defeated and killed by Earl of Richmond, later Henry VII.

    127.18   Dook Hookbackcrook...booseworthies

BOTANIC GARDENS (14–15/37).   In Glasnevin, adjoining Prospect Cem; founded in 18th cent by Royal Dub Soc; administered since 1901 by Dept of Agriculture
(14/37).

    622.36   How they housed to house you after the Platonic garlens!

BOTANY BAY.   (1) First Brit penal settlement in Australia, near Sydney, NSW;
subject of the song, "Botany Bay."   (2) Res court in Trinity Coll, Dub, so-called
since the 19th cent, presumably because of its bleak prison-like appearance. It is in
fact not within reach of a long drive ("boundary") from the TCD cricket pitch on
the other side of the grounds.

    543.04   I sent my boundary to Botany Bay
    601.17   they coroll in caroll round Botany Bay

BOTHNIA.   Form terr, now part of Swed and Fin. The Gulf of *B* is N part of Baltic Sea, btwn Swed and Fin.

    25.11   whole households beyond the Bothnians

BOULTER'S HILL (15/34).   18th-cent name of area now Henrietta St. Aka "Primates' Hill," because 4 Primates of the CI resided there btwn 1724 and 1794.

    ?136.35   looks like a moultain boultter

BOURNEMOUTH.   City and seaside resort on Eng Channel, Hampshire, 30 mi SW

of Southampton.
?578.25   Pont Delisle till she jumped the boom at Brounemouth

BOURSE.   The Paris stock exchange is the original for the *bourses* in other Eur
cities.
448.30   a bourse from bon Somewind
540.26   our bourse and politicoecomedy
589.09   weighty on the bourse

BOW LANE (13/33).   *B* Lane and *B* Bridge (a street) pass St Patrick's Hosp and
the Royal Hosp on rd to Kilmainham, roughly parallel to Conyngham Rd, on the
other side of the Liffey and the S boundary of Phoenix Park.
576.27   Bogy Bobow...cunnyngnest...Phenicia Parkes

BOWLING GREEN.   Bowling greens were more common once. The best-known
bowling green in Dub was on the site of Oxmantown (qv) Green. Stanislaus Joyce
mentioned to Patricia Hutchins that there was once a bowling green behind the Mullingar Hotel (HCE's Tavern) in Chapelizod. Visiting Nora's mother in Galway City,
JJ stayed at 4 Bowling Green. In Cork, the anti-Nationalist militia once drilled, presumably with muskets, on the Bowling Green. And, of course, Sir Francis Drake left
a bowling green to repel the Spanish Armada.
517.09   with his black masket off the bawling green

BOYNE RIVER.   Riv, E Ire; its source is at Trinity Well, Hill of Carberry, Co Kildare, and it flows NE into Ir Sea just below Drogheda. On 1 July 1690, Eng (Prot)
forces under Wm III defeated Jacobites under James II in Battle of the *B*, 3 mi W of
Drogheda. "Boyne Water" is an Orange song (98.22, 137.01).
"Foyne Boyne salmon" was once a Dub street cry. It was cockles and mussels
that were alive alive O (41.26, 538.21).
The Brugh of the Boyne (?136.22) near Slane, Co Meath, is an anc royal cem,
"burial place of kings."
8.22   the three lipoleum boyne
41.26   foyneboyne salmon alive
98.22   wangfish daring the buoyant waters
114.36   battle of the Boyne
126.22   shocked the prodestung boyne
130.13   buttle of the bawn
?136.22   king's brugh
137.01   boinyn water
211.34   Billy Dunboyne
341.06   Buckily buckily, blodestained boyne
361.25   budkley mister, bester of the boyne
372.07   barttler of the beauyne
538.21   saumone like a boyne alive O

BRABANT.   Former duchy; its terr was divided after 1830 btwn S Neth and N and
cen Belg; the Belg prov of *B* surrounds Brussels. "La Brabonçonne" is the nat anthem
of Belg.
138.12   a brabanson for his beeter

BRADOGE (BRADOGUE) RIVER (14/34–35).   A small Dub riv (or "Water"),
now entirely subterranean, flowing from the intersection of Grangegorman and NCR,
SE to Liffey near Arran St.
212.09   Melissa Bradogue

BRANDON MT.   Mt, Co Kerry, on Dingle Penin. *B* Head is just NE of *B* Mt. Connor Pass crosses Dingle Penin, from Dingle to bays of *B* and Tralee just S of *B* Mt. Named for St Brendan, one of St Patrick's 4 saints.
> ?81.14   in the saddle of the Brennan's (now Malpasplace?) pass
> 491.11   from Lismore to Cape Brendan, Patrick's

BRANDYWINE.   Small riv in Penn and Del, US. Site of defeat of Washington by Gen Howe on 11 Sept 1777.
> ?510.19   the brandywine bankrompers

BRATISLAVA.   Cap of prov of Slovakia, Czech.
> 219.14   the Brothers Bratislavoff (Hyrcan and Haristobulus)
> 424.01   Bruda Pszths and Brat Slavos

BRAY.   Coastal resort town ("The Ir Brighton") SE of Dub in Co Wicklow. *B* Head is a 793-ft hill projecting from the coast S of *B*. The short *B* Riv reaches the sea at *B*. There is also a *B* Head in Valencia Isl, W Co Kerry, and a Lough *B* near the Liffey source in Wicklow. *Bri*, Ir "hill."
> 53.30   Bri Head
> 203.11   not where the Braye [Riv] divarts the Farer
> 313.31   brayvoh, little bratton!
> ?325.33   Blass Neddos bray!
> 448.18   Who'll brighton Brayhowth
> 522.30   tonedeafs [see *Tonduff*]...from the sound, bray
> 537.34   to bray at by clownsillies
> ?550.27   drapier-cut-dean, bray, nap
> 624.32   your brothermilk in Bray

BRAZIL (BRASIL, BREASIL, BREASAIL).   *Hy Brasaille*, Ir "Enchanted Isle," the Ir Atlantis. St Brendan (d 578) of Clonfert (in Galway), one of St Patrick's 4 saints, was in legend the first to cross the Atlantic, and the discoverer of the "Promised Land of the Saints," or "Isle of the Blest," an isl W of Ire. From the 6th to as late as the 18th cent, geographers accepted its existence; it was sometimes identified with Labrador, sometimes with Atlantis.
St Brendan's Isle was in the middle ages confused with "brazil," a red dye-wood. It is for the latter that *B* in S Amer was named. As Port, it is alluded to at 316.28.
> 316.28   from Blasil the Brast to our povotogesus portocall
> 442.14   Brendan's...Kerribrasilian sea
> ?464.07   A leal of the O'Looniys, a Brazel aboo!
> 488.25   High Brazil Brandan's Deferred
> 549.26   the island of Breasil

BREFFNY.   Name of anc tribe, which survived as name of dists in Cos Cavan and Leitrim. E Breffny is associated with the O'Reilly's (*Breifne Uí Raghilligh*), while W Breffny is associated with the O'Rourkes (*Breifne Uí Ruairc*). Tullymongan (qv) is in E Breffny.
> 99.26   Breffnian empire...Tullymongan...rayheallach...O'Roarke
> 332.05   −uaragheallachnatullaghmongan− [in C-word]
> 373.30   Rorke relly

BREGIA, PLAIN OF.   Anc name for the plain btwn the Liffey and the Boyne, Co Meath. Named for Breagha, who came to Ire with Heremon and Heber and the other sons of Milesius. When Heremon and Heber divided Ire between them, *B* (and Teffia, qv) were in Heber's territory S of the Boyne, but were soon taken over by Heremon.

604.04   Heremonheber on Bregia's plane where Teffia lies

BRENNER PASS.   Alpine pass, btwn Austria and It. The lowest and one of the oldest of the important Alpine passes.
?81.14   the Brennan's...pass

BRETLAND.   In the Sagas, the name for Wales; later poetic for "Britain."
25.28   never a warlord in Great Erinnes and Brettland
228.19   Pencylmania, Bretish Armerica

BRICKFIELDS, THE   (18/32).   Area btwn Merrion and Sandymount, so-called in the 17th and 18th cents; aka Lord Merrion's Brickfields. Acc to early records quoted by Haliday, "The bank at the west end of Cock (or Cockle) Lake called Salmon Pool bank, running southwards to the Brick Fields is very high."
174.27   beyond the brickfields of Salmon Pool

BRIDE ST   (15/33).   *B* St and New *B* St run N–S, W of Stephen's Green. There is no Queen's Coll there, or anywhere in Dub, but the City of Dub Coll of Technology has been in Lwr Kevin St around the cor from *B* St, since the 19th cent.
388.27   neer the Queen's Colleges, in 1132 Brian or Bride street

BRIDEWELL.   Orig a London pris, later a generic term for any reformatory.
    In 1603, part of Hoggen Green (qv) was vested in trustees for erection of a Bridewell; in 1617 the house was sold to TCD and occupied as Trinity Hall. Another Dub Bridewell, opened in 1801, was in Smithfield, N of Arran Quay.
172.03   she knew the vice out of bridewell was a bad fast man

BRIDGES, DUBLIN.   The Liffey btwn Chapelizod and Dub Bay is spanned by 9 rd brs, 2 rlwy brs, and a footbridge. The following list shows location, from W to E, and other names; most have been renamed since the publ of *FW*. In each case the most common name known to JJ is given first. See individual entries.

Island Br (*ca* 1790).
   Sarah
   (Railway Br)
King's Br (1828).   Now Sean Heuston
Barrack Br (1704).   Now Rory O'More
   "Bloody" (1670)
   Victoria (1863)
Queen's Br (1768).   Now Queen Maev
   Arran (1683)
   Bridewell
   Ellis's
   Mellows
Whitworth Br (1818).   Now Father Mathew
   King John's (1210)
   Old (*ca* 1385)
Richmond Br (1816).   Now O'Donovan Rossa
   Ormond (1683)
Essex Br (1676; rebuilt 1755).   Now Grattan (1874)
Wellington Br (1816).   Now Liffey
   Cast Iron
   Metal
   Ha'penny

O'Connell Br (1880).
Carlisle (1794)
Butt Br (1879).
Swivel
Loop Line Rlwy

Other Dub brs span the Grand and Royal Canals and the Camac, Dodder, and Tolka rivs. Those named in *FW* (see individual entries) are: Annesley, Ball's (see *Ballsbridge*), Binns's, Cross Guns, Golden, Newcomen, Rialto, and Tolka.

BRIE.   Dist, NE Fr, in Depts of Aisne, Marne, and Seine-et-Marne; noted esp for its cheese.

"Brie-on-Arrosa/O'Briny rossies" presents a problem. The Arros R, a trib of the Adour, is in SW Fr (Dept of Gers); *arroser*, Fr "to water"; *bri*, Ir "hill"; Chateau Haut Brion (claret) is from Graves, S of Bordeaux. Take your pick.

95.04   the O'Moyly gracies and the O'Briny rossies
163.28   the Bure will be dear on the Brie [butter, cheese]
207.15   A call to pay and light a taper, in Brie-on-Arrosa

BRIGHTON.   Town and seaside resort, Sussex, S Eng, on Eng Channel. JJ was born in Brighton Sq, Rathmines (S of Dub).

320.21   Brighten-pon-the-Baltic
448.18   Who'll brighton Brayhowth
537.11   outbreighten their land's eng

BRINDISI.   It prov and port on Strait of Otranto, Adriatic Sea; wine and spirits are among its exports. Also, *brindisi*, It "a toast."

462.02   brindising brandisong

BRISTOL.   City, Glocs (now Avon), SW Eng, on Avon R 8 mi from the Severn estuary. Earlier spellings: Bricgstoc, Brigstow, Bristowe. In 1172, Henry II granted Dub to the city of *B* (the charter is parodied on *FW* 545). The hist of *B* is a hist of foreign trade, including slave-trading in the 16th and 17th cents (537.24). The wool-trade with Ire has existed since the time of Canute. The 17th-cent Christmas Steps, off Colston St, a stepped st of shops, is a *B* landmark. Name *B* is OE for "bridge"; see *Tavern, The* (Bridge Inn) for additional listings.

?133.29   tribute...schenkt publicly to brigstoll
?353.34   *birstol boys*
378.19   Bring forth your deed...Brystal Palace
?391.09   borstel her schoon...grooming her ladyship
392.31   the heights of Newhigherland heard the Bristolhut
405.27   the house the once queen of Bristol and Balrothery twice admired
421.13   Bloody Big Bristol
442.10   about their bristelings
537.24   Blawlawnd-via-Brigstow [see *Blaaland* (Africa)]
539.21   my brixtol selection here at thollstall
542.16   I downsaw the last of Christmas steps
545.20   the men of Tolbris, a city of Tolbris...Tolbris
606.17   if you know your Bristol
?624.33   you were bragged up by Brostal

BRITAIN.   See *England*.

BRITAIN COURT   (15/34).   Off Gt Brit (now Parnell) St (N side), btwn Gardiner

St and Temple St. Britain Quay, where the Grand Canal and the Dodder R enter the Liffey, is just across the Grand Canal from Charlotte Quay.

434.15   our Harlotte Quai from poor Mrs Mangain's of Britain Court

BRITAIN, LITTLE.   Fr *Bretagne* or Brittany, NW Fr; aka Armorica (qv). Tristram died there; Amory Tristram, first Lord of Howth, was born there, or so JJ believed. The "prow" of *LB* is Cap Finistère (see *Finisterre*). The *Matière de Bretagne* is the med Arthurian cycle. Ptolemy called Ire "Little Britain."

LB St (15/34) runs W off Capel St. Barney Kiernan's pub, in *U*, was at 8, 9, and 10.

62.36   hailing fro' the prow of Little Britain
152.05   lattlebrattons
157.33   *la princesse de la Petite Bretagne*
292.F2   Matter of Brettaine and brut fierce
313.31   brayvoh, little bratton
375.08   in the matter of Brittas more than anarthur
565.29   Poor little brittle magic nation

BRITISH BROADCASTING CORP.   Familiarly known as the BBC. Among other services of the BBC was the "London Regional Service." Acc to J S Atherton, Daventry, Eng (244.02) was a BBC transmitter which JJ could have heard in Paris. I don't know whether there was a program of "BBC Minstrels"; for the Moore and Burgess Minstrels and Christy Minstrels, see *Census*.

?39.07   Bold Boy Cromwell
62.30   the Boore and Burgess Christy Menestrels
?75.14   broadsteyne 'bove citie
244.02   Hear, O worldwithout...Daintytrees, go dutch
253.10   London's...regionals
342.33   *first sports report of Loundin Reginald*
343.03   Boyle, Burke and Campbell [+ "bell, book and candle"]
?489.03   *V.V.C.*
534.07   Big big Calm, announcer

BRITISH MUSEUM.   Lord Elgin brought the marble frieze and pediment of the Parthenon at Athens to the *BM* in London in 1816, and the "Elgin marbles" are there still.

549.15   Elgin's marble halles

BRITTAS.   Town, Co Wicklow, and riv, which drains Glen of Kilbride and flows S into Liffey just above Blessington Reservoir.

201.17   *my short Brittas bed*
375.08   in the matter of Brittas more than anarthur [+ "matter of Britain"]

BRIXTON.   (1) S London dist, btwn Clapham and Dulwich, part of borough of Lambeth. Oscar Wilde served his prison term in *B* Pris.   (2) Town, SE of Plymouth, Devon, Eng.

538.09   best Brixton high yellow

BROADSTONE STATION (14/35).   Now disused terminus of the form Midland Gt Western Rlwy, Phibsborough Rd. It was not yet in existence when George IV visited Dub in 1821 (568.23).

75.14   broadsteyne 'bove citie
568.23   shall receive Dom King at broadstone barrow

BROBDINGNAG.   Land of giants, in *Gulliver's Travels*.

491.21   Braudribnob's...lillypets
583.09   Bigrob dignagging his lylyputtana

BROCKEN, THE.   Highest point of the Harz Mts, N Ger; scene of the legendary witches' orgy on Walpurgis Night (229.16, 530.31), on the eve of 1 May (not 1 July).
    70.04   first deal of Yuly...swobbing broguen eeriesh myth brockendootsch
           [+ "broken German"]

BROKEN HILL.   Silver mine and mining town, NSW, on W border with S Australia, SE of Barrier Range.
There is also a *BH* (copper mine and mining town) in cen Rhodesia.
    182.24   Broken Hill stranded estate, Camebreech mannings

BROSNA.   Riv, Cos Westmeath and Offaly, flows into Shannon R. Mullingar (qv) is on the *B* (475.22). *Brosna*, Ir "faggot."
    212.07   Briery Brosna
    474.20   along the amber way where Brosna's furzy

BROWNE AND NOLAN   (16/33).   Printers, publishers, and booksellers; at 24-25 Nassau St at the turn of the cent, now in Dawson St, with works at Clonskeagh; owners of the Richview Press (qv).
This well-known firm provides a Dub habitation for JJ's preoccupation with Giordano Bruno of Nola ("the Nolan"), and "Browne" and "Nolan" become pseudonyms for Shem and Shaun. For the many Bruno allusions, see *Census*; listed below are only those clearly referring to the Dub firm.
    211.32   a jackal with hide, for Browne but Nolan
    268.08   Browne and Nolan's divisional tables
    412.36   my publickers, Nolaner and Browno
    488.04   Bruno and Nola...stationary lifepartners off orangey Saint Nessau Street
    503.34   Browne's *Thesaurus Plantarum* from Nolan's, The Prittlewell Press

BRUSSELS.   City, and cap of Belg, on Senne R; Fr *Bruxelles*. The Willibroek Canal makes *B* a seaport. The *Porte de Hal*, the only gate remaining from the anc walls, dates from 1381; it has been a mus since the 19th cent.
    17.06   brookcells...riverpool
    199.07   zwarthy kowse and weedy broeks
    535.05   whenby Gate of Hal
Like any tourist, *FW* forgets that *B* was Napoleon's objective when Wellington and his officers left the Duchess of Richmond's ball in *B* to ride for the field of Waterloo, and remembers, again and again, the Manneken-Pis, the stat (and fountain) of the pissing boy behind the Hôtel de Ville.
    17.02   Minnikin passe
    58.10   Mannequins pause!
    207.14   passe...minnikin
    267.F2   Mannequins' Pose
    ?268.15   a bodikin a boss
    329.04   mimmykin puss
    334.35   Millikin's Pass
    532.33   Mannequins Passe
    ?559.07   millikinstool
    576.15   my wee mee mannikin

BUCCLEUCH.   The estate of the Scott family in Selkirkshire, Scot. Gladstone contested Midlothian against the Duke of *B* in 1880, and won. Sir Walter Scott's *The Lay of the Last Minstrel* is about his ancestor and namesake (d 1552) at the battle of Pinkie.

    346.19   How Buccleuch shocked the rosing girnirilles

BUCHAREST (BUKHAREST).   City, cap of Romania, founded by Radu Negru (540.21). Kisilev Park, on the N side of *B*, is continuous with the Calea Victoriei.

    114.04   in the Nemzes and Bukarahast directions
    532.22   Kissilov's Slutsgartern
    540.21   Redu Negru may be black in tawn
    554.01   buckarestive bronchos

BUCKINGHAM.   Whether this is a Duke of *B* (eg, of Shakespeare's *Richard III*), the cen Eng co or town of *B*, or perhaps *B* Palace in London, depends on the un-identified quotation about the "sad slow march."

    318.21   with his sad slow munch for backonham

BUDAPEST.   City, cap of Hungary, on the Danube, which separates Buda (Ger, *Ofen*) on R bank from Pest on L. The Inner City of Pest is Belváros, containing the square *Eskü-Ter*.

    131.13   brought as plagues from Buddapest
    150.27   Judapest, 5688, A.M.
    199.08   the tits of buddy and the loits of pest
    424.01   Bruda Pszths
    541.16   Bulafests onvied me
    541.35   Escuterre ofen...Belvaros

BUENOS AIRES.   City, cap of Argentina.

    435.01   near the ciudad of Buellas Arias
    540.35   Blownose aerios we luft to you!

BUFFALO.   City, W NY State, US. But the allusion is not only to the *Buffalo Times* (founded 1885) but also to the bygone days in the American West before the buffalo (bison) were destroyed.

    275.L3   *From the Buffalo Times of bysone days*

BULAWAYO.   Town, former cap of Matabeleland, S Rhodesia, Afr. Until occupied by the Brit in 1893, it was the royal res of Matabele (a Zulu tribe) chiefs. The name means "Place of Slaughter" in Zulu.

    353.29   *Similar scenatas are projectilised from Hullulullu, Bawlawayo, em-pyreal Raum and mordern Atems*

BULGARIA.   Country, SE Eur. *Ezik Bulgarski*, Bulg "the Bulgarian lang" (346.24). The nat assembly was known as the Sobranje.

    54.08   sobranjewomen, storthingboys
    114.05   from Maliziies with Bulgarad
    339.19   *his bulgeglarying stargapers*
    346.24   Sayyessik, Ballygarry
    ?347.01   where the midril met the bulg, sbogom
    563.14   Are you not somewhat bulgar with your bowels?

BULL ALLEY (ST) (15/33).   Short st btwn St Patrick St and Bride St; it borders St Patrick's Park, which replaced the warren of tenements to the N of St Patrick's Cath.

    98.31   Cope and Bull go cup and ball

BULLOCK CASTLE   (26/27).   One of 7 castles in Dalkey, SE of Dub. The name is a corruption of its earlier Dan name, Blowick.

    135.14   changes blowicks into bullocks
    243.19   it was such a blowick day

BULL RING   (14/33).   An iron ring in a wall on Cornmarket, to which bulls for baiting were tied in the 16th-17th cents. A Mayor of the *BR* was elected annually by the citizens of Dub; he served as a captain of the unmarried men, and had authority to punish "unchaste places" such as disorderly tavs.

    534.19   Keisserse Lean...bullfist rings round him

BULL RUN.   Stream in Virginia, US; gave name to 2 Civil War battles (known to the Confederate side as Manassas). In Second *BR*, Pope (84.06) was a Union gen, Jubal Early (84.02) a Confederate.

    84.02   bull's run over the assback bridge

BULLS, NORTH AND SOUTH.   The "Bulls" were the great sandbanks N and S of the channel in inner Dub Bay, so-called "from the roaring of the surf against them when uncovered at low water" (Haliday, 234). Since the building of the South and Bull Walls, the S Bull is under water at all tides and the N Bull is an isl, connected with the mainland by a br (no longer wooden as in *A Portrait*), and paralleling the shore from Clontarf almost to Howth. Clontarf, "meadow of the bull," may have been named from the N Bull.

    17.09   Somular with a bull on a clompturf
    84.02   a bull's run over the assback bridge
    198.04   her bulls they were ruhring, surfed with spree
    448.19   brighton Brayhowth and bait the Bull Bailey

BULLY ACRE   (12/33).   Anc cem of Kilmainham, cor of SCR and Royal Hosp Rd, adjoining Royal Hosp. Closed 1832 after thousands of burials in cholera epidemic. The name is still in use.

    73.23   rochelly exetur of Bully Acre
    87.15   the bullycassidy of the friedhoffer [*Friedhof*, Ger "cemetery"]
    320.33   Infernal machinery...Bullysacre
    618.08   The thicks off Bully's Acre

BUMBAILIFF'S LANE   (15/33).   Since *ca* 1792 corrupted to Fumbally's Lane; off Blackpitts.

    568.23   bumbellye [with other lanes]

BUNCOMBE.   Co, N Carolina, US. The term "bunkum," "to waste an audience's time by talking of matters of interest only to a few," derives from a N Carolina Representative who explained a speech as "talking for Buncombe."

    ?254.35   prince of Bunnicombe
    316.14   the hot air of Montybunkum
    ?422.30   allus pueblows and bunkum
    608.04   what bunkum!

BUNKER HILL.   Hill, Charlestown area, Boston, Mass, US. Amer Revolutionary battle, 17 June 1775, known as "Bunker Hill," was actually on the adjacent Breed's Hill. The Royal Ir Regt was part of Brit force. No one, including *FW*, is sure whether Israel Putnam actually said, "Don't fire until you see the whites of their eyes."

    9.29   ousterlists dowan a bunkersheels
    542.25   who in hillsaide, don't you let flyfire till you see their whites of the
                  bunkers' eyes!

BURE RIVER.   In Norfolk and Suffolk, Eng; one of the rivs forming the Broads.
>   ?163.27   the Bure will be dear on the Brie

BURGAGE.   Name of Blessington (qv), Co Wicklow, until 1683. There is still a *B* on the Blessington-Donard rd. *B* Moat, in the tnld of Ballyknockan, on the Barrow R, S of Leighlinbridge, was an anc palace of the kings of Leinster. The name was once common, since it means "town."
>   358.08   happy burgages abeyance
>   ?539.20   taking bourd and burgage

BURGH QUAY   (16/34).   S side of Liffey, E of O'Connell Br and across from Eden Quay.
>   ?541.35   in the meckling of my burgh

BURNHAM LIGHTHOUSE.   Burnham-on-Sea, on the Severn estuary SW of Bristol, in Somerset, Eng, has 2 lighthouses, one a unique wooden construction on the sands.
>   71.21   *Burnham and Bailey*

BUSACO.   Sierra de *B*, Port, site of battle, 27 Sept 1810, in which Wellington repulsed a Fr attack.
>   10.19   Basucker youstead!

BUSHMILLS.   Town, Co Antrim; "Old Bushmills" whiskey is to N Ire what John Jameson and Son is to Dub.
>   292.F3   Bussmullah
>   357.04   Bismillafoulties
>   521.15   Bushmillah!
>   577.21   from Bushmills to Enos

BUTT BRIDGE   (16/34).   Aka Swivel Br. The last (and E-most) br as the Liffey flows except for the Loop Line Rlwy br. Erected 1879; named for the 19th-cent politician Isaac Butt.
>   6.07   butt under his bridge
>   11.19   rattlin buttins...bloodstaned breeks
>   13.14   see the old butte new
>   85.15   bare by Butt's, most easterly...of blackpool bridges
>   196.09   And don't butt me
>   ?208.20   alpheubett buttons
>   254.13   from Sara's drawhead...to Isaac's, the lauphed butt one
>   ?265.24   from contact bridge to lease lapse [Leixlip]
>   ?332.27   a bridge of the piers, at Inverleffy ["Liffeymouth"]
>   ?374.19   Batt in, boot! Sell him a breach contact
>   471.17   bridge...fouling her buttress for her but
>   525.35   if he pool her leg and bunk on her butt
>   580.32   O'Connell...butted...grattaned [all Liffey bridges]

BUTTER (BOATER) LANE   (15/33).   Aka Big Butter Lane; from *bóthar*, Ir "road." Now (since 1774) Bishop St.
>   ?210.33   Kitty Coleraine of Butterman's Lane
>   ?533.36   Big Butter Boost!

C

CABBAGE GARDEN GRAVEYARD (15/33).   The cem of this name was at the end of *CG* Lane (now Cathedral Lane) in the interior of the block S of Upr Kevin St. The name did not derive from "Capuchin." The DMP horse police barracks were just across Upr Kevin St from *CG* Lane.

Wm Smith O'Brien's hopeless insurrection in 1848 ended in the "Battle of Widow McCormack's Cabbage Garden," 4 mi N of Ballingarry.

568.28   that horse elder...the wise graveleek in cabbuchin garden

CABINTEELY.   Vill, Co Dub, S of Dun Laoghaire.
533.19   that cabinteeny homesweetened

CABMAN'S SHELTER (16/34).   The cabman's shelter of the Eumaeus chap of *U*, where Bloom and Stephen talk over undrinkable coffee, was on Custom House Quay by the Loop Line Br. There was another in O'Connell St.
542.14   coppeecuffs...as you pay in caabman's sheltar

CABRA.   Dist, NW Dub. The Joyce family lived at No 7 St Peter's Terr (now St Peter's Rd), Cabra, in 1902-04. Mrs Joyce died there. *C* Park is a res circle just N of the Joyce home but built since that time. *Cabrach*, Ir "bad land."
142.14   Cabra fields
370.07   like the cavaliery man in Cobra Park
420.36   7 Streetpetres. Since Cabranke
497.19   Cabraists
609.34   moveyovering the cabrattlefield of slaine

CAERLEON-ON-USK.   Vill, Monmouthshire (now Gwent), Wales, on Usk R, 3 mi NE of Newport. Famous in legend as the chief home of King Arthur and seat of his court. Est *ca* 50 AD as Isca Silurium, it became Castra Legionum, one of the 3 great legionary fortresses of Roman Brit, and was known as the "City of the Legions." It may be the site where 5 Kings of Cymry rowed Edgar on his barge to acknowledge his sovereignty (973 AD).
220.35   his pilgrimst customhouse at Caherlehome-upon-Eskur
277.21   city self of legionds
?341.19   *the worldrenownced Caerholme Event*

CAHERMOHILL.   Aka Cahermoyle, near Ardagh, Co Limerick; home of Wm Smith O'Brien. See *"Cattermole" Hill*.
?129.04   Cattermole Hill

CAIRO.   City, cap of Egypt. Arab, *Misr-al-Kahira*, or *Misr*.
One of the cens of *C* is the Place Atabeh, once the main point of intersection of tram-lines.
177.09   Kairokorran
509.19   Who kills the cat in Cairo
534.15   Misrs Norris, Southby
541.17   Atabey!

CALCUTTA.   City, form cap of Brit Ind and of prov of Bengal. Surrajah Dowlah

(492.21), the Nawab of Bengal, cast 146 persons into the "Black Hole of *C*" in 1756; only 23 survived.

The *Maidan* is the great park of *C*; it has a race course. *Maidan*, Sans "plain"; there are "Maidans" in many other Ind cities, in Iran, and elsewhere.

492.15	back haul of Coalcutter
502.27	parkiest...first fog in Maidanvale
541.17	Corkcuttas graatched
547.27	I had done abate her maidan race
549.05	blackholes

CALEDONIA.   (1) Lat and poet name for Scot. In Ptolemy, the sea N of Scot is called Duecalledonius.   (2) Caledon, town and ho, Co Tyrone.

187.07	at the caledosian capacity for Lieutuvisky
241.30	three Dromedaries of the Sands of Calumdonia
481.21	Smithwick, Rhonnda, Kaledon [Eng, Wales, Scot]

CALIFORNIA, GULF OF.   Form known as the Vermilion Sea; the arm of the Pacific O which extends NW btwn the Mex states of Baja California on the W and Sinura and Sinaloa on the E.

352.17	*volkar boastsung is heading to sea vermelhion*

CAMBRIDGE.   City, Cambridgeshire, Eng, and site of *C* Univ, Latinized *Cantabrigia*, colloq "Cantab." The form Entrance Examination was nicknamed the "Little Go" (279.F12, 507.09, 567.24). Girton Coll was the 1st (1873) women's coll at *C*.

182.24	Camebreech mannings...hogsford
211.01	a starr and girton for Draper and Deane [with "Stella" and Dean Swift]
279.F12	when I slip through my pettigo
463.13	Auxonian...cantanberous
467.31	he can cantab as chipper...oxon
507.09	slapping greats and littlegets
567.24	our littlego illcome faxes
?587.08	the snug at the Cambridge Arms of Teddy Ales

CAMDEN ST   (15/32).   The section N of the Grand Canal of the main rd from Dame St to Rathmines and Rathgar (not to Booterstown).

132.06	Baddersdown...made his end with the modareds that came at him in Camlenstrete

CAMEL, BATTLE OF THE.   Near Basra, Iraq, in 656 AD; Ali, 4th caliph succeeding Mohammed, defeated a rebellion instigated by Mohammed's widow Ayesha, in the "Battle of the Camel."

9.24	This is camelry...floodens

CAMELOT.   King Arthur and all that. It has been variously located at Caerleon-on-Usk (qv), Queen Camel in Somerset, Camelford in Cornwall (see *Tintagel*), etc.

143.07	camelot prince of dinmurk
?323.23	a hill of a camelump bakk
359.16	Rum Tipple...camelottery...lyonesslooting

CAMLAN.   Somewhere in Cornwall, possibly near Camelford, site of the battle (539 AD) in which King Arthur was killed, betrayed by his nephew Modred, who also was slain.

132.06	made his end with the modareds that came at him in Camlenstrete

CAMMOCK (CAMAC) RIVER   (11/32).   Small riv, R bank trib of the Liffey at Inchicore in Dub; it rises in the hills above Brittas and flows NE past Clondalkin and Drimnagh.
205.28   the cornerboys cammocking his guy
212.08   Zusan Camac

CAMOMILE ST.   London, off Bishopsgate, S of Liverpool St Sta (a short distance from Primrose St). The Roman wall ran along the N side. Named after the camomile plant, which in med times was gathered here.
553.05   Cammomile Pass cuts Primrose Rise

CANAAN.   In the *OT* the whole area of Pal W of the Jordan R (*Gen* 12:5; *Num* 33:51). The ancestor of the Canaanites was Canaan, son of Ham, who was cursed by Noah and condemned to be the servant of Shem and Japheth (*Gen* 9:25–27).
264.09   Even Canaan the Hateful
364.19   let him be asservent to Kinahaun!

CANADA.   Became a Brit Dominion in 1867; form called Brit N Amer. The Fr-speaking residents have long called themselves "Les Habitants." Around the turn of the cent, the Can Pacific Rlwy operated passenger liners to the Orient, the "Empress of India," "Empress of China," and "Empress of Japan"; there was no "Empress of Asia." The Brit battleship "Empress of India" was flagship of the Home Fleet around the turn of the cent.
548.02   Impress of Asias
604.25   Habitant and the onebut thousand insels

CANBERRA.   City, cap of Australia, SE NSW.
569.17   Cantaberra and Neweryork

CANDIA.   The Venetian name for Medit isl of Crete; also a name for Herakleion, Cretan port and form cap (until 1841); the Sea of *C* is the Medit btwn Crete and Cyclades Isls.
When Crete became independent after 7 cents of rule by the Venetians and then the Turks, it was governed autonomously from 1898 to 1906 by Prince George of Gr. But Giuseppe Mario, Count of *C*, a 19th-cent tenor, is called "prince of *C*" in *U* 506/517.
408.11   principot of Candia

CANISTER, THE.   House, Jamestown, St Helena, so named for its teacup-like shape. Napoleon is said to have turned off Main St at "The Canister" on his first day of exile, and since then this st has been known as Napoleon St.
?9.32   in the cool of his canister

CAN-MATHON.   In Macpherson's *Temora* (VII, 309), the name of a star.
329.14   Cannmatha and Cathlin sang together

CANNAE.   Battlefield near mod Barletta, in Apulia, S It, where in 216 BC Hannibal inflicted on Roman army a total and disastrous defeat.
?273.L3   *Old Kine's Meat Meal*

CANOSSA.   Vill, Ciano d'Enza, N It, where Henry IV submitted to Pope Gregory VII and did public penance, 1077; hence the phrase "going to Canossa," meaning "humble submission."
154.31   if I connow make my submission, I cannos give you up

CANTERBURY.   City, Kent, SE Eng, ecclesiastical cen of the Ch of Eng; the Archbishop of *C* is the primate of Eng (the Archbishop of York ranks second). *C* bells are
flowers of genus *Campanula* (601.16), allegedly named from bells carried by pilgrims
to *C*.
>310.29   canterberry bellseyes
>569.17   Cantaberra and Neweryork may supprecate...Monsigneur of Deublan

CANTON (KWANG-CHOW).   Chief port and city of S China; locale of origin of
"pidgin English"; the only Chinese trading port until 1842.
>?91.23   an Inishman was as good as any cantonnatal

CANTRELL AND COCHRANE'S (16/33).   Around the turn of the cent, this
manufacturer of mineral waters was at 2-11 Nassau Pl; Sir Henry Cochrane was one
of the owners.
>137.07   Hennery Canterel – Cockran, eggotisters, limitated

CAPEL COURT.   Colloq name for London Stock Exchange, which has occupied
premises in *CC* of Bartholomew Lane since 1773.
>515.21   cast your eyes around Capel Court

CAPEL ST (15/34).   Commercial st N of Liffey; named for Arthur Capel, 17th-
cent Earl of Essex (not for *capall*, Ir "horse"). JJ frequented the *C* St Lib.
>?51.27   the capelist's voiced nasal liquids
>448.09   See Capels and then fly
>?488.33   wellmet Capeler, united Irishmen

CAPRI.   Famous resort isl in Bay of Naples; It, "goat."
>?412.33   a pair of capri sheep boxing gloves

CAPRICORN.   The Tropic of *C* is the latitude, terrestrial and celestial (about 23°
28′ S; the Tropic of Cancer is same distance N) at which the sun reaches S-most
point; *C* is the 10th sign of the zodiac, beginning at this solstice. *C* is also a constellation of the S hemisphere. Lat, *Caper*.
>26.12   your crested head is in the tropic of Copricapron
>415.10   soturning...dance McCaper...retrophoebia [see *Saturn*]

CAPUCHIN FRIARY (14/34).   The old *C* (Franciscan) Convent was on the E side
of Bridge St; more recently the Friary ("St Mary of the Angels") is in Old Church St.
>?386.30   and the cappunchers childerun
>?390.12   as per the cabbangers richestore
>447.19   Mirist fathers'...White Friars...Compare them caponchin trowlers
>   with the Bridge of Belches
>?568.28   the wise graveleek in cabbuchin garden

CARBERRY HILL.   Hill, E Lothian, Scot, E of Edinburgh; Mary, Queen of Scots,
surrendered to barons there 15 June 1567.
      In Ire there are many place-names including "Carbery," esp on S coast of Mun-
ster and in Leinster.
>?228.18   He wholehog himself for carberry banishment

CARHAIX.   Town in Brittany, Dept of Côtes du Nord. In Bédier's *Tristan and
Isolde*, Tristan dies there after raising the siege of the cas and marrying Iseult of the
White Hands. The region to the W abounds in standing stones (menhirs), like Stone-
henge.
>5.31   carhacks, stonengens, kisstvanes
>?340.08   The field of karhags

CARLISLE BRIDGE.   See *O'Connell Bridge*.

CARLOW.   Co and town, Leinster prov. *Ceathramba-loch*, Ir "fourfold lake"; there
is no trace of the 4 lakes which acc to tradition were formed by the Barrow R.
Song: "Follow Me Up to Carlow." Baronies: Carlow, Forth, E and W Idrone, Rath-
villy, Upr and Lwr St Mullin's.
    129.01   cowcarlows
    214.30   your slur gave the stink to Carlow
    ?239.24   to teach Connie Curley
    334.36   Izd-la-Chapelle...the waters from Carlowman's Cup
    379.10   Fellow him up too, Carlow!
    ?382.22   Faugh MacHugh O'Bawlar
    382.30   Now follow we out by Starloe
    466.02   All folly me yap to Curlew!
    479.06   Follow me up Tucurlugh!
    538.28   The man what shocked his shanks at contey Carlow's
    595.13   curlews

CARMAN.   The anc name of the site of the triennial *C* Games, or Fair, of Leinster,
said to have been est by Dunchadh, King of Leinster. Despite the fame of this institution, its location is not certain; some say it was in S Co Kildare, others that it was
on the site of the present town of Wexford, Co Wexford.
    ?237.22   Leperstower, the karman's loki
    ?239.24   tip Carminia to tap La Chérie

CARMANHALL.   Tnld, par of Tully, bar of Rathdown, S Co Dub; just NW of the
adjoining tnld of Carmanhall and Leopardstown, which contains the Leopardstown
race course.
    237.22   Leperstower, the karman's loki, has not blanched at our pollution

CARMELITE (CALCED) CHURCH (RC)   (15/33).   In Aungier St; aka "White Friars Ch."
    447.18   Mirist fathers' brothers eleven versus White Friars
    601.27   S. Waidafrira's

CARMELITE (DISCALCED) CHURCH (RC)   (15/33).   In Clarendon St.
    601.22   S. Clarinda's

CARNSORE POINT.   Co Wexford; the extreme SE point of Ire.
    580.34   Carnsore Point

CAROLINA, NORTH AND SOUTH.   S US states. Song, "Dinah": "Dinah/ Is there
anyone finer/ In the state of Carolina?/ If there is and you know her/ Show her to
me..." A caroline hat (from "Carolina") is a stove-pipe hat.
    226.02   always down in Carolinas lovely Dinahs vaunt their view
    460.10   let me just your caroline for you

CARR, HENRY L   (15/35).   Confectioner, 44 Upr Dorset St, around the turn of
the cent.
    ?339.14   From Karrs and Polikoff's, the men's confessioners

CARRICK-ON-SHANNON.   Co town of Co Leitrim, across Shannon R from Co
Roscommon.
    526.28   the most broadcussed man in Corrack-on-Sharon, County Rosecarmon

CARRIGACURRA.   Tnld, par of Boystown, bar of Talbotstown, Co Wicklow; on the

Liffey. Also an estate SE of Blessington Reservoir.

Since Conway's Tav (qv) was in Blackrock, JJ may have invented his own Ir name from *carrig*, "rock" and *ciar*, "black." But C K Ogden's notes to his Basic Eng translation of this passage, prob on information from JJ, identify C as town "where Conway had a beer house."

    214.20   Conway's Carrigacurra canteen

CARRIGEEN.   *C* House is 3 mi W of Tallow, Co Cork. *C* is also a rocky islet and bay on Ireland's Eye, N of Howth, and there are Carrigeens or Carriganes in Cos Cork, Galway, Limerick, and Waterford. Since carrageen is a kind of edible seaweed, aka "Irish moss," the allusions may be to none of these places.

    ?108.19   the barbar of the Carrageehouse
    ?184.21   Carrageen moss

CARTHAGE.   Anc Phoenician city, N Afr, on coast NE of mod Tunis, noted for sea power and the Punic Wars with Rome. Cato the Elder proclaimed that Rome must destroy *C*: "Delenda est Carthago." An 18th-cent theory held that the Ir people was of Carthaginian origin.

    64.03   Delandy is cartager
    87.28   Carrothagenuine ruddiness
    90.36   punic judgeship strove with penal law
    156.03   the penic walls
    270.30   Hireling's puny wars
    344.15   like a brandylogged rudeman cathargic
    347.31   roaming cartridges
    ?468.31   beneath me corthage, bound
    538.12   roohms of encient cartage

CASABLANCA.   Port and once largest city of Morocco; Sp, "White House."

    ?342.09   *a middinest from the Casabianca*

CASHEL.   Town, Co Tipperary; form cap of the king-bishops of Munster. The cath-fortress (now ruins), on the "Rock of *C*," was burned in 1495 by Fitzgerald Mor (the Great Earl of Kildare) (cf *U* 228/231); also by the renegade Murrough O'Brien in 1647. *Caisel*, Ir "castle."

C was one of the orig ecclesiastical sees of Ire and is still one of the 4 RC provs (283.L1), although the see is now at Thurles. Orig name of the Great Southern and Western Rlwy (qv) was "*C* Rlwy."

    4.08   chance cuddleys, what cashels aired and ventilated
    228.26   Every monk his own cashel
    283.L1   *Non plus ulstra, Elba, nec, cashellum tuum*
    381.22   a blurney Cashelmagh crooner
    ?414.20   −cashl− [in C-word]

CASPIAN SEA.   Anc *Hyrcanum Mare*; a salt sea bordered by USSR and Iran, it receives the Volga (among other rivs) and has no outlet. The *C* Gates, on its W (USSR) shore, is a mt pass important for cents as a trade route btwn Asia and Eur.

    578.05   with the snow in his mouth and the caspian asthma

CASTLE, THE (15/33).   Dub Cas, now surrounded by cen Dub S of the Liffey, was first built on the site of an early Dan fortress by Henry de Londres, Archbishop of Dub and Eng viceroy, *ca* 1220; he also made St Patrick's Ch a cath (543.18). Orig a rectangular fortress, with 4 towers and a moat fed by the Poddle R (qv), it was extensively rebuilt, esp in the 18th cent, and only 2 of the orig towers survive:

Bermingham Tower (SW) and Wardrobe Tower, now called Record Tower (SE). Other towers were the Cork Tower (NW) and the Storehouse or Ordnance Tower (NE). The Bedford Tower was built with the present curtain wall and gates in the 18th cent.

Until 1921, the *C* was the official res of Lords Lt, the hqs of Brit administration, and the hated symbol of Brit rule. Spies were "in the pay of the *C*" or "*C* hacks" (see "Ivy Day in the Committee Room"). Poor Martin Cunningham, of *U* and "Grace," held a respectable job in the *C* (387.29).

The two chs of St Audoen and the ch of St Bride (qqv) are within short distances (569.11).

There are 3 castles on the Dub Coat of Arms (qv).

4.08	what cashels aired and ventilated
?21.13	flure of his homerigh, castle and earthenhouse
45.07	He was one time our King of the Castle
73.24	the siegings round our archicitadel
91.34	the halfkneed castleknocker's
92.01	had broken exthro Castilian
101.23	in the spy of three castles
301.27	laying siege to goblin castle
303.F3	Brownes de Browne-Browne of Castlehacknolan
387.29	poor Merkin Cornyngwham, the official out of the castle on pension
?440.03	despite the castle bar
471.16	the bridge a stadion beyond Ladycastle
543.17	William Inglis his house, that man de Loundres
560.09	The castle arkwright
569.11	Bride-and-Audeons-behind-Wardborg
582.21	Dyfflinsborg [*borg*, Dan "castle"]
?623.19	It's in the castles air

CASTLEBAR.   Town, Co Mayo. On 27 Aug 1798 a Fr and Ir army defeated the Eng garrison, who fled so fast and far that the event is known as the "Castlebar Races."

55.32	*Irish Field*...before they got the bump at Castlebar (mat and far!)
440.03	first in the field despite the castle bar

CASTLE BROWNE.   Orig one of the forts of the Pale, it was in the hands of the Browne family from 1667 until 1813, when it was sold to the Soc of Jesus and became nucleus of bldgs of Clongowes Wood Coll (qv) at Clane, Co Kildare.

37.22	studying castelles in the blowne...noran
303.F3	The Brownes de Browne-Browne of Castlehacknolan

CASTLE HOWARD.   Turreted ho on the heights above E bank of the Avonmore R, at the Meeting of the Waters (qv), Co Wicklow.

?242.33	Howarden's Castle, Englandwales
276.F1	He gives me pulpitixes with his Castlecowards

CASTLEKNOCK   (8/37).   Bar, par, and vill, W and NW of Dub. The bar of *C* includes Mulhuddart, Clonsilla, most of Chapelizod, 645 acres of Phoenix Park, and Finglas par. Rds from *C* Gate and Knockmaroon Gate, Phoenix Park, lead to the vill of *C*. *C* Coll is situated on the W side of the N extension of Knockmaroon Hill Rd; near the SE wing of the Coll is *C* Hill, with ruins of its cas, once the home of the Tyrrels (60.09). Across the rd from the Coll to the E lies Windmill Hill, surmounted by the ruins of an observatory. These 2 hills are the feet of HCE – Finn MacCool interred in the N Dub landscape – as Howth is his head (12.20, 595.03).

3.22	the knock out in the park
12.20	our review of the two mounds

91.34   the halfkneed castleknocker's
262.05   Thus come to castle. Knock.[1]
379.01   Kick nuck, Knockcastle!
447.15   strewing the Castleknock Road
?530.33   Tipknock Castle
595.03   Hill of Hafid, knock and knock...gives relief to the langscape

CASTLE MARKET   (15/33).   Short st btwn S William St and the Drury St entrance to the S City Market.
    The identification is very dubious, but it does suggest a route for mailman-Shaun along the main thoroughfare, successively named Richmond St, Camden St, Wexford St, Redmond's Hill, Aungier St, and Gt George's St, S, from Portobello Br to the S City Market.
    412.10   from Pontoffbellek till the Kisslemerched our ledan triz will be

CASTLEMORE.   Par and cas in the bar of Costello, N Co Roscommon, outside town of Ballaghaderreen. High King Roderick O'Connor was involved in a siege of the cas in which the walls were burnt down.
    72.05   *What He Done to Castlecostello*

CASTLE TIROWEN.   The cas of the O'Neills, kings of Tir Eoghain or Owen, which stood on Castle Hill above Dungannon, Co Tyrone, until destroyed without trace after the Battle of Benburb in 1646. "Castle Tirowen" is the air of T Moore's song, "Remember Thee!"
    230.35   Remember thee, castle throwen?

CASTLETOWN HOUSE.   This immense ho 1 mi NE of Celbridge, Co Kildare, was built 1722 for Wm Conolly, Speaker of the Ir House of Commons 1715-1729. Supposedly the largest private ho in Ireland, it is said to contain 365 windows, one for each day of the year.
    456.27   the roomiest house even in Ireland
    456.34   redletterday calendar, window machree
    457.01   before I'll quit the doorstep of old Con Connolly's residence

CASTLEWOOD AVENUE   (15/31).   In Rathmines, S Dub; the Joyce family lived at No 23 in 1884.
    420.31   3 Castlewoos. P.V.

CATALAUNIAN PLAINS.   S of Châlons-sur-Marne (chief town of anc Catalauni) in NE Fr, site of great battle in 451 AD in which Attila the Hun was defeated by the Roman Aetius and the Visigoth Theodoric.
    266.24   commencement catalaunic when Aetius check chokewill Attil's gambit [+ Catalan Gambit in chess]

CAT AND CAGE.   Tav in Drumcondra, then and now, on E side of Drumcondra Rd across from St Patrick's Coll.
    563.19   Donatus his mark, address as follows...From the Cat and Cage

CATHLIN.   In Macpherson's *Temora* (VIII, 309), the name of a star.
    329.14   Cannmatha and Cathlin sang together

CATTEGAT (KATTEGAT).   The strait connecting North and Baltic Seas btwn Swed and Den. Dan, "cat's throat."
    22.36   his cattegut bandolair
    197.10   Tvistown on the Kattekat [*tvis*, Dan "discord"]

507.10   his cattegut belts
548.15   had I not workit in my cattagut with dogshunds' crotts

CATTERICK.   Town, Yorkshire, Eng; the *C* racecourse is a cen of steeplechase racing. *C* Br was a junction of Roman rds in the N of Eng (not including Watling St).
?24.22   the Cottericks' donkey with his shoe hanging

"CATTERMOLE" HILL.   NPN: as Fritz Senn discovered, the actor Hill, described
as "that mountain of flesh," played Cattermole in the play "The Private Secretary"
(40.16) at the Gaiety Theatre in 1885.
129.04   Cattermole Hill, ex-mountain of flesh

CAUCASUS.   The region btwn the Black and Caspian seas, S USSR. The *C* Mts, 700
mi long, are trad considered the boundary btwn Eur and Asia.
162.14   the Coucousien oafsprung
344.20   some herdsquatters beyond the carcasses
?378.15   Coucous! Find his causcaus!
392.23   the king of the Caucuses

CAUDINE FORKS.   Two mt gorges (*Furculae Caudinae*) near town of Caudium in
Campania, S It, where 4 Roman legions were captured by the Samnite general Pon-
tius in 321 BC. Proverbial for a strategic trap.
273.L3   *All we suffered under them Cowdung Forks*

CAVAN.   Co, Ulster prov, N Ire, and its co town. Baronies: Castlerahan, Clankee,
Clanmahon, Upr and Lwr Loughtee, Tullygarvey, Tullyhaw, Tullyhunco.
150.21   Cavantry
?333.10   her complement of cavarnan men...corkedagains
482.09   chuam and coughan!...Maho
595.15   coffins

CAWDOR.   See *Dunsinane.*

CECILIA ST   (15/34).   Short st crossing the N end of Crow St, btwn Dame St
and the Liffey. Site of Crow St Theatre, which faced Crow St; in 1836 it became
Apothecaries' Hall, in 1852 the medical sch of the Nat Univ. JJ attended medical
sch briefly in Dub, prob at *C* St Sch (424.07). There is no par of St Cecilia in Dub.
St Cecilia is patron saint of music.
33.03   retired cecelticocommediant
41.33   parish of Saint Cecily
224.21   blabber...tynpan...skoll...Cicely, awe!
?279.F3   chants for cecilies
424.07   Then he went to Cecilia's treat on his solo to pick up Galen

CELBRIDGE.   Vill, on Liffey R 4 mi from Lucan. Form Kildrought (*Cill Droichid*,
Ir "church of the bridge"). The private house Marley Abbey (no connection with *C*'s
anc monastery of St Mochua) was bought by Bartholomew Vanhomrigh, and Swift
visited Esther V. ("Vanessa") there. Castletown Ho (qv) is 1 mi N, Hazelhatch (qv)
2 mi S.
129.09   was hatched at Cellbridge but ejoculated abrood
305.08   celebridging over the guilt of the gap

CELEBES.   Isl, Indonesia, form Dutch E Indies; separated from Philippine Isls on N
by *C* Sea.
?191.17   seducing every sense to selfwilling celebesty

CHALLENGER DEEP.   In the Mariana Trench, 200 mi SW of Guam I, Pacific O. The deepest spot yet discovered in any ocean: 38,500 ft.

    501.11   Challenger's Deep is childsplay to this...soundings

CHAMP DE MARS.   Orig market-gardens on the L bank of the Seine in Paris, it became a parade ground in the 18th cent, the site of exhibitions in the 19th, and is now a formal garden btwn the Eiffel Tower and the École Militaire.

    119.32   an Irish plot in the Champ de Mors
    551.10   I made nusance of many well pressed champdamors

CHAMPS ELYSÉES, AVENUE DES.   Ave and promenade btwn the Place de la Concorde and the Place de L'Étoile, Paris. The entrance from the former is framed by the statues of the Marly Horses, which were brought from the Marly Palace near Versailles in 1795.

    365.29   reyal devouts...marly lowease...spruce a spice for salthorse
    607.14   segnall for old Champelysied

CHAPELIZOD.   The ostensible site of Earwicker's pub (see *Tavern*) in *FW*, *C* is a vill W of Dub, on the Liffey and adjoining the SW area of Phoenix Park. Thom's *Directories* at the turn of the cent describe it as "a village partly in Palmerstown parish, Uppercross barony [262.03–.04], but chiefly in the parish of the same name, Castleknock barony [262.05–.06], Dublin county, three miles W from the General Post Office, Dublin [265.25–.28], comprising an area of 63 acres" (264.21).

    The name *C*, or "chapel of Isolde," is said to date back to Arthurian times, when La belle Isoult (or Izod) dwelt in the area. On Petty's map of Leinster, *Hiberniae Delineatio*, it appears as "Chapell Lizard" (242.28). For some reason, *FW* frequently conflates *C* with Lucan (qv), which is 6 mi farther up the winding Liffey.

    The par of *C* encompasses roughly ¼ of Phoenix Park (qv), in the S cen region, including the "Fifteen Acres." The vill lies SW of the *C* Gate, at the SW cor of the park. The Liffey at *C* is divided into 2 channels by the main Dub rd (209.24   her arms encircling Isolabella [It, "beautiful island"], then running with reconciled Romas and Reims [ie, Shem and Shaun as the banks of the Liffey]).

    J Sheridan Le Fanu made *C* the setting for *The House by the Churchyard*, an important sourcebook for *FW* allusions, and one of the 4 books in the elder Joyce's "library." The novel is set in 1767, as told by the narrator a cent later. Central to the action is the fact that a regt of artillery is stationed in *C*; its barracks lie along the N bank of the Liffey at the W end of the vill, and its officers are quartered at the King's Ho and carouse at the Phoenix. The artillery butt was in Phoenix Park in a circular enclosure of just 15 acres; the area of Phoenix Park now called the "Fifteen Acres" is very much larger than that.

    I.   Chapelizod Place-Names from The House by the Churchyard:

BRASS CASTLE.   Mr Dangerfield's ho and form an actual ho in *C*. The drawing in Frances Gerard's *Picturesque Dublin*, although identified as "Brass Castle, Chapelizod," is actually of a house of the same name in the Liberties.

    183.05   your brass castle...tyled house
    246.04   brass castle flambs with mutton candles

HOUSE BY THE CHURCHYARD, THE.   In the novel, Dr Sturk lives and dies there. Also called the Gray Stone Ho, the ho survives, sited btwn the 2 approaches to the CI ch.

    34.08   on the old house for the chargehard
    96.07   the old house by the churpelizod
    213.01   Lefanu (Sheridan's) old *House by the Coachyard*
    221.15   whouse be the churchyard or whorts up the aasgaars

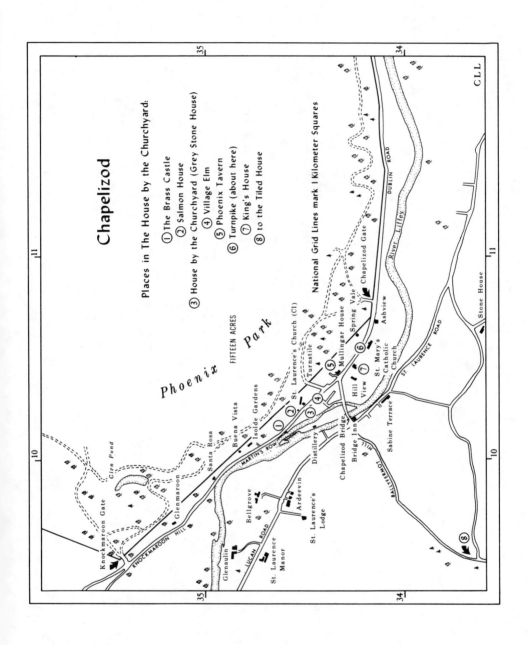

Chapelizod

Places in The House by the Churchyard:

① The Brass Castle
② Salmon House
③ House by the Churchyard (Grey Stone House)
④ Village Elm
⑤ Phoenix Tavern
⑥ Turnpike (about here)
⑦ King's House
⑧ to the Tiled House

National Grid Lines mark 1 Kilometer Squares

Phoenix Park

FIFTEEN ACRES

Glen Pond

Knockmaroon Gate

Santa Rosa

Buena Vista

Isolde Gardens

Glenmaroon

KNOCKMAROON HILL

MARTIN'S ROW

St. Laurence's Church (CI)

Turnstile

Distillery

Chapelizod Bridge

Bellgrove

Ardeevin

Glenaulin

LUCAN ROAD

St. Laurence Manor

St. Laurence's Lodge

Mullingar House

Spring Vale

Chapelizod Gate

River Liffey

DUBLIN ROAD

Ashview

St. Mary's Catholic Church

Bridge Inn

Hill View

Sabine Terrace

BALLYFERMOT HILL

ST. LAURENCE ROAD

Stone House

CLL

245.36   De oud huis bij de kerkegaard
371.25   hostillery With his chargehand
621.34   In the church by the hearseyard

KING'S HOUSE.   The orig King's Ho, near the present RC ch at the E end of
C, was in the 17th cent the res of Brit viceroys; Wm III stayed there after the Battle
of the Boyne. From *ca* 1726 it was the country res of Ir Primates, and in 1758 it
became officers' quarters for HM Regt of Artillery. Sold in 1832, the bldg was destroyed by fire and later replaced; its successor retained the name and survived as a
private res.

?32.26   that king's treat house
?70.19   houseking's keyhole
?136.23   from king's brugh to new customs [*brugh*, Ir "mansion, fort"]
?219.15   Before all the King's Hoarsers
264.32   with our king's house of stone
?567.17   to all the king's aussies...knechts tramplers and cavalcaders

PHOENIX TAVERN.   The "jolly old inn" of Le Fanu's novel was "as gone as
the guests" when the novel was written a cent later. It was sited just where the Mullingar Ho now stands. See *Tavern*.

265.08   the phoenix, his pyre

SALMON HOUSE.   The pub of Le Fanu's novel, demolished by the time of
writing, jutted into the high st from the N side and looked E down the road to Dub
past the Phoenix and the King's Ho.

25.14   over the bowls of memory...in the Salmon House

TILED HOUSE.   Actually S of *C* in Ballyfermot (qv), the Tiled Ho was Mr Mer-
wyn's ho in Le Fanu's novel, which mentions that it is spelled both "tiled" and
"tyled." W St J Joyce surmised that it is the ho more recently known as Ballyfermot
Lodge, located on the W side of Le Fanu Rd just N of the rail line (9/33).

183.05   your tyled house in ballyfermont

TURNPIKE.   Acc to Le Fanu, it was just E of the Phoenix Tav. Earwicker not
only keeps a public house in *C* but is in charge of the turnpike (31.01, 31.27). See
Turnpike.

VILLAGE ELM (10/34).   Le Fanu describes "the village elm" on p 3 of *HBC*;
acc to the narrator, it hadn't grown an inch in a hundred years. It stood by the high
st, btwn the Phoenix and the Salmon Ho.

?247.04   the hike from Elmstree to Stene and back
265.04   the loftleaved elm Lefanunian
293.14   the Turnpike under the Great Ulm
?507.36   at the Big Elm and the Arch
563.21   Gipsy Devereux...Lylian...why the elm

II.   *Private houses named in* FW *264–265.*

As Fritz Senn has *shown (AWN VIII.1, 88–89), the names of these houses, listed
here in order of appearance, are from a* Thom's Directory *of the 1920's or 1930's:*

Riverside House	264.23	By this riverside
Sunnybank	264.23	on our sunnybank
Buena Vista	264.24	how buona the vista
Santa Rosa	264.24	by Santa Rosa
Mayfield House	264.24	A field of May
Spring Vale	264.25	the very vale of Spring
Orchard Lodge	264.25	Orchards here are lodged
St Laurence House and Lodge	264.26	lodged; sainted lawrels
Hill View	264.27	hoig view
Ashview	264.27	hoig view ashwald

Glenmaroon	264.27	glen of marrons
Glen Thorn	264.27	glen...of thorns
Glenaulin	264.28	Gleannaulinn...purty glint

   (*Gleann Aluinn*, Ir "pretty glen"; Tim Healy lived here)

Ardeevin	264.28	Ardeevin...plaising height

   (*Ard Aoibhinn*, Ir "pleasant height")

Norman Court	264.29	Norman court
Boundary Villa	264.30	at boundary of the ville
Stone House	264.32	king's house of stone
Belgrove	265.01	belgroved
Mulberry Hill House	265.01	mulbrey
Auburn	265.06	Sweetsome auburn
Sabine Terrace	265.11	turrises of the sabines
The Cottage (in Castleknock near *C*)	265.12	the cottage
The Bungalow	265.12	the bungalow

III. Other Chapelizod Place-Names:

BANK, THE.   Name of 3 cottages, 1 on N bank and 2 on S bank of the Liffey.
   6.34   from Buythebanks to Roundthehead
BRIDGE INN.   See *Tavern.*
CARLISLE TAVERN and THE TAP.   Adjacent public houses under the same management; flourished from the 1910's through the 1930's.
   265.23   wine tap and warm tavern
CHAPELIZOD CHURCH (CI).   The med ivy-covered tower of St Laurence's Ch is much older than the body of the ch (rebuilt *ca* 1830). This ch is set back to the N of Martin's Row, at the W end of the vill.
   264.31   yon creepered tower of a church of Ereland
ISOLDE GARDENS.   Short st, NW of the CI Ch.
   265.13   Izolde, her chaplet gardens
MARTIN'S ROW.   Where the Dub Rd turns S to *C* Br in front of the Mullingar House, St Martin's Row continues NW up Knockmaroon Hill toward Knockmaroon Gate of Phoenix Park.
   ?6.34   from the foot of the bill to ireglint's eye
MT SACKVILLE (9/35).   In Castleknock just N of Knockmaroon gate, Phoenix Park. Once a country seat, since the 19th cent it has been a convent of the Order of St Joseph. "Yeomansland" suggests that it was earlier a hqs or barracks for the Yeomen, militia units which served with Brit regulars in suppressing rebellions, but I don't know of any such use.
   265.02   Kloster that was Yeomansland
   375.12   all the Misses Mountsackvilles in their halfmoon haemicycles
MULLINGAR HOUSE.   See *Tavern.*
PHOENIX PARK DISTILLERY.   Btwn Martin's Row and N bank of Liffey. Est in late 19th cent (the elder Joyce was an officer of the co) in bldgs form occupied by the *C* Mills, flax spinners and linen manufacturers.
   265.01   the still that was mill
ST MARY'S RC CHURCH.   Located S of the *C*-Dub Rd, at E end of vill. Not mentioned in *FW*?

IV. Chapelizod References:

6.33	Shopalist		32.16	Lucalizod
7.28	Seeple Isout		51.27	capelist's
26.17	chempel of Isid		62.35	Lucalizod
29.01	Shop Illicit		80.36	Issy-la-Chapelle

87.18	unlucalised	325.14	Capel Ysnod
87.29	Isod's towertop	334.36	Izd-la-Chapelle
96.08	churpelizod	370.29	Ship-le-Zoyd
101.11	Lucalizod	370.36	Capolic Gizzards
107.05	*Lucalizod*	372.13	the sheep was looset
110.08	Isitachapel-Asitalukin	385.25	Luvillicit
111.06	Cheepalizzy's	396.31	chapell-ledeosy
127.29	chapel exit	444.33	chapel...isod
178.09	Lucalizod	452.11	Hothelizod
209.24	her arms encircling Isolabella	487.32	Capalisoot
236.20	Chapelldiseut	527.01	Iscappellas
242.28	couple of lizards	560.27	iszoppy chepelure
255.01	Capellisato	565.33	Lucalised
265.13	Izolde, her chaplet gardens	571.11	chapelofeases...of Ziod
265.20	two barreny old perishers	571.18	littleeasechapel
290.02	La Chapelle, shapely Liselle	598.28	Ysat Loka
323.04	Ship Alouset	607.14	Champelysied...Chappielassies

CHARLEMONT MALL   (15/32).   St, bordering Grand Canal just E of Portobello. Charleville Mall borders the Royal Canal between N Strand Rd and Summerhill Parade.

   37.19   Charlatan Mall...darkenings of Grand and Royal
   ?147.22   out with the daynurse doing Chaperon Mall

CHARLES ST, GREAT   (16/35).   Btwn SE cor of Mountjoy Sq and the NCR. No 21 was the home of Dr Petrie and the office of his Topographical Branch of the Ir Ordnance Survey, where John O'Donovan, W F Wakeman, the poet Mangan, et al, compiled the archive of Ir antiquities.

   603.22   Dr Chart of Greet Chorsles street

CHARLOTTE QUAY   (17/33).   S side of Grand Canal Dock, where the Grand Canal joins the Liffey. Britain Quay is across the dock, but Britain Court (qv) is in N Dub.

   434.15   I buried our Harlotte Quai...Britain Court

CHARTERHOUSE.   Almshouse for elderly (uniformed) pensioners, and pub sch (moved 1872 to Surrey), endowed 1611 on site of Carthusian monastery W of Aldersgate, London.

   137.21   Elder Charterhouse's duckwhite pants

CHATTAHOOCHEE RIVER.   Rising in NE Ga, it flows SW to become the border btwn Ga and Ala, then btwn Ala and Fla. It is nowhere near Dublin, Ga.

   209.22   making chattahoochee
   ?552.04   attachatouchy floodmud

CHEAPSIDE.   St in City of London btwn Paternoster Row and Bank of Eng.
   577.30   at shipside, by convent garden

CHEEVERSTOWN.   Tnld, par and bar of Ratoath, Co Meath.
   97.09   Cheeverstown

CHELSEA.   Dist, SE London, fashionable res area. Song: "Elsie from Chelsea." Song: "Master Dilke Upset the Milk When Taking it Home to Chelsea."
   61.12   Jarley Jilke...couldn't get home to Jelsey
   587.26   the daintylines, Elsies from Chelsies

CHENONCEAUX. Vill, Dept of Indre-et-Loire, on Cher R, 20 mi E of Tours, Fr. The 16th-cent chateau astride the Cher was a gift from Henry II to his mistress Diane de Poitiers, taken from her by Catherine de Medici. There never was a duchess of *C.*

?229.33 the suchess of sceaunonsceau
?233.10 frenge...such as touch with show and show

CHEVY CHASE. One of the oldest Eng ballads, about the rivalry of neighboring families of Percy and Douglas. Hotspur Percy of Northumberland vowed he would hunt for 3 days in the lands of Earl Douglas without asking leave. The *Ballad of CC* mixes up this hunt with the battle of Otterburn, in which Percy was captured, Douglas killed. The Cheviot Hills, associated with the ballad, are on the border btwn Eng and Scot.

Chevychase Tnld (aka Derrynacarragh) is in the bar of Coolestown, Co Offaly.

30.14 Hag Chivychas Eve
245.35 Chavvyout Chacer calls the cup
335.10 the hundt called a halt on the chivvychace

CHICHESTER. City, W Sussex, Eng, with early Norman cath and a grammar sch founded 1497.

Arthur Chichester, Baron *C* of Belfast, who "planted" Ulster as Lord-Deputy of Ire 1604-1614, lived in Dub at the "Carye's Hospital" on Coll Green, which later was known as *C* Ho; and the 1st Ir Parl was convened there in 1661. In 1700, the lands of the Ir adherents of James II were sold by pub auction at *C* Ho (Gilbert III, 68). It was demolished in 1728 and the Parl House, now the Bank of Ire, was erected on the site.

390.18 half a Roman hat, with an ancient Greek gloss on it, in Chichester
        College auction

CHILTERN. Chiltern Hills, Bucks, Eng. The Stewardship of the *C* Hundreds of Stoke, Desborough and Burnham is a sinecure to which a Brit MP may be appointed as a way of giving up his seat.

105.02 *To Plenge Me High He Waives Chiltern on Friends*
359.04 ever the pelican huntered...chiltern
589.02 their chiltren's hundred

CHINA. Known in Eur in classical times as the "land of the Seres," in med times as Cathay, esp after Marco Polo's travel book (late 13th cent). Trad Chinese names are Shih-pa-shêng, "Eighteen Provinces"; Chung-kwo, "Middle Kingdom"; and Hwa-kwo, "Flowery Kingdom." From the time of the Chou dynasty (1122 BC) the Emperor was known as "the Son of Heaven" (110.04).

JJ was delighted to find that the Chinese symbol ⛰ means "mountain" and is pron "Chin," "the common people's way of pronouncing Hin or Fin" (*Letters* I, 250).

28.24 Opportunity fair with the China floods
89.24 a maundarin tongue
104.13 *Flee Chinx on the Flur*
106.19 *Chee Chee Cheels on their China Miction*
110.04 We who live under heaven...clovery kingdom...middlesins people
119.23 we have heard from Cathay cyrcles
131.34 confusianist...chinchin
213.05 pattern chayney...Hoangho, my sorrow
231.09 in Shina from Yoruyume
263.13 Hispano-Cathayan-Euxine

304.F2	Chinchin Childaman!
329.10	chenchen...bonzeye nappin
343.15	scoopchina's desperate noy's totalage
367.04	chinchinatibus
433.07	in china dominos [+ *in coena dominus*]
435.27	chine throws over jupan
461.24	soiedisante chineknees cheeckchubby
484.16	chunk your dimned chink, before avtokinatown
485.29	me speakee Yellman's lingas
485.36	chinchin chat
486.11	chink in his conscience...jape
486.13	psychosinology
490.28	your contraman from Tuwarceathay
533.06	chinatins...spekin
583.18	china's dragon...japets
611.05	islish chinchinjoss

CHIOS.   Gk isl off W coast of Asia Min. The anc sch of epic poets called the Homeridae claimed the isl to be Homer's birthplace; it was one of the 7 cities which made that claim in anc times.

129.24	pigeonheim to this homer...Quayhowth
481.22	humeplace...Childers

CHIPPING NORTON.   Town, Oxon, Eng, with woollen and glove factories and an agricultural market.

351.04	And as I live by chipping nortons

CHRISTCHURCH CATHEDRAL   (15/33).   The cath ch of the Prot archdiocese of Dub and Glendalough, in *CC* Place, the heart of Norse and med Dub. *Ca* 1038 Sitric MacAulaf (Sigtryggr Silkbeard), King of Dub and son-in-law of Brian Boru, gave land to Donagh (Donatus), 1st Bishop of Dub, for a ch on the site of the present *CC* (427.04). The orig ch was expanded and rebuilt as a cath by Strongbow and St Lawrence O'Toole, 1172. The latter died and is buried in Eu (qv), Normandy, but his heart is preserved in *CC*, in the Chapel of St Laud (613.15).

In 1871-78, *CC* was extensively rebuilt – rather than restored – at the expense of Henry Roe the distiller (211.25). Among the tourist attractions are Strongbow's Tomb in the S nave, with a recumbent effigy on which in med times debts and wagers were paid (343.04); and at one time a glass case with the mummified bodies of a cat and a rat which were discovered behind the organ-case (82.18).

26.22	grammarians of Christpatrick's ordered concerning thee in the matter of the work of thy tombing
82.19	as stuck as that cat to that mouse in that tube of that christchurch organ
138.26	chrysmed in Scent Otooles
179.12	mesa redonda of Lorencao Otulass in convocacaon
211.25	change of naves...Saint Lawrence
343.04	I'll gogemble on strangbones tomb
427.04	Mac Auliffe's, the crucethouse
552.03	twinminsters, the pro and the con
569.15	Greatchrist
613.15	Lo, the laud of laurens now orielising benedictively
625.20	Dom on dam ["cath on bank" (of Liffey)]

CHRISTIANIA.   See *Oslo*.

CHRISTIE'S.   London auction house for works of art.
    130.31   his whole means a slump at Christie's [Bud-Nil = "bid: nil"?]
    ?515.29   Let's have it, christie...bebattersbid

CIMMERIA.   Homer (*Odyssey* XI, 14) refers to the Cimmerians as inhabiting a land
of wintry gloom beyond the sea. As hist people the Cimmerians lived on the Black
Sea, whence "Crimea."
    504.07   Summerian sunshine...Cimmerian shudders

CINCINNATI.   City in Ohio, US. But all refs in *FW* are mainly or exclusively to
Lucius Quintus Cincinnatus, who returned to his plow after leaving it to save Rome.
    285.L1   *Finnfinnotus of Cincinnati*
    307.L1   *Cincinnatus*
    ?367.04   Here endeth chinchinatibus
    456.08   for kailkannonkabbis gimme Cincinnatis

CITIES OF THE PLAIN (OF JORDAN).   Sodom, Gomorrah, Admah, Zeboim, and
Zoar. Lot was spared in Zoar when Sodom and Gomorrah were destroyed for their
wickedness with fire and brimstone (*Gen* 19).
    188.23   while we all swin together in the pool of Sodom
    251.36   We've heard it aye since songdom was gemurrmal
    307.17   The Shame of Slumdom [paired with *Lot* in L margin]
    564.28   but it is a bad pities of the plain
    579.23   Gomorrha...Lots feed

CITY ARMS HOTEL   (15/35).   55 Prussia St, near the Cattle Market. Leopold and
Molly lived there (eg, *U* 300/305); the Joyce family never did.
    420.33   Return to City Arms

CITY HALL   (15/33).   On Cork Hill (junction of Dame and Parliament Sts); erected 1769-79 as the Royal Exchange. The Muniment Room contains municipal archives
going back to the 12th cent, and civic regalia including the Lord Mayor's collar of SS.
    94.25   upin their judges' chambers, in the muniment room, of their mar-
            shalsea
    ?595.22   vellumtomes muniment

CITY QUAY   (16/34).   S side of Liffey, E of Butt Br.
    535.07   first city's leasekuays

CLADDAGH.   Across the Corrib estuary from Galway City, it was orig a gathering
place of native Ir excluded by the Norman burghers of the city. Later a self-contained
fishing vill, preserving anc tradition, it survived until 1937, when its cottages were replaced by mod apartments. The *C* Ring, first fashioned by a 17th-cent Joyce, is a
ring of 2 hands clasping a heart.
    ?55.26   cladagain
    464.24   the Claddagh clasp
    497.33   the claddagh ringleaders
    606.32   her fancy claddaghs

CLANE.   Town, Co Kildare, on the Liffey. Bodenstown churchyard (Wolfe Tone's
grave) is in the vicinity. Clongowes Wood College (qv) is 2 mi N. Song: "The Rambler from Clare." See *Slane*.
    86.10   clanetourf...disguising himself
    212.25   for the honour of Clane

274.29   Clane's clean hometown ["Slane" in 1st Draft]
381.06   ramblers from Clane
509.36   pantoloogions...first perpersonal puetry...Cleaned
625.17   Clane turf

CLANRICKARD.   Clanricarde "castle" (1609, ruins) is in demesne of Portumna
Cas, Lough Derg, Co Galway. The C Burkes, Earls of C, were descended from Ulick
De Burgo, who seized Galway in the 14th cent. For 3 cents they ruled Galway and
fought the Eng whenever they weren't fighting the Mayo Burkes.
376.32   Clanruckard for ever!

CLARE.   Co, Munster prov, W Ire. Baronies: Upr and Lwr Bunratty, Burren, Clon-
deralaw, Corcomroe, Ibrickan, Inchiquin, Islands, Moyarta, Upr and Lwr Tulla.
C oysters are from S Galway Bay; see *Polldoody*. Song: "The Rambler from
Clare." The "poor Clares" are Franciscan nuns (226.10).
226.10   she'll stay daughter of Clare
381.06   the ramblers from Clane
381.22   that lerking Clare air, the blackberd's ballad [Moore's "The Lark in
                Clear Air"; air, "The Blackbird"]
479.06   claire oysters, Polldoody
488.25   midden Erse clare language
595.14   for clear goldways

CLAREGALWAY.   Vill, Co Galway, on Galway-Tuam rd.
?595.14   clear goldways

CLEAR ISLAND.   S of Roaringwater Bay, W Co Cork; Cape Clear, at the S tip, is
the S-most point of Ire.
580.34   from Malin to Clear

CLEOPATRA'S NEEDLE.   The 2 obelisks of this name were removed from Heliopolis to the Caesareum in Alexandria by Augustus, *ca* 14 BC. In the 1870's they were
given to London and NYC, where they now stand on the Victoria Embankment and
in Central Park.
104.20   *Cleopater's Nedlework Ficturing Aldborougham on the Sahara*

CLERY AND CO   (15/34).   Dept store, 21-27 Lwr O'Connell St – across the Liffey from Dame St.
?385.07   O'Clery, the man on the door
?386.20   in front of the place near O'Clery's...Dame street
459.08   cleryng's jumbles

CLIFDEN.   Town, on Atlantic coast of N Co Galway; site of trans-Atlantic Marconi
wireless sta, built 1910. Its sister sta was at Glace Bay, 14 mi E of Sydney, NS, Can.
Visiting Nora's relatives in Galway in Aug 1912, JJ went to C hoping to interview
Marconi or see the sta, prob for a *Piccolo della Sera* article like those he wrote on
Galway and the Aran Isls, but was unsuccessful (*Letters* II, 298–300).
?315.32   Cablen: Clifftop
407.20   the loftly marconimasts from Clifden sough...Nova Scotia's listing
                sisterwands
528.28   Longhorns Connacht, stay off my air!

CLONAKILTY.   Town, S Co Cork, W of Kinsale. Still known as "Clonakilty, God
Help Us!" from Famine days, when the workhouse was so appalling that the starving
who entered it were given up for dead.

57.09   I, says Clonakilty, God help us!

CLONDALKIN.   Vill, 12 mi SW of Dub; on the Grand Canal, but several miles S of the Liffey (201.26). *Cluain Dealgan*, Ir "thorn-meadow"; called Dun-awley by the Danes. It was a favorite res of Aulaffe, Dan King of Dub (532.13); burned by Ir 865 AD.

201.26   hazelhatchery...After Clondalkin the Kings's Inns
?370.35   Nomo clandoilskins cheakinlevers!
414.04   Mr van Howten of Tredcastles, Clowntalkin
532.13   Owllaugh...the meadows of Dalkin

CLONGOWES WOOD COLLEGE.   Jesuit sch for boys, Sallins, Co Kildare; founded 1814; alma mater of JJ and Stephen Dedalus. The 10th-cent Prosperous Crozier is preserved there (211.05). The orig bldg of the Coll was Castle Browne (qv).

211.05   a tibertine's pile with a Congoswood cross on the back for Sunny Twimjim
348.21   we were all under that manner barracksers on Kong Gores Wood together
453.15   Ole Clo goes through the wood

CLONLIFFE (16/36).   Dist and Rd, NE of Phibsborough. *C* House, still extant, was in early 19th cent the property of "Buck" Jones, and Jones Rd (16/35) was then "Buck Jones Rd," leading to it. Stephen Dedalus was beaten by schoolmates on *C* Rd, for preferring Byron to Tennyson.

210.18   Buck Jones, the pride of Clonliffe
?532.14   a cleanliving man...as cleanliving as could be

CLONMACNOISE.   NW Co Offaly; near Shannon R at ford of the anc Esker Rd. Extensive ruins of monastery and cen of learning founded in 6th cent by St Ciarán. The Dane Turgesius burned monastery 844 AD, and his wife Ota gave heathen oracles sitting naked on the altar.

31.21   the learned scholarch Canavan of Canmakenoise
?242.20   some make one noise
493.19   Ota...bumped her dumpsydiddle down
552.29   she sass her nach, chillybombom...upon the altarstane

CLONMEL.   Co town of Co Tipperary, on Suir R; *Cluain Meala*, Ir "honey-meadow." Laurence Sterne and George Borrow were natives. Cromwell suffered his worst defeat in the siege of *C*, 1650.
Clonmel St in Dub leads from Harcourt St to the grounds of Univ Coll S of Stephen's Green; they were in the 18th cent the gardens of Clonmell Ho in Harcourt St. Lord Clonmell was the notorious Copperfaced Jack Scott.

76.04   the Meadow of Honey is guestfriendly
443.10   stranger...meadow of heppiness...clonmellian
558.19   on his seven honeymeads

CLONSILLA.   Vill in Castleknock, NW of Dub.
537.35   bray at by clownsillies

CLONSKEAGH (17/30).   Dist and Rd SE of Milltown, S Dub. The ch alluded to at 601.25 may be the local RC ch or the chapel of Milltown Park, a Jesuit house of studies.

129.24   Kolonsreagh
601.25   S. Clouonaskieym's

CLONTARF   (20/35).   Dist, NE Dub, on Dub Bay; *Cluain Tarbh*, "bull-meadow."
The Battle of *C*, 1014 AD, was the great victory of Brian Boru and the Ir over the
Danes; the battle prob took place some distance to the N and W but the Vikings were
driven back to their ships on the beach at *C*. The aged Brian stayed during the battle
at Tomar's (Thor's) Wood (qv) and was slain there at the very end of the battle.
    C Isl, now submerged, lay S of *C*, and was used as a place of refuge during the
plague of 1650.
    See *Bulls, N and S.*
    16.22   Inns of Dungtarf
    17.09   Somular with a bull on a clompturf
    68.31   Tomar's Wood
    71.10   one clean turv
    71.33   *Thunder and Turf Married into Clandorf*
    73.23   Bully Acre...last stage in the siegings
    86.10   a clanetourf
    87.21   boer's trespass on the bull [see *Clonturk*]
    99.32   of the clontarfminded class
    201.18   *the plage au Clontarf*
    307.05   What Happened at Clontarf?
    315.31   clown toff, tye hug fliorten [*ti og fjorten*, Dan "ten and fourteen"]
    320.33   Bullysacre, dig care a dig [*deag ceathair a deag*, Ir "1014"]
    324.20   Clontarf, one love, one fear [*vier*, Ger "four"]
    353.13   a bull in a meadows
    376.08   after the Clontarf voterloost
    385.15   Boris O'Brien, the buttler of Clumpthump
    388.17   rising Clunkthurf over Cabinhogan
    497.20   bettlers of Clontarf
    539.28   slauchterday of cleantarriffs
    ?543.17   Thorstan's, *recte* Thomars Sraid
    618.08   The thicks off Bully's Acre
    625.17   Clane turf...batt on tarf...broin burroow

CLONTURK.   The entire area N of Dub btwn Glasnevin and Artane-Killester was
once known as *C*; later, the area now Drumcondra. *Cluain Tuirc*, Ir "boar-meadow."
C Ho (16/36), E side of Drumcondra Rd, *ca* 1819 was converted to a "Vauxhall"
and chalybeate spa. In 1894, the Joyce family lived at 2 Millbourne Lane (now Ave),
just across Drumcondra Rd from the *C* area (present *C* St) (420.30).
    51.27   average clownturkish
    87.21   boer's trespass on the bull [see *Clontarf*]
    ?353.11   Cocksnark of Killtork...bull in a meadows
    ?388.17   rising Clunkthurf over Cabinhogan
    420.30   Place scent on. Clontalk.

CLUSIUM.   Anc name of Chiusi, near Siena, It, one of 12 Etruscan cities. Horatius
held the br against Lars Porsena (83.07) of *C* (Macaulay, *Lays of Anc Rome*).
    84.15   nobiloroman review of the hugely sitisfactuary conclusium

COAL HOLE.   Off the Strand, London, it was a rather notorious "cellar singing-
room" which became fashionable about 1840 and was a predecessor of the music
hall. Later in the cent it became Terry's Theatre.
    ?194.18   to me unseen blusher in an obscene coalhole
    434.09   in flesh-coloured pantos instead of earthing down in the coalhole
    ?531.34   from Terreterry's Hole to Stutterers' Corner

COCKAIGNE (COCKAYNE).   Dutch, "Luilekkerland." Imaginary land of idleness and luxury; origin in 13th-cent Fr poem, *The Land of Cockaign*, in which "the houses were made of barley sugar cakes, the streets were paved with pastry, and the shops supplied goods for nothing." London, Paris, and Scot have been so called.
  ?56.36   leeklickers' land

COCK, THE.   18th-cent tav in Werburgh St, acc to Peter's *Dublin Fragments* (95), which identifies it with the Cock and Anchor described in J S Le Fanu's novel of that name.
  39.36   the Duck and Doggies...the Cock, the Postboy's Horn

COCK (COCKLE) LAKE.   Pool and form anchorage in Dub Bay SE of mouth of Liffey. Stephen Dedalus knows it by that name, *U* 49/50.
  ' 199.31   What harm if she knew how to cockle her mouth!

COCK LANE (15/33).   Mentioned as early as 1557, presumably near Cock Hill (see *Giglotte's Hill*). The allusion is rather to *CL* in Smithfield, London, the scene of pop excitement in 1762 over the "*CL* Ghost"; Dr Johnson joined the investigation of the mystery. It was exposed as a cock-and-bull story ("Gallotaurus").
  118.13   somebody...Coccolanius or Gallotaurus...wrote it all down

COCKSPUR ST.   In Westminster, London; leads from Trafalgar Square to Pall Mall.
  ?50.03   the iron thrust of his cockspurt start
  ?124.17   he venerated...at Cockspur Common

COCYTUS.   In Gk myth, a riv of the Underworld, flowing into Acheron (sometimes into Styx).
  ?56.04   listening to the cockshyshooter's...doomed
  198.22   For coxyt sake

CODLING LIGHTSHIP.   Form anchored off Wicklow Town btwn Codling Bank and India Bank.
  ?91.22   amreeta beaker coddling doom

COGNAC.   Town, on Charente R, SW Fr. Known not only for its brandy but also for the Treaty of *C* (1526), in which Francis I, the Pope, Venice, and Milan allied against Charles V.
  83.36   torgantruce...schmallkalled the treatyng to cognac

COLDSTREAM.   Border town, Berwickshire, Scot. The celebrated *C* (Foot) Guards were first raised there in 1659; later they became part of the Brit sovereign's Household Troops.
  58.25   of the Coldstream. Guards were walking

COLERAINE.   Town, Co Derry, at head of Bann R estuary; known for whiskey ("a wee drop of Cowlraine") and for the song, "Kitty of Coleraine," in which Kitty breaks her pitcher of buttermilk.
  ?68.08   soft coal or an array
  86.06   a pipkin ofmalt as he feared the coold raine
  210.33   for Kitty Coleraine of Butterman's Lane
  328.23   ill omens on Kitty Cole if she's spilling laddy's measure

COLLEGE GREEN (15/34).   Form Hoggen Green (qv), long a cen of Dub civic life. TCD faces *CG* on the E, Parl House (now Bank of Ire) on the N, and it contains the stat of Grattan and form of Wm III (qv); it was long the site of Unionist rallies.
  106.35   *Manyfestoons for the Colleagues on the Green*

388.35   oceanfuls of collegians green
550.06   Steving's grain for's greet collegtium

COLLEGE OF SURGEONS, ROYAL   (15/33)   W side of Stephen's Green; occupied by the Stephen's Green detachment and shelled in the Rising of 1916.
189.35   dynamitisation of colleagues
450.15   king's royal college of sturgeone

COLLOONEY.   Vill, Co Sligo, 7 mi S of Sligo. *C* Gap and Cas besieged by Red
Hugh O'Donnell, 1599; Col Vereker lost it to Gen Humbert in 1798, then took "Collooney" as his motto.
?624.24   parafume, oiled of kolooney

COLOPHON (KOLOPHON).   Once flourishing city of Ionia, N of Ephesus, now
only an archaelogical site, it was one of the 7 cities which claimed to be the birthplace of Homer.
129.24   pigeonheim to this homer...Kolonsreagh
481.21   humeplace...Kaledon

COLOSSUS OF RHODES.   Bronze stat of the sun-god Helios, completed *ca* 280 BC,
commemorating successful defense of Rhodes. It was one of the 7 Wonders of the
Anc World (qv) and prob stood *ca* 100 feet high. Destroyed by earthquake, 224 BC.
The story that it was built astride the harb and that ships could pass btwn its legs is
of 16th-cent origin. See *Rhodes.*
5.27   collupsus of his back promises
132.27   a Colossus among cabbages
241.08   Collosul rhodomantic
261.12   cacchinated behind his culosses
551.35   Newgade...kolossa kolossa!...porte...ghates (+ "Thalassa! Thalassa!"
           See *Constantinople*)
553.10   pyramidous...beaconphires...colossets
625.22   olympics...Steadyon, Cooloosus!

"COLUMBIA."   A US sailing vessel of Boston registry, it was the first US ship to
circumnavigate the globe, 1787-1790.
548.02   Impress of Asias and Queen Columbia

COMMITTEE ROOM NUMBER FIFTEEN.   The room of the Brit House of Commons in which in Dec 1890 the Ir MP's debated Gladstone's threat to resign as leader
of the Liberal party unless Parnell were ousted as chairman of the Ir Home Rule
party. With the scandal of Kitty O'Shea's divorce as only one of the issues, Parnell
was deposed by a majority including Davitt, Dillon, and Timothy Healy.
529.08   removal act by Committalman Number Underfifteen

COMO, LAKE.   In Lombardy, N It; celebrated as a resort since the time of Virgil
and Claudian.
?154.27   *Como? Fuert it?*
395.08   like the narcolepts on the lakes of Coma

CONA.   Riv and bay, mentioned in Macpherson's *The Battle of Lora.* Identified
in Campbell's notes to Macpherson as Campbelltown, Scot. In MacPherson's *Songs
of Selma*, Ossian is "the voice of *C.*"
228.13   A conansdream of lodascircles

CONCORD.   (1) Town, NH, US, on Merrimac R. Thoreau, of Concord, Mass, wrote

about the Merrimac R.   (2) Town, Mass, US, on *C* Riv. The "Minutemen" stood off the Brit there on 19 April 1775.
>   197.10   New Hunshire, Concord on the Merrimake

CONG.   Vill, Co Mayo, btwn Lough Mask and Lough Corrib, noted for connection with legends of the Firbolg. Site of 7th-cent monastery, rebuilt 12th cent, to which Rory O'Conor, the last high king of Ire, retired in old age. The jeweled "Cross of *C*" found at *C* is now in the Nat Mus, Dub.
>   87.25   local congsmen and donalds, kings of the arans and the dalkeys
>   167.16   with the cong in our gregational pompoms
>   211.05   with a Congoswood cross
>   306.06   Betwixt me and thee hung cong
>   325.32   bless madhugh, mardyk, luusk, and cong [= Connacht]
>   399.25   *By the cross of Cong*

CONGESTED DISTRICTS.   The *CD* Board of Ire was constituted in 1891 to improve conditions in the poorest areas; it encouraged emigration and the amalgamation of small holdings. In practice, "congested districts" means the W of Ire, esp Connacht.
>   580.03   were responsible for congested districts

CONGO RIVER.   The great riv of W cen Afr and the adjacent territory; its headwaters were explored by David Livingstone 1867-73 and the entire riv system by Henry Stanley 1874-84. Although one of the world's great rivs (2716 mi long), the *C* is not —as are the Nile, Amazon, and Mississippi — identified with Anna Liffey in *FW*.
>   165.21   wallopy bound...a congorool teal
>   211.05   a tibertine's pile with a Congoswood cross

CONN, LOUGH.   In N Co Mayo, connected with Lough Cullin; for the Moy "changing her minds," see *Cullin, Lough*.
>   203.12   where the Moy changez her minds twixt Cullin and Conn tween Cunn and Collin
>   549.33   Conn and Owel with cortoppled baskib

CONNA.   (1) *C* Cas (ruins) and vill, E Co Cork, on rock over Bride R 5 mi W of Tallow, Co Waterford.   (2) Old *C* Hill: house N of Old Connaught vill, near Bray, Co Wicklow; orig name of locality was Old *C*.   (3) Connahill, tnld, par of Kilnahue, bar of Gorey, Co Wexford.
>   160.12   East Conna Hillock

CONNACHT (CONNAUGHT).   W prov of Ire; its cos are Galway, Leitrim, Mayo, Roscommon, and Sligo. Its arms are a black eagle rampant (482.15) on a white ground, right, and a white sleeved arm with dagger, on a blue ground, left. Among the Four, it is the prov of Johnny MacDougall, and it represents West. The name is from *Connachta*, "the descendants of Conn." "Connacht" is the Ir spelling, "Connaught" the Brit; JJ uses both (although only the former is in *U*).

When Cromwell expelled the Ir from Leinster in 1653 he said that they could go "to Hell or Connaught." 2 cents later, the Connaught Rangers (disbanded 1922) were a crack regt in the Brit army (451.14).

The proverb (in the rest of Ire) "Cows in Connacht have long horns" means that stories about faraway things are exaggerated (528.28).

For indirect allusions to *C* as one of the 4 provs, see *Provinces*.
>   47.28   there's no true spell in Connacht or hell
>   71.29   *Go to Hellena or Come to Connies*
>   96.17   used her, mused her, licksed her and cuddled

180.15	Cardinal Occidentaccia
?227.27	no geste reveals the unconnouth
229.17	Leimunconnonnulstria
271.L1	*Ulstria, Monastir, Leninstar and Connecticut*
389.05	Ulcer, Moonster, Leanstare and Cannought
?390.31	the holymaid of Kunut
392.04	he attempted or, the Connachy, he was tempted
451.14	Connacht Rangers
467.30	Illstarred punster, lipstering cowknucks
482.15	Number four, fix up your spreadeagle
514.02	Normand, Desmond, Osmund and Kenneth
520.23	Nils, Mugn and Cannut
521.28	leinconnmuns
528.28	Longhorns Connacht, stay off my air!
528.33	there's moreen astoreen for Monn and Conn
536.27	I cannot let it. Kanes nought.
546.34	Chief Night Cloud by the Deeps

CONNECTICUT.   State, riv, NE US (which it represents among the other countries at 271.L1).
271.L1   *Connecticut*

CONNEMARA.   Coastal region, W Co Galway, known for its beauty and poverty. "Black-faced Connemara" is a breed of sheep.
76.01   posteriors, blackfaced connemaras not of the fold

CONN'S HALF.   *Ca* 200 AD, Conn "of the Hundred Battles" agreed with his southern rival Eoghan Mor (aka Mogh Nuadat) to divide Ire along the line of the Eiscir Riada (see *Esker*) btwn Dub and Galway. Henceforward the area N of this line was known as "Conn's Half" (*Leath Cuinn*) and the area S of it as "Mogh's Half" (*Leath Mogha*), qv.
475.06   one half of him in Conn's half...Owenmore's...[.22] esker ridge
549.33   Conn and Owel with cortoppled baskib

CONSTANTINOPLE.   On Eur side of Bosporus at latter's juncture with the Sea of Marmara. Before 330 AD called Byzantium; since 1930 named Istanbul (Stamboul). When Constantine the Great enlarged Byzantium and made it the seat of govt, it was named Nova Roma but styled *C*; the chief patriarch of the Gk ch still signs himself "Archbishop of Constantinople, New Rome" (155.05). Cap of Byzantine Empire 395-1453; of Ottoman sultans 1453-1922. The Ottoman seat of govt was the "Sublime Porte" (72.02, 551.35). Abdul Hamid II, Sultan from 1876, centralized all govt functions in the Yildiz Kiosk (135.18), a palace on the heights above the suburb of Beshiktash, and in fear of assassination withdrew behind its fortifications after the 1895 massacres.
Major dists of *C* are Stamboul, Pera, and Galata (33.36, 547.31), on opp sides of the Golden Horn, an arm of the Bosporus. Returning from the Anabasis, Xenophon's troops cried, "Thalassa! Thalassa!" when they reached the Bosporus across from Galata (547.32).
The Ch of St (Hagia) Sophia (552.07) was built 532-538 by Justinian. Among other chs and mosques is the Ch of the Pantocreator (551.07). Alti Mermer is a dist on Sea of Marmara side (551.04). Wyndham Lewis published "Constantinople Our Star" in *Blast* 2 (1915) (155.19).
33.36   abhout that time stambuling...tarrk record

72.02   *Sublime Porter*
74.11   our pantriarch of Comestowntonobble
135.18 yldist kiosk on the pleninsula
155.09 Novarome...constantinently
155.19 Cospol's not our star
294.27 One recalls Byzantium
357.30 the manmade Eonochs Cunstuntonopolies
?442.05 constantineal namesuch
547.32 Galata! Galata!
548.16 constantonoble's aim
551.04 she skalded her mermeries
551.07 were I our pantocreator
551.35 no porte sublimer benared my ghates
552.07 Hagiasofia of Astralia

CONSTITUTION HILL   (14/34).   St, contiguous with Phibsborough Rd on the N.
12.29   Constitutionhill

CONWAY'S PUB   (16/33).   Around the turn of the cent, the public house of James
Conway and Co, "grocers and wine merchants," was at 31-32 Westland Row, cor of
Lincoln Pl. Acc to Gorham, JJ frequented *C*'s. *U* 73/74, 84/86.
?214.20 Conway's Carrigacurra canteen

CONWAY'S TAVERN   (21/29).   Blackrock tav, cor of Rock Rd and George's Ave.
"People of quality went [to Blackrock] to stop at Conway's Tavern, which had a
great reputation for its ballroom" (Gerard, 378). Demolished in the 1870's. See *Carrigacurra.*
83.20   Conway's Inn at Blackrock
214.20 in Conway's Carrigacurra canteen

CONYNGHAM ROAD   (12–13/34).   From Parkgate W toward Chapelizod btwn
the S wall of Phoenix Park and the N bank of the Liffey. Roughly parallel to Bow Lane
on other side of Liffey.
576.28 Bobow...cunnyngnest couchmare...Phenicia Parkes

COOLE.   *C* Park, 2 mi N of Gort, Co Galway; the home of Lady Gregory, and subject of Yeats's "The Wild Swans at Coole"; demolished 1941. There is also a *C* Abbey, 4½ mi SE of Fermoy, Co Cork.
531.33 by the holy child of Coole
?622.01 they're cawing you, Coole!

COOLOCK   (19/39).   Dist, NE Dub, N of Artane on Dub-Malahide Rd.
73.31   Howth or at Coolock or even at Enniskerry
552.22 my sweet coolocked
616.02 the hartiest that Coolock ever

COOMBE, THE   (14/33).   St and working-class res area, W of St Patrick's Cath, in
the heart of The Liberties (qv); the name (*cum*, Ir "hollow") is from the riv vall of
the Poddle R, now subterranean.
73.30   Oxmanswold...up hill and down coombe...Howth
104.21 *the Coombing of the Cammmels*
243.23 sickling the honeycoombe
255.22 Dublin's capital, Kongdam Coombe
334.35 Donnicoombe Fairing

390.32   the haryman of Koombe
423.25   hag of the coombe
442.35   coomb the brash of the libs round Close Saint Patrice
506.12   when they lagged um through the coombe
516.13   take the coocoomb to his grizzlies
529.19   this hackney man in the coombe
542.03   libertilands...curraghcoombs

COPE ST   (15/34).   Short st btwn Anglesea St and Fownes St, along the back of Jury's Hotel, as it was, in Dame St.
98.30   Cope and Bull go cup and ball

COPENHAGEN.   Seaport city, cap of Den, on isl of Zealand; Dan, *Kjöbenhavn*. In the naval battle of *C*, 1801, the Dan fleet was destroyed by a daring maneuver by Nelson, the second-in-command. In 1807 the Brit took *C* in a land battle, with Wellington the second-in-command. "Copenhagen" was Wellington's favorite horse (223.16), a chestnut which he rode at Waterloo.
8.17   same white harse, the Cokenhape
10.02–.13   harse, the Capeinhope...Culpenhelp
10.21   How Copenhagen ended
46.18   Cookingha'pence, he bawls
143.10   old hopeinhaven
199.17   staynish beacons...cupenhave...Greenland's
220.34   The Rockery, Poopinheavin
223.16   Copenhague-Marengo
?248.25   to the cope of heaven
321.20   Copeman helpen
324.29   hear kokkenhovens ekstras
328.22   Coxenhagen
328.35   help of me cope
378.14   Kovenhow
388.17   rising Clunkthurf over Cabinhogan
478.16   hopenhaven
?530.34   He's cookinghagar
548.32   the cupandnaggin hour
568.28   Caubeenhauben
620.34   Dogging you round cove and haven

COPPINGER.   The identity and associations of Archdeacon J.F.X.P. Coppinger (55.18, 211.20 and see *Census*) are still a mystery. I list here place-names which I fear only deepen it.
(1) *C*'s Row (15/33), a short st btwn William and Clarendon Sts; named after Robert Copinger or Coppinger, who lived in William St, d 1715; "*C* Lane" in the 18th cent.   (2) *C*'s Cottages, Chapelizod. In his book on JJ, Budgen speaks of painting there, "south of the river, east of the bridge." No one else seems to have heard of them.   (3) *C*'s Court, a ruined 17th-cent mansion 2 mi WSW of Ross Carbery, Co Cork.   (4) The Chartulary of St Thomas's Abbey was known as *C*'s Register.
280.L2   *A shieling in coppingers*
294.F1   Ex jup pep off Carpenger Strate. The kids' and dolls' home
386.30   the cappunchers childerun
390.12   as per the cabbangers richestore
575.06   2 Coppinger's Cottages, the Doyle's country

CORK.   (1) Co, Munster prov, SW Ire.

Baronies: Bantry, Barretts, Barrymore, Bear, E and W Carbery, Condons and Clangibbon, Cork, Courceys, Duhallow, Fermoy, Ibane and Barryroe, Imokilly, Kerrycurrihy, Kinalea, Kinalmeaky, Kinnatalloon, Kinsale, E and W Muskerry, Orrery, and Kilmore.

(2) Founded by St Finbar (Finnbarr) in the 7th cent, *C* City was built on swampy land by the R Lee, hence *Corcaigh*, Ir "marsh," angl "Cork"; a section of the city is still called "The Marsh" (140.22). Wellington commanded 9000 men from *C* at Lisbon and Cadiz, July 1808 (9.23). Percy French's song, "Slattery's Mounted Foot": "You've heard of Julius Caesar, and the great Napoleon too,/An' how the Cork Militia beat the Turks at Waterloo" (451.13). *C* raised 24 companies of militia in the 1790's, and quartered 71 companies, to defend against foreign invasions.

Broad St Patrick's St, the main downtown thoroughfare, curves like a quarter of the circumference of a circle; the local saying is that "it would be the grandest street in the world if they could only take the bint outa the middle of it" (341.18, 491.12, ?576.20). The Mardyke is a tree-lined promenade btwn the N and S branches of the Lee, W of the city cen (325.32). The *Cork Examiner* is the daily newspaper (519.24). In the Ir office of arms for heraldry, the two Heralds are *C* and Dub (498.11).

The elder Joyce was from *C* (155.01, 197.05). JJ kept a painting of *C* City, framed in cork, in his Paris apartment. Many of the *FW* refs are to cork as used in bottling wine.

See *Blarney, Shandon.*

9.23	Willingdone, by the splinters of Cork, order fire
?52.03	Lili and Tutu, cork em
?85.35	a policeman's corkscrew trowswers
89.18	marsheyls...coke
95.11	There's three other corners to our isle's cork float
?116.11	We are not corknered yet, dead hand!
?121.23	ladywhite don a corkhorse
140.21	Dorhqk...as on the Mash
155.01	my corked father
160.27	Wilsh is full of curks
?176.30	kuskykorked
180.14	Cardinal Carchingarri ["Cork and Kerry" = Munster]
197.05	his corksown blather [= Munster]
221.35	(that's Cork!)
236.07	He's not going to Cork till Cantalamesse [Candlemas, 2 Feb, JJ's birthday]
?310.34	the turfeycork...out of Lougk Neagk
325.32	bless madhugh, mardyk [= Mark, Munster], luusk and cong
?333.11	cavarnan [?Cavan] men...corkedagains upstored
341.18	*Up to this curkscraw bind*
352.09	by the splunthers of colt
406.03	Corkshire alla mellonge
427.02	with corks, staves and treeleaves
?443.35	his lost angeleens is corkyshows do morvaloos
451.13	the Cork Milice
491.10	our straat that is called corkscrewed...Patrick's...bint out of the mittle
498.11	Munster's Herald
513.05	Marcus of Corrig [= Mark, Munster]
519.24	before your Corth examiner
541.17	Corkcuttas graatched

?576.20   corkscrewn perambulaups
577.34   strangfort planters...karkery felons
?588.11   his corkiness lay up two bottles
595.10   korps

CORK HILL   (15/33).   The area fronting City Hall (qv), where Dame St becomes Lord Edward St, and is intersected by Parliament St. Generally supposed to have been named after *C* House, built by the Earl of Cork, but it has also been derived from *Cuill-Choille*, Ir "hazel wood." Little Alf Bergan of *U* is a clerk in the subsheriff's office in City Hall.
12.27   shortlegged bergins off Corkhill

CORKSCREW ROAD.   (1) In Co Donegal, from Doochary Br through the Rosses to Dungloe. Descends from Doochary Hill to vall of Gweebarra R.   (2) Through the Burren, Co Clare, btwn Lisdoonvarna and Ballyvaughan.
?341.18   *Up to this curkscraw bind*
491.10   our straat that is called corkscrewed...Lismore to Cape Brendan
576.20   straxstraightcuts and corkscrewn perambulaups

CORNEILLE, GRAND HÔTEL DE.   Rue Corneille, Paris; despite its name, it was the cheapest lodging available when JJ lived there on his first trip to Paris during the winter of 1902-03, as a poverty-stricken student.
173.20   his entire low cornaille existence

CORNWALL.   Co, extreme SW Eng; Land's End (qv) is its SW tip. In the Tristan legend (Malory's *Morte d'Arthur*, 151.19), Mark is king of *C*. The Cornish lang, a form of Brythonic Gaelic like Welsh, became extinct in the 18th cent.
?49.13   on the field of Vasileff's Cornix inauspiciously...he perished
126.24   with Hirish tutores Cornish made easy
135.01   the king was in his cornerwall melking mark so murry
151.19   in accornish with the Mortadarthella
157.34   Mrs Cornwallis-West
?261.L3   *Ungodly old Ardrey, Cronwall* [*árd rí*, Ir "high king"]
291.01   Saint Yves by Landsend cornwer
387.28   poor Merkin Cornyngwham
388.02   Kram of Llawnroc
419.16   The blarneyest blather in all Corneywall!
581.09   he never was worth a cornerwall fark
586.27   yet singing oud his parasangs in cornish token

CORPUS CHRISTI CHURCH (RC)   (16/37).   In Home Farm Rd, Drumcondra.
601.24   S. Drimicumtra's

CORRY'S PUB.   Around the turn of the cent, there were two: John J Corry did business at 1 Fownes St (15/34), and Patrick Corry at 28 King St, N (14/34). The former is closer to the other pubs mentioned.
140.02   not Corry's not Weir's

CORSICA.   Fr Medit isl, Dept of Corse; cap is Ajaccio (89.10). Birthplace of Napoleon, the "Corsican upstart" (333.11). "The Corsican Brothers" is a 19th-cent play by Boucicault about twin brothers who experience directly what happens to each other even when they are separated.
8.14   Saloos the Crossgunn!
10.18   cursigan Shimar Shin
89.10   ajaciulations to his Crosscann Lorne...corso in cursu on coarser again

175.11   *the Emp from Corpsica*
?176.30   kuskykorked himself up tight
305.17   if you're not your bloater's kipper may I never curse again
333.11   the corkedagains upstored
465.16   like the corks again brothers
561.06   The Corsicos?

COVENT GARDEN.   St, market area, and opera house, N of the Strand, London. From the 1650's until the 1970's a market for fruit, flowers, and vegetables. *CG* Theatre (1858) is the chief seat of grand opera in London; there have been theatres on the site since 1733.
538.24   and I their covin guardient
577.30   at shipside, by convent garden

COVENTRY.   City, Warwickshire, cen Eng. Home of Lady Godiva (11th cent), wife of Leofric, earl of Mercia; she rode naked through the sts of *C* at noon (353.26) to fulfill a bargain whereby her husband would remit an unpopular tax imposed on the citizens. The forewarned citizens, except for Peeping Tom, looked the other way.
150.21   Jericho...I shall shortly be wanted in Cavantry
353.26   *coventry plumpkins...twelves of clocks*

CRAMPTON QUAY (15/34).   S side of Liffey, btwn Aston and Wellington Quays.
?204.36   not crampton lawn

CRAMPTON'S MONUMENT (16/34).   Erected 1862 in honor of Sir Philip Crampton (1777-1858), at junction of College, D'Olier, Townsend, and Gt Brunswick (now Pearse) Sts, on the site of the Steyne (qv); now demolished. This odd statue, with a face peering from what appeared to be brussels sprouts, was locally known as "the water-babe," "the pineapple," "the artichoke," and "the cauliflower"; there were 3 drinking fountains in the stone base with chained community cups (*U* 168/170). The inscription (quoted 132.30) read,
"This fountain has been placed here,
A type of health and usefulness,
By the friends and admirers
Of Sir Philip Crampton, Bart,
Surgeon General to Her Majesty's Forces.
It but feebly represents
The sparkle of his genial fancy,
The depth of his calm sagacity,
The clearness of his spotless honour,
The flow of his boundless benevolence."
132.30   [last 4 lines of inscription]
?204.36   not crampton lawn
542.09   sprouts fontaneously from Philuppe Sobriety in the coupe that's
           cheyned

CRAMPTON'S PEAR TREE (16/33).   An actual pear tree, planted in 1815 by the Philip Crampton of *C*'s Mon in front of the walled garden of his house at 14 Merrion Sq. It was famous in mid-19th cent. JJ may have confused the pear tree with Crampton's Mon (qv), which was "inseuladed" in the center of a roundabout.
291.05   so inseuladed as Crampton's peartree

CRÉCY.   Town, N Fr, Somme Dept; site 26 Aug 1346 of first decisive battle of Hundred Years' War, a victory for Edward III of Eng over Philip VI of Valois. The

Eng use of bombards was one of the earliest uses of artillery.

> 9.08   gonn boycottoncrezy

CREMONA.   City, Lombardy, It; cen of the making of violins, cellos, etc, by the Amati family and Antonio Stradivari, its name became generic for "fiddle." The crwth was an anc Brit stringed instrument. *Crónán*, Ir "drone."

> 41.22   crewth fiddle which, cremoaning and cronauning

CRIMEA.   Penin, S USSR, extending into the Black Sea; joined to mainland by isthmus of Perekop (qv). Known to anc Gks as the Tauric Chersonese (Gk, "peninsula") (347.09); the mod name is from the tribe of Cimerii (see *Cimmeria*). Russ, Ger, *Krim* (*Krimkrieg*, "Crimean War"). The Crimean War of 1853-56 was an intervention by Brit and Fr, and later Sardinia, in a Russ-Turk war; the Allies intended to immobilize the Russ Black Sea fleet by investing its base at Sevastopol (qv) on the SW coast of the *C*. The siege ended with the fall of the Malakov fort 8 Sept 1855, after earlier battles on the Alma R, at Balaclava (The Charge of the Light Brigade), Eupatoria and Inkerman (qqv). Peace was concluded Feb-Mar 1856.

Ir troops were present in large numbers in the Brit forces, Buckley among them.

> 8.30   This is the crimealine
> 49.05   the Crimean war
> 334.25   crimm crimms...woollied and flundered
> 339.09   Chromean fastion
> ?342.20   *the Creman hunter*
> 346.01   *the fictionable world in Fruzian Creamtartery*
> 347.09   Reilly Oirish Krzerszonese Milesia
> 347.10   Crimealian wall
> 347.32   Crummwiliam wall
> 350.28   crimsend daun
> 366.17   increaminated...assault of turk
> 478.15   crimeslaved cruxway
> 522.08   these two Crimeans
> 532.19   crim crig
> 539.11   cramkrieged
> 569.02   crimosing balkonladies

CRIPPLEGATE.   London dist, N of Guildhall. St Giles *C*, Fore St, is the burial place of Oliver Cromwell, John Milton, et al.

> 579.32   recrutched cripples gait

CRITERION THEATRE.   Literary readers of *FW* no doubt prefer to see an allusion to *The Criterion*, the journal edited by T S Eliot in the 1920's and 1930's, but the context suggests the *C* Theatre in Piccadilly Circus, London, next door to the *C* Restaurant from 1873.

> 150.04   Talis de Talis, the swordswallower, who is on at the Craterium

CROAGH PATRICK.   Mt, 6 mi SW of Westport, Co Mayo, on S shore of Clew Bay, where St Patrick is said to have fasted for 40 days and driven various demons, toads, and snakes from his presence. Site of annual pilgrimages, last Sun in July, *Domhnach Chrom Dubh*, "Crom Dubh's Sunday." *Cruach-Phadrig*, Ir "Rick of St Patrick," hence the local name, "The Reek." See also *St Patrick's Purgatory*.

> 53.30   Bri Head and Puddyrick
> 81.18   the attackler, a cropatkin...engaged the Adversary
> 301.30   on his laughside lying sack to croakpartridge

?344.03−.07   *croak in his cry*...partridge's last
?508.23   Clopatrick's cherierapest

CROKE PARK (16/35).   E of Jones's Rd, N Dub; hqs of Gaelic Athletic Assn, cen for hurling and Gaelic football. On "Bloody Sunday," 21 Nov 1920, Brit forces fired on the crowd at *CP*, killing spectators and a player after Michael Collins's men had killed Brit intelligence officers in their homes on Sun morning.
178.33   all the kules in Kroukaparka
301.30   goblin castle...lying sack to croakpartridge

CROM CRUACH.   Pagan idol ("Bloody Croucher") destroyed by St Patrick; some say he overturned it on the plain of Magh Slecht, Co Cavan, others that he took it from Tara and threw it into the Boyne R.
?22.14   curses of cromcruwell
173.25   tarabooming...cruaching three jeers (pah!) for his rotten little ghost of a Peppybeg
?526.20   Naif Cruachan [*Naomh* (pron "neav"), Ir "saint"]

CROMLEACH HILL.   See *Lubar River*.

CROMMAL HILL.   See *Lubar River*.

CROMWELL'S QUARTERS (13/33).   A short lane of steps btwn Bow Br (St) and Mt Brown (St); locally known as "Forty Steps." Before 1876 it was known as "Murdering Lane." No hist connection with Oliver Cromwell, but there are local legends that streams of blood flowed down the steps from a massacre under Cromwell.
68.15   Forty Steps...his perch old Cromwell's Quarters

CRONA RIVER.   Stream in Macpherson's *Ossian*, trib of Carron (Carun) R.
?376.34   Deaf to the winds when for Croonacreena
602.14   Croona is in adestance

CROOK (CROOKE).   Par and tnld on W side of inner Waterford Harb; not the site of a lighthouse. When Henry II visited Ire, he landed at "the Crook, over against Hook tower" (Warburton, Whitelaw and Walsh, I, 10). It is actually some distance up the estuary from Hook Head (qv).
     An apocryphal story derives the expression "by hook or by crook" from Henry's avowed intention to land "by Hook or Crook."
245.08   wextward warnerforth's hookercrookers
549.19   Wexterford's hook and crook lights

CROOM.   Town, Co Limerick, on Maigue R. Around the middle of 18th cent the poet Seán Ó Tuama of *C* summoned poets to a Court of Poetry which met at intervals until his death.
?156.06   all the mummyscrips in Sick Bokes' Juncroom

CROSS GUNS (15/36).   Br carrying Phibsborough Rd across the Royal Canal (aka Westmoreland Br); Crossguns pub, at the br.
?8.14   Saloos the Crossgunn!
?89.10   Crosscann Lorne

CROW ST THEATRE (15/34).   The theatre, actually on Cecilia St facing the N end of Crow St, opened as the Theatre Royal 23 Oct 1758 and closed 15 Jan 1820. In 1836 it became Apothecaries' Hall, in 1852 the medical sch of the Catholic U. See *Theatre Royal*.
105.27   *From Abbeygate to Crowalley*

CRUACHAN.   The present vill of Rathcroghan, Co Roscommon (526.28) preserves the name (*Cruachán*, Ir "little hill") of the anc royal seat of Connacht, home of Queen Maeve of the Red Branch cycle. The Cave of Rathcroghan was believed to be the entrance to the Otherworld. ½ mi SE is Reilig na Riogh, "Cemetery of Kings," form believed to be the burial ground of such royalty as Dathi, Conn of the Hundred Battles, and the queens Eire, Fodhla, and Banba.

 ?173.25 cruaching three jeers
 526.20 Naif Cruachan! Woe on woe, says Wardeb Daly

CRUMLIN (12/31).   Dist, SW Dub; *C* Rd continues Cork St. *C* was one of the 4 Royal Manors of Dub (qv). *Croim-ghlinn*, Ir "crooked glen"; it is the vall of the Cammock (Camac) R (qv). There is also a *C* in Co Antrim, W of Belfast.

 18.07 O'c'stle...crumbling
 73.06 for the honour of Crumlin
 142.13 Crumglen's grassy
 339.34 *in the minkst of the Krumlin*
 353.33 *wools gatherings all over cromlin*
 497.19 Krumlin Boyards
 536.10 in my krumlin
 555.13,15 esker, newcsle, saggard, crumlin
 586.29 crumlin quiet down from his hoonger

CRYSTAL PALACE.   S London football team. Its grounds are in Selhurst, Croydon; its connection with the edifice of the 1851 Exhibition, later removed to Sydenham and destroyed by fire in 1936, is tenuous.

 378.19 Brystal Palace agus the Walsall!

CUBA.   Largest isl of the W Indies; cap Havana (see *Appendix*). The name is aboriginal. *C* is known for tobacco and sugar, and was for hats; but not for stockings. "The Cubanola Glide" was a pop song (US) of 1909.

 208.12 her nude cuba stockings
 618.22 on Wanterlond Road with my cubarola glide

CUJAS, RUE DE.   A short st in the 5th Arr, Paris, from the Blvd St Michel past the Sorbonne to the Pantheon; site of the École de Droit. There has never been a Place de *C*. JJ lived at several addresses in the area. The Paris sch of medicine is a block away; JJ went first to Cecilia St (qv) medical sch in Dub, then tried Paris in 1902-03.

 41.32 house of call at Cujas Place...parish of Saint Cecily

CULLEN'S BARN.   Very likely this is only Boucicault's "Colleen Bawn" (as in *transition*) with an echo of Dolphin's Barn, but in the late 19th cent Wm Cullen was the proprietor of the Northern and Commercial Hotel at 78-79 Capel St (15/34).

 385.01 after an oyster supper in Cullen's barn

CULLENSWOOD (15/31).   The area btwn Rathgar and Ranelagh, including Rathmines, in S Dub. On Easter Monday 1209, the Bristol settlers were ambushed by Ir tribes from the mts while at sports. For cents after, the citizens marched out to the "Bloody Fields" on the anniversary of Black Monday to defy the tribes, and "banqueted" under a black standard on a dinner provided by the mayor and sheriffs.

 141.35 the blackcullen jam for Tomorrha's big pickneck
 ?385.01 oyster supper in Cullen's barn
 ?440.09 Carnival Cullen

CULLIN, LOUGH.   In N Co Mayo, S of the larger Lough Conn, with which it is connected by a short channel at Pontoon Br. Lough Conn drains into Lough *C*, which drains into the Moy R which flows N just E of the lakes and parallel to them. At one time there was occasionally a reverse flow from *C* to Conn; *FW* seems to think that the lakes are joined by the Moy.

    203.12   where the Moy changez her minds twixt Cullin and Conn tween
           Cunn and Collin

CULLINAN.   The *C* diamond, named after the owner of the diamond field in S Afr where it was found, was the largest ever found. It was divided into two stones called "Stars of Africa," both among the Brit crown jewels kept in The Tower of London.

    286.14   cardinhands...radmachrees and rossecullinans [hearts, diamonds, etc]

CURRAGH, THE.   Treeless plain E of Kildare, Co Kildare. *An Currach*, Ir "The Racecourse": there have been horseraces there since earliest times, and it is the hqs of Ir racing. Among the classic stakes races are the Ir Cesarewitch and the Ir St Leger in Sept, the Guinness Oaks in July, and the 1000 Guineas and 2000 Guineas in May. Long a military cen, earlier of the Brit garrison, now of the Ir Army. The surrounding country is hunted by the Kildare Foxhounds, known as "the Killing Kildares."

    160.06   as if there was howthorns in Curraghchasa
    202.29   a Curraghman...by the dykes of killing Kildare
    273.L1   *Curragh machree, me bosthoon fiend*
    322.19   how the whole blazy raze accurraghed
    342.15   *Thousand to One Guinea-Gooseberry's*
    387.01   the tercentenary horses and priesthunters, from the Curragh
    ?399.05   *In her curragh of shells*
    498.02   Cesarevitch...Sant Legerleger...oakses
    542.03   making free through their curraghcoombs

CURRAGH CHASE.   Demesne 5 mi SE of Arkeaton, Co Limerick; ancestral home of de Vere family, destroyed by fire, 1941.

    160.06   as if there was howthorns in Curraghchasa

CUSA.   For Nicholas of Cusa, see *Census*.

CUSH (25/40).   Point of land in Sutton, W of Howth.
    346.32   *cushlows of his goodsforseeking hoarth*

CUSTOM HOUSE (16/34).   One of Dub's great Georgian bldgs, the *CH* fronts the Liffey (*CH* Quay) on the N side just E of Butt and Loop Line Brs. Built 1781-1791, it was burned in May 1921 during the Troubles (189.36), later restored. Among other pieces of sculpture, there are carved stone heads over the doorways, representing Ir rivs – all male except for that of Anna Liffey (106.19). JJ kept a picture of the Liffey head in his Paris flat. Guinness vessels tie up at the *CH* Quay (136.26, 406.26). The "old" *CH* was on the S side of the Liffey, near Essex (Grattan) Br.

    55.13   then an excivily (out of the custom huts)
    106.19   *It Was Me...Lent my Dutiful Face to His Customs*
    136.23   from king's brugh to new customs
    189.36   levelling of all customs by blazes
    220.35   HUMP...engaged in entertaining in his pilgrimst customhouse at
           Caherlehome-upon-Eskur
    406.26   brown pride of our custard house quay

CUTHONE.   In Macpherson's *Fingal*, "dark winds pour it on rocky Cuthon."

190.30   the cuthone call...oozy rocks
?353.18   untuoning his culothone

CUT-PURSE ROW   (14/33).   The 18th-cent name of a lane now (since 1863) the W end of Cornmarket St.
42.30   young dublinos from Cutpurse Row

CUXHAVEN.   Seaport on Elbe R 70 mi NW of Hamburg, Ger; form terminal for the Ger transatlantic liners. Erskine Childers (see *Census*) won the DSO in WW I for his part in a successful attack on *C* by the Royal Naval Air Service, 1 Jan 1915.
Does the ref echo the spiritual "Oh, Dem Golden Slippers"? "...gonna walk all over God's Heaven."
60.22   there would be fights all over Cuxhaven

CYPRUS.   E Medit isl, off coast of Turk. *Cuprum*, Gk "copper."
460.23   the cyprissis and babilonias

CZECHOSLOVAKIA.   Rep formed 1918 by Czechs and Slovaks from parts of form Austro-Hungarian Emp; its regions included Bohemia (Czech, *Čechy*), Moravia, Slovakia, and Ruthenia (qqv). *Narodní dúm*, "national house": the Parliament. In 1618, Bohemian Prots living up to their name threw three of the king's counselors out of a window of the Hradčany Palace in Prague (?230.05). The nat anthem is *Kde Domov Muj*, "Where is my home?"
230.05   eggspilled him out of his homety dometry narrowedknee domum
332.36   Check or slowback. Dvershen [*dver*, Russ "door"]
411.18   Hek domov muy
423.36   Bro Cahlls and Fran Czeschs

D

DÁIL ÉIREANN.   The elected house of the Oireachtas, or legislature of the Ir Free State, later of the Rep of Ire. The first Dáil sat 1918. Pron "doyle."
256.28   what the doc did in the doil
309.14   their tolvtubular high fidelity daildialler
322.16   who did you do at doyle today
466.23   our own deas [Ir, "south"] dockandoilish
574.09   heard by Judge Doyle
574.32   were curiously named after doyles
575.06   Ann Doyle...the Doyle's country. Doyle (Ann)...doylish
575.32   Judge JeremyDoyler

DAILY EXPRESS.   Form publ by Maunsell and Co at 39-40 Parliament St. A conservative paper, it ceased publ in 1921.
500.15   Christ light the dully expressed!
501.20   Delhi expulsed

DAILY MAIL.   London mass-circulation newspaper, founded 1896 by Alfred Charles Harmsworth, later Lord Northcliffe, who incidentally was born in Chapelizod.
150.06   penscrusher...who runs his duly mile
177.05   *Daily Maily, fullup Lace!*

199.02   their debths in that mormon's thames...his berths in their toiling
moil

DAISY MARKET   (15/34).   Form the second-hand market in cen Dub, near Green
St Courthouse.

?158.02   fair...daisy's worth

DALKEY   (27/26).   Vill, SE of Dun Laoghaire, at S end of Dub Bay. *Deilginis*, Ir
"Thorn Island." JJ taught at Clifton Sch, Summerfield Lodge, *D* Ave, *D* for 4 months
in 1904. *D* was the S terminus of the *D*, Kingstown, and Blackrock Tram line (qv).

Offshore are *D* Isl (form St Benett's), and the smaller Muglins Isl. In the 18th
cent a convivial society in Dub called itself the "Kingdom of *D* Isl" and annually
elected "His Facetious Majesty, King of Dalkey, Emperor of Muglins,...Defender of
his own Faith and Respecter of all others, and Sovereign of the Illustrious Order of
the Lobster and Periwinkle" (87.25). It became political and was suppressed by the
Castle.

D claims, by a commemorative tablet and with more enthusiasm than evidence,
to be the birthplace of the composer John Dowland (570.03).

40.29   Dullkey Downlairy and Bleakrooky tramaline
87.25   kings of the arans and the dalkeys, kings of mud and tory
294.23   Blake-Roche, Kingston and Dockrell
317.05   Allkey dallkey
390.29   In Dalkymont nember to
?422.07   dalickey cyphalos
533.08   chaplain of Lambeyth and Dolekey
570.03   Deep Dalchi Dolando
582.32   dullakeykongsbyogblagroggerswagginline
616.11   three Sulvans of Dulkey

DALKEY, KINGSTOWN, AND BLACKROCK TRAM LINE.   Its route from Nelson's Pillar was Sackville (O'Connell) St, Westmoreland St, Grafton St, Nassau St,
Merrion Sq N, Lwr Mount St, Northumberland Rd, Pembroke Rd, Ballsbridge, Merrion Rd, Booterstown, Blackrock, Monkstown, Kingstown, Dalkey: a 9-mile ride.
Anna Livia remembers riding on it, 615.20−.21.

40.29   Dullkey Downlairy and Bleakrooky tramaline
294.22   Blake-Roche, Kingston and Dockrell
582.32   dullakeykongsbyogblagroggerswagginline

DALYMOUNT   (14/35).   Dist and park, N of NCR and W of Phibsborough Rd; *D*
Park is the main Association football (soccer) stadium in Dub, the site of international matches. See *Dollymount.*

375.23   A grand game! Dalymount's decisive
?390.29   In Dalkymont nember to

DALY'S CLUB   (15/34).   The chief resort for gambling and tippling by the aris-
tocracy and gentry in the 18th cent, it moved in 1791 from its bldg in Dame St to a
new edifice in College Green, next to the Parl Ho, and continued through the 19th
cent. The cen portion of the bldg survives, converted into offices.

42.35   nooning toward Daly's

DAMASCUS.   City, cap of Syria. Saul was converted and became Paul on the road
to *D*. Damask ("cloth of Damascus") is a self-patterned fabric.

131.12   he rowed saulely to demask us...appauling
404.27   the damasker's overshirt

DAME ST   (15/33).   From College Green (TCD) to Lord Edward St, at the Castle. The name (1610) is from Dame's Gate, the E gate of the city walls which adjoined the Ch of the BVM "del Dame" (see *St Mary del Dam*). In the 14th cent it was "the st of the Thing-mote" (see *Thing Mote*).

    135.11   dames troth
    386.21   beside that ancient Dame street
    387.07   colleges...Mr Dame James
  ?389.10   Janesdanes Lady Andersdaughter Universary
    548.13   in trinity huts they met my dame

DANA, PAPS OF.   The 2 hills of Slieve Luachra in Co Kerry have traditionally been called "the Paps of Dana." Dana (Anan, Ana, Danaan) was the goddess of the Tuatha Dé Danaan, whose queen Banba also became a personification of Ire. *Dana-dún*, Ir "Fort of Dana."

    19.29   dugters of Nan
  ?79.15   the first city (called after the ugliest Danadune)
  325.24   the two breasts of Banba are her soilers and her toilers
  469.01   twinn her ttittshe...Banbashore
  583.22   ninsloes of nivia, nonpaps of nan

DANELAGH.   The area of N and NE Eng settled by Danes and other Scandinavians in 9th and 10th cents, and subject to the Danelagh or Danes' Law, comprising kingdoms of Northumbria and E Anglia and the Five Boroughs of Leicester, Nottingham, Derby, Stamford, and Lincoln.

  334.13   the funst man in Danelagh
 ?353.31   *At someseat of Oldanelang's Konguerrig*

DANESBURY.   Vill just N of Welwyn Garden City, Herts, SE Eng; N of London. It is a little far from the Bow bells which told Dick Whittington to turn again.

  372.17   turned again weastinghome, by Danesbury Common

DANE'S ISLAND.   (1) Small isl 1 mi SW of Bunmahon, Co Waterford; form Illaunobric, "O'Bric's Isl," a limit of the terr of Ormond (E Munster). Site of anc fort, but no archimandrate (abbot) is associated with it.   (2) The arctic Danes Island is N of North-East Land in the Spitsbergen archipelago.

  496.08   an Archimandrite of Dane's Island and the townlands

DANUBE RIVER.   Riv, cen Eur. Ger, *Donau*; Hung, *Duna*; in its lwr course it was in anc times known as the *Ister* (214.01, 295.01). Despite Strauss's "The Blue Danube," the *D* at Vienna is brown.

   76.32   erst curst Hun in the bed of his treubleu Donawhu
   78.05   Donnaurwatteur! Hunderthunder!
  181.05   Shruggers' Country, Pension Danubierhome
  203.08   For the dove of the dunas!
  214.01   lost histereve
  295.01   istherdie forivor
  435.15   Suzy's Moedl's [*süsse Mädl*, Ger "pretty girls"] with their Blue
               Danuboyes!
  550.35   duncingk the bloodanoobs
  578.19   Donauwatter! Ardechious me!

DANZIG (GDANSK).   City, Baltic port, and prov, N Pol. Form Ger, after WW I it became a free city, and provided access to sea for Pol via the Pol Corridor. The Ger claim on *D* in 1939 was an occasion of WW II (89.28).

89.28   Are you not danzzling on the age of a vulcano?
?105.10   *his Notylytl Dantsigirls*
333.08   the danzing corridor

D'ARCY'S ANCHOR BREWERY (14/34).   In Usher St; John D'Arcy and Son, proprietors. Once the 2nd largest brewery in Ire, took over O'Connell's Ale from the Phoenix Brewery (qv), then in 1926 was taken over by Watkins, Jameson, and Pim.
333.08   darsey dobrey...pimpim him
?543.20   the darsy jeamses
?587.04   me and my auxy, Jimmy d'Arcy

DARGLE.   Vall and riv, from Enniskerry to Bray, S of Dub. The picturesque little riv runs through the Powerscourt Demesne. "Dargle" is also Dub slang for "picnic," as in the song, "The Waxies' Dargle."
206.17   the farest gargle gargle in the dusky dirgle dargle
327.18   making every Dinny dingle after her down the Dargul dale
460.15   The Dargle shall run dry

DARK LANE (13/31).   In Dolphin's Barn; now Sundrive Ave.
568.22   darklane

DARTRY ROAD (15–16/30).   S from Palmerstown Park Rd to the Dodder R. The entire locale has occasionally been called "Dartry."
305.07   Imagine it, my deep dartry dullard!

DAWSON ST (16/33).   Btwn Nassau St and Stephen's Green, N; with parks at both ends, no house looks along its length. It contains St Anne's Ch and the Mansion Ho. Nothing in it seems a very good candidate for the porterhouse (405.23) where Shaun stuffs himself.
?405.28   her frumped door looked up Dacent Street

DEAD SEA.   Btwn Israel and Jordan, it is 1300 ft below the level of the Medit. Called the Salt Sea in the *OT*; also the Sea of Sodom (*II Esdras*, 5:7).
29.24   the deadsea dugong
188.23   swin together in the pool of Sodom
392.06   he was dead seasickabed
416.30   Had he twicycled the sees of the deed

DEAF AND DUMB INSTITUTION.   (1) Claremont Inst for the Education of the Deaf and Dumb, form in Glasnevin (15/35).   (2) Catholic Inst for the Deaf and Dumb; in Cabra, at the intersection of Cabra, Navan, and Ratoath Rds, NE of Phoenix Park (13/36).

Each of these was known as "the deaf and dumb inst," and they were both so called in Thom's *Directories*. The ubiquitous "deaf and dumb" motif in *FW* has never been adequately explained. Shem and Shaun are mute and deaf (as Mutt and Jeff), HCE is often deaf and dumb (329.27), and the 12 Customers are sometimes deaf and dumb (175.25, 284.18).
73.20   in the directions of the duff and demb institutions
?593.21   in the domnatory of Defmut

DEANSGRANGE (20/27).   Area SE of Stillorgan; Dean's Grange Cem. In the ref, *D* represents the prov of Leinster.
57.09   I, says Deansgrange, and say nothing

DEE RIVER.   (1) In Aberdeenshire, Scot, flowing from Cairngorms to North Sea at

Aberdeen. (2) Dea R, the anc name of the Vartry R (qv), Co Wicklow. When St
Patrick returned to Ire, he landed at Inverdea (*inver*, Ir "rivermouth"). (3) Riv, Co
Louth, flowing into Dundalk Bay at Annagassan. (4) Riv, N Wales and W Eng.

    133.36   stood into Dee mouth
    198.26   she can't fiddan a dee
    226.15   In the Dee dips a dame
    327.10   a touch as saft as the dee in flooing
    525.33   He missed her mouth and stood into Dee

DEER PARK.   There are of course "Deer Park"s everywhere in the Brit Isles and N
Eur, but a few are most likely associated in the mind of *FW*'s dreamer: (1) Phoenix
Park (qv) was originally a deer park, and herds of deer graze there to this day.
(2) The Buddha lived for a while after his enlightenment in the Deer Forest, near
Benares, Ind.   (3) Dyrhaven is the royal Dan deer park, N of Copenhagen.

    244.29   In deerhaven
    ?553.23   the dyrchace

DELGANY.   Vill, Co Wicklow, 6 mi S of Bray, near Glen of the Downs. Sitric Mac-
Aulaf, Norse King of Dub, was routed by King Ughaine of Leinster, 1021 AD, at The
Battle of *D.*

    334.08   Mr 'Gladstone Browne'...from that 'man of Delgany'
    427.04   in the direction of Mac Auliffe's [1st Draft, "in the direction of
              Delgany"]

DELHI (DEHLI).   Ind city, form cap of Mogul emp, later of Brit Ind; seat of Ind
govt at New *D.* Chandni Chauk ("Silver Street") is a principal st. The Peacock Throne
(551.04), of gold inlaid with precious stones, stood in the Divan-i-Am or Hall of Public Audience until carried off by the Pers invader Nadir Shah in 1737.

    497.24   delhightful bazar
    501.20   Delhi expulsed [+ "Daily Express"]
    542.31   I dehlivered them
    542.33   with my chandner's chauk
    551.04   in paycook's thronsaale she domineered

DELIUM.   Anc seaport, Boeotia, E cen Gr; site of battle, 424 BC, in which Thebans
defeated Athenians.

    8.28   This is Delian alps

DELOS.   Smallest of the Cyclades Isls in Aegean Sea. Birthplace of Apollo and Artemis; site of the Delia, the quinquennial festival of Apollo. Highest "mt" is Mt Cyn-
thus (350 ft) on neighboring Gt *D* Isl.

    ?8.28   This is Delian alps
    ?208.29   the dowce little delia looked a bit queer

DELVILLE (15/37).   Estate in Glasnevin, on the Tolka R, built by Dr Patrick De-
laney, Dean of Down, and frequented by Swift, whose "Legion Club" satire was pri-
vately printed there. The site is most recently the Bon Secours Nursing Home.

    43.26   privately printed at the rimepress of Delville...Mr Delaney
    503.17   delville of a tolkar

DELVIN RIVER.   This small riv forms the boundary btwn Co Meath and Co Dub
for 7 or 8 mi, passing N of Naul to the sea at Lowtherstone, 1 mi N of Balbriggan.
The riv crossing known as the Ford of Fine (qv) is in Naul par. See *Devlin River.*
FW plays on the trad rhyme, "When Adam delved and Eve span, who was then

the gentleman?", to make Delvin = Adam = HCE, and Liffey = Eve = ALP.

21.06	when Adam was delvin...watersilts
106.26	*Exat Delvin Renter Life*
197.20	delvan first and duvlin after
566.20	two princes...daulphin and deevlin
622.35	to the Ford of Fyne on Delvin

DEMETRIAS.   Ruined city in NE Gr, near mod Volos; a res of Macedonian kings.

?319.05   bringing briars to Bembracken and ringing rinbus round Demetrius

DENMARK.   Kingdom, NW Eur. *Dansk*, Dan "the Danish lang"; *at alle taler dansk*, Dan "that everybody speaks Danish" (336.03). The Viking invaders and settlers of Ire from the 9th cent AD were sometimes indiscriminately called "Danes" by the natives, as in "this cold wind would perish the Danes" (452.02), sometimes discriminated as the dark foreigners (Ir, *dubh-gall*) from Den and the fair foreigners (Ir, *fionn-gall*) from Nor. The Order of the Dannebrog (549.01) is a Dan order of knighthood.

15.06	brittled the tooath of the Danes	?340.09	Warful doon's bothem
16.06	You tollerday donsk?	353.31	*Oldanelang's Konguerrig [konge-*
47.23	devil and Danes...deaf and		*rige*, Dan "kingdom"]
	dumb Danes	359.14	tyres onto Danelope boys
77.14	it was Dane to pfife	?369.12	Woovil Doon Botham
79.35	King Hamlaugh's gulden dayne	372.17	Danesbury Common
84.04	seven and four in danegeld	378.31	You talker dunsker's brogue
86.22	look his brother dane in the	385.16	the mad dane ating his vitals
	face	387.11	hayastdanars and wolkingology
105.18	*My Old Dansh*	?389.10	Janesdanes Lady Andersdaughter
129.12	gone the way of the Danes	420.29	Dining with the Danes
133.28	indanified...boro tribute	421.29	views of Denmark
139.22	Dann's dane, Ann's dirty	433.06	Danish spoken!
143.07	camelot prince of dinmurk	452.02	borting that would perish the
185.11	his own rude dunsky tunga		Dane
192.21	cockcock crows for Danmark	479.32	Draken af Danemork!
199.17	staynish beacons on toasc	480.10	From Daneland sailed the ox-
201.08	*my old Dane hodder dodderer*		eyed man
237.18	Daneygaul	496.08	Archimandrite of Dane's Island
255.15	Ivorbonegorer of Danamaraca	?503.21	Woful Dane Bottom
261.16	denary, danery	518.23	the expeltsion of the Danos
288.19	Gratings, Mr Dane! [Dubliners	549.01	order of the Danabrog
	greeting Dean Swift]	562.30	take his dane's pledges
?301.F5	going to Penmark	593.02	Calling all downs to dayne
323.36	gen and gang, dane and dare	593.11	Calling all daynes...daynes to
326.13	be danned to ye		dawn
330.06	Danno the Dane	?594.12	warful dune's battam
330.34	they barneydansked a katha-	594.27	Cur...Dane the Great
	reen	617.06	thank Danis
336.03	add all taller Danis	622.20	go dutc to Danegreven

DENMARK ST, GREAT   (15/35).   From Parnell Sq N to Gardiner Pl. The Jesuit Belvedere Coll, where JJ was a student, is on *GD* St. Hengler's Circus (qv) was just around the cor in Rutland (now Parnell) Sq.

529.35   coowner of a hengster's circus near North Great Denmark Street

DERBY.   Co and town, cen Eng. The "*D* Stakes" is a classic flat race for 3-year-olds, held not at *D* but at Epsom, S of London, since 1780. The Ir Sweeps Derby is held at the Curragh (qv) in Kildare.

Henry Woodfall's ballad "Darby and Joan" (1735) is purportedly about John Darby of Bartholomew Close and his wife, who is described as chaste and cold (454.32, 473.09).

180.15	in the dearby darby doubled...first over the hurdles
?446.20	till they'll bet we're the cuckoo derby
448.14	goldcapped dupsydurby houspill
454.32	neck and necklike Derby and June
473.09	rived by darby's chilldays embers...Juhn
577.28	him to the derby, her to toun

DERG, LOUGH.   (1) A lake of the Shannon R, N of Killaloe, Co Clare. *Loch Deirgdheirc*, Ir "lake of the red eye"; acc to legend the lake was reddened by the blood of King Eochy MacLuchta, who plucked out his only eye when asked for it by the poet Aithirne.   (2) Lake, Co Donegal, 3 mi N of Pettigo. *Loch Dearg*, Ir "red lake." Site of St Patrick's Purgatory (qv).

203.20	venersderg
582.28	Derg rudd face should take patrick's purge

DERRY.   Co and city, on Foyle Riv, Ulster prov, N Ire; aka Londonderry. *Doire*, Ir "oak grove." Founded as a monastery by St Columba in 6th cent. James I granted the city and co to a company of London merchants. The fortified walls of the city are reminders of the sieges it withstood in 1641, 1649, and by the forces of James II in 1689; hence the name "The Maiden City." Song, "I Dreamt I Was in Derry."

Baronies: Coleraine, Keenaght, Loughinsholin, NE Liberties of Coleraine, NW Liberties of Londonderry, Tirkeeran.

?6.02	the derryjellybies snooping
?45.20	my fine dairyman darling
?58.36	her cherryderry padouasoys
89.18	Lindendelly, coke or skilllies
180.13	Cardinal Lindundarri [Ulster]
197.04	his derry's own drawl
210.04	her...dribblederry daughters
295.13	I dromed I was in a Dairy
323.21	Drumadunderry
?411.08	home to dearies
416.11	bilking with durrydunglecks
484.33	Kelly Terry per Chelly Derry lepossette

DEUX MAGOTS, LES.   Literary and Bohemian café in the Blvd St Germain, Paris. Acc to Arthur Power, JJ didn't like to go there himself.

562.21	so tightly tattached as two maggots

DEVA.   Anc name of Chester (aka Devana Castra), city in Chester, NW Eng, on Dee R. It was the Roman "camp on the Dee" from 60 AD for several cents.

614.25	By dim delty Deva

DEVIL'S GLEN.   Vall and waterfall of the Vartry R, 2 mi NW of Ashford, Co Wicklow, below Roundwood Reservoir; it leads to the Devil's Punchbowl (qv). The ref describes the Liffey R, but there is no "Devil's Glen" on the course of the Liffey.

204.15	out by a gap in the Devil's glen

DEVIL'S PUNCHBOWL.   (1) In Devil's Glen (qv), Co Wicklow, a basin of the Var-

try R.   (2) Deep lake near the peak of Mt Mangerton, near Killarney, Co Kerry.
>   227.22   rocked the divlun from his punchpoll to his tummy's shentre
>   582.06   between the devil's punchbowl and the deep angleseaboard

DEVLIN RIVER.   Small riv, SE Co Meath; a trib of the Mattock R, which joins the
Boyne at Oldbridge, W of Drogheda. Gerald Nugent's (*ca* 1588) "Ode Written on
Leaving Ireland": "From thee, sweet Devlin [Dublin], must I part." See *Delvin River*.
>   ?3.23   since devlinsfirst loved livvy
>   24.25   To part from Devlin is hard as Nugent knew
>   197.20   delvan first and duvlin after
>   ?243.22   renownse the devlins in all their pumbs
>   566.20   two princes...daulphin and deevlin

DILMUN.   In Sumerian legend, the land and garden of Paradise, located on the E
shore of the Pers Gulf; in the same legends, the date palm is the tree of life.
>   136.01   was Dilmun when his date was palmy

DINGLE.   Town, Co Kerry, on S side of Corcaguiney (aka Dingle) penin.
>   ?327.17   every Dinny dingle after her
>   399.03   *sweet nymphs of Dingle beach*
>   499.29   the Dingle bagpipes

DIONYSIUS'S EAR.   In the anc palace of Dionysius, the tyrant of Syracuse (Sicily), there was a bell-shaped pris chamber connected by a passage to the palace, with
acoustic properties such that *D* could hear everything said by his prisoners.
>   70.36   that paradigmatic ear, receptoretentive as his of Dionysius

DIRTY DICK'S.   Tav in Bishopsgate, London. Named after Nathaniel Bentley's
18th-cent hardware store in Leadenhall St, notorious for its squalor; some of its con-
tents were bought for decor by the tav owner.
>   69.34   Rum and Puncheon (Branch of Dirty Dick's free house)

DOBBIN.   Song, "Dobbin's Flowery Vale": "I'll bid adieu to Armagh, you,/ and
Dobbin's Flowery Vale." If it's a real vall, I don't know where.
>   ?7.12−.14   foamous olde Dobbelin ayle...flowerwhite

DODDER RIVER.   The main riv of S Dub, it flows NW from its source not far
from the source of the Liffey in the Wicklow Hills, then NE through Rathfarnham,
Donnybrook, and Ballsbridge to join the Liffey just W of Ringsend. By bringing a
dependable supply of water from the mts, it made the growth of Dub possible, but
also ravaged its vall with periodic floods until fully confined *ca* 1796.
>   201.08   *my old Dane hodder dodderer*
>   283.L2   *Dondderwedder Kyboshicksal*
>   523.26   the Doddercan Easehouse

DODECANESE.   "12 islands," isl group in S Aegean Sea, including Patmos but not
Rhodes. *FW* associates it with the 12 Customers of HCE's Tav. For "Dodecanesian
baedeker" see *Phoenicia*.
>   100.30   few of his dode canal sammenlivers
>   123.27   a Punic admiralty report...saucily republished as a dodecanesian
>   baedeker
>   523.26   the Doddercan Easehouse

DOG AND DUCK TAVERN.   (1) Dog-and-Duck Yard, now Usher's Lane, off Usher's Quay, was named after a tav located there as early as 1709 (14/34).   (2) *D&D*

Tav on Temple Bar, *ca* 1745 (15/34).

The name derives from Eng sport of setting spaniels on ducks in a pond; there is still a *D&D* in the London docks. *Deoch an dorais*, Ir "a drink for the road."

    39.35   the Duck and Doggies
    73.26   Bar-le-Duc and Dog-an-Doras

DOGRA.   The predominant race and lang in Kashmir, Ind, and adjoining areas; also name given to country around Jammu, Ind.

    498.16   paunchjab and dogril

DOLE LINE.   Some people claim to remember it as a shipping line from the Hudson R docks in Manhattan, NYC, served by the rlwy line along Eleventh Ave, once known as "Death Ave"; see *NYC: Eleventh Ave.* But this is completely unconfirmed. In Brit, in the 1930's, of course, lines formed for the dole, like bread lines in the US.

    60.01   Dole Line, Death Avenue

DOLLYMOUNT.   Dist, NE Dub, btwn Clontarf and Raheny. Also the orig name of Mt Pelier Ho at the foot of Mt Pelier Hill, S of Tallaght. See *Dalymount.*

    294.21   Dolly Monks [+ Monkstown]
    ?327.25   dollimonde
    390.29   Dalkymont nember to [+ Dalkey]
    580.22   dollymount tumbling

DOLOMITE ALPS.   See *Alps.*

DOLPHIN HOTEL (15/34).   It was long at 45-49 Essex St, E; the bar was popular. No connection with Dolphin's Barn.

    376.11   Delphin dringing!

DOLPHIN'S BARN (13/32).   Dist, SW Dub. The name is anc, and the etymology is unclear; perhaps from *Cairn Uí Dunchada*, "Dunphy's Cairn."

    211.21   tenpounten on the pop for the daulphins born
    275.F6   for the nusances of dolphins born
    434.27   to joy a Jonas in the Dolphin's Barncar
    513.09   Delphin's Bourne
    601.22   S. Dolores Delphin's [Ch of Our Lady of Dolours]

DON.   (1) Riv, USSR, 1224 mi long; Tartar, *Duna.*   (2) Riv, Yorkshire, N cen Eng.   (3) Riv, Aberdeenshire (now Grampian), NE Scot.

    197.17   Don Dom Dombdomb
    ?365.16   from our Don Amir anent villayets...tarafs
    ?375.23   Don Gouverneur Buckley's in the Tara Tribune

DONABATE.   Town, N Co Dub, btwn Malahide and Rush; on penin off which Lambay Isl lies. Portraine Ho, 1 mi NE, was the home of Swift's Stella.

    547.27   till I had done abate her maidan race

DONEGAL.   Co and town, Ulster prov; the anc kingdom of Tír Connail. *Dún na nGall*, Ir "fort of the foreigners." Ptolemy knew it as *Boreum* (qv).

Baronies: Banagh, Boylagh, E and W Inishowen, Kilmacrenan, N and S Raphoe, Tirhugh.

    237.18   in all Daneygaul
    ?594.29   duan Gallus
    595.14   tunnygulls

DONNELLY'S ORCHARD   (16/36).   Orig part of "Buck" Jones's Clonliffe demesne, N of Croke Park, the name survived into the 20th cent, but is now virtually
unknown in the area. It was bounded by the present Clonliffe, Distillery, and Orchard Rds.
>   585.28   among Donnelly's orchard

DONNYBROOK.   Dist, SE Dub, scene of the notorious fair founded in 1204, abolished in 1855 because of its disorderliness. *Domhnach Broc*, Ir "Ch of St Brac."
>   142.12   Donnybrook prater
>   ?191.27   daybroken donning
>   323.09   Donnerbruch fire
>   334.35   Donnicoombe Fairing [+ song "Widdicombe Fair"]
>   353.31   *dawnybreak in Aira*
>   499.33   Donnerbruck Fire
>   514.25   Bonnybrook
>   537.35   to bray at by clownsillies in Donkeybrook Fair
>   563.26   the maryboy at Donnybrook Fair

DORA.   In Macpherson's poems, a hill near Temora (qv). The Brit WW I "Defense
of the Realm Act" was generally called "DORA" (*Letters* I, 340).
>   228.16   Brassolis...Gelchasser...Dodgesome Dora

DOUCE, MT.   Mt, Co Wicklow, 2½ mi SE of the source of the Liffey. There is also
a Mt *D* near Inchigeelagh, Co Cork. Miss Douce is one of the barmaids in the Sirens
chap of *U*; Joseph Douce was a champagne manufacturer whom JJ knew (and bor-
rowed money from) in Paris.
>   ?106.17   *Way for Wet Week Welikin's Douchka Marianne*
>   208.29   dowce little delia
>   462.09   champagne, dimming douce
>   577.06   dowser dour and dipper douce

DOWN.   Co, Ulster prov. Baronies: Upr and Lwr Ards, Upr and Lwr Castlereagh,
Duff Erin, Upr and Lwr Iveagh, Kinelarty, Upr and Lwr Lecale, Upr and Lwr Lordship of Newry, Mourne.
>   54.01   Downaboo! ["Up with Down"]
>   101.06   the ards and downs
>   482.29   up-in-Leal-Ulster and I'm-free-Down-in-Easia
>   612.35   apt the hoyhop of His Ards

DOWNPATRICK.   (1) Town, Co Down. The mouth of the Slaney R, where St Pat-
rick landed when he was first brought to Ire, is 1½ mi NE. The Norman John de
Courcy ruled Ulaidh (Ulster) from *D* from 1177 to 1203, and pretended to deposit
the bones of St Patrick, St Brigid, and St Columba in a vault in the cath.   (2) *D*
Head, Co Mayo (Connacht), near Ballycastle. If the ref names places in the 4 provs,
"Puddyrick" should be in Connacht; but the pattern isn't clear.
>   53.30   Gort and Morya and Bri Head and Puddyrick

DRACO.   Constellation, N hemisphere; "the Dragon."
>   343.02   *Draco on the Lour*

DRAGON VOLANT.   "The Room in the Dragon Volant" is a short story by J S
Le Fanu, one of the horror tales in *In a Glass Darkly* (1872). The locale is Paris and
Versailles.
>   24.05   he urned his dread, that dragon volant

DROGHEDA.   (1) St (15/34); orig name of Upr Sackville, now O'Connell, St. It didn't lead to the Liffey, as it does now. Henry, Moore, Earl, and *D* Sts, which intersect each other in the vicinity of the GPO, were all named after Henry Moore, Earl of *D*, the landholder who laid them out in the 17th cent. (There is also an Of, or Off, Lane.) Talbot St, constructed and named in the 19th cent, continues Earl St to Amiens St Sta.   (2) City and port on Boyne R, Co Louth. Anc name, *Inver Colpa*; *Droichead Átha*, Ir "Bridge of the Ford." In 1649 Cromwell besieged it and massacred virtually all its inhabitants.

    31.18   jubilee mayor of Drogheda, Elcock
    197.01   Reeve Drughad
    447.13   drawadust jubilee...Henry, Moore, Earl and Talbot Streets
    518.06   the Ruins, Drogheda Street
    566.11   duntalking [Dundalk]...dowan her droghedars

DRUMCOLLIHER.   Town, Co Limerick, S of Newcastle West. Percy French's song "Drumcolliher" praises *D* as a town which everyone should visit: "There's only one house in Drumcolliher/For hardware, bacon, and tea." Many lives were lost in a cinema fire in *D* in 1926 (540.12).

    176.10   *There is Oneyone's House in Dreamcolohour*
    540.09   *Drumcollogher*
    540.10   *Drumcollogher-la-Belle*
    540.11   *Drumcollogher*
    540.12   *Vedi Drumcollogher e poi Moonis*

DRUMCONDRA   (16/36).   Dist, Rd, N Dub, earlier known as Clontu.k (qv). *D* Rd is the main highway to Belfast and Derry. *Drom Conaire*, Ir "Connor's Ridge" (532.12).

    181.35   the excommunicated Drumcondriac, nate Hamis
    293.F1   Draumcondra's Dreamcountry
    420.33   2 Milchbroke...Traumcondraws [see *Millbourne Lane*]
    447.32   Drumgondola tram
    532.12   Condra's ridge
    601.24   S. Drimicumtra's [see *Corpus Christi Ch*]

DRUMSALLAGH.   *Drom salach*, Ir "miry ridge." There are *D*s in Cos Donegal and Down, and a Dromsallagh in Co Limerick. The land in Armagh given to St Patrick for his ch by Daire was called Drum-salach.

    ?239.31   a miry hill
    449.26   breezes zipping round by Drumsally

DRURY LANE.   Famous London st and theater; orig a cock-pit, it became a theater in 1663, and has been burned and rebuilt several times since. It was Garrick's theater, and later Sheridan's. "Buck" Jones was manager of Crow St Theatre in Dub (543.20).

    50.06   cockspur start...Disliken as he was to druriodrama
    79.28   in a dreariodreama setting
    491.30   He loves a drary lane
    543.20   the darsy jeamses, the drury joneses
    600.02   in this drury world of ours...lane

DUBBER.   Vill, N of Dub, near Huntstown. The *D* Hunt was a forerunner of the Ward Union Staghounds.

    333.35   from his dauberg den and noviny news from Naul

DUBH-GALL.   Acc to Thom's Annals of Dub, the terr S of the Liffey was once
called Dubh-gall ("land of the dark foreigners" = Danes) as that N of the Liffey was
called (as it still is) Fin-gall ("land of the fair foreigners" = Norse). The anc br across
the Liffey at the time of the battle of Clontarf (1014 AD) was called "Dubhgall's Br."

Doves (pigeons) are said to have no gall, since the dove sent from the Ark by
Noah burst its gall out of grief.

      21.23   warlessed after her with soft dovesgall ["loud finegale," 22.10]
      ?276.05   gale with a blost to him, dove without gall
      500.04   Dovegall and finshark, they are ring to the rescune

DUBLIN.   Like *FW* itself, Dub is a palimpsest of its hist. Unlike *U*, in which Dub's
hist appears only in the uncertain memories of Dub citizens in 1904, *FW* remembers
the many Dubs which lie buried beneath the mod city: the hypothetical Ir settlement
on the banks of the Liffey, the Viking stronghold, the Anglo-Norman walled town,
the Eng cap of the Pale, and the Georgian city of the Anglo-Irish Ascendancy. For
FW these are simultaneously present with the decaying provincial cap whose sts JJ
walked in the decade before 1904 and with the city of the Rising of 1916 and of the
Troubles of 1921-22.

Whether or not there was an Ir settlement on the site of Dub before the 9th cent,
there was certainly a ford of the Liffey on the highway from Tara to SE Ire. In 837
the first Vikings landed at the mouth of the Liffey, and later established themselves
on the S bank, setting up their Steyne at what is now the intersection of D'Olier,
Pearse, and Townsend Sts, their hill of assembly or Thing Mote at what is now St
Andrews St, and their harb at the point where the little Poddle R then joined the
Liffey.

The battle of Clontarf in 1014 AD marked the end of Scand rule although not of
Scand presence and intermarriage. It was at about this time that the "Ostmen" moved
across the Liffey to the area still known as Oxmantown. For a cent Dub was an Ir
city – the only Ir cent before the 20th. This came to an abrupt end in 1170 when
Dermot MacMurrough, King of Leinster, imported Richard De Clare ("Strongbow")
and his Anglo-Normans from Wales as allies in Dermot's Ir disputes, and together
they occupied Dub. Arriving as allies, the Anglo-Normans remained as masters, in
Dub and elsewhere. The cents of Eng rule were formally initiated in 1172, when
Henry II came to Ire and held court in a wickerwork pavilion in Dub. Henry's claim
to Ire was supported by the papal bull "Laudabiliter" by Adrian IV, the only Eng
pope; Dub itself was granted by Henry to his "men of Bristol," for whom the city
for more than a cent was a commercial colony, regularly raided by the O'Byrnes and
O'Tooles from their strongholds in the Wicklow Mts.

With the building of the Castle in the early 13th cent, Dub as the hqs of the Pale
became the cen of Eng rule. The city walls included the Castle at their SE cor, and
included Christchurch Cath (but not St Patrick's); only in 1312 were the walls extended to the riv. The late med city remained clustered within and outside the walls;
N of the Liffey there were only the Norse settlement in Oxmantown, and St Mary's
Abbey.

The physical geography of Dub remained much the same as it had been at the
time of the first Norse landing. The waters of Dub Bay lapped the shore at the present N Strand Rd, and the tidal Liffey washed as far as the present TCD grounds.
Only with the laborious walling of the Liffey in the early 18th cent did E Dub come
into being, with the extension of the N and S walls making possible a deep-water
channel to the city. The 18th cent was the great cent of Dub's physical development,
with the building of its Georgian pub bldgs, great private houses, chs, brs, and the
Royal and Grand Canals encircling and defining the city N and S. In 1801, however,

Dub's Georgian period came to an end with the Act of Union. With the Ir Parl abolished, the Ir peers who had contributed to Dub's elegance, if not to its social welfare, deserted the city and it began the slow decline into the city whose 19th-cent mons were the rlwys and the tramlines – the city of Bloom's Odyssey.

Like Leopold and Molly in bed, head to foot and foot to head, *FW*'s archetypal HCE lies interred in the landscape of N Dub, his head rising as Howth from Dub Bay, and his feet the 2 hills W of Phoenix Park – alongside the Liffey, who reaches Dub Bay feet first, her hair trailing "fifty odd miles" behind her. N Dub does in fact have a gentle ridge from Summerhill in the E across the N side of Rutland (now Parnell) Sq, through Constitution Hill and Arbour Hill and into Phoenix Park. The image of HCE as the sleeping giant Finn MacCool is however an invention of JJ's; there seem to be no legends connecting Finn with Dub.

HCE is of course all of Dub and its physical site. Geographically, as in other ways, Shem and Shaun are complementary aspects of the father: in this case Shem is S Dub, which is middle-class, Prot, and high-culture, with its universities, libraries, and museums, while Shaun is N Dub, which is working-class, Catholic, political, and low-culture (except for the Gate in Parnell Sq, Dub's theaters have been in S Dub, and its cinemas in N Dub). As rivals (Lat, *rivae*) Shem and Shaun are also the R and L banks of Anna Liffey.

Topographically, *FW*'s archetypal family is completed by Chapelizod (qv), named for Issy's namesake, Iseult. As Anna Liffey dies into the Ir Sea to be reborn in the rain falling on the Wicklow Mts, so Issy is the young Anna – upstream, as Chapelizod is upstream from Dub. Chapelizod is on both banks of the Liffey, as the brothers share incestuous fantasies of the sister, and by incidental analogy, the Liffey at Chapelizod is divided into channels by a long isl: "Shem and Shaun and the shame that sunders them"?

I. Names of Dublin:

AULIANA.   Acc to Wilson's *Post-Chaise Companion* (xv), in 155 AD King Alpinus changed the city's name from "Asch-cled" to Auliana, after his daughter, who drowned in the Liffey. Not in *FW*?

AVARI TÓM (AVARI LIRK).   "Shelta" name for Dub. Not in *FW*?

ALP UÍ LAOGHAIRE (EALP O'LAUGHRE).   "O'Leary's job," in "Mason's Slang" or "Rhyming Slang," *Béarlagair na Sáer* (BNS) (*Alp*, BNS "town").

?209.09   *...and the granite they're warming, or her face has been lifted or Alp*
           has doped
243.29   her shookerloft hat from Alpoleary
340.06   *Djublian Alps*
?478.10   landeguage in which wald wand rimes alpman
?595.19   You are alpsulumply wroght!

BAILE ÁTHA CLIATH.   Ir, "Town of the Ford of the Hurdles"; pron "Ballyclay." One of the most anc Ir names, it is the official Gaelic name of the mod city. The ford of the Liffey carried the anc Slighe Cualan from Tara toward SE Ire and was prob near the site of Dub's first br (now site of Whitworth Br).

14.02	blay of her Kish [*Baile Átha Cis*,	86.11	Mudford
	Ir "town of the ford of wick-	?99.12	bloody antichill cloak
	work"]	110.23	kischabrigies [*cis*, Ir "wicker"]
14.05	Hurdlesford	134.01	Baulacleeva
14.09	Ballyaughacleeaghbally	136.33	bally clay
29.01	haunt of the hungered bordles	138.10	ath...cleah
57.31	Ceadurbar-atta-Cleath	159.30	baileycliaver
71.17	*Blau Clay*	170.33	Balaclava
73.18	Hubbleforth	180.16	first over the hurdles

203.07	fordofhurdlestown	352.23	bullyclaver of ye
210.19	Ballyclee	353.23	*Hurtreford*
224.06	fourd...hurtled stones	393.09	Hungerford-on-Mudway
237.33	Labbeycliath	420.20	Baile-Atha-Cliath
277.21	Blath	447.24	Baughkley
279.07	athclete...bally	447.30	town of the Fords in a huddle
279.08	Towntoquest, fortorest...hurley	481.28	Huddlestown
285.25	bullyclavers	498.12	Athclee
288.28	Wickerworks...ford	512.31	O'Ford...hurdley
297.20	Hurdlebury Fenn	539.17	Athacleeath
310.12	Bauliaughacleeagh	547.18	Hurdlesford
314.21	Ballaclay	?570.05	crosshurdles
316.28	furt on the turn of the hurdies	570.21	Hurtleforth
326.25	Diaeblen-Balkley	570.32	ford...hurdley
335.13	Bullyclubber	576.26	hungerford
341.09	balacleivka	600.10	Cleethabala
342.18	*turn of the fourth of the hurdles*	608.29	hindled firth...hundled furth

DROM CUILL-CHOILLE.   Ir, "brow of a hazelwood" or "hazelwood ridge."
Acc to Harris's *History of Dublin* (1766), "Drom-Choll-Coil" was Dub's orig Ir name.
The ridge runs E and W on the S bank of the Liffey: the anc rd from Dub to the W.
Although the name conjures up a pastoral Ir pre-Dan Dub, George Little was unable
to find any anc ref to the name.

?4.07	Killykillkilly
60.08	Well done, Drumcollakill!
135.13	brow of a hazelwood
176.10	*There is Oneyone's House in Dreamcolohour*
?361.16	Kissykitty Killykelly!
372.14	kaillykailly...Brownhazelwood
?389.07	Killkelly-on-the-Flure
469.18	Hazelridge has seen me
540.09,10,11,12	*Drumcollogher*

DUBH-LINN.   Ir, "Black Pool," prob referring to the little harb once formed at
the point where the Poddle R joined the Liffey from the S. The Viking invaders
adopted and gave currency to this name. Various forms: Doolin, Dublin, Dyflin (eg,
in Snorri's *Heimskringla*); the area around Dub was called Dyfflinarsky (13.22), also
Dyflinarskidi (314.05).

3.08	doublin	37.03	dublnotch
3.23	devlinsfirst	39.04	Dublin
7.12	Dobbelin ayle	42.30	dublinos
13.04	Dyoublong	44.11	dub him Llyn
13.14	Dbln	61.02	Doveland
13.22	Dyfflinarsky	66.18	Dubblenn, WC
16.35	dabblin bar	72.34	diablen lionndub
17.12	Brian d' of Linn	74.13	Liverpoor [Riverpool]
18.07	Humblin! Humblady Fair	79.29	dumplan
19.12	durlbin	84.31	Dublin stone
20.16	Doublends Jined	85.15	blackpool bridges
21.06	delvin	87.30	macdublins
24.01	Novo Nilbud	88.34	leaftime in Blackpool
24.25	Devlin	91.22	Dublin
34.01	Dumbaling	97.09	doubling
35.16	Poolblack	98.28	Dub's

101.18	Dublin Wall	332.06	—debblen—dubblan— [in C-word]
113.18	dapple inn	332.10	Doolin
114.25	Dalbania	335.28	tublin
129.20	dub...limn	337.26	So these ease Budlim!
130.30	young rose [BUD]...French-	339.31	*Lubliner*
	Egyptian [NIL]	340.06	*Djublian*
130.34	you and I...surrented by...bldns	346.15	*dubrin*
	[dUblIns]	347.35	*durblinly*
135.14	pool in the dark	353.19	dobblenotch
136.02	Mudlin	362.02	Clandibblon
139.13	wan wubblin wall	362.36	**Dulby**
139.24	dabblin	364.25	duvlin
140.27	Nublid	365.18	double densed
153.18	Dubville	370.19	drooplin
158.04	dubliboused	372.02	Dublin
160.27	deblinite	372.16	dinnasdoolins
169.23	Shuvlin	373.19	Alddaublin
174.26	Tumblin-on-the-Leafy	373.20	Deblinity devined
177.28	dubbed	377.22	Dovlen
181.17	Dustbin's	382.06	Dublin
193.02	dulpeners	383.23	Dubbeldorp
196.08	dabbling	385.35	darblun
196.12	water black	410.11	Dublin river
197.05	doubling	413.25	doubling
197.18	Dombdomb	432.20	Dubloonik
197.20	duvlin	436.26	Dublin
202.08	diveline	437.06	Dunlob
204.18	stagnant black pools	443.16	Dumnlimn
210.19	Doolin	447.20	Dublin's
222.25	duvlin	447.23	Dufblin
227.22	divlun	448.11	d'lin
236.10	Dublin's	451.13	Dublin Fusees
243.22	devlins	462.19	doubling
248.07	Doubtlynn	469.21	Linduff
255.21	Dublin's capital	479.18	Dunlin
264.15	Eblinn	480.30	dob dob dobbling
266.03	Lynne	481.14	Tupling Toun
266.06	D'Oblong's	482.07	Dublinn
266.F1	Dublin	484.21	Aud Dub
290.16	doubling	488.26	Dublire
293.12	DVbLIn	489.21	Doubly Telewisher
295.31	doubling	490.17	doblinganger
309.13	Ibdullin	515.29	The Dublin own
310.07	antidulibnium	520.25	wabblin
311.16	dubble in	534.29	double inns
313.34	Lynn-Duff	539.24	Fort Dunlip
314.05	dyfflun's kiddy	546.17	dubildin
316.36	dobblins	546.34	Chief Brown Pool
326.34	Dybblin water	550.23	doveling
329.03	divlin's	550.34	dabblingtime
329.14	Dub	553.27	Dublin lindub
331.19	diublin's	555.14	wumblin...bumblin

569.20	Deublan	600.11	Libnud Ocean
578.14	doublin existents	602.19	Durban Gazette
580.22	tumbling	603.27	Debbling
582.21	Dyfflinsborg	603.29	dubbledecoys
585.21	Dublin	620.03	nill, Budd
586.15	Dupling	621.13	Blugpuddels
590.29	Rumbling	625.27	dumblynass
593.24	Ntamplin	625.36	Londub
594.05	We Durbalanars	626.31	dev...duv...div...linn
596.12	leery subs of dub		

EBLANA.   The Lat name appears on Ptolemy's map of Ire around the N part of what appears to be Dub Bay. There is no evidence that it refers to an anc settlement on the site of Dub, but it has been so often cited as the Lat name of Dub (cf *U* 619: "the farfamed name of Eblana") that *FW* dreams it too.

13.34	Blubby wares upat Ublanium
41.18	Ebblinn's
46.14	Eblana bay
49.22	a dour decent deblancer
57.32	Dablena Tertia
99.34	D. Blayncy's trilingual triweekly
135.28	ebblanes
138.23	a see in Ebblannah
139.36	Ebblawn Downes
215.27	*Eblanensis*
245.21	Hulker's cieclest elbownunsense
264.15	Eblinn
364.22	city of Analbe [backwards]
373.12	ebblynuncies
432.21	Dellabelliney
553.29	eblanite
612.15	Hump cumps Ebblybally
614.25	Eblania's
625.26	Eblanamagna

FORD OF THE HURDLES.   See *Baile Átha Cliath*.

II.   Dublin Allusions:

ANNAPOLIS.   The city of Anna (Liffey).

222.07	the ambiamphions of Annapolis
318.24	Annapolis, my youthrib city

DEAR DIRTY DUBLIN.   Lady Morgan's epithet becomes in *FW* a paradigm of punning. Before mod paving came in, Dub's sts were in fact notorious for their grime; something to do with the cobblestones and the soil in which they were laid.

7.05	teary turty Taubling
49.21	dour decent deblancer
60.35	Moirgan's lady...dirty dubs
76.25	dear dutchy deeplinns
95.10	dear divorcee darling
105.18	*Hear Hubty Hublin*
131.06	distinctly dirty but rather a dear
136.20	dire dreary darkness
180.15	dearby darby doubled
196.15	duddurty devil

199.14	dear dubber Dan
206.17	dusky dirgle dargle
215.13	Dear Dirty Dumpling
219.08	producer and daily dubbing
305.07	deep dartry dullard
317.34	dun darting dullemitter
319.24	double dyode dealered
333.33	dour dorty dompling
337.26	do, dainty daulimbs
366.24	dire daffy damedeaconesses
370.09	Dix Dearthy Dungbin
374.18	deep dorfy doubtlings
570.03	Deep Dalchi Dolando
614.25	dim delty Deva
615.12	Dear...Dirtdump

DUBLIN'S FAIR CITY.   In the song, "In Dublin's fair city/Where girls are so pretty," Molly Malone sells cockles and mussels, crying, "Alive, alive O."

| 41.18 | Ebblinn's chilled hamlet |
| 116.13 | Dumbil's fair city |

FINN'S TOWN.   Except in *FW*, no legend associates Dub with Finn MacCool, who was not an urban hero. *Fionn*, Ir "fair," "light," or "clear," may be intentionally contrasted with *dubh*, "black" or "dark."

There is a Finnstown House, S of Lucan (qv). Fintona is a town in Co Tyrone.

78.18	murdered Cian in Finntown
100.07	Fiounnisgehaven
265.28	Finntown's generous poet's office
617.06	We are all at home in old Fintona, thank Danis

HELIOPOLIS.   See separate entry. Timothy Healy became 1st Gov-Gen when Ir Free State was est.

HUMPHREYSTOWN.   The town of Humphrey Chimpden Earwicker. *Letters* I, 251: "Dring! Dring! Next stop Humphreystown."

| 270.13 | the Merry Mustard Frothblowers of Humphreystown Associations |
| 375.05 | Hunphydunphyville'll be blasted to bumboards |

LOCHLAUNSTOWN.   Norse Dub, from *Lochlainn*, the anc Ir name for Norway.

| 291.10 | and the O'Hyens of Lochlaunstown |

LORCANSBY.   A *FW* coinage: "the town of Lorcan," ie, Lorcan or Lawrence O'Toole.

| 448.19 | and never despair of Lorcansby |
| ?518.11 | Weepin Lorcans! |

POPLINSTOWN.   The specialty of Dub weavers, centered in the Liberties, was poplin, a fabric of silk and wool woven so that only the silk shows on the surface.

| 539.24 | Poplinstown |

ROCKY ROAD TO DUBLIN.   The rd of the well-known ballad may preserve a memory of the anc Slighe Cualan, which reached the ford of the hurdles from Tara by something like the route of Stoneybatter (qv); "batter" = *boher*, Ir "road." The rd of the ballad is from Tuam to Dub via Mullingar.

14.14	Blotty words for Dublin
64.03	the raglar rock to Dulyn
197.26	the quaggy waag for stumbling
244.24	a craggy road for rambling
287.05	royol road to Puddlin
315.23	the snarsty weg for Publin

323.35   the steerage way for stabling
328.03   wattling way for cubblin
341.17   The mlachy way for gambling
355.16   them rollicking rogues...rockery rides from. Rambling
372.20   rockers on the roads
514.05   the ranky roars assumbling
565.22   lucky load to Lublin
623.24   The rollcky road adondering

SEVENTH CITY OF CHRISTENDOM.   JJ jokes about the Seventh City in *Letters* I, 212. In *A Portrait*, Stephen, no joker, gazes poetically at "the image of the seventh city of Christendom" (167). An early use of this appellation – which JJ prob knew – was in Warburton, Whitelaw, and Walsh's *History of the City of Dublin* (I, 451); the first 6 cities are given there as London, Paris, Constantinople, Vienna, Moscow, and Naples.

53.03   this mimage of the seventyseventh kusin of kristansen
61.36   The seventh city, Urovivla

TOLKAHEIM.   From the Tolka R (qv) of N Dub.

52.09   far from Tolkaheim

MISCELLANEOUS ALLUSIONS.

?15.18   aspace of dumbillsilly [Dublin City]
79.04   bully on the hill
110.26   (dump for short)
211.23   from Lusk to Livienbad
404.30   Or for royal, Am for Mail, R.M.D. [Royal Mail, Dublin]
528.29   You've grabbed the capital
535.08   Nova Tara

John Pentland Mahaffy, a Provost of TCD, once quipped that in Dublin "the inevitable never happens, the improbable always."

110.11   where the possible was the improbable and the improbable the inevitable

McAlister's *Secret Languages of Ireland* gives "I saw pigeons bringing fire to boil meat at Dublin" as a trans of a sentence in BNS ("Mason's jargon").

239.31   a place where pigeons carry fire to seethe viands

DUBLIN BAR.   Before the construction of the N and S Walls, the mouth of the Liffey was blocked by a sandbar which vessels could cross only at high tide, signaled by a flag on the Poolbeg lightship.

?81.31   oblong bar
321.07   discoastedself to that kipsie point of its Dublin bar
512.26   from her gingering mouth like a Dublin bar in the moarning
607.30   Solsking the Frist...will processingly show up above Tumplen Bar

DUBLIN BAY.   Embraced by Howth on the N and Dalkey on the S, *D* Bay has often been compared with the Bay of Naples. Song by Alfred Perceval Graves, "O Bay of Dublin" (*Letters* III, 370). Place names listed separately include: Bulls, N and S; Cock Lake; Dublin Bar; Green Patch; Pigeonhouse; Poolbeg Light; Salmon Pool.

3.02   to bend of bay
29.22   *The Bey for Dybbling*
46.14   Eblana bay
71.19   *Gibbering Bayamouth of Dublin*
201.19   *to feale the gay aire of my salt troublin bay*
208.32   Making mush mullet's eyes at her boys dobelon

250.36   any dubble dabble on the bay
?266.06   Treetown Castle...D'Oblong's by his by
287.09   alp get a howlth on her bayrings
?290.16   doubling back, in nowtime,[5] bymby when saltwater
303.07   this is Doubbllinnbbayyates [+ W B Yeats]
333.33   dompling obayre
523.17   will stand at Bay (Dublin)

DUBLIN BREAD CO.   It had restaurants in Stephen's Green N, Lwr Sackville St,
and Dame St; in *U*, Haines and Mulligan meet in the Dame St *DBC*; "We call it D.B.
C. because they have damn bad cakes," says Mulligan (*U* 245/248).
149.25   as brisk as your D.B.C....coat of homoid icing
433.16   Dar Bey Coll Cafeteria
460.32   do be careful teacakes

DUBLIN BY LAMPLIGHT INSTITUTION   (17/32).   Modeled on the similar "London by Lamplight," this (Prot) charitable inst at 35 Ballsbridge Terr rescued fallen
women by putting them to work in its commercial laundry. Maria, in JJ's "Clay,"
worked there.
    In the 19th and early 20th cents, priests warned against "company-keeping," ie,
going steady. A companykeeper was on the way to becoming a demimondaine.
?438.30   a detestificated companykeeper on the dammymonde of Lucalamp-
          light

DUBLIN COAT OF ARMS.   The coat of arms displays 3 stone castles, flaming,
with draped female figures R and L as supporters. The origin of the iconography is
unknown. JJ had an 18th-cent woodcarving of the *DCofA* in the hall of his Paris
apartment (*Letters* I, 285).
18.06   O'c'stle, n'wc'stle, tr'c'stle, crumbling
22.34   three shuttoned castles
101.23   in the spy of three castles
128.17   shot two queans and shook three caskles
139.33   Ousterholm Dreyschluss
266.03   Treetown Castle under Lynne
?414.04   Mr van Howten of Tredcastles
526.16   three slots and no burners [*slot*, Nor "castle"]
551.31   triscastellated, bimedallised
?594.09   Heliotropolis, the castellated, the enchanting

DUBLIN COUNTY.   The Liffey divides not only Dub City but Co Dub into N and
S, the former stretching along the coastal plain to Balbriggan and including Fingal
and the anc Moyelta (qqv), the latter reaching up to the Dub Hills and Wicklow Mts.
The W boundary at Leixlip is that of the orig Viking enclave: "as far as the salmon
swim upstream."
    Baronies: E and W Balrothery, Castleknock, Coolock, Dublin, Nethercross, New-
castle, Rathdown, Uppercross.
446.35   We'll circumcivicise all Dublin country
583.25   to weight down morrals from county bubblin

DUBLIN GAZETTE.   Before 1921, it was publ twice a week at 87 Middle Abbey
St by Alexander Thom and Co for HM Printing Office.
602.19   the Durban Gazette, firstcoming issue

DUBLIN, GEORGIA.   Town, Laurens Co, Ga, US, on Oconee R. JJ explained to

Harriet Weaver (*Letters* I, 247) that it was founded by a Dubliner named Peter Sawyer (actually it was Jonathan Sawyer; see *Census*), and that its motto was "Doubling all the time." Amos Love, Jeremiah Yopp, and Hardy Smith were early settlers.

Dub's Amer "cousin-german" is one of no more than 10 US Dublins. Cosgrave's *North Dublin*, however, says (29, n1) "there are twenty-four Dublins in the US" (130.27).

3.08	Oconee...Laurens County's...doublin their mumper
130.27	twenty four or so cousins germinating in the United States of America
372.02	Dublin...Tuppeter Sowyer...thise citye...Amos Love...Jeremy Yopp...Hardy Smith
549.28	the tawny sprawling beside that silver burn [but Dublin, Ga is not at confluence of Oconee and Altamaha; Joyce's error?]

DUBLIN GULCH.   Locality in Silver Bow Co, Montana, US; near Butte. One of the fewer than 10 "Dublins" identifiable in the US.

254.17	A babbel men dub gulch of tears

DUBLIN HORSE SHOW.   The Royal Dub Soc holds this very famous event each Aug at its grounds in Ballsbridge (18/32).

32.35	on all horserie show command nights from his viceregal booth
159.28	Horoseshoew
246.23	The horseshow magnete draws his field
447.17	from Ballses Breach Harshoe up to Dumping's Corner
?595.23	hoseshoes, cheriotiers...bargainboutbarrows

DUBLIN INTELLIGENCER.   The shortlived "Dublin Intelligencer," the 1st issue of which appeared 30 Sept 1690, was the 2nd Dub newspaper (after the "Dublin News Letter," 1685). Gilbert's *History* records newspapers of this name, each with a different publisher, in 1705, 1717, 1724, and 1726; and the "Dublin Intelligencer" in 1728 was conducted by Swift and Dr Sheridan, and publ by the redoubtable Sarah Harding.

49.18	so says the Dublin Intelligence

DUBLIN METROPOLITAN POLICE.   Usually referred to as the "D.M.P.", it was noted for the giant size of its policemen. Until about the time of WW I, the famed *DMP* band gave regular Sunday concerts in the Hollow at Phoenix Park (565.04).

306.24	Dublin Metropolitan Police Sports at Ballsbridge
524.02	was...held by the metropolitan
532.28	toombs and deempeys
543.01	doubling megalopolitan poleetness
565.04	banders of the pentapolitan poleetsfurcers

DUBLIN MOTTO.   *Obedientia civium urbis felicitas*, "The obedience of the citizens is the felicity of the city."

23.14	Thus the hearsomeness of the burger felicitates the whole of the polis
76.09	the obedience of the citizens elp the ealth of the ole
81.01	the viability of vicinals if invisible is invincible
139.29	the true-to-type motto-in-lieu
140.06	Thine obesity, O civilian, hits the felicitude of our orb!
266.01	the boxomeness of the bedelias[1] makes hobbyhodge happy in his hole
277.08	To obedient of civicity in urbanious at felicity

347.35   *durblinly obasiant to the felicias of the skivis*
358.08   happy burgages abeyance would make homesweetstown...my mottu
            propprior
494.21   Obeisance so their sitinins is the follicity of this Orp!
540.25   Obeyance from the townsmen spills felixity by the toun
610.07   And the ubideintia of the savium is our ervics fenicitas

DUBLIN UNITED TRAMWAYS CO.   The tram-lines (orig horse-drawn) were instituted in Dub in 1865, and by the turn of the cent the *DUTC* operated to such distant suburbs as Dalkey, Howth, Lucan, and Terenure. Fitzpatrick's *Dublin* gives the
routes, 346-49.
256.30   where G.P.O. is zentrum and D.U.T.C. are radients
553.33   dutc cundoctor
622.20   Les go dutc to Danegreven

DUBLIN, WICKLOW, AND WEXFORD RAILWAY CO.   Its termini were Harcourt
St Sta (now closed) and Westland Row (now Pearse) Sta, with sep lines to the SE,
converging at Bray.
552.02   the Geenar, the Greasouwea, the Debwickweck

DUKE HUMPHREY'S WALK.   Part of old St Paul's Cath, London; so-called because
the stat of Sir John Beauchamp was pop mistaken for that of Humphrey, Duke of
Gloucester, son of Henry IV. "To dine with Duke Humphrey" was to walk up and
down (there) while others dined, ie, to go without.
32.15   good Dook Umphrey for the hungerlean spalpeens
405.18   that ne'er would nunch with good Duke Humphrey
441.07   Blesht she that walked with good Jook Humprey

DULWICH.   S London suburb, site of *D* Coll and *D* Picture Gallery.
352.12   after meath the dulwich

DUNBOYNE.   Town, par, and bar, Co Meath. See *Boyne* for King Billy, *Lambeg*
for Orange drums.
211.34   a big drum for Billy Dunboyne

DUNDALK.   Seaport at head of *D* Bay, Co Louth. The prehistoric fort, *Dún Dealgan* (now Castletown Hill), for which the city is named, is said to be the home of Cú
Chulainn, and guards the entrance to Ulster Gap, the Pass of Moyry.
91.08   what he would swear to the Tierney of Dundalgan
566.11   Katya to have duntalking...droghedars

DUNDRUM   (16/27).   Dist, S Dub. At the turn of the cent, it was still a sep vill.
36.14   tapped his chronometrum drumdrum
60.08   Well done, Drumcollakill!
135.31   from Rhoda Dundrums
?288.22   humdrum dumb and numb
?314.08   –drumstrum– [in C-word]
323.21   Skunkinabory from Drumadunderry
497.17   Dumstdumbdrummers
553.03   with myraw rattan atter dundrum
590.26   After having drummed all he dun
614.03   Annone Wishwashwhose...Doone of the Drumes [see *Manor Mill
            Steam Laundry*]

DUNDRUM BAY.   Inlet of Ir Sea, SE coast of Co Down. The Mourne Mts lie W of the S end of the bay, near Newcastle. *DB* may echo faintly in any of the refs to the Dub suburb of Dundrum (qv). See *Four Waves of Erin*.

    614.03   Doone of the Drumes...mournenslaund

DUN HILL (27/37).   On S side of Howth, near Sheilmartin; form a semaphore signal sta. There is also a *DH* 2 mi W of Tramore, Co Waterford, at Woodtown br, with a cas (ruins) of the Powers. The ref, however, is mainly to the tobacconists Dunhill of London; "dunhill" is almost generic for "pipe."

    50.30   snob of the dunhill

DUN LAOGHAIRE, DUNLEARY (KINGSTOWN) (24/28, etc).   Port and resort town SE of Dub; named for Laoghaire, High King of Ire, converted by St Patrick. The harb serves the mail boats from Holyhead, and it was connected to Dub by the Dalkey, Kingstown, and Blackrock tram line (qv). The main rd to Dub is the Rock Rd, via Blackrock.

    The town was renamed Kingstown in 1821, on the occasion of George IV's visit to Ire. An obelisk (566.36) on the waterfront, surmounted by a crown and oddly supported on four stone spheres, also commemorates the visit; the Ir did not fail to comment on the fact that the monarch's visit was commemorated at the point where he left Ire, rather than at Howth Harb, where he arrived. Renamed Dun Laoghaire (428.18), 1920.

    DL is hqs for most Dub yacht clubs, including the Royal George YC (151.29).

    40.30   a sidewheel dive somewhere off the Dullkey Downlairy and Bleak-
             rooky tramaline
    136.31   Baslesbridge...Koenigstein's Arbour
    151.29   royal gorge...hydrostatics and pneumodipsics
    294.22   Blake-Roche, Kingston and Dockrell auriscenting him from afurz
    367.12   When visiting Dan Leary try the corner house for thee
    370.19   it all flowowered your drooplin dunlearies
    428.18   Don Leary gets his own back from old grog Georges Quartos
    ?488.26   Dublire, per Neuropaths
    566.36   To the dunleary obelisk via the rock
    582.32   Thon's the dullakeykongsbyogblagroggerswagginline
    582.35   Leary, leary...he's plotting kings down for his villa's extension
    596.12   sire of leery subs of dub

DUNLECKNY.   Town, Co Carlow.
    ?416.11   bilking with durrydunglecks

DUNLOE, GAP OF.   Ravine btwn MacGillycuddy's Reeks (W) and the Tomies and the Purple Mt (E) W of Killarney, Co Kerry.
    229.24   her michrochasm as gap as down low

DUNMOW.   Market town in Essex, Eng. Little *D*, 2 mi E, has been known from the reign of King John for the custom of presenting a flitch of bacon to any couple who could prove that they had spent their 1st year of marriage in perfect harmony.
    579.01   Dunmow's flitcher with duck-on-the-rock

DÚN-NA-SCIATH.   The res of Malachy, Brian Boru's predecessor as King of Ire, on Lough Ennel, Co Westmeath. Ir, "fortress of the shields." Neither the fort nor the name survives on the site.
    ?185.11   his own rude dunsky tunga

DUNPHY'S CORNER (15/35).   Cor of Phibsborough Rd and NCR. Thomas Dunphy's public house at 161 Phibsborough Rd was taken over by John Doyle in the early 1890's, but it was many years before "Dunphy's Cor" came to be generally known as "Doyle's Cor." Bloom, in 1904, remembers when "the hearse capsized round Dunphy's" (*U* 97/98).

> ?375.05   old Hunphydunphyville'll be blasted to bumboards
> 447.17   from Ballses Breach Harshoe up to Dumping's Corner
> 549.02   mare's greese cressets at Leonard's and Dunphy's

DUNSINANE.   Macbeth, thane of Glamis, becomes thane of Cawdor as prophesied by the weird sisters, falls when Birnam Wood comes to his castle *D* as branches borne by Macduff's army.

> 250.16   burning would...dance inane...Glamours...Coldours
> ?600.36   by that look whose glaum is sure he means bisnisgels

DUNSINK OBSERVATORY   (10/38).   Est 1788, N of Castleknock, as the Obs of TCD. At one time it computed Dub time, about 25 min later than Greenwich time, and controlled the daily fall of the time ball on the Ballast Office (qv). The Obs ceased to function shortly after 1921, but was re-established in 1947.

> 359.36   Mooreparque...after Sunsink gang
> ?371.30   Dancingtree...Suttonstone
> 518.01   Dunsink, rugby, ballast and ball
> 550.35   duncingk the bloodanoobs...ballast
> 551.25   under astrolobe from my upservatory

DURBAN.   S Afr seaport, on Indian O; oldest Eur settlement in Natal. Named after Sir Benjamin D'Urban, gov of Cape Colony. There is no record of a *Durban Gazette*.

> ?594.05   We Durbalanars, theeadjure
> 602.19   for the Durban Gazette

DÜSSELDORF.   City, cap of N Rhine-Westphalia, Ger, on Rhine R, 21 mi NW of Cologne.

> ?383.23   Dubbeldorp, the donker

DVINA.   The name of 2 sep Russ rivs. The N (Little) *D*, *Dvina Syevernaya*, flows into the Gulf of Archangel (Archangel, qv, is associated with St Michael); the S *D*, *Dvina Zapadnaya*, flows from near the source of the Volga to the Gulf of Riga in the Baltic Sea.

If the "divine brethren" are St Michael and Lucifer, the N *D* = Chuff = Shaun = Stanislaus, while the S *D* = Glugg = Shem = JJ.

> 212.31   the cracka dvine
> 252.04   Dvoinabrathran, dare!

DYSART O'DEA.   Ruins of anc hermitage, founded 8th cent by St Tola, near Corofin, Co Clare. Site of decisive battle, 1318, in which the O'Briens routed Richard de Clare and arrested Norman conquest of Thomond.

> 13.27   o'brine a'bride, to be desarted. Adear, adear!

E

EAGLE AND CHILD, THE.   18th-cent Dub shop sign at the "abode of a chimney-sweeper" (Peter's *Dublin Fragments*, 154–55).

> 59.03   amongst the climbing boys at his Eagle and Child

EAGLE LIFE AND ANNUITY INSURANCE CO.   A Brit company est 1807, it was represented around the turn of the cent by several agents in Dub. In 1908 it was taken over by the Phoenix Assurance Co. John K James and Co, 9 Cavendish Row, Rutland Sq, represented both the Eagle and the Pelican (qv) insurance companies.
 ?197.19 Was his help inshored in the Stork and Pelican

EAGLE TAVERN.   Among Dub's tavs of this name were the *E* Tav on Eustace St (15/34), noted as early as 1565 as the meeting-place of the Corporation of Cooks and Vintners; the *E* Tav on Cork Hill (15/33), where the Hell Fire Club (qv) was founded in 1735; and the late-19th-cent *E* Hotel and Tav, 8 N Wall Quay (17/34), 2 blocks from St Laurence St (named for St Lawrence O'Toole), off Sheriff St.
 ?53.28 at Eagle Cock Hostel on Lorenzo Tooley street

EALING.   W suburb of London.
 446.21 when cherries next come back to Ealing

EASTCHEAP.   St, City of London, joining Cannon St and Gt Tower St. Orig the City's meat market.
 347.11 the freshprosts of Eastchept
 374.31 Orange Book of Estchapel

EASTMANS LTD.   Around the turn of the cent, a firm which operated butcher shops at more than a dozen different locations in Dub and suburbs. Thom's *Directories* invariably identify it as "Eastmans (Limited) Victuallers."
 67.18 Otto Sands and Eastman, Limericked, Victuallers

EASTMORELAND LANE   (17/32).   A short block off Haddington Rd, parallel to Upr Baggot St.
 553.30 eastmoreland and westlandmore

ECCLES ST   (15/35).   Btwn Dorset St and Berkeley Rd, N cen Dub; No 7 (now demolished) was the home of Leopold and Molly Bloom in *U* (the "Blue Book of Eccles," 179.27). Cardinal Cullen lived at No 59 and Isaac Butt at No 64. The Mater Misericordiae Hosp (qv) is at the Berkeley Rd end.
 N Gt George's St was known as Eccles Lane in 18th and early 19th cents. Belvedere Ho (later Belvedere Coll) on Gt Denmark St faced it.
 179.27 Blue Book of Eccles
 242.05 howthold of nummer seven
 514.14 Ecclesiastes...no hay in Eccles's hostel
 535.12 ecclesency
 567.27 Me Eccls!
 ?613.09 Feist of Taborneccles, scenopegia, come!

EDAM.   Seaport town, N Holland prov, Neth; known for *E* cheese.
 183.08 not Edam reeked more rare
 ?538.25 my ways from Haddem or any suistersees

EDDYSTONE LIGHTHOUSE.   14 mi SW of Plymouth, on *E* Rocks in Eng Channel.
 127.15 towers, an eddistoon

EDEN.   Form res of Adam and Eve. Co Wicklow is called the "Garden of Erin (or Ire)."
 18.23 Heidenburgh
 29.35 hubbub caused in Edenborough
 66.17 Edenberry, Dubblenn, WC
 69.10 garthen of Odin...eddams ended with aves

124.34   *L'Auberge du Père Adam*
?130.03   yeladst glimse of Even [Erin]
?183.08   Edam reeked more rare
203.01   garden of Erin
263.21   garden of Idem
282.18   Holy Joe in lay Eden
324.07   while Ede was a guardin
324.36   Giant crash in Aden
350.02   *tree of livings...middenst of the garerden*
354.22   When old the wormd was a gadden
370.07   Cobra Park
482.17   gander of Hayden
487.09   when I was in odinburgh...garden substisuit
597.35   You have eaden fruit

EDEN QUAY   (16/34).   E of O'Connell Br; N side of Liffey, across from Burgh Quay.

172.15   a coarse song and splash off Eden Quay
?278.F7   his Eddems and Clay's hat

EDINBURGH.   The Caledonian metropolis, in the heart of Midlothian (qv), cap of the latter and of Scot. Nicknames for *E* are "the mod Athens" and "Auld Reekie" – the latter presumably referring to the precipitous crag in the very cen of the city, bearing *E* Cas.

Except on the N, *E* is ringed by hills: Braid Hills, SW; Blackford Hill, SW; Calton Hill, E; Liberton Hill, SE; Craiglockhart Hills, SW; Corstorphine Hill, W; Arthur's Seat, SE (all named at 541.01 – .04); a viewpoint from Corstorphine Hill to the E is "Rest and Be Thankful" (?118.32, 543.13). Arthur's Seat has nothing to do with King Arthur; *Árd na said*, Gael "height of the arrows."

All of the local place-names alluded to in *FW* are mentioned in the 11th EB, "Edinburgh": Mons Meg is a 15th-cent cannon preserved in the Castle; the Cunzie House was the minthouse in the Old Town, now demolished (*howff*, Scot "place of resort," is mentioned in the same par in the EB); Echobank Cem is in S *E*. Hawthornden Ho (553.22) is 10 mi from *E*; when it was occupied by the poet Drummond, Ben Jonson walked there all the way from London to visit him.

Acc to J S Atherton (*Books*, 41–42), James Hogg's *Private Memoirs and Confessions of a Justified Sinner*, much of which takes place in *E*, is JJ's source for allusions to demonic possession.

18.23   Heidenburgh
29.35   Edenborough
66.17   Hyde and Cheek, Edenberry
?118.32   we ought really to rest thankful
183.08   Edam reeked more rare
353.29   *mordern Atems*
487.09   when I was in odinburgh
536.09   ould reekeries' ballyheart
537.34   my comic strip, Mons Meg's Monthly
538.16   tickey...coynds ore...cunziehowffse...Cash
541.01 – .04   Seven ills...Braid Blackfordrock, the Calton, the Liberton, Craig and Lockhart's, A. Costofino, R. Thursitt
543.13   Rest and bethinkful
547.31   from bank of call to echobank

553.22   a hawthorndene, a feyrieglenn
?577.28   long sizzleroads neath arthruseat

EDOM.   Anc name for the area S of Pal, btwn the Gulf of Aqaba and the Dead
Sea. The Edomites were the tribe of Esau (*Gen* 36:9). Leopold Bloom thought Edom
was one of the cities of the plain (*U* 61/61).
72.11   *Edomite*

EGLANTINE.   The sweet-briar plant, or the honeysuckle (as in Milton's "L'Alle-
gro"). In the 15th and 16th cents every town in the Low Countries had its own literary guild or "Chamber of Rhetoric," each with its own fanciful name. Many of
these were botanical names such as the "Violet" of Antwerp and the "Marigold" of
Gouda. The most celebrated and, in the late 16th cent, the literary center of Holland, was the "Eglantine" of Amsterdam.
39.34   Eglandine's choicest herbage

EGOIST, THE.   See *New Freewoman.*

EGYPT.   Rep, NE Afr. In the VIth dynasty, there were 2 pharaohs named Pepi
(415.36). A prayer from the pyramid of Pepi II reads in part "...the name of Pepi
shall flourish...shall flourish..." (Budge, *Book of the Dead*, xxviii, fn1). Little Egypt
was a dancer at the 1893 Chicago World's Fair (551.30). In the Exodus, the starving
Israelites pined for the fleshpots of *E*, *Exod* 16:3.
5.23   bedoueen the jebel and the jpysian sea
104.22   *and the Parlourmaids of Aegypt*
130.30   his second's French-Egyptian [ie, Nil]
192.29   the flushpots of Euston
198.01   you born ijypt...ptellomey...sheba...salomon
263.06   Egyptus, the incenstrobed, as Cyrus heard of him?
347.11   the freshprosts of Eastchept
355.23   land of engined Egypsians
364.18   captivities...parchment...apoclogypst
415.36   Beppy's realm shall flourish
551.30   rosetted on two stellas of little egypt
625.04   king of Aeships

EHREN ON THE RHINE.   Song about a soldier's goodbye: "When the war is o'er/
We'll part no more/ At Ehren on the Rhine" (*U* 324/330). There is no actual Ehren,
although Ehrenfeld is a suburb of Cologne, and Ehrenbreitstein is a town on the
Rhine across from Coblenz.
In 1937 JJ stopped at Rheinfelden, Switz, on his way to Zurich, and called it
"Erin on the Rhine" (*Letters* I, 396).
288.F6   his native Ireland from erring under Ryan
338.03   Germanon. For Ehren, boys, gobrawl!

EIFFEL TOWER.   Paris landmark.
4.36   a waalworth of a skyerscape of most eyeful hoyth entowerly
88.24   Holy Saint Eiffel
314.01   where the deiffel...scaffolding...babeling
541.06   by awful tors my wellworth building

ELBA.   Isl btwn Corsica and Ital mainland where Napoleon spent the period between his abdication in 1814 and his return for the "Hundred Days" of 1815.
52.25   his elbaroom surtout...woolselywellesly
?283.L1   *Non plus ulstra, Elba, nec, cashellum tuum.*

ELBERFELD.   City, NW Ger, on Wupper R; textile and dyeing center. In 1929 it merged with adjoining towns to become Wuppertal. The "Elberfeld horses," including "Clever Hans," tapped out the answers to simple sums with their hooves, and were exhibited in the years before WW I.
> 108.15   Elberfeld's Calculating Horses

EL DORADO.   Aka Manoa, the legendary city of gold, believed to be on the Amazon, which expeditions from Sp and Eng sought. Because of the gold once mined in Co Wicklow, Dub was sometimes called on the Continent "the El Dorado of Western Eur."
> 134.01   eldorado or ultimate thole
> 276.16   if Nippon have pearls or opals Eldorado

ELEPHANT AND CASTLE.   Dist, rd junction, and Undergound sta in Southwark, London; the name is from a local pub.
> 537.01   The elephant's house is his castle

ELLIOTT, THOMAS   (14/33).   25 Brown St, S; poplin and silk manufacturer.
> 43.09   and then Elliot and, O, Atkinson

ELLIS QUAY   (14/34).   N side of Liffey, btwn Barrack Br and Queen's Br.
> 205.07   Ellis on quay in scarlet thread

ELPHIN.   Vill, 10 mi SE of Boyle, Co Roscommon; an anc ecclesiastical cen, and associated with the childhood of Oliver Goldsmith.
> ?79.29   homelike cottage of elvanstone
> ?249.07   the glittergates of elfinbone

ELVERY'S ELEPHANT HOUSE.   Form the shop name of John W Elvery and Co, 46-47 Lwr O'Connell St; waterproof and gutta percha manufacturers. Now "Sport Outfitters" in different locations.
> 461.05   rainproof of...elephant's
> 537.01   The elephant's house is his castle

ELYSIAN FIELDS (ELYSIUM).   Paradise or abode of the blessed in Gk mythology and poetry.
> 379.17   he had the delysiums
> 453.32   the fieldnights eliceam, *élite* of the elect, in the land of lost of time
> 607.14   Champelysied

EMANIA (EMAIN MACHA).   Now known as Navan Fort, a circular rath of about 11 acres; 1½ mi W of Armagh, Co Armagh. Founded 300 BC by Queen Macha, it was the royal res of Ulster for more than 600 yrs; in the 1st cent AD it was the hqs of the Red Branch Knights. *Eamhuin*, Ir "brooch of the neck."
> ?410.23   Speak to us of Emailia
> ?412.08   *Buccinate in Emenia tuba insigni volumnitatis tuae* [*Ps* 80:4, "Buccinate in Neomenia [new moon] tuba, in insigni die solemnitatis vestrae"]
> 480.21   It's his lost chance, Emania. Ware him well
> 521.32   from exemple, Emania Raffaroo!

EMANIA OF THE APPLES.   *Emain Ablach*, the res of Manannan mac Lir beyond the sea. In the "Voyage of Bran," a silver branch of the apple tree from *E* of the Apples magically appears to him to invite his voyage.
> 504.24   Orania epples playing hopptociel bommptaterre

EMBANKMENT, THE.   N side of the Thames R, London, S of the Temple. *Recte*, Victoria Embankment.

    547.19   long rivierside drive, embankment large

EMPIRE THEATRE.   19th-cent music hall in Leicester Sq, London; alluded to in the song, "There's Hair, Like Wire, Coming out of the Empire."

    289.10   Derzherr, live wire, fired Benjermine Funkling outa th'Empyre
    516.15   bear's hairs like fire bursting out of the Ump pyre

ENGLAND.   Strictly, it does not include Scot or Wales; but historically and politically, esp from the Ir point of view, it has often been regarded as equivalent to Brit, or the United Kingdom, which for convenience are included here. In both Ir and Scot Gaelic it is "Sasana," and Eng people are "Sasanachs," terms which have become pejorative. *Beurla* is Ir for the Eng lang (17.13, 132.27, 467.25). Fr, *Angleterre*; Ger, *England*. The Ger warcry *Gott straf' England* is a motif in *FW* (9.28, 229.03, 340.24, 451.04).

    Napoleon (in exile at St Helena) is supposed to have called Eng "a nation of shopkeepers," but he was anticipated by Adam Smith (*The Wealth of Nations* II, iv, 7) (128.16, 229.08, 352.26, 539.06).

    "Hodge" (from "Roger") is a generic name for an Eng rustic (138.11). The familiar "John Bull" was popularized by Dr John Arbuthnot's *The History of John Bull* (255.13, 366.20).

    See *Albion, Anglo-Saxon Kingdoms, Saxony.*

    9.28   Goat strip Finnlambs!
    13.01   Here English might be seen
    16.06   You spigotty anglease?
    17.13   I can beuraly forsstand a weird
    19.14   triangular Toucheaterre beyond the wet prairie
    36.29   High Church of England
    36.32   my British to my backbone tongue
    49.04   the (Zassnoch!) ardree's [king's] shilling
    52.09   in a quiet English garden
    54.26   in ahoy high British quarters
    85.08   be British, boys to your bellybone
    93.02   murdered all the English he knew...scotfree...britgits
    104.14   *Groans of a Britoness*
    106.08   *Inglo-Andean Medoleys*
    116.26   the lingo...however basically English
    124.19   though plain English
    127.33   shows Early English tracemarks
    128.16   the man who had no notion of shopkeepers
    132.27   Banba [Ireland]...Beurla
    138.11   has a hodge to wherry him
    154.24   Irene [Ireland]...Los Angeles
    156.29   as british as bondstrict
    160.22   it is most unenglish
    170.32   Corner House, Englend
    171.02   Rosbif of Old Zealand!
    175.11   *forced the Arth out of Engleterre*
    178.06   alley english spooker
    181.01   stage Englesemen
    183.07   Angles aftanon browsing there
    185.10   an Anglican ordinal

188.16   your disunited kingdom
229.03   Gout strap Fenlanns!...Mary Inklenders
229.08   its nation of sheepcopers
233.14   them that won't leave ingle end
233.33   pure undefallen engelsk
241.22   in the benighted queendom
242.33   Howarden's Castle, Englandwales
255.13   The Bulljon Bossbrute
257.01   angelland all weeping bin
271.F3   your cumpohlstery English
275.F6   jinglish janglage
284.L1   *stodge Angleshman...eccentricity*
304.21   her dream of Endsland's daylast
306.26   Homely Anglian Monosyllables
327.23   over the wishtas of English Strand
340.24   Guards, serf Finnland
346.18   *pitchin ingles in the parler*
350.24   their sassenacher ribs
351.07   prettish...engrish
352.26   counterination oho of shorpshoopers
357.02   so splunderdly English
362.07   contracted out of islands empire
362.10   soldr of a britsh
366.20   Jambuwel's defecalties is Terry Shimmyrag's uppperturnity
386.28   angler nomads [Anglo-Normans]
387.05   scotobrit sash
403.23   greatbritish and Irish objects
447.06   the cokeblack bile that's Anglia's
451.04   cold strafe illglands
467.25   beurlads scoel...past participle
484.36   Anglicey [Fr, *anglais*]
485.12   speachin d'anglas landadge
485.29   Me no angly mo
512.23   Anglys cheers our ingles
520.22   Angly as arrows
524.14   J. P. Cockshott, reticent of England
528.23   aglo iris [Anglo-Irish]
532.10   Allenglisches Angleslachsen is spoken
539.06   Daunty, Gouty and Shopkeeper, A.G.
539.36   famine with Englisch sweat
552.29   she sass her nach
562.30   quit our ingletears
579.21   Herenow chuck english
595.03   knock and knock, nachasach
596.14   the sousenugh
609.15   inplayn unglish
613.01   Good safe firelamp!...Goldselforelump!

ENGLYSH, WILLIAM, HOUSE OF.   The White Book of Christchurch describes the route of "riding the franchises" in Dub in 1488: "...and so threw the strete southward till they come to William Englysh is [his] hous, and so...to the Combe."
543.17   from Huggin Pleaze to William Inglis his house

ENNELL, LOUGH.   3 mi S of Mullingar, Co Westmeath; about 6 mi E of Hill of Uisneach (qv).

Clive Hart identifies the Stone of Divisions on Uisneach (qv) with A∝ in fig on *FW* 293 (Mearingstone), and confirms this identification by the ref below to Lough *E*.

    293.15   Given now ann linch you take enn all

ENNISCORTHY.   Town, Co Wexford, near the Slaney R on the Ferns-Wexford Rd. Song, "When McCarthy Took the Flure at Enniscorthy" (*U* 85/86).

    310.13   the forty routs of Corthy
    514.06   when Big Arthur flugged the field at Annie's courting

ENNISKERRY.   Vill, Co Wicklow, 12 mi S of Dub in the Dargle vall.

    38.22   never have Esnekerry pudden
    73.31   at Howth or at Coolock or even at Enniskerry

ENNISKILLEN.   Town, Co Fermanagh, on an isl in the Erne R btwn Upr and Lwr Lough Erne.

The famous "Inniskillings" of the Brit army go back to 1689, when a cavalry and an infantry regt were raised in *E* to defend the town for Wm III against the forces of James II. The cavalry became the 6th (Inniskilling) Dragoons (now the 5th Royal Inniskillings), and the infantry became the 27th (Inniskilling) Regt, later the Royal Inniskilling Fusiliers. They both fought at Waterloo, and the Dragoons were in the Crimean campaign.

    8.23   inimyskilling inglis

ENOCH.   The 1st city, built by Cain in the land of Nod, east of Eden, and named after his eldest son (*Gen* 4:17−18).

    ?283.01   Foughty Unn, Enoch Thortig
    ?357.30   the manmade Eonochs Cunstuntonopolies
    442.06   like enoch to my townmajor ancestors
    535.21   Enouch!

EPHESUS.   Anc Ionian city, now ruins, on Aegean coast of Asia Min. An early Christian cen, it was visited twice by St Paul, whose *Epistle to the Ephesians* is directed to its ch. The Temple of Artemis (qv) was one of the 7 Wonders of the Anc World.

    124.35   old Huffsnuff, old Andycox [Antioch]

EPSOM DOWNS.   Racecourse, S of London; the site of the Derby (qv) and the Oaks.

    49.24   after life's upsomdowns
    139.36   Ebblawn Downes

EQUITABLE INSURANCE COS.   At the turn of the cent, there were 3 *E* Insurance Cos with Dub offices: *E* Fire Insurance Co, 61 Upr Sackville St; *E* Plate Glass Insurance Co, 14 Suffolk St; *E* Life Assurance Co (US), 70 Dame St.

    362.28   equitable druids and friendly or other societies

EREBUS.   In Gk myth, the subterranean region through which shades enter Hades; its entrance was placed in the mythical land of the Cimmerians.

    ?38.03   erebusqued very deluxiously
    239.30   wherebus...belchybubhub and a hellabelow

EREWHON.   The mythical land in the novel by Samuel Butler (who had NZ in mind), where money doesn't exist and physical ailment is a crime.

    ?46.01   He'll Cheat E'erawan

152.18   ere wohned
155.12   newwhere
213.15   erewone
?394.29   Huber and Harman orhowwhen theeuponthus...on this ourherenow
        plane
510.27   e'er a one

ERIE, LAKE.   One of the "Great Lakes" of midwestern US and Can; the only one
mentioned in *FW*, no doubt because its name is an anagram of "Eire."
?326.07   Ocean...Erievikkingr
601.06   that greyt lack...wasseres of Erie. Lough!

"ERIN'S KING."   In JJ's day, a ship which took tourists on 2-hour trips around
Dub Bay. *U* 66/67, 150/152, 373/379.
428.20   that goodship the Jonnyjoys takes the wind from waterloogged Er-
        in's king

ERNE.   (1) Riv, N Ire, flowing into Atlantic at Ballyshannon, Co Donegal; the anc
name was Samhair (qv).   (2) Upr and Lwr Lough *E*, Co Fermanagh.
198.05   erned his lille Bunbath
?324.03   erning his breadth
?382.28   Farvel, farerne!
433.31   Never dip in the ern

ERNE ST   (16/34).   Upr *E* St runs N from Hogan St to Gt Brunswick (now Pearse)
St; Lwr *E* St from the latter to Hanover St. *E* St is straight from one end to the other.
134.20   earned in Watling Street
459.18   round the elbow of Erne street Lower

ERNING (ERMINE) ST.   Along with Icknield St, Watling St, and Foss Way (qqv),
it was one of the 4 "royal rds" of anc Brit. *E* St was part of a line of Roman rds
leading N from London through Huntingdon to Lincoln.
42.26   *via* Watling, Ernin, Icknild and Stane
134.20   earned in Watling Street

ERRICK.   Name of 2 tnlds, Co Roscommon.
?530.21   magnon of Errick. Sackerson! Hookup!

ERZERUM.   Vilayet and anc city in NE Turkey-in-Asia (Armenia). The *E* Treaty of
1847 provided for the definition of the frontier btwn Pers and Turk. A Turk base in
the Crimean War, *E* was threatened but not taken by a Russ army.
?240.28   Jebusite, centy procent Erserum spoking
344.31   meac Coolp, Arram of Eirzerum

ESCORIAL.   Vast structure erected in 16th cent by Philip II, about 25 mi N of
Madrid, Sp, comprising palace, ch, mausoleum, coll, and monastery; known for its
works of art. JJ jokingly referred to the Euston Hotel in London, as the "Euston Escorial" (*Letters* III, 120).
550.24   in our saloons esquirial

ESKER.   (1) Vill, Co Dub, ¾ mi SE of Lucan; one of the 4 Royal Manors of Dub
(qv).   (2) The *E* Rd (Ir, *Eiscir Riada*) was the anc rd, prob the earliest Ir highway,
following the chain of gravel ridges, or "eskers," from Dub across cen Ire to Galway.
It marked the boundary in the anc division of Ire into "Conn's Half" and "Mogh's
Half" (qqv). Aka *Slighe Mór* ("Great Rd"), esp btwn Clonard and Galway. It was the

rd which refugees from Cromwell followed to Connacht.

   126.15   the esker of his hooth
   220.35   Caherlehome-upon-Eskur
  ?350.21   With askormiles' eskermillas
   475.22   Up to the esker ridge it was
  555.13,15 esker, newcsle, saggard, crumlin
  ?570.31   our national first rout, one ought ought one

ESPLANADE.   (1) The open area, once a drill ground, now a sports ground, btwn Albert (now Wolfe Tone) Quay and Barrack (now Benburb) St (14/34).   (2) Promenade in Bray; the Joyce family lived just off the *E*, at No 1 Martello Terr, from 1887 to 1891.

  ?553.12   esplanadas and statuesques and templeogues

ESSEX.   Co, SE Eng, one of the Anglo-Saxon Kingdoms (qv).

   291.26   dolightful Sexsex home, Somehow-at-Sea
   524.01   exess females

ESSEX BR (15/34).   Now Grattan Br, aka Capel St Br, at Capel St. Orig built in 1676 with stone from St Mary's Abbey, it collapsed in 10 yrs. Rebuilt 1753-55, again rebuilt and renamed, 1874. Acc to Cosgrave's *North Dublin*, 35, "It is as true as Essex Bridge" (125.17, 521.04) is "an old Dublin affirmation."

   125.17   as true as Essex bridge
  ?202.17   waterlows year, after Grattan or Flood
   521.04   Essexelcy...the Golden Bridge's truth
   580.32   kneed O'Connell...butted...grattaned

ESSEX ST (15/34).   An old st in cen Dub S of the Liffey, it was the site of the "Wooden Man" (qv). *E* St, Gate, Br, and Quay are all named after Arthur Capel, Earl of Essex, 17th-cent Lord Lt of Ire.

   535.04   my poplar Sexsex, my Sexencentaurnary...hostel of the Wodin Man
  ?611.35   his essixcoloured holmgrewnworsteds

ETNA, MT.   Active volcano in NE Sicily, It.

   318.12   Ethna Prettyplume, Hooghly Spaight [mt and riv]
   494.06   etnat athos? Extinct your vulcanology

ETRURIA.   Anc country, cen It, mod Tuscany and part of Umbria. Chief confederation consisted of 12 cities; its height of power was *ca* 500 BC; gradually absorbed by Rome. The Etruscan lang has never been deciphered.

   120.23   kakography affected for certain phrases of Etruscan stabletalk
   215.20   like any Etrurian Catholic Heathen

EU.   Town, NW Fr, Dept of Seine-Maritime, on Bresle R. St Lawrence O'Toole died and was buried at the monastery in Eu, but his heart was taken to Christchurch Cath (qv), Dub. JJ dictated to Frank Budgen that Book IV of *FW* is "a triptych...the third being St Lawrence O'Toole, patron saint of Dublin, buried in Eu in Normandy." There is still a ch of St Laurent in Eu.

   307.26   Eu
   307.F8   Eu, Monsieur?
   601.30   S. Loellisotoelles!...Euh! Thaet is seu whaet shaell one naeme it!

EUPATORIA.   Seaport, W Crimea, N of Sevastopol. In the Crimean War, Eng and Fr troops landed there in 1854; Turks defeated Russians in a short battle, Jan 1855.

366.21   increaminated...assault of turk against a barrakraval...Terry Shimmy-
            rag's upperturnity

EUROPE.   George IV of Eng was known as the "First Gentleman of Europe"
(300.F2).

3.06	Europe Minor
10.17	Pukka Yurap!
37.26	Iro-European
69.36	Zentral Oylrubber
70.01	Osterich, the U.S.E.
88.01	Waterhose's Meddle Europeic Time
133.02	though you rope Amrique
138.07	Europe
155.05	Tugurios-in-Newrobe...Ashies
171.06	lentils in Europe
191.04	Europasianised Afferyank
205.29	Evropeahahn cheic house
228.26	Euro pra nobis
263.08	Egyptus...A. Shaw...old Whiteman
300.F2	First Gentleman in youreups
?338.16	*with a yellup yurrup*
343.10	Orops and Aasas
?419.14	earopen
423.35	europicolas
466.13	europe
482.29	You're up-in-Leal-Ulster...Easia
488.26	per Neuropaths
497.12	Europa Parade
519.01	engels opened to neuropeans
595.20	perporteroguing youpoorapps
598.15	earopean
610.12	Eurasian

EUSTACE ST   (15/34).   Btwn E Essex St and Dame St. Other refs in *FW* (361.11,
535.26) are to the Eustachian tube of the ear. See *O'Reilly and Co.*

310.12   Eustache Straight, Bauliaughacleeagh

EUSTON.   (1) Rlwy Sta, *E* St, just off Marylebone Rd, London; terminus for trains
to Holyhead and Ire; now demolished, this architectural landmark was in the Egyptian style (192.29).   (2) Hotel, by *E* Sta; JJ called it the "Euston Escorial," and
liked to stay there because "I feel I am near Number Thirteen platform – the Irish
Mail." The manager was Mr E H Knight; JJ said he was a "very knice kman (*Letters*
I, 239).

192.29   the flushpots of Euston...Marylebone
245.30   troublebedded rooms...Mr Knight, tuntapster
578.30   Norwood's Southwalk or Euston Waste

EVENING WORLD.   Not a Dub or London newspaper; the only *EW* of note was
the NY daily newspaper publ from 1887 until it merged with the *NY Telegram* in
1931.

28.20   reading her Evening World
285.27   see Iris in the Evenine's World

EVEREST, MT.   Highest mt in the world, of course. Since HCE and ALP are mt and riv, Everest is HCE *in excelsis*.

    ?536.04   buttes? Everscepistic!

    548.09   I was her hochsized, her cleavunto, her everest

    ?619.36   here your iverol and everthelest your umbr

EVIAN-LES-BAINS.   Spa in Dept of Haute-Savoie, Fr, S of Lake Geneva. JJ stayed there at the Grande Hôtel, 6-16 July 1933.

    ?211.23   heftiest frozenmeat woman from Lusk to Livienbad

EXMOUTH.   Port town, Devonshire, SW Eng, at mouth of Exe R, 10 mi SE of Exeter. 1st seaside resort in Devon. There is no henge (circular earth fort) at Exmouth, but Exeter Cas is on the site of a great Brit earthwork.

    177.25   every lass of nexmouth

    ?595.01   Henge Ceolleges, Exmooth, Ostbys

F

FAEROE ISLANDS.   Dan, *Faerøerne*; isl group in N Atlantic O, 200 mi NW of Shetland Isls; a possession of Den since 1380 (self-governing since 1947).

    326.18   from osion buck fared agen fairioes feuded

    382.28   Farvel, farerne!

FAIRBROTHER'S FIELDS   (14/32–33).   Form name of the area bounded by the SCR, Clanbrassil St, The Coombe, and Cork St; named after Tom Fairbrother, Capt of the Liberty Boys of 1798. The name survived into the 20th cent as a local name for the area.

    585.29   lifelong the shadyside to Fairbrother's field

FAIRVIEW   (17/35).   Dist, NE Dub; because of the conformation of Dub Bay, it really is the SW part of NE Dub (447.20). *F* Park, on Dub Bay, is filled-in sloblands at the mouth of the Tolka R. The Joyce family lived at several addresses in the *F* area btwn 1896 and 1901 (420.25).

    420.25   Pulldown. Fearview

    447.20   Bridge of Belches [see *Ballybough (Br)*]

    541.25   I let faireviews in on slobodens

    601.25   S. Bellavistura's [see *Visitation, Ch of the*]

FAIRYHOUSE RACECOURSE.   2 mi S of Ratoath, Co Meath. The Ir Grand Nat Steeplechase is held at *F* on Easter Mondays. (The Eng Grand Nat is held at Aintree, just N of Liverpool.)

    13.32   the cycles of events grand and national

    39.04   hippic runfields...events national

    610.35   Peredos Last in the Grand Natural

FALLAREES COMMONS.   Tnld, par of Ballymore Eustace, bar of S Naas, Co Kildare. It is on the Liffey.

    214.13   Yonne there! Isset that? On Fallareen Common?

FANAGAN, WILLIAM   (15/33).   Funeral establishment, 54 Aungier St, around

the turn of the cent.
    ?537.34   Fanagan's Weck

FAREWELL, CAPE.   Dan, *Kap Farvel*; S-most point of Greenland.
    382.28   Farvel, farerne!

FARM ST.   St, Westminster, London, W of Berkeley Sq; site of Jesuit ch and house of study for Gt Brit.
    ?424.04   society of jewses...clericy...demonican...Hooley Fermers

FEAR, CAPE.   On Smith I, SE coast of N Carolina, US, mouth of Fear R. Not a very convincing identification, but neither is Cap de Fer, in NE Algeria. *Caer* is Welsh for "fort," as in the Welsh town (and cheese), Caerphilly.
    ?171.34   Caer Fere, Soak Amerigas

FENGYANG (FUNGYANG).   City, N Anhwei prov, China. Home of the Ming dynasty 1368-1644 AD.
    109.06   his greatest Fung Yang dynasdescendanced

FERMANAGH.   Co, Ulster prov; co town, Enniskillen.
    Baronies: Clanawley, Clankelly, Coole, Knockninny, Lurg, Magheraboy, Magherastephana, Tirkennedy. *Fir Monaigh*, Ir "Men of Monach."
    284.05   A Tullagrove pole[1] to the Height of County Fearmanagh
    595.15   fairmoneys

FERMOY.   Town, NE Co Cork, on Blackwater R.
    257.27   —fermoy— [in C-word]

FERN, LOUGH.   In Co Donegal. Ferns, a vill in Co Wexford, was in the 12th cent the see of a diocese and the royal seat of Leinster.
    212.09   Flora Ferns

FEZ.   City in N cen Morocco, one of the sacred cities of Islam. The Wad Fez, or Wad Fas, is the main trib of the Wad Sebu, which flows through the city. At one time all fezzes (44.02, 56.09, 83.36) were made in *F*, and dyed crimson from a local berry.
    28.22   Death, a leopard, kills fellah in Fez
    44.02   'Ductor' Hitchcock hoisted his fezzy fuzz
    56.09   this fez brimless as brow of faithful toucher of the ground
    83.36   turning his fez menialstrait in the direction of Moscas
    535.01   never see his waddphez again

FIFE.   Co, E Scot, btwn Firth of Tay and Firth of Forth. Long an independent kingdom, often called just The Kingdom. *Macbeth* V, i, 46: "The Thane of Fife [Macduff] had a wife: where is she now?"
    77.14   it was Dane to pfife

FIJI ISLANDS.   Isl group (more than 800 isls and islets) in SW Pacific O, SW of Samoa.
    546.18   of Feejeean grafted ape

FINDLATER, ALEXANDER, AND CO   (15/34).   Grocers, tea and wine merchants, form at 29-32 O'Connell St and other locations. Mr Findlater paid for the Presbyterian ch, often called "Findlater's Ch" (qv). Around the turn of the cent, *F* sold its own house brand of whiskey, called "A.1" (245.35). A chromo of the Charge of the Light Brigade — *F*'s Christmas print — hangs on the wall of HCE's tav (334.24−33).

170.32   Findlater and Gladstone's, Corner House, Englend
245.35   A's the sign and one's the number...cup...astirrup
334.33   thon print...how it came from Finndlader's Yule to the day
558.10   Adam Findlater, a man of estimation
619.03   to Adam, our former first Finnlatter and our grocerest churcher...for
          his beautiful crossmess parzel

FINDLATER'S CHURCH (15/35).   Presbyterian ch at NE cor of Rutland (now Parnell) Sq; the gift (1865) of Alexander Findlater, grocer and distiller. His brother Adam was a magistrate, his great-nephew Adam a managing director of Alexander Findlater and Co (qv), acc to Roland McHugh.

?170.32   Findlater and Gladstone's, Corner House, Englend
420.35   The Reverest Adam Foundlitter
533.23   my Kerk Findlater's, ye litel chuch rond ye coner
569.05   S. Presbutt-in-the-North
'619.03   Adam...Finnlatter and our grocerest churcher

FINGAL.   The plain N of Dub; it comprises the Co Dub parishes of Castleknock, Mulhuddart, Cloghran, Ward, St Margaret, Finglas, Glasnevin, Grangegorman, St George, and Clonturk. The name derives from the fairhaired Norsemen (*fionn-gall*) who settled it. The *F* Harriers are a well-known hunt (480.34).

Refs may be combined with "Fingal," Macpherson's name for Finn MacCool in the Ossianic cycle (eg, 329.14); with the mod political party, Fine Gael (?22.10); or with *fiongal*, Ir "fratricide" (564.30).

22.10   with a loud finegale
72.07   *Enclosed find the Sons of Fingal*
?106.17   *The Last of the Fingallians*
?138.11   a prince of the fingallian
?215.14   foostherfather of fingalls and dotthergills
329.14   In Fingal of victories
480.34   Find the fingall harriers
?496.18   I have it here to my fingall's ends
500.04   Dovegall and finshark
503.13   In Fingal too they met at Littlepeace
564.30   By feud fionghalian
?594.23   our peneplain by Fangaluvu Bight
596.36   rained never around Fingal
?622.06   the lodge of Fjorn na Galla of the Trumpets

FINGAL'S CAVE.   Legendary home of Fingal on isl of Staffa, in the Inner Hebrides; pop name for Mendelssohn's *Hebridean Overture*. Described by Scott in Canto IV of "Lord of the Isles."

198.33   deathcap mushrooms round Funglus grave
462.05   A stiff one for Staffetta mullified with creams of hourmony

FINGLAS (12/39).   Vill, NW Dub, on rd to Ashbourne, and the surrounding dist, which loosely includes Glasnevin (Prospect) Cem (198.33). In 1690, Wm III's army camped in *F* for several days after returning from the battle of the Boyne (75.16).

74.15   Fengless, Pawmbroke
75.16   a kingbilly whitehorsed in a Finglas mill
100.23   with suffusion of fineglass transom
142.14   Finglas fields
198.33   round Funglus grave

497.19   Cabraists and Finglossies
502.35   from Foxrock to Finglas
550.24   with fineglass bowbays
625.13   *Finglas since the Flood*

FINIAS, MURIAS, FÁILIAS, GORIAS.   Acc to Keating's hist of Ire, the Tuatha Dé
Danann migrated orig from Gr to Nor (Lochlann), where they dwelt a while in the 4
cities of Finias, Murias, Fáilias, and Gorias; thence they sailed for Ire, taking with
them their 4 talismans: the sword (from Gorias) and spear (from Finias) of Lugh
Lámhfada, the cauldron of the Daghda (from Murias), and the Lia Fáil (qv) (from
Fáilias). The actual location (if any) of these legendary cities is unknown.
       219.11   from the four coroners of Findrias, Murias, Gorias and Falias...Clive
                 Sollis, Galorius Kettle, Pobiedo Lancey and Pierre Dusort

FINISTERRE (FINISTÈRE).   (1) The NW point of mainland Fr; a dept, part of
old prov of Brittany.   (2) Cape *F*, NW tip of Sp, prov of Galicia.
     Acc to the *Book of Invasions*, the Celts came to Ire from the Fr Finistère, the
megalith builders from Sp Finisterre.
       17.23   from his Inn the Byggning to whose Finishthere Punct
       50.17   his funster's latitat to its finsterest interrimost
      ?228.28   Fuisfinister, fuyerescaper!
       516.35   photoplay finister started
       566.32   How is hit finister!

FINLAND.   Finn, *Suomi*. A Scand country, its lang is not Scand but Finno-Ugrian,
distantly related to Hungarian. *F* shares Lapland with Nor, Swed, and Russ. For some
reason, JJ associates *Gott Straf' England!* with *F*.
        9.28   Goat strip Finnlambs!
       17.14   forsstand a weird from sturk to finnic
       39.17   Finnish pork
       98.07   Arsa, *hod* S.S. Finlandia
      105.21   *Lapps for Finns*
      229.03   Gout strap Fenlanns!
      ?238.24   fools length finnishfurst
      ?245.16   a flip flap in all Finnyland
      ?257.36   Fionia
      285.22   the finish of helve's fractures [Finn words in preceding lines]
      287.F4   Basqueesh, Finnican, Hungulash
      325.12   Whilesd this pellover his finnisch
      329.02   a suomease pair
      340.24   Guards, serf Finnland
      362.12   is a finn as she...is a lap
      374.21   Finnish Make Goal!
      518.26   in finnish...in Feeney's
      ?589.22   'twas in fenland

FINN RIVER.   In Co Donegal; flows E to Lifford, where it joins the Mourne R to
form the Foyle R.
      203.09   Not where the Finn fits into the Mourne

FINN'S HOTEL   (16/33).   In Nassau St (actually 1 and 2 Leinster St). Nora Barnacle was working there when she and JJ met in 1904; JJ put up his Triestine cinema
partners there in 1909 and romantically visited Nora's room (330.24) (*Letters* II, 272).

330.24   pictures motion...eloping for that holm in Finn's Hotel Fiord, Nova
Norening
420.25   Vale. Finn's Hot.
?440.10   *Percy Wynns* of our S. J. Finn's
514.18   .i..'. .o..1.

FINSBURY.   Dist, just N of the City of London. In the 17th cent it was a cen of
entertainments and amusements; Pepys frequented it. Sadler's Wells Theatre preserves
the name of a former spa, where Grimaldi the clown appeared. Also the home of Mr
Pickwick and of John Wesley.
374.28   Finsbury Follies...batter see...regent

FINTONA.   Vill, Co Tyrone, btwn Omagh and Fivemiletown; once an O'Neill stronghold.
617.06   We are all at home in old Fintona, thank Danis

FINVARRA.   Vill, Co Clare. *F* Point is a promontory in S Galway Bay. Finnbhearra
was "King of the Connacht Fairies"; his Otherworld seat was Knockmaa, 6½ mi NE
of Headford, Co Galway.
621.11   I'll take me owld Finvara for my shawlders

FISHAMBLE ST   (15/33).   From Christchurch Cath to the Liffey.
61.14   granite cromlech setts of our new fishshambles
494.32   libels of snots from the fleshambles, the canalles
538.22   Lizzy and Lissy Mycock, from Street Fleshshambles

FITZGIBBON ST   (16/35).   Off NE cor of Mountjoy Sq; the Joyce family lived at
No 14 (now demolished) in 1894.
420.21   Tried Apposite House. 13 Fitzgibbets. Loco.

FIUME.   Adriatic seaport; disputed btwn Austro-Hung and It, it became Italian
1922-47; Yugo, and renamed Rijeka, since 1947. The refs may be simply to *fiume*,
It "river."
208.24   sommething quaint in her fiumy mouth
243.02   fiuming at the mouth
548.08   I chained her chastemate to grippe fiuming snugglers

FIVE LAMPS   (16/35).   An elaborate Victorian street light at the junction of N
Strand Rd, Portland Row, Killarney (now Sean MacDermott), Seville, and Amiens Sts
gave this intersection its pop name, which is still in use.
88.33   out of the five lamps in Portterand's praise

FLAMINIA, VIA.   The anc Roman rd to N It, built *ca* 220 BC. The 11th *EB* article ("Flaminia, Via") discusses in more detail than in the case of other Roman rds
the construction and preservation of brs along its length.
81.03   Fluminian!...Hannibal's walk
277.L1   *bridges span our Fluminian road*

FLEET STREET.   (1) In Dub, intersects Westmoreland St btwn O'Connell Br and
College Green (15/34).   (2) In London, continues the Strand E to Ludgate Hill and
St Paul's Cath; the cen of London newspaper offices.
5.32   streetfleets

FLEMINGSTOWN.   Tnld, par of Clonalvy, bar of Upr Duleek, Co Meath.
622.34   Flemingtown

FLODDEN.   Hill in Northumberland, Eng; site of Battle of *F* Field, 9 Sept 1513, in which Eng defeated Scots under James IV.
>   9.24   this is floodens

FLORIDA.   SE US state; Sp *F* was SE part of present US. Called "Florida" by Ponce de León who first saw it on Easter (1512), pop called *Pascua florida*, "flowery Easter." Acc to legend, St Brendan landed on the coast of *F*. There are other Floridas in Cuba, Uruguay, and the Solomon Isls.
>   158.02   carried her daisy's worth to Florida

FOCLUT (FOCHLAD).   Anc forest in vicinity of Killala Bay, N Co Mayo, possibly extending considerably to S. St Patrick dreamed of "The Voice of the Irish" prior to beginning his mission in Ire: "I imagined that I heard in my mind the voice of those who were near the wood of Foclut, which is near the western sea, and thus they cried, 'We pray thee, holy youth, to come and walk again amongst us as before'." *Faolchú*, Ir "wolf"; *fochla*, Ir "cave."
>   290.18   to mount miss (the wooeds of Fogloot!)
>   407.14   vote of the Irish, voise from afar
>   478.34   The woods of fogloot! O mis padredges!
>   479.13   The wolves of Fochlut!

FOLKESTONE.   Seaport on Dover Strait, 6 mi SW of Dover, Kent, Eng. Named for the *Lapis tituli* or "folkstone" at the landing place of the Saxons, similar to the Viking Steyne (qv) in Dub.
>   ?68.30   shaft...obelise...neither pobalclock neither folksstone

FOLLY.   Tnld, par of Palmerston, bar of W Balrothery, Co Dub; in Fingal.
>   503.15   Winning's Folly Merryfalls

FONTENOY.   Vill, SW Belg, 5 mi SE of Tournai; scene of battle 11 May 1745, in which Marshal Saxe's Fr army including the Ir Brigade defeated an Anglo-Allied army under the Duke of Cumberland in the War of the Austrian Succession.
>   *F* St (15/35) lies btwn Phibsborough Rd and Dorset St. JJ stayed at No 44 with his father and sister during his 2 visits to Dub in 1909.
>   9.06   for to fontannoy the Willingdone
>   ?212.14   Fountainoy Laura

FOOCHOW (FUCHOW).   Chinese seaport on Min R, cap of Fukien prov; aka Minhow. Long known as main port for export of black tea; one of first 5 treaty ports opened by Nanking treaty of 1842.
>   466.04   Lets have a fuchu all round
>   608.21   beckerbrose, the brew with the foochoor in it

FORD OF FYNE.   Local place-name, on Delvin R (qv), par of Naul, bar of Balrothery W, Co Dub.
>   ?330.24   Finn's Hotel Fiord
>   622.35   to the Ford of Fyne on Delvin

FORTH, FIRTH OF.   Estuary of the Forth R, E Scot. The exploits of Robert and Edward Bruce (596.15) were in W and cen Scot (and in Ire).
>   200.13   so firth and so forth
>   ?596.15   the big brucer, fert in fort
>   608.29   hindled firth and hundled furth

FORTY STEPS (13/33).   The pop local name for the st of steps, Cromwell's Quar-

ters (qv). There is another *FS* btwn York and Castle Sts.
> 68.14   her pitch was Forty Steps...Cromwell's Quarters

FOSS WAY.   One of the "4 Royal Rds" of Gt Brit (see *Erning.St*); it ran from Lincoln to Bath and mid-Somerset. The ref may be an oblique allusion to Med Lat *fossa*, "a bank of stones or earth."
> 42.26   *via* Watling, Ernin, Icknild and Stane

FOSTER PLACE   (15/34).   Dead-end st at W side of Bank of Ire, form Parliament Ho. Orig Turnstile Lane; it was renamed after John Foster, last speaker of House of Commons before the Act of Union in 1800. In the early 20th cent it was the site of pop oratory, eg by James Larkin, at political rallies.
> 490.23   in blessed foster's place
> 542.18   in Forum Foster I demosthrenated my folksfiendship

FOUR CANTONS.   Switzerland's Four Forest Cantons, which border on Lake Lucerne, Ger, *Vierwaldstättersee*, the "Lake of the Four Forest Cantons," are Lucerne, Schwyz, Uri, and Unterwalden. The latter 3 formed an alliance against the Hapsburgs in the 13th cent; Lucerne was more loosely allied and inclined toward sep action, esp in the 15th cent.
For JJ, of course, the 4 Cantons are inseparable from Ire's 4 provinces.
> 472.24   light lucerne...would it splutter to the four cantons
> 496.09   nor a one of the four cantins

FOUR COURTS   (15/34).   On King's Inns Quay; the mod Supreme Court has been added to the orig 4 courts: King's (or Queen's) Bench, Chancery, Exchequer, and Common Pleas. Moved 1608 from Castle to site near Christchurch Cath; the present bldg was begun 1776, badly damaged, and the Public Record Office destroyed by fire, when the *FC* was held by Republican forces and shelled by Free State troops in June, 1922; restored 1931.
> 5.36   his fore old porecourts
> 30.23   to the forecourts of his public
> 91.07   king's commons
> 91.19   pleas bench
> 91.30   exchequered
> 91.31   chancery
> 92.35   the four justicers
> 94.24   the four with them...upin their judges' chambers
> 94.31   The four of them and thank court
> 147.03   their whole four courtships
> 189.35   the reducing of records to ashes
> 232.13   her forecotes
> 422.04   before the four divorce courts...King's paunches
> 422.29   commonpleas
> 423.13   thank the Bench
> 423.14   chancery licence
> 423.19   that eggschicker
> 589.27   wrothing foulplay over his fives' court
> 602.15   Potterton's forecoroners

FOURKNOCKS.   Tnld, par of Stamullin, bar of Upr Duleek, Co Meath, 1 mi NW of Naul.
> 622.34   Four Knocks

FOUR SEES OF IRELAND.   The Synod of Kells, 1152 AD, est Armagh, Dublin, Cashel, and Tuam as the 4 ecclesiastical sees of Ire. They remain the 4 provs of the RC Ch in Ire.

    138.23   easier to found a see in Ebblannah

    283.L1   *Non plus ulstra, Elba, nec, cashellum tuum*

FOUR WAVES OF ERIN.   The 4 legendary *tonns* or waves, whose roar was believed to forebode the death of a king, were the Wave of Tuath, at the mouth of the Bann, Co Derry (Wave of the North); the Wave of Rory (Rudhraidhe) in Dundrum Bay, Co Down (Wave of the East); the Wave of Cleena (Chliodhna) in Glandore Harbor, Co Cork (Wave of the South); and the Wave of Scéina in Kenmare Bay btwn Co Cork and Co Kerry (Wave of the West).

In Welsh legend, the death of the hero Dylan was lamented by the Wave of Erin, the Wave of Man, the Wave of the North, and the Wave of Brit.

Sometimes the 4th wave is omitted, as by P W Joyce, who identifies the Three Waves of Erin (*Social History of Ancient Ireland*, II, 18). *FW* identifies the 4 Waves with the 4 Old Men, but when it names them (254.02) it gives only the first three, and not in the usual order of NSEW. See O Hehir, *Gaelic Lexicon*, 385–86.

    23.27   wave of roary...hooshed...hawhawhawrd...neverheedthem—

    254.02   Rurie, Thoath and Cleaver

    373.08   Waves

    384.06   four maaster waves of Erin...Matt Gregory...Marcus Lyons

    384.08   four waves

    390.15   the four of the Welsh waves

    424.29   talking to the four waves

FOX AND GEESE (9/31).   Vill, 3½ mi SW of Dub, on Naas Rd.

    124.33   fox and geese still kept the peace

    ?446.19   wildflier's fox into my own greengeese

    ?514.33   Gaa. And then the punch to Gaelicise it. Fox. [*gaas*, Dan "goose"]

    557.14   goodmen twelve and true at fox and geese

FOXROCK (21/25).   Vill, 6 mi SE of Dub; site of Leopardstown race course.

    502.35   from Foxrock to Finglas

    547.01   the foxrogues

"FRAM."   The ship used both by Fridtjof Nansen in his N polar explorations, 1893-96, and by Roald Amundsen in his S polar expedition, 1910-12. It is now preserved, as a tourist attraction, in its own bldg in Oslo. The name means "Onward."

    312.07   the Norgean run...fram Franz José Land

    313.27   the frameshape of hard mettles

    ?317.09   Afram

    ?596.07   fram choicest of wiles with warmen and sogns

FRANCE.   Since "Eng's difficulty is Ire's opportunity" (366.20), the Ir view of *F* from the 17th cent into the 19th was as a haven for Ir exiles and a potential source of military aid, by sea. As Eng and Ger poets and adventurers were drawn to It and the Medit, the Ir were drawn to Paris, JJ among them.

In the late 1920's, the Dub Corp employed a Fr firm of st cleaners (138.12). There was a French Coll (qv) at Blackrock. Percy French (495.03) was the great Ir songwriter. *FW* quotes also evoke Fr pastry and cooking, the Fr Revolution, and the Fr lang; a "Fr leave" is "absence without leave." Marianne, a symbol for *F* as Uncle Sam is for the US, derives from a republican secret soc of that name formed *ca*

1852. She is usually represented wearing the Phrygian cap of liberty (?257.06). Fr, *Gaule*, Lat, *Gallia*. See *Gaul*.

?12.06	we all like a marriedann because she is mercenary
15.14	pollyfool fiansees
50.09	all the French leaves unveilable
83.30	his friend's leave
83.31	French hen
?106.17	*Wet Week Welikin's Douchka Marianne*
127.29	brain of the franks
130.30	French-Egyptian
?134.26	frankeyed boys
138.12	a frenchy to curry him
146.20	an engindear from the French college
192.15	ordinary emetic French
198.18	Tell us in franca langua
226.09	a son to France's [ie, a Franciscan]
233.09	Find the frenge for frocks
246.32	Brune is bad French for Jour d'Anno
256.19	Fine's French phrases
311.33	his fringe sleeve
315.36	lauwering frankish for his kicker who, through the medium of gallic
343.28	allafranka
346.18	*pollyvoulley foncey*
352.25	race of fiercemarchands
363.19	friends' leave
372.08	frankling
388.18	Frankish floot of Noahsdobahs
392.15	exchullard of ffrench and gherman
412.19	That's not French pastry
420.09	from Francie to Fritzie
423.36	Fran Czeschs
462.34	after his French evolution
464.36	french davit
465.12	almeans...my frank incensive
478.19	perfrances...dans votre boche
479.30	The Frenchman, I say, was an orangeboat
486.17	blackfrinch pliestrycook
495.03	skirriless ballets in Parsee Franch
495.27	Wwalshe's ffrenchllatin
498.01	French wine stuarts and Tudor keepsakes
606.20	franklings by name
625.01	Our native night when you twicetook me for some Marienne Sherry ["Marianne, chérie"]

FRANKFURT.   (1) Frankfurt-am-Main, in Hesse, Ger. An imperial city; most emperors were crowned there btwn 12th and 19th cents. The daily *Frankfurter Zeitung* has been noted since the 19th cent for its commercial and business reporting. (2) Frankfurt-an-der-Oder, in Brandenburg, Ger.   (3) The Trieste restaurant "Alla città di Francoforte," on the Via Mercadante, was a favorite of JJ's.

70.05	Frankofurto Siding, a Fastland payrodicule
332.08	frankfurters on the odor
533.15	Frankfurters, numborines, why drive fear? [eins, zwei, drei, vier]

FRANZ JOSEF LAND.   Uninhabited arctic archipelago E of Spitsbergen, btwn 80° and 82° N, the most northerly land in E hemisphere. Discovered by Julius Payer in 1873, explored by Leigh Smith in yacht "Eira" in 1881-82.
>   312.07   fram Franz José Land til Cabo Thormendoso

FREEMAN'S JOURNAL.   Recte, *Freeman's Journal and National Press*; its offices were in 4-5 N Prince's St and 83-84 Middle Abbey St. It ceased publ in 1925.
>   ?291.F6   See the freeman's cuticatura by Fennella
>   500.15   Christ hold the freedman's chareman!
>   501.19   Vehement Genral
>   ?546.20   my natural born freeman's journeymanright

FRENCH COLLEGE   (20/29).   Now Blackrock Coll (RC), Castledawson Rd, Williamstown, near Blackrock. Form called *"FC"* because it was founded by Fr and Alsatian priests of the Holy Ghost Fathers, in 1860.
>   146.20   I was always meant for an engindear from the French college, to be musband

FRIEDLAND.   Commune in E Prussia, since 1945 Pravdinsk, Pol. Napoleon defeated Russians under Gen Bennigsen, 14 June 1807.
>   14.31   eirenical...our fredeland's plain!

FRIEDRICHSHAFEN.   Town, Württemberg, Ger, on E shore of Lake Constance; formed by Frederick I from the towns of Buchhorn and Hofen. Cen for the manufacture of zeppelins through the 1920's.
>   529.21   a papersalor...carrying his ark, of eggshaped fuselage and made in Fredborg

FRISIA.   (1) Anc name (during Frankish emp) of country roughly corresponding to mod Neth.   (2) Friesland, prov, N Neth; dairy farming.   (3) Frisian Isls in N Sea, off coasts of Den (Jutland, 327.01), Ger, and Neth; N *F* Isls are Ger and Dan, E and W *F* Isls are Dutch.
>   327.01   smukklers he would behave in juteyfrieze
>   ?346.01   *the fictionable world in Fruzian Creamtartery*

FRY AND CO   (14/33).   115-116 Cork St; carriage lace, silk, and trimming manufacturers.
>   43.09   Peter Pim and Paul Fry

FUKIEN.   Prov, SE China; cap, Foochow.
>   468.03   to be a coach on the Fukien mission

G

GAELIC ATHLETIC ASSOCIATION.   Founded 1884 by Michael Cusack (the "Citizen" of *U*) as an athletic-political assn to advance Ir games (hurling, Gaelic football) and eschew Brit sports (cricket, rugby).
>   175.31   gaasy pure, flesh and blood games
>   323.13   Free kicks...Capteen Gaascooker
>   332.14   the gaauspices (incorporated)
>   332.26   the fiounaregal gaames of those oathmassed fenians
>   514.33   Gaa. And then the punch to Gaelicise it

GAIETY THEATRE   (14/34).   48-49 S King St. Opened 1871 by John and
Michael Gunn, and still in operation; home of Dub Pantomime, for which Edwin
Hamilton (513.21) wrote librettos. "Turko the Terrible" (98.10; see also 132.18,
205.29, 520.02) is the one *FW* remembers.

32.26	king's treat house...footlights
98.10	as Turk of the theater (first house all flatty: the king, eleven sharps)
180.04	in their gaiety pantheomime
219.15	Before all the King's Hoarsers with all the Queen's Mum
285.L2	*Arthurgink's hussies and Everguin's men*
285.15	MPM brings us a rainborne pamtomomiom
411.15	Geity's Pantokreator
455.25	Hereweareagain Gaieties of the Afterpiece
513.22	Edwin Hamilton's Christmas pantaloonade...at the Gaiety
?567.17	all the king's aussies

GALWAY.   (1) Co, Connacht prov. *Gaillimh* (pron "golliv"), Ir "foreigner." Baro-
nies: Athenry, Ballymoe, Ballynahinch, Clare, Clonmacnowen, Dunkellin, Dunmore,
Galway, Kilconnell, Killian, Kiltartan, Leitrim, Longford, Loughrea, Moycullen, Ross,
Tiaquin.

A "Galway jury" is an independent-minded one; from the incident when Thomas
Wentworth, Lord Deputy of Ire, claimed all the lands of Connacht for the King, and
among the co juries only that of *G* found against the claim.

(2) Co town of Co *G*, at head of *G* Bay. In the early 13th cent Richard de Burgh
(Burgo) (372.30, 543.19) and his Anglo-Normans seized the surrounding territory
from the O'Flaherties and built a cas on the site of *G* city. For cents the city was
an Eng stronghold; the native Ir were excluded by an anc ordinance, acc to which
"Neither 'O' nor 'Mac' shall strutte ne swagger thro' the streets of Galway" (543.19).
Outside the city to the SW grew up the Ir quarter called the Claddagh (qv). Prospect
Hill (?541.02) is a st running NE from the central Eyre Sq. For Bohermore **Rd** and
Cem, see *Bohermore*.

G was sometimes called the "City of the Tribes" for the 14 "tribes" or families which were its med oligarchy: Athy, Blake (563.13), **Bodkin**, Browne, Darcy
(?543.20), Deane, ffont, ffrench (495.29), Joyce, Kirwan, Lynch, Martin, Morris, and
Skerrett. Lynch's Cas (16th cent) in Shop St (now a bank) is named for the Lynch
family, 84 of whom were mayors btwn the 15th and 17th cents. A doubtful story
has it that James Fitzstephen Lynch, mayor in 1493, hanged his own son for killing
a Sp guest named Gomez in a fit of jealousy (372.30, 495.11, 545.32). The once-
extensive sea trade with Sp is remembered by Sp Parade and Sp Arch, a remnant of
the city walls, leading to Sp Place (141.01).

In 1912, JJ wrote two articles on *G* in *Il Piccolo della Sera* (Trieste): "The City
of the Tribes" and "The Mirage of the Fisherman of Aran." Among other things, he
recounts the Lynch story and discusses the "Transatlantic Scheme" to make *G* a
great Brit port. Nothing came of it. Nora Barnacle was from *G*, and in 1912 JJ visited
her family there, at 4 Bowling Green.

89.07	Gallwegian
140.36	Dalway
141.01	down Spanish Place...Galway's grace
160.28	Mr Wist...wist
190.29	Boulanger from Galway
197.06	gullaway swank
343.10	Galwegian caftan
372.30	lyncheon partyng of his burgherbooh

458.09   think galways
?482.09   Macdougal, Atlantic City
495.11   Lynch Brother...Warden of Galway
?541.02   seaventy seavens for circumference inkeptive are your hill prospect
543.19   foeburghers...strutting oges and swaggering macks...darsy
545.32   the game for a Gomez, the loy for a lynch
594.23   peneplain by Fangaluvu Bight [?Galway Bay]
595.14   goldways

GAPING GHYL.   A deep vertical cave in Yorks, Eng.
36.35   Gaping Gill...Heidelberg mannleich cavern
37.08   he shall gildthegap Gaper

GARDEN CITY.   The "Garden City" concept of planning for new cities in Eng began with Ebenezer Howard's book *Tomorrow* in 1898. The 1st Garden City was Letchworth, Herts, 1903.
Norwich, Eng, and Chicago, US, are both nicknamed "The Garden City."
553.09   lecheworked lawn, my carpet gardens of Guerdon City

GARDENS OF SEMIRAMIS.   The "Hanging Gardens" or "Terraces" of anc Babylon; one of the 7 Wonders of the Anc World (qv).
192.29   hanging garments of Marylebone
261.10   pondered the pensils ["pensile": hanging or suspended]
347.12   dangling garters of Marrowbone
553.11   carpet gardens...pensilled turisses...of the summiramies

GARDINER'S MALL (15/34).   When Luke Gardiner widened Drogheda St in the 1740's and named it Sackville St (now O'Connell St), the 48-ft wide promenade down the cen was called *GM*, later just the Mall.
?260.09   Long Livius Lane, mid Mezzofanti Mall
547.19   by...Gardener's Mall

GARRYOWEN.   Suburb of Limerick City; song, "Garryowen" (Air: "We May Roam Through This World"): "...From Garryowen to Thomond Gate/ For Garryowen and glory."
372.28   to corry awen and glowry
588.02   Carryone, he says, though we marooned through this woylde

GASCONY (GASCOGNE).   Region and form duchy, SW Fr; cóntested by Eng and Fr during 100 Years War. Proverbial for poverty and braggadocio.
403.08   gorsecone...Gascon Titubante [*titubo*, Lat "stagger"] of Tegmine –
            sub – Fagi [*Sub tegmini fagi*, "beneath the beech-tree," Virgil's
            1st Eclogue]

GASOMETER (17/34).   In JJ's day, the cylindrical gasometer on Sir John Rogerson's Quay (S bank of Liffey) was the most noticeable feature of the Dub skyline.
67.09   the gasbag where the warderworks
95.08   why would he heed that old gasometer with his hooping coppin...
            southside
221.09   the Gugnir, his geyswerks, his earsequack
559.24   paralleliped homoplatts, ghazometron pondus

GATES OF HORN AND IVORY.   NPN. False dreams pass through the Ivory Gate, those which come true through the Gate of Horn. Based on 2 puns in Gk: *elephas*, "ivory," and *elephairo*, "to cheat with empty hopes"; *keras*, "horn," and *karanoo*,

"to accomplish." *Odyssey* 19:562; *Aeneid* 6:894 ff.
    192.27   those hornmade ivory dreams you reved

GATE THEATRE   (15/35).   In Rutland (now Parnell) Sq, E, part of the Rotunda (qv) bldgs. Still in operation.
    105.26   *From Abbeygate to Crowalley*
    569.30   Play actors...crash to their gate

GATH.   Bibl city of the Philistines, N edge of Negev Desert. Mod *G* founded 1942.
    286.06   bagdad...begath, and the arab in the ghetto

GAUL.   Anc country of Eur, commonly the part S and W of the Rhine, W of Alps, and N of Pyrenees, inhabited *ca* 600 BC by Celtic race (Lat, *Galli*); divided into 3 early divisions: Cisalpine *G*; Transalpine *G*, almost all of mod Fr (qv); and Galla Narbonensis, now Provence. In Gaelic, *gall* is "foreigner"; see *Fingal*.
    43.36   as men of Gaul noted
    70.01   Gaul save the mark!
  ?134.22   land of younkers...gale of his gall
    176.20   the grand germogall allstar bout...roth, vice and blause
    185.33   gallic acid on iron ore
    237.18   in all Daneygaul
  ?267.07   gael, gillie, gall
    281.05   *la jacinthe se plaît dans les Gaules*
    288.24   galloroman
    291.23   its gaulish moustaches
    315.36   frankish...through the medium of gallic
    321.23   geil as gaul
    326.08   forfor furst of gielgaulgalls
    377.05   eye of a gull
  ?406.06   gaulusch gravy and pumpernickel
    509.20   Who kills the cat in Cairo coaxes cocks in Gaul
    604.22   The primace of the Gaulls, protonotorious...Gael warning
    615.04   all-too-ghoulish and illyrical

GAWILGHUR.   Fortress in N Ind, S of Taptec R. Wellington took it by assault, 15 Dec 1803, in his campaign against the Mahrattas, shortly after battle of Argaum (qv).
    8.25   A Gallawghurs argaumunt
  ?493.13   mayarannies...rawjaws...in his gulughurutty

GAZELLE PENINSULA.   NE end of New Britain Isl in Bismarck Archipelago; separated by a channel from New Ireland Isl to N and E, but no maps name it Gazelle Channel or anything else.
  ?595.04   as he strauches his lamusong untoupon gazelle channel

GEHENNA.   The Valley of Hinnom (*Ge-Hinnom*) just S of anc Jerusalem, orig a place for the disposal of the dead, later conflated with the place of eternal torment (*Jer* 19:6).
    78.09   buried burrowing in Gehinnon
    434.19   get to henna out of here

GENERAL POST OFFICE (GPO)   (15/34).   W side of O'Connell St, btwn Henry St and N Prince's St; present bldg erected 1818 (former GPO's in High St and Fishamble St, then in College Green until 1818); hqs of Ir Volunteers during Easter Rising of 1916, from which proclamation of Ir Rep was issued, Easter Mon, 24 Apr

1916. In the 19th and early 20th cents, distances from Dub were reckoned from the *GPO* (256.29). It's also the cen of mailman Shaun's universe (454.16, 602.36).

256.29	where G.P.O. is zentrum
265.28	a Finntown's generous poet's office
?294.F1	Ex jup pep off Carpenger Strate
364.06	post puzzles deparkment
369.34	parting parcel of the same goumeral's postoppage
412.22	past purcell's office
454.16	O Jaun, so jokable and so geepy, O
567.02	to the general's postoffice
602.36	geese and peeas and oats

GEMINI.   "The twins," one of the constellations of the Zodiac. The twins are the stars named for Castor and Pollux. See *Census.*

409.01	Piscisvendolor...But, Gemini, he's looking frightfully thin!

GENOA.   Seaport, NW Italy; It, *Genova*; Lat, *Genua*. In early med times, Geneva was also sometimes called "Genua," confusing scholars if not the inhabitants. An appellation of *G* is "La Superba" (*Letters* I, 298). Christopher Columbus (513.16) was Genoese.

113.21	any Genoaman against any Venis
274.F2	the both of him is gnatives of Genuas
513.20	Crashedafar Corumbas...Prisky Poppagenua
545.29	I debelledem superb

GEORGIA.   SE state, US. See *Dublin, Georgia.*

3.08	Laurens County's gorgios
?562.29	By gorgeous...quit our ingletears...wend him to Amorica

GERMANY.   Country, cen Eur; partitioned into E and W *G* since WW II. Ger, *Deutschland*; Fr, *Allemagne*; Russ, *nemtsy*, "Germans"; Albanian, *nemc*, "Austrians or Germans" (114.04); Dan, *Tyskland* (37.08, 427.22). Alliance of Fascist states of It and Ger called "Axis" as early as 1936 (423.04).

The Ger firm of Siemens Schuckert (qv) installed the hydroelectric works at Ardnacrusha on the Shannon R (138.13, 485.07). "Fritz," a German (138.13, 420.09).

"Cousin-German" – first cousin, or first cousin once removed – is from Med Fr *germain* and has actually nothing to do with Ger.

20.03	his cousin charmian
37.08	his Tyskminister
83.28	bully German grit
114.04	in the Nemzes and Bukarahast directions
127.13	three germhuns
130.28	twenty four or so cousins germinating in the United States
135.08	Dutchlord, Dutchlord, overawes us ["Deutschland, Deutschland über alles"]
138.13	a fritz at his switch
176.20	the grand germogall allstar bout
230.33	germane faces
235.29	Our cousin gourmand, Percy, the pup
289.10	Benjermine Funkling
316.05	thane and tysk and hanry
338.03	the rackushant Germanon. For Ehren
352.11	an Almagnian Gothabobus

355.22	in Moltern Giaourmany
?363.08	Almayne Rogers
392.15	exchullard of ffrench and gherman
410.08	new hikler's highways [the Autobahnen built in the 1930's]
416.05	chairmanlooking...wisechairmanlooking
420.09	from Francie to Fritzie
420.13	Feefeel! [*Wieviel*, Ger "how much"] And the Dutches dyin loffin
423.04	when he feraxiously shed ovas in Alemaney
?427.22	to the inds of Tuskland where the oliphants scrum
464.28	the Beer and Belly
465.11	by almeans at my frank incensive
467.27	twickly fullgets twice as allemanden huskers
478.20	perfrances...votre boche provenciale
?479.35	Allmaun away
485.07	Or in alleman: Suck at! [Siemens Schuckert]
485.13	sprakin sea Djoytsch
497.35	German selver geyser [Kaiser]
543.25	work on German physics
550.11	swinespepper and gothakrauts
?594.34	rob with Alliman, saelior
625.02	your Jermyn cousin who signs hers with exes

GHAZIPUR.   Town, N Ind, on Ganges R 40 mi NE of Benares; form cen for processing opium; scent distilleries. For the Dub character Frank "Ghazi" Power, see *Census*.

?369.10	The View, Gazey Peer

GHENT (GENT).   City, cap of E Flanders prov, NW cen Belgium. Birthplace of John of Gaunt (Ghent), son of Edward III. R Browning, "How They Brought the Good News from Ghent to Aix." "Roland," the bell of St Bavon's Cath, is the subject of "The Great Bell Roland," by Theodore Tilton (1835-1907): "Toll! Roland, toll!/In old St Bavon's Tower/At midnight hour..."

10.18	Willingdone, bornstable ghentleman
56.15	olover his exculpatory features, as Roland rung
74.05	his mighty horn skall roll, orland, roll
278.L5	*How he broke the good news to Gent*
353.15	tolfoklokken rolland allover ourloud's lande
381.13	his Ghenter's gaunts

GIANT'S CAUSEWAY.   Formation of prismatic basaltic columns on N coast of Co Antrim, N Ire, making a rough platform extending for 300 yds along the coast and at one point 500 ft into the sea. Acc to legend, the columns were the stepping-stones of the Fomorians btwn Ire and Scot.

80.02	Bryant's Causeway
198.32	giant's holes in Grafton's causeway
284.F5	A gee is just a jay on the jaunts cowsway
343.06	giant's hail over the curseway
391.18	sculling over the giamond's courseway
503.01	All effects in their joints caused ways
576.18	boomooster giant builder of all causeways

GIBBET MEADOW (16/34).   Aka Gibbet's Mead, aka Ellen Hore's Meadow. It was near Gallows Hill at the end of the present Lwr Baggot St, on the site of E Mes-

pil Rd.
      568.22   gibbetmeade

GIBEON.   Before the Temple was built in Jerusalem, the Israelites sacrificed to the
Lord in the "high places" around Jerusalem, chief of which (the "great high place")
was called G (I *Kings* 3:4, I *Chr* 21:29).
      331.18   on this mounden of Delude, and in the high places of Delude of
                Isreal, which is Haraharem

GIGLOTTE'S (GIGLOT'S) HILL   (15/33).   Mentioned as early as 1541, later
known as Cock Hill and now St Michael's Hill, btwn Cook St and High St, W of
Christchurch Cath. "Giglotte," "giglot," "a wanton woman."
      532.22   in Kissilov's Slutsgartern or Gigglotte's Hill

GILEAD.   Bibl city and region, now NW Jordan. The resin from "balm of G" trees
was used as both perfume and medicinal panacea; *Jer* 8:22. Hymn, "There Is A Balm
in Gilead."
      442.24   bringthee balm of Gaylad

GILL, M H AND SON   (16/35).   Booksellers and publishers, 50 Upr Sackville St
(now O'Connell St). *U* 196/198.
      440.14   two best sells...set up by Gill the father, put out by Gill the son
                and circulating disimally at Gillydehooly's Cost

GINNUNGA GAP.   In Norse myth, the eternal region of chaos btwn Niflheim, N
region of mist and cold, and Muspelheim, S region of heat. Localized as the N Atlantic btwn Greenland and Labrador.
      14.16   the ginnandgo gap between antediluvious and annadominant
      ?90.13   Guinney's Gap...between what they said and the pussykitties

GIPSY BAR.   Ellmann, 529: "Wyndham Lewis was much in Paris and would often
join Joyce at the Gipsy Bar near the Panthéon or at a small café" [*ca* 1921].
      177.23   in the porchway of a gipsy's bar

GLADSTONE, STATUE OF.   Nat mon, The Strand, London, by W H Thornycroft.
There are no statues of Gladstone in Dub, although in 1887 the Lord Mayor of Dub,
T D Sullivan, began a subscription for a Gladstone stat, later thought better of it.
      ?41.35   statue of Primewer Glasstone [1st Draft: "Parnell's statue"]

GLAMIS.   See *Dunsinane.*

GLASHABOY.   (1) Riv, Co Cork.   (2) Brook, Co Wicklow; from W shoulder of
Tonelagee Mt to Kings R, which once was a trib of the Liffey, now flows into Poulaphuca Reservoir from the S.
      209.30   The rivulets ran aflod to see, the glashaboys, the pollynooties

GLASNEVIN (14/37).   Former vill, now N Dub dist; named for a streamlet which
once flowed through the Delville estate into the Tolka R by the br. *Glas-Naoidhean,*
Ir "Naoidhe's little stream"; a common but false etymology accepted by *FW* is *glasín-
aoibhinn,* "pleasant little green" (252.07), or "pleasant little field" (135.18) (so trans
by Warburton, Whitelaw, and Walsh). In the 6th cent, a monastery was established on
the banks of the Tolka by St Berchán, nicknamed Mo-Bhi (252.07).
      G Cem (RC) is *recte* Prospect Cem. The grave of Daniel O'Connell is marked by a
round tower 160 ft high (56.12, 69.06). Parnell's grave, now marked by a rough boulder, had no mon in JJ's time (198.33?).

56.12   overgrown leadpencil...monumentally...Molyvdokondylon...his mausoleum...O'dan stod tillsteyne [*molybdos*, Gk "lead-pencil"]

69.06   Where Gyant Blyant fronts Peannlueamoore [*peann-luaidhe mór*, Ir
"big lead-pencil"; *blyant*, Dan "pencil"]

81.05   unemancipated...The mausoleum lies behind us...*multipopulipater*...
milestones

135.18   his burialplot in the pleasant little field

198.33   Funglus grave and the great tribune's barrow all darnels occumule

252.07   Saint Mowy of the Pleasant Grin

252.08   everglass and even prospect

?362.34   with greenhouse in prospect

?476.11   the watchers of Prospect

?504.27   with their underhand leadpencils...overthrown milestones

601.27   S. Glacianivia's [chapel of Prospect Cem]

GLASSHOUSE (15/34).   The "Round Glass-house in Mary's Lane" was a glass
factory est *ca* 1690; it prob bordered Mary's Lane btwn George's Hill and Bradogue
Lane (now Halston St).
"Glasshouse" is Brit slang for "prison," Ir slang for "privy."

?27.01   Tom Bowe Glassarse

409.22   a pair of men out of glasshouse...factory life

?428.08   ladymaid at Gladshouse Lodge

537.01   nosty mens in gladshouses they shad not peggot stones

?589.30   his plateglass housewalls

GLASTHULE (25/27).   Rd and res area, E end of Dun Laoghaire. Thom's *Directories* around the turn of the cent listed Belle Alliance (see *Waterloo*) as a "hackney
set-down" in *G.* Park Rd (*Bóthar na Pairc*, or Bohernapark) runs along the W side of
People's Park, in the Glasthule area (321.08).

321.08   Glasthule Bourne or Boehernapark Nolagh

529.23   like a Glassthure cabman

GLENAGEARY (24/27).   Rd in Dun Laoghaire. *Gleann na gCaoirigh*, Ir "valley of
the sheep"; the ref is also to the "glengarry," a Scottish cap.

529.26   Glassthure cabman [see *Glasthule*]...with their glenagearries

GLENASMOLE.   Vall of Dodder R in Dub Hills; now contains Bohernabreena Reservoir. Ir, "glen of the thrush." *G* was a hunting ground of Finn MacCool, and a
boulder at *G* Lodge S of the reservoir is still called "Finn MacCool's Stone." When
the hero Oisin (223.18) returned to Ire from the Land of Youth, he remained on
horseback so as not to touch the land, but at *G* he fell and immediately became aged
and withered. Afterward, he encountered St Patrick.

223.17   since in Glenasmole of Smiling Thrushes Patch Whyte passed O'Sheen
ascowl

GLENDALOUGH.   "Valley of the Two Lakes," in Co Wicklow, with extensive remains of the monastery est early in the 6th cent by St Kevin, who sought solitude
but attracted a multitude of followers.
The 2 lakes are unnamed except as "Upper" and "Lower." The monastery contained 7 chs, the best known of which is pop called St Kevin's Kitchen. (There are
also 7 chs at Clonmacnoise, qv, and on Inishmore in the Aran Isls, 7 pilgrimage chs
in Rome, and the 7 Chs of the Marshland, btwn King's Lynn and Wisbech, Eng.) St
Kevin's Bed is a cave in the cliffs of the Upr Lake; acc to a trad story, Kevin was
pursued to this hermit abode by the lady Kathleen, who fell or was pushed to her

death in the lake below. Other *G* landmarks apparently not mentioned in *FW* are the Round Tower, St Kevin's Cross, St Kevin's Well, and the Deer Stone.

No birds will fly over the *G* lakes, acc to a trad immortalized in Moore's "By That Lake, Whose Gloomy Shore" ("Skylark never warbles o'er"), which tells the story of Kathleen's fatal pursuit of Kevin (600.36).

Lawrence O'Toole, who as a boy had been rescued from Dermot MacMurrough by the Bishop of *G*, was appointed Abbot of *G* from 1153 until he became Archbishop of Dub in 1162. In 1214, King John united the dioceses of *G* and Dub, and they remain united to this day (433.06) in the CI (in the RC Ch, *G* is only a par). By tradition, 7 visits to *G* are equivalent to one pilgrimage to Rome, but the "pattern" which attracted so many pilgrims was suppressed in 1862.

40.36	the Saint Kevin's bed in the Adelaide's hosspittles
59.16–.18	dustman nocknamed Sevenchurches...prairmakers, Glintalook... thankeaven
62.35	not a Lucalizod diocesan or even of the Glendalough see
130.33	buyshop of Glintylook, eorl of Hoed
248.30	my lord of Glendalough benedixed the gape for me
433.05	dietcess of Gay O'Toole and Gloamy Gwenn du Lake
525.17	all amanygoround his seven parish churches
?589.20	a change of a seven days license...his early parishlife
600.36	by that look whose glaum is sure
601.32	Ascend out of your bed, cavern of a trunk, and shrine! Kathlins is kitchin
605.11	our own midmost Glendalough-le-vert...lone navigable lake

GLEN OF THE DOWNS.   Wooded area, a vall without a riv, 1 mi W of Delgany, Co Wicklow, on the Dub-Wicklow Rd.

221.08	Glen of the Downs
623.28	the moon of mourning is set...Over Glinaduna

GLIBB, THE (14/33).   18th-cent tav in Thomas St, acc to Peter's *Dublin Fragments* (95). "The Glib" was an artificial riv created as a water supply through Thomas St in 1670.

63.24	the Glibt

GLOBE THEATRE.   Burbage's theatre on the Bankside in Southwark, London, erected 1599; burned 1613 during a performance of *Henry VIII* when a peal of ordnance was discharged at the entry of the king; rebuilt 1614. Shakespeare had a share in the theatre and acted there.

455.26	Royal Revolver of these real globoes lets regally fire

GOA.   Former Port colony on W coast of Ind, 250 mi S of Bombay.

?8.09	Mind your hats goan in!
?10.22	Mind your boots goan out
233.27	Gau on!

GOAT AND COMPASSES, THE.   A common tav sign, it is pop derived (as by P W Joyce, *Irish Names* I, 39) from "God encompasseth us." The phone no, written in the Fr style (cf 308.02), is the birth-year of Wellington, for some reason.

275.16	their palace of quicken boughs hight The Goat and Compasses ('phone number 17:69...)

GOATSTOWN (18/28).   SE Dub dist, btwn Dundrum and Stillorgan.

15.01	the duskrose has choosed out Goatstown's hedges

?329.25   by Ghoststown Gate
?390.03   Lally, the ballest master of Gosterstown

GOBELINS.   Ave, factory, mus, and Métro sta, 13th Arr, Paris; locus of tapestry
and carpet manufacturers. "Gobelins" is also a Paris telephone exchange (308.01,
501.19).
?183.22   solid objects cast at goblins
308.01   Gobble Anne: tea's set, see's eneugh! ["dix, sept, six et neuf"; cf
           275.17]
?357.29   natural sins liggen gobelimned theirs before me
501.09   I gotye. Gobble Ann's Carrot Cans ["quarante quinze"]
552.13   gobelins...tileries

GODDAMENDY.   Tnld, par of Mulhuddart, bar of Castleknock, Co Dub; in Fingal.
503.17   Godamedy, you're a delville

GODTHAAB (GODTHAB).   Town, main settlement and cap of Greenland, on SW
coast. Dan, "Good Hope." See *Good Hope, Cape of.*
312.19   whol niet godthaab...off his Cape of Good Howthe

GOERZ (GÖRZ, GORIZIA).   Town and resort, 74 mi NE of Venice; form Austrian, since 1919 an It prov and town.
577.22   to Goerz from Harleem

GOG AND MAGOG.   (1) Bibl: *Gen* 10:2, Magog, son of Japhet, son of Noah; *Ezek*
38–39, Gog from "the north parts," the land of Magog his territory; *Rev* 20:7–9, *G*
and *M* represent the nations of the earth that are deceived by Satan. Acc to an old
legend, the Ir are descended from Magog.   (2) In cycle of legends relating to Alexander the Great, *G* and *M* are allies of Ind King Porus, shut off by the great wall
built by Alexander in the Caucasus.   (3) Acc to Brit legend, *G* and *M* were giants
captured and brought to London. Their effigies, several times destroyed but replaced,
have stood at the Guildhall since the 15th cent. In another version, Gogmagog, chief
of the giants of Albion whom Brute destroyed, wrestled with Corineus and was
thrown into the sea. The statues *G* and *M* have also been said to represent Gogmagog
and Corineus.   (4) Gogmagog Hill, 3 mi SE of Cambridge, Eng, is referred to in
Kingsley's *Hereward the Wake.* Acc to legend, the giant Gogmagog was changed into
the hill.
6.19   Agog and magog and the round of them agrog
71.26   *Magogagog*
73.06   Gog's curse to thim
136.01   can be as noisy as a sonogog
?169.14   from his megageg chin
222.14   The whole thugogmagog
?246.05   Gadolmagtog!

GOLDEN BALL.   Vill, S Co Dub, on the Dub-Enniskerry Rd. 3 balls are of course
the trad sign of a pawnshop.
?589.08   three golden balls

GOLDENBRIDGE (12/33).   Ave and dist S of Kilmainham. Golden Bridge spans
the Camac R btwn Tyrconnell Rd and Emmet Rd.
234.09   coton breiches, the whitemost, the goldenest
521.05   Essexelcy [Bridge]...the Golden Bridge's truth

GOLDEN FALLS.   On the Liffey, 1 mi W of Poulaphuca, Co Wicklow; now the site

of a dam and hydroelectric power sta.
    214.31   Near the golden falls

GOLDEN GATE.   (1) The entrance from the Pacific O to San Francisco Bay, US,
through which sailed the goldrushers of 1849.   (2) The entrance to the Golden
Horn, the port of Constantinople (Istanbul).   (3) All that remains of the 11th-cent
walls of Kiev, USSR.
    ?433.32   silver key through your gate of golden age
    493.27   Let Eivin bemember for Gates of Gold

GOLDEN SPURS, BATTLE OF THE.   In the battle of Courtray, 11 Jul 1302, the
Flemish routed the Fr and hung 700 golden spurs as trophies in the ch at Courtray.
    8.18   in his goldtin spurs

GOLIAD.   City, 22 mi W of Victoria, S Texas, US; scene of battles in Mex revolt
against Sp, 1812-13, and in revolt of Texas, 1835.
    8.20   goliar's goloshes

GOMORRAH.   See *Cities of the Plain.*

GOOD HOPE, CAPE OF.   SW coast of Cape Prov, Rep of S Afr; orig named Cabo
Tormentoso (Cape of Storms) by Bartholomeu Diaz, 1488. The ship of the Flying
Dutchman was usually sighted in the latitudes of the *C* of *GH.* See *Godthaab.*
    10.02   his big white harse, the Capeinhope
    312.08   fram Franz José Land til Cabo Thormendoso
    312.19   godthaab...Cape of Good Howthe

GOODMAN'S LANE   (15/33).   The character of Fox Goodman (see *Census*) appears often in *FW,* always with bells or chs; perhaps as the sexton of the "speckled
ch" (qv). Prob unknown to JJ, there was in the 19th cent a Goodman's Lane in the
shadow of St Patrick's Cath, btwn St Patrick's Close and Walkers Alley. Other doubtful allusions are at 328.26, 360.11, 369.08, 511.09, 515.02, 557.13, 603.32, and
621.35.
    ?35.30   old Fox Goodman, the bellmaster

GOOD WOMAN, THE   (18/33).   Inn at Ringsend; noted for oysters, shrimps and
cockles, as early as beginning of 18th cent.
    83.19   into the Good Woman at Ringsend

GOOSE GREEN AVE   (17/37).   Rd, now Grace Park Rd, in Drumcondra. The
whole adjacent area was once called *GG.* St Mary's Asylum and Reformatory, High
Park Convent (on *GG* Ave), was the 1st reformatory for juvenile offenders in Ire
(1859).
    ?446.19   wildflier's fox into my own greengeese again
    533.19   cagehaused duckyheim on Goosna Greene

GOREY.   Town, N Co Wexford; the insurgents of 1798 stormed *G* on 3 June but
their victory was short-lived. Song, "The Croppy Boy": "At the siege of Ross did my
father fall/And at Gorey my loving brothers all." Also, *gorey,* Basque "red."
    246.04   All's quiet on the felled of Gorey
    ?310.32   Culsen, the Patagoreyan

GORT.   (1) Town, Co Galway; near Lady Gregory's Coole Park.   (2) Vill, Co Roscommon.
    Both of these are in Connacht, which at 53.30 comes 1st among the provs, instead
of its usual last, as at 89.19.

53.30   the bannocks of Gort and Morya and Bri Head and Puddyrick
89.19   Lindendelly, coke or skilllies spell me gart

GORTEEN.   Vill, 3 mi W of Ballymahon, Co Longford (Leinster). Goldsmith's Lissoy or "Sweet Auburn" is a few mi S. Many Ir vills and tnlds, eg, Gortin in Co Tyrone (Ulster), bear this name; Ir, "little field."
?53.30   the bannocks of Gort and Morya and Bri Head and Puddyrick
379.28   that Missus with the kiddies of sweet Gorteen

GOTA RIVER.   In SW Swed; *Göta Elv*, Swed "Göta Riv." Flows into Cattegat Strait at Gothenburg. Known to Vikings simply as "The Elv."
198.13   Gota pot!
262.F1   his beelyingplace below the tightmark, Gotahelv!

GOTHAM.   Vill, Notts, Eng, once proverbial for the stupidity of its inhabitants, "the wise men of *G*." Acc to trad, King John intended to maintain a hunting lodge near the vill, but the villagers, afraid of the cost of supporting the court, feigned idiocy and thereby caused the king to build his lodge elsewhere. Among other examples of idiocy, the villagers joined hands around a thornbush to shut in a cuckoo so that it would sing all year.
NYC was dubbed *G* by Washington Irving in *Salmagundi* (1808).
538.33   I liked his Gothamm chic! Stuttertub! What a shrubbery trick to play!

GOTHENBURG (GÖTEBORG).   City and port, SW Swed, on Göta R, just above point where it flows into the Cattegat Strait. The Kungspark contains Johann Peter Molin's famous group of statuary, the "Belt-Bucklers" (*Bältespännere*).
534.31   Allare beltspanners

GOUGANE BARRA.   Lake, W Co Cork; source of R Lee. Named for St Finbarr, or Barra, who founded a monastery there (*Letters* I, 462). Often called "Lone Gougane Barra" as in the poem by J J Callanan: "There is a green island in lone Gougane Barra/Whence Allua of songs rushes forth like an arrow."
88.31   Long's gourgling barral...more gargling bubbles
93.28   from lone Coogan Barry his arrow of song

GRAFTON ST (15/33).   Dub's fashionable shopping st, from College Green to Stephen's Green. The city assessment of 1712 records an allocation "for making a crown causeway through Grafton St" (cf *U* 165/168).
198.32   giant's holes in Grafton's causeway

GRAMPIAN HILLS.   Mt system of Scot, NE to SW Scot, boundary btwn Highlands and Lowlands. John Home, *Douglas*, II.1: "My name is Norval; on the Grampian hills/My father feeds his flocks..."
569.36   My name is novel and on the Granby in hills
570.01   Mine name's Apnorval and o'er the Grandbeyond Mountains

GRAND CANAL.   Begun in 1765, it encircles S Dub from Ringsend to Kilmainham, and extends W to the Shannon R at Shannon Harbor and the Barrow R near Athy.
37.20   the quiet darkenings of Grand and Royal
207.12   her boudeloire maids...Ciliegia Grande and Kirschie Real
494.32   the fleshambles, the canalles
551.23   my tow tugs steered down canal grand...Regalia Water

GRAND TURK ISLAND.   Isl, largest of the Turks isl group in the Brit W Indies, politically part of Jamaica. The name comes from a local cactus which resembles a turbaned head. The allusion, however, is primarily to the Sultan of Turkey, Sp *El Gran Turco*.

    132.29   Gran Turco, orege forment

GRANGEGORMAN.   Tnld and form vill in NW Dub, including NE part of Phoenix Park. *G* Rd (14/34) runs parallel to Phibsborough Rd; site of *G* Female Convict Prison and Richmond Lunatic Asylum (aka *G* Mental Hosp).

    236.24   held ragtimed revels on the platauplain of Grangegorman

GRAUBÜNDEN (GRISONS).   Canton in E Switz; contains the sources of the Rhine R.

    ?190.31   the cuthone call over the greybounding slowrolling amplyheaving
                 metamorphoseous
    ?577.15   basal [?Basle] curse yet grace abunda

GRAVESEND.   Town on S bank of Thames R, E of London; within commuting distance of London, but that doesn't seem to be the point.

    434.34   Not before Gravesend is commuted

GRAY, SIR JOHN, STATUE (15/34).   In O'Connell St, by Thomas Farrell (1879). The inscription commemorates his services as head of Dub's waterworks (1863-75) in providing Dub with water from the Vartry R.

    553.13   Jean de Porteleau

GREAT BELT.   The strait dividing the isl of Zealand from the rest of Denmark, and connecting the Cattegat with the W Baltic Sea.

    35.09   his...great belt

GREAT BRUNSWICK ST (16/34).   Now Pearse St. Along N side of TCD grounds.

    578.04   in his chrismy greyed brunzewig

GREAT NORTHERN RAILWAY CO.   The main line btwn Dub and Belfast. Its terminus was Amiens St (now Connolly) Sta.

    552.02   the Geenar, the Greasouwea, the Debwickweck

GREAT SOUTHERN AND WESTERN RAILWAY CO.   The main line btwn Dub and Cork. Its terminus was Kingsbridge (now Heuston) Sta. Its tracks roughly parallel the Liffey on the S as far as Sallins, then on the N to Newbridge (Droichead Nua) where they diverge.

    203.02   with the great southerwestern windstorming her traces
    552.02   the Greasouwea, the Debwickweck, the Mifgreawis
    ?604.12   greek Sideral Reulthway

GREECE.   Anc Hellas, mod Gk Ellas. *FW* alludes most often to anc *G*, bracketing it with Rome, but also remembers its long occupation (1456-1829) by the Turks (181.22).

    The Uniate Ch (43.13) follows the forms of the Gk Orthodox Ch but acknowledges the Roman pontiff.

    Aeneid II, 48: "Timeo Danaos et dona ferentis," "I fear the Greeks, though they bear gifts" (94.14).

    11.35   Gricks may rise and Troysirs fall
    43.13   the roman easter...and greek uniates
    94.14   Ah, furchte fruchte, timid Danaides!
    113.02   the lapins and the grigs

120.19	crisscrossed Greek ees
125.15	little laughings and some less of cheeks
155.27	gresk, letton and russicruxian
170.34	Grex's
171.01	greekenhearted yude
181.22	Turk, ungreekable in purscent of the armenable
214.22	creakorheuman
220.19	Grischun scoula
226.06	Hey, lass!...pooripathete [Aristotle's "Peripatetic" School]
235.17	Turkish hazels, Greek firs
242.13	glycorawman arsenicful femorniser
263.14	Espanol-Cymric-Helliniky
267.04	thou fountain of the greeces
343.17	*he was in a greak esthate phophiar an erixtion*
390.18	half a Roman hat, with an ancient Greek gloss on it
409.19	bed as hard as the thinkamuddles of the Greeks
419.20	Greek!...nobly Roman
419.27	hellas
464.29	Not forgetting the oils of greas [Byron's "Isles of Greece" in *Don Juan*]
509.19	what seemed sooth to a Greek
518.23	Irish Ruman...the expeltsion of the Danos
561.18	Grecian language
564.09	grekish and romanos
581.31	grippes and rumblions
604.12	greek Sideral Reulthway
620.30	merry as the gricks...ledden

GREENHILLS   (10/29).   Vill, SW of Dub, on rd to Tallaght.

194.35	by Tallaght's green hills
?480.08	far away from those green hills

GREENLAND.   Dan, *Grønland*; a Dan colony and since 1953 a prov. Cap, Godthaab (qv). Orig discovered and colonized by Eric the Red in 10th cent.

199.18	a cupenhave so weeshywashy of Greenland's tay
378.11	nonirishblooder that becomes a Greenislender...Kovenhow
?469.16	whaler went yulding round Groenmund's Circus

GREEN MAN.   A common pub sign (representing a green-clad forester) in Eng but not in Ire. Peter's *Sketches of Old Dub* (91) mentions an 18th-cent *GM* in Bride St, but it was a linen draper's, not a tav. *Green Man Rise-O* is a very old London st game resembling hide-and-seek.

74.02	in his valle of briers of Greenman's Rise O
469.16	hill of a whaler went yulding round Groenmund's Circus
507.04	down at the Green Man...drinking gaily

GREEN PATCH   (18/34).   A pool and anchorage in Dub Bay just off Ringsend, before the S Wall was extended in the 18th cent. About 1710 it was decided that the S Wall should run "from Mr Mercer's (formerly Vanhomrigh's) house to Green Patch" (Haliday, *Scandinavian Kingdom*, 235n).

174.27	from Mr Vanhomrigh's house at 81 bis Mabbot's Mall as far as Green Patch

GREEN STREET COURTHOUSE   (15/34).   25 Green St, btwn Little Britain St and N King St; built 1792 on site of former Little Green; Robert Emmet delivered here his famous speech from the dock, 19 Sept 1803 (but was sent to Newgate and Kilmainham Jails, not Mountjoy Pris).

    45.09   from Green street he'll be sent...To the penal jail of Mountjoy
    575.26   little green courtinghousie

GREENWICH.   Town and suburb, SE London; site of Royal *G* Obs; the *G* meridian serves as basis for standard time throughout the world, although into the 20th cent Dub had its own time, 25 min later than *G* Mean Time.

    517.25   Grinwicker time

GRESHAM HOTEL (15/34).   In Upr Sackville St (now O'Connell St).
    376.11   Delphin dringing! Grusham undergang!

GRETNA GREEN.   Vill, Dumfries Co, Scot, near the Eng border, 12 mi N of Carlisle; long famous as marrying place of runaway couples from Eng. In 1931, JJ concocted the story that he and Nora were married after they went to Trieste, and she gave the name of "Gretta Greene" (*Letters* III, 222).

    94.01   the wedding on the greene, agirlies, the gretnass of joyboys
    212.10   Fauna Fox-Goodman and Grettna Greaney
    533.19   cagehaused duckyheim on Goosna Greene

GRIFFEEN RIVER.   Small riv rising E of Newcastle and flowing N into the Liffey at Lucan, Co Dub. "Dapping" is fly-casting.

    450.14   dapping my griffeen, burning water in the spearlight

GRIMSTAD.   Town, Nor, where Ibsen worked as a druggist's apprentice, and fathered an illegitimate child; *grim stad*, Nor "ugly city." Before the age of steamships it was a shipbuilding cen and home port for a large fleet.

    ?602.35   of the Grimstad galleon, old pairs frieze

GUADIANA RIVER.   Major riv in Sp and Port, 515 mi long, from S cen Sp W to Port border, where it flows S to the Gulf of Cadiz, as the border btwn Sp and Port for much of its length. The Guadiana Menor ("Lesser") is a trib of the Guadalquivir R.

    294.29   our callback mother Gaudyanna

GUINNESS'S BREWERY (14/34).   Arthur Guinness, Son, and Co (Ltd), aka St James's Gate Brewery; it occupies the entire area bounded by James's St, Watling St, Victoria Quay, and Steevens' Lane, with offices in James's Gate. Sir Benjamin Lee Guinness (1798-1868) restored St Patrick's Cath (qv). For members of the Guinness family, see *Census*.

Export Guinness is transported from the brewery to ships at the Custom House Quay and other quays below Butt Br by a fleet of Liffey barges (204.09; cf 549.34); in the days of steam barges, their stacks were hinged for passing under the Liffey brs (136.22). Motto: "Guinness is Good for You." John Joyce thought JJ should take a clerk's job with *G*'s (190.17, 299.30).

    9.01   Awful Grimmest Sunshat Cromwelly. Looted
    16.31   Ghinees hies good for you
    29.04   the height of Brewster's chimpney
    71.04   flight of his wild guineese
    90.13   Guinney's Gap
    99.03   no concern of the Guinnesses
    106.30 *Allfor Guineas, Sounds and Compliments Libidous*
    136.22 puffing...to new customs, doffing...to every breach
    140.01 not Benjamin's Lea

140.11	most expensive brewing industry in the world
140.32	Irish in my east hand and a James's Gate in my west
190.17	Guinness's, may I remind, were just agulp for you
204.09	bulgic porterhouse barge
258.08	on our jambses, in his gaits
?285.L2	*Arthurgink's hussies and Everguin's men*
299.30	Ever thought about Guinness's?
307.01	Visit to Guinness' Brewery
309.01	concern of the Guinnesses
325.04	Art thou gainous sense uncompetite! Limited.
333.17	jammesons...juinnesses
345.22	*power...another guidness*
361.05	Shares in guineases!
373.25	Broree aboo! Run him a johnsgate down jameseslane
382.03	Guiness's or Phoenix brewery stout it was
407.04	a bottle of ardilaun
414.12	Mooseyeare Goonness's...barrels
420.22	B.L. Guineys, esqueer
443.32	with a good job and pension in Buinness's
510.13	from Gunner Shotland to Guinness Scenography
521.14	either Jones's lame or Jamesy's gait
549.34	Noeh Guinnass...his bargeness
565.10	guineeser...beutel of staub
593.17	genghis is ghoon for you

GUJARAT (GUJRAT). State, NW Ind; also the larger area of Gujarati-speaking Hindus. In 1849, Lord Gough (see *Phoenix Park: Gough Statue*) crushed the Sikh rebellion in the battle of *G*, city now in Pakistan, making possible Brit annexation of the Punjab (qv).

| ?493.13 | mayarannies...rawjaws...in his gulughurutty |
| 498.17 | paunchjab...gougerotty |

GULF STREAM. The great current of warm tropical water which flows N past Florida and the E coast of N Amer, and turns E to keep Ire green.

| 319.27 | trombsathletic [transatlantic] like the marousers of the gulpstroom |
| 547.32 | malestream in shegulf |

GWALIOR. Town, Madhya Pradesh state, N cen Ind; overlooked by Port of *G*, med Hindu fort lost to Brit in Mahratta Wars.

| 8.20 | bangkok's best and goliar's goloshes |

H

HADES. In Gk myth, the abode of departed spirits; a place of gloom, but not necessarily a place of punishment. The 6th chap of *U* – Paddy Dignam's funeral in Glasnevin Cem – is the "Hades" chap, corresponding to Odysseus's descent into *H* in Book XI of the *Odyssey* (229.13).

| 183.35 | fresh horrors from Hades |
| 229.13 | Had Days |

289.14   Bill Hayses's...Ellishly Haught's
?366.27   Houtes, Blymey and Torrenation
547.29   Heaven...Heydays

HAGUE, THE.   City, seat of Dutch govt, SW Neth. Meeting place of International
Peace Conferences, 1899, 1907. The Palace of Peace (1913) has housed the Permanent Court of Arbitration (the "Hague Tribunal") and its successors (?54.10). Baruch
Spinoza, for whom space ("extension") was the physical aspect of God, lived in The
H (150.08).
54.10   its bleak and bronze portal of your Casaconcordia
150.08   spinosis an extension lecturer on The Ague...Dr's Het Ubeleeft
?223.16   Copenhague-Marengo
367.05   With a haygue for a halt on a pouncefoot panse
436.30   Hill or hollow, Hull or Hague

HALFMOON AND SEVEN STARS, THE   (14/35).   Peter's *Dub Fragments* (154)
refers to this as an 18th-cent shop in Francis St where "Irish poplin was to be had."
The same passage also mentions paduasoys and other goods at the Blackamoor's Head
(qv) and cherry-derries (no shop mentioned for these).
59.01   in her cherryderry padouasoys, girdle and braces by the Halfmoon
and Seven Stars

HALLEY'S COMET.   The Brit astronomer Edmund Halley (1656-1742) observed
the comet of 1682, in 1704 calculated that it was identical with comets of 1531,
1607, and 1682, and accurately predicted its return in 1758. Its period is about 76
years.
54.08   like sixes and seventies as eversure as Halley's comet

HAMBLEDON.   Town, Surrey, Eng, where one of the earliest and most famous
cricket clubs met, 1750-1791. At that time all cricketers were gentlemen (586.11).
?483.36   crouched low entering humble down
584.18   treading her hump and hambledown
586.11   humbledown jungleman

HAMBURG.   City and seaport, W Ger, on the Elbe R. The Sankt Pauli dist is the
waterfront area, notorious for its sailors' bars and bordellos. See also *Bad Homburg*.
?117.24   Pieter's in Nieuw Amsteldam and Paoli's where the poules go
?560.07   The old humburgh...head

HAMMAM   (15/34).   The Hammam Hotel and Turkish Baths (*humoun*, Pers "sweat-
ing bath") was at 11-12 Upr Sackville St. In London, a 17th-cent Turkish Bath called
Hummums gave its name to the hotel later built on its site at Covent Garden.
?205.30   hamman now cheekmee
?416.02   Hummum

HAMMERFEST.   Nor city and port for Arctic sealing and whaling fleets; N-most
city in Eur.
46.13   hooker of that hammerfast viking

HAMMERSMITH.   (1) Dist, W London, N of Thames R. The famous St Paul's Sch
moved to H from the precincts of St Paul's Cath in 1884.   (2) H Pl (17/32), old
name for the S section of Pembroke Rd, from its intersection with Northumberland
Rd to Ballsbridge.
43.05   an aged hammersmith who had some chisellers by the hand [*chiselur*,
Dub slang for "child"]

HANGING TOWER   (15/33).   In the anc walls of Dub SE of Newgate, near intersection of Back Lane and High St.
    534.34   Eristocras till Hanging Tower!

HANKOW.   City and port, E cen China, on N bank of Yangtsze R; commercial city
after 1861, burned in Revolution in 1911, captured by Nationalists Dec 1926. *H* was
not involved in the Boxer Rebellion of 1900 (which was mainly in Peking and Tien-
tsin). Neither was Sun Yat-sen, although he was the leader of the 1911-12 Revolution
which overthrew the Manchus.
    89.36   But, why this hankowchaff...son-yet-sun...buxers

HAPI.   Egyptian name of Nile R (qv), and also name of ape-headed god.
    416.01   Heppy's hevn shall flurrish

HARBOURSTOWN.   Tnld, par of Stamullin, bar of Upr Duleek, Co Meath.
    622.34   Harbourstown

HARCOURT ST RAILWAY.   Officially the "Dublin and South-Eastern Railway,"
its terminus (now a warehouse) was in *H* St at Adelaide Rd (15/32). The rlwy ran to
Bray through the Wicklow hills.
    236.22   along that hercourt strayed reelway

HARDANGER FJORD.   Inlet of N Sea on SW coast of Nor.
    579.28   brought Thawland within Har danger

HARDWICKE ST   (15/35).   Parallels Upr Dorset St, ending at St George's Ch in
Hardwicke Pl. The Joyces lived at No 29 (now demolished) in 1894.
    420.19   29 Hardware Saint

HARLEM (HAARLEM).   City, 12 mi W of Amsterdam, W Neth.
    577.22   to Goerz from Harleem

HARLOCKSTOWN.   Tnld, par and bar of Ratoath, Co Meath.
    97.07   Horlockstown

HAROLD'S CROSS   (14/31).   S Dub dist, S of Grand Canal; site of Mt Jerome
Cem (Prot).
    252.11   Saint Jerome of the Harlots' Curse
    ?570.05   forain dances and crosshurdles and dollmanovers
    574.15   in the name of Wieldhelm, Hurls Cross

HARRODS LTD.   Dept store in Brompton Rd, London; founded 1848.
    127.11   outharrods against barkers
    159.15   by hopeharrods
    536.35   Harrod's be the naun

HARROGATE.   City and resort N of Leeds, Yorks; noted for its sulphur spring,
once recommended for anemia.
    ?149.32   sorrogate...harrogate and arrogate

HARROW-ON-THE-HILL.   NW London suburb; highest elevation in Co of Middlesex; known particularly for Harrow Sch, whose most spectacular sinner was Byron.
    The ref is combined with the "harrowing of hell," the descent of Jesus into Hell
btwn Good Fri and Easter Sun to redeem the righteous who died BC.
    355.16   the Hersy Hunt they harrow the hill

HASTINGS.   Town, E Sussex, S Eng; scene of battle 14 Oct 1066, in which Normans under Wm the Conqueror defeated Saxons under King Harold. Sir Arthur Welles-

ley, Duke of Wellington, was appointed to the Brigade at Hastings after his Ind campaigns.

9.02   This is the jinnies' hastings dispatch for to irrigate the Willingdone

30.22   Harold...hasting to the forecourts of his public...[31.14] William the Conk

HATTERAS, CAPE.   Promontory and isl on coast of N Carolina, US, notorious for dangerous seas.

?10.16   madrashattaras

HAUSSMANN, BOULEVARD.   Paris blvd, major artery E of Place de l'Étoile. Baron Haussmann was a 19th-cent city planner of Paris, laying out sts, parks, brs, etc.

129.16   but a no street hausmann when allphannd

205.35   This is the Hausman all paven and stoned

HAVRE, LE.   Seaport, Seine-Maritime Dept, N Fr, on Eng Channel, N side of Seine estuary.

416.31   come to hevre...gone to hull

HAWARDEN.   Town, Flintshire (now Clwyd), N Wales; site of Gladstone's country home, Castle *H*. Gladstone retired and died there. His "*H* Manifesto" of 1885 announced his partial support of Parnell's demand for Ir independence.

242.33   she not swop her eckcot hjem for Howarden's Castle, Englandwales

515.35   You were ever the gentle poet, dove from Haywarden

HAWKINS ST   (16/34).   Btwn Burgh Quay and D'Olier St. See *Leinster Market*.

34.09   Roche Haddocks off Hawkins Street

HAYES, CONYNGHAM, ROBINSON.   Dub chemists and chain of pharmacies, at 12 Grafton St (15/33) and other locations.

434.12   Hayes, Conyngham and Erobinson

HAY HOTEL   (15/34).   In Cavendish Row, around the turn of the cent.

?514.15   there is no hay ["A"] in Eccles's hostel

HAZELHATCH.   House and demesne, 5 mi W of Clondalkin, 2 mi SE of Celbridge, on Gt Southern and Western Rlwy and Grand Canal, but not on Liffey (201.25). Thomas F Kelley, an Amer millionaire who lived in Celbridge (qv), subsidized Padraic Colum. JJ walked from Cabra to Celbridge (and back) to ask for some support too, but wasn't even admitted. "The Holy Office" on Colum: "Or him who plays the ragged patch/To millionaires in Hazelhatch."

129.09   was hatched at Cellbridge but ejoculated abrood

201.25   Well, now comes the hazelhatchery part. After Clondalkin the King's Inns

HEARTS OF OAK.   Brit life assurance co; it did not have offices in Dub in JJ's time. Also the name of 18th-cent Ir rural patriotic secret soc, like the Ribbonmen, but the "Oakboys" (cf 385.09) don't seem to be included in the allusion.

545.36   Hearts of Oak, may ye root to piece!

577.22   to Hearths of Oak from Skittish Widdas

HEATHTOWN.   Tnld, par of Clonalvy, bar of Upr Duleek, Co Meath.

622.34   Heathtown

HEBRIDES.   Aka Western Isles, isls in Atlantic O, W of Scot. The Inner *H* includes Iona (see sep listing), Mull (462.05), Islay (462.15), Staffa (see *Fingal's Cave*) (462.05),

Jura (?536.33), Skye (424.04), Soay (200.13), and Eigg. The "Singing Sands" (548.03), a well-known beach on the N side of Eigg, are so-called because they make a sibilant sound when walked on.

The Hebrides, Mendelssohn's overture, was inspired by Fingal's Cave on Staffa (462.05, 548.03). Macpherson's *Temora* (VIII, 320) refers to "I-mor" (547.35) as one of the *H.*

200.13	soay and soan
263.14	Castilian-Emeratic-Hebridian
424.04	demonican skyterrier
462.05	Staffetta mullified with creams of hourmony
462.15	gullaby, me poor Isley
?536.33	my jurats
547.35	igone, imorgans
548.03	the singing sands for herbrides' music

HEIDELBERG.   City, W Ger, on Neckar R. The bones of anc "*H* Man" were found in the Mauer Sands near *H* in 1907.

18.23	meandertale...old Heidenburgh
37.01	hypertituitary type of Heidelberg mannleich cavern ethics

HEJAZ.   The coastal prov of Saudi Arabia along the Red Sea from the Gulf of Aqaba to Yemen; contains the sacred cities of Mecca and Medina.

533.26	while still to hedjeskool...Caulofat's bed
?571.10	by hedjes of maiden ferm

HEKLA, MT.   Volcano, SW Iceland; Iceland's best-known volcanic mt, it had erupted 18 times in recorded hist through the 19th cent.

494.08	in erupting, hecklar!

HELGOLAND.   Isl in N Sea off W coast of W Ger, attached to the N Frisian Isls (see *Frisia*); Dan possession to 1807, now Ger. Ibsen play: *The Vikings of Helgoland.* *H* Bucht (or Bight) is the arm of N Sea SE of *H*, the scene of battle 28 Aug 1914 btwn Brit and Ger navies.

388.19	the Frankish floot...from Hedalgoland, round about the freebutter year

HELIOPOLIS.   Gk name ("City of the Sun") of 3 anc cities: (1) Bibl *On*, Egyptian *Annu*; now ruins 6 mi NE of Cairo; dedicated to worship of Sun-god, Ra (or Aton); temple was a depository for hist records, where priests established the authorized version of the *Book of the Dead.* Cleopatra's Needles (qv) originated here.
(2) Anc Egyptian city, destroyed 5000 BC, R bank of Nile, 15 mi S of Cairo.
(3) Anc name of Baalbek, E Lebanon; in anc times a Syrian city, later a Roman colony, dedicated to worship of semitic sun-god Baal, and notorious for its licentiousness.

In *FW*, *H* is also Dub. Timothy Healy was the first and last Ir Gov-Gen under the Treaty of 1921; "Healiopolis" is a not entirely friendly nickname for Dub. When Healy occupied it, the Vice-Regal Lodge in Phoenix Park (qv) was nicknamed "Uncle Tim's Cabin" by Dubliners.

24.18	you'd only lose yourself in Healiopolis now
?143.03	to be on anew
311.12	comer forth from Anow...from Thenanow
530.16	under the noses of the Heliopolitan constabulary
594.08	Even unto Heliotropolis, the castellated, the enchanting
609.16	Brancherds at: Bullbeck, Oldboof...

HELL.   See *Amenta, Erebus, Gehenna, Hades, Inferno, Sheol, Tartarus, Tophet, Unterwelt*; and *"Hell."*

The "harrowing of Hell" (355.16) was Jesus' descent into *H* btwn crucifixion and resurrection to redeem the righteous who died BC. Oliver Cromwell ordered the propertied Irish of E Ire to resettle W of the Shannon R: they could choose btwn going "to Hell or Connacht" (71.29, 525.06).

29.21	in a hull of a wherry
71.29	*Go to Hellena...Connies*
107.36	who in hallhagal
108.26	Siam, Hell or Tophet
116.23	punch hell's hate into his twin nicky
117.06	tell hell's well
190.02	O hell, here comes our funeral!
208.27	Hellsbells, I'm sorry I missed her!
225.24	Hellfeuersteyn
228.06	hells where
231.21	Holihowlsballs
234.04	looked like bruddy Hal
239.33	hellabelow...Helldsdend, whelldselse
245.25	hellpelhullpulthebell
258.02	Hlls vlls
289.14	Ellishly Haught's
299.F1	Hen's bens, are we soddy we missiled her?
323.23	hell of a hull of a hill
326.12	hellsinky of the howtheners
349.26	Hll
354.12	*too foul for hell* [*Teufel*, Ger "devil"]
355.16	the Hersy Hunt they harrow the hill
393.28	come out to hell
416.32	to hull with the poop
432.15	hell in tunnels
449.27	till heoll's hoerrisings
454.33	our snug eternal retribution's reward (the scorchhouse)
502.20	hellstohns
518.35	houlish like Hull hopen for christmians
519.01	hellish like engels
520.20	hell's flutes
525.06	Tallhell and Barbados wi ye
535.28	lived true thousand hells
609.18	Hillewille and Wallhall

"HELL" (15/34).   The passage leading from Christchurch Cath to the old Four Courts, near the present SW cor of Fishamble St, was widely known as "Hell," prob from a 17th-cent wine cellar; it was obliterated by the widening of Fishamble St. An image over the gate was supposed to represent the devil. An 18th-cent advt cited by J T Gilbert and others: "To be let, furnished apartments in *Hell*. N.B. They are well suited to a lawyer." Robert Burns, "Death and Doctor Hornbook": "It is just as true as the Deil's in Hell,/Or Dublin city." Peter's *Dublin Fragments*, on "Taverns," notes "The Parrot" (qv) was in "Hell" (63.23).

63.23	the Parrot in Hell
535.05	Gate of Hal

HELLESPONT.   Anc name of Dardanelles, the narrow strait btwn Eur and Turkey-in-Asia; with the Sea of Marmara and the Bosporus (qqv) it connects the Medit with the Black Sea. Leander (203.13) swam it to see Hero (328.19).

135.17   his birthspot lies beyond the herospont [+ O'Connell Br]
328.19   the breath of Huppy Hullespond swumped...mallymedears'
583.03   Poor little tartanelle...the strait's she's in

HELL FIRE CLUB.   Clubs of this name were drinking and gambling assns of rake-hells, chiefly in early 18th-cent London. In Dub, the 18th-cent *HFC* met at the Eagle Tav in Cork Hill, later at Daly's on College Green. A structure on Mountpelier Hill near Lough Bray, Co Wicklow, has trad been pointed out (on very little authority) as a site of *HFC* revels. The bldg was erected in 1725 as a res by Wm Conolly (?457.01), Speaker of the Ir House of Commons.

409.23   shuffled hands...from the Headfire Clump
436.29   meeth...Kellsfrieclub
?457.01   old Con Connolly's residence
514.09   a hellfire club kicked out
552.27   slub out her hellfire

HELSINKI.   Seaport, and cap of Fin since 1812; Swed, *Helsingfors.* The harb is pro-tected by Sveaborg fortress, on one of the isles at entrance to the harb.

326.12   out of the hellsinky of the howtheners
?552.16   arcane celestials to Sweatenburgs Welhell [+ Emanuel Swedenborg]

HENGLER'S CIRCUS (15/34).   Bldgs on E side of Rutland (now Parnell) Sq (around the cor from Gt Denmark St); used temporarily as GPO when Sackville St bldg was badly damaged in 1916. Various Brit cities had a *HC*; in London it was in Argyll St, on the site on which the Palladium was built in 1940.

307.08   Hengler's Circus Entertainment
529.34   coowner of a hengster's circus near North Great Denmark Street

HENLEY.   City, on Thames R, 35 mi W of London; site since 1839 of the annual *H* Royal Regatta, incl (since 1844) the Diamond Sculls for single scullers.

464.08   shaved his rough diamond skull for him
498.14   his diamondskulled granddaucher

HENRIETTA ST (15/34).   Leads to the King's Inns, the law sch and law library of Dub.

447.08   vocational scholars...for Henrietta's sake..life of jewries

HEYTESBURY ST (15/32).   S part of main N-S thoroughfare btwn St Patrick's Cath and SCR. Hatch St is only a few blocks to the E, btwn Harcourt and Leeson Sts.

80.33   Hatchettsbury Road
578.26   Hatesbury's Hatch

HICKEY'S.   (1) Peter's *Dublin Fragments* (155) mentions Noah Hickey's 18th-cent confectionery shop "The Golden Ring" in the same context as such Dub delights as "Turkey coffee and orange shrub."

43.09   tassing Turkey Coffee and orange shrub in tickeyes door

(2) Michael Hickey, bookseller, 8 Bachelor's Walk (at the end of the Wellington or Metal Br) (15/34). In "The Dead," Gabriel is described as frequenting it.

286.10   book...to be hacked at Hickey's, hucksler, Wellington's Iron Bridge

HILLBOROUGH.   After a drinking bout at Bidford, Shakespeare refused to return next day with his friends, saying: "Piping Pebworth, Dancing Marston, Haunted Hillborough, Hungry Grafton, Dadgeing Exhall, Papist Wicksford, Beggarly Broom, and Drunken Bidford" (E K Chambers, *William Shakespeare*, II, 292). These are all places within 12 mi of Stratford-on-Avon.

H is also a town in Co Down, near Cromore Cas.

    340.34   from Piping Pubwirth to Haunted Hillborough

HILL 60.   In WW I, an important feature of the Ypres salient, SE of Ypres, 8 mi N of Armentières. Changed hands many times in 1st (Oct-Nov '14) and 2nd (Apr '15) Battles of Ypres (not 3rd).

    7.33   this belles' alliance beyind Ill Sixty, ollollowed ill!

HIMALAYA MOUNTAINS.   Mt system, S Asia. Name from Sans *hima*, "snow," and *alaya*, "abode."

    5.01   the himals and all
    329.32   Cymylaya Mountains
    502.05   In hilly-and-even zimalayars
    ?627.03   Imlamaya

HINDUSTAN.   The Pers name of Ind, used variously to describe either the entire Ind penin, or the smaller area in the upr basin of the Ganges R. Also the Hindustani dialect.

    492.17   I hindustand

HIPPO.   Roman Afr city, diocesan city (396-430 AD) of St Augustine, who as a determinist didn't believe in accidents. Now ruins just S of Bône, Algeria.

    38.30   accident...Ecclectiastes of Hippo

HODGES FIGGIS AND CO.   Publishers and booksellers, in JJ's day at 104 Grafton St; now at Stephen Court and 6 Dawson St.

    347.19   Hajizfijjiz

HOEY'S COURT (15/33).   Btwn Werburgh St and Castle St; a block of 17-cent houses, now demolished, erected by Sir John Hoey. Jonathan Swift was born in No 9, 30 Nov 1667.

An older Hoey's Court was a tennis court at the rear of the "Pyed House" on E side of Winetavern St (15/34). Yet a third, still in existence, is off S Townsend St (16/34).

    ?5.34   the hoyse
    563.27   the godolphinglad in the Hoy's Court

HOGGEN GREEN (15/34).   The old name of College Green (qv), E of Dame St. The name was from Norse *hauge*, "mound," ie, the little hill of the Thing Mote (qv) which stood just to the S. The ch of St Mary del Hogges was built *ca* 1147.

    292.10   young catholick throats on Huggin Green
    386.26   James H. Tickell, the jaypee, off Hoggin Green
    543.17   and from Huggin Pleaze to William Inglis his house [ie, from College
              Green W on Dame St toward the Castle]

HOG HILL (HOGGES HILL) (15/33).   The old name of St Andrew St (S of College Green). The name survived into the 18th cent, when the st was for a while called Church St, and from *ca* 1772 St Andrew St. See *Hoggen Green*.

    568.22   hoghill

HOLMPATRICK.   (1) Par in bar of E Balrothery, Co Dub; contains the town of Skerries.   (2) St Patrick's Isl, off Skerries, Co Dub, was earlier called Holm Patrick,

alleged to be the res of Ire's patron saint. See *Census* for Lady Holmpatrick.
> ?31.31   the roadside tree the lady Holmpatrick planted

HOLY LAMB, THE   (14/33).   18th-cent tav in the old Corn Market, acc to Peter's
Dublin Fragments (96).
> 63.24   the Holy Lamb

HOME'S HOTEL   (14/34).   19th-cent hotel on Usher's Quay, well-known and fashionable around the middle of the cent.
> ?586.18   Here is a homelet not a hothel

HONG KONG   (HONGKONG).   Brit crown colony and trading port, SE China.
Consists of *HK* Isl, Kowloon Penin, and the New Territories, an enclave of Kwang-
tung prov, China.
"Hongkong and so long" (446.11) was a snappy repartee in the early 20th cent.
> 25.29   sung king or hung king
> 119.25   siangchang hongkong sansheneul
> 306.06   Betwixt me and thee hung cong
> ?374.34   Hung Chung Egglyfella
> 446.11   hong, kong, and so gong
> 457.07   Hungkung! Me anger's suaged! Hangkang!

HONOLULU.   Seaport city, isl of Oahu, Hawaii, US, in N Pacific O; royal res (1803-
11) of Kamehameha the Great.
> 353.28   *Hullulullu*

HOOGHLY (HUGLI) RIVER.   W channel of Ganges R, W Bengal, NE Ind, and a
town and dist in Bengal near Calcutta.
> 207.33   her hoogly igloo
> 318.12   Ethna Prettyplume, Hooghly Spaight ["spate": flood or inundation]

HOOK HEAD (THE HOOK).   Promontory with lighthouse at E entrance to Waterford Harb. Crook (qv) is on the opp side of the harb.
> 245.08   warnerforth's hookercrookers
> 549.19   Wexterford's hook and crook lights

HOPE BROTHERS.   London outfitters, in Regent St.
> 159.15   hopeharrods
> ?461.07   Hope Bros., Faith Street, Charity Corner

HOPKINS AND HOPKINS   (15/34).   1 Lwr Sackville (now O'Connell) St; gold-
smiths, jewellers, and watchmakers.
> 26.02   But as Hopkins and Hopkins puts it

HORN AND HOUND.   Eng hunting journal, irreverently nicknamed the "Bugle and
Bitch."
> 379.04   with Bugle and the Bitch pairsadrawsing

HORNIMAN MUSEUM.   Hist mus with gardens, opened 1901, occupying summit
of hill near Lordship Lane Sta in Dulwich, S London. JJ may conceivably have been
interested in its collection of old musical instruments, but *FW* only sniggers at the
name. For the Miss Horniman who was a patron of the Abbey Theatre, see *Census*.
> 61.23   your two velvetthighs up Horniman's Hill

HORROCKS, LTD.   Textile firm (sheets, towels, etc) in Lancs, Eng.
> 326.01   Horrocks Toler

491.32   resting between horrockses' sheets

HORSEPASS BRIDGE.   Before the Liffey was dammed to form the Blessington Reservoir, *H* Br (built 1820, replacing earlier br) spanned *H* Ford, 4 mi S of Blessington.
203.02   she'd lave Kilbride and go foaming under Horsepass bridge

HOSPICE FOR THE DYING   (14/32).   In Harold's Cross, adjacent to Mt Jerome Cem.
24.04   auspice for the living
392.07   housepays for the daying
514.25   the Auspice for the Living, Bonnybrook
555.18   under all the auspices

HOSPITAL FOR INCURABLES   (16/34, later 17/31).   Founded 1744 by the Charitable Musical Soc led by Garrett Wellesley (41.01), Lord Mornington. Orig in Fleet St, it moved in 1753 to Lazy (Lazar's) Hill (now Townsend St), then in 1792 exchanged premises with the Lock Hosp in Donnybrook Rd, where it continued throughout the 19th cent.
41.01   from these incurable welleslays...uncarable wellasdays...Lazar
197.25   and the rest of incurables and the last of immurables

HOUSE OF BLAZES, THE   (15/34).   17th-cent tav on Aston's Quay, acc to Peter's *Dublin Fragments* (93).
63.23   the House of Blazes

HOUSE OF COMMONS.   Until the Act of Union in 1801, Ire had its own House of Commons in Parliament Ho on College Green. Eamon DeValera was sometimes called "the long fellow"; the elected house of the Ir nationalists (from 1918), later of the Ir Free State and the Rep of Ire, was the Dáil. "*H* of *C*" was slang for "privy" (Grose, *Dictionary*).
261.F2   Longfellow's Lodgings, House of Comments III, Cake Walk
380.07   melumps and mumpos of the hoose uncommons

HOUSE OF THE SEVEN GABLES, THE.   In Nathaniel Hawthorne's novel of this name (1851), the house is occupied by the long-suffering Hepzibah Pyncheon, who is reduced to opening a shop.
100.16   from the seventh gable of our...buttertower

HOWITT MOUNTAINS.   Mt range in the Kimberley Dist of W Australia; in the area of the Kimberley Goldfields.
?15.24   that saying is as old as the howitts

HOWTH.   Aka *H* Head, the hilly promontory NE of Dub which forms the N boundary of Dub Bay; connected to the mainland by the "neck" or isthmus of Sutton (qv). In *FW* it is the head of the sleeping giant Finn MacCool, whose body stretches across the landscape of Dub N of the Liffey to his toes beyond Phoenix Park.
Names: Howth (Hofda, Houete, Howeth) from *hoved*, Dan "head." The anc name was Ben Edar (*Beinn Éadair*, Ir "Eadar's Peak). Ptolemy's map shows it as an isl called Edri Deserta (Gk, *Edrou Heremos*), "Desert of Edar" (309.09, ?505.03). JJ mentions (*Letters* I, 247) the belief of "old geographers" that it was an isl (17.18).
In 1177, Armoricus (Armory or Almeric) Tristram from Brittany (qv) defeated the Dan inhabitants at Evora on the N side of *H*; since the battle was on St Lawrence's Day (10 Aug), he thereafter assumed the name of St Lawrence, and the St Lawrence family were Lords of *H* into the present cent; the male line ended in 1909 with the death of the 30th Baron.

Early in the 19th cent, *H* harb on the N side was developed as a major port, and it became the mail packet sta for vessels from Holyhead, Wales in 1809; but the harb silted up swiftly and irretrievably, and port functions were transferred to Dun Laoghaire, where they remain. With the building of a rail line from Amiens St Sta, and later of a tram line, *H* became a favorite Dub resort for the likes of Molly and Leopold Bloom; in her dying soliloquy Anna Livia imagines an expedition to *H* (622.20–624.26).

I. Howth Place-Names

BAILEY LIGHTHOUSE.   See sep listing.

BALSCADDEN BAY (29/39).   Bathing beach E of harb on N side of *H*.

    326.34   from Ballscodden easthmost till Thyrston's Lickslip

BLACK LINN (28/27).   The highest (560 ft) point of *H*. Acc to Weston St J Joyce (336), on clear days the mts of Wales can be seen from *BL*.

    17.12   sutton...did Brian d'of Linn [*dubh*, Ir "black"]

    ?447.16   till the first glimpse of Wales

    ?626.33   As duv herself div. Inn this linn

DOLDRUM BAY (28/36).   SE shore of *H*, btwn Bailey Lighthouse and Drumleck Pt; lined with bluffs, not a landing-place.

    51.34   the southeast bluffs of the stranger stepshore...amid the devil's one
          duldrum

DRUMLECK POINT (28/36).   S tip of *H*.

    623.26   heathery benn...Out from Drumleek

DUNCRIFFAN (29/36).   SE promontory, on which the Bailey Lighthouse (qv) stands. Criffan (*Crimthann*) was an Ir king, *ca* 5th cent. The circumvallation of the fort (*dun*) attributed to him was visible until the present lighthouse was erected, 1814.

    622.20   Les go dutc to Danegreven, nos?

EVORA (28/39).   The Br of *E* crossed a small stream near the present rlwy sta, known as the "Bloody Stream" after the conjectural battle of 1177 in which Armoricus Tristram is supposed to have conquered *H*. (*E* is also a seaport in Port in which the insurgent population was massacred by the Fr in the Peninsular War.)

    ?539.22   mean straits male with evorage fimmel

    623.27   It was there Evora told me I had best

HOWTH CASTLE (27/38–39).   On the N slopes of *H* and W of the vill, the present cas was built 1564 and has been greatly altered and extended. Acc to legend, the pirate-queen Grace O'Malley (*Gráinne Ní Mháille*) of Clare I in W Ire abducted the young heir of the St Lawrences in revenge for finding the cas gate closed at dinner time. She returned him on the promise that *HC* would forevermore be hospitable to the traveler (the story, much embroidered, is at *FW* 21.05–23.15), and it is said that to this day an extra place is always set at the St Lawrence table (623.06–.07).

The gardens and demesne, which includes the ruins of 16th-cent Corr Cas, are especially noted for their rhododendrons (*U* 767/782).

    3.03   Howth Castle and Environs

    12.35   the macroborg of Holdhard [*borg*, Dan "castle"]

    21.13   his homerigh, castle and earthenhouse

    22.34   his three shuttoned castles

    135.18   yldist kiosk on the pleninsula...unguest hostel

    135.29   Hewitt Castello...Rhoda Dundrums

    ?414.04   Mr van Howten of Tredcastles

    623.19   It's in the castles air

NOSE OF HOWTH (30/38).   The NE tip of *H*.

    577.11   nazil hose and river mouth

    624.26   Even in Houlth's nose

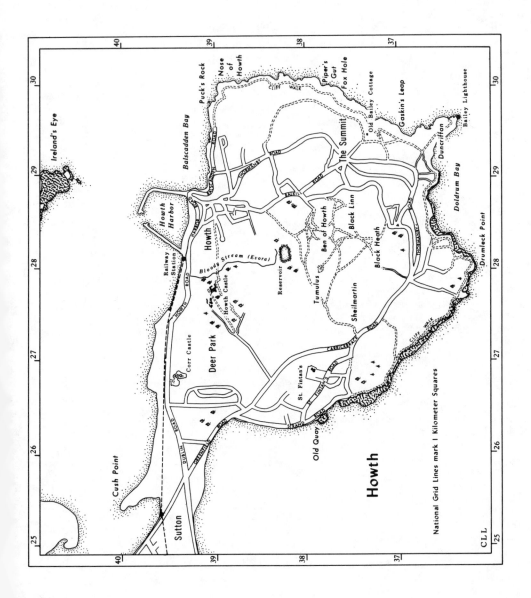

Ireland's Eye

Cush Point

Sutton

Howth Harbor

Railway Station

Balscadden Bay

Puck's Rock

Nose of Howth

Piper's Gut

Fox Hole

Old Bailey Cottage

Gaskin's Leap

Bailey Lighthouse

Duncriffan

Doldrum Bay

Drumleck Point

The Summit

Black Linn

Black Heath

Ben of Howth

Howth

Bloody Stream (Evora)

Reservoir

Howth Castle

Tumulus

Sheilmartin

Corr Castle

Deer Park

St. Fintan's

Old Quay

Dublin Road

Howth Road

Greenfield Road

Carrickbrack Road

Thormanby Road

Balkill Road

Kilrock Road

Howth

National Grid Lines mark 1 Kilometer Squares

CLL

ST FINTAN'S (26/37).   A tiny 9th-cent oratory (ruins) in W part of *H*; also *St F's* Rd.

624.18   For the loves of sinfintins!

SHEILMARTIN (Shelmartin) (28/37).   Hill in cen *H*, 2nd in height (550 ft) to Black Linn. *Siol-Martin*, Ir "seed (posterity) of Martin."

624.21   Blessed shield Martin!

SPECIES SLOPE (28/37).   Together with The Summit, one of the best views from *H*.

?318.27   To slope through heather till the foot

SUMMIT, THE (29/37).   Not the highest point of *H*, but one of the best-known views; the intersection of the main Thormanby Rd with Balkill and Bailey Green Rds, in SE area of *H*.

624.11   Scale the summit!

II.   Howth References:

3.03	Howth Castle and Environs	253.32	Lucanhof
3.20	the humptyhillhead of humself	264.05	Horn of Heatthen
4.05	Hoodie Head	276.26	hoodie hearsemen
4.11	how hoth sprowled	287.09	howlth
4.36	most eyeful hoyth entowerly	309.09	Etheria Deserta
6.33	baronoath	310.06	howdrocephalous
6.34	Roundthehead	312.19	Cape of Good Howthe
7.28	Benn Heather	315.30	a penincular fraimd of mind
7.30	Whooth	317.32	promonitory...headth of hosth
10.27	houthse of a month and one windies	324.20	Hoved politymester
		326.13	howtheners
12.35	macroborg of Holdhard	326.18	Edar
15.24	howitts	340.06	*Hoofd Ribeiro*
17.18	this albutisle	?346.26	Thingman placeyear howed
27.27	Be nayther angst	346.31	*his goodsforseeking hoarth*
30.11	Hofed-ben-Edar	357.32	howthern folleys
36.26	make my hoath	?359.25	a hofdking or a hoovthing
42.18	col de Houdo humps	?383.15	Overhoved
53.12	how on the owther	385.33	his crusted hoed
73.31	Howth	394.28	Earl Hoovedsoon's
?77.21	hoofd	433.12	hog of the howth
?81.12	howe's	?448.02	hoyth of number eleven
81.16	traums halt (Beneathere! Benathere!)	448.18	Brayhowth...the Bull Bailey
		452.11	Hothelizod
106.33	*Manorlord Hoved*	497.07	houthhunters
116.15	oldowth guns	506.19	capocapo promontory
126.15	cap onto the esker of his hooth	514.23	A Little Bit of Heaven Howth
128.23	hoved by	525.24	*between Howth and Humbermouth*
129.24	Quayhowth		
130.33	eorl of Hoed	535.26	Old Whitehowth...poor whiteoath
?131.07	hoveth chieftains evrywehr	?536.14	haute white toff's
135.29	Hewitt Castello...from Rhoda Dundrums	538.34	oathhead
		540.17	the hold of my capt...till the mortification
175.15	*from on Hoath*		
197.03	howeth	?556.23	nowth upon nacht
223.29	hoothed fireshield	560.18	begraved beneadher
242.05	howthold of nummer seven	588.16	hofd a-hooded

594.28	Edar's chuckal humuristic	623.06	a proper old promnentory
595.03	Hill of Hafid	623.10	say hoothoothoo
607.27	to the hothehill	623.25	the heathery benn
619.12	himp of holth	624.26	Houlth's nose
619.25	man of the hooths		

HULL.   Aka Kingston-upon-Hull; city, E Riding, Yorks, N Eng, on Humber and *H* Rivs.

   29.21   in a hull of a wherry
 245.25   hellpelhullpulthebell
 416.32   to hevre...to hull with the poop
 436.30   Hill or hollow, Hull or Hague!
 518.35   Hull hopen for christmians

HUMBER RIVER.   Estuary on E coast of Eng, formed by confluence of Ouse and Trent Rivs 8 mi E of Goole. Flows into North Sea.

 198.29   old Humber
 525.25   *wet lissy between Howth and Humbermouth*

HUME ST   (16/33).   A single, once-elegant Georgian block btwn Stephen's Green, N, and Ely Place (which was once called Hume Row). Its ladies would have gone to Anglican, not RC, mass.

  43.01   massgoing ladies from Hume Street in their chairs
?481.21   re humeplace of Chivitats Ei

HUMPHREYSTOWN.   Tnld, par of Boystown, bar of Talbotstown, Co Wicklow. The name is old; it appears on Petty's 1685 map of Co Wicklow. "Humphreystown" is for *FW* a kenning for Dub and/or Chapelizod: HCE's town.

?270.13   Merry Mustard Frothblowers of Humphreystown Associations

HUNGARY.   Rep, form kingdom, cen Eur; once the terr of the Magyars (*ca* 893-901), later part of the "dual monarchy" of Austria-Hungary (1867-1918). Ger, *Ungarn*; Russ, *Vengerskey*; Lat, *Pannonia*; Hung, *Magyar*.

    Arthur Griffith, the founder of Sinn Féin, saw a close analogy btwn Ire's relation to Brit and *H*'s to Austria; his book *The Resurrection of Hungary* (1904) defended the "Hungarian policy," ie, a dual monarchy, which became the policy of Sinn Féin and led to the Treaty of 1921.

    St Margaret of *H* (460.26), daughter of King Bela IV (13th cent), built a convent on the (now) Margaret Isl in the Danube R at Budapest. *FW* often conflates *H* with Bartholomew Vanhomrigh (see *Census*), and esp Vanhomrigh's house (qv): 406.30, 535.02, 623.16. The Hung lang (Magyar) is non-Indo-European and is related to Finnish (but not to Basque or Cornish) (287.F4).

  56.36   orfishfellows' town or leeklickers' land or panbpanungopovengreskey
             [ie, Hungary = Ireland]
  66.19   inbursts of Maggyer
?101.35   cadet and prim, the hungray and the anngreen
?126.22   killed his own hungery self in anger
 171.25   magyansty
 287.F4   Basqueesh, Finnican, Hungulash and Old Teangtaggle
 406.30   At the sign of Mesthress Vanhungrig
 460.26   reflections in words over Margrate von Hungaria
 464.27   old Auster and Hungrig
?535.02   Barktholed von Hunarig
 623.16   magyerstrape...Bomthomanew vim vam vom Hungerig

HUNGERFORD.   Name of 3 Eng vills and towns, none on or near the Medway R (qv). There is also a *H* rlwy br, across Thames R to Charing Cross Sta, London.

> 393.09   in old Hungerford-on-Mudway
>
> 576.26   perils behind swine and horsepower down to hungerford

HUNGRY HILL.   Mt, W of Glengarriff, Co Cork. Acc to P W Joyce (*Irish Names of Places*, III, 391), the Ir name is *Cnoc-déud*, "Angry Hill," although the usual meaning of *déud* is "tooth, jaw, set of teeth"; which prob caused the change from "Angry Hill" to "*HH*."

> ?465.16   the corks again brothers, hungry and angry

HUNG-TSE HU.   Lake in E China, Anhwei and Kiangsu provs; traversed by Hwang Ho R (qv).

> 322.12   he pouly hung hoang tseu

HWANG HO (HOANGHO) RIVER.   The great riv of N China, the "Yellow R," aka "China's Sorrow" because of its disastrous floods. The course of the lwr riv has changed many times; before 1852, it emptied into the Yellow Sea, but flooding over the Shantung plains it seized the bed of the Tsing R (485.28) for a new outlet hundreds of miles to the N.

If Anna Liffey has a sister, handmaiden, or incarnation on every continent (Amazon, Mississippi, Nile), the Hwang Ho may be her Asian avatar. For a longer list of conjectural identifications, see Adaline Glasheen, "Hwang Ho," *AWN* XII (1975), 94.

> 4.28   pon the banks for the livers by the Soangso
>
> ?63.22   too much hanguest or hoshoe fine to drink
>
> 213.06   chayney...Hoangho, my sorrow
>
> 322.12   he pouly hung hoang tseu
>
> 442.03   a tongser's tammany hang who
>
> 468.36   her Orcotron is hoaring ho
>
> 485.28   Ho ha hi he hung! Tsing tsing!
>
> 611.30   a hunghoranghoangoly tsinglontseng
>
> 627.31   Amazia...Niluna...Ho hang! Hang ho!

HWANG P'U RIVER.   Chinese riv whose mouth is the port of Shanghai.

> 297.F5   Whangpoos the paddle and whiss whee whoo

HYDE PARK.   Park, W cen London; site of Apsley House, the Wellington Mus (qv). For Lud, see *London*.

> 540.34   Me ludd in her hide park seek Minuinette

HY KINSELAGH.   The terr of the Macmorroughs, overlords of Leinster, until the 13th cent. It included the N part of Wexford.

> 549.19   Wexterford's...to the polders of Hy Kinsella

HY MANY (HY MAINE, UÍ MÁINE).   Form kingdom in E Connacht, since the 11th cent aka "the O'Kelly's country." It extended from the Shannon R on the E to a line running S from Tuam through Athenry and Gort, on the W. Acc to legend, it was Firbolg terr given to Máine Mór by his relative, the Milesian king of Tara.

> 261.15   Hymanian Glattstoneburg
>
> 309.14   Hiberio-Miletians...and as for Ibdullin what of Himana
>
> ?600.35   the pirigrim from Mainylands beatend

HYPERBOREAN OCEAN.   Aka Iperboreus, Ptolemy's name for the sea N of Ire; he called the NW promontory of Ire "Boreum." The Hyperboreans were mythical people connected with the worship of Apollo, who were pop supposed to dwell "beyond the north wind."

?484.15   a mockbelief insulant, ending none meer hyber irish [*Meer*, Ger
            "sea"]

487.01   by a stretch of your iberborealic imagination

I

IBERIAN PENINSULA.   3 penins jut out from *FW*: Howth, the Crimea, and the *I*
Penin, where Napoleon's generals fought the Sp and Port successfully and Wellington
unsuccessfully, in the "Peninsular War" of 1808-1814.

3.06   to wielderfight his penisolate war

23.01   furframed panuncular cumbottes

ICELAND.   Dan, Icelandic, *Island*; isl btwn N Atlantic and Arctic Os. Discovered by
Scands *ca* 850 AD, it had previously been the site of an Ir colony of Culdees. Queen
Aud, widow of Olaf the White of Dub, settled there with many of her clan around
900 AD. The Parl of *I* is the Allthing; it was first held in 930 AD in Thingvellir (qv).

40.19   the bunk of iceland

129.27   looks like Iceland's ear

133.35   calls upon Allthing when he fails to appeal to Eachovos

139.20   the bergs of Iceland

?290.18   when saltwater he wush him these iselands

316.32   kumpavin on iceslant

323.20   feof fife of Iseland

536.31   Thing of all Things

ICKNIELD ST.   One of the 4 "royal rds" of anc Brit (see *Erning St*); *I* St was the
Saxon name of a prehistoric (not Roman) "ridgeway" from London along the Berk-
shire downs and the Chilterns, ending near Tring or Dunstable.

42.26   *via* Watling, Ernin, Icknild and Stane

ILLYRIA.   Anc Balkan country comprising E Adriatic coast and its hinterland; setting of Shakespeare's *Twelfth Night*. Illyricum was a Roman prov̌ with frequently
shifting boundaries; in anc *I*, now roughly coextensive with W Yugo. The Illyrian
Provs were a part of Napoleon's emp formed from Austrian lands acquired in 1809,
reconquered by Austria 1813-1815.

281.06   *la pervenche en Illyrie*

?415.01   inscythe his elytrical wormcasket...Dehlia and Peonia

615.04   Pervenche...all-too-ghoulish and illyrical

IMMACULATE HEART OF MARY CHURCH (RC)   (16/34).   On City Quay.

601.22   S. Immecula's

INCHICORE   (11/33).   Dist, W Dub, btwn Grand Canal and S bank of the Liffey.

590.27   Worked out to an inch of his core

INCHIGEELAGH.   Vill and angling resort, Co Cork, at E end of Lough Allua, an
expansion of the Riv Lee.

407.18   from Inchigeela call the way how it suspired (morepork! morepork!)

INDIA; WEST INDIES.   Christopher Columbus confused *WI* with *I*; *FW* occasionally conflates the two as well, and refs to either or both are listed here.

106.08	*Inglo-Andean Medoleys*
?156.03	the penic walls and the ind
215.03	my Garry come back from the Indes
215.21	turkiss indienne mauves
224.03	injine ruber
289.06	not allfinesof greendgold that the Indus contains
292.07	indiapepper edition
307.25	Outcasts in India
390.25	the wettest indies
403.13	becco of wild hindigan
?427.22	inds of Tuskland
483.08	dipdip all the dindians
496.11	nor nogent ingen meid
497.29	durbar...indiarubber umpires
541.33	fluted up from the westinders
598.16	earopean end meets Ind
612.08	enamel Indian gem

INDIANA.   Midwestern state, US, but in *FW* just a pun on "Indian blue," a name for indigo.

285.F6	served with Indiana Blues on the violens

INDUS RIVER.   The great riv of NW Ind (now W Pakistan), flowing from Tibet to the Arabian Sea. The Jholung goldfields are on its upr reaches.

289.06	not allfinesof greendgold that the Indus contains

INFERNO.   Hell (qv), as in Dante's *Divine Comedy*. Derives from Lat *infernus*, "of the realms below." Jean Cocteau's *The Infernal Machine* (1934) is a re-telling of the Oedipus story.

300.07	dampned...one of these invernal days
?320.33	Infernal machinery
497.23	*Uisgye ad Inferos!*
505.04	barking their infernal shins
552.15	oathiose infernals to Booth Salvation

INKBOTTLE HOUSE   (15/37).   The inkbottle house, appropriately enough, is Shem's dwelling (176.11), and perhaps any ho where JJ wrote. But there was an *IH*, a schoolhouse in Glasnevin, said to have been named by Swift; it was demolished in 1901. There is a picture of it in Cosgrave and Strangways, 112.

?93.16	biss Drinkbattle's Dingy Dwellings
176.31	in his inkbattle house
182.31	house O'Shea...known as the Haunted Inkbottle
?263.24	on excellent inkbottle authority

INKERMAN.   Vill, mt, and vall near mouth of Chernaya R, just E of Sevastopol; scene of Crimean War battle, 5 Nov 1854, in which Brit and Fr (including Zouave infantry) defeated a Russ attack.

48.10	amid those zouave players of Inkermann
71.08	the collision known as Contrastations with Inkermann
356.02	redoubtedly...each and ilkermann
433.09	pen of our jocosus inkerman militant

INNISFREE (INISHFREE).   Isl, Lough Gill, Co Sligo. Yeats's "The Lake Isle of Innisfree" made it famous.
> 204.19   she laughed innocefree
> ?211.04   for Oliver Bound a way in his frey
> ?605.17   its supreem epicentric lake Ysle

INNISHMACSAINT.   Isl, 5½ mi NW of Devenish, Co Fermanagh, in Lwr Lough Erne. Site of monastery founded in 6th cent by St Ninnidh.
> 267.F1   For Rose Point see Inishmacsaint

INSUPPRESSIBLE, THE.   Dub journal publ 1890-91 continuing Wm Smith O'Brien's suppressed *United Ireland.*
> 568.16   It stands in *Instopressible*

INVALIDES, HÔTEL DES.   On left bank of Seine R in Paris; built 17th cent as barracks to house 7000 disabled soldiers, it became site of Napoleon's tomb and of the great Musée de l'Armée.
> 8.06   Redismembers invalids of old guard

IONA.   Isl, Inner Hebrides (qv), Scot, off SW tip of Mull Isl. St Columcille's (Columba's, Columb's) main monastery was est there *ca* 563 AD.
> ?358.24   bejetties on jonahs
> 463.31   as snug as Columbsisle Jonas wrocked in the belly of the whaves
> ?569.08   Iona-in-the-Fields
> 594.08   semitary of Somnionia

IONIA.   Anc dist on W coast of Asia Minor bordering the Aegean Sea, colonized by Gk cities. The Ionian cities produced the earliest Gk philosophy and the Ionian order in architecture.
> ?594.08   amid the semitary of Somnionia

IPSUS.   Vill, S Phrygia, NW of modern Aksehir, Asia Minor. Scene of decisive battle, 301 BC, in Wars of the Diadochi, which precipitated the break-up of the Greco-Macedonian world.
> ?8.29   Mont Tipsey

IRAN.   The mod (since 1935) name of Persia (qv). The Indo-European peoples who occupied the Iranian plateau called themselves Aryans (Zend, *Airya*) and the country Ariana (Zend, *Airyana*), which became Eran and then Iran. *FW* accepts the pun on "Erin" without so much as a thank you.
> 129.34   the oldest creater in Aryania
> 144.18   turkish...Come big to Iran
> ?275.14   Airyanna and Blowyhart...that royal pair
> 310.20   the man of Iren...Nur
> 358.21   the sens of Ere with the duchtars of Iran
> 491.36   the bold bhuoys of Iran wouldn't join up
> 493.13   Yran for parasites with rum for the turkeycockeys

IRELAND.   Ire is divided into provs (see *Ireland: The Five Fifths*; *Provinces*), cos, bars (listed under cos in this *Gazetteer*), pars, and tnlds (60,462 in the 1901 Census). By one trad classification, 10 acres = 1 gneeve, 2 gneeves = 1 sessiagh, 3 sessiaghs = 1 ballybo, 2 ballyboes = 1 tnld (or ballybetagh), and 30 tnlds = 1 barony. In fact, there is considerable variation in the size of tnlds, pars, and bars. None of these have been functioning administrative units in the 20th cent.

For the most part *FW* embraces all of the isl of Ire, but it occasionally acknowl-

Ireland

------- Country Borders
··········· Province Boundaries
·-·-·-·- County Lines

edges the division, consequent upon the Treaty of 1921, into the "26 cos" (see *Irish Free State*) and the "6 cos" of Northern Ire (see *Ulster*); cf "twenty six and six," 264.22.

Ire is of course both macrocosm and microcosm ("Oh Kosmos! Ah Ireland!" 456.07) in *FW*; its hist, geography, and lang stand in for all hist, all geography, and every lang. In this entry, only refs to the names and epithets of Ire are collected. No other country has a richer stock. They form, in fact, one of the structures of the Ir imagination.

Several names and kennings for Ire have not been clearly identified in *FW*. They are: "Fodhla" (for a legendary queen, like Banba and Eire); "The Four Green Fields" (for the 4 provs); "Matula Jovis" (for Ire's dampness); "Ogygia," Plutarch's name for Ire; "The Old Woman (or Old Hag) of Beara"; "Rilantus" (Shelta for "Ire"); and "Silk of the Kine."

I. Names of Ireland:

EIRE, ERIN, IRELAND.   The Eng name has been variously derived from *Iar*, Ir "west"; from a mythical ancestor named "Iar"; and from the anc Celtic name of Ire, "Iverio." Its Ir name, "Eire" (Old Ir, Ériu), has also been derived from "Iverio," as well as from Eire, the legendary queen of the Tuatha Dé Danann at the time the Milesians arrived. "Erin" has been derived from *Iar-innis*, Ir "west island," from the Lat name "Ierne," and from *Érainn*, the Ir form of the Lat "Iverni," an Ir tribe identified by Ptolemy.

Eriugena, Lat "Ireland born," is best known by way of the 9th-cent Johannes Scotus Erigena. *Éire go bráth*, Ir "Ireland till Judgment [Day]" is a well-known battle-cry (as at 338.03). Among expressions which recall cents of Eng domination are "mere Irish" (484.15), "murdering Irish" (63.21, etc), and "shanty Irish" (312.30, etc).

4.36	erigenating	55.24	airish chaunting car
8.27	Hairy O'Hurry	62.19	common or ere-in-garden casta-
9.36	Dalaveras fimmieras		way
13.01	Behove this sound of Irish sense	62.25	premier terror of Errorland
13.23	Eire's ile	63.21	muttering Irish
14.30	how paisibly eirenical	69.08	Ere ore or ire in Aaarlund
16.21	Whose poddle? Wherein?	70.04	broguen eeriesh myth
17.23	Let erehim ruhmuhrmuhr	71.34	*Stodge Arschmann* ["stage Irish-
21.16	fireland was ablaze		man"]
21.24	come back to my earin	72.12	*an Irish Nature*
21.26	somewhere in Erio	?73.02	he had left Hyland
22.10	come back with my earring	78.26	New South Ireland and Vetera
22.13	somewhere in Erio		Uladh
25.17	the toethpicks ever Eirenesians	86.01	the royal Irish vocabulary ["Con-
	chewed		stabulary"]
25.27	Great Erinnes and Brettland	86.20	Irish Angricultural...brother dane
28.01	Like the queenoveire	88.30	aleland
37.25	Irish saliva	89.25	pounderin jowl
37.26	Iro-European ascendances	91.22	an Inishman was as good as any
38.24	their Irish stew		cantonnatal
42.15	his lay of the vilest bogeyer	93.05	britgits
48.16	Eyrawyggla saga	93.30	Suffering Dufferin
49.07	the Irish whites	100.06	Paisdinernes
49.29	the last straw glimt his baring	111.23	ancient Irish pleasant pottery
53.04	the wineless Ere...mere eerie	112.33	she has a heart of Arin
53.07	an Irish visavis	119.32	an Irish plot in the Champ de
53.13	maymay rererise in eren		Mors

353.16	allover ourloud's lande	431.04	Irish legginds
353.19	that instullt to Igorladns	431.35	our erigenal house
353.32	*by dawnybreak in Aira*	446.21	come back to Ealing
354.25	mouldhering iries	447.04	Burn only what's Irish
358.21	sens of Ere...duchtars of Iran	449.30	wireless harps of sweet old Aerial
359.26	pinginapoke in Oreland	452.27	overking of Hither-on-Thither
360.32	eeriewhig airywhugger		Erin
361.07	twisters in tongue irish	452.29	Ireland
362.22	yearin out yearin	453.06	clambake to hering
364.20	water of Elin	456.07	Oh Kosmos! Ah Ireland!
367.33	that eyriewinging one	456.28	roomiest house even in Ireland
371.36	hugon come errindwards	462.04	Erin go Dry
374.19	Our island, Rome and duty!	463.25	every distinguished Ourishman
378.06	mannork of Arrahland	463.26	a Yourishman
378.09	the rollorrish rattillary	465.27	a queen's earring false
379.11	Aerian's Wall	465.31	irish
380.13	last preelectric king of Ireland	467.32	your Erin's ear
380.18	last king of all Ireland	469.21	Lood Erynnana, ware thee wail
380.20	eminent king of all Ireland	470.33	Irish frisky
380.20	last preeminent king of all Ire- land	472.35	joyful Ireland
		481.05	in *Dies Eirae*
380.34	waterproof monarch of all Ire- land	482.13	worst curst of Ireland
		484.14	uppish...meer hyber irish
381.29	what the Irish, boys, can do	488.33	united Irishmen
387.29	Erin Isles	491.36	bold bhuoys of Iran
389.04	Eringrowback	493.13	Yran for parasites
389.06	the matther of Erryn	493.27	Let Eivin bemember for Gates of
391.01	in or aring or around		Gold
391.16	through Herrinsilde	496.15	old Eire wake
391.28	upon your Ire	498.15	murdering Irish
392.27	oxsight of Iren	501.23	in holy Ireland
392.31	the heights of Newhigherland	503.23	gan greyne Eireann
394.34	hear, O hear, Caller Errin!	508.02	none Eryen blood in him
396.08	ancient Irish prisscess	510.27	comeback for e'er a one
397.02	woman the owneirist	514.36	The eirest race, the ourest nation,
398.05	heroest champion of Eren		the airest place that eresta-
403.23	Irish objects nonviewable		tioned
404.18	indigo braw	518.22	caractacurs in an Irish Ruman
404.19	an Irish ferrier collar	522.04	Gently, gently Northern Ire!
405.19	without a sign of an err in hem	524.20	school of herring
406.11	praties sweet and Irish too	524.26	them errings
407.14	vote of the Irish	525.06	your Errian coprulation!
408.08	trod sod of Erin	525.21	*Herrin Plundehowse*
410.33	sixty odd eilish mires	525.30	his tear make newisland
411.12	On the continent as in Eironesia	528.31	all the difference in Ireland
412.25	I was thinking of her in sthore	530.18	arianautic sappertillery
421.14	Came Baked to Auld Aireen	530.21	magnon of Errick
421.27	into impulsory irelitz	532.01	eirenarch's custos
425.18	arrah go braz	533.05	Evans's eye
427.06	ere in	537.07	after the Irishers
428.07	Sireland calls you	537.10	*Ehren til viktrae!*
429.17	through Ireland	538.01	irished Marryonn Teheresiann

538.18	My herrings!	598.28	Hearing
538.26	heiresses of theirn	600.33	goodbroomirish
539.18	Athacleeath...Irrlanding	601.06	wasseres of Erie
541.19	If they had ire back of eyeball	604.08	alcove makes theirinn
542.02	pletoras of the Irish shou	605.04	ysland of Yreland
546.33	men of Earalend	605.05	yrish archipelago
555.18	irishsmiled	608.14	This Mister Ireland?
559.02	empty Irish grate	608.25	royalirish uppershoes
565.17	Thunner in the eire	610.32	Erinmonker
566.25	Herein	611.05	islish chinchinjoss
567.22	by aryan jubilarian	613.01	Good safe firelamp...Goldselfore-
571.19	rather than Ireland		lump!
580.34	Eryan's isles	616.03	A nought in nought Eirinishmhan
582.25	he sod her in Iarland	620.06	pooraroon Eireen
583.20	helpless Irryland	621.06	Gustsofairy
593.03	Eireweeker	626.28	invision of Indelond
595.10	Newirgland's premier		

ERSE.   An early Scot word for "Irish," from Old Nor *Irskr*; since the 18th cent it has been used as an Eng name for Scot Gaelic and increasingly also or only for Ir Gaelic.

3.20	erse solid man	354.10	*Old Erssia's*
117.15	ereperse and anythongue	364.14	Ears to hears!
178.07	english spooker...the face of the	375.19	It will wecker your earse
	erse	484.09	then ersed irredent
208.36	Mersey me!	488.25	midden Erse clare language
221.09	his earsequack	490.18	pick the erstwort out of his
240.28	Erserum spoking		mouth
253.01	ersebest idiom	507.22	word of ur sprogue
268.L4	*as daff as you're erse*	530.19	his morse-erse wordybook
273.28	piebold hoerse	534.18	Keisserse Lean
285.11	the ersed ladest mand[3]	540.11	*Be suke and sie so ersed* ["Be-
314.27	noirse-made-earsy		suchen Sie zuerst"]
319.04	the ersewild aleconner	575.24	Mack Erse's Dar
339.18	*Perssiasterssias*	596.05	hailed chimers' ersekind
346.23	Vaersegood!	620.09	somebrey erse
353.18	an exitous erseroyal *Deo Jupto*		

HIBERNIA.   The Lat name has been derived from the anc Celtic name "Iverio," as well as from the Iverni (Hiberni), an Ir tribe identified by Ptolemy. *Pacata Hibernia* (1633) is by Thomas Stafford (275.04).

55.20	a pullwoman of our first trans-	388.30	(hello, Hibernia!)
	hibernian	396.01	(Eburnea's down, boys!)
104.14	*Rebus de Hibernicis*	440.12	bishops of Hibernites
138.11	a hiberniad of hoolies	484.15	meer hyber irish
212.21	Hibernonian market	497.06	panhibernskers
275.05	Pacata Auburnia	551.32	Hibernska Ulitzas
297.05	a son of Sibernia	567.35	beseem Sibernian and Plein Pe-
316.15	hiberniating after seven oak ages		louta
335.26	hibernian knights underthaner	605.15	orders hibernian [Ancient Order
381.04	Hauburnea's liveliest vinnage on		of Hibernians]
	the brain	616.05	Hibernia metal

IBERIO, IBERIU, IBERIA.   The most direct form of the Celtic name "Iverio";

as *Hiberes* it also became the Gk and Lat name for "Spaniards," and survives in the name of the Iberian Penin.

    78.25   both Celtiberian camps
    309.11   Hiberio-Miletians

IERNIA, IUVERNA.   From the anc Gk name for Ire. Ptolemy called a riv in SW Ire "Iernus."

    ?207.21   Spitz on the iern
    ?242.34   alleance of iern
    455.08   Iereny allover irelands
    547.33   I thumbed her with iern of Erin

IRENA.   Female personification of Ire in Book V of Spenser's *Faerie Queene*. *Irene*, Nor "the Irish."

    23.19   these will not breathe upon Norronesan or Irenean
    154.23   Let Pauline be Irene

IRIS.   JJ could have learned from Warburton, Whitelaw, and Walsh's *History of Dublin* that Diodorus Siculus (and no other) gave this name to Ire. *Iris*, Ir "faith."

    285.27   see Iris in the Evenine's World
    318.34   from the irised sea
    489.31   S. H. Devitt, that benighted irismaimed
    528.23   aglo iris ["Anglo-Irish"]
    612.20   Iro's Irismans ruinboon pot before

IRSK.   Dan, "Irish."

    70.30   irsk irskusky
    132.33   Irskaholm [*holm*, Dan "islet"]

IWERDDON.   The Welsh name ("west valley") for Ire. Spelled "Yverdon" in Gerard Boate's 17th-cent *Natural History of Ireland*.

    407.18   a brieze to Yverzone
    ?559.13   Flagpatch quilt. Yverdown design

OINCIU.   Bog Latin, "Ireland."

    90.34   Meirdreach an Oincuish! [*méirdreach*, Ir "whore"]

SCOTIA.   The most common med name of Ire; the most commonly contrived etymology (eg, by Keating) was that the Milesians were called "Scotti" because they came from Scythia. By one of history's ironies, Scotland is named for the "Scots" who invaded and settled the W coast of Scotland from their native Ire, or *S*.

    43.29   the united states of Scotia Picta
    164.05   the one the pictor of the other and the omber the *Skotia* of the one
    412.24   Scotic Poor Men's Thousand Gallon Cow Society

    II. Epithets for Ireland:

BANBA.   One of the 3 queens of the Tuatha Dé Danann (acc to Keating); the others were Eire and Fodhla. Sovereignty rotated annually among the 3 kings, and each year the country took the name of the ruling queens. Since Eire was queen when the Milesians arrived, they knew Ire by her name alone.

    132.26   Banba prayed...Beurla missed [*Beurla*, Ir "English"]
    ?198.05   He erned his lille Bunbath hard
    ?273.L4   *a bombambum for the nappotondus*
    294.F4   Banbasday was lost on one
    325.24   two breasts of Banba
    ?330.21   With her banbax hoist
    389.12   Bambam's bonniest
    468.36   'Bansheeba peeling hourihaared

469.06   far away from Banbashore
596.08   wiles with warmen and sogns til Banba, burial [*Beurla*, see 132.26
           above] aranging

CATHLEEN NI HOULIHAN.   Poetic personification of Ire. AE wrote, "The generations for 700 years fought for the liberation of beautiful Cathleen ni Houlihan, and when they set her free she walked out, a fierce vituperative old hag." Kate, the Earwickers' slavey, is certainly one of her avatars (see *Census*), and another is the heroine of Yeats's play *The Countess Cathleen* (1892, produced by the Ir Nat Theatre 1899), who sells her soul to the devil to feed the starving Irish. Yeats's *Cathleen ni Houlihan* (1902) is about the 1798 insurrection.

39.29   the land of counties capalleens
189.11   cantreds of countless catchaleens
330.35   a kathareen round
441.11   Comtesse Cantilene
448.10   Cowtends Kateclean, the woman with the muckrake

INIS EALGA (ELGA).   Ir, "noble island"; acc to Keating, a name of Ire during the time of the Firbolgs.

596.22   when no crane in Elga is heard

INISFAIL, INNISFALLEN.   An old epithet for Ire: "island of the [Lia] Fáil" (qv). T Moore's song, "Sweet Innisfallen, fare thee well." Both Ireland's Eye (qv) and an isl in the Lwr Lake near Killarney were once called Innisfallen.

72.07   *Swayed in his Falling*
244.06   Shopshup. Inisfail!
462.08   though Shaunathaun is in his fail!
476.13   that personer in his fallen
510.33   for songs of Inishfeel

LITTLE DARK (BLACK) ROSE.   Ir, *Roisin Dubh*. Another female personification, best known through James Clarence Mangan's poem, "My dark Rosaleen, do not sigh, do not weep...."

?15.01   the duskrose has choosed out Goatstown's hedges
92.18   Oirisher Rose
93.27   From dark Rosa Lane a sigh and a weep
96.01   The rose is white in the darik!
277.16   a little black rose a truant in a thorntree
351.09   and pithy af durck rosolun
583.22   jettyblack rosebuds

PIG ISLAND.   Not a common name, but included in Keating's list of names as a "Milesian" name, *Muicinis*.

51.30   pig's older inselt
86.21   Irish muck

SHAN VAN VOCHT.   Ire as the "Poor Old Woman," *Sean Bhean Bhocht*, who has seen all its troubles; a revolutionary song of 1798, "The French are on the sea, says the Shan van Vocht...."

13.25   A shoe on a puir old wobban
48.03   Bigamy Bob and his old Shanvocht!
54.04   Poolaulwoman...Ann van Vogt
77.14   the Ryan vogt it was Dane to pfife
323.34   O, the wolf he's on the walk, sees his sham cram bokk!
372.30   The Shanavan Wacht

TÍR NA BHFIONN.   Ir, "Land of the Fair." There may be an echo of this epithet in all *FW* refs to Finland (qv). The allusions cannot of course be separated from

"Finn's Land" or "The Island of Finn [MacCool]."
       9.28   Goat strip Finnlambs!
     245.16   in all Finnyland
    ?257.36   Fionia is fed up
     340.24   Guards, serf Finnland
     398.16   Fionnachan sea
     510.24   ehren of Fyn's Insul
  TÍR NA SIMEARÓIG.   Ir, "Land of the Shamrock."
     366.21   Terry Shimmyrag's upperturnity
     472.01   Shamrogueshire
  MISCELLANEOUS ALLUSIONS.
       3.06   Europe Minor
      37.18   between Druidia and the Deepsleep Sea
      48.05   Humidia
      51.25   sisterisle
      51.30   pats' and pigs' older inselt [+ G B Shaw's play, *John Bull's Other Island*]
      51.30   southeast bluffs of the stranger stepshore [St Patrick landed in SE Ire]
      62.11   Emerald-illuim
     110.04   clovery kingdom
     111.18   whollyisland
     124.24   waterungspillfull Pratiland
     135.19   Saint Scholarland
     169.23   Shuvlin, Old Hoeland
     188.10   two easter island [until the Synod of Whitby, 664 AD, Ire computed
                   the date of Easter differently from the Roman system; cf 210.35]
    ?229.08   nation of sheepcopers
     264.22   twenty six and six [Eire and Northern Ire]
     320.21   back to Brighten-pon-the-Baltic
     325.31   our quadrupede island
     378.11   Greenislender
     387.12   our seaborne isle
     447.27   the greenest island
     491.32   welshtbreton ["West Briton"]
     506.26   this socried isle
     528.30   the lion's shire since 1542 [Henry II declared himself King of Ireland
                   in 1542; before, his rule was by papal donation]
     589.22   'twas in fenland
     593.05   Haze sea east to Osseania ["land of Ossian"]
     615.04   our mutter nation

IRELAND: THE FIVE FIFTHS.   The division of Ire into the 4 provs of Ulster, Munster, Leinster, and Connacht is cents old; but the Ir word for "province," *cúige*, means "a fifth." Thereby hangs a tale.

The Ulster epics describe pre-Christian Ire as divided into 5 coordinate kingdoms, without a cen monarchy. Acc to older historians such as Keating, these were Ulster, Leinster, Connaught, and 2 Munsters, E and W. Eoin MacNeill has argued that the 5 Fifths were Ulster, Munster, Connaught, and 2 Leinsters (which by the 5th cent had become 7 kingdoms).

In later times, when the high king ruled at Tara, the "five fifths" were the present provs, plus Royal Meath — now absorbed into Leinster. By tradition, the common meeting point of the provincial boundaries was the Hill of Uisneach (qv), SW of Tara.

43.29	the five pussyfours green
323.20	the feof fife of Ireland
353.35	*fullfour fivefirearms*
370.28	of the feof of the foef of forfummed Ship-le-Zoyd
394.17	the five fourmasters
396.26	four...fiveful moment...poor [four] old timetetters
?440.01	five wits to the four verilatest
475.07	in Owenmore's five quarters [see *Mogh's Half*]
513.34	consecutive fifth...four wise elephants
?589.27	wrothing foulplay over his fives' court
596.16	one of the two or three forefivest fellows

IRELAND'S EYE   (28/41).   Small isl N of Howth; aka Inis Mhic Neasáin, "Island of the Son of Nessan." The name is from *ey*, old Dan "island." *IE* was the site of the murder of Mrs Kirwan by her husband (*ca* 1860), who was convicted when it was proved he was the only other person on the isl at the time (?254.10). Acc to F E Ball (*Howth and its Owners*, 130), *IE* was "for samphire famed" (?601.11); one spot on *IE* is called Samphire Hole.

6.35	ireglint's eye
129.27	looks like Iceland's ear
162.32	the green moat in Ireland's Eye
?254.10	Irenews eye-to-eye ayewitnessed
466.35	not so much green in his Ireland's eye
?601.11	Longsome the samphire coast
604.24	Inoperation Eyrlands Eyot

IRISH AGRICULTURAL ORGANIZATION SOCIETY.   Founded in 1894 by Horace Plunkett, *et al*, it was and is the moving force of the agricultural cooperative movement in Ire. Its hqs were at 2 Stephen's Green, N. George Russell (AE) edited its publ, *The Homestead*, from Plunkett Ho in Merrion Sq.

86.20	convened by the Irish Angricultural and Prepostoral Ouraganisations

IRISH FIELD.   Publ weekly in Dub, it was known from 1870 to 1894 as *The Irish Sportsman and Farmer*, from 1894 to 1933 as *The Irish Field and Gentleman's Gazette*, from 1933 as *The Irish Field*.

55.31	the Archicadenus, pleacing aside his *Irish Field*

IRISH FREE STATE.   Saorstát Éireann, the "Free State" or "Republic" of Ireland, was proclaimed by the Sinn Féin Dáil in Jan 1919, and was recognized by Gt Brit in the Treaty of 1921, which was supported by Free Staters and opposed by Republicans.

69.15	the drema of Sorestost Areas, Diseased
117.34	we in our wee free state...prestatute in our charter
242.01	sorestate hearing, diseased
310.08	from the antidulibnium onto the serostaatarean
329.31	Freestouters and publicranks...swearing threaties
?352.33	frustate fourstar
406.19	in their green free state
482.29	I'm-free-Down-in-Easia
?596.31	sorensplit and paddypatched
604.23	the free state on the air

IRISH INDEPENDENT.   Main office was at 12 St Andrew St. Both the *Irish Daily Independent* and the *Irish Weekly Independent* were Nationalist and Parnellite.

118.02   however unfettered our Irish daily independence
500.14   Christ on the airs independence!
501.19   The ales is Penzance
602.17   an independant reporter

IRISH RACE AND WORLD.   There was no publ by this or a similar name. (*The Racing World* was publ in London from 1887 to 1929.) Whether there was an "Irish Racing World" program on Radio Éireann or the BBC, as the context suggests, I do not know.

341.20   *presentment...has been being given by* The Irish Race and World
342.32   From Topphole to Bottom *of* The Irish Race and World

IRISH RUGBY UNION   (18/33).   Its hqs and stadium are in Lansdowne Rd, Beggarsbush (qv). Among the leading clubs of the *IRU* have been Blackrock, Clontarf, Lansdowne and Bective Rangers (451.10), Monkstown, Old Wesley (377.13), University, and Wanderers (377.13).

Acc to Wm G Fallon, a Dub friend, JJ attended the rugby International matches held in Paris in the Stade Colombes btwn Fr and Ir (IRU) teams. "I had to go and see the boys in green jerseys," JJ told Fallon (U O'Connor, *The Joyce We Knew*, 53).

377.13   A wing for oldboy Welsey Wandrer
446.17   in that united I.R.U. stade...wildflier's fox into my own greengeese
          again
616.33   Order now before we reach Ruggers' Rush!

IRISH SEA.   Btwn Ire and Brit, it is separated from Eng in the S by St George's Channel (qv) and from Scot in the N by North Channel (see *Moyle, Sea of*). On Ptolemy's map of Ire, it is called the "Ivernian Ocean." *Muir Meann*, Ir "Limpid Sea" (628.06).

197.29   from the harbourless Ivernikan Ocean
318.34   his spectrem onlymergeant crested from the irised sea
471.26   the highroad of the nation, Traitor's Track
600.11   Libnud Ocean, Moylamore
628.06   Onetwo moremens more

IRISH TIMES.   Main office at 31 Westmoreland St. In JJ's day it was the main Anglo-Ir newspaper.

327.31   good airish timers
424.03   the *Ikish Tames*
498.01   tyrent of ourish times
500.14   Christ in our irish times!
501.19   The isles is Thymes

IRON GATE.   Gorge and rapids of Danube R, on Romanian-Yugo boundary.
?69.24   the iron gape, by old custom left open

ISKER.   Anc Tatar town, by Cossacks called Sibir (origin of "Siberia"), near Tobolsk, Siberia. The *I* (Iskr) Riv in NW cen Bulg is a trib of the Danube R.
213.04   My hands are blawcauld between isker and suda

ISLAND BRIDGE (ISLANDBRIDGE)   (12/34).   Aka Sarah Br, after the Countess of Westmoreland, who laid the first stone in 1791; spans the Liffey near the SE entrance (*IB* Gate) to Phoenix Park. The area S of the riv and W of the br is known as *IB*. The Liffey is tidal to *IB* (103.01, 578.25). There is a weir just W of the br (626.07).
103.01   *At Island Bridge she met her tide*

170.29   between Leixlip and Island Bridge
254.12   from Sara's drawhead [*droichead*, Ir "bridge"]...to Isaac's [Butt
            Br, qv]
567.03   to Sara's bridge good hunter and nine to meet her
578.25   She tired lipping the swells at Pont Delisle
?600.05   Saras the saft as
626.07   Here, weir, reach, island, bridge

ISOD'S (IZOD'S, ISEULT'S) TOWER (15/34).   Part of the med Dub walls along
the Liffey, in (now) Essex St. Demolished 1675 for construction of Essex Gate. Isod's
Lane, later Scarlet Lane, led from the tower to Cork Hill.
87.29   Isod's towertop
353.34   *is it her tour*

ISTANBUL.   See *Constantinople*.

ITALY.   Although Ital was the lang of JJ's household, *FW* is remarkably uninter-
ested in It geography, hist, politics, or culture. Uppermost in its Ir mind is the It
dominance of the RC hierarchy. *Il bel paese*, It "the homeland"; the cheese of this
name has a map of *I* on the wrapper (129.27).
    "Ital warehouses," shops selling Ital groceries, were pop i.1 Dub around the turn
of the cent; there were more than 50 in Dub and suburbs.
31.20   Italian excellency named Giubilei
89.35   pontiff's...an ital on atac
129.27   reeks like Illbelpaese
151.08   neoitalian or paleoparisien schola
182.27   inky Italian moostarshes
407.17   more numerose Italicuss
456.08   Italian...ciccalick cheese
464.28   the Boot and Ball [Italy *cum* Sicily]
498.30   in an italian warehouse
504.18   italiote interfairance
569.29   What, no Ithalians?

IVAR ST (14/34).   St just N of Arbour Hill, and N of Olaf and Sitric Rds (qqv),
at right angles to them but not intersecting. Ivor is the legendary Dan founder of
Limerick.
12.31   Ivor's on the lift

IVEAGH.   Barony (Upr and Lwr *I*), Co Down; a home of the Guinness family. The
name was taken as his title by Edward Cecil Guinness, Lord Iveagh. His brother Arthur was Lord Ardilaun.
    Among other civic improvements by the Guinness family in Dub are the *I* Baths
(swimming pool) in cen Dub (408.28).
29.04   yardalong [Ardilaun] (ivoeh!)...Brewster's
408.28   Guinness gala in Badeniveagh
418.02   Artalone the Weeps...Highfee the Crackasider
498.14   gemmynosed sanctsons in epheud and ordilawn
557.11   tocher of ivileagh
588.04   his old face's hardalone

J

JACKSON'S ISLAND.   In *The Adventures of Tom Sawyer*, Tom, Huck, and Joe
Harper set off to begin their pirate career there: "Three miles below St. Petersburg,
at a point where the Mississippi River was a trifle over a mile wide...a long, narrow,
wooded island...far over toward the further [Illinois] shore..." (Ch XIII). In *The Adventures of Huckleberry Finn*, Huck goes there to get away from Pap, and meets runaway Jim (Ch VII).
    245.24   while Jempson's weed decks Jacqueson's Island

JACOB, W AND R, CO   (15/33).   Dub bakers, Bishop St.
    26.30   Jacob's lettercrackers
    138.14   casts Jacob's arroroots
    ?300.12   sweet...marie to reat from the jacob's[3]
    303.16   that Jacoby feeling...puppadums [pappadums are Indian biscuits]
    433.20   bisbuiting His Esaus and Cos
    542.30   biscums...jacobeaters

JAFFA (JOFFA, JOPPA).   Seaport, cen Israel. Cen for fruitgrowing, esp of *J* oranges; also exports olive oil, barley, wine.
    406.32   menuly some ham and jaffas

JAMBU.   Acc to B P Mishra (*AWN* I.6, Dec '64, p 9), the Sans name of the "continent" whence came the "Vipra," a Brahman, Markandeya.
    596.29   Jambudvispa Vipra

JAMESON, JOHN, AND SON (LTD)   (14/34).   Distillery, Bow St, off S side of
N King St. *FW* regularly pairs Power's whiskey and Guinness's stout (qqv) because
of their addresses at John's Lane and James's Gate, but it does not neglect Jameson's
holy water, which is pop called "J.J. and S."
    ?3.13   malt had Jhem or Shen brewed
    42.05   stimulants in the shape of gee and gees
    83.03   to buy J. J. and S.
    126.05   Messrs Jhon Jhamieson and Song
    229.23   malters among the jemassons
    ?257.36   fed up with Fidge Fudgesons
    305.17   that pint I took of Jamesons
    325.17   jonjemsums both
    333.16   jammesons...juinnesses
    382.04   John Jameson and Sons
    424.27   a slug of Jon Jacobsen
    425.06   Shamous Shamonous, Limited
    470.33   a Juan Jaimesan *hastaluego*
    523.16   groomed by S. Samson and son

JAMESON, PIM AND CO   (15/34).   Brewers and maltsters, 25-30 N Anne St (also
4 Beresford St and 21 Mercer St, Lwr), around the turn of the cent.
    ?106.20   *Pimpimp Pimpimp*
    ?305.17   that pint I took of Jamesons

333.09   darsey dobrey...pimpim
533.33   Pimpim's Ornery forninehalf ["Guinness's Ornery" in 1st Draft]

JAPAN.   Jap, *Nippon*. *FW* regularly pairs *J* with China, but there seems little reason to connect this with other important pairings in *FW*, despite the fact that by JJ's own account the dialogue between Archdruid Berkeley and St Patrick (611–13) represents them as speaking pidgin and "Nippon English" respectively. Gilbert and Sullivan's *Mikado* (233.35) is about *J*.

81.33   Nippoluono
90.27   yappanoise language
233.35   Makoto! Whagta kriowday!
276.15   if Nippon have pearls
329.10   a bonzeye nappin
339.01   *his lipponease longuewedge*
435.27   when chine throws over jupan
467.14   japlatin
485.36   chinchin chat with nipponnippers
486.12   chink...jape
583.18   china's dragon snapping japets

JARAMA RIVER.   Chief trib of the Tagus R in Sp.
602.13   Be thine the silent hall, O Jarama!

JAVA.   Isl, Indonesia (Malaysia). "*J* Man" was the name given to the fossil remains of *Pithecanthropus erectus*, discovered at Trinil by Eugen Dubois.
152.12   As none of you knows javanese
254.25   Java Jane, older even than Odam Costollo
351.35   Mellay...by Jova

JEDBURGH.   Cap of Roxburghshire, Scot. The highwaymen who infested the Eng-Scot border in the neighborhood were when captured often executed first, tried afterward, giving rise to the expression "Jedburgh justice."
57.36   sentenced pro tried with Jedburgh justice

JEHOSHAPHAT, VALLEY OF.   Bibl name for the vall of the Kidron R btwn Jerusalem and the Mt of Olives where, acc to *Joel* 3:2,12, the Last Judgment will take place.
255.12   Jehosophat, what doom is here!

JENA.   City, E Ger, on Saale R; site of victory of Napoleon over Pruss and Saxon armies, 14 Oct 1806.
10.04   This is hiena hinnessy

JERICHO.   Now the Arab vill of Ariha, Jordan, 14 mi NE of Jerusalem; site of the anc city where Joshua made the walls come tumbling down. In Eng idiom, "*J*" is used to mean "anywhere but here," as in "He's gone to *J*" ("I don't know where he is").
150.20   the reason I went to Jericho
210.21   Jerry Coyle
470.18   roseway anjerichol

JERUSALEM.   The Holy City of Jews, Christians, and Muslims; cap of Pal, now of Israel. Solomon's Temple was prob on the site of the 7th-cent Mosque of Omar, in the enclosed area now known as the Haram (331.19, 532.32). The only remaining wall (the "Wailing Wall") of the Temple of Herod, destroyed 70 AD, is revered by

Jews as a symbol of the past glories of Israel and the lamentations of the Dispersion (469.09, 542.04).

"Jerusalem-farers" were the crusaders; King Sigrid Magnusson (25.36), the most famous of the Northmen Crusaders, was known as the "Jerusalem-farer" (26.04). The 18th-cent Dub eccentric Buck Whaley won a small fortune in wagers on his spur-of-the-moment bet that he could walk to Jerusalem and back within a year, and was thereafter known as "Jerusalem" Whaley.

See *Gibeon, Kedron, Olivet,* and *Zion, Mt.*

26.04	since he went Jerusalemfaring in Arssia Manor
105.06	*He's my O'Jerusalem*
124.35	old Jeromesolem...Huffsnuff...Andycox...Olecasandrum
192.35	pleasegoodjesusalem
258.08	Mezouzalem
331.19	high places of Delude of Isreal, which is Haraharem
355.11	In alldconfusalem
368.09	woking around jerumsalemdo at small hours
469.09	from Jehusalem's wall
532.32	out of haram's way
542.04	hurusalaming before Wailingtone's Wall

JERVIS STREET HOSPITAL   (15/34).   Founded 1721 as Inns Quay Charitable Infirmary; removed to *J* St 1728, rebuilt 1803 and 1887. The st is named for Sir Humphrey Jervis, 17th-cent Sheriff of Dub.

40.35	through Sir Humphrey Jervis's

JOHANNESBURG.   City in Witwatersrand, Rep of S Afr; largest city in sub-Saharan Afr; gold-mining (not diamond-mining) cen.

Johannisberg, Ger, is a vill on the Rhine R known as the cen for Johannisberger wine.

453.33	Johannisburg's a revelation!...diamants...Drink it up

"JOHN JOYCE."   In 1937 someone sent JJ a throwaway advertising 3-hour cruises from Dun Laoghaire on the steamer "John Joyce." He tried to find out more about it and asked Frank Budgen to help, but no trace of the ship was ever found (Ellmann, 718).

428.20	that goodship the Jonnyjoys takes the wind from waterloogged Erin's king

JOMSBORG.   Viking settlement, *ca* 970-1098, on isl off mouth of Oder R; its site was near mod town of Wolin. The fortress was on the "silver hill" often mentioned in the sagas. See *Wolin.*

310.03	Thorpetersen and Synds, Jomsborg, Selverbergen

JORDAN RIVER.   'In the *OT*, it separated the wilderness of the world from the Promised Land; its water is holy, and in mod spirituals ("Roll, Jordan, Roll," 74.05) "crossing over *J*" means going to heaven, or achieving freedom. Crusaders and pilgrims brought back water from *J* in a "*J* bottle"; this term was later used by alchemists for a mixing pot, and still later for a chamber pot.

74.05	roll, orland, roll
103.08	let naaman laugh at Jordan
117.04	iordenwater
210.30	jordan vale
228.31	othersites of Jorden
287.24	*Jordani et Jambaptistae...fluvii...fluere*

497.31   jordan almonders

JOTUNFJELL.   "Giant mountains," mt range in S cen Nor, containing Galdhøpig-
gen (8100 ft). Aka *Jotunheim*, Nor "giants' home."
>   57.14   one Jotnursfjaell

JUBALAND.   Aka Trans-Juba; region of SW Somalia, E Afr. The Juba R, 1000 mi
long, flows through E Afr S across SW Somalia into Indian O.
>   338.17   tillusk, unt, in his jubalant tubalence

JUDE'S HOTEL   (16/33).   19th-cent hotel, 5 S Frederick St; Horatio T Jude, prop.
The Ouzel Galley Society (qv) met there in early 19th cent. In the mid-18th cent, *JH*
was in Grafton St.
>   205.25   Jude's Hotel

JUGGERNAUT.   Jagannath, or Puri, town and dist of Bengal, Ind. *Jagannatha*, Sans
"Lord of the World," ie, Vishnu, whose temple at *J* is a great pilgrimage site. The an-
nual Car Festival, in which the *J* Car is drawn through the sts, gave rise to spurious
Western stories about the number of pilgrims crushed beneath its wheels.
>   342.13   *the lost Gabbarnaur-Jaggarnath. Pamjab!*

JULIAN ALPS.   See *Alps*.

JUNGFRAU.   Cleft mt S of Interlaken, Switz, a favorite tourist excursion by rlwy
which climbs above 11,000 ft to the Jungfraujoch.
>   318.09   Her youngfree yoke stilling his wandercursus
>   ?460.20   my Jungfraud's Messongebook

JUPITER.   The largest planet of the solar system, 5th in order from the sun. It has
12 satellites, 4 of which – Io (583.10), Europa (cf 583.04, .08), Ganymede (583.11),
and Callisto – were first sighted by Galileo in 1610, and were the only ones known
until 1892, when a 5th was sighted through the great telescope at Lick Obs, Calif
(241.34). The 6th, 7th, and 9th were discovered at Lick Obs in 1904 and 1914 and
the 8th at Greenwich in 1908. The last 3 were discovered btwn 1938 and 1951.
>   Jupiter is surrounded by a vaporous envelope (426.21) with changing belts and
spots, esp the Great Red Spot (582.31), whose size varies regularly.
>   241.34   lick their lenses...negatise a jom petter from his sodalites
>   426.21   pansiful heathvens of joepeter's gaseytotum
>   582.31   Redspot his browbrand
>   583.02   his juniper arx
>   583.10   io, io...ganymede, garrymore

JUPITER TONANS, TEMPLE OF.   Capitoline Hill, Rome; acc to Tacitus, it was ap-
proached by 100 steps, "centum gradibus." Richard Kain has suggested that this may
explain why the thunder-words in *FW* have 100 letters (*AWN* VIII [1971], 15).
>   ?504.19   Tonans Tomazeus

JURA.   Mt range and region btwn Fr and Switz. *J* is also an isl in the Hebrides
(qv). Besides "studied law" and "read metaphysics," the quotation pairs mountains.
and (Mississippi) river.
>   356.08   if they had steadied Jura...raced Messafissi

JURY'S HOTEL   (15/34).   Until the 1970's, it was at 7-8 College Green. The cli-
entele in its bar was a cut above JJ's lower-middle-class Dub. No one in *U* drinks there.
>   91.20   the gentlemen in Jury's
>   257.23   the panch of the ponch in jurys

JUTLAND.   N Eur penin including the Dan mainland and part of Schleswig-Holstein, Ger. The Jutes who invaded Brit in the 5th cent and est kingdoms in Kent and Hampshire, alongside the Angli and the Saxons, may or may not have come from *J.*
>16.07   Comestipple Sacksoun...'Tis a Jute
>141.22   jublander or northquain bigger prefurred
>175.12   *Not yet have the Sachsen and Judder on the Mound of a Word made Warre*
>327.01   smukklers he would behave in juteyfrieze ["duty free"]
>600.25   Saxenslyke...Anglesen, free of juties

K

KADESH.   Aka Kadesh-barnea, Lat, Gades, the desert oasis in the Negeb desert S of Beersheba, Pal, where the Israelites spent much of their wilderness sojourn before entering Canaan.
>258.05   Kidoosh!...let us extol Azrael
>470.17   Oasis, palmost esaltarshoming Gladdays! [*Quasi palma exaltata sum in Gades*]

KANE AND CO   (15/34).   11 Aston Quay; portmanteau and trunk makers.
>448.03   Aston's...quaith...number eleven, Kane or Keogh's

KANSAS.   Midwestern state, US; called the "Sunflower State" after its official state flower.
>509.21   sunflower state
>509.24   Putawayo, Kansas, Liburnum

KAPILAVASTU.   Birthplace of the Buddha; cap (at that time) of the Sakiya clan, which occupied area roughly that of mod Nepal.
>24.19   your roads in Kapelavaster...calvary

KAPP AND PETERSON   (15/33).   Tobacconists, pipe manufacturers; around the turn of the cent, at 53 Grafton St and 56 S King St.
>221.29   Kopay pibe by Kappa Pedersen
>?529.30   pfuffpfaffing at his Paterson and Hellicott's

KARAKORUM.   Anc cap (ruins) of the Mongolian khans, 200 mi SW of Ulan Bator; est early 13th cent by Genghis Khan, cap transferred to near Peking late 13th cent by Kublai Khan, abandoned by 16th cent.
>177.09   whole continents rang with this Kairokorran lowness

KARS.   Prov, cap city, and riv in Transcaucasia, USSR, on Turk border. The fortified city was often besieged; during the Crimean War, the Turk garrison withstood a bloody siege by the Russians but capitulated in Nov 1855, toward the end of the war.
>339.14   Karrs and Polikoff's, the men's confessioners
>365.17   villayets...kuschkars tarafs

KATTY GOLLOGHER.   Pop name for the hill over the Ballycorus lead mines, near Enniskerry, Co Wicklow; corrupted from Carrickgollogan, "Hoolahan's Rock."
>90.10   That it was wildfires night on all the bettygallaghers

KEDRON (KIDRON).   Stream and vall, in Jordan (Bibl Judaea), btwn Jerusalem and the Mt of Olives. The word "cedar" has been alleged to derive from the name *K*.
    171.11   the kcedron, like a scedar, of the founts, on mountains

KEHOE, DONNELLY AND PAKENHAM   (14/33).   Ham and bacon curers, 12-14 Brabazon St.
    39.17   theft of a leg of Kehoe, Donnelly and Packenham's Finnish pork
    379.36   Keyhoe, Danelly and Pykemhyme, the three muskrateers

KELLS.   Town, NW of Navan, Co Meath; site of important anc Columban monastery: origin of *Book of Kells* (begun in Iona, qv, and brought to *K* in 806 AD to escape Vikings), Crozier of *K*, and other treasures of anc Christian Ire. Anc Kenlis, Ir Ceanannus Mor ("head fort").
    122.23   *Tunc* page of the Book of Kells
    436.29   meeth in Navan till you try to give the Kellsfrieclub the goby
    482.33   our book of kills

KELLY, TERENCE   (15/34).   Pawnbroker, 48 Fleet St, around the turn of the cent.
    206.19   Tirry and Killy's mount of impiety
    484.33   Kelly Terry per Chelly Derry lepossette

KENNEDY, PETER   (16/35).   Baker, form at 39-40 Lwr Buckingham St and 127-28 Gt Britain (now Parnell) St. The bakery was and is in the latter st.
    7.11   A loaf of Singpantry's Kennedy bread
    317.01   on a doroughbread kennedy's for Patriki
    498.19   at Kennedy's kiln she kned her dough

KENT.   Co, SE Eng, known for its hops, which are dried in oasthouses. The "Holy Maid of Kent" was the 16th-cent Elizabeth Barton, who resisted the Reformation, prophesied the doom of Henry VIII, and was hanged for her pains in 1534. See *Old Kent Rd* (London).
    390.31   As the holymaid of Kunut said to the haryman of Koombe
    553.19   Chesterfield elms and Kentish hops

KEOGH, AMBROSE   (15/34).   12 Aston Quay; woollen draper and military tailor.
    448.03   Aston's...quaith...number eleven, Kane or Keogh's

KERRY.   Co, Munster prov; co town Tralee. Baronies: Clanmaurice, Corkaguiny, N and S Dunkerron, Glanarought, Iraghticonnor, Iveragh, Magunihy, Trughanacmy.
    15.16   Elsekiss thou may, mean Kerry piggy?
    76.24   a fairly fishy kettlekerry
    82.22   joking and knobkerries all aside
    89.19   Lindendelly, coke or skilllies ["Londonderry, Cork or Kerry"]
    180.14   Cardinal Carchingarri ["Cork and Kerry" = Munster]
    247.14   hamo mavrone kerry O
    258.34   the kerrybommers in their krubeems [cherubim]
    442.14   the Kerribrasilian sea
    ?469.26   Watllwewhistlem sang to the kerrycoys
    513.33   the Kerry quadrilles
    ?515.24   homer's kerryer pidgeons
    577.25   till their cozenkerries
    595.13   curries

KEVIN ST   (15/33).   *K* St Upr and Lwr intersect at Bride St. Kevin's Port was once a gate in Wexford St (15/33); that part of *K* St was pop called "Kevin's Port" into the

20th cent.
>   ?64.24   the honour of Keavens pike
>   ?547.18   whimpering by Kevin's creek ["Kevin's port" in 1st Draft]

KEW.   The Royal Botanic Gardens, including *K* Palace, on the Thames R in Richmond, SW London.
>   469.18   Squall aboard for Kew, hop!

KEYSAR'S LANE   (14/33).   Lane btwn Cook St and Cornmarket (then Newgate) as early as 1610; variously spelled Keyzar's, Keizer's, Cazer's, DeKeyzar's, etc, and pop called Kissarse Lane.
>   61.27   about their three drummers down Keysars Lane
>   534.18   tobtomtowley of Keisserse Lean

KHORASAN.   NE prov of Persia. Mountainous but includes Jovain plain in N, the saline desert of the Great Kavir in cen and W part.
>   347.03   on the plain of Khorason as thou goest from the mount of Bekel,
>   Steep Nemorn

KHYBER PASS.   Pass in Safed Koh range S of Mohmand Hills on border btwn Afghanistan and Pakistan; traversed for cents by armies and peoples invading Ind.
>   464.10   khyber schinker escapa sansa pagar!
>   577.23   via mala, hyber pass

KIEL.   Seaport city, Ger, at head of *K* Harb on Baltic Sea.
>   ?160.31   Houdian Kiel vi fartas, mia nigra sinjoro?

KIEV.   Cap of *K* state in USSR; on W bank of Dnieper R. *K* was seized in 864 AD, the year of its founding, by 2 Scandinavians, Askold and Dir; 18 years later it was conquered by Oleg. The early rulers were sometimes called Rhossisti. In the 10th cent it became the seat of the 1st Christian ch in Russ under Prince (St) Vladimir.
>   310.16   the Askold Olegsonder Crowds of the O'Keef-Rosses and Rhosso-
>   Keevers of Zastwoking

KILBARRACK   (23/38).   The ruins of *K* Ch, with its churchyard where Francis Higgins the "Sham Squire" is buried, stand on the shore of N Dub Bay btwn Raheny and Sutton. "Kilbarrack" may be taken as *Cill Breac*, or "Speckled Church" (qv), but the name actually is from its founder, St Berach of Roscommon. It was once called the chapel of Mone (315.28).
      Also *K* Rd, *K* Ho, and Upr and Lwr *K* tnlds. *U* 486/496: "What did you do in the cattle creep behind Kilbarrack?" Bloom: "Spare my past."
>   35.32   in the speckled church
>   315.28   mone met the Kidballacks...suttonly...strandweys
>   327.24   when Kilbarrack bell pings saksalaisance

KILBRIDE.   "Bridget's Church"; the name of many places in Ire, but esp the vill on the Brittas R just N of Blessington Reservoir, Co Wicklow. It is not quite laved by the Liffey, which just S of *K* turns from NW to SW and enters the Reservoir.
>   203.02   before she ever dreamt she'd lave Kilbride
>   ?576.06   Hal Kilbride *v* Una Bellina

KILDARE.   Co and town, Leinster prov. *Cill Dara*, Ir "church of the oak," ie, the oak under which St Bridget set up her cell. The "Killing Kildares" are a foxhunt, still in existence. The 12th Earl of Kildare, who d 1597 fighting against the Tyrone rebels, was known as "Henry of the Battleaxes" (516.05). *FW* associates *K* with cocks; I don't know why. See also *Curragh, The.*

Baronies: Carbury, Clane, Connell, Ikeathy and Oughterany, Kilcullen, Kilkea and Moone, N and S Naas, E and W Narragh and Reban, E and W Offaly, N and S Salt.

In Dub, the *K* St Club (?436.31) was founded in 1782.

202.31	oaktrees...down by the dykes of killing Kildare
427.34	out there in Cockpit...Biddyhouse
436.31	wet cocktails in Kildare
516.05	MacSmashall Swingy of the Cattelaxes...with a cock on the Kildare side of his Tattersull
571.08	cull dare
595.13	cold airs

KILKELLY.   Vill, 18 mi E of Castlebar, Co Mayo.

?4.07	Killykillkilly: a toll, a toll
?361.16	Kissykitty Killykelly!
?389.07	Killkelly-on-the-Flure [= Connacht?]

KILKENNY.   (1) Co, Leinster prov. *Cill Cainnigh,* Ir "Canice's ch." Baronies: Callan, Crannagh, Fassadinin, Galmoy, Gowran, Ida, Iverk, Kells, Kilculliheen, Kilkenny, Knocktopher, Shillelogher.

(2) *K* city, co town of Co *K.* Before the Normans, it was the cap of the kingdom of Ossory. Song, "The Boys of *K* " (4.07). *K* cats (142.04), as everyone knows, will fight until they eat each other up entirely.

4.07	Whoyteboyce of Hoodie Head...Killykillkilly
142.04	who let the kilkenny stale the chump
?595.17	kilalooly

KILLADOON.   House and area on W bank of Liffey, 1¼ mi SW of Celbridge, Co Kildare. Also, a vill in Co Sligo.

456.26	ryuoll on my usual rounds again to draw Terminus Lower and Killadown

KILLALA.   Vill, N Co Mayo, on W shore of *K* Bay; name from a ch founded by St Patrick (?83.34), now site of St Patrick's Cath (CI). Fr forces under Gen Humbert landed nearby in Aug, 1798.

15.11	on the eve of Killallwho
83.34	hillelulia, killelulia, allenalaw
?595.17	kilalooly

KILLALOE.   Town, Co Clare: *Cill Dhá Lúa,* Ir "Ch of (St) Dalua." Anc royal seat of Brian Boru and his descendants (the O'Briens) and later an important ecclesiastic cen of Munster. See *Kincora.*

15.11	the eve of Killallwho
83.34	hillelulia, killelulia, allenalaw
?595.17	kilalooly

KILLARNEY.   Town, Co Kerry, near the Lakes of *K*; the lakes have long been known as "Heaven's Reflex." In *FW,* Benedict's opera, *The Lily of Killarney,* steals the show from the scenic landscape. The song, "By Killarney's Lakes and Fells," is by Balfe and Falconer.

32.35	*The Lily*
246.18	lily of Bohemey
427.01	by Killesther's lapes and falls
433.13	your linen of Killiney

450.29   the lillabilling of killarnies
467.03   billyboots...were laking like heaven's reflexes

KILLDROUGHALT.   NPN? "Killdroughalt Fair" is the air for Moore's "O, Arran-more." Kildrought is the old name of Celbridge (qv), but it was never noted for a fair.
?378.10   —allucktruckalltraum—
588.29   Since Allan Rogue loved Arrah Pogue it's all Killdoughall fair

KILLESTER   (19/37).   Dist, NE Dub, N of Clontarf. The "lakes and fells" are those of Killarney (qv); there are none in *K*.
427.01   by Killesther's lapes and falls

KILLINEY   (25/25).   Coastal vill S of Dalkey. *K* Hill, rising from the Ir Sea, pairs with Howth on the other side of Dub Bay.
295.F1   the Jukes of Kelleiney
433.13   howth...your linen of Killiney
?624.24   oiled of kolooney...Houlth's nose

KILLORGLIN.   Town, near E end of Dingle Bay, Co Kerry; known for its annual "Puck Fair and Pattern," Aug 10-12, when the Puc, a large goat, is enthroned and presides over the livestock fair.
87.26   goat king of Killorglin
?596.01   at milchgoat fairmesse

KILLTORK.   As very local names, there are Kilturks in Cos Fermanagh and Wex-ford, and Kiltorkin (Kiltorcan) in Co Kilkenny. *Coill tuirc*, Ir "wood of the boar." However, the pairing of boar and bull suggests Clonturk and Clontarf ("meadow of the bull") (qqv).
353.11   as Cocksnark of Killtork can tell...Ursussen...bull in a meadows

KILMAINHAM   (12/33).   *K* Jail (now a mus) and surrounding dist, S of Island-bridge; includes the Royal Hosp (504.31). The area, including that of Phoenix Park, across the Liffey, belonged to the House of Knights Templars founded by Strongbow; from the suppression of the Templars in 1307 to the Dissolution of 1541 it belonged to the Knights of St John, aka Hospitallers. The leaders of the 1916 Rising were exe-cuted in *K* Jail; the last prisoner incarcerated there was the late President De Valera.
74.15   Fengless, Pawmbroke, Chilblaimend and Baldowl
223.20   from all Saint Joan's Wood to kill or maim him
504.31   the killmaimthem pensioners

KIMMAGE   (13/30).   Dist, SW Dub, btwn Crumlin and Terenure.
72.20   ring up Kimmage Outer 17.67
142.13   Kimmage's champ
507.02   Kimmage, a crofting district

KINCORA (KINKORA).   Anc seat on Shannon R in Co Clare of the kings of the Dalcassians and of Thomond — Brian Boru and his descendants; fortress destroyed 1088, but *K* remained a royal seat. Allegedly located near the churchyard of the pre-sent RC ch at Killaloe (qv), Co Clare. T Moore's song, "Remember the Glories of Bri-en the Brave": "Though lost to Mononia, and cold in the grave,/ He returns to Kin-kora no more!"
6.21   Some in kinkin corass, more, kankan keening
316.13   in the old walled of Kinkincaraborg [*borg*, Dan "castle"]
367.32   kingcorrier of beheasts

471.15   kingscouriered round with an easy rush

KING'S AVENUE (16/35).   Short res st btwn Ballybough Rd and N Strand Rd.
The name "Basil" is from *Basileus*, Gk "king."
374.32   Basil and the two other men from King's Avénance

KING'S BRIDGE (13/34).   Br over Liffey E of Phoenix Park. Built 1828, named
after George IV; now Sean Heuston Br.
136.22   from king's brugh to new customs
471.15   kingscouriered round...by the bridge

KING'S COUNTY.   See *Offaly*.

KING'S HEAD.   (1) 17th-cent inn in Winetavern St (15/34).   (2) 18th-cent inn
off Capel St (15/34).   (3) 18th-cent inn off Exchequer St (15/33).   (4) 17th-cent
inn in Ringsend (18/33). The notorious Brennans hid out there.
90.05   from the king's head to the republican's arms

KING'S HOSPITAL (14/34).   In Blackhall Pl. Officially The Hosp and Free Sch of
King Charles II; pop known as the Blue-Coat Sch. Orig chartered 1671; now a public
sch.
43.06   two bluecoat scholars
193.19   Mull took it from a Bluecoat schooler
543.21   redmaids and bleucotts

KING'S INNS (15/34).   Since 1795, at the NW end of Henrietta St, facing Constitution Hill; law sch and court, now used as dining hall for law students and Registry
of Deeds. As early as 1610, "The Inns" stood on the Liffey, E of Church St, at the
present Inns Quay, the site now occupied by the Four Courts (qv).
94.28   Accourting to king's evelyns
369.18   a rudrik kingcomed to an inn court
539.31   our good kingsinnturns

KING'S INNS QUAY (15/34).   N side of Liffey; site of Inns of Court, 17th-18th
cents, since late 18th cent of Four Courts.
201.26   After Clondalkin the Kings's Inns

KINGSTOWN.   See *Dun Laoghaire*.

KING STREET, NORTH (14/34).   Runs off W side of Church St. Sammon's (qv)
grocery was at No 167.
557.36   outside Sammon's in King Street

KING STREET, SOUTH (15/33).   Off S end of Grafton St. The Gaiety Theatre
(qv) is at Nos 48-49.
32.26   in that king's treat house...footlights

KINSALE, OLD HEAD OF.   Promontory, Co Cork; one of the S-most points of Ire.
?609.25   Old Head of Kettle

KINVARA.   Vill, Co Galway, on S Galway Bay. The ballad-writer Francis A Fahy
was a native of *K*; his song "The Oul' Plaid Shawl" begins "Not far from old Kinvara,
in the merry month of May..."
621.11   I'll take me owld Finvara for my shawlders

KIPPURE, MT.   Mt S of Dub on boundary btwn Co Dub and Co Wicklow. The Liffey rises just SE of *K*.

204.13   on the spur of the hill in old Kippure
207.11   His Affluence

KISH LIGHTSHIP.   First anchored in 1811 E of Dub Bay btwn the Bennet and Kish Banks; replaced by a lighthouse in 1965.

Other *FW* refs to "kish" are to the trad Ir wicker basket (Ir, *cis*) used for many purposes. In the walling of the Liffey in the 17th cent, kishes filled with stones were sunk in Dub Bay before pilings were driven. *FW* prob also remembers that Saul was the son of Kish. .

7.08   pool the begg and pass the kish
?14.01   a wickered Kish...under the blay of her Kish
215.02   Poolbeg...a fireboat coasting nyar the Kishtna
316.06   Kish met...a coast to moor
512.08   He came, he kished, he conquered...beam in her eye

KLONDIKE.   Region in Yukon Terr, Can; site of gold rush 1897-99.
181.04   klondykers from Pioupioureich

KNOCK.   Vill, Co Mayo, 7 mi NE of Claremorris; *Cnoc Mhuire*, "Mary's Hill." A place of pilgrimage ever since apparitions were seen on the gable of the ch, 21 Aug 1879; sometimes called "the Lourdes of Ire."
186.25   Knockmaree, Comty Mea

KNOCKMAROON (9/35−36).   Locality just W of Phoenix Park; *K* Hill is the rd from Chapelizod to *K* Gate at the SW cor of the park.
3.22   the knock out in the park
15.04   the mayvalleys of Knockmaroon

KNOCKNAGOW.   Not primarily a place-name, but the title of Charles Kickham's novel about 19th-cent rural life in Tipperary. Kickham was born in 1828 at Knick-eenagow, Mocklershill, 3 mi E of Cashel, Co Tipperary.
228.32   cashel...make one of hissens with a knockonacow

KNOCKNAREA.   Hill, Co Sligo, 4 mi SW of Sligo town. Aka Hill of Executions. On the top is a cairn attributed to Queen Maeve.
?186.25   Knockmaree, Comty Mea

KNOCKPATRICK.   Hill, tnld, 1 mi S of Foynes, Co Limerick. Remains of med ch, also "Patrick's Seat" on hill.
81.28   patrecknocksters

KOHINOR.   This great Ind diamond was "acquired" by the East India Co and presented to Queen Victoria in 1850; in 1911 it was set in a royal crown now in the Tower of London. Name is Pers, "mountain of light." It was once used as the eye of a peacock in the Peacock Throne of the Moguls in Delhi (qv).
398.27   she haihaihail her kobbor kohinor sehehet on the praze savohole
          shanghai

KOVNO (KAUNUS).   City, Lith SSR, at confluence of Neris and Neman Rivs. Cap of Lith 1920-1940.
531.36   the Kovnor-Journal and eirenarch's custos

KREUGER AND TOLL.   Through his Swedish Match Co, Ivar Kreuger lit up the world by controlling through state monopolies more than 65% of the world's match production before the collapse of his financial empire after 1929.
221.28   Limes and Floods by Crooker and Toll

KYOTO (KIOTO).   City, W cen Honshu, Jap; for more than 1000 years the res of the imperial family; cap of Jap from 794 to 1868.
     534.02   Kyow! Tak.
     550.28   kiotowing

L

LACE LAPPET, THE.   18th-cent shop in Capel St, specializing in lace garments, acc to Peter's *Dublin Fragments* (156).
     43.13   a lace lappet head

LADBROKE.   Mainly Ragnar Ladbrok, the Viking chief slain in Northumbria *ca* 865 (see *Census*). Ladbroke's is the famous Eng betting house, and *L* Rd, Sq, and Grove are in Kensington, London.
     22.36   ladbroke breeks
     313.23   Meanly in his lewdbrogue take your tyon coppels token
     343.31   I heard his lewdbrogue reciping his cheap cheateary gospeds

LAD LANE   (16/32).   Off Lwr Baggot St.
     51.08   Slypatrick, the llad in the llane
     568.23   beaux and laddes [other lanes in context]
     ?600.04   every lad and lass in the lane knows

LADY'S ISLAND.   Isl, Co Wexford, 5 mi S of Rosslare, at head of *L I* Lake (saltwater lagoon); "ey" in place names is (old) Dan "island." Song, T Moore's "To Ladies' Eyes a Round" (air, *Faugh a ballagh*).
     ?398.18   vogue awallow...sing a lovasteamadorion to Ladyseyes

LADYSMITH.   Town, W Natal, S Afr. The Brit garrison was besieged from Oct 1899 through Feb 1900 by a Boer force commanded by Piet Joubert, who died on 28 Mar 1900. But for "MacJobber" see *Majuba Hill*.
     178.22   vying with Lady Smythe to avenge MacJobber

LAFAYETTE.   Town, Louisiana, US, W of Baton Rouge. In *Huckleberry Finn*, the duke lies to Huck that Jim has been sold to Abram G. Foster, "forty mile back here in the country, on the road to Lafayette" (Buffalo workbooks VI B 46).
     26.16   the loamsome roam to Laffayette

LAGAN RIVER.   The Lagan R flows N through Co Down and Belfast to Belfast Lough. *FW* associates it with lighthouses, for reasons I don't understand. *Laigin* is the anc name for Leinster. Song: "My Lagan Love."
     292.17   tongues laggin too...search lighting
     345.19   *lagan on lighthouse*
     390.04   the Lagener, in the Locklane Lighthouse
     ?530.15   him and his lagenloves were rampaging the roads

LALOUETTE, HENRY.   Funeral establishment, 11 Tyrone Pl (12/33) and 68 Marlborough St (15/34). Song: "O, Twine Me a Bower."
     ?450.16   O twined me abower in L'Alouette's Tower

LAMB ISLAND.   Tiny islet, just N of Dalkey Isl, with Maiden's Rock (off which

there is a drowning, *U* 45/46) and Clare Rock.
?294.04   Lambday¹: Modder ilond

LAMBAY ISLAND.   Isl N of Howth; it dominates the seascape N of Dub. St Columcille founded a monastery, now vanished, on the isl, and Archbishop Ussher wrote
most of his works in a castle incorporated in present *L* Cas.
208.03   did you ever pick a Lambay chop
294.04   strayedline AL...stops ait Lambday
?390.16   in their Lumbag Walk
?398.30   The Lambeg drum...Lombog...Lumbag...Limibig
410.13   isolate i...on the spits of Lumbage Island
464.35   did you like the landskip from Lambay?
?502.36   A lambskip for the marines!
533.08   private chaplain of Lambeyth and Dolekey, bishop-regionary
?600.30   His showplace at Leeambye

LAMBEG.   Vill, Co Antrim. The big drums made in *L*, which thunder in Orange pa-
rades in Ulster, were called "Lambegs."
?390.16   in their Lumbag Walk
398.29   The Lambeg drum, the Lombog reed

LAMBETH.   Dist, SW cen London on S bank of Thames R. Contains *L* Palace, London res of Archbishops of Canterbury. The "*L* Walk" was a dance craze of the 1930's.
390.16   in their Lumbag Walk
533.08   private chaplain Lambeyth and Dolekey, bishop-regionary

LANCASTER.   Cap of Lancashire, Eng, on the Lune R 46 mi N of Liverpool. Most
allusions are to the wars btwn the Red Rose of *L* and the White Rose of York (qv).
In the War of the Roses, the Ir Geraldines supported *L*; the Butlers, York.
     The Royal *L* Regt (infantry) distinguished itself at Waterloo (348.28, 500.11) but
was then known as the 4th Corps of Foot.
95.18   Lankyshied
348.28   Up Lancesters!
374.07   Torkenwhite Radlumps, Lencs.
442.09   lanky sire
465.33   Be Yorick and Lankystare
485.12   Rose Lankester and Blanche Yorke
500.11   Redshanks...Up Lancs!
567.36   yerking at lawncastrum

LAND'S END.   SW tip of Brit, in Cornwall. Sorrento (qv) at S end of Dub Bay, was
once called "The Land's End."
?279.F24   Trestrine von Terrefin
291.01   Saint Yves by Landsend cornwer
?304.21   her dream of Endsland's daylast
535.15   First liar in Londsend!
537.12   outbreighten their land's eng

LANGUEDOC.   Before 1790 the SW prov of Fr; name (13th cent) from *langue d'oc*,
the tongue whose word for "yes" was *oc* rather than *oil*, later *oui*. A hotbed of heresy,
site of persecution of Albigensians (173.13) in the 13th cent and of Prots in 16th-
18th cents. Allusions to the lang (Shem's is *langue d'oc*, Shaun's *langue d'oil*) but not
to the prov are at 83.15, 256.27, 286.30, 287.F3, 427.13, 466.23, 478.20, and 485.29;
and see *Provence*.
70.23   break the gage over his lankyduckling head

LANSDOWNE (17/32).   Rd in Beggarsbush, SE Dub. Dub's rugby football grounds and hqs of the Ir Rugby Union (qv) are in *L* Rd.

Madame Blavatsky lived in *L* Rd, London, and Yeats attended her séances there.

506.24   Now you are mehrer the murk, Lansdowne Road

LAOIS (LEIX, LAOGHIS).   Co, Leinster prov. Form Queen's Co (1556), after Mary, Queen of Scots. The co town Maryborough (577.14) is now Port Laoise. Baronies: Ballyadams, Clandonagh, Clarmallagh, Cullenagh, E and W Maryboro, Portnahinch, Slievemargy, Stradbally, Tinnahinch, Upperwoods.

31.18   lord of Leix and Offaly
124.30   in the Kvinnes country with Soldru's men
446.25   queens
577.15   leaks
578.36   queensh countess
595.13   leekses

LAPLAND.   The region comprising N Nor, N Swed, N Fin, and the Kola Penin in NW Russ, all N of the Arctic Circle.

66.18   lappish language...Maggyer
105.21   *Lapps for Finns this Funnycoon's Week*
362.13   hun of a horde, is a finn as she, his tent wife, is a lap

LARACOR.   Vill, ¾ mi SE of Trim, Co Meath; Swift was incumbent of its ch 1700-1714; he was often an absentee. "Dearly beloved Roger" was clerk. Stella lived nearby at Knightsbrook.

228.21   quit to hail a hurry laracor...regain that absendee tarry easty

LARNE.   Lough *L*, a sea-inlet, Co Antrim, btwn mainland and penin of Island Magee. The *L* R empties into it.

149.06   a diffle to larn and a dibble to lech

LATIN QUARTER.   The students' dist of Paris, around the Sorbonne, 5th Arr, on the left bank of the Seine. The name comes from the fact that until 1789 Lat was the Univ lang.

205.27   from Porta Lateen to the lootin quarter

LA TOUCHE'S BANK (15/33).   Castle St; during 18th and 19th cent, the oldest bank in Ire. No longer in existence.

450.36   what sensitive coin I'd be possessed of at Latouche's

LATVIA.   Before it was absorbed by the USSR it was a rep. N Eur, at E end of Baltic Sea. Ger, *Lettland*.

78.28   moors or letts
382.13   Litvian Newestlatter
548.01   from Livland, hoks zivios, from Lettland, skall vives!

LAUDERDALE MANSIONS.   In *L* Ave, Maida Vale, London. Yeats took JJ to visit Arthur Symons at No 134, and Symons wrote to JJ from this address in 1904.

620.21   From the Laundersdale Minssions

LAURENS COUNTY.   Co in cen Ga, US; co seat is Dublin; the Oconee R flows through co from NW to SE and through Dublin.

3.08   Laurens County's gorgios...doublin
?613.15   the laud of laurens now orielising

LAZY (LAZAR'S) **HILL** (16/34).   Present Townsend St, at Tara and Luke Sts.

Before the 17th cent, this was the tidal S bank of the Liffey, and was the Dan landing place near where they erected the "Steyne" (qv). As early as the 13th cent it was
a leper (lazar's) hosp, the gathering place of pilgrims waiting to embark for the shrine
of St James (Iago) of Compostella (Spain), patron saint of lepers; pilgrims wore scal-
op- or cockle-shells in their hats. The site was occupied by the Hosp for Incurables
from 1753 to 1792, and by the Westmoreland Lock Hosp after that date.

    41.02   Saint Iago by his cocklehat, good Lazar, deliver us!
   209.03   North Lazers' Waal
   429.06   weir by Lazar's Walk
 ?484.25   loups of Lazary

LEANDER BOAT CLUB.   Eng rowing club on the Thames R, London.
   203.13   Neptune sculled and Tritonville rowed and leandros three bumped

LEBANON.   Rep at E end of Medit Sea, N of Israel; named for the *L* (anc Libanus)
Mts. "The Cedars of *L*" are often mentioned in the *OT*; they provided the paneling
for Solomon's Temple. The Maronite sect of Christianity survives in *L*, and its ritual
is parodied on *FW* 470 (*Letters* I, 263–4; JJ adds that *libanos* is also Gk for "incense").

   171.12   the kcedron, like a scedar...of Lebanon
   460.22   libans...babilonias
   470.15   Oasis, cedarous esaltarshoming Leafboughnoon!

LECAN (LACKEN).   Ruined cas 3 mi N of Inishcrone, Co Sligo; once home of the
MacFhirbhisigh family, hereditary poets and chroniclers, who compiled the *Yellow
Book of Lecan* (now in TCD) and the *Great Book of Lecan* (now in the Royal Ir Acad).

 ?53.24   pluk to pluk and lekan for lukan
 255.21   that Buke of Lukan in Dublin's capital

LECH RIVER.   Trib of the Danube, flowing through Ger and Austria.
   149.07   a diffle to larn and a dibble to lech
   209.26   on like a lech to be off like a dart

LEE RIVER.   Rising in Gougane Barra in W Co Cork, it flows E through Cork City.
Called "Luvius" by Ptolemy.

   210.07   bann...barrow...for Gipsy Lee
 ?226.35   before the Luvium doeslike
 ?250.22   your lep's but a loop to lee
 ?315.24   so was his horenpipe lug in the lee
   487.31   Out of my name you call me, Leelander
 ?512.12   Wilt thou the lee?
 ?619.16   Alma Luvia

LEEDS.   City in W Riding, Yorks. Only about 18 mi from York, it is 10 times as large.
   576.22   as different as York from Leeds

LEFT AND RIGHT BANK, PARIS.   The quarters on opp banks of the Seine in cen
Paris have long had distinctive atmospheres. The Rîve Gauche, with the Sorbonne and
the Latin quarter, is bohemian and Shemlike. The Rîve Droit is commercial, fashionable, conservative, Shaunlike.

   197.01   Reeve Gootch was right and Reeve Drughad was sinistrous [*droichead*,
             Ir "bridge"]

LEGHORN (LIVORNO).   Seaport in Tuscany, cen It. It was seized by Napoleon
in 1796.

    8.31   jinnies with their legahorns

LEGO.   A lake in Ulster, aka Leno, often mentioned in Macpherson's poems as a source of mist and vapors. Campbell's notes to Macpherson point out that Macpherson confused it with the lake of Lano in Scand, proverbially the source of pestilential mists in autumn.
　　131.26   the lakemist of Lego

LEINSTER.   E prov of Ire. Ir, *Laighain*. Its cos are Carlow, Dublin, Kildare, Kilkenny, Laois, Longford, Louth, Meath, Offaly, Westmeath, Wexford, and Wicklow. Its arms are a gold harp on a green ground. Among the 4, it is the prov of Luke Tarpey. For indirect allusions to *L* as one of the 4 provs, see *Provinces*.
　　42.21   overflow meeting of all the nations in Lenster
　　68.13   come leinster's even
　　96.17   licksed her
　　180.14   Cardinal Loriotuli
　　202.24   a dynast of Leinster
　　229.17   untired world of Leimuncononnulstria
　　271.L1   *Leninstar*
　　288.14   when he landed in ourland's leinster
　　351.06   the loyal leibsters [the Leinster Regt (infantry) of the Brit Army]
　　381.16   the heart of Midleinster
　　389.05   Leanstare
　　442.30   like Leary to the Leinsterface
　　467.29   lipstering cowknucks
　　514.02   Osmund [with other provinces]
　　520.22   Nils, Mugn and Cannut
　　521.28   leinconnmuns
　　528.32   the leinstrel boy to the wall is gone
　　546.34   Chief Brown Pool
　　550.08   my barelean linsteer

LEINSTER HOUSE   (16/33).   Btwn Kildare St and Merrion Sq W. Begun 1745 by the 20th Earl of Kildare, later the 1st Duke of Leinster, it attracted the fashionable from N Dub to S Dub. Occupied for a cent by the Royal Dub Soc, it has been the meeting pl of the Ir Parl since 1921.
　　In the last quarter of the 18th cent, the corps of the Dub Volunteers drilled on the "Duke of Leinster's Lawn" (aka Duke's Lawn and Leinster Lawn) btwn *LH* and Merrion Sq. The 2nd Duke of Leinster was Gen of the Volunteers from their formation.
　　140.30   my own owned brooklined Georgian mansion's lawn to recruit upon

LEINSTER MARKET   (16/34).   Btwn D'Olier St and Hawkins St, it was a fish market in the 19th cent.
　　?34.09   Roche Haddocks off Hawkins Street

LEIPZIG.   City, Saxony, E Ger. Napoleon was defeated at *L* in 1813 by Pruss-Russ-Swed-Austrian army.
　　10.05   lipsyg dooley

LEITRIM.   Co, Connacht prov. Baronies: Carrigallen, Dumahaire, Leitrim, Mohill, Rosclogher.
　　595.13   late trams

LEIX.   See *Laois*.

LEIXLIP.   Vill, Co Kildare; the Liffey crosses here from Co Kildare to Co Dublin.

Lax-hlaup, old Dan "salmon leap." *L* marked the W boundary of Dub's occupation by the Scandinavians who acc to their custom claimed terr "as far as the salmon swims upstream." The salmon is associated with HCE, as with Finn MacCool. The Lat name of Leixlip, *Saltus Salmonis*, gave its name to the baronies of Salt in Kildare.

The New Bridge across the Liffey was built at least by 1308 and is possibly the oldest in Ire (13.14, 63.14).

13.14	old butte new
20.24	lettice leap...strubbely beds
63.14	hir newbridge is her old
69.34	Laxlip (where the Sockeye Sammons were stopping...)
79.11	salmon of his ladderleap
?132.29	lachsembulger, leperlean
170.29	between Leixlip and Island Bridge
242.02	laxtleap
265.25	from contact bridge to lease lapse
280.07	Satadays aftermoon lex leap smiles on the twelvemonthsminding
310.05	lackslipping...liffing
314.17	luck's leap to the lad at the top of the ladder
326.35	Dybblin water...easthmost till Thyrston's Lickslip
451.15	leip a liffey
460.29	Sarterday afternoon lex leap will smile on...twelvemonthsmind
525.10	leixlep
540.31	lepers lack
547.17	from lacksleap up to liffsloup, tiding down
558.22	nine with twenty Leixlip yearlings
597.20	lucksloop

LEMAN, LAC (LAKE GENEVA).   Lake in SW Switz; traversed E to W by Rhone R. City of Geneva near S tip. No connection with *leman*, archaic Eng "lover."

100.03	or Macfarlane lack of lamentation?
?302.R1	WHEN THE ANSWERER IS A LEMAN
571.22	with limmenings lemantitions [*limnus*, Lat "lake"]
601.04	our lake lemanted, that greyt lack

LENA (MOY-LENA, MOILENA).   The scene of almost all of Fingal's battles in Macpherson's *Fingal* and *Temora*. Toscar was one of Ossian's companions in *Fingal*. The "plain of Lena," the valley of the Lubar R (qv), now the Six Mile Water, is just NE of Lough Neagh.

?25.27	eye of Tuskar sweeps the Moylean Main

LEONARD'S CORNER   (14/32).   SE cor of Clanbrassil St, Upr, and S Circular Rd; site of store of Francis Leonard, "grocer, ironmonger, purveyor, glass, delft, haberdasher, coal and gen. mer."

549.02	mare's greese cressets at Leonard's and Dunphy's

LEOPARDSTOWN   (10/25–26).   Town and racecourse, Co Dub, in tnld of Carmanhall-and-Leopardstown, S of Stillorgan. The name is a corruption of "Leperstown," from the Ir *Ballymalour*, "town of the lepers."

237.22	Leperstower, the karman's loki
462.24	don't encourage him to cry lessontimes over Leperstown

LES EYZIES.   Vill in the Tayac dist, Dordogne, Fr. Skeletons of Cromagnon man were discovered in the Cromagnon cave near the vill in 1868.

20.07	Gutenmorg with his cromagnom charter

154.05   awn and liseias? Ney?

530.21   Sickerson, the lizzyboy! Seckersen, magnon of Errick

LETHE.   The riv of forgetfulness in the underworld of Gk myth. Also in Gk myth, the daughter of Eris (but not a Muse).

78.04   lethelulled

214.10   husheth the lethest zswound

272.F3   the lethemuse

L'ÉTOILE, PLACE DE.   Paris landmark; the Arc de Triomphe (see *Arch of Triumph*) stands at its cen, and 12 aves radiate from it.

?546.06   At the crest, two young frish, etoiled, flappant

LETTERANANIMA.   Hill, Co Donegal; "Hill-side of the soul."

456.27   Lettermuck to Littorananima

LETTERMUCK.   Vill, Co Derry; "Hill-side of the pigs."

456.27   Lettermuck to Littorananima

LETTERNOOSH.   Vill, Co Galway; "Hill-side of the fir-wood."

456.26   Letternoosh, Letterspeak

LETTERPEAK.   Vill, Co Galway; "Hill-side of the peak."

456.26   Letterspeak, Lettermuck

LETTREEN.   Tnld, Co Roscommon; "Little hill-side."

?276.07   lettereens she never apposed a pen upon

LEVANT.   The terr on the E shore of the Medit btwn Gr and Egypt. From Fr *lever*, referring to the E or (sun) rising. The levant wind is the E wind, the ponent wind the W. "To levant," meaning to abscond, is not connected with the *L* but is from *levantar*, Sp "to break up" (eg a household).

84.02   levanted off with tubular jurbulance

480.10   come to the midnight middy on this levantine ponenter

LEWES.   The co town of Sussex, Eng. After Simon de Montfort defeated Henry III on 14 May 1264, he extracted from Henry the document called the "Mise of Lewes," in which Henry promised to abide by the Magna Carta and other documents and customs limiting royal prerogative.

87.20   ever since wallops before the Mise of Lewes

LIA FÁIL.   The "Stone of Destiny," a monolith at anc Tara (qv) which shrieked at the coronation of rightful high kings, and caused "black spot" on any guilty man seated on it. Acc to one legend it was brought to Ire by the Milesians; acc to another it was brought by the Tuatha Dé Danaan together with the sword of Nuad, the cauldron of the Dagda, and the spear of Lug (219.11–12). Later taken to Scot, where it was called the "Stone of Scone," it is now in Westminster Abbey, London, beneath the throne on which Brit monarchs are crowned.

6.24   Sharpen his pillowscone

25.31   hoist high the stone that Liam failed

40.19   pillowed upon the stone of destiny

131.10   his Tiara of scones...Liam Fail felled him in Westmunster

219.11   Falias...Pierre Dusort

227.35   Tartaran tastarin toothsome tarrascone

331.04   though that liamstone deaf do his part

518.10   headlong stone of kismet

600.13   Viggynette Neeinsee gladsighted her Linfian Fall

LIBERTIES, THE.   Roughly the area of Old Dub S of the Liffey bounded E and W by the Castle and St James's Gate, N and S by the Quays and Blackpitts. Orig, the Liberties were jurisdictions, civil and ecclesiastical, independent of the city of Dub and for the most part outside the walls, esp the Liberty of Donore, the Archbishop's Liberty (or St Sepulchre), which included the Coombe, and the Liberty of St Patrick's. Others were the Earl of Meath's Liberty (aka Liberty of Thomas Court) and the tiny Liberty of Christchurch.

In the anc ceremony of "riding the franchises" (or "fringes," 548.19, ie, of the liberties), the Lord Mayor carried the sword along the "mears and bounds" (292.26, 316.06–.07) separating the City from the adjoining Liberties.

The Liberty Lads (or Boys) (542.02, 577.34) were from the Huguenot and other European weavers who settled in the Liberties in the late 17th cent and made the area the cen of the city textile industry. Fierce and bloody battles raged in the 18th cent btwn the Liberty Boys and the Ormonde Boys, who were butchers' apprentices from across the Liffey.

        ?17.01   Here where the liveries, Monomark
        40.04   Pump Court, The Liberties
        371.34   to Rochelle Lane and liberties
        442.36   coomb the brash of the libs round Close Saint Patrice
        542.02   libertilands making free through their curraghcoombs
        548.19   enfranchised her to liberties of fringes
        577.34   the leperties' laddos railing the way

LIBERTY AND CO.   London store in Regent St, famed for fabrics and ladies' wear.
        ?179.33   ladies tryon hosiery raffle at liberty
        ?226.24   libertyed garters

LIBERTY HALL   (16/34).   Eden Quay hqs of James Connolly's Transport and Gen Workers' Union and of his Ir Citizen Army; destroyed in the 1916 rising by a Brit gunboat on the Liffey.
        Goldsmith, *She Stoops to Conquer*: "This is Liberty-Hall, gentlemen."
        ?338.20   amaltheouse for leporty hole!

LIBNIUS RIVER.   Ptolemy's hearsay map of Ire shows tribes and rivs, but is so inaccurate that few of the latter can be certainly identified. The W coast is especially sketchy. It shows in NW Ire, S of the unidentified "Nagnata City," the riv "Libnius." (No name is given to the riv flowing into what is evidently Dub Bay – "Eblana.") *FW* seems to think that Ptolemy called the Liffey "Libnius," as did the historian D'Alton (see *Liffey*).
        250.20   Lolo Lolo liebermann you loved to be leaving Libnius
        310.07   liffing...the antidulibnium
        540.07   the famous river, called of Ptolemy the Libnia Labia

LIBURNIA.   Region and inhabitants of N Illyria (Yugo).
        Laburnum is a leguminous tree with yellow flowers; cf Kansas, "the sunflower state."
        509.24   Kansas, Liburnum

LICK OBSERVATORY.   See *Jupiter*.

LIDO.   Of the many Lidos, the best known is the isl reef outside the Lagoon of Venice, It.
        417.17   a baskerboy on the Libido

LIFFEY.   The little riv of Dub rises in a glen on the S side of Mt Kippure, Co Wicklow, btwn Upr Lough Bray and Crockan Pond, and W of Sally Gap. The source is 12 mi from Dub in a straight line (207.17), but by various estimates is btwn 40 and 82 mi by the circuitous course the *L* follows (50-odd mi, acc to *FW*, 208.26). The riv first flows westward, receiving from the S a number of its early tribs from the 3 mts, Giravale, Duff, and Mullaghcleevaun. It turns N to join the Brittas R at Kilbride, just N of Blessington, then SW into the Blessington or Poulaphuca Reservoir (built 1938-39) at Blessington. The King's R flows into the reservoir from the S and the *L* exits at the W end, near Ballymore Eustace, where it flows along the boundary btwn Co Wicklow and Co Kildare for 2 mi, plunging over the waterfall of Poulaphuca. It flows N, then NE, through Kildare to enter Co Dublin at Leixlip, where before the recent building of a dam it formed the waterfall of Salmon Leap, and flows due E through Dub, about 12 mi from Leixlip to Dub Bay at Ringsend. The R Griffeen joins at Lucan, and the tribs in Dub are the Cammock (S), the Poddle (S), and the Bradogue (N), a streamlet NE of Phoenix Park. The Dodder R joins the *L* at Ringsend, just before it enters Dub Bay. The *L* is tidal to Island Br (103.01).

The old name of the *L* is Rurthach (Ruirtheach); the Lat name is Amnis Livia, Ir *Lifé*. It is called Auenlith in King John's charter, "aquam de Amliffy versus boream" in Richard II's charter; in the *Annals of the Four Masters* it is *Abhainn* [River] *Liphte*. Although Ptolemy's map of Ire shows the Libnius (qv) in NW Ire, *FW* follows D'Alton's statement (*History of the Co Dublin*, 666) that the *L* is the Libnius of Ptolemy and the Labius of Richard of Cirencester (540.07).

Anna Liffey is represented on the arch keystone of Four Courts (qv), and with other riverine heads on the Custom House (qv).

Acc to D'Alton's *History of the Co Dublin* (669), the *L* was completely frozen over in 1338, 1739, and 1768, and the citizens frolicked on the ice.

626.25   And I'd frozen up and pray for thawe. Three times in all.

In the great fire of 9 Aug 1833 which consumed the warehouses E of the Custom Ho, flaming rum and molasses ran into the riv and (acc to Irwin's *Dublin Guide*) "presented the extraordinary appearance of 'the Liffey on fire'." "He'll never set the Thames on fire" has exact analogues for the Tiber, the Seine, and the Rhine, so why not the *L*? In *FW*, it is HCE who does set the *L* on fire (131.13, 137.24). Shem denies trying (172.19), and Shaun warns against it (426.03). Other examples of the motif are at 52.21 and 570.06, with echoes at 12.09–.11, 190.26, 327.32, 466.09, and 542.22.

In *Letters* I, 261, JJ discusses his difficulty in working in the passage from the *Annals* (1452 AD) about the *L* at Essex Br being completely dry for 2 minutes.

204.01   While you'd parse secheressa she hielt her souff' [*sécheresse*, Fr
          "drought"; *souffle*, Fr "breath"]

625.28   If I lose my breath for a minute or two...Once it happened...[.32]
          I'll begin again in a jiffey

The list of citations below does not include all allusions to Anna Livia Plurabelle (for which see *Census*) — only those whose context is to some degree riverine or watery.

3.01	riverrun	23.20	Livia Noanswa
3.18	life	26.08	Liffey
3.24	livvy	26.16	Laffayette
7.01	livvylong	41.22	levey
7.35	lyffing-in-wait	42.18	Riau Liviau
11.05	liv	42.25	liffeyside
11.32	livving...laffing	55.05	Life
13.30	leaves of the living	57.11	alplapping streamlet
14.29	*Liber Lividus*	63.14	ann...liv
17.34	alp	64.17	liffopotamus

86.09	any luvial	283.17	alliving...allaughing
88.34	laving his leaftime	287.07	Anny liffle
106.26	*Life*	287.09	alp get a howlth on her bayrings
126.13	liffeyette	287.21	*chartula liviana*
128.14	Anna Livia	289.28	Liv's
131.14	living a fire	293.19	liv
137.24	lymphyamphyre	297.25	appia lippia pluvaville
139.19	Ann alive	308.20	livvey
146.23	leapy like	309.05	wades a lymph
153.02	*Amnis Limina Permanent*	310.05	liffing
154.04	aulne and lithial...awn and liseias	311.01	lift-ye-landsmen
159.12	Missisliffi	317.32	obliffious
172.19	Liffey	318.04	live
174.26	Tumblin-on-the-Leafy	327.06	anny livving plusquebelle
175.23	*Rillstrill liffs*	328.17	Lif, my lif
181.25	Sniffey	332.17	lifflebed
195.04	Anna Livia	332.28	Inverleffy
196.03−.05	Anna Livia...Anna Livia	333.04	anni slavey
198.10	Anna Livia...Anna Livia	337.08	annapal livibel
199.11	Anna Livia	340.22	annal livves
200.16	Anna Liv	342.25	*Leavybrink*
200.36	Anna Livia's	355.32	An-Lyph
203.06	lifey	361.18	o'liefing
204.05	Livvy	361.26	leavely of leaftimes
204.14	livvly	372.16	labious banks
207.19	Anna Livia	373.34	mummur allalilty
207.28	Amnisty Ann	380.03	Liffey
208.05	Liviam Liddle	382.13	Litvian
209.24	her arms encircling Isolabella	382.27	Liff
	[see *Chapelizod*]	387.09	Strathlyffe
210.18	Clonliffe	404.01	affluvial
213.32	Allalivial, allalluvial	410.11	Dublin river
215.12	Anna Livia	420.34	Laffey
215.24	Anna...Livia	425.20	Lief
215.33	liffeying	445.34	Liffalidebankum
215.35	Livia's	447.23	liffe
224.29	Madama Lifay	451.15	liffey...annyblack
230.25	liffe	452.18	annals...livy
231.12	googling Lovvey	463.10	anny living
236.17	Anneliuia	495.21	lifing
242.28	Avenlith	496.27	Abha na Lifè
245.11	Liffeyetta's	512.06	liffey
245.23	Livmouth	512.16	antelithual paganelles
254.11	livvying	513.05	Amnis Dominae
264.06	Brook of Life	526.01	liffeybank
265.14	liefest	527.11	my lickle wiffey
266.03	Rivapool	540.07	called of Ptolemy the Libnia Labia
268.L1	*annaryllies*	547.17	liffsloup
268.F6	Mrs Lappy	547.34	lieflang
273.11	Hanah Levy	548.06	Appia Lippia Pluviabilla
275.12	lavy	549.16	Livania's
277.L1	*Fluminian road*	553.04	Livvy

562.07	Allaliefest	600.08	river of lives
564.22	liveside	600.13	Linfian Fall
568.04	livlianess	608.14	And a live
570.06	pyrolyphics	614.24	liffeyism
576.01	Liffey	619.16	Alma Luvia
576.36	neoliffic	619.20	leafy
577.01	wiffeyducky	619.29	leafy
577.11	constant lymph	619.30	life
577.12	river mouth	624.22	Leafiest
580.25	ambling limfy	625.33	jiffey
583.21	Liv	627.27	allaniuvia pulchrabelled
597.07	livesliving	628.07	Lff!
600.05	Innalavia		

LIFFEY ST   (15/34).   From Liffey R at Wellington Br to Henry St.
 L St, W ("New Livius Lane"?), is a short st off Benburb St near the entrance to Phoenix Park (14/34).
>   260.09−.13   Long Livius Lane...by New Livius Lane
>   387.09   from Strathlyffe and Aylesburg [*strath*, Scot "valley"]

LILLIPUT.   Land of the little people, in Swift's *Gulliver's Travels*.
>   22.08   all the lilipath ways to Woeman's Land
>   284.24   Aysha Lalipat...Big Whiggler
>   491.22   Braudribnob's...lillypets on the lea
>   583.09   Bigrob dignagging his lylyputtana

LIMA.   City, cap of Peru, on Rimac R. "Lima" is a Sp corruption of the Quichuan word *Rimac*.
>   ?376.01   the lovablest Lima

LIMBO.   Suburb of Hell, the abode of unbaptized infants and the righteous who died BC.
>   224.17   that limbopool which was his subnesciousness
>   256.23   why is limbo where is he

LIMERICK.   Co, Munster prov, and city on both banks of the Shannon R. The dams (183.23) of the Shannon Hydro-Electric Scheme are upstream from *L* City. *L* is famous for hams and for the "Broken Treaty" of 1691 by which the city surrendered to Wm III's forces commanded by Ginkel. A Ger colony from the Palatinate (qv) was settled btwn *L* City and Newcastle West in 1709. Baronies: Clanwilliam, Upr and Lwr Connello, Coonagh, Coshlea, Coshma, Glenquin, Kenry, Kilmallock, Owneybeg, N Liberties, Puddlebrien, Shanid, Small County.
>   67.18   Otto Sands and Eastman, Limericked, Victuallers
>   183.23   limerick damns
>   410.21   from franking machines, limricked
>   434.21   ribbons of lace, limenick's disgrace
>   444.36   as sure as there's a palatine in Limerick
>   595.12   limericks

LIMMAT.   Riv, Zurich, Switz, flowing through the city from L Zurich. In its upper reaches on the other side of the lake it is called Linth.
>   198.13   Yssel that the limmat?
>   208.05   The linth of my hough

LINEN HALL   (15/34).   Erected 1726 in Lurgan St, near W end of Bolton St; later the barracks of the Dub Fusiliers. Another hall erected 1728, N end of Capel St, modeled on Blackwell Hall (drapers' market), London. Disused, 1828; used later as barracks, burned in 1916 rising.

    458.02   in second place of a linenhall valentino

LISBON (LISBOA).   The name of the Port cap is from Olisipo or Ulyssippo, after a legend that Ulysses founded a city in Iberia. The royal palace, Paço das Necessidades, is on the site of a chapel dedicated to Nossa Senhora das Necessidades. *L*'s water is provided by 2 aqueducts: the Abviella and the Aqueducto das Aguas Livres.

    442.09   Old Father Ulissabon Knickerbocker
    553.18   lisbing lass
    553.21   pampos animos and (N.I.) necessitades iglesias and pons for aguaducks

LISMORE.   Town, Co Waterford. There are also vills of this name in Co Galway and Co Tyrone.

    491.11   from Lismore to Cape Brendan

LISDOONVARNA.   Town, Co Clare, and Ire's best-known spa.

    472.06   Come to disdoon blarmey

LISIEUX.   City, NW Fr, dept of Calvados. St Thérèse lived in Carmelite convent here.

    432.29   Where the lisieuse are we

LISTOWEL.   Town, Co Kerry.

    513.33   Kerry quadrilles and Listowel lancers

LITHUANIA.   The area S of the Gulf of Riga in the W Baltic; Lith, *Lieutuva*. Polit-ically independent in the late mid ages, it was united with Pol in the 16th cent, and divided btwn Pol and Russ since the 16th cent. The Letts, with their own lang, have lived in *L* and Livonia (Livland, qv), esp the Courland penin, in recent cents. There are clusters of Lith words on *FW* 186–87 and 511–12 (Hodgart, in *A Wake Digest*, 59–61).

    187.08   the caledosian capacity for Lieutuvisky [*Kaledos*, Lith "Christmas"]
    338.19   laut-lievtonant of Baltiskeeamore
    548.01   from Livland...from Lettland

LITTLE BIG HORN.   Riv, Montana, US, on which Gen Custer made his last stand against the Sioux on 25 June 1876.

    84.08   anywheres between Pearidge and the Littlehorn...confederate

LITTLE GREEN (15/34).   Bounded by N King St, Capel St, Little Britain St, and (present) Halston St. Earliest mention 1719. Later site of Newgate Pris (erected 1773-1780), and of the *LG* Market: eggs, butter, and fowl. See *Green St Courthouse*.

    15.08   Little on the Green
    575.26   little green courtinghousie

LITTLEPACE.   Tnld, par of Mulhuddart, bar of Castleknock, Co Dublin.

    503.13   Littlepeace aneath the bidetree

LIVERPOOL.   City and port, Lancs, NW Eng. 200 yrs of emigration have made it as Irish as Dub. The *L* Summer Cup is a Brit racing fixture (342.16) and the Grand National is Eng's leading steeplechase (448.14).

    17.07   the brookcells by a riverpool
    74.13   Liverpoor? Sot a bit of it!

?224.17   in that limbopool
266.03   Rivapool? Had a brieck on it!
342.16   *Thousand to One Guinea-Gooseberry's Lipperfull Slipver Cup*
379.13   His lights not all out yet, the liverpooser!
437.11   liver asprewl
448.13   l'pool and m'chester...grandnational
533.35   Livpoomark lloyrge hoggs

LIVLAND (LIVONIA).   Form Baltic prov of Russ, lying W of the Gulf of Riga. Main city Riga, main riv the Dvina (Duna). The trad lang of the Livs, related to Finnish, was replaced in the 19th cent by a dialect of Lettish. From the 13th to the 16th cent, the Livonian Order ("Brothers of the Sword") waged uninterrupted war to dominate the whole E Baltic area.

81.17   versts...where livland yontide meared with the wilde
338.19   laut-lievtonant of Baltiskeeamore
548.01   from Livland...from Lettland
549.16   through all Livania's volted ampire

LIZARD, THE.   In Cornwall; the S-most point of the Brit Isles. The lighthouse is one of the main landmarks of the Eng Channel.

324.04   picking up the emberose of the lizod lights

LLOYD'S OF LONDON.   The London insurance brokerage cen.

?326.19   the loyd mave hercy on your sael
?373.04   sailalloyd donggie
413.05   the Loyd insure her!
590.05   honest policist...swore on him Lloyd's

LOCHLANN (LOUGHLINN).   The anc Ir name ("country of lakes") for the Country of the Ostmen, ie, Nor, and for the Scands themselves. *FW* uses the term to refer to the Scand ancestry of HCE (370.28, 600.29), of HCE's man-of-all-work (141.08), and of Dub itself (291.10).

100.06   Lochlanner Fathach I Fiounnisgehaven
141.08   Whad slags of a loughladd
268.F6   Leap me, Locklaun
291.10   Lochlaunstown...Staneybatter
370.28   the marringaar of the Lochlunn gonlannludder
390.04   the Lagener, in the Locklane Lighthouse
541.18   Brien Berueme to berow him against the Loughlins
596.36   Loughlin's salts
600.29   *Homos Circas Elochlannensis*
626.06   Ludegude of the Lashlanns

LODA.   The mossy "stone of power" in Scand folklore; also a circle of stones used prob as a place of worship; associated with Odin.

228.13   a conansdream of lodascircles

LOIRE RIVER.   Longest riv in Fr; rises in SE Fr, flows N to Orleans, then W to Bay of Biscay.

207.11   boudeloire
?419.12   How farflung is your fokloire

LOMBARD ST.   (1) In the cen of the City of London, it was the hqs of the Lombard bankers before the 17th cent, and still stands for high finance.   (2) In Dub, *L*

St runs from Pearse St to Townsend St (16/34), and *L* St W runs btwn Arnott St and Clanbrassil St Lwr (15/32). Bloom and Molly were happy there (*U* 153/155).

    72.02   *Bombard Street Bester*
    207.23   Not for the lucre of lomba strait

LOMOND, LOCH.   Lake, S cen Scot; largest lake in Gt Brit. "By the bonny, bonny banks of Loch Lomond" is where me and my true love will never meet again.

    340.09   the lomondations of Oghrem
    520.27   on the bibby bobby burns of...ye lamelookond fyats

LONDON.   Co, city, SE Eng, cap of Brit Emp. Called Lud's Town (152.28) from mythical King of Brit: "And on the gates of Lud's town set your heads" (Shakespeare, *Cymbeline* IV, iii). Roman name was Londinium, used by Tacitus, from uncertain Celtic root. Bog Lat for *L* is Ondlosbu (244.07). A slang term for *L* is "Romeville," (*U* 47/48, 188/191) (6.04). *L* was also until recently called (esp in the rest of Brit) "The Big Smoke" or "The Smoke." Songs: "While London Sleeps"; "London Bridge is Falling Down." Dick Whittington did turn again and became Lord Mayor of *L*.
    Places in *L* are listed separately in this gazetteer.

    ?6.04   ville's indigenous romekeepers
    12.05   while Luntum sleeps
    20.19   many a smile to Nondum
    58.10   Longtong's breach is fallen down
    ?143.05 fatigued by his dayety in the sooty ["duty in the City"]
    152.28   set off from Ludstown
    178.01   teashop lionses of Lumdrum
    239.34   Lonedom's breach lay foulend up
    244.07   For all in Ondslosby
    244.34   While loevdom shleeps
    253.10   a London's alderman...regionals [BBC Regional Service]
    307.17   The Shame of Slumdom
    331.09   Lludd hillmythey
    342.33   *Loundin Reginald* [BBC Regional Service]
    353.27   *Landaunelegants of Pinkadindy*
    409.01   futs dronk of Wouldndom
    535.15   First liar of Londsend
    540.34   Me ludd in her hide park
    541.16   Daniel in Leonden
    ?568.33 youghta kaptor lomdom noo [..."kappa lambda"...]
    577.12   big smoke and lickley roesthy
    602.28   scuity, misty Londan
    625.36   laud men of Londub

LONG ACRE.   St in Holborn, London, from St Martin's Lane to Drury Lane. The Piccadilly Line Tube runs directly underneath its entire length.

    579.33   recrutched cripples gait and undermined lungachers

LONG ENTRY   (14/33).   A place, off Tripoli St (form N part of Pimlico), near the Coombe.

    248.31   lord of Glendalough benedixed the gape for me that time at Long
             Entry

LONGFORD.   Co, and town, cen Ire. There are other Longfords in Cos Offaly and Tipperary and in Tasmania, Australia.

Baronies: Ardagh, Granard, Longford, Moydow, Ratheline, Shrule.
?222.31   athletes longfoot
595.14   lungfortes

LOOP LINE BRIDGE   (16/34).   Rlwy br across the Liffey alongside Butt Br (qv).
E-most of the Liffey brs, it carries the Loop Line joining Amiens St (now Connolly)
and Westland Row (now Pearse) Sta.
?551.01   duncingk...interloopings...ballast
569.05   S. Mark Underloop [see St Mark's Ch]

LOOS.   Town, N of Arras, Fr. The battle of L, 25-28 Sept 1915, was the largest
Brit offensive to that date against Ger trenches.
8.14   Saloos the Crossgunn!

LORA.   In Macpherson's poems, a hill overlooking Lena (qv), the vall of the Lubar
R, across the vall from the hill of Mora. Fingal spends a lot of time on Mora, his various opponents on L. Campbell's notes to Macpherson identify L as Lisle or Lysle
Hill, S of the Six Mile Water in Co Antrim.
Also a riv in "The Battle of Lora." Macpherson's note: "probably one of the little
rivers in Argyleshire."
131.23   Mora and Lora had a hill of a high time

LORD'S CRICKET GROUND.   See Marylebone Cricket Club.

LORETO (LORETTO).   (1) House of L, aka the Santa Casa, reputed house of Mary
at Nazareth. Miraculously moved to Dalmatia in 1291, to Recanati in 1294, to near
Ancona in 1295 (to prevent destruction by Turks). From lauretum, Lat "grove of
laurels," in which it stood in Recanati. Final site 14 mi from Ancona belonged to a
Lady Lauretta.   (2) The "Ladies of Loreto," an order of teaching nuns, founded in
Dub in 1822 by Mary Teresa Ball; named after the House of L. There are a number
of L convents and schs in and around Dub, the largest in Rathfarnham.   (3) Notre
Dame de Lorette, Paris. "Lorette" was Paris slang for "whore" in the 1920's because
the prostitutes went to church there.
?67.33   Lupita Lorette
312.20   trippertrice loretta lady
340.18   nose easger for sweeth prolettas
359.14   laurettas
528.01   convent loretos
538.01   irished Marryonn Teheresiann

LOS ANGELES.   City, S Calif, US, founded 1781 as El Pueblo de Nuestra Señora
la Reina de los Angeles de Porciuncula.
154.24   And let me be Los Angeles

LOTTS   (15/34).   The embankment of the Liffey in the 17th and 18th cents reclaimed the tidal flats behind the quays E of Butt Br, and these areas, parceled into
lots, were known as North L and South L. The name survives in S L Rd, near Ringsend, and in the L, a st btwn Liffey St and Williams Row, parallel to Bachelor's Walk.
Lots Rd in London W of Chelsea is the site of Lots Rd Power Sta.
203.06   the barleyfields and pennylotts of Humphrey's fordofhurdlestown
321.17   old lotts have funn
436.24   And at 2bis Lot's Road
625.25   Neighboulotts for newtown

LOUGHLINSTOWN.   (1) Tnld, par and bar of Ratoath, Co Meath (97.10).

(2) The better-known *L* is a vill S of Dub, btwn Dalkey and Bray, form a cen for hunting.

  97.10   Loughlinstown
  291.10   the O'Hyens of Lochlaunstown

LOUISIANA.   S state, US; orig the whole Mississippi R area, as in the "*L* Purchase"; no special connection with shirts.

  ?368.32   Peaky booky nose over a lousiany shirt

LOURDES.   Town, near Tarbes, SW Fr; one of the chief shrines of pilgrimage in Eur, famous for reputed apparitions of the Virgin (Our Lady of *L*) to Bernadette in 1858.

  299.06   My Lourde! My Lourde!

LOUTH.   Co, Leinster prov. Anc name Oriel or Uriel. *Lughbhadh*, Ir "pertaining to Lugh" (leader of the Tuatha Dé Danaan).

  The hazy assn with Lucan (290.24, 295.19) seems to pun on "Lux upon Lux," which in JJ's "Grace" Cunningham says was the motto of Leo XIII. Baronies: Ardee, Drogheda, Upr and Lwr Dundalk, Ferrard, Louth.

  ?23.31   the louthly one whose loab we are devorers of
  49.15   mouther-in-louth
  ?132.23   our lurch as lout let free
  290.24   Arklow Vikloe to Louth super Luck
  295.19   mudland Loosh from Luccan
  329.33   louthmouthing after the Healy Mealy...Tarar
  336.06   the louthly meathers, the loudly meaders, the lously measlers
  ?460.11   How he stalks to simself louther and lover
  595.12   louts

LOVE LANE.   4 Dub sts have borne this name at various times. (1) From Cork St S past W end of Brown St to SCR; now Donore Ave (14/33).   (2) Btwn York and King Sts, W of Stephen's Green; now Mercer St, Upr (15/33).   (3) Off Lwr Mount St (E *LL*) (16/33).   (4) Off Ballybough Rd (N *LL*; now Sackville Ave) (16/35).

  LL in London is several blocks NW of the Bank of Eng on Threadneedle St, and the same distance NE of the Old Bailey (site of the form Newgate Pris) on Newgate St.

  ?260.09   Long Livius Lane
  ?260.13   by New Livius Lane
  551.34   made...Threadneedles and Newgade and Vicus Veneris to cooinsight
  578.27   head under Hatesbury's Hatch and loamed his fate to old Love Lane

"LOVELY PEGGY," THE.   A notorious prison-ship which was anchored off Ringsend from 1798 to 1805.

  291.05   ship me silver...the poour girl, a lonely peggy

LUBAR RIVER.   Acc to Macpherson, the old name of the Six Mile Water, Co Antrim, which flows W into NE cor of Lough Neagh from the hills N of Belfast. Hugh Campbell's notes to Macpherson identify it as rising on Cromla or Crommal Hill, now Cave Hill NW of Belfast. Brewer's *Reader's Handbook*: the *L* "flows between the two mountains Cromleach and Crommal." See *Lena*.

  132.24   Cromlechheight and Crommalhill were his farfamed feetrests when
            our lurch as lout let free into the Lubar heloved

LUBLIN.   City, E Pol, 95 mi SE of Warsaw.
  130.29   namesake with an initial difference in the once kingdom of Poland
  339.31   *like aleal lusky Lubliner*

565.22   the lucky load to Lublin

LUCAN.   Suburban vill 9 mi W of Dub, at the confluence of the Griffeen and Liffey Rivs; on the S bank of the Liffey, crossed by a single-arched br. *Leamhchan*, Ir "place of mallows." Once a spa (sulphur spring); site of the *L* Hydropathic Spa and Hotel (565.33, 580.25). The hotel seems to be one of the metamorphoses of HCE's inn (see *Tavern*), which spends most of its time in Chapelizod. A steam tram ran from Dub to *L* via Chapelizod (80.36, 482.07).

For the Dub journalist Charles Lucan (419.35) see *Census*. For the Earls of *L* (253.32, ?255.21, 452.29, 620.08), see *Census*. Patrick Sarsfield, created Earl of *L* by James II, may have been born there; the mod earls (Brit title dating from 1795) never lived there.

32.16	Lucalizod
37.32	Lukanpukan pilzenpie
48.12	Coleman of Lucan
51.26	lucal odour
53.24	lekan for lukan
62.35	Lucalizod diocesan
80.36	Any lucans, please? [tram conductor to passengers]
87.18	unlucalised, of no address
101.11	folkrich Lucalizod
107.05	*Lucalizod*
110.08	Isitachapel-Asitalukin
143.17	spot lucan's dawn
178.09	every doorpost in...Lucalizod
203.15	Lucan Yokan
253.32	laird of Lucanhof
255.21	Buke of Lukan
290.24	Louth super Luck [see *Louth*]
295.20	mudland Loosh from Luccan [see *Louth*]
324.32	lucal drizzles
359.28	Lets All Wake Brickfaced In Lucan
419.35	Charley Lucan's
438.30	the dammymonde of Lucalamplight
452.29	lived a lord at Lucan
474.07	locks of a lucan tinge
482.07	Haltstille, Lucas and Dublinn!
497.18	Luccanicans
521.06	a glass of Lucan
545.33	I revolucanized by my eructions
564.33	Archfieldchaplain of Saint Lucan's
565.33	Lucalised, on the sulphur spa...stop at his inn
580.25	his hydrocomic establishment
598.28	Ysat Loka
620.08	an earl was he, at Lucan?

LUCCOMBE.   Vill, N Somerset, Eng. In the middle ages the area which includes *L* was the site of Exmoor Forest.

235.16   Oncaill's [*on-caill*, Ir "great damage"] plot. Luccombe oaks, Turkish hazels, Greek firs

LUCERNE, LAKE.   The *Vierwaldstättersee* or Lake of the Four Forest Cantons (see *Four Cantons*), Switz.

472.23   Thy now paling light lucerne we ne'er may see again...four cantons

LUGGELA (LUGGALA) LAKE.   Lake in Wicklow Mts, 16 mi S of Dub; aka Lough Tay. Fed by Annamoe R, it empties into Lough Dan to the S. This is where St Kevin ran first to escape Cathleen before going to Glendalough. *L* Lodge (built for Sir Philip Crampton) is at the N end of Lough Tay. Moore's "No, Not More Welcome the Fairy Numbers" is set to the old air "Luggala."

141.14   nor his hair efter buggelawrs
203.17   You know the dinkel dale of Luggelaw?
305.R1   LIGGERILAG, TITTERITOT, LEG IN A TEE, LUG IN A LAW
315.24   lug in the lee
?531.04   Log Laughty

LUGNAQUILLA, MT.   Highest mt in Co Wicklow, S of Dub, pop called "Lug."
?130.04   the Lug his peak has, the Luk his pile
204.07   Lugnaquillia's noblesse pickts

LUKE'S MT.   Mt, Co Down, W of Newcastle on Dundrum Bay; N spur of Mourne Mts.
?130.04   the Lug his peak has, the Luk his pile

LUND.   City, SW Swed. The mythological builder of *L* Cath was the giant, Finn MacCool, at the request of St Lawrence. If the saint did not guess the builder's name by the time the ch was built, Finn would get his eyes. Lawrence guessed it as the last stone was put in place.
137.09   built the Lund's kirk
320.22   Brighten-pon-the-Baltic, from our lund's rund turs bag

LUSK.   Vill, N of Dub, W of Rush.
211.23   from Lusk to Livienbad
325.32   madhugh, mardyk, luusk [= Leinster] and cong
339.31   *aleal lusky Lubliner*
541.19   Lusqu'au bout
576.03   the Eaudelusk Company

LUTSK.   City, now in Ukrainian SSR; belonged to Lith-Pol until 1791, Russ until 1919, Pol until 1939. Pol, *Luck* (pron "Loosk").
339.31   *strangling like aleal lusky Lubliner*
565.22   Gothgorod...the lucky load to Lublin

LUXEMBOURG.   Country and cap city, btwn Belg and Fr. The city fortress (demolished in the 1860's) was located on the cliffs above the Alzette R.
    Aldborough Ho (qv) in Dub became a sch called "Luxembourg."
132.29   lachsembulger, leperlean
330.09   for Laxembraghs was passthecupper to Our Lader's
578.35   that Luxuumburgher evec cettehis Alzette

LUXOR.   Egyptian town on Nile R in Upr Egypt; site of anc Thebes. The obelisk in the Place de la Concorde, Paris, was brought from *L*.
548.27   loomends day lumineused luxories on looks

LYDIA.   Anc kingdom in W part of Asia Min; now part of Turk.
294.20   raucking his flavourite turvku in the smukking precincts of lydias
348.01   *smolking his fulvurite turfkish in the rooking pressance of laddios*

LYNCH, ANNE, AND CO.   Tea merchants, with shops at 162 N King St and several other locations in Dub. *U* 659/675.

293.15   ann linch
325.04   Anna Lynchya Pourable
392.32   alfred cakes from Anne Lynch
406.27   Anne Lynch...Tea is the Highest
506.34   Anna Lynsha's Pekoe

LYNDHURST TERRACE.   In Hampstead, London.
?351.29   soeurs assistershood off Lyndhurst Terrace, the puttih Misses Celana
           Dalems

LYONESSE.   Legendary tract of land in which was the City of Lions, btwn Land's
End and the Scilly Isles, later submerged under "forty fathoms." Arthur came from
this fabled land, and it was the birthplace of Tristram, acc to Spenser's *Faerie Queene*.
?229.10   the lalage of lyonesses [*lalage*: type name for classic beauties]
359.16   Arser of the Rum Tipple...lyonesslooting

LYONS.   (1) Fr, *Lyon*; city, cap of Rhône Dept, at confluence of Rhône and Saône
rivs. The "poor men of Lyons," or Waldenses, were followers of Peter Waldo, who
gave away his wealth and preached poverty in the late 12th cent. Edward Bulwer Lyt-
ton's play *The Lady of Lyons* (449.11) is laid in *L*. The Irvings, father and son, starred
for 35 years in *The Lyons Mail* (465.15), about an innocent man convicted of a mail
robbery because he looked like one of the robbers (the same actor played both parts).
(2) Newcastle (qv) of *L*, SW of Dub, was one of the 4 Royal Manors of Dub (qv) est
by Henry II. *Dun Liamhnas*, the Hill of *L*, is on the anc rd from Dub to Naas.
229.10   malady...lalage of lyonesses
371.36   that poor man of Lyones, good Dook Weltington
387.14   the manausteriums of the poor Marcus of Lyons
449.11   my lady of Lyons
465.15   as the lyonised mails

LYONS CORNER HOUSES.   The showplaces of the form chain of Lyons tea-shops
and restaurants, London; est btwn 1910 and 1928, Messrs Gluckstein and Salmon,
owners. Lyons's waitresses were called "Nippies."
170.32   Findlater and Gladstone's, Corner House, Englend
177.36   with all the teashop lionses of Lumdrum
367.12   try the corner house for thee
449.11   the nippy girl...my lady of Lyons...gastronomy

M

MAAM.   Vill, Co Galway.
85.23   a child of Maam, Festy King

MABBOT'S MILL.   In the 17th and early 18th cents it stood on N bank of Liffey,
about the present Talbot St (16/34). Built by Gilbert Mabbot, whose name survived
in Mabbot Lane and Mabbot (now Corporation) St, in the heart of the (erstwhile)
brothel district.
    JJ's 1st Draft had "82 Dublin Square." In *transition* and in the first 3 printings
of *FW* this was changed to "82 Mabbot's Mall," and in the "Correction of Misprints"
and succeeding printings to "81 bis...." Numbers in Mabbot St and Lane never ran

into the 80's, but Bella Cohen's establishment was at 82 Lwr Tyrone St, around the cor from Mabbot St. At *U* 466/475 Bloom asks, "Is this Mrs. Mack's?" and Zoe replies (incorrectly): "No, eightyone. Mrs. Cohen's." (Mrs Mack's was in reality at No 85.)

    174.26   Mr Vanhomrigh's house at 81 bis Mabbot's Mall

MACAO.   Form Port colony on *M* Isl, in delta of Pearl R, Kwangtung Prov, SE China. (Camoëns lived there, St Francis Xavier died there.)

    233.27   Gau on! [Goa] Micaco!

MACCLESFIELD.   Town S of Manchester, Eng. It produced silk textiles and silk-covered buttons as far back as the 17th cent.

    ?381.14   Macclefield's swash

McGILLYCUDDY'S REEKS.   Mt ("reek") range W of Killarney, Co Kerry. Boucicault's Colleen Bawn had her cottage there. The hereditary title of the chief is "The M'Gillycuddy of the Reeks." *Letters* I, 389: JJ makes a joke about "Fr. McGillicuddy of the Breeks."

    92.26   Gentia Gemma of the Makegiddyculling Reeks
    228.02   the MacSiccaries of the Breeks
    518.09   So wreek me Ghyllygully!

MACHPELAH, CAVE OF.   Acc to *Gen* 25:9 and 50:13, the burial place of Abraham, and also of Sarah, Isaac, Rebecca, and Leah.

    77.25   a stone slab with the usual Mac Pelah address of velediction

MADAGASCAR.   Large isl off E coast of SE Afr; since 1958 the Malagasy Rep. The Malagasy people, inhabitants of the isl, are derived from Malayo-Polynesian and Melanesian stocks, with much Arab intermarriage.

    207.26   Duodecimoroon?...Malagassy?

MADAME TUSSAUD'S (WAXWORKS) EXHIBITION.   In Marylebone St, London. The chamber of horrors, celebrating famous murderers, is in the basement.

    57.20   Madam's Toshowus waxes largely more lifeliked
    455.05   Toussaint's wakeswalks experdition...chamber of horrus

MADELEINE, LA.   Dist in lwr Vézère, the Dordogne, Fr, whose relics give its name to the Magdalenian, or late Paleolithic period.

    153.36   wherry whiggy maudelenian woice
    576.36   neoliffic...magdalenian jinnyjones

MADRAS.   City and state, SE Ind. The Mahratta Confederation, defeated by the Brit in the 18th cent, governed terr farther N, though there was a Mahratta attack on *M* in 1741. *M* was not involved in Wellington's engagements nor in the Sepoy Mutiny of 1857.

    11th *EB*, "Madras": "The European 'compounds' or parks...make Madras a city of magnificent distances."

    10.16   seeboy, madrashattaras, upjump and pumpim
    539.25   now city of magnificent distances

MADRID.   Cap city of Sp. The Buen Retiro Park, E of the Prado, is *M*'s principal park.

    ?313.34   towerds Meade-Reid and Lynn-Duff
    536.21   *Buen retiro!*
    553.36   madridden mustangs

MAELSTROM.   Orig, a strong current running past the S end of Moskenes Isl, W coast of Nor; aka *Moskenström.* Now a generic term for "whirlpool."

    547.32   malestream in shegulf

MAGAZINE FORT, PHOENIX PARK   (12/34).   At the SE cor of the "Fifteen Acres," on St Thomas's Hill in the Park, built on the site of the old Phoenix or Fionn Uisge House in 1801. The bldgs of the Magazine are surrounded by a ditch and wall. Even in his madness, Swift quipped: "Behold a proof of Irish sense,/Here Irish wit is seen;/When nothing's left that's worth defence,/They build a magazine." The "Starfort" (see *Phoenix Park: Starfort*) was a different fortification, to the N of the *MF.* The crash (Fimfim Fimfim, etc) which usually appears with refs to the Magazine Wall is the fall of Humpty Dumpty and of HCE. Strongbow had nothing to do with Phoenix Park or the *MF*, but acc to the 11th *EB*, "Dublin," he died "of a mortification in one of his feet" (540.18).

As the ammunition dump for the Dub garrison, the *MF* has been a target of mod rebellions. On Easter Mon 1916 it was captured by a party of Ir Volunteers and Fianna Éireann pretending to play football near the gate. They failed to blow it up because their fuses didn't work. In 1939 the IRA successfully raided the *MF* and took many truckloads of arms and ammunition – all recovered in a few days.

7.31	magazine wall...maggy seen all
12.36	from the macroborg of Holdhard [Howth Cas] to the microbirg of Pied de Poudre
13.14	mausolime wall
44.27	*Mag-a-zine Wall*
44.28	*Mag-a-zine Wall*
45.04	Magazine Wall
48.16	merrymen all
58.13	ring and sing wohl
116.18	makeussin wall
?137.17	a footprinse on the Megacene
139.13	wan wubblin wall
176.04	*Moggie's on the Wall*
262.26	Bacchus e'en call
273.01	By old Grumbledum's walls
294.25	magmasine fall
310.02	magazine battery
314.13	muddies scrimm ball
314.13	maidies scream all
331.30	imageascene all
334.24	mizzatint wall...chromo for all
437.10	abdominal wall
497.25	magazine hall, by the magazine wall
540.18	the mortification that's my fate
553.24	magicscene wall
560.15	maggies in all
567.11	Courtmilits' Fortress
615.31	margarseen oil

MAGDALEN.   There were *M* Asylums (for fallen women or "magdalens") in Donnybrook and Leeson St Lwr. In 19th-cent Dub, fallen women were "saved" by putting them to work as laundresses; hence for *FW* the Two Washerwomen are the "maggies," as at 586.13–.15 and *passim.*

The *M* R is in Can, and the Magdalena R in Colombia. The Isis R (upr Thames) flows by Oxford's *M* (pron "maudlin") Coll. Paris's Madeleine (the Ch of St Mary-Magdalen) looks down the Rue Royale to the Obelisque in the Place de la Concorde.

    211.08   Olona Lena Magdalena [all rivs]
    ?237.36   toutes philomelas as well as magdelenes
    289.20   leathercoats for murty magdies
    434.16   Harlotte Quai...Britain Court...the feast of Marie Maudlin
    586.09   and what do you think my Madeleine saw?
    586.12   the maudlin river then gets its dues
    586.15   brownie Mag Dillon

MAGELLAN, STRAIT OF.   The winding strait, 350 mi long, btwn S tip of S Amer and Tierra del Fuego, connecting Atlantic O and Pacific O.

    512.05   Megalomagellan of our winevatswaterway...[.15] the stricker the
             strait...puttagonnianne

MAGELLANIC CLOUDS.   Astronomical term for 2 cloud-like condensations of stars in the S constellation of Mensa; similar in constitution to the Milky Way.

    358.14   my travellingself, as from Magellanic clouds
    ?512.05   brustall to the bear [?Ursa Major], the Megalomagellan of our wine-
             vatswaterway

MAGENTA.   Town in Lombardy, N It: site of victory of Napoleon III in 1859 over Austrians in It War of Liberation. Marshal Macmahon received title of Duke of *M* for his victory there.

    8.18   grand and magentic

MAHRATTA WAR.   The *M* Confederation, which replaced the Mogul Empire, was the main force opposing Brit colonialization in Ind throughout the 18th cent. In the decisive *M* War of 1803-1805, Wellington won victories at Assaye (qv) and elsewhere.

    10.16   Willingdone...madrashattaras

MAIDA VALE.   Main rd in NW London; continues Edgware Rd NW through Paddington. Named after battle of Maida (Brit defeated Fr), 1806, near town of Maida in Calabria, It. See *Lauderdale Mansions*.

    ?110.09   in this madh vaal of tares
    ?267.02   let us missnot Maidadate
    340.21   the grizzliest manmichal in Meideveide [*medvyed*, Russ "bear"]
    502.27   of the first fog in Maidanvale?
    581.19   shedropping his hitches like any maidavale oppersite orseriders

MAIN DRAIN.   Anyone who has smelled the Liffey at low tide knows that it is a main drain.

    The Rathmines and Pembroke *MD* embankment, running to the S Wall from the shoreline in SE Dub, reclaimed much land once sea.

    In "The Holy Office," JJ described himself as the *MD* of Dublin's literati: "That they may dream their dreamy dreams/I carry off their filthy streams."

    214.02   a side strain of a main drain
    541.09   mains...drains
    623.31   I prays for be mains of me draims

MAINLY ABOUT PEOPLE.   London weekly, known as "M.A.P.," publ 1898-1911 by Thomas Power ("Tay Pay") O'Connor, Ir politician and journalist.

    260.L2   *Menly about peebles*

MAJUBA HILL.   Mt in Natal, S Afr, 160 mi N of Durban. The 1st Brit defeat of

the Boer War was the rout, on 27 Feb 1881, of the Brit force occupying *MH*.
>   178.22   vying with Lady Smythe to avenge MacJobber

MALAHIDE.   Seaside town, N Co Dub. Song: "The Bridal of Malahide," about Maud Plunkett, who was maid, wife, and widow in one day, when her husband was killed by robbers just after their wedding. Her effigy is in the abbey near *M* Cas.
>   141.13   kirkpeal, foottreats given to malafides
>   566.16   maidbrides all...joybells to ring
>   583.21   malahide Liv and her bettyship...county bubblin

MALAKHOF, THE (MALAKOFF).   Fortification whose capture by Fr on 8 Sept 1855 decided the fate of Sevastopol, in the Crimean War. Named after warrant-officer of Russ navy who committed suicide there.
>   339.11   his malakoiffed bulbsbyg

MALAYSIA.   The Malay Archipelago, now mostly Indonesia; aka Sunda Isls. Great Sunda Isls: Sumatra, Java (qv), Borneo (qv), Celebes (qv), etc; Little Sunda Isls: Timor (qv), Bali, Flores, etc. There is no "Malay Strait" as such; the Strait of Malacca separates Sumatra from the Malay Penin.
>   ?295.07   she give me the Sundaclouths
>   343.01   *tasing the tiomor of malaise*
>   350.33   we chantied on Sunda schoon
>   351.32   medams culonelle on Mellay Street...by Jova

MALIN HEAD.   Co Donegal; the N-most point in Ire.
>   ?380.05   Malincurred Mansion
>   525.29   Longeal of Malin, he'll cry before he's flayed
>   580.34   from Malin to Clear and Carnsore Point to Slynagollow

MALL, THE.   London's ceremonial ave joining Trafalgar Sq and Buckingham Palace, separating St James's Park from Green Park.
>   373.28   dizzy...Gladstools...ride as the mall
>   540.33   midday's mallsight...hide park seek

MALLOW.   Town, Co Cork. Its former eminence as a spa is commemorated in the pop song "The Rakes of Mallow"; the allusions are to the song.
>   199.28   *The Rakes of Mallow*
>   553.20   rigs of barlow

MALPAS (15/33).   St, from New St to Blackpitts. *M* Pl is off *M* St. Colonel John Mapas erected a large obelisk, still standing, on Killiney Hill S of Dub to make work after the "hard frost" of 1741-42.
>   81.15   in the saddle of the Brennan's (now Malpasplace?) pass

MAN, ISLE OF.   Isl in Ir Sea off NW coast of Eng. Called by Ptolemy, "Monada" ("further Mona") to distinguish it from Anglesea, Roman "Mona." But on Ptolemy's map it appears as Mona. Called by Pliny, "Monabia"; by Orosius and Bede, "Menavia"; by Gildas, "Eubonia." The name "Mona" (qv) is still used allusively.
     The name "Man" is from Manannan, the wizard who kept the isl hidden in mist when it was threatened by marauders. He had 3 legs on which he rolled along: the origin of the 3-legged figure on the Manx arms. This is the *triskelion*, "The Three Legs of Man."
     Finn MacCool dug the *I of M* with one stroke of his spade and hurled it into the Ir Sea, leaving Lough Neagh (310.31−.34). *M* has no lakes (76.23). The Calf of *M* is a rocky isl just off its SW coast. The elective branch of the anc Manx legislature is

called the "House of Keys"; the other branch is the Council, and sitting together the 2 branches constitute the Tynwald (262.F3) Court. Its courts of common law are administered by 2 "deemsters." The common law of *M* was called "breastlaw" (464.34), because, unwritten, it was held in the breasts of the deemsters and keys.

Frank Budgen said that JJ told him the Four's donkey is, among other things, the *I of M*, once owned by Ire (214.33).

26.29	Diet of Man
76.23	Isle of Man...limniphobes
78.19	three monads...dreyfussed as ever
85.36	cymtrymanx bespokes
91.22	an Inishman was as good as any cantonnatal
?150.31	endswell of Man
159.32	isle of manoverboard
214.33	dwyergray ass them four old codgers owns
252.05	manchind's parlements
262.F3	A goodrid croven in a tynwalled tub [for King Godred Crovan, see *Census*]
287.15	There's the isle of Mun, ah!
?291.09	till the ives of Man
310.31	ale of man...turfeycork...out of Lougk Neagk
331.08	The threelegged man
339.27	calves of Man
?353.04	his all of man
391.29	old Manx presbyterian
433.19	*Minxy was a Manxmaid when Murry wor a Man*
462.16	me poor Isley!...innerman monophone
464.32	Mona, my own love...you made your breastlaw
496.08	a minx from the Isle of Woman
?525.31	Three threeth...Manu ware!
529.20	Manofisle
576.03	Calif of Man
?595.26	the topaia that was Mankaylands
616.30	His giantstand of manunknown [Manannan]

MANCHESTER.   Manufacturing city in Lancs, NW Eng. The "*M* Martyrs" were 3 young Irishmen hanged for attempting the rescue of Fenian prisoners in *M* in Nov 1867; they were Wm Allen, Michael O'Brien, and Michael Larkin. (Acc to John Garvin, Murphy, Hernon, and Dwyer were the 3 City Commissioners appointed to replace the Dub City Council, 1924-1930.)

The Manchester Guardian, most famous of Eng daily newspapers outside of London, did not lose its reputation and local name until long after JJ's death.

42.29	landwester guardian
73.14	his manjester's voice
446.31	Up Murphy, Henson and O'Dwyer, the Warchester Warders!
448.14	l'pool and m'chester

MANDALAY.   City, Upr Burma. In the context of rds, the *FW* ref is to the song, "On the Road to Mandalay" ("Where there ain't no ten commandments, and a man can raise a thirst").

577.24   after many mandelays

MANHOOD, HUNDRED OF.   An anc territorial division in Sussex, Eng; it contains the town of Sidlesham (qv). The *H of M* appears in *FW* in HCE's genealogy (30.06):

"the Glues, the Gravys, the Northeasts, the Ankers and the Earwickers of Sidlesham in the Hundred of Manhood."

    30.08   Sidlesham in the Hundred of Manhood
    54.25   yorehunderts of mamooth
    98.01   with missiles too from a hundred of manhood
   264.20   for a four of hundreds of manhood
   329.09   a hulldread pursunk manowhood
   375.09   wholes poors riches of ours hundreds of manhoods
   596.02   hundering...plundersundered manhood

MANOR MILL STEAM LAUNDRY   (15/33).   In Dundrum, around the turn of the cent. Office: 13 Castle Market.

   614.02–.13   Annone Wishwashwhose...Doone of the Drumes...mannormillor clipperclappers [*clipeclash*, Ir Eng "gossip"]

MANSION HOUSE   (16/33).   In Dawson St; the official res of Lord Mayors of Dub since 1715. It has no lawn or park, but in the 19th cent Stephen's Green at the end of Dawson St was used as a paddock for the Lord Mayor's horses (617.22).

   ?22.21   by the ward of his mansionhome
  ?140.30   brooklined Georgian mansion's lawn
   491.18   *He drapped has draraks an Mansianhase parak*
   617.22   Manchem House Horsegardens

MANTUA.   Cap of *M* prov, Lombardy, N It. Birthplace of Virgil. Mantuanus was a writer of Lat eclogues used in schs in Elizabethan times.

   113.02   postmantuam glasseries

MAPLE'S HOTEL   (16/33).   Form at 24-28 Kildare St; F Maple, prop.

   155.25   a cloister of starabouts over Maples

MAPPA MUNDI.   Lat, "map of the world"; *mappa*, Lat "napkin," ie, a painted cloth. NPN, although in early usage it referred to the world itself, not only to a representation of it. But it seems relevant to a gazetteer, esp since *FW* vaguely links it to the mound from which the hen scratches up the letter.

JJ explained "Shaun's map" (211.30) as the map of Ire on postage stamps of the Ir Free State, which despite Partition showed the entire isl (*Letters* I, 213).

   211.30   a sunless map of the month, including the sword and stamps, for Shemus O'Shaun the Post
   253.05   the mappamund has been changing pattern as youth plays moves from street to street
   464.26   marauding about the moppamound [followed by allusions to Eur countries]

MARATHON.   Plain, 25 mi N of Athens; scene of victory of Athenians under Miltiades over Persians in 490 BC.

    9.33   marathon merry

MARBLE ARCH.   Victoria mem, roundabout, and Underground sta at NE cor of Hyde Park, London; former site of Tyburn gallows. Also the name of a well-known natural fountain in Florence Court, S of Enniskillen, Co Fermanagh.

   264.F2   dreamt that you'd wealth in marble arch do you ever think of pool beg slowe
   540.15   Tyeburn throttled, massed murmars march: where the bus stops

MARE INFERUS.   Anc name for Tuscan Sea, W of It.

136.08   leapt the Inferus, swam the Mabbul

MARENGO.   Vill, SE Piedmont, NW It; site of Napoleonic victory over Austrians in battle of 14 June 1800. "Marengo" was a favorite (white) horse of Napoleon; he rode it at Waterloo, as Wellington rode "Copenhagen."
223.16   no such Copenhague-Marengo

MARIENBAD.   Spa and town, Bohemia, W Czech; once one of the most frequented watering-places of Eur. Its mineral springs belonged to the adjoining abbey of Tepl.
333.36   toplots talks from morrienbaths

MARINE SCHOOL (ROYAL) (17/34).   On Sir John Rogerson's Quay; chartered 1775 for educating "orphans and sons of seafaring men." The bldg is now almost destroyed.
?548.33   a school of shells of moyles marine to swing their saysangs

MARINO (17/36).   Dist, NE Dub; named after *M* House, country seat of the Lord Charlemont who built Charlemont Ho in Rutland (now Parnell) Sq; the Greek temple ("Casino") in the grounds was built by the Earl and furnished at tremendous cost.
    William Carleton the novelist lived at 3 *M* Terr in the area, in the mid-19th cent.
607.01   The old Marino tale

MARIST FATHERS.   Around the turn of the cent, the house of the Fathers of the Society of Mary was at 89 Lwr Leeson St, where they operated a sch. The *M* Fathers and *M* Brothers now have houses in a number of suburbs.
447.18   Mirist fathers' brothers eleven versus White Friars

MARITZA (MARITSA) RIVER.   Anc, Hebrus; Gk, Evros; Turk, Meriç; flows from Bulgaria S into Aegean btwn Gr and Turk.
205.16   Mericy Cordial [Meriç]
205.29   Evropeahahn [Evros]
469.14   my olty mutther, Sereth Maritza

MARKLAND.   Portion of N Amer coast discovered by Norse explorers about 1000 AD. Variously located but most prob Newfoundland. Name means "woodland." See *Vinland.*
213.35   Markland's Vineland

MARLBOROUGH BARRACKS (13/35).   Btwn Blackhorse Ave and the Phoenix Park Zoo; now McKee Barracks.
5.35   the merlinburrow burrocks

MARLBOROUGH GREEN (16/34).   In the 18th cent, a small green E of *M* St, bounded roughly by Gardiner and Talbot Sts and Beresford Lane. It was a fashionable promenade, with a bowling green, tea-booths, singers, and bands.
57.35   on Marlborough Green as through Molesworth Fields

MARLBOROUGH PLACE (16/34).   A mews off E side of *M* St.
132.22   and then he tore up Marlborough Place

MARMORA, SEA OF.   The sea btwn the Black Sea and the Medit, separating Turkey-in-Europe from Turkey-in-Asia, fed by the Bosporus and emptying through the Dardanelles (Hellespont).
254.18   The mar of murmury mermers

MARROWBONE LANE (14/33).   Btwn Thomas St and Cork St. None of the following allusions are at all clearly to *ML*. The derivation of the name is uncertain, but it may be Dub's counterpart to London's St Mary-le-Bone (see *Marylebone*).

　?16.03　these kraals of slitsucked marrogbones
　?192.29　Euston...hanging garments of Marylebone
　?347.12　Eastchept...dangling garters of Marrowbone
　?391.32　on his two bare marrowbones
　?550.10　rich morsel of the marrolebone...Saint Pancreas

MARS.　The 4th planet from the sun, next in order from the Earth. For the Roman deity, see *Census*.

　494.12　Ers, Mores and Merkery
　581.14　the dipper and the martian's frost

MARSEILLES.　Fr city, Medit port. "The Marseillaise" was composed in 1792, adopted by a *M* battalion, suppressed by Napoleon, later became the Fr nat anthem.

　64.13　martiallawsey marses of foreign musikants'
　176.22　our pettythicks the marshalaisy
　464.21　a bawlful of the Moulsaybaysse and yunker doodler

MARSHALSEA.　Name of 2 Dub jails, the City *M* (dating from 1704) and the Four Courts *M* (dating from 1580), both for petty debtors. Both had a number of locations; the Four Courts *M* was in Werburgh St, near the present City Hall and its Muniment Room, when the Four Courts were adjacent, by Christchurch Cath. Into the 19th cent, turnkeys preyed on prisoners and sheriffs on turnkeys (456.32).

　89.17　dtheir gcourts marsheyls
　94.25　[the Four] upin their judges' chambers, in the muniment room, of
　　　　　their marshalsea
　?132.24　mareschalled his wardmotes
　456.32　milking turnkeys and sucking the blood out of the marshalsea
　?539.27　martiell siegewin

MARSH'S LIBRARY　(15/33).　Next to St Patrick's Cath, in St Patrick's Close; founded 1702 by Narcissus Marsh, Archbishop of Dub.

　212.31　estheryear's marsh narcissus
　?442.36　coomb the brash of the libs round Close Saint Patrice

MARYBOROUGH.　Now Port Laoise, Co Laois. Orig name after Mary, Queen of Scots, who changed the name of the co from Leix to Queen's.

　577.14　Miryburrow, leaks

MARYLEBONE.　London bor (St Mary-le-bone), W of Regent's Park. It contains *M* Cricket Club (qv) and *M* rlwy sta, but Euston and St Pancras stas are in the borough of St Pancras E of Regent's Park. All 3 rlwy stas are on *M* Rd.

　192.29　Euston...hanging garments of Marylebone
　347.12　Eastchept...dangling garters of Marrowbone
　550.10　rich morsel of the marrolebone...Saint Pancreas

MARYLEBONE CRICKET CLUB.　The MCC is the arbiter of world cricket; hqs at Lord's Cricket Ground, St John's Wood, Marylebone, London. The area opp the pavilion at Lord's is known as the "Nursery" end.

　71.34　*Cumberer of Lord's Holy Ground*
　?433.14　Never play lady's game for the Lord's stake
　584.09　till the empsyseas run googlie
　584.16　his norsery pinafore

MAS D'AZIL.   Town, Ariège Dept, S Fr, for which the Azilian culture of the mesolithic period is named.
    152.36   from his azylium

MASON'S RESTAURANT (14/34).   Mrs Mason's oyster saloon was at 12 S King
St, opp the Gaiety Theatre. Acc to Vivian Mercier, it was known as "Mother Mason's."
    223.05   the Mutther Masons

MASSACHUSETTS.   See *Boston*, *Salem*.

MATER MISERICORDIAE HOSP (15/35).   At Eccles St and Berkeley Rd (qqv).
    ?205.16   Mericy Cordial
    229.15   Mother of Misery
    260.F2   Mater Mary Mercerycordial of the Dripping Nipples
    392.08   housepays for the daying at the Martyr Mrs MacCawley's

MATHEW, FATHER THEOBALD, STATUE (15/34).   The 19th-cent temperance
priest is commemorated by Mary Redmond's stat (1893) in the cen of Upr O'Connell St.
    553.13   Fra Teobaldo

MATTERHORN.   Peak in the Pennine Alps on the Sw-It border. Dathi, the last pagan king of Ire (5th cent), invaded Gaul and was killed by lightning in the Alps for
(acc to Keating) having plundered the sanctuary of a holy hermit.
    274.07   Dathy...on the Madderhorn...daring Dunderhead

MAUNSELL AND CO (15/34).   Printing firm in Parliament St, publisher of the
Daily Express and other newspapers. George Roberts, the managing director, had bit-
ter disputes with JJ over deletions after the sheets of *Dubliners* were printed, and in
Sept 1912 the sheets were destroyed – JJ said by burning, Roberts said by "guillo-
tining and pulping."
    185.01   when Robber and Mumsell, the pulpic dictators...boycotted him

MAUSOLEUM AT HALICARNASSUS.   One of the 7 Wonders of the Anc World (qv).
    ?13.14   By the mausolime wall
    261.13   before a mosoleum
    553.10   mousselimes

MAXWELLTOWN.   Part of Dumfries in Dumfries Co, S Scot. Maxwelton's braes are
bonnie, in William Douglas's "Annie Laurie" (38.21).
    38.09   knee Bareniece Maxwelton

MAYNOOTH.   Town, Co Kildare. Best known for St Patrick's Coll, Ire's main RC
seminary, it is also the site of the great cas (now ruins) of the Fitzgerald Earls of Kildare. In 1535 the forces of Silken Thomas surrendered to the Eng after a siege in
which siege guns were used for the first time in Ire; the execution of the survivors
made the "Pardon of *M*" a by-word – which *FW* associates with the clerical hounding
of Parnell (553.13).
    370.34   Fyre maynoother endnow! [*Fire minutter endnu*, Dan "four minutes
             to go"]
    371.26   she been goin shoother off almaynoother onawares
    553.13   Pardonell of Maynooth

MAYO.   Co, Connacht prov. Baronies: Borrishoole, Carra, Clanmorris, Costello, Er-
ris, Gallen, Kilmaine, Murrisk, Ross, Tirawley.
    141.01   the first down Spanish Place, Mayo I make

?197.35   Pilcomayo!
479.03   in or about Mayo
482.11   Macdougal...Jong of Maho
589.07   mayom and tuam

MAYO OF THE SAXONS.   Monastery, now ruins and site of vill of Mayo 3 mi S of Balla, Co Mayo; est 7th cent by St Colman for Eng monks from Inishbofin following disputes btwn Ir and Eng monks there. Ir, *Mag nEó na Sachsen.*
85.25   in old plomansch Mayo of the Saxons·

MAYPOLE.   The phallic maypole was once erected in Ire as in Eng. Mayday Festival was trad kept on Oxmantown Green, but was abolished after Mayday Riot of 1733, when soldiers attempted to pull down the maypole. In 1798 Major Sirr took down the maypole on Harold's Cross Green because it was crowned with the Phrygian (Liberty) Cap. The maypole in Finglas survived into the 19th cent.

In *FW* "maypole" may allude to the Wellington Mon, since the Duke of Wellington may have been born on the 1st of May (though both his date and place of birth are disputed).

"Gilligan's maypoles" seem to be wireless antennae, but who Gilligan was I don't know.
44.04   our maypole once more where he rose of old
249.26   one maypole morning
358.34   discrimination for his maypole
421.32   from Rooters and Havers through Gilligan's maypoles
503.33   grawndest crowndest consecrated maypole
589.01   maypoleriding and dotted our green
596.21   broking by the maybole gards

MEANDER RIVER.   Now known as Menderes, in W Turk, flowing into the Aegean Sea, it was known in anc times for its wanderings. The anc Scamander R, which flowed past Troy, is now aka Menderes.
18.22   The meandertale, aloss and again
19.25   What a meanderthalltale
?123.10   a meandering male fist
209.05   meander by that marritime way

MEARINGSTONE.   Through the 17th cent, "mearing stones" marked the mears (boundaries) of municipal land and liberties. Gilbert's *History* (II, 8) notes a mearing stone set in the wall of Cork Ho, near the Castle, *ca* 1660. It is unlikely that boundaries in the area of Chapelizod would have been so marked.
?247.04   the hike from Elmstree to Stene
293.14   the Great Ulm (with Mearingstone in Fore ground)

MEATH.   Co, Leinster prov. Form 5th prov (see *Ireland: The Five Fifths*), "Royal *M*," when Tara was the seat of Ir kings. The "Royal *M*" foxhunt is still in existence. *Midhe*, Ir "middle"; Lat, Media.

Baronies: Upr and Lwr Deece, Upr and Lwr Duleek, Dunboyne, Fore, Upr and Lwr Kells, Lune, Morgallion, Upr and Lwr Moyfenrath, Upr and Lwr Navan, Ratoath, Upr and Lwr Slane.
?49.15   rawl chawclates for mouther-in-louth
51.25   Meathman or Meccan?
67.25   meatman's
87.24   they could not say meace, (mute and daft) meathe
?186.25   Knockmaree, Comty Mea

?284.01	Show that the median...County Fearmanagh...County Monachan
?313.34	Meade-Reid and Lynn-Duff
336.06	the louthly meathers, the loudly meaders, the lously measlers
340.21	the grizzliest manmichal in Meideveide
352.12	after meath the dulwich
436.28	We won't meeth in Navan
474.02	mead of the hillock
475.23	a mead that was not far
?479.09	Meads Marvel, thass [in context, the 5th prov]
595.17	larksmathes...homdsmeethes...quailsmeathes

MECCA.   Holy city of Islam, and chief town of the Hejaz in Saudi Arabia. Birthplace of Mohammed, who consecrated the Kaaba (named for its resemblance to a die or cube), form a heathen temple. The chief sanctuary of Islam, aka the "Ancient House," it contains the sacred Black Stone which was white when it fell from heaven, but turned black from the sins of those who have touched it. The Great Mosque contains the Kaaba, also the well Zemzem (Zamzam), by legend the well from which Hagar drew water for her son, Ishmael. Also in the temple were collected 360 images of *djinns*, one for each day of the lunar year (597.13). The area immediately surrounding *M*, a place of pilgrimage and sanctuary since before the Prophet, is known as the Haram. See *Arafat*.

5.14	cubehouse...arafatas...whitestone...heaven
34.08	alicubi on the old house for the chargehard
51.25	Meathman or Meccan?
84.01	fez...in the direction of Moscas
105.07	*By the Stream of Zemzem*
?143.27	seem seeming
323.21	till the rumnants of Mecckrass
471.14	bucketing after meccamaniac
518.10	the headlong stone of kismet
532.32	out of haram's way
542.13	meckamockame
597.13	Moskiosk Djinpalast

MECKLENBURG.   Form Ger state, a duchy since 14th cent, divided into grand duchies of Mecklenburg-Schwerin and Mecklenburg-Strelitz in 1701.

| 329.29 | as if he was the Granjook Meckl |
| 541.35 | in the meckling of my burgh |

MECKLENBURGH ST   (16/34).   Form Gt Martin's Lane (1756). Renamed *M* St in 1765 after Charlotte Sophia, Princess of Mecklenburg-Strelitz, who married George III in 1761. It was the heart of Dub's brothel dist; already (1887) renamed Tyrone St when Bella Cohen lived at No 82 and Annie Mack at No 85, it is now called Railway St. *U* 425/432: "Metaphysics in Mecklenburg St."

5.35	the mecklenburk bitch bite at his ear
90.31	—moecklenburgwh— [in C-word]
?329.29	the Granjook Meckl
541.35	in the meckling of my burgh Belvaros was the site forbed

MEDIA.   Anc country in area now NW part of Iran; became part of Pers emp under Cyrus, 6th cent BC. *Dan* 5:25: "Thy kingdom is divided, and given to the Medes and Persians."

| 18.22 | Thy thingdome is given to the Meades and Porsons |
| 286.07 | anymeade or persan |

MEDITERRANEAN SEA.   The highway of the anc world and the scene of Ulysses'
wanderings assumes no particular or symbolic importance in *FW*.
>120.29 of an early muddy terranean origin
>263.F2 we float the meditarenias
>289.20 blameall in that medeoturanian world
>324.30 through the middelhav of the same gorgers' kennel [*middelhav*, Nor
>   "Mediterranean"]

MEDWAY RIVER.   In Kent, Eng. There is no Hungerford (qv) on it.
>209.21 not knowing which medway or weser to strike it
>393.09 Hungerford-on-Mudway

MEETING HOUSE LANE   (15/34).   Off Mary's Abbey St. Named after Presbyterian congregation which met here 1667-1864.
>354.17 *after Meetinghouse Lanigan has embaraced Vergemout Hall*

MEETING OF THE WATERS.   The confluence of the Avonmore and Avonbeg Rivs
to form the Avoca R near Castle Howard, S of Rathdrum, Co Wicklow. The "Second
Meeting of the Waters" is the confluence of the Avoca and Aughrim Rivs at Wooden-
bridge, farther down the Vale of Avoca. T Moore said he wrote "The Meeting of the
Waters" ("There is not in the wide world a valley so sweet") at neither end of the
"Sweet Vale of Avoca" but prob had the First Meeting in mind.
 Moore's stat at the intersection of College and Westmoreland Sts at College Green
is over a public convenience. "They did right to put him up over a urinal: meeting
of the waters," Bloom thinks (*U* 160/162). See *Avoca*.
>96.14 meeting waters most improper
>?159.34 meeting of mahoganies, be the waves
>203.15 whereabouts in Ow and Ovoca?
>305.28 Ovocation of maiding waters
>345.30 Theres scares knud in this gnarld warld a fully so svend
>446.14 the mingling of our meeting waters
>466.35 Sweet fellow ovocal
>472.01 sweet wail of evoker
>?505.30 weeping of the daughters
>537.06 filthered Ovocnas
>587.25 meeting of the waitresses
>605.12 amiddle of meeting waters

MEGALOPOLIS.   Generically "great city," but specifically the Peloponnesian city
founded 370 BC as the Arcadian cap, with inhabitants drawn from about 40 towns,
as a defense against Sparta; destroyed 222 BC by Cleomenes III.
>128.03 is a quercuss in the forest but plane member for Megalopolis

MEISE.   The name of one of the Zurich guilds as well as of their Zunfthaus.
>568.12 so a sautril as a meise...Tix sixponce! Poum!

MELANESIA.   The region of isls N and NE of Australia. Includes the Bismarck Archipelago (qv).
>158.10 Metamnisia was allsoonome coloroform brune
>601.36 Milenesia waits. Be smark
>?604.25 Eyrlands Eyot, Meganesia, Habitant

MELES RIVER.   Homer was called "son of Meles," after the stream which flowed
through old Smyrna, on the border btwn Aeolia and Ionia.
>34.12 cabful of bash indeed in the homeur of that meal

MELLIFONT ABBEY.   4½ mi NW of Drogheda, Co Louth. First Cistercian Abbey in Ire, founded 1140 by King (of Uriel) Donchadh O Carroll for St Máel M'Áedhóg (Malachy) Ó Morgair, Bishop of Down. Seat of Moore family (later Earls of Drogheda) from 16th cent, now ruins.
    477.30   moor...melding mellifond indo his mouth

MELL OF MOY.   Anc Ir elysium; *Magh Meall*, Ir "honey plain." A name for the Otherworld.
    131.01   Mount of Mish, Mell of Moy

MELMOTH.   Town, Rep of S Afr (form Zululand), N of Durban. Zululand was NE part of prov of Natal.
    587.21   bugler Fred, all the ways from Melmoth in Natal

MEMPHIS.   Anc cap of Egypt, now the vill Mit Rahina 14 mi S of Cairo. Sacred to the worship of Ptah.
    516.29   whelp the henconvention's compuss memphis he wanted

MENAI STRAIT.   The channel of the Ir Sea which separates Anglesey from Caernarvonshire (now Gwynedd), the mainland of Wales. It's crossed on every trip btwn Ire and Brit *via* Holyhead, by suspension rd br ("assbacks," 84.03) or "tubular" rlwy br (84.02) (latter rebuilt after WW II).
    83.36   turning his fez menialstrait
    84.02   with tubular jurbulance...over the assback bridge
  ?300.F4   What a lubberly whide elephant for the men-in-the straits!
    539.22   for mean straits male

MENDICITY INSTITUTION (14/34).   On Usher's Isl; once Moira Ho, the elegant res of the Earl of Moira, it became in 1826 a hostel and public wash-house for mendicants.
    541.27   I bathandbaddend on mendicity

MERCER'S HOSPITAL (15/33).   In Mercer St; founded 1734 by Mary Mercer.
    260.F2   Mater Mary Mercerycordial

MERCHANT'S QUAY (14–15/34).   S side of Liffey. Site of Adam and Eve's Ch (qv).
    536.31   marchants grey

MERCIA.   A kingdom of Anglo-Saxon Eng, orig in the upr vall of the Trent R, later extended to all territories btwn the Humber and the Trent except E Anglia. Vortigern was king of Britons when the Saxons under Hengest and Horsa arrived—actually much earlier than any record of Mercian reigns.
  ?385.18   The ladies have mercias!
    565.12   Vortigern, ah Gortigern! Overlord of Mercia!

MERCURY.   The planet whose orbit is closest to the sun. For the Roman deity, see *Census*.
  ?454.20   swifter as mercury...starnly...sternish
    494.12   Ers, Mores and Merkery

MERMAID TAVERN.   It stood in Bread St, London. Sir Walter Raleigh started the early Eng club (Friday St Club) frequented by Shakespeare, Donne, Seldon, Beaumont & Fletcher. The *FW* ref is to the bar of the Ormond Hotel in *U*, where Miss Douce and Miss Kennedy are the barmaids.
    229.15   From the Mermaids' Tavern

MERRION.   (1) The coastal area of S Dub Bay btwn Sandymount and Blackrock;
M Strand was form a favorite bathing place. A convent of the Sisters of Charity
(?538.01) is in *M*. The section of the "Rock Road" (Dub-Blackrock) btwn Ballsbridge
and Booterstown is called *M* Rd (18/32).   (2) Mt *M*, res dist in SE Dub, inland from
M (19/29).   (3) *M* Sq (16/33), largest res sq in S Dub. Despite the number of emi-
nent people who have lived there, it's doubtful whether any of the *M* allusions other
than 285.F4 include it.

129.23	Smerrnion
177.02	monkmarian
285.F4	fraywhaling round Myriom square
294.20	Mary Owens
333.36	toplots talks from morrienbaths
497.17	Merrionites
538.01	irished Marryonn Teheresiann
615.20	between Williamstown and the Mairrion Ailesbury

MERRYFALLS.   Tnld, par of St Margaret, bar of Coolock, Co Dub; in Fingal.
   503.15   Winning's Folly Merryfalls

MESOPOTAMIA.   The region in SW Asia btwn the Tigris and Euphrates Rivs, from
Asia Min to the Persian Gulf. In the Bible, known as Paddan-Aram; site of early civilization. Acc to Vico, 100 yrs after the Flood the earth dried off enough in *M* to give
off exhalations producing lightning and the thunder that drove the descendants of
Noah into caves, thus beginning civilization.

318.25	my protectors unto Mussabotomia
559.35	like old mother Mesopotomac
607.09	Jakob...with Essav of Messagepostumia

MESPIL.   (1) Rd, S Bank of Grand Canal btwn Upr Leeson St and Upr Baggot St
(16/32).   (2) House, *M* Rd and Leeson St (16/32). Sarah Purser, famous for her sa-
lons, lived there in the 19th cent.

497.13	Vico, Mespil Rock and Sorrento
535.24	Give us your mespilt reception, will yous?

MÉTROPOLITAIN.   The underground rlwy system of Paris, usually called the "Métro." A number of *M* stas are named for places which are alluded to in *FW*, but it
does not seem that JJ deliberately included any list of *M* stas as such.

41.20	where our tubenny habenny metro maniplumbs below the oberflake underrails
128.22	went by metro for the polis

MICK'S HOTEL.   Percy French's song: "Has anybody ever been to Mick's Hotel,/
Mick's Hotel by the salt say water?/...Never again for me."

50.34	whoever's gone to mix Hotel by the salt say water...he's never again to sea

MIDGAARD.   In Norse myth, the abode of the first pair, parents of the human
race; it was joined to Asgard (qv) by the rainbow br Bifrost. See *Utgard*.
   424.20   —mudgaard— [in C-word]

MIDLAND BANK.   Brit banking co, with branches throughout Eng but none in Dub.
   235.11   a bank midland mansioner

MIDLAND GREAT WESTERN RAILWAY OF IRELAND CO.   The main rlwy line
btwn Dub and Galway. Its terminus was Broadstone Sta. Its tracks roughly parallel

the Liffey on the N as far as Leixlip, where they diverge.

    203.03   the midland's grainwaster asarch for her track
    447.33   the midlimb and vestee
    552.02   the Greasouwea, the Debwickweck, the Mifgreawis

MIDLOTHIAN.   Co, SE Scot, containing Edinburgh. Scott's *The Heart of Midlothian*
gave its name to a London-Edinburgh train and to a football team. Gladstone was
MP from *M*.
    381.16   poor he, the heart of Midleinster

MILE END ROAD.   In Stepney, E London, the "cockney Piccadilly."
    ?200.19   farmerette walking the pilend roads

MILESTONES.   Acc to Tindall's *Reader's Guide*, milestones in Ire were erected by
order of Oliver Cromwell, but this seems very early. The milestones along the main
Dub-Belfast rd date only from 1812. For the "overgrown milestone," see *Wellington
Monument*.
    322.33   millestones of Ovlergroamlius

MILKY WAY.   The band of light across the night sky made up by the Galaxy (*gala*,
Gk "milk") to which the solar system belongs. Lat, *via lactea*.
    148.13   the juliettes in the twinkly way
    215.06   shines high where the blue milk's upset
    341.17   The mlachy way for gambling
    395.01   murky whey, abstrew adim
    426.26   the spheres sledding along the lacteal
    432.05   my galaxy girls
    441.05   hoist Mikealy's whey
    461.03   wagon [Ursa Major]...star...way for spilling cream
    555.18   irishsmiled in his milky way
    604.14   vialact...milk train...gallaxion

MILLBOURNE LANE   (16/36).   Now *M* Ave, in Drumcondra. The Joyce family
lived at No 2 in 1894. At that time there were 2 dairies in this st.
    420.33   2 Milchbroke. Wrongly spilled. Traumcondraws

MILL ON THE FLOSS, THE.   In George Eliot's novel, the Floss is an imaginary
riv. The allusion is to an old joke about a catalogue of books which listed the books
by J S Mill and George Eliot in this way.
    213.02   Mill (J.) *On Woman* with *Ditto on the Floss*

MILLTOWN   (16/30).   Form vill, now res dist, S Dub, in the Clonskeagh area. *M*
Park is not a recreation ground but a Jesuit house of studies in Sandford Rd.
    71.07   the humours of Milltown
    96.10   in Milton's Park under lovely Father Whisperer
    601.25   S. Clouonaskieym's

MINA.   Vill, NE of Mecca (qv). A stop on the pilgrimage to Mecca where pilgrims
throw stones at pillars.
    ?318.18   veils of Mina!

MINSK.   Now cap of Belorussian SSR, it was Lith and then Pol until acquired by
Russ in the 1793 partition of Pol.
    339.34   *pallups barn in the minkst of the Krumlin...monkst of the vatercan*

MIRAMAR (MIRAMARE).   Seaside cas, 4 mi NW of Trieste, It, built and occupied by the Archduke Maximilian before he left for Mex in 1867.

    55.03   Ilyam, Ilyum! Maeromor Mournomates!
    ?247.27   moramor maenneritsch

MISERY HILL (17/34).   From Cardiff's Lane to Forbes St, through the Gas Works; 1 block S of and parallel to Sir John Rogerson's Quay.

    12.28   the bergincellies of Miseryhill
    ?239.07   with your lutean bowl round Monkmesserag

MISSISSIPPI RIVER.   Major US riv, called "Father of Waters." Its main tribs are the Missouri and the Ohio.

    159.12   her muddied name was Missisliffi
    207.13   respecks from his missus, seepy and sewery
    214.12   Father of Otters
    ?268.F6   you ran away to sea, Mrs Lappy
    ?305.R1   TILL OHIO OHIO IOIOMISS
    356.09   when they had raced Messafissi

MIZEN HEAD.   Tip of Crookhaven penin in W Co Cork; SW-most point of Ire. A rail line runs through Cork from Youghal (terminus) almost to *MH*; from *MH* to Youghal is the entire S coast of Co Cork.

    582.26   Iarland...from Maizenhead to Youghal

MIZPAH.   Several "Mizpah"s are referred to in the *OT*, but particularly *M* of Gilead (*Gen* 31:49) where Jacob and Laban marked their reconciliation by setting up a pillarstone, called *M* (that is, "watchpost") and by the "*M* benediction," "The Lord watch between thee and me, while we are absent one from the other." See also 23.12.

    306.07   Betwixt me and thee...Item, mizpah ends
    588.24   Mizpah low, youyou, number one

MOAB.   Bibl land and people, just E of Dead Sea.

    ?547.01   some prolling bywaymen from Moabit

MOATE.   Vill, Co Westmeath. Its name derives from the nearby Mote of Grania. A "Muldoon's picnic" is a chaotic mess.

    94.03   a slickstick picnic made in Moate by Muldoons

MOGGY'S ALLEY (15/34).   An 18th-cent lane off Temple Bar. Omitted here are the many refs to Maggy and the Maggies, for which see *Census*.

    79.30   old dumplan...stinkend pusshies, moggies' duggies

MOGH'S HALF.   About 200 AD, Eoghan Mór (aka Mogh Nuadat, "worshiper of [the god] Nuadat"), king of Munster, agreed with his northern rival Conn of the Hundred Battles to divide Ire along the line of the Eiscir Riada (see *Esker*) btwn Dub and Galway; their areas of influence were henceforward known as "Conn's Half" and "Mogh's Half." Eoghan's own kingdom of Munster was itself divided into 5 parts called "Eoghanacht."

    475.07   Conn's half...the whole of him nevertheless in Owenmore's five quarters...esker ridge
    549.34   Conn and Owel with cortoppled baskib

MOHER, CLIFFS OF.   Famous Atlantic cliffs, Co Clare, N of Liscannor Bay. At the S end is Hag's Head; there is no "Moher Head."

    373.05   he was berthed on the Moherboher to the Washte
    ?426.08   broke down on the mooherhead

MOLESWORTH FIELDS   (16/33).   Until the early 18th cent, the uninhabited marshy rectangle bounded by what are now Grafton and Nassau Sts, Stephen's Green, N, and Upr Merrion St. The 20th Earl of Kildare built the 1st great house S of the Liffey (Leinster Ho, now the Ir Parl Ho) and said "They will follow me wherever I go." Fashionable Dub did.
  57.35 on Marlborough Green as through Molesworth Fields

MOLYNEUX ASYLUM FOR BLIND FEMALES.   In Peter St. It opened in 1815 in bldgs form occupied by Astley's Amphitheatre (qv).
  214.14 Astley's Amphitheayter...Throw the cobwebs from your eyes, woman

MONA.   Anc name (eg, in Tacitus and Pliny the Elder) for Anglesey (Wales), which is separated from the mainland by the Menai Strait (qv). The Isle of Man (qv) was often confused with the Welsh *M* by anc geographers. Ptolemy thought *M* was a large isl off the SE cor of Ire.
  ?61.01 drabs downin their scenities, una mona
  287.15 There's the isle of Mun, ah!
  ?462.16 gullaby...Isley...me innerman monophone
  464.32 Mona, my own love...Lambay
  ?498.18 his oels a'mona nor his beers o'ryely
  ?502.12 whether Muna, that highlucky nackt, was shining
  ?628.03 moyles and moyles of it, moananoaning

MONAGHAN.   Co, Ulster prov, and co town, NW of Dundalk. Baronies: Cremorne, Dartree, Farney, Monaghan, Trough.
  261.F2 Salt Hill, Co. Mahogany, Izalond
  284.07 Lower County Monachan
  ?334.11 the 'ground old mahonagyan'
  595.15 moonyhaunts

MONASTIR.   The second city of Macedonia, form Turk, now Yugo; aka Bitol. There is also a *M* on the coast of E Tunisia, N Afr.
  271.L1 *Ulstria, Monastir, Leninstar*

MONKSTOWN   (22/28).   Dist and rd, SE Dub, btwn Blackrock and Dun Laoghaire. The area is also called Salt Hill (qv).
  294.21 Mary Owens and Dolly Monks seesidling...Blake-Roche
  532.13 Monkish tunshep

MONS.   City in Flanders, Belg, W of Charleroi. It anchored the right wing of Wellington's outpost line on the eve of Waterloo. In WW I it was the site of the 1st battle of the Brit Expeditionary Force, 23 Aug 1914.
  8.29 Grand Mons Injun
  113.19 a Mons held by tentpegs and his pal whatholoosed

MONTE CARLO.   Cap of the principality of Monaco, with its famous gambling Casino. All *FW* refs are to the song, "The Man Who Broke the Bank at Monte Carlo."
  90.24 bruck the bank in Multifarnham
  232.03 blinks you blank is mostly Carbo
  274.02 broke the ranks on Monte Sinjon
  538.28 shocked his shanks at contey Carlow's

MONTE DE PIETÀ.   NPN, but It (and Fr) slang for "pawnshop."
  206.19 Tirry and Killy's mount of impiety
  541.13 to Madame of Pitymount I loue yous

MONTENOTTE.   (1) Dist, NE Cork City.   (2) Vill, E of Genoa, It. 1st battle of Napoleon's It campaign, 11 April 1796, where he defeated the Austrians.
>   21.07   when mulk mountynotty man was everybully

MONTGOMERY ST (16/34).   Now Foley St, running W from Amiens (now Connolly) Sta to Mabbot St. The entrance to the once brothel dist, often called "Monto."
>   58.26   three...of the Coldstream. Guards...in...Montgomery Street
>   ?525.07   Remonstrant Montgomeryite!
>   ?543.28   new departure in Mountgomery cyclefinishing

MOONEY'S.   Mooney and Co has operated a chain of pubs in cen Dub since the 19th cent.
>   17.01   There where the missers moony, Minnikin passe
>   540.12   *e poi Moonis*

MOORE, THOMAS, STATUE OF (16/34).   At junction of College Green and Westmoreland and College Sts. The entrance to a gentlemen's convenience is just behind it; "Meeting of the Waters," Bloom thinks (*U* 160/162). "Eiligh": *eilig*, Ger "urgent," *heilig*, Ger "holy"; "ediculous": *édicule*, Fr "small bldg on public st"; piss if you can, pass if you can't.
>   553.14   the eiligh ediculous Passivucant

MOOR PARK.   Sir Wm Temple's estate in Surrey, Eng. Swift went there as secretary to Temple, 1689; met Esther Johnson there. There is also a Moore Park (Ho) 2 mi S of Duleek, N Co Dub.
>   359.35   from Mooreparque, swift sanctuary seeking
>   407.19   morepork! morepork!
>   407.21   mauveport! mauveport!
>   433.11   mere pork
>   449.31   moor park! moor park!

MORA.   In Macpherson's poems, one of a chain of hills overlooking Moi-lena (see *Lena*), the vall of the Lubar R, and the hill of Lora across the vall. Fingal spends most of his time there watching battles in the vall. In *Temora*, Malthos is one of Fingal's enemies.
>   131.23   Mora and Lora had a hill of a high time
>   231.28   Malthos Moramor
>   247.27   moramor maenneritsch

MORAVIA.   Form part of Bohemia, later of Austria, finally of Czech. The Hussite Moravian Brethren began in Bohemia, later flourished in Ger.
>   172.11   moravar [other heresies on p 173]
>   416.07   muravyingly wisechairmanlooking

MOREEN.   Form name of locality near Dundrum, S Dub. Acc to an old legend, 2 families feuded desperately there, then made peace and built a ch together.
>   528.32   there's moreen astoreen for Monn and Conn

MOREHAMPTON ROAD (17/32).   St in SE Dub, continuing Leeson St.
>   354.16   *S. E. Morehampton makes leave to E. N. Sheilmartin*

MORGAN, JOSEPH, MRS.   Hat manufacturer, 9 Grafton St, around the turn of the cent. *Hovedpine*, Dan "headache."
>   127.31   a block at Morgen's and a hatache
>   221.30   Hoed Pine hat...by Morgen

MORNING POST.   (1) London daily newspaper; merged with the *Daily Telegraph*, 1937.   (2) Dub daily newspaper; merged with the *Dublin Times*, 1832.

    36.05   stood stated in Morganspost

    617.22   shown in Morning post as from Boston transcripped

MOROCCO.   Kingdom, NW Afr; Rom prov of Mauretania.

    460.23   libans [Lebanon]...sickamours...babilonias

MORT HOMME, LE.   Aka Dead Man's Hill; aka Hill 295. Hill 6 mi NW of Verdun, NE Fr; scene of bloody battles when captured by Germans, May 1916, recaptured by French, Aug 1917.

    352.32   dead men's hills

MORVEN.   In Macpherson's poems, Fingal's Caledonian kingdom in NW Scot, usually called "streamy *M.*" *M* is part of Argyllshire, now the Highlands Region, Scot.

    131.28   Mora...Lora...the streamy morvenlight calls up the sunbeam

MOSCOW.   City, cap of Russ; Russ, *Moskva*; on the Moskva R. The city comprises 4 concentric circles, roughly marking the expanding fortifications. In the cen is the Kremlin, the seat of both Czarist and Soviet govt, adjacent to the Kitay-Gorod, surrounded by the Byelyi-Gorod and the Zenilyanoy-Gorod.

    84.01   in the direction of Moscas...hurooshoos

    140.02   gnot Antwarp gnat Musca

    339.34   *pallups barn in the minkst of the Krumlin*

    347.15   if moskats knows whoss whizz...San Patrisky

    416.17   pickopeck of muscowmoney

    497.19   Krumlin Boyards

    536.10   in my krumlin

    541.31   musky moved

    597.13   On the sourdsite...the Moskiosk Djinpalast

    ?622.24   The moskors thought to ball you out

MOUNT ANVILLE   (18/28).   Dist and ho btwn Milltown and Dundrum, S Dub. Since the 19th cent, *Mt A* House has been a Sacred Heart convent and boarding sch for girls.

    235.18   the hypsometers of Mount Anville

MOUNT CASHEL.   *Mt C* House, 70 Stephen's Green. Lord Mt Cashell entertained Swift, Berkeley, and others here. B L Guinness bought the house and No 72. Ruins of Mountcashel cas (Ballymudcashel) are 2 mi N of Sixmilebridge, Co Clare.

    ?228.26   Every monk his own cashel

MOUNT JEROME   (14/31–32).   Prot cem near Harold's Cross in S Dub.

    252.11   Saint Jerome of the Harlots' Curse

MOUNTJOY.   (1) Prison, btwn NCR and Royal Canal, E of Phibsborough Rd (15/37). Named after the *M* who succeeded the Earl of Essex as Lord Deputy for Ire in 1600.   (2) Sq (16/35) in N cen Dub, once fashionable, beginning to decay even at the turn of the cent. Named after Luke Gardiner, Viscount *M*, who, with his son, also Viscount *M*, developed it.

    There was also *M* Barracks in W Phoenix Park, now the Ordnance Survey Office. The ship *Mountjoy*, together with the *Phoenix*, raised the siege of Londonderry in 1689. I don't know whether a brand of cigarettes was called "Mountjoy" (587.06).

    45.10   To the penal jail of Mountjoy...Mountjoy

    76.04   the Mountain of Joy receives, of a truly criminal stratum

192.35   Templetombmount joyntstone
460.09   poor fool's circuts of lovemountjoy square
587.06   a couple of Mountjoys and nutty woodbines

MOURNE.   (1) The subject of Percy French's song, the Mountains of *M* "sweep down to the sea," in S Co Down, btwn Carlingford Lough and Dundrum Bay. Topazolites are in fact found in the *M* Mts (549.17).   (2) *M* Riv, Co Tyrone; flows N to join the Finn R at Lifford to form the Foyle R.

?55.04   Maeromor Mournomates!
203.10   Not where the Finn fits into the Mourne
247.18   Highly momourning
277.07   the mountain mourning his duggedy dew
331.06   the damp off the mourning
462.32   coming home to mourn mountains
549.17   from the topazolites of Mourne
614.08   Doone of the Drumes...mournenslaund
?623.27   When the moon of mourning is set and gone

MOUSTIER, LE.   Cave, Dordogne Dept, S Fr, on the Vézère R above Les Eyzies (qv), where important archeological remains were found. The Mousterian period of paleolithic culture marks the culmination of the Neanderthal race.

15.33   mousterious...brain pan...dragon man
154.03   maudelenian...my dear mouster

MOY.   Town on the Blackwater R about 12 mi SW of Lough Neagh. *Magh*, Ir "plain."

76.21   Moyelta of the best Lough Neagh pattern
310.33   moyety...Lougk Neagk
?340.16   rath...mines...selo moy

MOY RIVER.   Rising in the Ox Mts in Co Sligo, the *M* flows SW and then N to Killala Bay, for some of its length paralleling Loughs Cullin and Conn; for "changing her minds," see *Cullin, Lough.*

?131.01   Mount of Mish, Mell of Moy
201.30   meanacuminamoyas
203.11   where the Moy changez her minds twixt Cullin and Conn
215.10   moyvalley way
?340.16   Eh, selo moy!
418.17   *Moyhammlet...Mount* [river and hill]
?478.21   *Moy jay trouvay*

MOYELTA.   The plain running N and NE from Dub was anc called the *Sean Magh* [angl "Moy"] *Ealta Éadair*, the "Old Plain of the Bird Flocks of Howth." Acc to Keating, it was the 1st part of Ire to be cleared of forest; acc to the Four Masters, when Parthalon arrived in Ire it was the only open plain. Later Parthalon and his followers died in *M* and were buried in Tallaght (qv). The vill Shanmoy in Co Tyrone is prob not included in the allusions.

17.18   olde ye plaine of my Elters
76.21   a protem grave in Moyelta
205.03   only parr with frills in old the plain
427.27   we in the country of the old, Sean Moy, can part you for

MOYLE, SEA OF.   Poetic name for the N Channel of the Ir Sea, btwn Co Antrim and Scot. JJ thought (*Letters* III, 339) it was St George's Channel, btwn Wexford and Wales, which *is* swept by the Tuskar Lighthouse (25.27); it is true that at one time (eg, on Boazio's 1599 map of Ire) the entire Ir Sea was sometimes called St George's Channel. The enchanted children of Lir had to spend 300 years on it as swans. Ir, *Sruth na Maoile*. Title of opera, 1923, by G Molyneaux Palmer, who also set some of JJ's poems as songs. T Moore's song: "Silent, O Moyle" (546.02).

25.27	the millioncandled eye of Tuskar sweeps the Moylean Main!
86.15	They were on that sea by the plain of Ir
95.03	O'Moyly
136.09	and flure the Moyle
199.02	his berths in their toiling moil
315.12	butting back to Moyle herring
?372.34	at their wetsend in the mailing waters
?384.05	Moykle ahoykling!
428.21	Moylendsea
546.02	Sigh lento, Morgh!
548.34	moyles
600.11	Libnud Ocean, Moylamore
628.03	moyles and moyles

MOYLIFFEY.   *Magh Lifé*, Ir "Plain of the Liffey"; the plain in Co Kildare through which the Liffey R flows.
    54.24   moyliffey eggs

MOYNE.   There are vills named *M* in Co Wicklow, N of Tinahely, and in Co Mayo, N of Headford. *M* Cas and the ruined *M* Abbey are also in Co Mayo.
    ?469.11   It's Winland for moyne, bickbuck!

MOYRA.   Vill, Co Donegal, E of Ballyness Bay.
    53.30   Gort and Morya and Bri Head and Puddyrick

MOYVALLEY (MOYVALLY).   Town, on the Liffey, in Co Kildare; there are also Moyvalleys in Co Meath and Co Carlow. *Magh Bhealaigh*, Ir "Plain of the Path."
    15.03   the mayvalleys of Knockmaroon
    ?110.09   madh vaal of tares
    215.10   moyvalley way

MUCKROSS.   One of the lakes of Killarney, Co Kerry; aka Middle Lake. The ruins of *M* Abbey (15th cent) are nearby.
    290.F1   Muckross Abbey with the creepers taken off
    323.21   from Drumadunderry till the rumnants of Mecckrass

MUD ISLAND.   Until the mid-19th cent, the area btwn N Strand Rd and Ballybough Rd N of Royal Canal. Acc to W St J Joyce, it was "a locality of evil repute...inhabited by desperadoes of every description, and ruled by a hereditary robber chief rejoicing in the title of 'King of Mud Island' " (87.26). For 200 years, until mid-19th cent, it was a sanctuary from the police. *U* 219/222: Fr Conmee doesn't like walking past it.
    87.26   kings of mud and tory
    ?294.04   Modder ilond there too

MUGGLETON.   Fictional vill in Dickens' *Pickwick Papers*, scene of the cricket match btwn All-Muggleton and Dingley Dell.
    312.26   he, with Muggleton Muckers...grace

MULHADDART.   Vill NW of Dub, 2 mi NW of Blanchardstown; ½ mile NE is Our Lady's Well.
    206.18   the holy well of Mulhuddart

MULLAFARRY.   Tnld, Co Mayo, SW of Killala. Acc to P W Joyce (*Irish Names* I, 206), the name "hill of the meeting place," indicates the site of a tribal meeting place even before the time of St Patrick. But no battle is associated with it.

> 580.12   the battle of Multaferry

MULLET PENINSULA.   A near-isl (cf *ey*, Dan "island") in NW Co Mayo, connected to mainland by a narrow neck of land and separated from it by Blacksod Bay. Off the SW point is Duvillaun More Isl.

> 208.32   mush mullet's eyes at her boys dobelon

MULLINAHOB.   House, 2 mi SE of Ratoath, Co Meath.

> 97.03   of Humfries Chase from Mullinahob

MULLINGAR.   Town, Co Westmeath; it is in *M* par. The Hill of Uisneach (476.06) is·10 mi to the SW, on the *M*-Athlone Rd.

In *U*, Milly Bloom is a photographer's assistant in *M*. In *FW*, however, the name is important primarily as the *M* Ho in Chapelizod, a real locus of HCE's imaginary tav. See *Tavern, The: Mullingar House.*

> 475.22   Mallinger parish, to a mead that was not far

MULLINGAR HOUSE.   See *Tavern, The: Mullingar House.*

MULTYFARNHAM.   Vill and Franciscan abbey, Co Westmeath, N of Mullingar, btwn Lough Owel and Lough Derravaragh. In Sept 1798, the United Irishmen were routed by the Eng at Bunbroona, 1 mi SW.

> 90.24   bruck the bank in Multifarnham
> 580.12   the battle of Multaferry

MUNSTER.   S prov of Ire; Ir, *Mumha.* Its cos are Clare, Cork, Kerry, Limerick, Tipperary, and Waterford. Its arms are 3 gold crowns on a blue ground (521.07); this is also the emblem on the badge of the Order of St Patrick. Among the Four, it is the prov of Mark Lyons, and it represents South.

In the 2nd cent, Eoghan Mór (aka Mogh Nuadat) divided Ire with Con Ceadcathach ("Conn of the Hundred Battles"), the former taking S Ire ("Mogh's Half") and the latter N Ire ("Conn's Half"). Eoghan Mór divided *M* into 5 provs under his 5 sons; this dynasty, with its royal seat at Cashel, ruled *M* until displaced by the O'Briens.

In the 17th and 18th cents, the Eng spelling was often "Mounster," eg, "Mounster Provinc" on Petty's Down Survey map. "Momonian" (387.18) is artificial Lat for *M.*

Even before the Normans, subkingdoms of *M* were Thomond˙(Co Clare and at times much of Co Limerick), Osmond (most of Co Tipperary), and Desmond (roughly Co Cork) (*deas*, Ir "south").

"The Munster Mare" is the air of T Moore's "She Sung of Love, While O'er Her Lyre" (276.08). In the Ir office of arms of heraldry, the 2 Heralds are Cork and Dublin (498.11).

For indirect allusions to *M* as one of the 4 provs, see *Provinces.*

> 96.16   mused her
> 131.10   Westmunster
> ?178.16   Monster Book of Paltryattic Puetrie
> 180.14   Cardinal Carchingarri [Cork and Kerry]
> 229.17   Leimuncononnulstria
> 271.L1   *Ulstria, Monastir,...*
> 276.08   sung of love and the monster man
> 387.18   in the olden times Momonian
> 389.05   Ulcer, Moonster...

?454.09	westminstrel
467.29	Illstarred punster...
475.07	Owenmore's five quarters
498.11	Ulster Kong and Munster's Herald
514.02	Normand, Desmond...and Kenneth
520.23	Mugn and Cannut
521.07	the three crowns round your draphole
521.28	leinconnmuns
528.28	my Moonster firefly
528.33	Monn and Conn
546.33	Chief Goes in Black Water
?606.25	the monster trial

MURMANSK.   Seaport city and oblast on Kola Penin, NW USSR; largest city N of Arctic Circle. The name is from *murman*, a corruption of the Norman word for "coast." Separated from Novaya Zemlya (qv) by S Barents Sea.

  317.34   its zembliance of mardal mansk

MUSIC HALL.   Dub's music halls have been an important part of its life since the 1st was opened in 1731 in Crow St (15/34). In 1741 the Bull's Head Musical Soc erected a Music Hall in Fishamble St (15/33), where Handel performed in 1741-42, with the 1st performance of *The Messiah* in 1742; it was later used for public drawings for state lotteries. In the mid-19th cent, the Music Hall was in Abbey St, opp the W front of the Custom House. In 1879, Dan Lowry opened his Star of Erin Music Hall, later Dan Lowry's Palace of Varieties, later the Empire, finally the Olympia, in Dame St. *FW* refs are prob to no specific music hall.

  408.26   musichall pair
  450.19   to pipe musicall airs
  588.09   musichall visit

N

NA'AMAN RIVER.   Aka Belus; flows into Bay of Acre just S of Acre, N Pal.

  103.08   let naaman laugh at Jordan
  204.05   Nautic Naama's now her navn

NAAS.   Town, Co Kildare, anc res of kings of Leinster and meeting place (*Nás na Riogh*) of royal assemblies.

  Nas, Arab "men," is the last word in the *Koran*, and the title of its last Sura, or chapter.

  ?344.29   shkewers me gnaas me fiet
  516.11   was ever so terribly naas

NAGASAKI.   Seaport city, SW Japan, on Kyushu Isl. The shogun (Jap "general") was for several cents the *de facto* ruler of Japan until 1867, when the mikado was restored to power.

  315.22   nogeysokey first, cabootle segund
  ?535.19   Noksagt!...shugon

NANNYWATER.   Riv, N Co Dub, flowing through Duleek to sea at Laytown, N of

Balbriggan. Often used as boundary line: as the boundary of Viking power; in early Eng charters; and into the 20th cent as the boundary of admiralty jurisdiction.

    ?7.27   piddle med puddle, she ninnygoes nannygoes nancing by
    205.26   from Nannywater to Vartryville

NAPLES.   City, S It. Dub Bay is often compared with the Bay of *N*. Anc *N* was called *Parthenope*, after the Siren who threw herself into the sea for love of Ulysses and was cast up in the Bay of *N*. Napoleon created in *N* the "Parthenopean Republic," which lasted for 5 months in 1799. The pop expression "See Naples and then die" means you can't beat it.

    106.24   *Seen Aples and Thin Dyed*
    172.23   *Anzi*, cabled...from his Nearapoblican asylum
    448.09   See Capels and then fly
    494.11   Prisca Parthenopea
    ?540.12   *Vedi Drumcollogher e poi Moonis*
    542.21   the maugher machrees and the auntieparthenopes

NASSAU.   (1) Ger duchy until 1866. Wm the Silent, founder of the Dutch Rep, inherited the title of *N*-Dillenburg from his father, of Orange-Chalons from his cousin, was 1st prince of Orange-Nassau (21.20). (2) *N* St, along S side of College Park, TCD (16/34). Name first used 1756 from Wm III's title, Count of *N*. Form St Patrick's Well Lane. Raised to above level of College Park by material from Thingmote mound in Suffolk St. JJ first met Nora in *N* St. The publishers Browne and Nolan (qv) were at 24 and 25 *N* St.

    21.20   handworded her grace in dootch nossow
    135.12   towards dames troth...like the prince of Orange and Nassau...trinity
                left behind him
    178.29   luminous to larbourd only like the lamps in Nassaustrass
    488.05   Bruno and Nola...off orangey Saint Nessau Street

NAST, KOLB, AND SCHUMACHER.   Roman bank, Via S Claudio at the Piazza Colonna, where JJ worked unhappily as a clerk for 6 months, 1906-07.

    510.21   bank lean clorks...nasty blunt clubs

NATAL.   E prov, Rep of S Afr. Named Terra Natalis because sighted by Vasco de Gama on Christmas Day, 1497. Chief port *N*, renamed Durban in 1835. Melmoth (qv) is N of Durban.

    ?91.23   an Inishman was as good as any cantonnatal
    587.21   from Melmoth in Natal

NATION, THE.   Dub nationalist newspaper, 1842-1900, when incorporated with the *Irish Weekly Independent*. Lady Wilde contributed poetry and prose to it as "Speranza," 1845-48, when it was suppressed and its editor prosecuted, in part for her published appeal to Irishmen to take up arms.

    297.F1   Doña Speranza of the Nacion

NATIONAL GALLERY.   In Trafalgar Sq, London. From its completion in 1837, its architecture was ridiculed as "The National Cruet Stand" because of the appearance of its "pepperpot" domes. The adjacent Nat Portrait Gallery contains portraits of about 3000 notables, including Lewis Carroll – and JJ.

The Nat Gallery of Ire is in Merrion Sq, W.

    57.21   our notional gullery...an exegious monument, aerily perennious...that
                exposure of him [Lewis Carroll] by old Tom Quad
    165.16   my goulache...which...ornates our national cruetstand

NATIONAL LIBRARY   (16/33).   In Kildare St; it remains more or less as JJ knew
it. For William Archer, who designed the *NL* catalogue, see *Census*.
    440.05   William Archer's...cathalogue...the route to our nazional labronry

NATIONAL UNIVERSITY OF IRELAND.   A federation of the Univ Colls of Dub,
Cork, and Galway, and St Patrick's Coll, Maynooth (the RC seminary). Founded 1908
by Ir Universities Act, it replaced the Royal Univ (1879) and absorbed the Catholic
Univ (1854). The bldgs of Univ Coll, Dub, as JJ knew it, were (and are) at 85 and
86 Stephen's Green, S.
    551.28   unniversiries, wholly rational and gottalike

NAUL, THE.   (1) Vill, 6 mi SW of Balbriggan, Co Dub; on Delvin R. The hunt on
FW 622 moves through tnlds in the vicinity of *N*.   (2) Tnld, par of Clonalvy, bar
of Upper Duleek, Co Meath.
    310.13   cunduncing Naul and Santry
    333.36   noviny news from Naul
    622.25   Bugley Captain, from the Naul

NAVAN.   Town, Co Meath, NE of Trim; *An Uaimh*, Ir "the hollow."
    ?204.05   Naama's now her navn
    436.29   We won't meeth in Navan

NAZARETH.   Town, in Galilee, N Pal, now Israel. Home of Joseph and Mary and
of Jesus ("The Nazarene") in his childhood.
    154.19   woshup my nase serene

NAZE, THE.   (1) Cape on E Essex coast, Eng, just S of Stour R, btwn Harwich and
Walton-on-the-Naze. The *N* Tower has been a lighthouse since 1720.   (2) S tip of
Norway, aka Lindesnes.
    156.28   The Pills, the Nasal Wash (Yardly's)
    ?208.28   Was her naze alight
    524.21   herring...by the Bloater Naze

NEAGH, LOUGH.   The largest lake in the Brit Isles, bordered by Cos Antrim, Derry,
Tyrone, Armagh, and Down. There are only a few small isls (76.21); Coney Isl is the
largest. There are several legends concerning its formation, apparently by some sort
of eruption at the end of the 1st cent. Giraldus says it was formed by the overflow
of a fairy fountain, and that round towers can be seen below the water (as in Moore's
"Let Erin Remember": "On Lough Neagh's bank as the fisherman strays [393.29]/...
He sees the round towers of other days/In the wave beneath him shining [248.08]").
See also *Tír na Thuinn*. The water of *LN* is pop believed to petrify wood (23.29).
Another well-known legend has it that Finn MacCool scooped out a great sod of turf
and threw it in the Ir Sea, leaving *LN* and creating the Isle of Man (76.24, 310.34)
(*Letters* III, 348). Eochaidh Mac Maireda, the Munster chieftain, took possession of
the terr around *LN* and was subsequently drowned in the eruption which formed the
lake: *Loch-Neachach*, Ir "Eochaidh's Lake," thus Lough Neagh.
    23.29   Landloughed by his neaghboormistress...perpetrified
    48.14   *Fenn Mac Call and the Serven Feeries of Loch Neach*
    76.21   a protem grave in Moyelta of the best Lough Neagh pattern...miso-
            nesans ["island-haters"]
    76.24   fairly fishy kettlekerry, after the Fianna's foreman had taken his
            handful
    196.20   And how long was he under loch and neagh?
    241.24   lochkneeghed forsunkener

248.08   Arise, Land-under-Wave!
310.34   when he pullupped the turfeycork by the greats of gobble out of
          Lougk Neagk
338.36   *laugh neighs banck*
393.29   like knockneeghs bumpsed by the fisterman's straights
?584.21   laugh...neigh, neigh

NEANDERTHAL.   Vall E of Düsseldorf, W Ger, where stone age fossil skeletons of
N man were found.
18.22   meandertale...of our old Heidenburgh
19.25   What a meanderthalltale to unfurl

NEBO, MOUNT.   (1) Properly, Mt Pisgah, the ridge of the Abarim Mts in anc Pal, E
of N end of the Dead Sea; *N* was the alternative name for it or its top. *Deut* 34: 1–3
tells of Moses viewing Canaan from *Mt N*, opp Jericho.   (2) *Mt N* in Co Wexford, 3
mi NW of Gorey. Song, "I'll Travel to Mt Nebo."
?11.05   No nubo no! Neblas
11.16   Come nebo me and suso sing the day we sallybright
235.16   boskiest of timber trees in the nebohood
?270.27   from Nebob ...see you never stray...nehm the day
?590.17   Nuah-Nuah, Nebob of Nephilim!

NEFER-SENT.   Egyptian city mentioned in *The Book of the Dead*.
415.33   Nefersenless

NELSON'S PILLAR   (15/34).   In O'Connell St at its intersection with Earl and Henry Sts, until blown up, 8 Mar 1966. Erected in 1808 to commemorate the victory of
Trafalgar in 1805, it was a Doric column surmounted by a monumental statue of Lord
N. Tramcar routes started from the Pillar.
    The *N* Mon, or *N* Column, in Trafalgar Square, London, also a colossal statue on a
high column, dates from 1843.
322.32   from the pillary of the Nilsens
422.30   Nelson his trifulgurayous pillar
553.13   Nielsen, rare admirable

NEPHIN.   Mt, Co Mayo.
?376.17   Neffin

NEPTUNE.   The 8th planet of the solar system. Its satellite Triton was discovered
only a month after the planet in 1846. A 2nd satellite, Nereid, which *FW* appears to
prophesy at 267.24, was discovered in 1949.
?203.12   where Neptune sculled and Tritonville rowed
585.02   Neptune's Centinel and Tritonville Lightowler...round the whole uni-
          verse

NEPTUNE ROWING CLUB.   One of several rowing clubs whose boathouses were on
Thorncastle St, Ringsend, only a few blocks from Tritonville Rd, around the turn of
the cent. The Dub rowing clubs later moved to Islandbridge.
203.12   where Neptune sculled and Tritonville rowed
391.18   a Neptune's mess...sculling
585.02   next eon's issue of the Neptune's Centinel and Tritonville Lightowler

NETHERLANDS.   Kingdom, NW Eur on N Sea, also called Holland; Fr, *Les Pays Bas*.
The historian J L Motley wrote *The Rise of the Dutch Republic*. Song: "My Old Dutch."
105.18   *My old Dansh*

105.23   *From the Rise of the Dudge Pupublick*
117.31   caldin your dutchy hovel
126.16   his hullender's epulence
?181.05   Pioupioureich, Swabspays, the land of Nod
244.02   Daintytrees, go dutch!
314.22   dutchuncler mynhosts
319.17   Ampsterdampster...netherlumbs
327.23   flyend of a touchman ["Flying Dutchman"]
385.09   Nodderlands Nurskery
420.13   the Dutches dyin loffin
430.14   the boer...in his Dutchener's native
459.05   poor old dutch
541.14   Paybads floriners...hugheknots
622.20   Les go dutc

NEWCASTLE.   Vill, Co Dub, 12 mi SW of Dub; aka *N* of Lyons. It was one of the
4 Royal Manors of Dub (qv). Other Newcastles in Cos Down, Limerick, Meath, Tipperary, and Wicklow are prob not included in the allusion.
    18.06   O'c'stle, n'wc'stle
?230.15   Casanuova
555.13,15   esker, newcsle, saggard, crumlin

NEWCOMEN BRIDGE   (16/35).   Over the Royal Canal at N Strand Rd, just S of
the Tolka R.
    130.21   atolk of New Comyn

NEWFOUNDLAND.   Isl in Atlantic O SE of Quebec, a prov of Can since 1949. Discovered 1497 by John Cabot, but prob the "Markland" (qv) of the Norse explorers
ca 1000.
    412.04   New worlds...scotographically...by a scripchewer in whofoundland

NEW FREEWOMAN.   Journal founded by Dora Marsden in 1913; title was changed
to *Egoist* in 1914, and Harriet Weaver shortly afterward became editor. JJ's *A Portrait* was publ in installments, 1914-15. Until 1917, the editorial offices were in Oakley House, in Bloomsbury St, London.
    ?52.01   his sole admirers...with Anny Oakley deadliness
145.29   that New Free Woman with novel inside
488.16   Mutemalice, suffering unegoistically
488.21   my allaboy brother, Negoist Cabler [Shem]

NEWGATE GAOL   (15/34).   Dub's 1st jail was an old cas on the town wall, over
gate leading from Cut-Purse Row to Thomas St. New bldg (1773) in Green St, next
to Green St (Criminal) Courthouse; demolished 1877.
    The name was from London's New Gate, the W gate of the City of London, whose
gate-house was a pris as early as the 12th cent; enlarged by Richard Whittington, burnt
in 1780 and rebuilt, demolished and replaced by Cen Criminal Court in 1902.
    551.34   Threadneedles and Newgade and Vicus Veneris

NEW GUINEA.   Large isl N of Australia; form divided among the Neth (now Indo-
nesian W Irian), Ger and Gt Brit (now administered by Australia).
    182.25   Broken Hill [Australia]...brandnew two guinea dress suit

NEW HAMPSHIRE.   State, NE US. Its cap is Concord (qv), on the Merrimack R.
    197.10   New Hunshire, Concord on the Merrimake

NEW HOLLAND.   (1) Delta at confluence of Swan Water, Dodder R, and Liffey, SE Dub (18/33); embanked and reclaimed 1792; pop called *NH*, perhaps because desperadoes lived there; the orig *NH* was a convict colony.   (2) *NH* iron mills, Chapelizod.

   ?169.23   Phig Streat III, Shuvlin, Old Hoeland

NEW IRELAND.   Isl, E of New Guinea, in the Bismarck Archipelago (qv) in the isl chain of Melanesia (qv).

   ?78.26   New South Ireland...Vetera Uladh [mainly: the 26 cos, separated from
         the 6 of N Ire]
   ?392.31   the heights of Newhigherland
   595.10   It's a long long ray to Newirgland's premier
   601.35   who farshook our showrs from Newer Aland...Milenesia waits. Be
         smark

NEW ISLAND.   A pop Ir name for the US in the 19th and early 20th cents. Title of a W B Yeats book: *Letters to the New Island* (1934).

   ?348.16   the whole inhibitance of Neuilands!
   ?392.31   the heights of Newhigherland
   525.30   his tear make newisland
   595.10   It's a long long ray to Newirgland's premier [De Valera (b in US)?]

NEW SOUTH WALES.   State, SE Australia; cap is Sydney. Discovered 1770 by Capt Cook; a penal colony was est 1788 at Botany Bay (qv); more than one Ir patriot was transported there.

   489.13   The Workings, N.S.W.
   497.13   Noo Soch Wilds

NEW YORK CITY.   Largest city in US; not the cap of New York State (which is Albany); on New York Bay at entrance of Hudson R, and at W end of Long Island Sound. Its 5 boroughs are Manhattan, Bronx, Brooklyn, Queens, and Richmond (Staten Isl). Personified as "Father Knickerbocker" (139.06, 442.08); also nicknamed "Gotham" (qv). First colonized by the Dutch West India Co in 1624; in 1626 Peter Minuit (?540.34) bought Manhattan Isl from the Indians. The tiny settlement was càlled Ft Amsterdam, later New Amsterdam (117.24, 509.24). Peter Stuyvesant (550.31) was director-general from 1647 to 1664, when he surrendered the colony to the Brit, who renamed it New York.

   The dreamer of *FW* may dream the cosmos, but virtually everything he knows about NYC is in the 11th *EB* article, "New York (City)"; see *AWN* III (1966), 119, and IV (1967), 72−76. Some of these places (eg, Niblo's Garden, or Wallabout Market) are totally unknown to contemporary New Yorkers.

    I. New York City Place-Names:

AVENUE C.   On the Lwr East Side of Manhattan.
   549.20   avenyue ceen my peurls ahumming
BATTERY PARK.   On the S tip of Manhattan.
   497.18   Batterysby Parkes
BOWERY, THE.   St in Lwr Manhattan, SE of Greenwich Vill; it has long been a cen for vagrants ("bums" in Amer Eng).
   153.01   Saint Bowery's-without-his-Walls
   553.20   bowery nooks and greenwished villas
BROADWAY.   Major Manhattan thoroughfare and cen of NYC's theatrical dist.
   565.36   snugger to burrow abed than ballet on broadway
CLEOPATRA'S NEEDLE.   See separate listing.

CONEY ISLAND.   The famous beach and amusement park on S Long Island.
    553.06   and Coney Bend bounds Mulbreys Island

ELEVENTH AVENUE.   In W Manhattan, along the Hudson R piers. It was once known as "Death Ave" because of the numerous traffic fatalities caused by heavy rlwy traffic on tracks in the cen of the st.
    60.01   Dole Line, Death Avenue

ELEVENTH ST.   In Lwr Manhattan; W 11th St (W of Fifth Ave) is at the N edge of Greenwich Vill.
    ?274.12   Number Thirty two West Eleventh streak looks on to that...datetree

GRAMERCY PARK.   At Lexington Ave and 21st St in cen Manhattan.
    534.13   by gramercy of justness

GREENWICH VILLAGE.   In Lwr Manhattan, NW of the Bowery.
    553.20   bowery nooks and greenwished villas

LITTLE CHURCH AROUND THE CORNER.   Pop name for The Ch of the Transfiguration, W 29th St, 1½ blocks from Lwr Broadway in Manhattan; from the late 19th cent it was known for the actors who attended it and for the number of marriages performed there.
    67.13   brick and tin choorch round the coroner
    533.23   Kerk Findlater's, ye litel chuch rond ye coner

MORNINGSIDE HEIGHTS.   Area in NW Manhattan, site of Columbia U. The subway runs underneath, with a sta at 116th St.
    481.14   Morning de Heights...rambling undergroands

MULBERRY BEND PARK.   At the bend of Mulberry St, behind the Criminal Courts in Lwr Manhattan; now known as Columbus Park.
    553.06   and Coney Bend bounds Mulbreys Island

NIBLO'S GARDEN.   A well-known 19th-cent music hall, razed 1895.
    552.19   and ruffles through Neeblow's garding

PALISADES, THE.   The cliffs on the New Jersey shore across the Hudson R from N NYC; but also the name of the rude fortification of New Amsterdam which gave its name to Wall St in Lwr Manhattan.
    539.26   goodwalldabout...palisades

RIVERSIDE DRIVE.   On the upr W side of Manhattan, overlooking the Hudson R.
    547.19   long rivierside drive

ROXY THEATER.   In Cen Manhattan; NYC's biggest and best-known movie theater in the 1920's and 1930's.
    513.21   *Oropos Roxy and Pantharhea* at the Gaiety

SHERIDAN SQUARE.   At 7th Ave and 4th St in cen Manhattan.
    545.35   in Sheridan's Circle my wits repose

SPUYTEN DUYVIL.   The channel connecting the Harlem and Hudson Rivs at the N end of Manhattan; and the adjacent shore areas.
    535.15   The spiking Duyvil

TAMMANY HALL.   Democratic party hqs on 14th St, Manhattan; long a symbol for corrupt machine politics, esp under "Boss" Tweed. It was named for a political club, in turn named for a patriotic soc of the Amer Revolution, which adopted the name of a Delaware Indian chief.
    ?106.08   *from Tommany Moohr*
    131.08   baases two mmany
    379.34   Tem for Tam at Timmotty Hall
    442.03   I don't care a tongser's tammany hang

TOMBS, THE.   Until recently the main NYC pris, in Lwr Manhattan adjacent to the Criminal Courts.

    532.28   through toombs and deempeys

WALLABOUT BAY, WALLABOUT MARKET.   Inlet of East R and adjacent shore area, across the channel from SE Manhattan; long the site of the Brooklyn Navy Yard.

    539.26   goodwalldabout...palisades

WALL STREET.   Named for the 17th-cent palisades on the N side of New Amsterdam, now Lwr Manhattan; site of NY Stock Exchange and cen of the financial dist.

    3.17   fall...of a once wallstrait oldparr

WOOLWORTH BUILDING.   In Lwr Manhattan; one of the first skyscrapers and for many years the world's tallest bldg.

    4.35   a waalworth of a skyerscape
    72.14   *Woolworth's Worst*
    127.35   three wellworthseeing ambries
    ?357.03   arsoncheep and wellwillworth a triat
    ?398.23   so wellworth watching
    539.05   mostmonolith...longstone erectheion...wordworth's
    541.06   by awful tors my wellworth building

YONKERS.   See separate listing.

    II.   Allusions to New York City:

117.24   Pieter's in Nieuw Amsteldam
137.32   won the freedom of new yoke
139.06   a hoar father Nakedbucker in villas old as new
308.22   through their coming new yonks
442.08   Old Father Ulissabon Knickerbocker
509.24   New Aimstirdames
534.02   Abbreciades anew York gustoms
536.13   bronxitic in achershous
539.02   minhatton
569.18   Cantaberra and Neweryork

NEW ZEALAND.   Independent state SE of Australia. Became a Brit crown colony in 1840 when by Treaty of Waitangi the native Maori chiefs ceded lands to Brit; colonial status ended 1907. Consists of N Isl, S Isl, and a no of smaller isls. Cap is Wellington, on N Isl.

A well-known Polynesian *haka* begins "Ko Niu Tiireni, e ngunguru..." "It is New Zealand, rumbling here" (see *AWN* No 8, Dec '62, p 8).

In his *Edinburgh Review* essay on Ranke (1840), Macaulay imagined the future time "when some traveller from New Zealand shall...take his stand on a broken arch of London Bridge to sketch the ruins of St Paul's."

    111.01   puteters out of Now Sealand
    130.08   on Christienmas at Advent Lodge, New Yealand
    156.30   broken-arched traveller from Nuzuland
    ?171.02   Rosbif of Old Zealand
    335.13   vastelend hosteilend, neuziel and oltrigger some
    335.16   Ko Niutirenis...Ko Niutirenis
    335.17   Wullingthund sturm...maomaoring...Wellingthund sturm

NICE.   Medit seaport and resort, Alpes-Maritimes Dept, SE Fr.
    ?532.24   anniece...nieceless
    608.08   your two cozes from Niece

NIÈVRE RIVER.   Riv, Dept of Nièvre, cen Fr; joins Loire R at Nevers.
206.08   you niever heard
273.12   Hanah Levy...nievre anore

NIFLHEIM.   "Mist-home"; in Norse myth, the region of endless cold and everlasting
night, in far N; contained 9 worlds and its spring Hvergelmir was source of 12 streams.
?590.17   Nebob of Nephilim

NIGER RIVER.   Rises in the bulge of W Afr, flows in a great curve NE and E, then
SW through Nigeria to reach the Gulf of Guinea through a great swampy delta with
many outlets. Called Nigris by Pliny; believed as late as 19th cent to be a branch of
the Nile. How the N reached the sea was not known until 1830; Mungo Park discovered its upper reaches but lost his life on the riv in 1805 while attempting to find its
outlet. Major James Rennell, the geographer of Brit's African Assn, which sent out
Park and other explorers to track the N's course, believed it had no mouth and ended
by evaporation.
101.29   the upper reaches of her mouthless face
208.16   natural nigger boggers
212.01   Laagen or Niger
537.23   a mouthless niggeress, Blanchette Brewster from Cherna Djamja,
          Blawlawnd-via-Brigstow [*Blaaland*, old Nor "Africa"]

NIGERIA.   Country, form Brit colony, W Afr.
181.13   pothooks (a thing he never possessed of his Nigerian own)

NILE RIVER.   Riv in N and NE Afr; the longest riv in the world. The 6 "cataracts,"
or rapids, are non-navigable portions; the 1st cataract is just N of Aswan (Assuan),
Egypt, where early Medit civilization ended (332.29). The Aswan Dam was completed
in 1902. The Blue N (Bahr-el-Azrak) and White N (Bahr-el-Abiad) join above the 6th
cataract at Khartoum. The White N, btwn its junction with the Bahr-el-Ghazal and
Lake Albert, is called Bahr-el-Jebel ("mountain river") (5.23). The source of the N, a
mystery for cents, was not determined until the 1860's; it was the issue of a famous
dispute btwn Richard Burton and John Speke, the latter of whom guessed (correctly)
that Lake Victoria (Victoria Nyanza) was its source; exploration up the N was blocked
by the huge region of floating vegetation known as the Sudd (215.17). The Battle of
the N, in which Nelson destroyed the Fr fleet (328.22), was fought at Abukir Bay on
1 Aug 1798. Fr, Ger, *Nil*.
    In *FW*, the N's associations with fertility are used to suggest the Liffey (qv), as in
364.20. See *Albert Nyanza, Victoria Nyanza*.
5.23   bedoueen the jebel and the jpysian sea
?24.01   to play cash cash in Novo Nilbud
75.02   nenuphars ["water-lilies"] of his Nile
130.30   his second's French-Egyptian ["*Nil*"]
202.19   **Nieman from Nirgends found the Nihil**
215.17   Sudds for me
254.16   abu abiad [*abu*, Arab "father"; part of many place-names]
328.22   till the brottels on the Nile
332.29   nilly...first cataraction...assuan damm
364.20   water of Elin...city of Analbe
494.34   She's askapot at Nile Lodge
598.06   Nuctumbulumbumus wanderwards the Nil...Lotus spray
620.03   lotust...second to nill, Budd
627.30   Amazia...haughty Niluna

NIVE RIVER.   Riv, SW Fr. Wellington forced the passage of the *N* toward Bayonne against Fr resistance on 9 Dec 1813.

11.03   She niver comes out
203.36   he warned her niver to

NIXNIXUNDNIX.   In the fable of the Ondt and the Gracehoper (414–19), it is the home of the Ondt (= Shaun, Kevin, Stanislaus Joyce, etc); the name is *inter alia* the response of the provident ant to the begging grasshopper.

?27.06   Kevin's...bag of knicks
183.05   Niggs, niggs and niggs again
231.02   next, next and next
343.20   Ichts nichts on nichts!...antiants their grandoper
?361.02   nought...nil...nix...nothing
415.29   his windhame, which was cold antitopically Nixnixundnix
416.17   Nichtsnichtsundnichts!
488.25   midden Erse clare language, Noughtnoughtnought nein

NIZHNIY-NOVGOROD.   Area and town at confluence of Oka and Volga Rivs, 270 mi E of Moscow. Famous for its great fair. When Ivan the Terrible devastated Novgorod in 1570, thousands of families were transported to Moscow and *N-N*.

240.18   hiking ahake like any nudgemeroughgorude all over Terracuta
344.14   that tourrible tall with his nitshnykopfgoknob
346.02   *The neatschknee Novgolosh*

NOBLETT, LEONARD AND CO.   Confectioners, around the turn of the cent at 34 Lwr Sackville St (15/34), and 72 Grafton St (15/33).

306.04   sweetmeats...his Noblett's surprize

NOD, LAND OF.   When Cain was driven out of Eden, he went to the land of *N*, east of Eden, found a wife who bore Enoch, and built the 1st city (*Gen* 4:17–18).

181.05   Pioupioureich, Swabspays, the land of Nod
287.12   cain...able...Amicably nod
288.25   what was beforeaboots a land of nods
385.09   four collegians on the nod, neer the Nodderlands Nurskery

NOLA.   For Bruno of Nola, see *Census*.

NOLAGH.   Town, Co Cavan.
?321.08   Glasthule Bourne or Boehernapark Nolagh

NONESUCH (NONSUCH).   (1) Palace of Henry VIII, given as 'a gift by Charles II to his mistress Barbara Villiers, Duchess of Cleveland, who razed it (1670). She was also promised Phoenix Park in Dub, but the transaction was not completed.   (2) In *Huckleberry Finn*, the "duke" and the "king" bill their theatrical performances as the "Royal Nonesuch."   (3) Prob not intended is the tnld of Nonsuch, par of Mayne, bar of Fore, Co Westmeath.

143.15   such a none...twain
?442.05   a constantineal namesuch of my very own
534.23   to my nonesuch, that highest personage...throne

NORE.   (1) Riv, rises in Co Tipperary, flows E along S vall of Slieve Bloom Mts, then S (203.10) through Kilkenny to New Ross.   (2) Sandbank in cen of the Thames R estuary, SE Eng, 3 mi NE of Sheerness; at E end is *N* Light. The *N* was the scene of a famous mutiny of Brit sailors in 1797.

?21.01   we are in rearing of a norewhig

?67.13	Norewheezian tailliur
203.10	not where the Nore takes lieve of Bloem
273.12	Hanah Levy...nievre anore skidoos
?330.25	Finn's Hotel Fiord, Nova Norening
?359.03	the orenore under the selfhide [iron sulfide]
446.25	through suirland and noreland
?535.10	Noreway

NORFOLK.   Eng co, in E Anglia. Weybourne Crag, a glacial formation in *N*, is prob not included in the allusion. For the wey as a unit of measure, see *Suffolk*.

    ?283.14   weys in Nuffolk till tods of Yorek

NORMANDY.   Region, NW Fr. The Normans landed in Eng in 1066 and in Ire in 1170, but more recently the tourist traffic has gone the other way.

    443.33   what about our trip to Normandy style conversation
    510.20   trou Normend fashion

NORMAN'S WOE.   A reef off the vill of Magnolia on Cape Ann, Mass, US. Scene of legendary wreck of the "Hesperus." "Like a sheeted ghost, the vessel swept/Towards the reef of Norman's Woe" (Longfellow, *The Wreck of the Hesperus*).

    306.27   the Wreck of the Hesperus
    321.14   Lifeboat Alloe, Noeman's Woe
    387.21   after the wreak of Wormans' Noe
    557.06   the wrake of the hapspurus

NORTH CIRCULAR ROAD (NCR).   With the S Circular Rd (qv), and the adjacent canals, it was orig intended to mark the limits of the city boundary. At one time herds of cattle were driven along the NCR from the cattle market at Prussia St to the docks (284.F5); one of Leopold Bloom's schemes was to lay tracks so that they could be transported by tram.

    256.32   N.C.R. and S.C.R.
    284.26   NCR
    284.F5   on the jaunts cowsway
    295.31   our twain of doubling bicirculars
    310.07   circumcentric megacycles
    321.13   east circular route
    547.33   ringstresse
    553.30   my nordsoud circulums

NORTH, J H AND CO (15/33).   Dub auctioneers, then and now; in JJ's time at 110 Grafton St.

    529.13   service books in order and duly signed J.H. North and Company

NORTH POLE.   Everything is S of it. Hibernian polo can be found in Phoenix Park on Sun afternoons.

    435.12   icepolled globetopper...equator
    567.35   Polo north will beseem Sibernian

NORTH, SOUTH, EAST, WEST.   As the citations indicate, the pattern of the cardinal points of the compass is pervasive in *FW*. In every case there is some degree of allusion to Ire's 4 Provinces (qv) and to the Four Old Men who represent them.

    Trad, Ir peasants regard "east" as "straight ahead," and refer to things on their left and right as "north" and "south," no matter what their true direction.

    42.28   northern tory, a southern whig, an eastanglian chronicler and a land-
                wester guardian

95.05−.09   North Mister...southside

114.03   more than half of the lines run north-south...while the others go west-east...cardinal points

140.15,21,27,36   Delfas...Dorhqk...Nublid...Dalway

160.27   billfaust. .curks...deblinite...Mr Wist

251.14   If he spice east he seethes in sooth and if he pierce north he wilts in the waist

340.18   nose easger...sweeth...swooth

372.36−373.01,03,05   Bothersby North...Poors Coort, Soother...The Eats... Moherboher to the Washte

390.14   nangles, sangles, angles and wangles

418.26−.30   *Has Aquileone nort winged to go syf...heartseast...Wastenot*

494.14   Noth, Haste, Soot and Waste

523.34−524.15,21,26   norsect's...Soussex...Naze [Essex]...Wissixy

534.15   Misrs Norris, Southby, Yates and Weston, Inc

546.33   Chief North Paw and Chief Goes in Black Water and Chief Brown Pool and Chief Night Cloud by the Deeps

553.30   my nordsoud circulums, my eastmoreland and westlandmore

557.02   Norreys, Soothbys, Yates and Welks

569.05   S. Presbutt-in-the-North, S. Mark Underloop, S. Lorenz-by-the-Toolechest, S. Nicholas Myre [these 4 chs are in N, S, E, and W Dub]

578.30   Norwood's Southwalk or Euston Waste

NORTH STRAND ROAD (16/35).   Main thoroughfare which continues Amiens St NE toward Fairview and Clontarf; before the walling of the Liffey, it ran along the tidal strand of N Dub Bay. JJ's Aunt Josephine (Murray) lived at No 103.

315.30   suttonly...endnew strandweys...clown toff

534.27   He walked by North Strand with his Thom's towel in hand

NORTHUMBERLAND.   (1) Rd, SE Dub, from Grand Canal (Mount St) to Pembroke Rd; runs into Merrion Rd and Anglesea Rd (17/33).   (2) N-most Eng co, btwn Newcastle and Scot border, on N Sea. In early 7th cent, King Edwin briefly annexed Anglesea and Man. After 940, Anlaf son of Sitric extended terrs as far as Watling St. King Ella is said to have slain Ragnar Lodbrok there, *ca* 865.

24.19   the North Umbrian

387.09   from...Aylesburg and Northumberland Anglesey

NORTH WALL QUAY (17/34).   The embankment of the Liffey E from Custom House Quay along the docks into Dub Bay. At one time passenger trains of 2 different rlwys ran from stas on the *NWQ*, connecting with passenger ships.

95.14   heaving up the Kay Wall by the 32 to 11

141.22   northquain bigger

209.03   North Lazers' Waal

?621.18   next you go to Market Norwall

NORWAY.   Kingdom, NW Eur, W Scand penin. Nor, Swed, *Norge*. The old Ir name for *N* was *Lochlann* (qv). HCE is of Nor descent, and one of his roles is that of the Nor Captain in the story of the Nor Captain and Kersse the Tailor, at 311−332; omitted here are refs only to the Nor Captain, for which see *Census*.

Of the forms of the Nor lang to which the complicated hist of lang reform has given rise, *riksmaal* is closer to Dan, *landsmaal* to Old Nor (292.27, 323.06, 577.07).

16.06   You tolkatiff scowegian?

21.01	in rearing of a norewhig
23.11	sweet unclose to the Narwhealian captol
23.19	Norronesen or Irenean
28.27	*The Novvergin's Viv*
46.21	Norveegickers moniker...Norveegickers...Norwegian
49.28	a Northwegian and his mate
64.02	attracted by the norse of guns
67.13	Norewheezian tailliur
106.04	*Norsker Torsker Find the Poddle*
157.16	that Skand...in Norwood's sokaparlour...Voking's Blemish
203.07	a landleaper, wellingtonorseher
279.F20	my old nourse Asa...vicking
292.27	march of a landsmaul
309.11	Argloe-Noremen
312.05	Norgean run
314.27	noirse-made-earsy
323.06	raw lenguage...the lumbsmall of his hawsehole
327.30	Norgeyborgey
329.07	his farther was the norse norse east
329.11	an olewidgeon
376.09	O'Bryan MacBruiser [Brian Boru] bet Norris Nobnut
385.09	Nodderlands Nurskery
436.12	svarewords like a nursemagd
452.36	I'm not half Norawain for nothing
480.01	Norsker [ship]
530.19	his morse-erse wordybook
530.31	Norganson
533.22	Nowhergs
535.10	yeddonot need light oar till Noreway
547.26	domfine norsemanship
552.04	stavekirks wove so norcely [in Norse Dub]
577.07	norsebloodheartened and landsmoolwashable
590.22	sweetish mand...easteredman
618.34	Nollwelshian
626.04	that wind as if out of norewere

NORWOOD.   Dist and rlwy junction in S London, NE of Croydon.

?157.16	in Norwood's sokaparlour
578.30	Norwood's Southwalk

NOVARA.   (1) Ave in Bray, Co Wicklow; also *N* Terr, *N* Ho.   (2) Town, prov, and episcopal see in Piedmont, It; the town (anc Novaria) was founded by Celts.

191.10	Novena Lodge, Novara Avenue, in Patripodium-am-Bummel [boot-shaped It, poised for kicking?]

NOVA SCOTIA.   E-most Canadian prov. The 1st transatlantic wireless service was est by the Marconi Co in 1907 btwn Clifden (qv), in Connemara, and Glace Bay, 14 mi W of Sydney, *NS*.

407.21	from Clifden...to Nova Scotia's listing sisterwands
?595.33	Listening, Syd!

NOVAYA ZEMLYA (NOVA ZEMBLA).   Isl archipelago off NW coast of USSR (Archangel Oblast) in Arctic O; Russ, "new land." Separated from Murmansk by S

Barents Sea.
    317.33   its zembliance of mardal mansk

NOVGOROD.   City and region of NW USSR; ruled by Alexander Nevski in 13th cent; came to rival Moscow, but was conquered by Ivan III and devastated by Ivan IV; it later declined as St Petersburg rose. See *Nizhny-Novgorod:*
    ?565.21   Gothgorod father godown

NUBIA.   Never a political division; generally, the area S of Egypt and btwn the Red Sea and the Libyan Desert. "Nubian" was a 19th-cent euphemism for "slave" or "black African."
    559.28   Nubian shine

NUMANTIA.   Hill fortress, later Roman town, in N Sp, prov of Soria (Old Castile); prominent in war btwn Romans and Spaniards (143-133 BC); captured by Scipio the Younger. The allusions quote the Quinet sentence (281.04 –.13).
    281.07   *sur les ruines de Numance*
    615.04   illyrical and innumantic

NUMIDIA.   Anc N Afr country; its terr was about that of modern Algeria. Its most important city was Augustine's Hippo (Bône).
    ?48.05   kingsrick of Humidia

NUR.   Region in Mazandaran, N Iran; iron mining. The nomadic Lur tribe inhabited the area in W Iran on the Turk border (Luristan).
    310.24   man of Iren...a lur of Nur

NUREMBERG.   City, Bavaria, Ger, 90 mi NW of Munich. A "*N* egg" is an early and bulky portable timepiece, globular in shape. The absent-minded professor of the joke boils his watch while holding his egg.
    151.13   Professor Levi-Brullo...Nuremberg eggs in the one hands and the
                 watches cunldron

NUTTSTOWN.   Tnld, par of Kilbride, bar of Dunboyne, Co Meath. There is a tnld of Nutstown in the par of Ballymadun, bar of Balrothery West, Co Dub, but it doesn't fit the route of the foxhunt on *FW* 97.
    97.10   Nutstown

O

O'BRIEN, WILLIAM SMITH, STATUE   (15/34).   Orig at S end of O'Connell Br, moved to O'Connell St in 1920's; by Thomas Farrell (1870). "In 1928 [JJ] was thrilled to know that the statue of Smith O'Brien had been moved from O'Connell Bridge and was now lined up with the other statues in O'Connell St. 'Why has nobody told me that before?' he said rather petulantly" (E Sheehy, *The Joyce We Knew*, 35). In *FW* it is on its orig site. The cylindrical marble mass which supports the back of the stat looks something like a cabbage stalk (Lat, *caulis*). Smith O'Brien was leader of the "cabbage patch rebellion" in 1848.
    553.14   Guglielmus Caulis

OCEANIA.   Collective name for the isls of cen and S Pacific O, including Micronesia,

Melanesia and Polynesia (which includes the Society Islands), sometimes also Australia and New Zealand. *FW* puns on "ocean" and *Oisín*, pron "usheen," angl "Ossian."

125.03	to oceanic society [+ Ossianic Society]
593.05	Haze sea east to Osseania

OCONEE.   Riv and co, Ga, US; it flows through Laurens Co and its co seat, Dublin (qqv). In SE Ga, the Oconee unites with the Ocmulgee R to form the Altamaha R (549.28).

3.07	topsawyer's rocks by the stream Oconee
140.35	from Atlanta to Oconee
211.28	an oakanknee for Conditor Sawyer
277.01	Ochone! Ochonal!
297.11	Ocone! Ocone!
549.28	where bold O'Connee weds on Alta Mahar

O'CONNELL BRIDGE   (15/34).   Spanning the Liffey from O'Connell St to Westmoreland St, it is as broad as it is long. The 1st br on this site was built 1791-94 and called New Br, later Carlisle Br after the Earl of Carlisle, Lord Lt when it was erected. It was widened and renamed *O'C B* in 1880.

13.14	old butte new
63.14	hir newbridge is her old
135.17	his birthspot lies beyond the herospont [ie, S of the Liffey]
514.26	by the river and A. Briggs Carlisle
580.31	kneed O'Connell...butted...grattaned [see *Butt Br, Essex* (Grattan) *Br*]

O'CONNELL STATUE   (15/34).   The bronze statue of Daniel O'Connell, "the Emancipator," in his great cloak is at the S end of O'Connell St facing O'Connell Br. By John Henry Foley; unveiled 1882.

277.F2	his lucreasious togery [fn to 277.02 "Ochonal"]
386.22	the statue of Mrs Dana O'Connell...emancipated statues
553.14	Conall Gretecloke

O'CONNELL STREET   (15/34).   Dub's principal thoroughfare, sometimes called "the world's widest st" (140.12), it runs from Parnell Sq to the Liffey at O'Connell Br. The broad promenade down the cen is lined with stats, which are enumerated from N to S at 553.12−.14.

   Upr *O'C* St was in the 17th cent Drogheda St (qv). In the 1740's it was widened by Luke Gardiner and renamed Sackville St; the promenade down the cen was called Gardiner's Mall (qv). From 1784 on, the st was extended to the Liffey as Lwr Sackville St, and in 1924 the whole st was renamed *O'C* St. The mod st is largely rebuilt after the artillery shelling and fires of 1916 and 1921.

14.03	sackvulfe of swart
81.09	So more boher O'Connell!
140.12	most expansive...thoroughfare in the world
507.26	Lower O'Connell Street...Laura Connor's treat
514.24	Sackville-Lawry
626.11	Shackvulle Strutt

OCTROI.   Medieval Fr law surviving into the 20th cent, authorizing municipalities to impose duty on goods, esp food, brought into the city for sale; also the name of the posts at the city gates where officials collected the tax, as in JJ's "come-all-ye" about the (1937) Thanksgiving turkey at the Jolas's: "When we reached the gates of Paris cries the boss at the Octroi:/ Holy Poule, what's this I'm seeing. Can it be Grandmother Loye?"

538.07   to have ochtroyed to resolde or borrough by exchange

ODDI.   The settlement in SW Iceland which was the home of Snorri Sturlason and Saemund the Wise, compilers of the Eddas.
597.06   in eddas and oddes bokes

ODER RIVER.   In cen Eur; its lwr course is the border btwn Ger and Pol. See *Frankfurt: Frankfurt-an-der-Oder.*
204.34   the scent of her oder
332.08   frankfurters on the odor
?538.31   Odor...rivulverblott

OETZMANN AND CO   (15/33).   Cabinet makers and house furnishers, 60-61 Grafton St; and London, Brussels, and Constantinople, acc to Thom's *Directories* of early 20th cent.
66.31   the hardware premises of Oetzmann and Nephew, a noted house of the gonemost west...funeral requisites

OFFALY.   Co, Leinster prov; form King's Co, after Philip of Sp, husband of Mary, Queen of Scots. Orig an Ir kingdom, including parts of Tipperary, Kildare, and Queen's Co (now Laois, qv). The co town is Tullamore.
Baronies: Ballyboy, Ballybrit, Ballygowan, Clonlisk, Coolestown, Eglish, Garrycastle, Geashill, Kilcoursey, Upr and Lwr Philipstown, Warrenstown.
31.18   lord of Leix and Offaly
?329.28   as owfally posh
446.25   kings country
?465.32   Be inish. Be offalia. Be hamlet
548.35   king's count
577.15   leaks and awfully
578.36   konyglik shire
595.14   orphalines
?619.32   Stout Stokes would take you offly

OHIO.   State, N cen US. The *O* Riv is a trib of the Mississippi R.
305.R1   TILL OHIO OHIO IOIOMISS

OLAF ROAD   (14/34).   Short st just N of Arbour Hill, parallel to Sitric Rd. Olaf was the legendary founder of Dan Dub. See also *Ivar St, Sitric Rd.*
12.31   Olaf's on the rise

OLD BAILEY.   St, City of London; former site of Newgate Pris, now of the Central Criminal Court, nicknamed "the *OB*"; Oscar Wilde was tried there (350.12). *FW* conflates the *OB* with the Bailey Lighthouse (qv) on Howth, and with HCE as Bill Bailey, perhaps because of HCE's unnamed crime.
85.26   haled up at the Old Bailey
177.24   old Belly
350.12   *Mr Lhugewhite Cadderpollard...at Oldbally Court*
?448.19   bait the Bull Bailey
480.18   Bill of Old Bailey!

OLDBAWN   (10/26).   Vill on Dodder R, SW of Dub.
590.25   Who now broothes oldbrawn...scalp...drummed...dun...inch of his core

OLDCASTLE.   Town, Co Meath, 64 mi from Dub, NW of Kells. See *Royal Manors of Dublin.*
18.06   O'c'stle, n'wc'stle, tr'c'stle, crumbling!

OLD CURIOSITY SHOP.   In Dickens' novel, Little Nell's grandfather loses it to the monstrous Quilp.

    434.30   old cupiosity shape

OLDHAM.   Industrial suburb NE of Manchester, Eng. Harriet Weaver was from *O* and the money with which she supported JJ was made there.

    616.04   May all similar douters of our oldhame story have that fancied wid-
               ming! [*Widmung*, Ger "dedication"]

OLD KENT ROAD.   In Southwark, London. Song: "Knocked 'Em in the Old Kent Road."

    359.19   sock him up, the oldcant rogue
    584.06   for bricking up all my old kent road

OLD MEN'S HOME (16/32).   In Northbrook Rd, Ranelagh (S Dub); opened 1812 as "Old Man's Asylum," for "respectable but reduced Protestant men."

    197.24   auld min's manse
    397.14   Old Man's House, Millenium Road

OLD MOLYNEUX CHURCH (CI) (15/33).   In Bride St.

    569.10   S. Molyneux Without

OLD SARUM.   N of Salisbury, Wilts, Eng. Anc Brit fortress, later town and bishop-ric; declined after New Sarum (Salisbury) built in 13th cent. Before the Reform Bill of 1832, *OS* sent members to Parl but had no voters at all – the worst of the rotten boroughs.

    552.01   Oi polled ye many but my fews were chousen...early voter, he was
               never too oft for old Sarum

OLD SOT'S HOLE (15/34).   18th-cent tav near Essex Gate at S end of Essex (now Grattan) Br. It was in the par of St Werburgh. In 1757, the idea for the "Wide Streets Commissioners" originated in a discussion in the *OSH*, which later (1762) was torn down with other houses for the widening of the lane into Parliament St.

    41.32   the Old Sots' Hole in the parish of Saint Cecily
    147.05   The Old Sot's Hole that wants wide streets to commission

OLD VIC (16/32).   Theater in Waterloo Rd, London, famous for its Shakespearian productions. (Named Royal Victoria Hall, 1833.)

    62.05   ostmen's dirtby on the old vic

OLIVET.   Aka Mt of Olives; ridge E of Jerusalem and sep from it by the vall of the Kedron (qv).

    160.11   an olivetion such as East Conna Hillock

OLT RIVER.   Trib of the Danube R; flows from S Transylvania, Romania, to the Danube opp Nikopol, Bulg.

    469.14   my olty mutther, Sereth Maritza

OLYMPIA.   Anc rel cen and sanctuary on Alpheus R, in NW Peloponnese, Greece. Quadrennial Olympic games (races were held in the *stadion*, 625.21) first celebrated in 776 BC, which became date of origin for chronology; periods were known as Olym-piads. The Statue of Zeus by Phidias (?) was one of the 7 Wonders of the Anc World (qv) (261.11, 553.12).

    84.31   olympiading even until the eleventh dynasty
    261.11   ogled the olymp
    553.12   statuesques

        613.28   olympically optimominous
        625.21   olympics...Steadyon

OLYMPUS, MT.   In Thessaly, NE Gr; mythical home of the gods.
        167.22   thundering legion has stormed Olymp
        613.28   olympically optimominous

OPERA HOUSE   (15/34).   Dub's only theater called "Opera House" was in Capel
    St in the 18th cent; used for public drawings in the state lottery.
        179.35   an entire operahouse

OPHIUCUS.   Northern constellation in anc astronomy, "the serpent-bearer." In
    mod astronomy, extends N and S of the equinoctial near Scorpio.
        494.09   Ophiuchus being visible above thorizon

ORAN.   Port City, NW Algeria. The Grand Mosque was erected in 18th cent with
    money paid as ransom for Christian slaves.
        390.10   Mahmullagh Mullarty, the man in the Oran mosque

ORANGE.   Town and region, now in Dept of Vaucluse, S Fr. The title was inher-
    ited by Wm the Silent, 1st prince of *O*-Nassau, and founder of the Dutch Rep. The *O*
    Soc, *O* "Toast," and *O* drums are all named after Wm III, prince of *O*-Nassau and
    Eng king, but nothing in Dub bears the name (see *Nassau St*).
        135.12   prince of Orange and Nassau
        488.05   orangey Saint Nessau Street
        498.08   houses of Orange and Betters M.P

ORANGERIE.   The small pavilion in the Tuileries Gardens, Paris, at the Place de la
    Concorde; now used for exhibitions of contemporary art. The Orangery in Kew Gar-
    dens, London, is also well-known.
        ?110.27   afterwards changed into the orangery
        ?246.26   on that old orangeray, Dolly Brae
        ?477.36   prehistoric barrow 'tis, the orangery
        ?478.01   in your orangery

ORANGE TREE, THE   (15/33).   18th-cent tav in Castle St, acc to Peter's *Dublin
    Fragments* (95).
        63.23   the Orange Tree

ORDOVICES.   Anc Welsh tribe; inhabited area of Denbigh, Flint, and Montgomery
    (now Clwyd and N Powys). Mainly, the stratum of rock from the Ordovician geologi-
    cal period, which came btwn the Cambrian and the Silurian.
        51.29   craogs and bryns of the Silurian Ordovices
        215.23   Ordovico or viricordo

O'REILLY AND CO   (15/34).   "Mantle manufacturers," at 16 Eustace St, around
    the turn of the cent. Nothing to do with ears, though.
        310.10   monofractured by Piaras UaRhuamhaighaudhlug, tympan founder,
                    Eustache Straight

ØRESUND.   The strait btwn Den and SW Swed.
        315.23   as he made straks for that oerasound

ORION.   Constellation, seen by the ancients as the legendary hunter Orion girdled
    by 3 esp bright stars and carrying a sword and club. Its early rising heralded summer;
    rising at midnight it signalled the season of vintage. *O* was also known as *O nimbosus*,

"of the raincloud," because its setting in Nov heralded stormy weather.
>?107.14   the eternal chimerahunter Oriolopos
>185.24   *cum divi Orionis iucunditate*...faked O'Ryan's
>?254.03   Orion of the Orgiasts

ORKNEY ISLANDS.   Archipelago off NE coast of Scot. *O* horses are rather larger than Shetland ponies.
>554.06   skewbald awknees

ORMOND QUAY   (15/34).   N side of Liffey; Upr *OQ* is W of Capel St, Lwr *OQ* is E.
>105.02   *Oremunds Queue Visits Amen Mart*

OROPUS.   Anc Gk city btwn Boeotia and Attica. The site of the Oracle of Amphiaurus nearby contained a theater, whose proscenium is well-preserved.
>513.21   *Oropos Roxy and Pantharhea* at the Gaiety

ORTHEZ.   Town, SW Fr, where in 1814 Wellington defeated the Fr under Soult.
>9.26   Arthiz too loose!

OS.   Town and port, S of Bergen, W Norway. *Os*, Nor "rivermouth."
>?53.04   kristansen is odable to os...tingmount

OSLO.   Cap of Nor, in Akershus Co (*fylke*), S Nor. Founded by Harald Sigurdsson (aka Harald Haardraade) (?530.20) in 1048 AD as Opslo (553.32), it was renamed Christiania (Kristiania) after it was rebuilt after the great fire of 1624; JJ wrote to Ibsen at his home in "Christiania." Officially named *O*, 1925.
      The local place-names in *FW* are mostly mentioned in the 11th *EB*, "Oslo": Akershus (536.13) is not only the co, but a promontory extending into *O* Harb, containing the form royal palace and fortress, later an armory and now a mus. Björvik (550.18) is the main part of *O* Harb, separated by the Akershus promontory from the smaller Pipervik harb. The Dampkjökken (550.15) was the public kitchen, founded in 1858, where meals were provided for the poor; a dispute about sanitary conditions there may have contributed to Ibsen's *Enemy of the People*. Holmenkollen (533.33) is a hilly quarter in N *O*, known for skiing and its ski jump. The Oscarshall (536.21) is a "pleasure palace" in the Bygdöy section, built 1847-52 by King Oscar of Nor and Swed. The Storting (Storthing) (54.09, 553.32) is the Nor parl and its bldg in cen *O*.
>?17.33   olso th'estrange
>23.11   a sweet unclose to the Narwhealian captol
>53.04   kusin of kristansen...os...tingmount
>53.08   Jehu will tell to Christianier
>54.09   storthingboys and dumagirls
>317.16   or this ogry Osler will oxmaul us all
>329.06   lifebark *Ulivengrene* of Onslought
>331.32   by neuhumorisation of our kristianiasation
>340.17   Bernesson Mac Mahahon from Osro
>533.11   olso haddock's fumb
>533.33   hiemlancollin...Holmstock
>536.13   to die bronxitic in achershous
>536.21   our zober beerbest in Oscarshal's winetavern
>537.06   Browne umbracing Christina Anya
>550.14   potted fleshmeats from store dampkookin [*stor*, Nor "big"]
>550.18   Biorwik's powlver and Uliv's oils [*öl*, Nor "beer"]
>553.32   hearsemen, opslo! nuptiallers, get storting!

OSSA, MT.   Mt in Thessaly, Gr. See *Pelion, Mt.*
128.36   piles big pelium on little ossas

OSTIA.   Resort town at mouth of Tiber R, It; once the port of Rome, now its Lido. The Ostian Way ran (and runs) to Rome from the sea.
371.09   Ostia, lift it!...Ostia...From the say!...reromembered

OSTIAK VOGUL.   Nat Dist in W Siberia, USSR; since WW II called Khanty-Mansi. The Ostiak were a nomadic tribe occupying the region of Tobolsk; the Vogul were a nomadic tribe found on both sides of the Ural Mts.
162.15   *Ostiak della Vogul Marina!*

OSTROV.   Russ, "island." There are numerous Ostrovs in the USSR, Romania, and Turkey, but *FW* apparently refers only to the generic meaning.
136.08   bored the Ostrov
289.16   ostrovgods

OTTAWA.   City, Ontario, Can; the cap of Can since 1858. The nearby Rideau (Fr, "curtain") Falls and Riv have given their name to the Rideau Canal through the city, Rue Rideau/Rideau St, and Rideau Hall, the res of the gov-gen.
544.21   ottawark and regular loafer
?551.06   on Rideau Row Duanna dwells

OTTOMAN EMPIRE.   Sultanate of the Osmanli Turks in Eur, Asia, and Afr, replaced 1920 by the Rep of Turkey. The *O* lang was Turk; the phrase at 419.26 is a quotation from James Clarence Mangan. An ottoman is a couch, usually without end-pieces.
263.10   hope of ostrogothic and ottomanic faith converters
284.27   an ottomanitic turquo-indaco of pictorial shine
419.26   Persse transluding from the Otherman [ie, the *O* lang; cf the anc
               Oscan lang (.25) and the Coptic lang (.26)]
451.30   on the electric ottoman

OUDH.   NE portion of Uttar Pradesh; overrun by Moslem invaders in 11th cent, held by Brit 1756-1856, then annexed to Brit dominions.
10.08   fromoud of the bluddle filth

OUR LADY OF DOLOURS CHURCH.   (1) In Dolphin's Barn (RC) (13/32). (2) In Glasnevin (RC) (15/37).
588.14   Whose dolour, O so mine!
601.22   S. Dolores Delphin's
601.27   S. Glacianivia's

OUR LADY OF REFUGE CHURCH (RC)   (15/31).   In Rathmines.
601.23   S. Rhodamena's

OUZEL GALLEY SOCIETY.   A forerunner of the Dub Chamber of Commerce, it was founded in 1705 and dissolved in 1888. In 1695 the merchant ship "Ouzel Galley" left Dub and for several years nothing was heard of her. She was presumed lost and the insurance was paid. In 1700, she returned to Dub with valuable cargo and a story of having been captured by Algerian pirates and later recaptured by her Ir crew. Both owners and insurers claimed ship and cargo, and after the case dragged through the courts for years without resolution, a committee of merchants arbitrated the case to everyone's satisfaction. Inspired by this extralegal success, merchants formed the *OG* Soc to settle commercial disputes without lawyers, and it did so for many years, gradually turning into a convivial and fraternal soc.

Among the many meeting places (205.24) of the *OG* Soc were the Rose and Bottle, Dame St (1765), the Phoenix Tav, Werburgh St (1748), Power's in Booterstown (1776), and Jude's Hotel, S Frederick St (early 19th cent).

Dhuine uasail, Ir "gentleman."

    35.16   Guinness thaw tool in jew me dinner ouzel fin? (a nice how-do-you-do in Poolblack...)

    205.24   the Rose and Bottle or Phoenix Tavern or Power's Inn or Jude's Hotel

?332.33   Kenny's thought ye, Dinny Oozle!

    546.14   in ouzel galley borne

OVAL, THE.   (1) Public house, 78 Middle Abbey St (15/34).

    140.03   not The Uval

(2) Cricket ground in S London, home of the Surrey co team.

    144.10   so ovally provencial at Balldole

    435.18   Slip your oval out of touch

    584.19   like a maiden wellheld, ovalled over

OW.   Riv, Co Wicklow; rises S of Lugnaquilla Mt, flows into Aughrim Riv W of Avoca (qv).

    203.14   whereabouts in Ow and Ovoca?

OWEL, LOUGH.   Lake, Co Westmeath, 3 mi NW of Mullingar. In 845, King Malachy drowned the invading Viking Turgesius in the lake.

    549.34   Conn and Owel with cortoppled baskib

OWENKEAGH RIVER.   In Co Cork. *Abhainn Caoch*, Ir "blind river."

    66.24   with Owen K. after her

OXFORD UNIVERSITY.   Abbreviations and nicknames: Oxon ("Oxoniensis"); Jesus Coll: "Jagger"; Pembroke Coll: "Pemmer"; Christ Ch Coll: "The House" (from its Lat name, "Aedes Christi"); its bell is Great Tom, in Tom Tower, by Tom Quad, and it was C L Dodgson's coll.

Brasenose Coll was the home of Walter Pater, of whom it was said that the center of his life and influence was his rooms at Brasenose. On the main gate of Brasenose is a doorknocker in the form of a head with an exaggerated brazen nose; JJ sent a postcard of it to Stanislaus with the message, "Herewith W. Pater's photograph" (*Letters* III, 201).

Other Oxford Colls mentioned in *FW* are Magdalen (pron "maudlin"), All Souls (which has no undergraduates, and therefore no sports teams), and Balliol.

O's Literae Humaniores program is pop known as "Greats" (507.09).

    57.24–.27   Tom Quad...maugdleness

    125.20   the showering jestnuts of Bruisanose

    175.05   All Saints beat Belial!

    182.26   Camebreech...hogsford

    210.12   a brazen nose and pigiron mittens for Johnny Walker Beg

    301.02   Where's Dr Brassenaarse?

    301.09   Christ's Church varses Bellial!

    320.29   baken be the brazen sun, buttered be the snows

    398.30   the Limibig brazenaze

    463.07   Auxonian aimer's ace...cantanberous

    467.31   he can cantab as chipper as any oxon

481.36   Tam Tower...jagger pemmer...the house of Eddy's Christy, meaning
          Dodgfather, Dodgson and Coo
507.09   greats and littlegets

OXMANTOWN (OSTMANTOWN).   When the Anglo-Normans took over Dub after 1170, the Dan inhabitants were relegated to the area N of the Liffey, called *villa Ostmannorum*. The "town of the Ostmen," corrupted to "Oxmantown," adjoined *O* Green, covering most of the area btwn the riv and the NCR. *O* Green covered the area now bounded by Arbour Hill, N King St, Queen St, Benburb St, and the Collins Barracks. King's Hosp (Bluecoat Sch) is built on its W half. The par ch is St Michan's (243.26).

47.22   And we'll bury him down in Oxmanstown
62.05   the ostmen's dirtby on the old vic [*O* is *across* the Liffey from Victoria Quay]
73.28   many a door beside of Oxmanswold
135.25   repulsed from his burst the bombolts of Ostenton
243.26   hang herself in Ostmannstown Saint Megan's
288.11   and filthily with bag from Oxatown
355.24   where an oxmanstongue stalled stabled
543.16   from my fief of the villa of the Ostmanorum
?595.01   Henge Ceolleges, Exmooth, Ostbys for ost
621.14   Oaxmealturn, all out of the woolpalls!

P

PACIFIC OCEAN.   The name was first given to it by Magellan, who found it so after the passage of Cape Horn.

85.07   liberties of the pacific subject [.20 atlantic]
502.11   Peace, Pacific!

PADUA.   City, NE It, noted among other things for its manufacture of silks (59.01). Once supposed to be a cen for necromancy; in Scott's *Lay of the Last Minstrel* (I, xi) it is said of the Earl of Gowrie, "He learned the art that none may name/ In Padua, far beyond the sea." *Giacomo Joyce*, p 3: "Padua, far beyond the sea."

59.01   in her cherryderry padouasoys
463.04   a home cured emigrant in Paddyouare far below on our sealevel

PALACE OF THE QUICKEN TREES.   In the Ir tale of this name, Finn and his companions are imprisoned in an enchanted palace by the treacherous Midac. The site is the bar of Kenry, Co Limerick, on the S bank of the Shannon W of Limerick City. The quicken tree is the mountain-ash or rowan.

275.15   palace of quicken boughs

PALATINATE, THE.   Area btwn Adare and Rathkeale, Co Limerick. Calvinist refugees from the Rhenish Palatine were settled in this area, early 18th cent, by Lord Southwell.

444.36   as sure as there's a palatine in Limerick
?596.25   as of young a palatin

PALE, THE.   Since the 12th cent, the area of Eng domination and defense around

Dub, which with the contiguous parts of Kildare, Louth, and Meath, was incorporated by King John as the Eng *P*. The included tnlds were divided among Eng nobles; the following were "walled and good towns" of the *P*: Dublin, Swords, Balrothery, Howth, Newcastle, Bray, Clondalkin, Fieldstown, and Tallaght. By 1537 the *P* was much shrunken from the boundaries of the Counties (Dublin, Meath, Kildare, and Louth) as defined in 1488 by an Act of Parl. The boundary towns were Ardee, Kells, Athboy, Trim, Kilcock, Clane, Naas, Harristown, Ballymore-Eustace, Tallaght, and Bullock (in Dun Laoghaire). In the 17th cent, Gerard Boate described Ire as "divided into two parts: The English Pale, and the land of the mere Irish."

22.03	nipped a paly one
?26.02	you were the pale eggynaggy
42.34	a brace of palesmen
78.27	New South Ireland and Vetera Uladh, bluemin and pillfaces
128.13	pinkun's pellets for all the Pale
136.36	some lumin pale...boinyn water
?143.24	pales as it palls
209.23	the cree of the pale and puny
?269.08	a pale peterwright
289.08	old Pales time
323.30	bunch of palers on their round
332.11	you'll peel as I'll pale
483.33	verted embracing a palegrim
539.26	pale of palisades
563.11	within the pale

PALESTINE.   The land btwn the E end of the Medit Sea and the Jordan R; Bibl Canaan; successively Hebrew, Assyrian, Chaldean, Persian, Roman, Muslim, and Ottoman; under Brit mandate 1920-48, and since then Israel and part of Jordan.

289.08	flash and crash habits of old Pales time
?407.14	no purer puer palestrine e'er chanted [+ Palestrina]

PALL MALL.   London st, in Westminster, btwn St James St and Trafalgar Sq.

547.02	wher in pellmell her deceivers sinned

PALMERSTON PARK (16/30).   In Rathgar, S of Rathmines; site of the "Bloody Fields," where the massacre of Easter Mon took place in 1209.

P is also a vill on the Liffey NW of Chapelizod; no *P* Park except the grounds of *P* Ho, now the Stewart Inst.

383.06	*speckled trousers around by Palmerstown Park*

PANNONIA.   Prov of Roman emp embracing SW Hung, Austria, Croatia, and Slovenia. Attila the Hun was from there, Chopin (437.29) was not.

437.30	who he's kommen from olt Pannonia on this porpoise

PANTELLERIA (PANTELLARIA).   Volcanic isl, 60 mi SW of Sicily. Its quasirhyolitic rocks are so unusual that the type is called "pantellarites."

387.13	explutor...andesiters...two pantellarias

PAPA WESTRAY ISLAND.   N-most of the Orkney Isls. The name "Papa" in several of the Orkneys derives from the Ir missionaries, or *papae*, of St Columba's time (6th cent).

26.07	the priest of seven worms and scalding tayboil, Papa Vestray

PARAGUAY.   Rep, cen S Amer. *Paraguas*, Sp "umbrella."

?338.07	*byway of paraguastical solation*

520.15   her tocher from paraguais

PARIS.   The Fr cap was orig a settlement of the Parisi tribe on the marshy isls of the Seine R. Caesar called it *Lutetia Parisiorum* (*lutum*, Lat "mud"). JJ made an impecunious visit to *P* in 1903, passed through it with Nora on the way to Zurich (228.22) in 1904, and lived there from 1920 to 1939. He frequented among other cafes the Brasserie Lutétia and stayed at the Hôtel Lutétia from Oct to Dec 1939: his last address in *P*. The Rue de Lutèce is on the Île de la Cité.

The "Paris Funds" (192.08) were Ir Nationalist deposits in *P* whose administration was disputed after the split over Parnell in 1890.

Henry IV, trimming religion to politics, is supposed to have said, "Paris vaut bien une messe" (199.08). "Paname" was a slang term for *P*, used by JJ (228.22). Parisite is a rare crystalline mineral, named after its finder, JJ Paris, in the 19th cent.

Local place-names in *P* are listed separately in this gazetteer.

14.14	Caddy went to Winehouse
21.17	in her petty perusienne
?93.14	that fenemine Parish Poser [Wilde? Joyce?]
102.13	her Parisienne's cockneze
131.09	outpriams all his parisites
143.36	her best Perisian smear
151.09	neoitalian or paleoparisien schola of tinkers and spanglers
155.16	Parysis, *tu sais*, crucycrooks, belongs to him who parises himself
184.21	blaster of Barry's
192.08	Parish funds
199.08	was Parish worth thette mess
207.08	Annushka Lutetiavitch Pufflovah...boudeloire
228.22	Paname-Turricum
230.13	their trist in Parisise
287.22	*letitiae...situm lutetiae*
307.F3	pim money sans Paris
418.01	parisites
453.25	Paris
464.17	Paris addresse
536.10	aroundisements
?542.29	raped lutetias in the lock

PARIS BRIDGES.   Mr J S Atherton discovered the names of most of the brs of Paris in the pp btwn 7.12 and 17.08; "Royally," 13.02, and "mitchel," 13.09, were the only allusions in the 1st Draft; all the others were added in *transition* or later.

7.12	Dobbelin	Pont Au Double
7.36	clouds	Pont de St Cloud
8.01	national	Pont National
8.06	invalids	Pont des Invalides
8.25	petty	Petit Pont
9.01	phillippy	Pont Louis Philippe
9.25	solphereens	Pont de Solferino
9.28	ousterlists	Pont d'Austerlitz
9.35	royal	Pont Royal
9.36	pettiest	Petit Pont
10.04	hiena	Pont d'Iena
11.23	allmicheal	Pont St Michel
11.35	solly	Pont Sully

12.06	marriedann	Pont Marie
12.30	several	Pont de Sèvres
13.02	Royally	Pont Royal
13.09	Mitchel	Pont St Michel
13.14	old butte new	Pont Neuf
13.27	desarted	Pont des Arts
13.32	national	Pont National
14.18	billy	Pont de Billy
16.03	marrogbones	Pont Mirabeau
16.33	Louee, louee	Pont St Louis, Pont Louis Philippe
17.08	Allmarshy	Pont d'Alma

PARLIAMENT HOUSE   (15/34).   On College Green, a complex of bldgs built
btwn 1729 and 1787, sold to Bank of Ire in 1802. See: *Bank of Ireland, Chichester:*
Chichester House, House of Commons.
    189.34   auguries of rooks in parlament

PARNASSUS.   The mt near Delphi sacred to Apollo and the Muses, and to Bacchus;
a symbol for poetry and music. *Gradus ad Parnassum,* "Steps to Parnassus," was the
title of a pop dictionary of Latin prosody and of several treatises on music, eg, by
Fux (1725) and Clementi (1817).
    467.34   false steps ad Pernicious

PARNELL MONUMENT   (15/34).   At N end of O'Connell St, a granite shaft with
bronze stat by St Gaudens. Finished 1911, it is the only O'Connell St stat which JJ
did not know as a Dubliner. Inscription: "No man has the right to put a stop to the
march of a nation" (614.17).
    ?41.35   statue of Primewer Glasstone setting a match to the march of a maker
    553.12   the Pardonell of Maynooth

PARROT, THE   (15/33).   18th-cent tav in the area near Christchurch Cath known
as "Hell" (qv), acc to Peter's *Dublin Fragments* (95).
    63.23   the Parrot in Hell

PARTEEN.   Tnld and vill, Co Clare, 2½ mi N of Limerick on Shannon R; *pairtín,*
Ir "little port." This stretch of the Shannon btwn Limerick and Killaloe was known
for the best salmon fishing in Ire before the Ardnacrusha dam was built.
    100.13   Parteen-a-lax Limestone. Road

PARTICK.   Manufacturing town (with a large Ir population) near Glasgow, Scot.
"Partick Thistle" is its football (soccer) team.
    378.18   Partick Thistle

PASSAU.   Town in Bavaria, Ger. Charles V was pursued by Moritz, the Elector of
Saxony, until he signed the Treaty of Passau in 1552, granting full liberty of worship
to Protestants.
    ?13.32   bring fassilwise to pass how

PASS-IF-YOU-CAN.   In context, the ref is to the stat of T Moore (qv). But there
may be an allusion to places called "Pass-if-you-can": (1) Crossroads, once a tav,
btwn Finglas and St Margaret's, N of Dub.   (2) Gap 3 mi NE of Mullingar, Co
Meath, on Delvin Rd. In 1642 the Ir blocked the Eng retreat from Athlone at this
point.   (3) Tnld, par of Leixlip, bar of Newcastle, Co Dub.
    ?553.15   the eiligh ediculous Passivucant

PATAGONIA.   The S tip of S Amer, from the Limay and Negro Rivs to the Strait of Magellan; divided btwn Chile and Argentina. *Patagón*, Sp "big foot"; named by Magellan from the huge footprints he saw. (HCE as Finn MacCool has big feet, 78.05 megapod.) The natives, now extinct, were very tall.

> 310.32   for Culsen, the Patagoreyan, chieftan of chokanchuckers and his
>   moyety joyant
> 512.18   an absquelitteris puttagonnianne

PATERNOSTER ROW.   Before it was destroyed by bombs in 1940, it ran btwn Ave Maria Lane and St Paul's Churchyard, City of London. Acc to tradition, the clergy of old St Paul's recited the Lord's Prayer at this point of the Corpus Christi day procession around outside of cath.

> 444.29   Rosemiry Lean and Potanasty Rod

PATERSON AND CO   (14/34).   Match manufacturers of Belfast; its Dub works were and are in Hammond Lane.

> 421.01   Buy Patersen's Matches
> 529.30   pfuffpfaffing at his Paterson and Hellicott's

PATMOS.   Isl, Aegean Sea, in the Dodecanese; the place of banishment of St John the Evangelist.

> 526.18   Walker John Referent? Play us your patmost!

PATRICK ST   (15/33).   The st which runs N-S past the W front of St Patrick's Cath. *Slighe*, Ir "road, way."

> 51.08   Slypatrick, the llad in the llane

PEACOCKSTOWN.   Tnld, par and bar of Ratoath, Co Meath.

> 97.04   Peacockstown

PEA RIDGE.   The battle of Pea Ridge, in S Illinois, US, 7-8 Mar 1862, was a Union victory in the W theater of the Civil War.

> 84.07   anywheres between Pearidge and the Littlehorn...confederate

PEBWORTH.   Vill 7 mi SW of Stratford-on-Avon, Eng. See *Hillborough*.

> 340.33   from Piping Pubwirth to Haunted Hillborough

PEEBLES.   Co, SE Scot, and city on Tweed R. Mungo Park lived there between his Afr expeditions.

The Manor, *P*, is the trad site of "Macbeth's Castle"; by sheer coincidence, the *P* Bldgs were located on Manor St (14/34) in Dub. Peter Peebles is a pauper litigant in Scott's *Redgauntlet*.

> ?260.L2   *Menly about peebles*
> 390.26   *fell in with a lout by the name of Peebles*
> 537.13   glueglue gluecose, peebles

PEKING.   City, NE China, and cap of China for cents except 1928-49, when its name was changed to Peiping. Marco Polo made it known to Eur as Cambaluc. The Inner City contains Hwang Cheng, known as the "Imperial City" or "Forbidden City." Just N is the artificial hill, King Shan, known as "Prospect Hill"; it has 5 summits, with a temple on each, and is surrounded by a wall more than a mile around.

> 130.35   Elin's flee polt pelhaps but Hwang Chang evelytime
> 322.06   hwen ching hwan chang
> ?374.34   Hung Chung Egglyfella
> 507.28   picking pockets...the Pekin packet

533.06   chinatins...spekin tluly
541.02   seaventy seavens for circumference inkeptive are your hill prospect

PELICAN LIFE INSURANCE CO.   A Brit company est 1797, its Dub offices were at 53 Dame St.
197.19   Was his help inshored in the Stork and Pelican

PELION, MT.   Mt in Thessaly, Gr. The brothers Ephialtes and Otus (493.23–.24) tried to scale heaven by piling *P* on Ossa (*Odyssey* XI); hence, the phrase means any enterprise without hope of success.
128.35   piles big pelium on little ossas

PELOPONNESE.   The S mainland of Gr; it contained Sparta, not Athens. The Peloponnesian War (431-404 BC) btwn Athens and Sparta and their allies ended in the surrender of Athens and the brief transfer of leadership of Gr to Sparta.
8.20   pulluponeasyan wartrews

PEMBROKE.   The old name for the SE quarter of Dub, after the Earl of *P*. The *P* Estate includes the present Merrion and Fitzwilliam Sqs, and stretches S of the Grand Canal. *P* (now Sarsfield) Quay is on the N bank of the Liffey W of Barrack Br.
74.15   Fengless, Pawmbroke

PENMARK (PENMARC'H).   Point Penmarc'h, vill and penin in Dept of Finistère, Brittany, Fr, 18 mi SW of Quimper. The Phare d'Eckmuhl stands on the Point de Penmarc'h. Tristan watched for Iseult's sail from the cliffs of *P*.
P is also a town in Wales, 12 mi SW of Cardiff.
189.06   trysting by tantrums, small peace in ppenmark
?238.01   drawpairs with two pinmarks
301.F5   Very glad you are going to Penmark
421.18   the penmarks used out in sinscript
?606.26   arky paper, anticidingly inked with penmark, push

PENNSYLVANIA.   State, NE US.
228.19   banishment care of Pencylmania, Bretish Armerica

PENRITH.   In 1926, JJ suggested that Harriet Weaver "order" a piece for *Work in Progress*. She sent a picture of the "Giant's Grave" at the ch of St Andrew's, *P*, and asked for "grave account of his esteemed Highness Rhaggrich O'Hoggnor's Hogg Tomb." The 1st par of *FW*, JJ said, was his filling of the "order" (Ellmann, 594).
P is a town in Cumberland (now Cumbria), Eng. Miss Weaver's attention was attracted to the Giant's Grave by a pamphlet by the Rev James Cropper.
It may be significant that despite this early instance of *genius loci* there is no specific allusion by name to *P* or the Giant's Grave in *FW*.

PENTAPOLIS.   Anc name for the area on E coast of It btwn Rimini and Arcona and btwn the Adriatic coast and the mts. The name has been used for many groups or confederations of 5 cities; the Gk isl of Lesbos, for example, was called *P* for that reason. There may even be an allusion to the "Five Towns" (comprised by Stoke-on-Trent, Eng) of Arnold Bennett's novels.
565.04   the banders of the pentapolitan poleetsfurcers

PENZANCE.   Town, Cornwall, SW Eng, on Eng Channel 65 mi SW of Plymouth. Gilbert and Sullivan's *Pirates of Penzance*, of course.
The allusion is mainly to the Dub daily newspaper, the *Irish Independent*.
501.19   ales is Penzance

PEREKOP.   Town, S USSR, the main town on the isthmus of the same name from
which the Crimea "hangs" as one sees it on the map.
    339.13   his perikopendolous gaelstorms

PÈRE LACHAISE CEMETERY.   In E Paris, 20th Arr; Oscar Wilde is buried there,
among many other notables.
    76.36   its architecht, Mgr Peurelachasse

PERGAMUM (PERGAMOS).   Anc city, Asia Min, mod Bergama, Turk. A cen of
Gk culture, it was famed for its library, until Antony gave it to Cleopatra. Acc to
Pliny, parchment (Lat, *pergamena*) was invented at *P* when the Ptolemies, jealous of
its library, prohibited the export of papyrus from Egypt.
    303.23   writings...triperforator awlrite blast through his pergaman

PERSIA.   Now (since 1935) Iran (qv); kingdom, anc and mod, SW Asia.
    Daniel interprets the handwriting on the wall (135.16) to Belshazzar to mean:
"Thy kingdom is divided, and given to the Medes and Persians" (*Dan* 5:28). Mon-
tesquieu's *Persian Letters* (1721) is a critique of Fr insts (183.10). Persian blinds
(583.14) are shutters with moveable slats. Persian slippers (532.02) are carpet slippers.
    18.22   Thy thingdome is given to the Meades and Porsons
    38.11   no persicks and armelians for thee, Pomeranzia!
    ?48.16   Of the persins sin this Eyrawyggla saga
    135.16   handwriting on his facewall...exprussians
    ?141.25   inmoodmined pershoon
    162.12   Persic-Uraliens hostery
    183.10   persianly literatured
    ?224.02   he was goodda purssia
    280.15   A lovely...pershan of cates
    286.08   anymeade or persan...exerxeses
    339.18   *Perssiasterssias*
    ?353.24   *Parsuralia*
    357.09   hamid and damid...comequeers this anywhat perssian
    358.20   Perseoroyal...Iran
    419.24   in shunt Persse transluding from the Otherman [Ottoman]
    532.02   Off with your persians! Search ye the Finn!
    583.14   Casting such shadows to Persia's blind!

PERU.   Rep, S America. The lang is Sp.
    253.01   stammer up in Peruvian

PETERBOROUGH.   Town, Northants, Eng. The *P Chronicle* was compiled by monks
of *P* Abbey, suspended 1131, resumed and brought up to date 1154. Additions for
1132-1154 are earliest examples of Middle Eng. (J M Morse, "1132" *JJQ* III [1966],
272-75.)
    442.11   as true as there's a soke for sakes in Twoways Peterborough

PETER ROBINSON.   London dept store, in Oxford Circus.
    65.15   her Peter Robinson trousseau

PETIT PALAIS.   Ave Alexandre III, Paris, btwn the Seine and the Champs-Elysées.
Built, with the facing Grand Palais, for the Exhibition of 1900, it became the Art
Mus of the City of Paris. Not on a "crossknoll."
    ?552.23   her paddypalace on the crossknoll with massgo bell

PETTIGO.   Vill, Co Donegal, on Termon R 1 mi from where it flows into Lough

Erne. Cen for pilgrimages to St Patrick's Purgatory in Lough Derg.

The "Little Go" was the nickname of the former Entrance Examination for undergraduates at Cambridge (qv) U.

 ?279.F12 when I slip through my pettigo

PHAROS AT ALEXANDRIA. One of the 7 Wonders of the Anc World (qv) (553.10), generically (as in Fr *phare*), any lighthouse. See *Alexandria*.

?76.34	an inversion of a phallopharos
215.01	Poolbeg flasher beyant, pharphar
339.24	*farused...allasundery*
553.10	beaconphires...pensilled turisses
?625.03	Pharaops...[.21] olympics...Cooloosus

PHIBSBOROUGH (PHIBSBORO) (14–15/35). Dist and Rd, N Dub. The cen of the *P* dist is the intersection of *P* Rd and the NCR, a few blocks from Berkeley Rd: "Gainsborough Carfax" (260.12)? The ch of St Peter or *P* Ch (RC), on Cabra Rd and NCR, is 19th-cent Gothic, with a spire (highest in Dub). All Saints Ch (CI), on *P* Rd, is surmounted by a dome.

24.20	the Fivs Barrow and Waddlings Raid [Watling St]
147.26	by Fibsburrow churchdome [All Saints]
?260.12	Berkeley Alley, querfixing Gainsborough Carfax
569.08	S. Phibb [either ch]
601.21	S. Phibia's [St Peter's]

PHILADELPHIA. Wm Penn's City of Brotherly Love in Pennsylvania, US, attracts 2 kinds of allusions in *FW*: the not-so-loving brother-pair of Shem and Shaun and their metamorphoses, and the song "Off to Philadelphia in the Morning," about the Ir emigration to the US.

73.18	loff a falladelfian in the morning
93.33	Op. 2 Phil Adolphos the weary O
320.20	off for Fellagulphia in the farning
378.36	aped to foul a delfian in the Mahnung
418.22	*castwhores pulladeftkiss if oldpollocks*˙
530.27	upped their frullatullepleats with our warning
?572.25	two or three philadelphians

PHILADESPOINIS (ILL). NPN? Persephone was called *Despoina*, "mistress"; the title was common to (female) underworld divinities (eg, Artemis). There was a Temple of Despoina at Lycosura in Arcadia.

 165.28 Professor Ebahi-Ahuri of Philadespoinis (Ill)

PHILIPPI. Town, Macedonia, where in 42 BC Octavian and Anthony defeated Brutus and Cassius; also place where St Paul first preached in Eur.

 9.01 me Belchum sneaking his phillippy

PHILIPSBURGH AVE (17/36). In Fairview, NE Dub. The Joyce family lived at several addresses (see *Fairview*) within a block of *P* Ave btwn 1896 and 1901, but there is no record of their living in *P* Ave itself. JJ may have thought of "*P*" as naming the dist, as at 497.19.

420.29	Removed to Philip's Burke
497.19	Phillipsburgs, Cabraists

PHOENICIA. Anc country on E shore of Medit; flourished esp 1200-1000 BC. Its cap was Tyre (qv). Phoenicians were leading traders, sailors, navigators of anc world; Phoenician manuals for navigators (123.24–.27) were, acc to Victor Bérard, Homer's source for the travels of Odysseus. The alphabet was introduced into Eur by the Phoenicians.

68.29   from Phenicia to Little Asia
85.20   the atlantic and Phenitia Proper
123.25   Punic admiralty report
197.31   the gran Phenician rover
221.32   Phenecian blends
608.32   Ashias...the Phoenician wakes

PHOENIX BREWERY.   *P* Porter Brewery Co, in James's St, across Watling St from Guinness's. *Ca* 1820 the brewery was owned by Daniel O'Connell, Jr, later by John Brennan, O'Connell's manager, who renamed it the *PB*. Until it went out of business before WW I, the *PB* brewed "O'Connell's Ale." Its premises were taken over by Guinness, and the brewing of O'Connell's Ale by D'Arcy's Anchor Brewery (qv).

7.12   U'Dunnell's foamous olde Dobbelin ayle
38.04   bottle of Phenice-Bruerie '98
?70.29   after ten o'connell
310.28   to be unbulging an o'connell's
311.18   honour thee. O Connibell, with mouth burial!
382.04   Phoenix brewery stout...O'Connell's famous old Dublin ale
406.10   her old phoenix portar

PHOENIX FIRE INSURANCE CO.   Around the turn of the cent, its Dub office was at 41 Lwr Sackville St; David Drimmie and Sons, Secretaries.

590.05   policist...by Phoenis, swore on him Lloyd's

PHOENIX PARK.   Dub's great park, in the NW area of the city, is the largest enclosed park in Europe, covering an area of 1752 acres, and surrounded by a wall 7 mi in circumference, with 9 main gateways which permit access to the park rds. The Main Entrance, or Parkgate, is at the SE cor of the park; counting clockwise from the Main Gate are Islandbridge, Chapelizod, Knockmaroon, White's, Castleknock, Ashtown, Cabra, and NCR Gates.

The name of the park is derived from a misunderstanding by Eng speakers of *fionn uisge*, Ir "clear water," a spring in the park. The transliteration *Feenisk* was corrupted to "Phoenix," and the mistake is commemorated by the stately bird atop the *P* Pillar (see esp 135.15).

The area including the present park and stretching across the Liffey to the S once belonged to the Knights of St John of Jerusalem; it was surrendered to the Crown in 1541. Subsequently, it was used as the official res of the Brit Viceroy; following frequent attacks against the exposed residence by the O'Tooles and the O'Byrnes, it was vacated and leased to Sir Edmund Fisher in 1611. Fisher built a new res on St Thomas's Hill (on the site now occupied by the Magazine Fort), which was called Phoenix House, after the spring nearby.

Fisher's *P* Ho was surrendered to the Crown in 1617, and became the viceregal res: "His Majesty's house near Kilmainham, called the Phoenix"; it was demolished in 1731. In 1671, the Duke of Ormond purchased the "Phoenix and Newtown lands" in trust for Charles II, and made it into a deer park, extending the estate as far as Chapelizod, Ashtown, and Castleknock. By 1711, in the reign of Queen Anne, the park was known as "the Queen's garden at the Phoenix" (394.27, 553.24). To avoid the loss of deer through poaching and injury, the size of the park was reduced by building a wall to the N of the Liffey; by 1671, the park had reached its present size. In the 18th cent it was much improved by Lord Chesterfield when he was Lord Lt; he laid out roadways, planted avenues of trees, and erected the *P* Pillar.

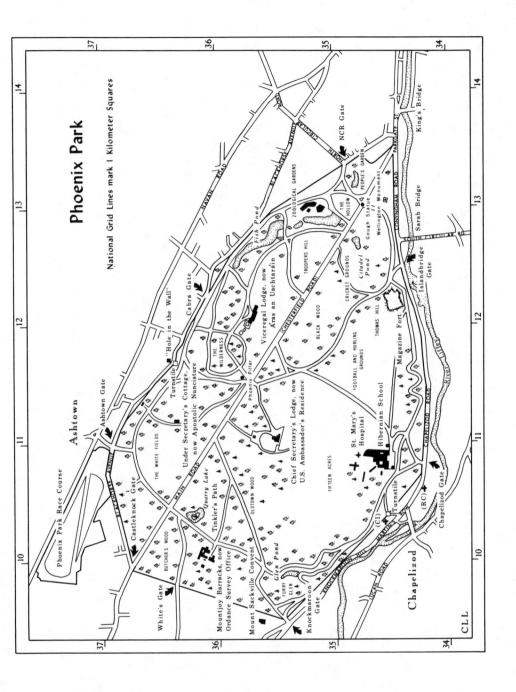

Phoenix Park

National Grid Lines mark 1 Kilometer Squares

One of the most famous episodes in the park's history is that of the *PP* Murders
(329.35, 617.12), on 6 May 1882, in which members of the secret society called the
"Invincibles" murdered Lord Cavendish and Thomas Burke, the Chief Secretary and
the Under-Secretary of Ire, in the vicinity of the *P* Pillar. *PP* has been the site of many
important meetings, notably the Ecumenical Congress of 1932 (attended by about 1
million people), numerous monster rallies, duels, and temperance, political, land league,
Ir Lang Week, and Fenian Movement meetings through the years. The park is maintained by "Rangers" (587.25), supervised by the Chief Ranger.

Since *PP* is conflated in *FW* with the Garden of Eden, and is the scene of HCE's
unnamed sin involving the two girls and the three soldiers, the name "Phoenix" is often punned with *felix culpa*, Augustine's phrase for original sin as the "happy fault"
without which there would be no divine redemption.

I. Place-Names in Phoenix Park:

BEAU-BELLE WALK.   The old name for the area where the *P* Pillar now stands,
in the cen of the park, just N of the Main Rd. Once a promenade for Dub gentry.

?405.13   the Bel of Beaus' Walk
?584.29   As the belle to the beau

BUTCHER'S WOOD.   S of Castleknock Gate. In Le Fanu's *The House by the
Churchyard*, Dr Sturk (cf 17.14) is bludgeoned and left for dead in *BW* by Paul Dangerfield (alias Charles Archer), who is overheard by Charles Nutter, agent for Lord
Castlemallard's Ir properties, as Dangerfield is his Eng agent. Fireworker O'Flaherty, of
the artillery regt stationed in Chapelizod, is not involved.

80.08   Phornix Park...dangerfield circling butcherswood where fireworker
oh flaherty engaged a nutter of castlemallards and ah for archer
stunned's turk

CHESTERFIELD ROAD.   Laid out as a serpentine rd the length of the park
and lined with elms by Lord Chesterfield, it was straightened in the 19th cent; like
other rds in the park, it is now officially nameless, but usually called the Main Rd, 3
mi from Main Gate to Castleknock Gate.

553.19   I fenced it about with huge Chesterfield elms
564.10   The straight road down the centre (see relief map) bisexes the park

CHIEF SECRETARY'S LODGE.   Now the US Ambassador's Res, on the S side
of the Main Rd near the cen of the park.

564.15   chief sacristary's residence

DRUIDS ALTAR.   Discovered many years ago in a sandpit near Chapelizod,
later re-erected in the Zoological Gardens, it consists of 3 supporters, a floating stone,
and a roof. Another anc burial tomb is located on a hill above Chapelizod Gate W of
Hibernian Sch.

?279.F27 Drewitt's altar

FIFTEEN ACRES.   The largest open area of the park, S of Main Rd at the W
end. Once a favorite spot for duels and meetings, it now contains sports grounds, and
herds of deer and cows graze there. Actually contains over 150 acres; the origin of
the name is almost forgotten, but is explained by Le Fanu in *The House by the Churchyard*, 82: "You all know the artillery butt. Well, that was the centre of a circular enclosure containing just fifteen acres..."

135.21   his great wide cloak lies on fifteen acres

FIONN UISGE SPRING.   The eponymous "well" for which the park is named.
The exact location is unknown, but was prob near the W boundary wall of the former
Viceregal Lodge, behind the *P* Pillar. The spring was covered by stonework in the early
19th cent, and was famous as a chalybeate spa. With the construction of main drains
in the area, the spring was contaminated and reduced to a small pool. It gradually lost

popularity, and in 1877 its thatched covering burnt, and later the stonework was removed. See 6.27, 80.07, 100.07, 135.15, 380.09, 571.02, 605.19.

FURRY GLEN.   A scenic and secluded area at W end of park, near Knockmaroon Gate. Aka Furzy Glen and Hawthorn Glen.

135.02	feeling fain and furry...midst the hawthorns
340.09	Here furry glunn...Their feery pass
357.32	golf stature [Gough Statue]...howthern folleys
?375.32	Between Furr-y-Benn and Ferr-y-Bree
526.22	the trefoll of the furry glans
553.22	a hawthorndene, a feyrieglenn, the hallaw vall

GOUGH STATUE.   The bronze equestrian stat of Sir Hugh (later Lord) Gough (pron "Goff") stood at the cor of People's Gardens (which Gough didn't give). He was "conqueror of the Punjab" at the battle of Gujerat, 1849. The stat was removed some years ago.

?211.25	gouty Gough
271.29	that grew in the garden Gough gave
334.18	our own one's goff stature
357.31	a general golf stature

HOLE IN THE WALL.   Public house, aka Blackhorse Tav, halfway btwn Cabra Gate and Ashtown Gate in Blackhorse Lane (now Ave), which runs along N wall of PP. The name is prob from the turnstile in the park wall, although Chart's *Dublin*, 319, repeats a pop explanation that voters there passed an empty hand through the wall and withdrew it filled with guineas. Nancy Hand was the proprietress from 1896 (Thom's *Directory*); she is conflated with Anna Livia (244.20, 621.21) and a Guinness vessel (382.27). *U* 656/672: "hole in the wall at Ashtown gate."

?5.30	wallhall's
69.05	turn wheel again to the whole of the wall
69.07	such a wallhole did exist
?78.03	whaling away the whole of the while
90.21	alluding to the whole in the wall
244.20	At house, to's pitty. With Nancy Hands
?365.16	wholenosing at a whallhoarding
382.27	So sailed the stout ship *Nansy Hans*. From Liff away
?587.15	weld the wall...belt and blucher him afore the hole
621.21	Mineninecyhandsy

THE HOLLOW.   Opp the main entrance to Zoo. Before WW I, concerts by the DMP band and other military and civilian bands were held on Sun afternoons, but interest declined after 1914.

34.20	in the swoolth of the rushy hollow
67.31	those rushy hollow heroines
136.34	in the hollow of the park
319.01	Hillyhollow
371.35	perked on hollowy hill
421.06	Park Bogey...Hollow and eavy
553.22	the hallaw vall
565.02	a depression called Holl Hollow...banders
607.27	to the hothehill from the hollow

MAGAZINE FORT.   On St Thomas's Hill, at the SE cor of Fifteen Acres, built on the site of the old *P Ho*. See separate listing.

MOUNTJOY BARRACKS.   Bldg included in the present Ordnance Survey offices, at the W end of the park, once used as a barracks. See *Mountjoy*.

PEOPLE'S FLOWER GARDENS, PEOPLE'S PARK. A scenic area at the E end of the park, near the Main Gate, surrounded by oak trees and walkways, with lakes at the cen. Bishop's Wood lies at the N side of the area, near the NCR Gate.

33.27 people's park
346.32 *pimple spurk*
564.35 royal park...gardeenen, is open to the public

PHOENIX PILLAR. Erected by Lord Chesterfield, a 30-foot high fluted stone pillar surmounted by a phoenix. Sometimes called the "eagle monument." It has been moved a short distance from its orig site, and is now at the intersection of the Main Rd, W of Viceregal Lodge, at the cen of the park. See esp 135.15.

STARFORT. Begun but never completed as an extensive fortified enclosure NE of site of the later Magazine Fort on the initiative of the Duke of Wharton; intended as a refuge in the event of a rebellion in Dub. It was known to Dubliners as "Wharton's Folly" (a name often mistakenly ascribed to the Magazine Fort, which was built years after Wharton's death).

12.23 playing Wharton's Folly, at a treepurty on the planko in the purk
246.04 Between the starfort and the thornwood brass castle flambs

UNDER SECRETARY'S COTTAGE. Now the Apostolic Nunciature, N of the Main Rd btwn Ashtown Gate and Cabra Gate.

VICEREGAL LODGE. Now *Áras an Uachtaráin*, the res of the President of the Ir Rep, N of the Main Rd, vicinity of Cabra Gate. Built in 1751, it was the Viceregal Res 1782-1922. Tim Healy occupied it as 1st Gov-Gen of the Ir Free State ("Uncle Tim's Cabin") in 1922. The "*PP* Murders" of 1882 were committed not far away; the driver of the murderers' carriage was called "Skin-the-Goat."

?209.34 artesaned wellings...vicereine's levee
329.36 Healy Mealy...The grandest bethehaily...Scape the Goat [*bethel*, Heb "house"]
564.13 vinesregent's lodge
622.07 Uncle Tim's Caubeen...Viker Eagle

WELLINGTON MONUMENT. *Recte*, Wellington Memorial; near the Main Gate, S of Main Rd, a granite obelisk, sometimes called the "overgrown milestone." See separate listing.

ZOO. *Recte*, Zoological Gardens; N of Main Rd, at E end of the park. It encircles 2 unnamed lakes, part of serpentine chain of lakes (resembling the Serpentine in London's Hyde Park but never called by that name) along NE boundary of the park. Known for its success in breeding lions; many of the lions in Eur zoos are Dubliners.

75.01 the lion in our teargarten [*Tiergarten*, Ger "zoo"]
488.14 lionroar...the zoohoohoom of Felin make Call
564.06 white and gold elephant in our zoopark

II. Phoenix Park Allusions:

3.22	knock out in the park	68.29	Phenicia
4.17	secular phoenish	80.06	Phornix Park
6.27	finisky	80.07	Finewell's Keepsacre
12.24	purk	85.20	Phenitia Proper
17.14	from sturk to finnic	88.24	Holy Saint Eiffel, the very phoenix!
17.23	Finishthere Punct		
33.27	people's park	100.07	Fathach I Fiounnisgehaven ["giant in clear water"]
35.08	our greatest park		
39.17	Finnish pork	116.17	parks...fornix
55.28	phoenix in our woodlessness	128.35	phoenix be his pyre
60.25	park	130.11	comminxed...phoenished

135.15	well of Artesia...bird of Arabia	506.03	midhill of the park
136.35	vaguum of the phoenix	520.01	feelmick's park
140.10	most extensive public park	524.06	our beloved naturpark
196.11	Fiendish park	534.12	Pynix Park
283.F3	Slash-the-Pill...Phoenix	553.24	Queen's garden of her phoenix
322.20	spark to phoenish	564.08	Finn his park
324.07	sphinxish pairc	564.35	this royal park
331.02	pahymix cupplerts	571.02	clear springwell...of our park
332.31	phoenix his calipers	576.28	Phenicia Parkes
373.20	the pairk	580.28	fenian's bark
380.09	Glenfinnisk-en-la-Valle	583.24	park's police
394.27	parkside pranks of quality queens	587.25	Phoenix Rangers'
		605.19	Yshgafiena and Yshgafiuna [*fionn uisge*]
454.34	felixed...parked		
461.10	Finest Park	617.12	pork martyrs
473.18	phaynix...sphoenix spark	621.01	Phoenix

PHOENIX TAVERN.   (1) 18th-cent Chapelizod public house; see *Chapelizod*.
(2) Cor of Werburgh St and Skinner's Row; kept by James Hoey until closed after his death in 1773, it was a favorite spot for meetings of clubs and political societies, including the Freemasons and the Ouzel Galley Soc (qv).
>   205.25   Phoenix Tavern
>   321.16   lit by night in the Phoenix
>   514.08   schappsteckers of hoy's house

PICCADILLY.   *P* Circus in London, and the thoroughfare btwn that and Hyde Park Cor. *FW* may conflate "Piccadilly" with "peccadillo" because London prostitutes once congregated around the statue of Eros in *P* Circus.
"Pinkindindies" were 18th-cent Dub bravos who enjoyed "pinking" passers-by with the sword-points projecting beyond their scabbards.
>   336.29   peckadillies at his wristsends...dovessoild
>   353.28   *the Landaunelegants of Pinkadindy*
>   577.05   martial sin with peccadilly

PICKARDSTOWN.   Tnld and vill, N Co Dub, on the Naul rd, 6 mi N of Dub. The Boot Inn was and still is in the vill.
>   262.21   as the Boote's at Pickardstown

PIEPOWDER COURT.   Trad court of justice held at fairs to settle disputes between buyers and sellers. From *pied-poudreux*, Fr "dustyfoot" or "wayfarer." That JJ knew the allusion, whether he intended it in the citations below, is shown by his use of the phrase "the court of pye poudre" in the 1st Draft of the text now *FW* 580; it was deleted before publication in *transition*.
>   12.36   from the macroborg of Holdhard to the microbirg of Pied de Poudre
>   545.30   I...domstered dustyfeets in my husinclose

PIERIAN SPRING.   Pieria is the area, with Mt Pierus, N of Mt Olympus, Gr, where the Muses (called the Pierides) were worshipped. Pope's *Essay on Criticism*: "A little learning is a dang'rous thing;/ Drink deep, or taste not the Pierian spring."
>   301.25   Sink deep or touch not the Cartesian spring!

PIGALLE.   St, Pl, and Métro stop below Montmartre in the 9th Arr, Paris; named after Jean Baptiste Pigalle, 18th-cent sculptor. *P* is a cen for nightclubs and other entertainments.
>   143.35   you perfect little pigaleen...Perisian

PIG AND WHISTLE.   A common pub name in Eng, pop derived from "piggin and wassail"; but not, apparently, a Dub pub or a common name in Ire.

    303.R2   FIG AND THISTLE PLOT A PIG AND WHISTLE

PIGEONHOUSE, THE   (18/33).   *P* Rd begins at Ringsend, contiguous with the S Wall, and extends E along the wall into Dub Bay. The old *P* Fort, halfway along *P* Rd, is now an electric generating and drainage sta. In the 18th cent, a man named Pidgeon was caretaker of the supply house erected at that spot, and made it an inn, "Pidgeon's House," then *P*. A *P* Hotel was erected at the spot in 1790, purchased by the govt in 1813, and incorporated in the construction of the *P* Ft, which was dismantled in 1897.

    ?129.23   seven dovecotes cooclaim to have been pigeonheim
    197.32   they made the pigeonhouse
    444.24   civil tongue in your pigeonhouse

PIGOTT AND CO   (15/33).   Music and Pianoforte Warehouse, 112 Grafton St, around the turn of the cent.

    43.32   king of inscrewments, Piggott's purest...Mr Delaney (Mr Delacey?), horn
    282.F4   his whisper waltz I like from Pigott's with that Lancydancy step

PIKE COUNTY.   Missouri co on the Mississippi R, N of St Louis; site of the imaginary town of St Petersburg (qv), home of Tom Sawyer and Huck Finn. In an introductory note to *Huckleberry Finn*, Mark Twain refers to the care he has taken with the "ordinary 'Pike County' dialect" and its variants.

    25.28   no, nor in all Pike County

PILE ENDS.   In the 18th cent, the outer end of the S Wall pilings was known as the "Pile Ends"; what later was the Pigeonhouse (qv) Rd would have been the *PE* Rd.

    ?200.19   wensum farmerette walking the pilend roads

PILLARS OF HERCULES.   The 2 promontories at the E end of the Strait of Gibraltar: Rock of Gibraltar, in Eur, and Jebel Musa at Centa in Afr.

    16.04   the pillory way to Hirculos pillar
    128.36   big pelium on little ossas like the pilluls of hirculeads

PILTDOWN COMMON.   Vill, Sussex, Eng. Pieces of human skull found there btwn 1908 and 1915 were supposed evidence of a new genus, *P* Man, until exposed as a hoax in 1953.

    10.30   wagrant wind's awalt'zaround the piltdowns

PIM, BROTHERS (LTD)   (15/33).   Manufacturers of poplin, and linen and woolen drapers and silk mercers, at 75-88 Gt George's St, S, around the turn of the cent.

    43.09   Peter Pim and Paul Fry
    ?533.33   Pimpim's Ornery forninehalf
    548.26   the peak of Pim's and Slyne's and Sparrow's

PIMLICO   (14/33).   Short st btwn Marrowbone Lane and The Coombe, in the Liberties. The N section was earlier called "Tripoli" (qv). In 1799-1800, Vincent Dowling satirized Ir Parl debates in a periodical called "Proceedings and Debates of the Parliament of Pimlico."

    The orig *P* was a pleasure garden in Hoxton, SW London; the name later came into use for an area of Westminster, London, noted for its pleasure gardens, including Ranelagh.

    135.08   he wanted to sit for Pimploco

PINCHGUT LANE   (15/35).   Off Phibsborough Rd; an obscure lane, but noted in Thom's *Directories* around the turn of the cent.
>   568.22   pinchgut

PISCES.   In astronomy, a constellation, and also the 12th sign of the zodiac, represented by 2 fishes tied together by their tails.
>   408.36   Piscisvendolor...Gemini
>   494.10   the pisciolinnies Nova Ardonis and Prisca Parthenopea
>   600.06   Deltas Piscium...Sagittariastrion

PLYMOUTH.   City, Devon, SW Eng. The evangelical sect known as the *P* Brethren was founded in *P* in 1830 by the Rev J N Darby, b 1800 in London but educated in Dub at TCD. He was a curate in Wicklow 1825-27, left Anglicanism and went to Dub where he associated with a small group who called themselves "Brethren," a name he carried along to *P*.
>   389.01   old trinitarian senate and saints and sages and the Plymouth brethren

PO RIVER.   Riv, N It. "Po" is slang for chamberpot.
>   105.07   *I'm his Po*
>   ?453.22   Sh the Po [Shaun the Post]

PODDLE RIVER.   Flows N into Liffey, underground from Harold's Cross until it emerges from a pipe in the wall of Wellington Quay (not .Wood Quay, as *U* says, 249/252). The Coombe (qv) marks its orig course. Its junction with the Liffey formed the harb called by the Dan settlers *Dubh-linn* or Black Pool, and it later was diverted into the moat around the city walls and Castle. The growing city was built over more and more of it, until Wakeman could call it, in 1887, "That mysterious River, Poddle, which runs under a good portion of Dublin, and which, at least in modern days, is only known, even by name, to one out of thousands of our citizens..." (*Old Dublin* I, 5). The little *P* St in the Coombe has been Dean St since 1827.
>   16.21   buttle...Whose poddle?
>   106.05   *Norsker Torsker Find the Poddle*
>   208.30   Lotsy trotsy, mind the poddle!
>   ?297.F5   Whangpoos the paddle
>   600.08   a poddlebridges in a passabed

POHLMAN AND SON   (16/33).   Around the turn of the cent, this firm's "Music and Pianoforte Warehouse" was at 40 Dawson St.
>   278.F3   I'll do that droop on the pohlmann's piano

POLAND.   Rep, cen Eur, it was a kingdom until dismembered by Russ, Pruss, and Austria in late 18th cent; and again from 1815 until it lost autonomy to Russ after Pol Revolt of 1830-31. The *Izba* was the Pol Chamber of Deputies.
>   101.27   holenpolendom...Szpaszpas
>   130.30   the once kingdom of Poland
>   281.F2   Translout...turfish...poliss it off
>   335.03   has madjestky who since is dyed drown reign before the izba
>   390.35   when Carpery of the Goold Fins was in the kingship of Poolland

POLARIS.   The Pole Star or North Star, the sailor's guide since the Phoenicians, is the end of the "handle" of the constellation Ursa Minor, the Little Bear, or Little Dipper.
>   255.15   Bearara Tolearis, *procul abeat*!
>   267.L2   *The Big Bear bit the Sailor's Only*

317.06   as deep as the north star
602.30   his polar bearing, steerner among stars

POLLANALTY.   Tnld, Co Roscommon. There is also Pollanoughty Tnld in Co Mayo,
and Pollaghnahoo in Co Cavan, where the riv disappears into a cavern.
?209.31   rivulets...the glashaboys, the pollynooties

POLLDOODY.   Stream, N Co Clare, on Galway Bay. The Red Bank oyster bed is
just off *P.*
479.06   the place for the claire oysters, Polldoody, County Conway

POLYNESIA.   Isls of cen Pacific O, incl Hawaii and New Zealand.
106.09   *The Great Polynesional Entertrainer Exhibits Ballantine Brautchers*
with the Link of Natures

POMERANIA.   Form Ger prov bounded by Baltic Sea (N), Mecklenburg (W), Brandenburg (S), and W Prussia (E). "Pommern" or "Pomore," "on the sea." Orig occupied by Celts, then Teutonic, later Slavonic tribes, united 1625 under Duke Bogislaus
XIV. See *Wolin.*
?31.25   how our red brother of Pouringrainia would audibly fume
38.11   no persicks and armelians for thee, Pomeranzia! [*Pomeranze*, Ger
"orange"]

POMEROY.   Town, Co Tyrone, near Armagh and Dungannon. The allusions suggest
a ship, perhaps at the Brit naval victory of Portobello (qv), but I know of no such ship.
27.26   since Portobello to float the Pomeroy
290.F5   Pomeroy Roche of Portobello, or the Wreck of the Ragamuffin

POMPEII (POMPEI).   The Roman city, destroyed by eruption of Vesuvius, 79 AD.
Bulwer Litton wrote *The Last Days of Pompeii,* 1834.
64.15   the third last days of Pompery
329.25   like Pompei up to date

POOLBEG.   Deep anchorage (Ir, "the little hole") in Dub Bay beyond the Pigeonhouse. The *P* lighthouse is at the end of the S Wall. Before the lighthouse (1767), a
P lightship marked the anchorage.
For James Begg the fishmonger (7.07), see *Census.*
7.07   So pool the begg and pass the kish
46.18   Where from? roars Poolbeg
215.01   Poolbeg flasher beyant, pharphar
264.F2   pool beg slowe
?369.29   laughing that Poulebec would be the death of her
525.35   if he poql her leg and bunk on her butt

POPOCATEPETL.   Dormant volcano, still giving off steam and fumes, in state of
Puebla, Mex. Name is Aztec, "mountain that smokes."
294.24   our papacocopotl.. magmasine...lavas
379.20   pappappoppopcuddle, samblind daiyrudder
386.35   like hopolopocattls, erumping

PORTARLINGTON.   Town, Co Laois, NE of Port Laoise.
406.02   Portarlington's Butchery

PORTERSTOWN.   Tnld, par and bar of Castleknock, Co Dub. (Other tnlds of this
name are in Cos Kildare, Meath, and Westmeath.) Since "Mr Porter" is one of HCE's
pseudonyms (560.24, etc) the allusions may be merely to "HCE's city."

276.L5   *Superlative absolute of Porterstown*
?602.15   Potterton's forecoroners

PORTLAND ROW   (16/35).   Btwn Summerhill and the intersection ("Five Lamps,"
qv) of Amiens, Killarney, and Seville Sts. *P* Pl runs E off Lwr Dorset St, and *P* St N
connects *P* Pl with the NCR.
88.33   out of the five lamps in Portterand's praise
?602.17   "Mike" Portlund, to burrow

PORTOBELLO.   (1) Seaport vill, Caribbean coast of Panama; in 17th cent the
strongly fortified port for Sp treasure convoys. Its capture by a Brit fleet in 1739,
although a minor victory, excited Brit patriotism and was the source of the following
"Portobellos."   (2) *P* Br, form canal boat harb on Grand Canal at S Richmond St,
and the surrounding dist.   (3) *P* Rd, Kensington, London, site of well-known market.   (4) Locality near Leith, Scot; Carlyle walked the beach btwn Leith and *P.*
P is also a game resembling billiards.
27.26   since Portobello to float the Pomeroy
134.18   Portobello, Equadocta, Therecocta, Percorello
290.F5   Pomeroy Roche of Portobello, or the Wreck of the Ragamuffin
?412.10   Pontoffbellek
?549.22   bellomport

PORTSMOUTH.   Seaport and naval base, Hants, S Eng. Its Lat name was "Portus
Magnus"; in Brit sailors' slang it was long known as "Pompey." "Portus Magnus" was
also the Lat name of Almería, seaport city in SE Sp, at the head of the Gulf of Almería.
?484.35   by Pappagallus and Pumpusmugnus
?536.16   and his puertos mugnum

PORTUGAL.   Rep, former kingdom, in W Iberian Penin. "My Husband's a Journey
to Portugal Gone" is the air of T Moore's "Ne'er Ask the Hour, What Is It to Us." Brazil
(qv) in S Amer was a Portuguese colony, and its lang is Portuguese (316.28).
?54.16   Ismeme de bumbac e meias de portocallie
104.18   *My Hoonsbood Hansbaad's a Journey to Porthergill gone and He*
    Never Has the Hour
114.25   a portogal and some buk setting out on the sofer
316.28   from Blasil the Brast to our povotogesus portocall
463.19   I love his old portugal's nose

POSEN.   Form prov, and its cap city, of Pruss (1793-1918), now Poznań, prov and
city of Pol.
?70.17   deposend

POST HOUSE   (15/33).   The 1st Dub *PH*, in the 17th cent, was located in High
St; in 1656, the Council employed Evan Vaughan to manage posting btwn Dub and
Eng, and he later became Deputy Postmaster.
482.19   Evan Vaughan, of his Posthorn in the High Street

POTOMAC RIVER.   Riv, E US; Washington DC is located on it.
?254.22   Potollomuck Sotyr or Sourdanapplous the Lollapaloosa [for Ptolemy
    Sotyr and Sardanapalus, see *Census*]
559.35   old mother Mesopotomac

POULAPHUCA.   Picturesque waterfall of the Liffey below the dam of present Blessington Reservoir, Co Wicklow, on Blessington-Hollywood Rd; *Poll an Phuca*, Ir "Goblin's Hole." The pooka (= Puck) is a malicious sprite (102.15, 338.32).

194.36   pools of the phooka...Blessington
?369.26   the secretary bird...Paullabucca...chilikin puck...Poulebec would be
the death of her

POULARD, MÈRE.   Hotel and 1-star restaurant, at Mont-Saint-Michel, NW Fr; its specialty is Omelette "Mère Poulard."
A Mme Puard was JJ's clinic nurse in Paris (*Letters* I, 237, 280).
184.31   oogs with somekat on toyast à la Mère Puard

"POURQUOI PAS?"   In 1908-10 the Fr explorer Charcot explored the Antarctic coast W of the Palmer Archipelago in the "Pourquoi Pas?", a steamer.
315.34   by pounautique, with pokeway paw
479.28   The *Pourquoi Pas*, bound for Weissduwasland, that fourmaster
barquentine

POWERSCOURT.   (1) Demesne, near Enniskerry, Co Wicklow; known for its gardens, waterfall, and park.   (2) Right-angled st btwn Lwr Mount St and Warrington Pl (16/33).   (3) *P* House, in S William St, erected by the Marquis of *P* 1771-74; one of Dub's great Georgian houses, now a commercial bldg (15/33).
FW connects one or all of these with Mark Lyons, the 2nd of the Four Old Men; all are relatively south, which is Mark's point of the compass.
373.01   number two digged up Poors Coort, Soother
386.18   like the old Merquus of Pawerschoof
388.15   Porterscout and Dona, our first marents
391.14   poor Mark or Marcus Bowandcoat

POWER'S DISTILLERY   (14/33).   John Power and Son, 4-12 John's Lane, W; it was often referred to as the "John's Lane Distillery." *FW* pairs Power's with Guinness's, whose works lie only a few blocks to the W, at James's Gate, by their addresses.
The label of Power's whiskey was and still is trademarked by 3 swallows. Power's never used as an advertising slogan the old Lat proverb "One swallow does not make spring," but *FW* does (319.11).
140.31   Irish in my east hand...James's Gate
319.11   He made one summery...of his the three swallows
321.01   liquorally no more powers to their elbow
345.19   *words of silent power...another guidness*
373.25   distillery...Run him a johnsgate down jameseslane
408.33   Take this John's Lane
495.04   smells cheaply of Power's spirits
521.13   either Jones's lame or Jamesy's gait

POWER'S INN.   18th-cent public house in Booterstown, SE Dub. The Ouzel Galley Soc (qv) met there in and around 1776. Power's (Royal) Hotel in Kildare St is better known, but all the tavs at 205.24 –.25 were meeting-places of the Ouzel Galley Soc.
205.25   Power's Inn

PRAGUE (PRAHA).   Cap of Czech and prov of Bohemia; on both sides of Moldau (Vltava) R. The form coll of the Ir Franciscans, founded 1629, is in Hibernská Ulice ("Irish St") (551.32). The old town of *P* is Staré město (539.21); it was fortified by King Wenceslaus I (539.29). The banks of the Moldau were connected very early by a br (?539.21 brixtol), later by Charles IV's famous "Br of *P*." Příkopy (Ger, *Graben*) is the main thoroughfare in cen *P* (554.03); the name means "ditch"; it follows orig wall and ditch fortification, and is continuous with Ovocna Ulice (537.06). Petrin (135.10) is the highest hill in *P*.

For the Defenestration of *P*, see *Czechoslovakia.*

135.10	Pitre-le-Pore-in Petrin
?333.28	Podushka be prayhasd
537.06	by virchow of those filthered Ovocnas
539.21	starrymisty...brixtol
541.24	I made praharfeast upon acorpolous
551.32	Hibernska Ulitzas
554.03	my priccoping gents

PRESQUE ÎLE.   There are towns, rivers, bays, and points in Maine, Michigan, Pennsylvania, and Canada named *PI*. The allusion may be mainly to Howth (qv), which is "almost an island" (this albutisle, 17.18).

56.28   quasi-begin to presquesm'ile to queasithin'

PRIMROSE ST.   In City of London, off Bishopsgate, N of Liverpool St Sta (a short distance from Camomile St); the st bridges the rlwy tracks for its entire length. The boundary of the City lies just N.

P Hill is N of Regent's Park, London. There is also a *P* Hill in Co Kildare, just SE of Celbridge; and a *P* Hill, now called Wickham, near Dundrum.

?361.22   Lodewijk is onangonamed before the bridge of primerose
553.06   Cammomile Pass cuts Primrose Rise

PRINCE'S ST.   N *P* St intersects O'Connell St at the GPO (15/34). S *P* St runs btwn City Quay and Townsend St (16/34). The former contained the offices of the *Freeman's Journal* (and also Thom's), but neither has connections with tinkers or with hymns.

363.04   when all the perts in princer street set up their tinker's humn

PRISONS.   See *Bridewell, Kilmainham, Marshalsea, Mountjoy, Newgate Gaol, Provost, The.*

139.02   the option of three gaols

PRO-CATHEDRAL.   The RC Pro-Cathedral, officially the Metropolitan Ch of St Mary, on Marlborough St is thus called because the other 2 Dub caths, St Patrick's and Christchurch, are Prot.

552.03   twinminsters, the pro and the con
569.14   Marlborough-the-Less, Greatchrist and Holy Protector

PROSPEROUS.   Vill, Co Kildare, on the Grand Canal, named for its flourishing cotton industry in the late 18th cent. The 10th-cent *P* Crozier, found in a bog near *P*, is at Clongowes Wood Coll (qv). Very questionable whether the allusions are to the vill, but it provides the occasion to note that there has never been a *P* St (230.35) in Dub.

?230.35   Remember thee, castle throwen? Ones propsperups treed, now stohong baroque
?428.11   may the mosse of prosperousness gather you rolling home!

PROVENCE.   In the 2nd cent AD the Provincia Romana; generally the region of S Fr btwn the Rhône R and the Alps. Old Provençal (sometimes called, as by Dante, the *langue d'oc* as distinguished from the *langue d'oui*) was the lang of literary composition from the 11th to the 14th cents. It preserved the Lat diphthong *au*, which became *o* in other Romance langs, and pronounced the Lat *o* as *oo* (Fr, *ou*).

144.10   so ovally provencial at Balldole
230.05   why they provencials drollo eggspilled him...(osco de basco de pesco de bisco!)

256.29   its denier crid of old provaunce
478.20   Vous n'avez pas d'o dans votre boche provenciale, mousoo

PROVIDENCE WOOLLEN MILLS.   Manufacturers of tweed; founded 1891 and still conducted by the Ir Sisters of Charity in Foxford, Co Mayo.
404.22   his jacket of providence wellprovided woolies

PROVINCES.   The 4 (mod) provs of Ulster, Munster, Leinster, and Connacht (qqv) represent and are represented by (almost invariably in that order) the Four Old Men, Matt Gregory, Mark Lyons, Luke Tarpey, and Johnny MacDougall, and their respective compass points, N, S, E, and W (qv). The ass which brings up the rear is sometimes the missing 5th prov (see *Ireland: The Five Fifths*), sometimes the Isle of Man (qv). Patterned allusions to the 4 provs are collected here for reference, since they are less apparent in the sep listings.
57.08   Armagh...Clonakilty...Deansgrange...Barna
89.18   Lindendelly, coke or skilllies [Skerries, Leinster]...gart [Gort, Connacht]
96.16   how they used her, mused her, licksed her and cuddled
140.15,21,27,36   Delfas...Dorhqk...Nublid...Dalway
160.27   billfaust...curks...deblinite. Mr Wist
180.13   Cardinal Lindundarri and Cardinal Carchingarri and Cardinal Loriotuli and Cardinal Occidentaccia
197.04   derry's...corksown...doubling...gullaway
203.09   Finn...Mourne [Ulster]...Nore...Bloem [Munster]...Braye [Leinster]... Moy...Cullin...Conn [Connacht]
229.17   He would bare to untired world of Leimunconnonnulstria
270.L4   *Ulstria, Monastir, Leninstar and Connecticut*
283.L1   *ulstra, Elba...cashellum tuum*
325.32   bless madhugh, mardyk, luusk and cong!
389.05   four trinity colleges...of Ulcer, Moonster, Leanstare and Cannought
398.33   *Ulster*...[399.03] *Dingle*...[399.14] *Balbriggan*...[399.25] *Cong*
451.13   the Ulster Rifles and the Cork Milice and the Dublin Fusees and Connacht Rangers
467.29   Illstarred punster, lipstering cowknucks
498.11   Ulster Kong and Munster's Herald with Athclee [Leinster] and Athlone [Connacht] Poursuivant
514.02   Normand, Desmond, Osmund and Kenneth
520.22   ["Northern Ireland" speaking]: Nils, Mugn and Cannut
521.24–.28   illconditioned ulcers...leinconnmuns
528.31   ["Northern Ireland" speaking]: leinstrel boy...moreen astoreen for Monn and Conn
546.33   Chief North Paw and Chief Goes in Black Water and Chief Brown Pool and Chief Night Cloud by the Deeps
569.05   S. Presbutt-in-the-North, S. Mark Underloop, S. Lorenz-by-the-Toolechest, S. Nicholas Myre
577.33   strangfort...karkery...leperties'...slogo
580.34   Malin to Clear and Carnsore Point to Slynagollow

PROVOST, THE   (14/34).   The military pris of the Royal (now Collins) Barracks just E of Phoenix Park. The rebels of 1798 were courtmartialed here; and Wolfe Tone died here.
534.13   Pynix Park...to provost myself, by gramercy of justness

PRUDENTIAL ASSURANCE CO.   Around the turn of the cent, its offices were at 11 Upr Sackville St.

    514.31   loans...purely providential

PRUSSIA.   Form Ger state, NE Ger. Created as a kingdom in 1701 from the duchy of Brandenberg, *P* became the dominant power in the formation of the Ger Emp in 1871. For Albert the Bear, see *Berlin*. Gen Blücher's Prussian army was crucially engaged against the Fr at the Battle of Waterloo (8.10–.14).

    8.10   Prooshious gunn...flag of the Prooshious
    8.13   flag of the Prooshious...flag of the Prooshious
    135.16   the cryptoconchoidsiphonostomata in his exprussians
  ?224.02   goodda purssia
    539.30   the prusshing stock of Allbrecht the Bearn
    608.10   bledprusshers

PUGH'S GLASS FACTORY   (16/34).   T and R Pugh, flint glass manufacturers, in Potter's Alley off Marlborough St in the 19th cent. JJ knew a member of the family (*Letters* III, 313).

    76.11   The teak coffin, Pughglasspanelfitted

PUMP COURT.   (1) Not a Dub place-name, but old maps of Dub mark the location of communal pumps in the inner courts of bldgs in The Liberties.   (2) *PC*, a 17th-cent sq off Middle Temple Lane, London, figures in Dickens' *Martin Chuzzlewit*. Edward Martyn, Ir playwright and friend of George Moore, lived there.   (3) The famous Pump Room in Bath, Eng (and other spas) is prob not alluded to.

    40.04   housingroom Abide With Oneanother at Block W.W....Pump Court, The Liberties
    49.10   the marble halls of Pump Court Columbarium, the home of the old seakings

PUNCHESTOWN.   Racecourse, Co Kildare (qv, for St Bridget [Bride]), 3 mi SE of Naas; site of annual Kildare and Nat Hunt Race Meeting.

    194.25   bride leaves her raid at Punchestime, stud stoned before a race-courseful

PUNJAB.   Form prov, NW Brit Ind, now prov of NW Ind Union. The major lang is Punjabi. Gen Hugh Gough, later Lord Gough, whose stat stood in Phoenix Park (qv), was commander-in-Chief of Brit forces in Ind in the 1840's, conducting successful campaigns against the Sikhs in the *P*. The Gov-Gen, Lord Hardinge, volunteered to serve under Gough's command.

  ?209.31   Out of the paunschaup on to the pyre
    342.14   *lost Gabbarnaur-Jaggarnath. Pamjab!*
    342.19   *Bumchub!*
    498.16   boom companions in paunchjab and dogril and pammel and gouge-rotty

PUNT (PUONI).   Anc country, somewhere on E coast of Afr; the Egyptians sent expeditions there to bring back incense, also gold.

    263.F2   the isle we love in spice. Punt.
    437.17   Your Punt's Perfume's

PURDON ST   (16/35).   Form in Nighttown or "Monto" (*U* 443/451), it ran parallel to and just S of present Railway St, but has disappeared in the redevelopment of the area. JJ sarcastically gave the name to the businessman's priest in "Grace."

    537.36   unpurdonable preempson

PUTAMAYO (PUTUMAYO).   Riv (known as Ica in Brazil), forming boundary btwn
Columbia and Peru, flows E through Brazil to Amazon R; also the area of the riv ba-
sin. Roger Casement served in *P* as a Brit civil servant investigating the Anglo-Peruvian
Amazon Co, and was knighted for his services there and in the Congo.
> 509.24   After Putawayo, Kansas, Liburnum
> 565.15   Putshameyu!

PYRAMIDS.   In Egypt, esp at Giza, near Cairo. One of the 7 Wonders of the Anc
World (qv). The 1st which can be definitely attributed is that of Cheops or Khufu,
the Great Pyramid of Giza.
> 261.09   conned the cones
> 553.10   chopes pyramidous

PYRENEES.   Mts separating Fr and Sp. Wellington drove Fr out of Sp in the Battles of the *P*, 25 Jul-2 Aug, 1813.
> 199.21   till her pyrraknees shrunk to nutmeg graters
> 330.09   no more Tyrrhanees

Q

QUAYS.   When the Danes first sailed up the Liffey to shelter in the little harb (later known as the Pill) formed by the mouth of the Poddle R, the tides washed on
what are now Amiens St and N Strand Rd and as far as Townsend St on the S; Ringsend was virtually an isl, often cut off by the flooding Dodder R.

With the embankment of the Liffey in the 17th and 18th cents, Dub's little riv now
flows btwn quays and walls from Kingsbridge into Dub Bay, and the quays are main E-
W thoroughfares. *FW* notices most of them, and for the most part in Book I, Chap
8, appropriately enough. As rivals (*rivae*, Lat "banks") Shem and Shaun flank their
hydraulic mummy as right (S) bank and left (N) bank. The quays are named below
in order from W to E. See separate listings.

North Bank	Bridges	South Bank
	Kingsbridge	
Albert		Victoria
now Wolfe Tone		
Pembroke		
now Sarsfield		
	Barrack	
Ellis's (205.07)		Usher's Island (?52.17; 206.35)
	Queen's	
Arran (204.31; 601.23)		Usher's (206.35)
	Whitworth	
(King's) Inns (201.26; 539.31)		Merchant's (536.32)
	Richmond	
Upper Ormond (105.02)		Wood (11.21; ?200.02)
		Essex
	Essex	
Lower Ormond (105.02)		Wellington (203.07)
	Wellington	
Bachelor's Walk (214.03;		Crampton (?204.36)
516.04)		Aston (205.13; 447.35)

North Bank	Bridges	South Bank
Eden (172.15; ?278.F7)	O'Connell	Burgh (?541.36)
	Butt	
	Loop Line	
Custom House (406.26)		George's
North Wall (95.14; 141.22;		City
209.03)		Sir John Rogerson's (?211.16)
North Wall Extension		(Dodder R)
		York Rd
		Pigeonhouse Rd (to Poolbeg
		Light)

QUEEN'S BRIDGE   (14/34).   Across the Liffey, joining Queen's St and Bridgefoot St. Arran Br, erected at this site in 1683, was swept away in 1763, rebuilt 1764-68. At various times since it has been called Bridewell Br, Ellis's Br, and Mellows Br, and it is now Queen Maev Br.
>   ?204.31   Arran, where's your nose?

QUEEN'S COLLEGES.   The Queen's Colls in Cork, Galway, and Belfast were found-ed by the Brit govt in 1845. In 1908, the Ir Universities Act created Queen's Univ in Belfast and the Nat Univ of Ire; the Queen's Colls of Galway and Cork bacame Univ Colls of the latter, with Univ Coll, Dub.
>   All of the Queen's Colls had medical schs (389.06 Killorcure, etc). None was or is on "Brian or Bride St."
>   385.13   Queen's Ultonian colleges
>   388.26   neer the Queen's Colleges...Brian or Bride street
>   389.04   in the four trinity colleges...of Ulcer, Moonster, Leanstare and Can-
>   nought, the four grandest colleges

QUEEN'S HEAD   (15/33).   A fashionable 18th-cent inn in Bride St. The ref may be entirely to Brit postage stamps, which throughout Victoria's reign bore the queen's profile.
>   ?101.24   that queen's head affranchisant

QUEEN'S ROAD.   (1) The waterfront rd at Dun Laoghaire Harb. It was laid out and named after Queen Victoria's 1st visit to Ire (24/28).   (2) Queen's Quay Rd in Belfast runs along the E side of the Lagan R. The quotation, addressed by "Roman Catholic" to "Northern Ireland," alludes primarily to this more commercial cen.
>   521.35   Tell Queen's road I am seilling...Buy!

QUERSCHNITT, DER.   Journal publ in Frankfurt am Main. In 1923 it publ several of JJ's poems.
>   67.15   a right querrshnorrt of a mand

QUILTY.   Fishing vill, Co Clare, btwn Kilkee and Milltown Malbay. Coillte, Ir "woods."
>   ?212.07   Peggy Quilty

QUIMPER.   Town in Finistère, Brittany, Fr; fishing, pottery manufacturing. Letters I, 220 (cf II, 106): "We leave for Quimper...on Monday."
>   149.04   guffalled quith a quhimper, made cold blood a blue mundy

QUI SI SANA.   In dreaming of owning his own home, Bloom aspires to more than "a terracehouse or semidetached villa, described as Rus in Urbe or Qui si Sana..." (U

697/712). Apparently an accepted name (Lat, "who would be healthy") for a country or suburban house, but I do not know of any specific house so called.

183.01   full and forty Queasisanos

R

RADIO ÉIREANN.   The 1st public radio broadcast from the Rep of Ire was on 1 Jan 1926 from a studio of the "Dub Broadcasting Corp" in Little Denmark St. The call sign of the new service was 2RN – chosen, believe it or not, as resembling the final words of "Come Back to Erin." The main transmitting sta of *RE* was later built 2 mi E of Athlone (qv). In Paris in the 1930's, JJ spent a good deal of time listening to "Radio Athlone." The BBC opened a sta in Belfast in Sept 1924.

?324.18   Rowdiose wodhalooing
528.28   And 2 R.N. and Longhorns Connacht, stay off my air!

RAGLAN ROAD   (17/32).   Off Clyde Rd in Ballsbridge.
132.21   first he shot down Raglan Road

RAHENY   (21/38).   Dist, NE Dub, N shore of Dub Bay opp N Bull Isl.
17.13   Boildoyle and rawhoney
129.24   Ratheny
142.15   the feels of Raheny
497.20   Raheniacs

RAILWAYS.   Before amalgamation, 4 rlwys had terminals in Dub:

Great Northern (to Belfast)	Amiens St (now Connolly) Sta
Great Southern and Western (to Cork)	Kingsbridge (now Heuston) Sta
Midland Great Western (to Galway)	Broadstone Sta (now closed)
Dublin, Wicklow and Wexford (or	Harcourt St Sta (now closed) &
Dub and South-Eastern)	Westland Row (now Pearse) Sta

The Loop Line (1891) joined all of these stas except Harcourt St, with a br across the Liffey just E of Butt Br. Another br and a tunnel under Phoenix Park connect the N and S lines W of Kingsbridge Sta. Ire's 1st rlwy, the Dub and Kingstown (1824), seems absent from *FW*.

See individual entries for rlwys and stas.

RANELAGH   (16/31–32).   The area S and E of Charlemont Br over the Grand Canal. *R* Rd continues Charlemont St. The site of the Black Monday massacre at Cullenswood (qv). Richmond Hill (542.04) is in Rathmines, just E of *R*.

The name of the famous *R* pleasure gardens in London actually originated in Ire. The Jones family of Co Wicklow took as their title, Ranelagh (*Raghnallach*, Ir "belonging to family Raghnall"); they moved to London in early 18th cent, where they built a house in Chelsea which became *R* Gardens in 1742. In 1766, one Hollister started a pleasure garden at Cullenswood, modelled after the one in London, and called it *R* Gardens, from which the current name of the area has been taken.

There is also a Rue de *R*, and *R* Métro Sta, 16th Arr, Paris.

235.19   the wych elm of Manelagh
334.13   the funst man in Danelagh
481.35   the furst man in Ranelagh, fué! fué!

542.05   I richmounded the rainelag in my bathtub of roundwood

RANGOON.   Port and cap city of Burma. The main suburbs are Kemmendine and Pazundaung; 11th *EB*, "Rangoon": "Electric tramways run to Pazundaung in one direction and to Alôn and Kemmendine in the other."
?256.26   whatfor paddybird notplease rancoon
541.34   ourangoontangues
542.08   in my Putzemdown cars to my Kommeandine hotels

RATHANGAN.   Town, Co Kildare, 6 mi NE of Kildare town. There is also a *R* tnld in Co Wexford.
497.11   from Rathgar, Rathanga, Rountown and Rush

RATHDOWN.   Vill, btwn Greystones and Bray, Co Wicklow; ruins of ch and cas. The sand banks along the coast btwn Bray and Wicklow were once called Rath Down. There is also Rathdowny, a town in Co Laois, 18 mi SW of Port Laoise.
?93.08   fortytudor ages rawdownhams tanyouhide

RATHFARNHAM   (14/29).   Form vill, now S Dub dist.
74.17   than raindrips to Rethfernhim
532.12   Farnum's rath or Condra's ridge

RATHGAR   (15/30).   Form vill, now S Dub dist. JJ was born in Brighton Sq, *R*, in 1882; within 2 years the family moved to Castlewood Ave, *R*. He omits his birthplace from the list of his addresses on 420-21, but alludes to it at 231.24.
231.24   forforgetting his birdsplace
497.11   Rathgar, Rathanga
499.33   Rawth of Gar and Donnerbruck Fire
541.26   ranked rothgardes round wrathmindsers
601.23   S. Ruadagara's [Ch of the Three Patrons, qv]
619.06   their demb cheeks, the Rathgarries

RATH HILL.   Tnld, par of Dunshaughlin, bar of Ratoath, Co Meath.
97.11   Ye Hill of Rut

RATHMINES   (15/31).   Dist, S Dub. Site of 1649 battle btwn Royalist army (Duke of Ormonde) and Parl forces (Col Michael Jones).
16.27   rath in mine mines
?27.16   the redminers riots
215.11   Towy I too, rathmine
340.16   Oh day of rath! Ah, murther of mines!
541.26   ranked rothgardes round wrathmindsers
601.23   S. Rhodamena's [Our Lady of Refuge Ch, qv]

RATOATH.   Vill, par, and bar in Co Meath. Richard Pigott, forger of the letters implicating Parnell in the Phoenix Park murders, b 1828 in the vill of *R*. Fairyhouse Racecourse (qv) is 2 mi S of *R*. The Ward Union Staghounds have hqs at Ashbourne, 4 mi E (*U* 158/160).
97.02   View! From his holt outratted

RAVEN AND SUGAR LOAF, THE   (15/34).   Grocer's shop in Essex St, *ca* 1740, acc to Peter's *Dublin Fragments* (54).
521.13   some staggerjuice or deadhorse, on strip or in larges, at the Raven and Sugarloaf

RAYSTOWN.   Tnld, in par and bar of Ratoath, Co Meath.

97.07   Raystown

RECHABITE AND TOTAL ABSTINENCE LOAN AND INVESTMENT SOCIETY
(16/34).   Founded in Dub in 1864, with hqs at 6 Townsend St around the turn
of the cent. In the *OT*, the *R* order abstained from wine; also from living in houses
and from sowing grain (*Jer* 35:1–11).
    546.01   Rechabites obstain!

RED BANK.   (1) Well-known oyster bed in S Galway Bay, offshore from the Burren in N Co Clare (see *Polldoody*). *U* 325/331.   (2) *RB* Oyster Tavern, form at 19-
20 D'Olier St (16/34). *U* 91/92.
    "Basket of Oysters" is the air of T Moore's "O Could We Do With This World of
Ours" (277.F7).
    83.17   foretaste of the Dun Bank pearlmothers
    277.F7   that redbanked profanian with his bakset of yosters

RED COW.   "At the foot of [Tallaght Hill] on the Blessington side, there stood an
inn, called the Red Cow, which, in the month of December, 1717, was the scene of a
sanguinary encounter between a party of rapparees...and the forces of the Crown"
(Ball, *Hist of Co Dub* III, 39). There is also a crossroads N of Tallaght on the Dub-
Naas rd, still called Redcow after a different inn.
    83.19   the Ruadh Cow at Tallaght
    344.18   renewmurature with the cowruads in their airish pleasantry

REDRUTH.   Chief mining town (tin) of Cornwall, Eng. The mineral copperglance, a
copper ore, is also known as redruthite.
    58.31   Wroth mod eldfar, ruth redd stilstand [*Wappenstillstand*, Ger "truce"]

RED SEA.   Anc *Sinus Arabicus*, inland sea btwn Arabia and NE Afr.
    ?352.17   *sea vermelhion*
    387.27–.30   the red sea...the red sea
    392.06   after eten a bad carmp in the rude ocean
    492.10   as the Crasnian Sea [*krasnii*, Russ "red"]

REGENT CIRCUS.   When Nash built London's *R* St, in 1816-20, the circus at the
intersection with Piccadilly St was called *RC*, and only later in the cent did it become universally known as Piccadilly Circus. A second *RC* was at the intersection of
R St and Oxford St, now Oxford Circus.
    132.01   he wallowed round Raggiant Circos

REGENT'S.   (1) Park, London. Laid out by Nash for the Prince Regent *ca* 1814; a
royal park, it was opened to the public only in 1838.   (2) Canal, London; from the
Thames at Stepney N and then W to Shoreditch, then through *R* Park.
    132.01   he wallowed round Raggiant Circos
    228.30   by dear home trashold on the raging canal
    374.29   Finsbury...batter see...regent refutation

REILIG NA RIOGH.   Anc "Cemetery of the Kings," near Rathcroghan, Co Roscommon, one of the 3 royal burial places of anc Ire (with Tailteann and Brugh). 2
mi S is the inauguration mound of the O'Connors, anc kings of Connacht.
    99.27   rayheallach royghal raxacraxian variety

REIMS (RHEIMS).   City, NE Fr, 100 mi NE of Paris. The anc capital of the Remi,
who after the Roman conquest remained faithful to Rome during the Gallic insurrections.
    209.25   reconciled Romas and Reims

REVUE DES DEUX MONDES.   A journal of literature, hist, art, and science, publ in Paris since 1831.

    12.19   our review of the two mounds

REVUE HEBDOMADAIRE.   Weekly journal of literature and the arts, publ in Paris since 1892.

    71.16   *Hebdromadary Publocation*
    581.27   so grunts a leading hebdromadary

RHAETIA (RAETIA).   Anc Roman prov, roughly mod Tyrol, Austria, and Grau-bünden (qv) or Grisons, Switz; the latter canton was orig "Raetia," and the name survives in, eg, the cantonal rlwy, the Rhätische Bahn.

    I am not at all confident about *FW*'s mysterious "rheda road," but the main anc rd crossing the Alps in Sw terr was the Rhaetian rd across the Splügen and Julier passes; the Brenner pass rd (81.14) was also in anc *R*.

    The lang of the area is Romansch or Rhaeto-Romansch (199.34, 327.11; cf 243.16).

    Rheda is a Lat word of Celtic origin, for a 4-wheeled carriage. For "Rhoda," see *Census*.

    81.09   Hannibal's walk...the past has made us this present of a rhedarhoad... Brennan's...pass
    199.34   riding the ricka and roya romanche
    327.11   rheadoromanscing long evmans invairn
    434.07   Rhidarhoda and Daradora
    467.34   read the road roman
    469.34   biga triga rheda rodeo
    478.13   alpman...no rheda rhoda
    551.06   on Rideau Row Duanna dwells

RHINE RIVER.   The great riv of W Eur barely figures in *FW*. "Die Wacht am Rhein," Ger nat song, dates from 1840; *Rhine vogt* (77.14), Dan "Rhine Watch." In the *Nibelungenlied*, the treasure of the Nibelungs eventually is buried in the *R* (Rhein-gold), guarded forever by the *R* Maidens. In Wagner's "Ring," Alberich steals the gold and forges a magic ring, later taken by Wotan who gives it to Fafnir, and so on and on. Rheingold is also a US beer. "Rhino" is 18th-cent slang for "money," as well as the Gk for "nose." Song, "Ehren on the Rhine" (see *Ehren*).

    77.14   holding with the Ryan vogt it was Dane to pfife
    207.07   rhunerhinerstones
    ?245.01   Rhinohorn...him ist gonz wurst [+ Siegfried's horn?]
    288.F6   to his native Ireland from erring under Ryan
    372.30   Shanavan Wacht...O'Ryne
    ?406.20   a fingerhot of rheingenever
    414.01   some rhino, rhine, O joyoust rhine
    578.23   rhaincold draughts to the props of his pubs

RHODES.   Gk isl, and its cap city, in S Sperades, off SW coast of Turk. Site of the anc Colossus of *R* (qv), one of the 7 Wonders of the Anc World. "FERT" was the motto of the Order of the Annunziata, orig the Order of the Collar, the highest order of Knighthood of the It Kingdom; it is rather uncertainly derived from *Fortitudo Ejus Rhodum Tenuit*, an allusion to defense of the isl of *R* by an anc Count of Sa-voy. (The motto is also derived from "fert," Lat "he bears.") In anc times, *R* was one of the 7 cities claimed as the birthplace of Homer (129.23, 481.21).

    53.17   fortitudinous ajaxious rowdinoisy tenuacity
    93.08   fortytudor ages rawdownhams tanyouhide

127.10	wrote F.E.R.T. on his buckler
129.23	pigeonheim to this homer...Rhoebok
?208.26	behind her lungarhodes
258.04	Fulgitudes ejist rowdownan tonuout
350.05	*pontofert*
369.12	Fert Fort
481.21	humeplace...Rhonnda
515.09	*Fortitudo eius rhodammum tenuit?*
596.15	fert in fort
610.06	Fulgitudo ejus Rhedonum teneat!

RHONDDA. City, and coal-mining vall, in Glamorgan, SE Wales.

| 481.21 | Smithwick, Rhonnda, Kaledon [Eng, Wales, Scot] |

RHONE RIVER. Lat, *Rhodanum* – which JJ substitutes for *Rhodum*, Rhodes in the Savoyard motto *Fortitudo Ejus Rhodum Tenuit.* See *Rhodes.*

53.17	rowdinoisy
93.08	rawdownhams
207.07	rhunerhinerstones
210.32	outflash Helen Arhone
258.04	rowdownan
515.09	*rhodammum*
610.06	Rhedonum

RIALTO (13/33). Br carrying the SCR over the Grand Canal; and the adjacent dist. The orig Rialto is the Venice quarter containing both the *R* Br and the Exchange.

| 84.07 | some rival rialtos...between Pearidge and the Littlehorn |
| 130.20 | rialtos, annesleyg, binn and balls |

RICHMOND. One of the most ubiquitous Dub place-names, all originating in the 2nd decade of the 19th cent, after Charles Lennox, 4th Duke of *R*, Lord Lt of Ire 1807-1813. In addition to *R* Ave, N and S, and *R* St, N and S, there is or was *R* Bridewell (later Wellington Barracks), *R* Lunatic Asylum, *R* Penitentiary (later Grange-gorman Pris), *R* Barracks, *R* Hosp, and *R* Inst for the Blind.

Listed below are allusions not clearly attributable to *R* Basin, *R* Br, or *R* St, N (qqv). I do not know of a rugby or other sports team called the *R* Rovers.

207.06	richmond and rehr
375.21	Good for you, Richmond Rover!
?515.04	No more than Richman's periwhelker

RICHMOND BASIN (15/32). In Portobello, just W of Portobello Harb on the Grand Canal; aka City Basin. Opened 1812, to supply water to SE Dub.

| 542.04 | I richmounded the rainelag in my bathtub of roundwood...through my longertubes of elm |

RICHMOND BRIDGE (15/34). Just E of Four Courts, it connects Winetavern St with Chancery Pl; aka Winetavern St Br. Ormond Br, 1683, was destroyed by flood in 1802; rebuilt 1813-16, it was named after Charlotte, Duchess of *R*. Now O'Dono-van Rossa Br.

207.06	richmond and rehr
?410.14	deep in my wineupon ponteen
?542.04	I richmounded the rainelag

RICHMOND STREET, NORTH (16/35). Cul-de-sac off the NCR. The Joyce family lived at No 17 in 1895. The st is described in JJ's "Araby." The Joyces also occupied part of a house in *R* Ave, Fairview, from late 1899 to May 1900.

420.23   Not known at 1132 a. 12 Norse Richmound

RICHVIEW PRESS.   Form in cen Dub, it moved to Clonskeagh in 1935 after its printing works were destroyed by fire. Now owned by Browne and Nolan (qv).

284.F3   Come all ye hapney coachers and support the richview press

RIDLEY'S.   A pop name for a mental inst (eg, the Richmond Lunatic Asylum in Grangegorman), but I don't know why. The London anatomist Humphrey Ridley (d 1708) wrote a treatise on the brain. A Dub ballad about a belle of the Coombe called "The Pride of Pimlico" ends, "Or soon beyond in Ridley's, a sight of awful woe,/ You'll see 10,000 victims of the Pride of Pimlico."

49.18   Paul Horan...by the doomster in loquacity lunacy...was thrown into a Ridley's for inmates in the northern counties

RIESENGEBIRGE.   "Giant mountains"; mt range, part of Sudetic Mts, along the boundary btwn SW Pol (form Pruss) and N Czech.

5.06   Wassaily Booslaeugh of Riesengeborg
133.06   ex-gardener (Riesengebirger)

RINGSEND   (18/33).   Dist, S bank of Liffey, where it enters Dub Bay. The name is a mixture of Dan and Eng; *reen*, Dan "a spit of land." The Dodder R joins the Liffey just above *R*. Before the embankment of the rivs in the 19th cent, the Dub-*R* Rd was regularly inundated and the brs carried away. The Lord Mayors when "riding the franchises" threw a spear or dart into the sea from *R* to mark the limits of city jurisdiction (547.20). St Matthew's Ch (CI) (328.25, 601.26) was form a shore chapel for seamen.

83.20   the Good Woman at Ringsend
?137.17   hetman unwhorsed by Searingsand
225.02   atvoiced ringsoundinly
328.25   Sing Mattins in the Fields, ringsengd ringsengd
547.20   to Ringsend Flott and Ferry...my dart to throw
567.04   to the point, one yeoman's yard
585.09   patient ringasend as prevenient
601.26   S. Ringsingsund's

RIO DE JANEIRO.   Seaport on Guanabara Bay, SE Brazil; form cap of Brazil. Not as spectacular as other peaks in and around the city, the Livramento Hill is N of the old city (545.24).

536.01   from the Rivera in Januero
545.24   Struggling forlongs I have livramentoed

RIO GRANDE.   Riv, border btwn US and Mex (where it is called Rio Bravo), flowing into Gulf of Mex. There are other rivs so named in Afr, S Amer, the Philippines, etc. Sp, "big river."

232.36   as her lucky for the Rio Grande

RIVIERA.   Scenic coast of Medit Sea in SE Fr and NW It.

?289.25   page Ainée Rivière!
467.22   down on the river airy

ROBENHAUSEN.   Vill at S end of Lake of Pfäffikon, E of Zurich, Switz, noted for remains of anc lake-dwellers. The neolithic Robenhausian period immediately preceded the Bronze Age.

154.08   robenhauses

ROCHELLE, LA.   City and port, Charente-Maritime Dept, W Fr, on Bay of Biscay. In the 16th cent, it was the chief stronghold of the Huguenots; besieged by Richelieu 1627-28, it capitulated after great suffering.

"My Love and Cottage Near Rochelle" is a 2nd act aria in the opera "The Siege of Rochelle" by Balfe; cf *U* 348/354.

> 73.23   this rochelly exetur of Bully Acre...siegings
> 179.32   a roseschelle cottage by the sea
> 466.25   My loaf and pottage neaheaheahear Rochelle
> ?472.07   see again the sweet rockelose

ROCHELLE LANE   (15/33).   The orig name of Back Lane (qv) in the Liberties; aka Rochestrete.

> 73.23   this rochelly exetur of Bully Acre
> 371.33   enrouted to Rochelle Lane and liberties

ROCKABILL LIGHTHOUSE.   Off E coast of Ire at Skerries (qv), 18 mi N of Dub.

> 104.06   *Rockabill Booby in the Wave Trough*
> 463.31   Jonas wrocked in the belly of the whaves

ROCK ROAD   (20/36).   The main Dub-Blackrock Rd, along the shore of S Dub Bay.

> 497.14   Vico, Mespil Rock and Sorrento
> 567.01   To the dunleary obelisk via the rock

ROCKY MOUNTAINS.   The mt range running N-S in W Can and US. The allusion is partly to the Baalfires (Balefires; no connection with the Canaanite Baal) which in Celtic custom were lit on hilltops on ceremonial occasions, eg, on Midsummer Eve.

> 198.31   bales allbrant on the crests of rockies

ROEBUCK   (17–18/29).   Dist and rd btwn Milltown and Mt Merrion, SE Dub. *R* Lodge, near Clonskeagh, was the home of Maud Gonne MacBride.

> 70.12   such as roebucks raugh at pinnacle's peak
> 90.26   The rudacist rotter in Roebuckdom
> 129.23   Rhoebok
> 142.12   Roebuck's campos

ROE'S DISTILLERY   (14/33).   Roe and Co, distillers, were at 157-159 Thomas St; the premises are now incorporated in Guinness's Brewery. There seems to be no record of a major fire at Roe's.

> 122.12   since Roe's Distillery burn'd
> 543.33   getting on like Roe's distillery on fire
> ?589.36   an explosium of his distilleries

SIR JOHN ROGERSON'S QUAY   (17/34).   S side of Liffey; the E-most of the Liffey quays.

> ?211.16   a Rogerson Crusoe's Friday fast

ROLLRIGHT STONES.   Anc stone circle on the border of Oxfordshire and Warwickshire, Eng, near Chipping Norton.

> 5.30   rollsrights, carhacks, stonengens

ROME.   City, S cen It, on Tiber R; cap of Roman Emp, later of the States of the Ch, since 1870 of It. Called "Eternal City" (532.06), "Holy City," "City of the Seven Hills" (469.04, 541.01). The early city was built on 7 hills enclosed by Servian Wall. The orig 7 hills were: Palatium, Caelian (latter are the summits of the Palatine

Hill), Velia, Oppius, Cispius (latter 2 are spurs of the Esquiline Hill), Fagutal, and Sucusa. The list usually given of the Roman Hills is: Palatine, Caelius, Aventine, Capitoline (Mons Tarpeius or Mons Saturni), Esquiline, Quirinal, and Viminal. *R* is not the only city with 7 hills; others are Edinburgh (541.01) and Constantinople.

"Romescot" is OE for Peter's Pence, the medieval papal tax of a penny per household (159.19). The *Gesta Romanorum* (361.32) was a med collection of pop tales in Lat. Chaucer, Shakespeare, and others drew on its tales; the Eng edition was publ by Wynkyn de Worde (249.04) *ca* 1510. "A Tuscan tongue in a Roman mouth" (89.25, 518.24), ie, Roman pronunciation and Tuscan syntax, is a definition of good Italian.

The citations below include refs to the Holy Roman Emp and the RC Ch (see also *Vatican*), but omit occurrences of the term "Roman Catholic"; the latter occur at 27.02, 50.24, 91.35, 239.21, 440.04, 485.01, 486.02, 519.26, and 611.24. In *FW*, the term usually refers to the Ir faith more than to the universal ch, and is most often associated with St Patrick.

I.   Place-Names in Rome:

CAPITOLINE HILL.   Orig called Mons Saturnius; of its 2 peaks, the S peak was the Capitolium, orig Mons Tarpeius; site of the Temple of Jupiter Capitolium. On the N peak, called Arx (Lat, "citadel") was the Temple of Juno Moneta, so-called because it was used as a mint. See *Tarpeian Rock*, below.

    538.01   by Juno Moneta!
    583.02   the heave of his juniper arx

CARCER.   The small pris NE of the Forum where criminals were held pending trial. From med times called the "Mamertine prison." Remains are preserved beneath the ch of San Giuseppe dei Falegnami. Both Peter and Paul were confined there, and it was prob in the dungeon that Catiline awaited execution. The *C* was not so bad, but the dungeon beneath it was connected directly to the Cloaca Maxima.

    85.36   the prisoner...in the mamertime
    577.34   the karkery felons dryflooring it

CATACOMBS.   Orig a dist in S *R*; the name was later applied to the pilgrimage tombs of the Basilica of San Sebastiano, in that dist, and eventually "catacombs" became generic for all underground sepulchres. The Christian catacombs of *R* are mainly in the S and SE, but others are N and NE, none very near either the Vatican or the Villa Borghese (152.28).

    152.28   borgeously letout gardens...currycombs
    542.03   I heard my libertilands making free through their curraghcoombs

COLISEUM (COLOSSEUM).   The great Flavian amphitheatre of anc *R*, said to be named from the colossal stat of Nero that stood close by in the Via Sacra. "While stands the Coliseum, Rome shall stand; when falls the Coliseum, Rome shall fall" (Byron, *Childe Harold* IV, cxlv; quoting Gibbon, *Decline...*, chap LXXI; who is quoting Bede). Cf *Letters* II, 145.

    129.09   while stands his canyouseehim frails shall fall

FORUM.   The Forum Romanum, with its wealth of temples, arches, and stats, occupied low ground btwn the Capitoline and Palatine Hills. It contained a temple of Saturn, built against the Capitoline Hill.

Imperial fora were also built in *R* by Julius, Augustus, Vespasian, Domitian, and Trajan.

    97.34   Saturnalia his goatservant had paraded hiz willingsons in the Forum

LUPERCAL.   The "cave of Lupercus" is on the W side of the Palatine Hill, where by trad Romulus and Remus were suckled by the wolf. The Lupercalia was an anc festival celebrated until the 5th cent on Feb 15; the rites involved thongs (*februa*), and women struck by them escaped sterility. The festival was in honor of Lupercus (protector against wolves), the Lycaean Pan.

    ?67.36   the other soiled dove...Luperca Latouche

    444.36   I'll homeseek you, Luperca as sure as there's a palatine in Limerick

PORTA LATINA.   One of the gates (now closed) in the Aurelian walls of *R*.

    205.27   from Porta Lateen to the lootin quarter

REGINA COELI.   "Queen of Heaven," main pris in *R*.

    64.19   be the chandeleure of the Rejaneyjailey

ST JOHN LATERAN.   San Giovanni di Laterano, in SW *R*; the Cath (It, *Domo*) of *R*.

    152.36   Shinshone Lanteran

    ?299.16   domefool...belested loiternan's lamp

ST PAUL'S-WITHOUT-THE-WALLS.   San Paolo Fuori le Mure, on Via Ostiense, S of *R*. Largest ch in *R*.

    153.01   Saint Bowery's-without-his-Walls

SPQR.   The abbreviation for the Roman motto, *Senatus Populusque Romanus*, was carved on bldgs and borne before the legions on their standards.

    ?37.33   senaffed and pibered him ["senate and people"?]

    229.07   S.P.Q.R.ish

    454.35   seanad and pobbel queue's remainder

    455.28   properly SPQueaRking

    484.22   W.X.Y.Z. and P.Q.R.S. of legatine powers

SUBURRA.   St and dist in anc *R*, now the area around the Piazza della Suburra, E end of Via Cavour. D'Alton's *History* (523) calls Barrack (now Benburb) St in Dub "That vilest of streets...once the Suburra of Dublin."

    454.30   the suburrs of the heavenly gardens

TARPEIAN ROCK.   The site for execution of traitors, a cliff on the Capitoline facing towards the Forum. Named after Tarpeia, who betrayed the Capitol to the Sabines, or Tarpeius, identified with one Tarquinius or another of the legendary kings of *R*.

    167.18   No! Topsman to your Tarpeia!...stormed Olymp

    526.30   my Tarpeyan cousin

VILLA BORGHESE.   Aka Villa Umberto I, in N *R*. Known for the extensive and parklike Borghese Gardens, which contain art museums (It, *pinacoteca*) and fountains, but no waterfalls (It, *cascata*).

    152.27   borgeously letout gardens...cascadas, pintacostecas, horthoducts, and currycombs

    II.   *Rome Allusions*

    6.04   his ville's indigenous romekeepers

    43.12   roman easter

    70.02   these wholly romads!

    72.24   rowmish devowtion...howly rowsary

    84.15   in nobiloroman review

    89.25   A maundarin tongue in a pounderin jowl ["Tuscan tongue in a Roman mouth"]

    96.03   all rogues lean to rhyme

    98.31   rome and reme round e'er a wiege

    113.02   the lapins and the grigs

    129.26   acknowledging the rule of Rome

    143.03   basking again in the panaroma of

    151.10   revolscian from romanitis [the Volscians, in the terr S of Latium, were bitter enemies of *R*]

153.23	in roaming run through Room
185.05	romeruled stationery
209.25	reconciled Romas and Reims
214.22	creakorheuman
236.19	the days of Roamaloose and Rehmoose
241.25	all ameltingmoult after rhomatism
242.13	glycorawman
243.33	for the hnor of Hrom
277.F4	the lays of ancient homes [Macaulay's *Lays of Ancient Rome*]
281.23	if she love Sieger less though she leave Ruhm moan [Shakespeare, *Julius Caesar*, III, ii: "Not that I loved Caesar less, but that I loved Rome more."]
286.F1	As Rhombulus and Rhebus went building rhomes one day
287.21	*lingua romana*
288.24	that same galloroman cultous
298.33	thoughts of that eternal Rome
299.31	the regrettable Parson Rome's advice
302.25	And i Romain, hup u bn gd grl
307.17	The Roman Pontiffs and the Orthodox Churches
344.15	rudeman cathargic
346.04	*Hebeneros for Aromal Peace*
347.31	and his roaming cartridges
353.29	*empyreal Raum*
361.32	gestare romanoverum
371.11	Ostia...reromembered [see *Ostia*]
374.19	Our island, Rome and duty!
388.32	in the Latimer Roman history
389.19	*arma virumque romano*
390.17	in their half a Roman hat...ancient Greek gloss
391.31	confession...at the rim of the rom
409.19	Greeks...as bare as a Roman altar
419.22	nobly Roman as pope and water could christen me
445.13	*Aveh Tiger Roma*
465.35	there's no plagues like rome
467.34	to read the road roman
469.04	Seven oldy oldy hills
469.25	this panromain apological
481.16	Romeo Rogers
487.22	imitation Roma now or Amor now
489.16	castor and porridge...roamin I suppose
518.22	their caractacurs in an Irish Ruman
518.24	Limba romena in Bucclis tucsada ["Tuscan tongue in a Roman mouth"]
525.33	Romunculus Remus
530.11	to turn a Roman
532.06	Eternest cittas, heil!
538.12	the mightyevil roohms of encient cartage
541.01	Seven ills so barely as centripunts
553.35	Roamer Reich's rickyshaws [*Römer Reich*, Ger "Roman empire"]
564.09	the stranger ones, grekish and romanos
581.31	grippes and rumblions
582.33	Lootherstown...Onlyromans

586.25   roamer's numbers ell a fee and do little ones [LVII: the time is 57 minutes past 2 AM]

ROOSKY.   Town, Co Roscommon, on Shannon R. The allusion at 335.24, however, is mainly or entirely to *po-rooski*, Russ "in the Russ lang."
?89.07   Rooskayman
?335.24   Paud the roosky

ROSAMOND'S BOWER.   Banqueting room built in the 18th cent by Lord Charlemont in the grounds of Charlemont Ho, NE Dub, "near some ornamental water." The well-known Casino was built later in the same grounds.
?245.18   Rosimund's by her wishing well

ROSCOMMON.   Co, Connacht prov, and its co town. Baronies: N and S Athlone, N and S Ballintober, Ballymoe, Boyle, Castlereagh, Costello, Frenchpark, Moycarn, Roscommon.
89.07   Rooskayman...Gallwegian
?436.36   raise cancan and rouse commotion
526.28   Corrack-on-Sharon, County Rosecarmon
595.16   rogues comings

ROSE AND BOTTLE   (15/33).   18th-cent tav (until 1773) in Dame St, on site of later Commercial Bldgs; meeting-place of many socs, incl the Ouzel Galley Soc (qv), *ca* 1765.
205.24   the Rose and Bottle

ROSEMARY LANE.   (1) Now Skippers Alley (15/34), site of W front of Adam and Eve's ch (qv). In the 17th and early 18th cents it led to the undercover RC chapels of Adam and Eve's and SS Michael and John. In 1815 the latter moved to a new ch in Exchange St, and in 1832 a new Adam and Eve's was built on the joint sites. (2) *RL* in Belfast is the site of the 17th-cent Presbyterian meeting house; at that time only Prot chs were permitted inside the city walls.   (3) *RL* in London, later Windmill Court, from Pie Corner to King St; St Bartholomew's Hosp now occupies the site.
In the citation, Shaun conflates secret sex and secret religion in his accusation of Issy.
444.29   Up Rosemiry Lean and Potanasty Rod you wos, wos you?

ROSETTA.   Egyptian town at the W or "Rosetta" mouth of the Nile R. The *R* Stone, or stele, inscribed in hieroglyphic, Greek, and demotic langs, was found near the town in 1799 and given up to the Eng at the surrender of Alexandria in 1801.
551.30   rosetted on two stellas of little egypt...rockcut readers, hieros, gregos and democriticos

ROSSES POINT.   Promontory, 5 mi NW of Sligo, Co Sligo. *Ros*, Ir "headland." Now known for golflinks and sea bathing, it was once associated with Manannan Mac Lir (see *Census*).
?267.F1   For Rose Point see Inishmacsaint

ROSS'S.   Around the turn of the cent a number of Dub restaurants were known as "Ross's"; Jane Ross, 124 Lwr Sackville St; John Ross, 1 Upr Sackville St; R Ross and Co, 49 S Gt George's St; Robert Ross, 11 Eden Quay; and Thomas Ross's private hotel, 9-11 Haddington Terrace, Dun Laoghaire (then Kingstown).
Wheatley's was a non-alcoholic beverage.
443.29   sipping some Wheatley's at Rhoss's on a barstool

ROTTERDAM.   Seaport city, W Neth.
   17.15   patwhat as your rutterdamrotter

ROTUNDA (15/34).   Maternity Hosp, Parnell Sq. In 1757 Dr Bartholomew Mosse erected the present bldgs as a charitable lying-in hosp, on a site form known as the Barley Fields. The *R* proper (now a cinema, in the late 19th cent used for skating) is a circular bldg adjacent to the hosp, with extensive gardens known at first as "New Gardens" and later as "Mosse's Gardens." The proceeds from balls and other entertainments in the fashionable *R* and Gardens were used to support the hosp.
   For Dr Bethel Solomon, a president of the *R* Hosp, see *Census.*
      43.03   adjacent cloverfields of Mosse's Gardens
     ?55.36   garrickson's...axiomatic orerotundity
    203.06   in the barleyfields and pennylotts
    205.33   triple tiara busby rotundarinking round his scalp
   ?295.24   gyre O, gyrotundo
    542.28   in my bethel of Solyman's I accouched their rotundaties

ROUEN.   City, Seine-Maritime Dept, N Fr. Joan of Arc was sentenced and executed at *R*. There is no Hôtel de *R* in *R* (or in Paris). *FW*'s pun is Fr as well as Eng: *aller à Rouen*, "to go to ruin."
    283.F2   Gamester Damester in the road to Rouen
   ?289.26   Lady Elisabbess, Hotel des Ruines

ROUNDWOOD.   Vill, Co Wicklow, aka Togher. The *R* Reservoir, fed by the Vartry R, was built in 1863 as the main S Dub water supply. By that time, the elm waterpipes of Dub (see *Waterworks*) had all been replaced.
    542.05   richmounded the rainelag in my bathtub of roundwood...through
          my longertubes of elm

ROYAL CANAL.   A financial disaster from the start, the *RC* was begun in 1789 to run N of the Liffey, roughly paralleling the course of the rival Grand Canal to the S. Its route was from the N Wall docks in Dub, W through Meath to Mullingar in Co Westmeath, then through Co Longford to the Shannon R.
    37.20   the quiet darkenings of Grand and Royal
   207.12   her boudeloire maids...Ciliegia Grande and Kirschie Real
   494.32   the fleshambles, the canalles
   551.24   canal grand...Regalia Water

"ROYAL GEORGE."   (1) Brit man-of-war which sank at Spithead in 1782 with the loss of 800 lives; subject of Wm Cowper's poem "The Loss of the Royal George." (2) *RG* Yacht Club in Dun Laoghaire (qv).
   151.29   asousiated with the royal gorge...hydrostatics and pneumodipsics...
         grapple away

ROYAL HIBERNIAN HOTEL (16/33).   In Dawson St.
   376.12   the Real Hymernians

ROYAL HOSPITAL (13/33).   In Kilmainham, its grounds bounded by Military, St John's, and S Circular Rds and Kilmainham Lane. The *RH* was pop known as the "Old Man's House" (*U* 710/725). Built 1680-84 "for old and maimed soldiers," its last pensioners lingered until 1927 and it is now used as a storehouse. Acc to Maurice Craig, the often repeated story that it was designed by Christopher Wren is not true; but JJ may have believed it (431.13).
   The great gothic gate, aka Richmond Tower (by Francis Johnston), was orig erected at the E end of Victoria Quay at Barrack Br, in 1816. Becoming an impediment

to traffic in 1846, it was removed stone by stone to its present site in the SCR.

 197.24   auld min's manse
?260.12   under Guido d'Arezzo's Gadeway
 397.14   Old Man's House, Millenium Road
 504.31   the killmaimthem pensioners

ROYAL LEG, THE.   18th-cent shop for stockings, acc to Peter's *Sketches of Old Dublin* (89).

 536.15   so buckely hosiered from the Royal Leg

ROYAL MANORS OF DUBLIN.   The 4 Royal Manors of Co Dub, est under Henry II, were Esker, Newcastle, Saggart, and Crumlin. All are W of Dub City and S of the Liffey.

 18.06   O'c'stle, n'wc'stle, tr'c'stle, crumbling!
555.13   esker, newcsle, saggard, crumlin
555.15   esker, newcsle, saggard, crumlin

ROYAL MARINE HOTEL   (24/28).   Gresham Terr, Dun Laoghaire, off Royal Marine Rd.

 30.16   rere garden of mobhouse, ye olde marine hotel, when royalty

ROYAL TERRACE   (24/27).   St in Fairview dist, NE Dub, later renamed Inverness Terr. The Joyce family lived at No 8 in 1901.

 420.28   Q.V. 8 Royal Terrors. None so strait

ROY'S CORNER.   This sounds like a real name in Dub pop usage, but no one seems to remember it. In the later 19th cent, George Roy's fish stores were at the cor of George's St, E, and George's Quay (16/34). The name might be a pun on "King's Corner," and W King, printer and stationer, was at the cor of Charles St and Ormond Quay, Upr (15/34).

 62.31   by the old spot, Roy's Corner

RUE DE L'ABBÉ DE L'EPÉE.   Paris st, 5th Arr, btwn the Blvd St Michel and the Rue Gay Lussac. Site of the Inst Nat des Sourds-Muets, founded 1791 to continue work of Charles-Michel, Abbé de l'Epée, who originated the instruction of deaf-mutes in sign lang.

 329.30   old dummydeaf...Paster de Grace on the Route de l'Epée

RUE DE LA PAIX.   Paris st, 2nd Arr, btwn the Opéra and the Place Vendôme.

 329.30   Paster de Grace on the Route de l'Epée

RUGBY.   Town, Warwickshire, Eng. *R* Sch, founded in the 16th cent, is known *inter alia* as the place where rugby football was invented. The Temple Obs of *R* Sch was founded in 1872.

 449.35   followed through my...neviewscope the rugaby moon
 518.01   Dunsink, rugby, ballast and ball

RUHMKORFF, RUE DE.   Paris st, 17th Arr. H D Ruhmkorff invented the mod induction coil, 1851.

?250.04   He simules to be tight in ribbings round his rumpffkorpff

RUHR.   Dist, W Ger, the vall of the Ruhr R and a major mining and industrial area.

 82.03   tipperuhry Swede

RUNNYMEDE.   The meadow on the bank of the Thames R near Egham, Surrey, Eng, where King John signed the Magna Carta in 1215.

?10.09   waxing ranjymad
286.07   nor anymeade
525.13   this ruttymaid fishery
525.19   For a runnymede landing...*Magnam Carpam*
566.14   runameat farums...magnum chartarums

RUSH.   Vill and seaside resort, Co Dub, 18 mi N of Dub.
15.02   sweet Rush, townland of twinedlights
?105.22   *Buckling Shut at Rush in January*
322.02   Boildawl...rushirishis Irush-Irish
497.11   Rountown and Rush
526.06   tulipbeds of Rush below
589.04   rushroads to riches

RUS IN URBE.   The phrase (orig from Martial's *Epigrams*) may be only general in *FW*, but JJ must have often seen the motto carved on the portico of Aldborough Ho (qv) in Gloucester (now Sean MacDermott) St (16/35). There is also a Rus in Urbe Terr in Dun Laoghaire, off Glenageary Rd (24/27).

Leopold Bloom's dream of owning his own house aspires beyond "a terracehouse or semidetached villa, described as *Rus in Urbe* or *Qui si Sana*" (*U* 697/712).
?40.07   the tale of the evangelical bussybozzy and the rusinurbean
332.34   suburbiaurealis in his rure
551.24   And I built in *Urbs in Rure*

RUSSIA.   Form kingdom and emp, now USSR, E Eur and N and W Asia. The pre-USSR Russ parl was called the Duma (54.09).

Omitted here are all refs to the Russ Gen shot by Buckley, for which see *Census*.
54.09   storthingboys and dumagirls
72.04   *Sur of all the Ruttledges*
155.27   gresk, letton and russicruxian [RC and Orthodox Chs]
250.03   rossy banders
253.03   Russky...slove
290.F7   The bookley with the rusin's hat is Patomkin
329.20   Holyryssia
335.24   Paud the roosky [*po-rooski*, Russ "in Russian"]
339.11   varnashed roscians
340.35   the sur of all Russers
344.33   Saur of all the Haurousians
347.31   orussheying
352.22   Oholy rasher, I'm believer!
352.33   frustate fourstar Russkakruscam
353.19   instullt to Igorladns
391.30   as red as a Rosse is
461.14   russians
463.24   red in Rossya
464.31   Peadhar the Grab
492.09   singing him henpecked rusish
494.19   bullsrusshius
509.07   rooshian mad
509.13   rooshiamarodnimad
596.12   forebe all the rassias

RUTHENIA.   Form Czech prov, now part of Ukrainian SSR, USSR. The Ruthenians are Little Russians whose terr has been governed by Lith, Pol, and Austro-Hung. *Rutene*, Russ "Ruthenian." The Ruthene lang resembles Ukrainian. The 1st par on *FW* 340 contains a number of Ruthenian words, incl *lis*, "wood"; *luhy*, "meadow."

    340.05   *pinkpoker pointing out in rutene...towards Lissnaluhy*

RUTLAND SQUARE   (15/35).   Now Parnell Sq, at the N end of Sackville (now O'Connell) St. Orig called the Barley Fields (qv), purchased by Dr Mosse for his Rotunda (qv) hosp and gardens in the mid-18th cent. The sq and its boundary sts slope upward from S to N.

    42.36   mallardmissing on Rutland heath
    97.11   he last was lost, check, upon Ye Hill of Rut
  ?148.08   For Rutland blue's got out of passion
  ?260.10   diagonising Lavatery Square
  437.05   up windy Rutland Rise

RYE RIVER.   Whether "Coming Through the Rye" refers to a field of grain or to a stream, I have not found a Scot riv or brook of that name. (Another faint echo of the song is at 578.32.) Ire has its own Rye R, however; it forms part of the boundary btwn Cos Kildare and Meath, and flows into the Liffey at Leixlip.

  200.33   the wyerye rima she made
  329.22   mabbing through the ryce

S

SAGGART.   Vill, SW of Dub on Naas Rd. *S* was one of the 4 Royal Manors of Dub (qv) (555.13,15). Brian Boru routed allied Norse-Leinster forces at the battle of Glenmama on the slope of *S* Hill, to the SW.

    The name is a corruption of *Teach Sacra*, Ir "priest's house," the monastery founded late 7th cent by St Moshacra. Most *FW* refs may be just to "saggart," or priest.

  ?98.16   he saw the family saggarth
 ?135.36   he swarms with saggarts
 555.13,15   esker, newcsle, saggard, crumlin

SAGITTARIUS.   Constellation, N hemisphere; "the Archer." 9th sign of zodiac.

  343.01   *orients by way of Sagittarius*
  600.06   Deltas Piscium and Sagittariastrion

SAHARA.   Vast desert region, N Afr. *FW* conflates the infertile desert with Abraham's elderly Sarah, who conceived Isaac against the odds.

  60.14   caveman chase and sahara sex
 104.20   *Aldborougham on the Sahara*
 127.26   sorrow of Sahara, oxhide on Iren
 336.15   awebrume hour, her sere Sahara

The Dub habit of colloquially omitting "Saint" from place-names ("Stephen's Green" rather than "St Stephen's Green") has been noticed for more than a cent, but such names are nevertheless sanctified in their alphabetical listing in this Gazetteer whenever it is formally a part of the name, however little used in common speech.

It has long been a Dub habit as well to identify chs by the st of their location; eg, "Gardiner St ch" for the Jesuit ch of St Francis Xavier. This practice is evident in FW, esp in the lists of chs given on FW 569 and 601.

ST AGATHA'S CHURCH (RC) (16/35).   In N William St.
     569.14   Agithetta
     601.21   S. Wilhelmina's

ST ANDREW'S CHURCH (CI) (15/33).   In St Andrew's St, S of Dame St. There has been a ch on this site since the 12th cent. The 18th-cent *St A's*, commonly called the Round Ch, burned in 1860 and was replaced by the present edifice.
     ?147.26   Sainte Andrée's Undershift
     ?277.18   And Sein annews

ST ANDREW'S or ALL HALLOWS CHURCH (RC) (16/33).   In Westland Row.
     ?147.26   Sainte Andrée's Undershift
     569.09   S. Weslen-on-the-Row
     601.21   S. Veslandrua's

ST ANDREW UNDERSHAFT, CHURCH OF.   City of London, at foot of St Mary Ave. The name is apparently from the Maypole set up annually until 1517. Andrew Undershaft of Shaw's *Major Barbara* was a foundling named after the ch.
     147.26   Sainte Andrée's Undershift

ST ANNE'S (ANN'S) CHURCH (CI) (16/33).   In Dawson St, facing S Anne St. There was never a tollgate near this cen Dub site. I doubt whether any of the allusions are to this st or ch, but it is an occasion to point out that there is no other ch in Dub named for Anne or Annona. As the *Census* notes, Annona was a Roman female deity, the personification of the harvest; *annona* is also It for "supply of food, esp grain." But there must be some further explanation of Anna Livia's appearance as Annona.
     ?44.06   by the old tollgate, Saint Annona's Street and Church
     ?199.34   Annona, gebroren aroostokrat Nivia

ST AUDOEN'S CHURCH (14/33).   Dub's 2 chs of this name are neighbors in High St: the ch (CI) of *St A*, St Michael, and St Nicholas Within, and the mod *St A's* Ch (RC). The wards of Dub do not include a *St A's* (484.03).
     484.03   attaching Audeon's prostratingwards
     528.06   St Audiens rosan chocolate chapelry
     569.11   Bride-and-Audeons-behind-Wardborg

ST AUSTELL.   Town and resort, Cornwall, 30 mi W of Plymouth. For the tenor Ivan St Austell (*U* 648/664), see *Census*.
     48.12   Ivanne Ste Austelle (Mr J. F. Jones)

ST BARBARA'S.   There is no ch of *St B*, or other relevant place, in Dub. In the "Circe" chap of *U* (583/599), Fr Malachi O'Flynn and Mr Hugh C Haines Love, M.A., celebrate a black mass on the "field altar of St Barbara."
     335.27   half for the laugh of the bliss it sint barbaras

ST BARTHOLOMEW-BY-THE-EXCHANGE.   Ch, City of London. It was burned in the Great Fire, rebuilt by Wren, demolished in 1841 to make room for the new Royal Exchange. Aka *St B* the Less to distinguish it from *St B* the Great (qv).
     135.10   Barth-the-Grete-by-the-Exchange

ST BARTHOLOMEW THE GREAT.   Ch, N side of Smithfield Close, W Smithfield, London.

135.10   Barth-the-Grete-by-the-Exchange

ST BRICIN'S HOSPITAL.   Military hosp adjacent to (now) Collins Barracks, btwn Arbour Hill and Benburb St. It incorporates part of the bldgs formerly the Provost Marshal's Pris, where Wolfe Tone died and the bodies of executed 1916 leaders were buried in quicklime.

390.01   the mossacre of Saint Brices

ST BRIDE'S CHURCH (CI)   (15/33).   Form in Bride St, several blocks S of St Audoen's and St Werburgh's; aka St Bridget's. It was united to St Werburgh's in 1886, and demolished in 1898.

569.11   Bride-and-Audeons-behind-Wardborg

ST BRIGID'S.   The school-coven of the 29 leapyear girls to whom Shaun-Jaun preaches in *FW* III.2 is no doubt a *St B's* sch in a generic sense, but any or all of the following may be echoed.

(1) *St B's* Schs of the Holy Faith, for boys and girls, were in the care of the Sisters of the Holy Faith, at 116-117 The Coombe (14/33).   (2) *St B's* Schs, for boys and girls, were conducted by the Sisters of Faith in Little Strand St (15/34). (3) *St B's* Orphanage, for boys and girls, was and is operated at 46 Eccles St by the same order (15/35).   (4) *St B's* Nat Sch was and is in Castleknock (8/37).   (5) The Convent of *St B* was est in the 7th cent by St Brigid by an oak said to have been on the hill where Kildare Cath now stands. It was, unusually in Ire, a double monastery for both monks and nuns.

220.03   St. Bride's Finishing Establishment, demand acidulateds
427.36   becoming back to us way home in Biddyhouse
430.02   Benent Saint Berched's national nightschool
562.13   common marygales that romp round brigidschool

SAINTE-CECILE, ÉGLISE DE.   Ch, 46 Rue des Pyrénées, 20th Arr, Paris. There is no par of St Cecilia in Dub.

?41.33   the Old Sots' Hole in the parish of Saint Cecily

ST COLUMBA'S CHURCH (RC)   (15/36).   In Iona Rd, Glasnevin.

569.08   Iona-in-the-Fields

ST DIZIER.   Town, NE Fr; founded 3rd cent, named after Bishop St Didier, whose relics were brought there. The feast of *St D* is 23 May. Napoleon defeated Blücher in the battle of *St D*, 27 Jan 1814.

408.22   tomorry, for 'twill be, I have hopes of, Sam Dizzier's feedst

ST DOOLAGH (DOULAGH).   Vill, with 13th-cent stone-roofed ch, NW of Baldoyle. *FW* associates it with horseracing, but it's 2 mi from Baldoyle racecourse.

39.09   Baldoyle...roe hinny [Raheny, qv] Saint Dalough
341.27   *shrineshriver of Saint Dhorough's*

ST DUNSTAN-IN-THE-EAST.   London ch, Gt Tower St and Lwr Thames St; damaged in 1940 blitz and not rebuilt.

135.09   dunstung in the Yeast

ST EDMUND, KING AND MARTYR.   London ch, N side of Lombard St, in the City. Edmund was king of E Anglia, killed by Danes in 870 AD.

135.09   Headmound, king and martyr

ST FIACRE.   Hôtel *St F*, Rue St Martin, Paris. Vehicles for hire in Paris are called "fiacres" after the hackney coaches which once were stationed at the hotel.

There is a commemorative plaque to *St F* in the ch of St Mathurin in Paris. JJ mentions it in "Ireland, Island of Saints and Sages," *Critical Writings*, 158.

    81.11   in the fane of Saint Fiacre

ST FRANCIS XAVIER'S CHURCH (RC)   (15/35).   The Jesuit ch in Gardiner St, Upr.

    569.07   S. Gardener
    601.21   S. Gardenia's

SAINT-GABRIEL, ÉGLISE DE.   Paris ch (RC), Rue des Pyrénées, 20th Arr.

    ?184.27   oewfs à la Madame Gabrielle de l'Eglise

ST GEORGE'S CHANNEL.   The S part of the Ir Sea, btwn Wales and SE Ire.

    324.31   through the middelhav of the same gorgers' kennel
    492.34   a basketful of priesters crossing the singorgeous

ST GEORGE'S CHURCH (CI)   (15/35).   In Hardwicke Place, off Dorset St. There are no chs in Gt George's St, N or S.

    569.07   S. George-le-Greek

ST GEORGE'S-IN-THE-EAST.   London ch, Cannon St Rd. In 1860, "No Popery" protesters filled the ch Sunday after Sunday, interrupting the services by singing "Rule Britannia," throwing orange peel and walnut shells during services, etc.

    541.34   while from gorges in the east came the strife of ourangoontangues

ST HELENA.   Brit isl, S Atlantic O; site of Napoleon's exile, 1815-21; detention camp for Boer prisoners of war, 1899-1902.

    71.29   *Go to Hellena or Come to Connies*

ST IVES.   Town, NW coast of Cornwall, Eng. In the riddle-rhyme "As I was going to St Ives, I met a man with seven wives," the answer is "One."

Saint Yves is also the Eng name of Setúbal, a seaport and form royal res in S Port. St Yves (1253-1303) is the patron st of lawyers.

    147.10   holly...mistle and it Saint Yves
    291.01   Unic bar None, of Saint Yves by Landsend cornwer
    523.08   the deponent, the man from Saint Yves

ST JOHN'S ROAD   (12–13/33).   From Kingsbridge (Heuston) Sta to SCR in Kilmainham.

St John's Wood is a well-known res area in London, NW of Regent's Park.

    223.20   from all Saint Joan's Wood to kill or maim him

ST JOSEPH'S CHURCH   (RC).   (1) In Berkeley St (15/35).   (2) In Portland Row, at NCR (16/35).

    569.07   S. Barclay Moitered
    601.22   S. Perlanthroa's

ST JOSEPH'S NIGHT REFUGE   (14/33).   In Brickfield Lane, Cork St, around the turn of the cent; for homeless women and children. The many refuges and asylums in Dub in the 19th and early 20th cents testify to the extent of misery among the homeless poor as much as they do to charitable benevolence. With 145 beds, St Joseph's, run by the Sisters of Mercy, was one of the largest.

    555.21   hurrying to be cardinal scullion in a night refuge

ST JUDE'S CHURCH (CI)   (12/33).   In Inchicore Rd, Kilmainham, near the gate of the Royal Hosp.
    569.09   S. Jude-at-Gate

ST JUST.   Town, Cornwall, 4 mi N of Land's End; contains amphitheater where miracle plays were performed in the Middle Ages. For the tenor Hilton St Just (*U* 648/664), see *Census*.
    48.11   Hilton St Just (Mr Frank Smith)

ST KEVIN'S CHAPEL (RC)   (15/33).   The chapel of the Nat Univ, in Stephen's Green, S.
    601.24   S. Una Vestity's

ST KEVIN'S HOSPITAL   (13/33).   On SCR, NE of Rialto Br.
    40.36   Saint Kevin's bed

ST LAWRENCE'S CHURCH (RC)   (16/34).   In Seville Place; named for St Lawrence O'Toole. Around the turn of the cent, the Seville Engineering Works was 2 doors away (569.06).
    138.26   chrysmed in Scent Otooles
    569.06   S. Lorenz-by-the-Toolechest
    601.28   S. Loellisotoelles

SAINT-LAZARE.   The Paris prison to which prostitutes were sent was known as "Saint-Lago" in local slang.
    203.08   Alesse, the lagos of girly days!

ST MARK'S CHURCH (CI)   (16/39).   In Gt Brunswick (now Pearse) St, under the Loop Line Rlwy.
    569.05   S. Mark Underloop

ST MARTIN'S IN THE FIELDS.   London ch, NE cor of Trafalgar Sq, Westminster.
    328.24   Sing Mattins in the Fields

ST MARY DEL DAM (DAME)   (15/33).   The ch which gave its name to Dame's Gate and the present Dame St was orig on the site of the present City Hall. The ch was founded by the 12th cent and perhaps even earlier. It ceased to function as a ch in the late 16th cent, and was demolished by the Earl of Cork to build his mansion known as "Cork House." The name has been variously explained as deriving from the dammed millpond in the vicinity of the orig ch, or from "Notre Dame."
    206.06   Par the Vulnerable Virgin's Mary del Dame!
    520.19   N.D. de l'Ecluse [*écluse*, Fr "mill-dam"]

ST MARY-LE-BOW.   London ch, on Cheapside; totally burnt out in 1940 blitz. Only someone born within sound of its bells is a true cockney. The Bow Bells said "Turn again, Lord Mayor of London" to Dick Whittington.
    372.01   belles bows...londmear of Dublin
    584.28   bill...bowe...belle...beau
    626.02   turn agate, weddingtown...if you le, bowldstrong

ST MARY OF THE ANGELS CHURCH (RC)   (14/34).   Franciscan Capuchin ch, Church St, called "Brown Friars."
    569.09   Bruno Friars
  ?588.13   my old brown freer
    601.25   S. Churstry's

ST MARY'S CHAPEL OF EASE (CI)   (15/35).   Among many "chapels of ease," the best-known in Dub is *St M's* in Mountjoy St at *St M's* Pl; it has always been pop known as the "Black Ch."

    ?495.10   a froren black patata, from my church milliner

ST MARY'S CHURCH (RC)   (17/33).   In Haddington Rd.

    601.26   S. Heddadin Drade's

ST MARY'S HOSPITAL   (10/34).   In Phoenix Park, N of Chapelizod Gate. Form the Hibernian Military Sch.

    260.F2   Mater Mary Mercerycordial

ST MICHAN'S CHURCH.   (1) (CI) Church St (14/34). Dates from 1554; until 1700 the only Dub ch N of the Liffey. The mummified cadavers in its vaults (455.18, 601.25) are for some reason a tourist attraction.   (2) (RC) Btwn Halston St and N Anne St (15/34).

    Both are in "Ostmannstown" or Oxmantown (qv), the area N and W of the Four Courts.

    36.29   Bishop and Mrs Michan of High Church of England
    243.27   hang herself in Ostmannstown Saint Megan's
    ?378.19   Partick Thistle agen S. Megan's
    443.35   Michan and his lost angeleens
    455.18   Here we moult in Moy Kain
    541.05   I raised a dome on the wherewithouts of Michan
    601.25   S. Misha-La-Valse's

ST NESSAN'S CHURCH.   Ruined ch on Ireland's Eye (qv); all that remains of the abbey founded in the 6th cent by St Nessan, moved to Howth in the 13th cent. The illuminated *Garland of Howth*, now in TCD, was begun at *St N's*.

    26.34   attending school nessans regular, sir

ST NICHOLAS OF MYRA'S CHURCH (RC)   (14/33).   In Francis St.

    569.06   S. Nicholas Myre

ST NICHOLAS WITHIN, CHURCH OF (CI)   (15/33).   In Nicholas St, near High St, near Christchurch Cath and St Michael's Ch.

    541.04   The chort of Nicholas Within was my guide

ST OLAVE'S   (15/33).   The ch of St Olaf (king and nat saint of Nor) stood at the lwr end of Fishamble St. In 15th-cent documents the par is styled that of "St Olave the King"; later corrupted into "St Tullock's."

    138.25   was dipped in Hoily Olives

ST PANCRAS.   London borough, incl Camden Town. In the 17th-18th cents *St P* was a spa whose mineral waters were reputed a cure for digestive troubles, scurvy, and leprosy. *St P* Rlwy Sta is on Marylebone Rd.

    550.13   marrolebone...come the feast of Saint Pancreas

ST PATRICK'S CATHEDRAL (CI)   (15/33).   In Patrick St, bounded by *St P's* Close, N (now *St P's* Park) and *St P's* Close, S (now Guinness St). Acc to trad, a small ch was built on this site by St Patrick in 448 AD. In any case, an existing ch was rebuilt as a collegiate ch in 1191 by Archbishop Comyn; his successor, Henry de Londres, made it a cath in 1213, to rival Christchurch. It has been rebuilt many times but is basically Early Eng (?127.33) in style. After the fire of 1363, Archbishop Minot rounded up "straggling and idle fellows" to repair the nave and build a steeple

(128.32, 287.18). In the 1860's Sir Benjamin Lee Guinness financed a general rebuilding, much of it from the ground up. The "convenience" (51.24, 530.10) is in the Park.

During the Wars of the Roses, the Earls of Kildare and Ormond were reconciled in *St P's* but suspiciously would not approach each other until a hole was chopped in the door of the Chapter House through which they shook hands (248.23). The door is still preserved in the S transept.

Jonathan Swift became a pop hero in Dub (288.21) while Dean of *St P's* (1713-1745); he is buried in the S aisle.

26.22	the grammarians of Christpatrick's
51.24	in Loo of Pat
128.32	three hundred sixty five idles to set up one all khalassal
248.23	Shake hands through the thicketloch!
287.18	a spirit spires...dean of idlers
288.21	(Gratings, Mr Dane!)...that other familiar temple
326.25	Domnkirk Saint Petricksburg
530.10	a litterydistributer in Saint Patrick's Lavatory
552.23	her paddypalace on the crossknoll with massgo bell
569.15	Greatchrist and Holy Protector

ST PATRICK'S CHURCH (RC) (18/33).   In Ringsend.
    601.26   S. Ringsingsund's

ST PATRICK'S CLOSE.   In JJ's day, *St P's* Cath was bounded to the N by *St P's* Close, N (now absorbed by *St P's* Park) and to the S by *St P's* Close, S (now Guinness St) in which were the Deanery and Marsh's Library (qv).

JJ was delighted to discover the vineyard Clos S Patrice, by his account the oldest *vignoble* in Provence (*Letters* III, 178). He didn't drink its wine because it was red, but sent cases of it to Ir friends. It is still bottled, the only Fr wine with a label bordered with shamrocks.

    442.36   coomb the brash of the libs round Close Saint Patrice

ST PATRICK'S HOSPITAL (13/33).   In James's St, btwn Bow Lane and Steeven's Lane. Aka Swift's Hosp; it was founded by a bequest from Swift, opened 1757; 1st lunatic asylum in Ire, now a mod psychiatric cen.

?124.07	the circumflexuous wall of a singleminded men's asylum
197.24	Maisons Allfou
?221.01	St. Patricius' Academy for Grownup Gentlemen
?289.18	gigglehouse...molniacs' manias and missions for mades
294.16	to Swift's, alas, the galehus! [Dan, "lunatic asylum"]
?422.01	drapery institution [cf Swift's *Drapier's Letters*]
618.11	in the Sweeps hospital

ST PATRICK'S PURGATORY.   Cave on Station Isl in Lough Derg, Co Donegal. Acc to legend it was the last stronghold of the devil in Ire until St Patrick drove the devil out by 40 days of fasting and prayer. As the name indicates, it has also been believed to be the entrance to Purgatory. A pilgrimage site still, it was immensely pop in the middle ages with pilgrims from all over Eur, who ignored even the order by Alexander VI in 1497 (later revoked), forbidding pilgrims to visit it.

80.07	filthdump...Finewell's Keepsacre...tautaubapptossed Pat's Purge
177.04	his pawdry's purgatory
352.36	*pungataries of sin praktice*
530.10	a litterydistributer in Saint Patrick's Lavatory

582.29   Derg rudd face should take patrick's purge
618.15   a good allround sympowdhericks purge

ST PATRICK'S TRAINING COLLEGE   (16/37).   (1) In Belvidere Ho, Drumcondra.   (2) *St P's* Coll in Maynooth, the principal Ir seminary for the training of the
diocesan priesthood.
221.01   St. Patricius' Academy for Grownup Gentlemen, consult the annuary

ST PAUL'S CHURCH.   (1) In N King St (CI) (14/34).   (2) On Arran Quay (RC)
(14/34). Usually known as "the Arran Quay ch."
569.08   Paull-the-Aposteln
601.23   S. Errands Gay's

ST PAUL'S COLLEGE   (14/31).   In Mt Argus House, S of Mt Jerome cem, Harold's
Cross; home of the Passionist Fathers. The ref is to the chapel.
601.24   S. Mintargisia's

ST PETER-LE-POER.   London ch, W side of Old Broad St, demolished *ca* 1912.
135.10   Pitre-le-Pore-in Petrin

ST PETERSBURG.   Second largest city of USSR, and cap 1712-1917; on delta of
Neva R at E end of Gulf of Finland; built by Peter the Great in 1703. Renamed
Petrograd (1914), Leningrad (1924). Wellington as diplomat lost ground in the Pro-
tocol of *St P*, 4 Apr 1826. The Prospekt Nevskiy (442.11) is a main thoroughfare,
cutting across the bend of the Neva. Among the most noted bldgs are the Winter
Palace (551.01), the Peter and Paul Fortress, now a pris (277.10), and the Cath of
St Isaac of Dalmatia (326.25). Lenin's (351.28) arrival at the Finland Sta from Zurich in 1917 was the crucial event of the Bolshevik Revolution.
     Mark Twain characters Huck Finn and Tom Sawyer lived in the "poor shabby vil-
lage" of *St P*, Missouri (549.24).
162.30   as were the wholeborough of Poutresbourg to be averlaunched over
            him pitchbatch
205.34   Pate-by-the-Neva or Pete-over-Meer
277.10   he's head on poll and Peter's burgess
326.25   Domnkirk Saint Petricksburg
351.14   S. Pivorandbowl
351.24–.27   sunpictorsbosk...reptrograd leanins
442.11   Twoways Peterborough...newsky prospect
549.24   sankt piotersbarq...a sawyer
551.01   in our windtor palast it vampared for elenders

ST PETER'S CHURCH (RC)   (14/35).   In Cabra Rd, Phibsborough (qv).
569.08   S. Phibb
601.21   S. Phibia's

ST PETER'S, PAUL'S WHARF.   London ch, mentioned *ca* 1767 as St Peter de la
Wodenwarve (Wood Wharf), destroyed in Great Fire, par united with St Benet's,
Paul's Wharf. In the 15th cent, the area S of St Benet's was ceded to St Paul's Cath,
and a wharf in the Thames R was built for unloading goods bound to the cath.
580.04   rolled olled logs into Peter's sawyery and werfed new woodcuts on
            Paoli's wharf

ST PETER'S TERRACE   (14/35).   N side of Cabra Rd near its intersection with
NCR. The Joyce family lived at No 7 in 1902-1903; JJ's mother died there. Later
renamed St Peter's Rd.

420.35   7 Streetpetres. Since Cabranke

ST SEPULCHRE'S   (15/33).   Palace of the Dub Archbishops, built shortly after St Patrick's Cath to the S of the cath; vacated as archepiscopal res 1822, then used as courthouse and pris for the pars of St Kevin and St Nicholas Without. Its remains were incorporated in the DMP horse police barracks in Kevin St. The Cabbage Garden graveyard was in the 19th cent just adjacent to the site of St Sepulchre's on the S. Like other foundations of the same name, it was named after the Ch of the Holy Sepulchre in Jerusalem.

?28.28   bluebells blowing in salty sepulchres

343.05   camp camp camp to Saint Sepulchre's march

?568.27   We but miss that horse elder yet cherchant of the wise graveleek in cabbuchin garden

ST STEPHEN'S GREEN   (15–16/33).   The beautiful park in S cen Dub was once the site of a lazar hosp and ch, which were destroyed in the Reformation. Once called Rapparee Fields, it was first enclosed in 1670, and became fashionable as a promenade in the 18th cent; the N side was called Beaux' Walk, with Monk's Walk on the E, Leeson Walk on the S, and French Walk on the W. In 1880 the park was railed and landscaped by Lord Ardilaun. Among its notable bldgs are the Shelbourne Hotel (qv) on the N, the Royal Coll of Surgeons on the W, and the bldgs of the Nat Univ (qv), attended by JJ, on the S.

550.06   Steving's grain for's greet collegtium

ST SULPICE.   Paris ch, Pl St Sulpice, 6th Arr.

?254.08   chroncher of chivalries is sulpicious save he scan

ST SWITHIN'S CHURCH.   London ch opp Cannon St rlwy sta. There is no *St S's* in Dub.

520.16   midnight mask saints withins

604.07   hourly rincers' mess [early risers' mass]...in close. Withun

ST TERESA, MONASTERY OF   (14/30).   Carmelite convent in Mt Tallant Ave, Harold's Cross (not in Merrion, qv).

538.01   irished Marryonn Teheresiann

ST THOMAS, CHURCH OF (CI)   (15/34).   In Marlborough St at Findlater Pl. The 18th-cent ch, modelled on Palladio's Redentore in Venice, was badly damaged in 1922 and a new ch built in 1931-32.

?53.31   a starchboxsitting in the pit of his St Tomach's

ST THOMAS À BECKET, ABBEY OF   (15/33).   Founded in 1177 AD by Henry II, on the site of what is now St Catherine's Ch (CI) in Thomas St. St Thomas's became one of the Liberties of Dub. None of the Abbey bldgs survive. The Chartulary of *St T's* Abbey was known as Coppinger's Register.

390.12   as per the cabbangers richestore, of the filest archives

601.27   S. Thomassabbess's

ST WERBURGH'S, ST JOHN'S, AND ST BRIDE'S CHURCH (CI)   (15/33).   In Werburgh St; known usually only as "St Werburgh's." It stands just W of the Castle (qv) (*borg*, Dan "castle"); in 1810 the Castle authorities, nervous about the ch spire as a vantage-point overlooking the Castle, declared it unsafe and had it taken down. The 2 chs of St Audoen (qv) are a short distance to the W, and the ch of St Bride a short distance to the S.

569.11   Bride-and-Audeons-behind-Wardborg

SALAMANCA.   Sp prov and city; site of Wellington's victory over Fr in the Penin War, 22 Jul 1812.
>   9.13   Salamangra

SALAMIS.   Anc city and port on the Gk isl of Cyprus. (Not the *S* of the Gk-Pers naval battle of 480 BC.) One of the 7 cities claimed in anc times as the birthplace of Homer.
>   129.24   pigeonheim to this homer...Seapoint
>   481.22   humeplace...Salem (Mass)

SALEM.   City, NE Massachusetts, US, 14 mi NE of Boston; scene of witchcraft hysteria 1692, in which 20 persons were executed.
>   481.22   Salem (Mass)

SALISBURY.   Aka New Sarum; city, Wiltshire, S Eng. *S* Plain, N of *S*, has been used for Brit military maneuvers.
>   541.28   whom I filled ad liptum on the plain of Soulsbury

SALLY GAP.   Pass in the Wicklow mts S of Mt Kippure. Water from the N side of *SG* flows into the Liffey, from the S side into the Annamoe R (thence through Luggela to Lough Tay and Lough Dan). In the allusion at 195.01 the course of the Liffey is traced backwards to its source.
>   195.01   Tallaght's...pools of the phooka...Blessington...slipping sly by Sally-
>   noggin
>   204.15   she sideslipped out by a gap...while Sally her nurse was sound asleep

SALLYNOGGIN   (24/26).   Res area just S of Dun Laoghaire and W of Dalkey; it is nowhere near the Liffey R.
>   195.01   Tallaght's...Blessington and slipping sly by Sallynoggin

SALMON POOL.   Channel of the Liffey btwn the Dodder R and Poolbeg; an anchorage before the S and N Walls were built into Dub Bay. Haliday, 237n: "The bank at the west end of Cock [or Cockle] Lake called Salmon Pool bank, running Southwards to the Brick Fields..."
>   174.28   beyond the brickfields of Salmon Pool

SALO.   Town, Lombardy, N It, 40 mi NW of Mantua; site of Fr defeat by Austrians in Napoleon's siege of Mantua during the Fr Revolutionary War, 29 Jul 1796.
>   8.14   Saloos the Crossgunn

SALT, BARONY OF.   The Baronies of N Salt and S Salt form the cor of Co Kildare, containing Maynooth, Leixlip, and Celbridge. The name is from the Lat name of Leixlip, *Saltus Salmonis*. Henry de Londres, 13th-cent Dub Archbishop, had no connection with Leixlip, but in the 18th cent the Archbishop of Armagh, Primate of Ire, had his Dub country seat there.
>   543.18   William Inglis his house, that man de Loundres, in all their barony
>   of Saltus

SALT HILL.   (1) Another, now little-used name for Monkstown (qv), SE Dub, btwn Blackrock and Dun Laoghaire (22/28).   (2) Suburb and seaside resort W of Galway City.
>   261.F2   Amusing Avenue, Salt Hill, Co. Mahogany

SAMARIA.   Anc city and the surrounding country, cen Pal. The story of the "good Samaritan" is in *Luke* 10.
>   228.34   Cernilius slomtime prepositus of Toumaria

556.06   the beautiful Samaritan

SAMHAIR (SAMER).   The old name of both the Erne R (qv) and the Morning
Star R in Co Limerick (the latter by corruption to *Camhair*, "break of day," acc to
P W Joyce). Inishsamer is an isl near the Erne R at Ballyshannon, Co Donegal. Also
a woman's name, root and origin unknown.
242.20   like hear samhar tionnor falls some make one noise

SAMMON'S (14/34).   James Sammon, grocer, 167 N King St; Sammon's Horse
Repository was at No 35.
557.36   he tells me outside Sammon's in King Street

SAMOA.   Isl group, SW cen Pacific O; part of Polynesia. Btwn 1860 and 1889 the
isls were contested by Brit, Ger, and US; divided 1889 into Amer *S* and Western *S*
(Ger), the latter mandated to New Zealand 1919.
428.02   Palmwine breadfruit...Our people here in Samoanesia
?603.19   shadows, nocturnes or samoans

SAMPHIRE ISLAND.   Small isl just off N shore of Tralee Bay, 7 mi W of Tralee,
Co Kerry. There are no cliffs along this lowlying coast.
?601.11   cliffs...Longsome the samphire coast

SANDGATE.   St (in Newcastle, Eng) named in folk song, "As I came through Sandgate.../I heard a lassy cry/Oh, weel may the keel row/That my laddy's in" (Atherton).
?329.21   What battle of bragues on Sandgate where met the bobby mobbed
                his bibby

SANDHURST.   *S* Royal Military Coll, in Berks, Eng. Wellington Coll (public sch)
is nearby.
162.08   never quite got the sandhurst out of his eyes
347.09   Milesia [militia] asundurst...Woolwichleagues [Wellesley]

SANDYMOUNT (18/32).   Dist, SE Dub, on Dub Bay. In *U*, Stephen walks on *S*
Strand in the morning, Bloom watches Gerty MacDowell there in the afternoon.
?247.34   dandymount to a clearobscure
323.02   shandymound
601.26   S. Santamonta's [Stella Maris Ch, qv]

SAN FRANCISCO.   Hist Calif city and port, on the S side of the Golden Gate (qv).
Most Eur and Amer cities have Chinatowns (though Dub doesn't), but since the city
refs in *FW* 532–554 are so largely culled from the 11th *EB*, it may be relevant that
SF's Chinatown is the only one there described and indexed.
?533.06   the smallest shoenumber outside chinatins

SANITÀ, VIA.   St in Trieste, It. JJ and family lived at No 2 in 1919-1920.
?60.16   A wouldbe martyr, who is attending on sanit Asitas

SANTRY (17/39).   Dist, N Dub. The *S* Riv flows into Dub Bay at Raheny.
14.13   Primas was a santryman
142.15   Santry fields
310.13   cunduncing Naul and Santry
343.32   sintry and santry and sentry and suntry

SARAH PLACE (12/34).   Small st, now obliterated by housing estate, on N bank
of Liffey, just W of *S* Br (aka Island Br).
570.29   sairey's place
571.24   saarasplace

SARDINIA.   Large isl in Medit Sea W of S It penin. Orig settled by Phoenicians and Gks.

    221.32   Phenecian blends and Sourdanian doofpoosts [*sourd*, Fr "deaf"]

SATURN.   The 6th planet from the sun, unique in its "rings" and notable for its satellites. In order of distance from *S*, they are Janus (discovered 1966), Mimas, Enceladus, Tethys, Dione, Rhea (583.17), Titan (583.17), Hyperion, Japetus (583.18), and Phoebe (583.19). Phoebe is by far the most distant, and the last to be discovered (1898) when *FW* was publ. Until 1928, it was believed to be unique in the solar system for its retrograde motion (415.09).

Saturn was an anc It god; the Romans identified him with the Gk Cronus, who acc to legend came to It after he was deposed by his son Zeus, and ruled in the Golden Age. Many towns and places, esp mts, were named after *S*. The Roman festival of Saturnalia, noted for its license and gifts of dolls, which Varro believed represent earlier human sacrifices, began on Dec 19 (later Dec 17) and lasted for several days.

At 90.17 and 137.09, *S* is combined with Percy French's song, "Slattery's Mounted Foot."

90.17	the unfortunate class on Saturn's mountain fort
97.33	For the triduum of Saturnalia...in the Forum
137.09	round sadurn's mounted foot
264.05	two lunar eclipses...three saturnine settings
355.26	the sat of all the suns which are in the ring of his system
366.15	of Saturnay Eve
415.09	soturning...retrophoebia
415.14	*Satyr's Caudledayed Nice*
449.02	onsaturncast eyes in stellar attraction
494.10	occluded by Satarn's serpent ring system
583.17	jealousjoy titaning fear...rumour rhean...japets
583.19	Satyrdaysboost besets Phoebe's nearest

SAUL.   Town, 2 mi NE of Downpatrick, Co Down. Acc to legend, St Patrick built his 1st ch in Ire at *S. Sabhal Padraic*, Ir "Patrick's Barn."

    ?14.03   be me sawl

SAUNDERS' NEWS LETTER.   Dub newspaper, founded 1754 (renamed from *Esdaile's News Letter*, 1744), it became a daily in 1777 and lasted until 1879.

?369.28	Schelm the Pelman to write somewords to Senders
389.36	for the seek of Senders Newslaters
534.20	he is cunvesser to Saunter's Nocelettres

SAVILE ROW.   London st, near Piccadilly; famous for men's clothing and tailoring establishments.

320.07	civille row faction
353.04	In sobber sooth and in souber civiles?
353.09	In sabre tooth and sobre saviles!

SAXE-WEIMAR-EISENACH.   Form grand duchy, largest of the Thuringian states, SE of Prussia. Cap, Weimar; chief univ town, Jena.

    151.11   Levi-Brullo, F.D. of Sexe-Weiman-Eitelnaky

SAXONY.   The mod *S* (Ger, *Sachsen*) in E Ger is quite distinct from the earlier *S* in NW Ger, whose very name disappeared after the 12th cent. The earlier Saxons were a Teutonic seafaring people occupying Schleswig and offshore isls. In the 5th cent, under Hengest and Horsa (see *Census*) they aided the Britons to repel the northern Picts and Scots, then settled down and took over. The Angli do not seem to have been distinct from the Saxons by the time of the invasion of Brit, although Bede refers to the kingdom of Angulus as well as to the territories of the Saxons and the Jutes. Alfred, "rex Anglorum Saxonum," united all the kingdoms in 886. See *Anglo-Saxon Kingdoms*.

FW conflates the invasions of Brit with the invasions of Ire (esp 15.35, 16.07ff), although the Saxons, Angli, and Jutes never reached the coast of Ire. "Saxon" is a pejorative Ir term for "Englishman."

15.35	Comestipple Sacksoun
16.07	You phonio saxo?...'Tis a Jute
?22.35	bullbraggin soxangloves
58.24	saxonlootie...cockaleak...Coldstream. Guards [Eng, Wales, Scot]
85.25	old plomansch Mayo of the Saxons
88.22	Saxon
175.12	*Not yet have the Sachsen and Judder on the Mound of a Word made Warre*
281.L4	*A saxum shillum for the sextum*
363.35	hintering influences from an angelsexonism
411.30	Down with the Saozon ruze!
495.27	noblesse of leechers at his Saxontannery
532.10	Allenglisches Angleslachsen is spoken
565.35	the pickts are hacking the saxums [*saxum*, Lat "rock"]
600.24	Saxenslyke our anscessers thought...Anglesen, free of juties...white alfred

SCALDBROTHER'S HOLE   (14/34).   A subterranean bldg once in Oxmantown (qv), referred to by Stanihurst; named after a thief who lived there until he was caught and hanged. The entrance was from "Bailey's Timber Yard."

99.13	antichill cloak...found nigh Scaldbrothar's Hole
223.19	Arrest thee, scaldbrother!

SCALP, THE.   Picturesque defile on the Dundrum-Enniskerry Rd, S of Dub.

497.06	scalpjaggers and houthhunters
590.26	The nape of his nameshielder's scalp...drummed all he dun

SCANDINAVIA.   Anc name for the land of the Norsemen, incl the *S* Penin and the present Den. For Turgesius the Viking, who first landed in Ire, *ca* 830, see *Census*.

47.21	the brave son of Scandiknavery
254.33	in all the aisles of Skaldignavia
323.20	the wholeabelongd of Skunkinabory
324.27	the allexpected depression over Schiumdinebbia
464.32	Tower Geesyhus [in context of Eur countries]
510.28	the depredations of Scandalknivery

SCATTERY ISLAND.   Isl in the Shannon estuary, off Kilrush, Co Clare; ruins of the Monastery of St Seanán (6th cent). Repeatedly attacked by marauding Scands in the 9th and 10th cents. Pebbles from *S* were believed to protect against shipwreck. *Inis-Cathaige*, Ir "island of Cathach" – a demon exorcised by St Seanán.

86.24	gathering...of a scattery kind...ballybricken
?343.06	scattering giant's hail over the curseway

SCEAUX.   SW suburb of Paris. The park (form of the chateau) contains the Allée de la Duchesse.

?229.33	the suchess of sceaunonsceau

?233.10 frenge...such as touch with show and show

SCHMALKALDEN. City, E Ger, where in 1531 Lutheran princes formed the League of *S* against Charles V; it lasted until 1547, when Charles defeated its leaders and destroyed its power.

83.35 schmallkalled the treatyng

SCOTCH HOUSE, THE (16/34). Public house on Burgh Quay. In Dub pubs, the "snug" is a private partitioned alcove.

140.03 The Dotch House
454.33 our snug eternal retribution's reward (the scorchhouse)

SCOTLAND. Ironically, its name derives from Ir invaders (Skotia or Scotia, anc name of Ire). Anc names Alba (in Ir records this was sometimes applied to whole of Brit), Albania (generally the region N of the Clyde). Ger *Schottland*, Fr *Ecosse*. Includes the isls of the Hebrides, Orkneys, and Shetlands (qqv).

Orig occupied by Picts before the 1st cent Roman invasion, by the 5th cent *S* included the northern Pictish kingdom, a Scots kingdom in the W highlands, and in the S the kingdom of Strathclyde and part of Anglo-Saxon Northumbria. Picts conquered Scots, 9th cent. Eng wars resulted in independence after Bannockburn (1314); united with Eng 1707. See also *Ireland: Scotia*.

43.29 the united states of Scotia Picta
66.11 Letters Scotch, Limited
93.03 English...scotfree...britgits
108.15 Bruce...Scotch spider
?114.25 disheen of voos from Dalbania
163.08 Caseous, the brutherscutch
204.06 scoutsch breeches...pickts
206.33 butterscatch and turfentide
210.27 picked and scotched
245.28 Marely quean of Scuts
352.01 scutt's rudes unreformed
366.27 Houtes...upkurts and scotchem
387.05 scotobrit sash
391.04 Johnny of the clan of the Dougals, the poor Scuitsman
404.21 the scotsmost public and climate
412.03 scotographically
422.06 seeing Scotch snakes
?463.24 red in Rossya, white in Alba
487.15 a half Scotch and pottage
510.13 from Gunner Shotland to Guinness Scenography
518.21 Picturshirts and Scutticules
521.11 scotty pictail
537.29 two punt scotch
565.35 pickts are hacking the saxums
593.13 albas Temoram
600.22 scainted to Vitalba...Saxenslyke...Anglesen
619.11 pigs and scuts

SCOTLAND YARD. The Criminal Investigation Dept of the London Metropolitan Police; orig in Gt Scotland Yard, Whitehall, it has moved twice since 1891 but remains "the Yard" wherever it goes.

97.35 the Yardstated

124.08   Yard inquiries pointed out
374.25   Darby's in the yard...the whispering peeler

SCOTTISH WIDOWS' FUND AND LIFE ASSURANCE SOCIETY (15/34).   Its Dub
offices were at 41 Westmoreland St; named in Rowntree's *Poverty*, along with Hearts
of Oak Life Assurance Co (qv).
577.22   to Hearths of Oak from Skittish Widdas

SCULLABOGUE HOUSE.   At foot of Carrickbyrne, 2 mi SE of Old Ross, Co Wexford. *Scealbóg*, Ir "piece of kindling."
In the 1798 rebellion, 35 men were massacred at *S* by the insurgents and their
100 women and children were burned alive when the barn in which they were imprisoned was set on fire after the defeat of the insurgents in the battle of New Ross.
528.37   Ye've as much skullabogue cheek on you now as would boil a cal-
dron of kalebrose

SCULLOGUE GAP.   Btwn Mt Leinster and Blackstairs Mt, on the border btwn Co
Carlow and Co Wexford. *Scológ*, Ir "farm laborer."
?398.03   beeves and scullogues, churls and vassals

SCYLLA AND CHARYBDIS.   *S* was the legendary monster opposite the whirlpool
of *C*, supposedly in the Straits of Messina, btwn Sicily and It. The ref is to the "Scylla
and Charybdis" chap of *U*; as Bloom leaves the National Library, he passes btwn Stephen and Buck Mulligan as Ulysses escaped the peril of *S* and *C* in *Odyssey* XII.
229.14   Skilly and Carubdish

SEAFORTH HIGHLANDERS.   This famous Brit regt is named, not for a place, but
for the last Earl of Seaforth (d 1781), who raised the orig regt, later the 2nd Battalion of the Seaforths. The band of the 2nd played in College Park, TCD on 16 June
1904, and the viceroy hears "My Girl's a Yorkshire Girl" as his cortège passes (*U*
250/254).
39.22   while the Seaforths was making the colleenbawl

SEAPOINT (22/29).   Res area btwn Blackrock and Monkstown, SE of Dub. The
name survives mainly in *S* Ave.
129.24   Seapoint, Quayhowth
588.15   Following idly up to seepoint
594.34   a turnkeyed trot to Seapoint

SÉGUR.   Paris telephone exchange. In the late 1920's, JJ's telephone no was Ségur
95.20 (*Letters* III, 167).
233.31   zingo, zango, segur ["cinque-O, cinque-O, Ségur"]
501.08   Hello! Are you Cigar shank and Wheat? ["Ségur cinquante-huit"]

SEINE RIVER.   Riv, N Fr, the Liffey of Paris; Lat, *Amnis Sequana*. JJ called it
"Anna Sequana" (*Letters* I, 230).
208.17   her...joseph was sequansewn and teddybearlined
213.15   senne eye or erewone
?277.18   And Sein annews

SEKHET HETEP.   The Egyptian version of the Elysian Fields, or "Field of Peace,"
the abode of Horus and Set, supposed to be N of Egypt. "Sekhet Aaru," "Field of
Reeds," formed one part of *SH*.
360.16   Secret Hookup
415.34   Seekit Hatup...Suckit Hotup!

418.06   sekketh rede
454.35   Seekit headup!
530.22   Sackerson! Hookup!

SELFRIDGE'S.   London dept store in Oxford St.
137.34   peddles...selfridgeousness
497.36   to himsilf so silfrich

SELMA.   Fingal's royal res in Morven, in Macpherson's poems. In *Dar-Thula*, it is a
cas in Ulster, which Campbell conjectured as on the shore of Belfast Lough btwn Belfast and Carrickfergus.
254.31   she's a quine of selm ashaker

SELSKAR.   Abbey founded in late 12th cent near W gate of Wexford City. The
name is a corruption of "St Sepulchre." Henry II did penance there in Lent, 1172,
for the death of Becket.
FW's association of *S* with the bluebells and periwinkles of the Quinet sentence
is obscure. The conflation with *elskere*, Dan "lovers," is perhaps more relevant. It is
said in Wexford that the bells of *S* Abbey were taken by Cromwell's soldiers to Liverpool, where they still are in a River St ch.
For Selskar Gunn, see *Census*.
?28.26   *Les Loves of Selskar et Pervenche*...There'll be bluebells blowing in
salty sepulchres [*sel*, Fr "salt"]
388.06   So mulct per wenche is Elsker woed
?580.18   Pervinca calling, Soloscar hears
?626.19   while blubles blows there'll still be sealskers

SENDAI.   City, N Honshu, Japan. Also the Sendai R (*Sendaigawa*).
196.19   What was it he did a tail at all on Animal Sendai? [+ *Anima Mundi*]

SERBONIAN BOG.   Anc lake and swamp btwn Suez and Nile delta, proverbial for
hopeless inextricability. Milton, *Paradise Lost*, ii, 592: "A gulf profound as that Serbonian bog/ Betwixt Damiata and Mount Casius old..."
539.25   hole of Serbonian bog

SERENDIP (SERENDIB).   Form name of Ceylon (now Sri Lanka). The word "ser-
endipity" was coined from H Walpole's fairy tale "The Three Princes of Serendip."
191.03   you...semi-semitic serendipitist

SERETH (SIRET) RIVER.   Trib of Danube R, flows from Carpathian Mts through
Romania.
469.14   my olty mutther, Sereth Maritza

SERINGAPATAM.   Town in Mysore, S Ind; form cap of Mysore and site of palace
of Tippoo Sahib, killed in siege by Brit, 1799.
The Mahratta princes (but Tippoo Sahib was not a Mahratta) were called "lords
of the umbrella."
?344.30   solongopatom
492.23   1001 Ombrilla Street, Syringa padham, Alleypulley

SERPENTINE.   (1) Although the long pond which curves from one end of the Zoo
in Phoenix Park to the other resembles the *S* lake in Hyde Park, London, it has no
name, official or pop. The ave of elms laid out by Lord Chesterfield along the line of
the present Main Rd was serpentine.   (2) *S* Ave (also *S* Rd and *S* Park) in Sandymount, SE Dub (18/32). The register of the "Academy of St Thomas," Univ Coll,

shows JJ's address in 1901 as "60 Sandy Serpentine Avenue, Sandymount"; there's no other record that JJ roomed there.   (3) In Clongowes Wood Coll, the *S* Gallery leads to the Rector's office; in *A Portrait*, Stephen Dedalus follows it to the office.

    80.06   filthdump near the Serpentine in Phornix Park

   ?121.20   strange exotic serpentine [the letter "S"]

   ?206.34   turfentide and serpenthyme

   365.07   any old cerpaintime...virginial water

SEVASTOPOL.   City and port on bay of Akiar in Crimea, USSR; port built as Russ naval base; named 1784 by Catherine II: *Sevastos*, Gk "august" + *polis*. In the Crimean War, the siege of *S* by the Allies lasted 322 days before it fell, 11 Sept 1855.

   ?104.06   *Augusta Angustissimost for Old Seabeastius' Salvation*

   338.14   Sea vaast a pool!

   365.09   a lieberretter sebaiscopal

SEVEN DIALS.   The intersection of 7 sts in Holborn, E of Shaftesbury Ave, London, an area once notorious for vice, crime, and balladmongers. The pillar with 6 sundials was moved to Weybridge Green in 1773, but the area retains the name.

   551.32   my sevendialled changing charties...Threadneedles

SEVEN SISTERS.   (1) Rd in Tottenham, NE London, named after famous old elm trees in one of Tottenham's greens, removed 1840.   (2) The 7 yew trees in the vall of the Skell R, Yorks, under which lived the Cistercian monks of St Mary's Abbey while they were building Fountain Abbey, 3 mi SW of Ripon, in 1132 AD. That's right, 1132.

    Other "Seven Sisters" prob not alluded to are the Pleiades; the 7 cannon used by the Scots in the battle of Flodden; the chalk cliffs btwn Beachy Head and Cuckmere Haven on the Sussex coast, Eng; and a circle of 6 (!) stones in Lissyviggeen, Co Kerry, 2 mi E of Killarney.

   248.35   Seven Sisters is my nighbrood

   579.33   cripples gait...manplanting seven sisters...warmwooed...scrubbs

SEVEN WONDERS OF THE ANCIENT WORLD.   This list of anc tourist attractions circulated in several versions during the Alexandrian era. Earliest extant list is 2nd cent by Antipater of Sidon; also a slightly different list by Philo of Byzantium. The Pyramids are the oldest of the Wonders and the only ones to survive into mod times. See *Babylon, Colossus of Rhodes, Gardens of Semiramis, Mausoleum at Halicarnassus, Olympia, Pyramids, Temple of Artemis (Diana) at Ephesus.*

   261.09   conned the cones and meditated the mured and pondered the pensils and ogled the olymp and delighted in her dianaphous and cacchinated behind his culosses, before a mosoleum

   553.09   with chopes pyramidous and mousselimes and beaconphires and colossets and pensilled turisses for the busspleaches of the summiramies and esplanadas and statuesques and templeogues

SEVILLE.   City, SW Sp. Marmalade (223.08) is made from *S* oranges. Dub's *S* Pl runs from Amiens St to Sheriff St, just NE of Amiens St Sta; the origin of its name is unknown.

   223.06   Rose, Sevilla nor Citronelle

SHACKLETON, GEORGE, AND SONS, LTD   (13/33).   Flour millers, corn merchants, 35 James St. The co also owned the Anna Liffey mills in Lucan (*U* 235/239).

   317.15   Shackleton Sulten!...ham

   392.33   Shackleton's brown loaf

393.01   the smell of Shakeletin
397.17   bowl of brown shackle and milky
?512.28   shekleton's my fortune...I hurdley chew you

"SHAMROCK."   Around the turn of the cent, Sir Thomas Lipton, the tea magnate, repeatedly and unsuccessfully attempted to win the America Cup for yacht races with a succession of boats, all named "Shamrock." The allusion conflates these gallant failures with the arrival in Ire of Strongbow, the Norman Earl of Pembroke, brought to Ire by Dermot MacMurrough, the King of Leinster, who handed over his daughter Eva in marriage to Strongbow.
288.15   off Lipton's strongbowed launch, the *Lady Eva*

SHANAVON.   Acc to P W Joyce, *S* or Shanowen is a common local name for small rivs, esp in S Ire. *Seán Abhainn*, Ir "old river." The allusion refers to Anna Liffey, conflated with the Shan van Vocht, perhaps the Shannon R, and an echo of "Die Wacht am Rhein."
?372.30   The Shanavan Wacht

SHANDON.   An area on the N side of Cork City, noted for the bells of St Ann's Ch (CI) and the poem by "Father Prout": " 'Tis the bells of Shandon/That sound so grand on/The pleasant waters of the River Lee." There are 8 bells, each of which sounds at the end of 141.07.
140.22   such good old chimes
141.05   A bell a bell on Shalldoll Steepbell...Shand...gon...*Shandeepen... Aequalllllllll!*
393.27   inside their poor old Shandon bellbox
483.06   'Tis the bells of scandal that gave tune to grumble over him

SHANGHAI.   Main port of cen China, in prov of Kiang-su; on W bank of Hwang-p'u R, 12 mi from its outlet in estuary of Yangtsze R.
398.28   on the praze savohole shanghai
485.24   be shanghaied to him

SHANNON RIVER.   The longest (230 mi) riv in Ire, it rises in Co Cavan and flows S and W to the Atlantic O.
211.09   for Nancy Shannon a Tuami brooch
213.34   that same brooch of the Shannons
451.14   I'd axe the channon...liffey...annyblack water

SHARON.   The fertile plain of Pal btwn Joppa and Mt Carmel. The "Rose of Sharon" of *Song of Solomon* 2:1 has been identified with various flowers, such as the crocus and narcissus.
34.29   Rosasharon
?340.27   *roshashanaral*
526.28   Corrack-on-Sharon, County Rosecarmon
620.04   Rosensharonals

SHEELIN, LOUGH.   Lake at junction of Cos Cavan, Meath, and Westmeath, S of Cavan Town. "Lough Sheeling" is the air to T Moore's "Come, Rest In This Bosom" (527.04).
526.33   Lough Shieling's love

SHELBOURNE HOTEL   (16/33).   On Stephen's Green, N; where in *U* Bloom buys black drawers from Mrs Dandrade (*U* 158/160, 524/536). It has long been Anglo-Ir, elegant.

?134.19   softclad shellborn

SHELBOURNE ROAD   (17/32).   In SE Dub. When JJ left his father's house at 7
St Peter's Terr, Phibsborough, in March 1904, he lived until Sept in a furnished room
at 60 *S* Rd. *S* is also the name of one of the 1st Association football (soccer) teams
formed in Dub, in the 1890's (377.07).
    377.07   The Shallburn Shock
    421.04   60 Shellburn

SHELLY BANKS   (19/33).   Old name of shallows in Dub Bay, off the S Wall beyond the Pigeonhouse.
    ?231.12   feastking of shellies by googling Lovvey

SHELMARTIN   (17/36).   Ave (also Terr) in Fairview, NE Dub, named after Sheilmartin on Howth (qv).
    354.16   *S. E. Morehampton makes leave to E. N. Sheilmartin*

SHEOL.   Hebrew "Hell," the afterworld.
    78.10   sheol om sheol
    83.08   thorntree of sheol
    177.10   Sheols of houris in chems upon divans
    228.17   sheolmastress
    228.33   gheol ghiornal [+ John Mitchell's *Jail Journal*]
    449.27   till heoll's hoerrisings

SHETLAND ISLANDS.   Archipelago off N Scot, 50 mi NE of Orkney Isls; known
for its miniature horses, or ponies. Aka Zetland. The Marquess of Zetland was Lord-
Lt of Ire from 1889 to 1892.
    ?510.13   Now from Gunner Shotland
    544.01   marquess of Zetland
    554.06   piebald shjelties

SHILLELAGH.   Vill, S Co Wicklow, on *S* Riv; it gave its name to the blackthorn
club. In the fight that breaks out in the ballad "Finnegan's Wake," "Each side in war
did soon engage;/'Twas woman to woman and man to man;/Shillelagh law was all the
rage,/And a bloody ruction soon began."
    25.15   our supershillelagh...manument
    114.12   shillelagh as an aid to calligraphy
    361.20   black thronguards from the County Shillelagh
    511.15   she laylylaw was all their rage

SHINAR.   The city and tower of Babel (qv) were built on a "plain in the land of
Shinar," *Gen* 11:2. Aka Sumer, the anc name of Babylonia. Cf *U* 672/688.
    ?10.06   hinndoo Shimar Shin
    ?10.18   the cursigan Shimar Shin
    ?320.03   the shines he cuts, shinar, the screeder
    504.06   In Summerian sunshine...Cimmerian shudders

SHIP HOTEL AND TAVERN   (16/34).   It was at 5 Lwr Abbey St. In *U*, Stephen
is to meet Buck Mulligan there (*U* 23/24), but doesn't.
    63.25   Ramitdown's ship hotel
    460.08   just there beside the Ship...poor fool's circuts of lovemountjoy square

SHIP ST   (15/33).   *S* St, Gt, runs S, *S* St, Little, runs W, from the SW corner of the
Castle. The name is from anc *Vicus Ovium*, "Sheep St."

?148.10   the boy in sheeps' lane knows that
?481.06   ere bawds plied in Skiffstrait

SHOOLBRED'S.   London dept store of James Shoolbred and Co, in Tottenham Court Rd; ceased business in 1935, bldg demolished 1936.
127.11   to the shoolbred he acts whiteley

SIAM.   Country in SE Asia, now Thailand. *FW* is interested only in the orig Siamese twins, Chang and Eng (1814-74), like Shem and Shaun a musichall pair.
66.20   that siamixed twoatalk
108.26   Siam, Hell or Tophet
235.30   Seemyease Sister, Tabitha
329.02   suomease pair and singlette
344.08   *scimmianised twinge*
354.24   samuraised twimbs
408.27   swimmyease bladdhers
411.13   so I am
425.16   soroquise the Siamanish
425.22   soamheis brother

SIANG-CHANG-KIANG.   Riv (*kiang*) in cen China; flows into Po-yang lake in Kiang-si prov. The Siang-kiang is a riv farther W, which flows into the great Tung-t'ing lake in Hunan prov.
119.24   siangchang hongkong sansheneul

SIBERIA.   N USSR btwn Ural Mts and Pacific O. The Trans-Siberian rlwy was built 1891-1906.
55.20   a pullwoman of our first transhibernian...intouristing
297.05   You've spat your shower like a son of Sibernia
424.09   Tiberia is waiting on you...Chaka
567.35   Polo north will beseem Sibernian

SICILY.   Largest isl in the Medit Sea, W of extreme S point of It penin; the ball to Italy's boot.
354.14   *hurdly gurdly Cicilian concertone*
464.28   the Boot and Ball

SICK AND INDIGENT ROOMKEEPERS SOCIETY   (15/34).   Founded 1790 as a philanthropic relief soc, its offices are still at 2 Palace St, off Dame St.
6.04   ville's indigenous romekeepers

SIDLESHAM.   Town, SE Eng, S of Chichester, Sussex, in the Hundred of Manhood (qv). Prof Clive Hart discovered that Earwickers have long lived there and are buried in the local churchyard. JJ may have visited it on a summer holiday in 1923.
30.07   the Earwickers of Sidlesham in the Hundred of Manhood
98.05   hundred of manhood...sidleshomed

SIEMENS SCHUCKERT.   Ger electrical equipment firm; it constructed the power sta of the Shannon hydroelectric works at Ardnacrusha (qv), and *FW* credits it also with the lighthouses at Arklow and Wicklow (245.08, 549.18) and the electrification of Dub (or the Dub tram system?) (?138.13).
138.13   a fritz at his switch
245.08   Lights...Hanoukan's lamp...arcglow's seafire siemens lure
485.07   Or in alleman: Suck at!
549.18   Wykinloeflare, by Arklow's sapphire siomen's lure and Wexterford's hook and crook lights

SIHL RIVER.   Zurich's 2nd riv (the 1st is the Limmat, qv). The Sihlpost, Zurich's main post office, is on its banks.
>   75.04   sigilposted...brievingbust [*Brief*, Ger "letter"]
>   200.22   sillypost
>   200.24   legging a jig or so on the sihl

SILKEBORG.   City in Jutland, Den. Butter churns from Paasch and *S* have long been widely used in Ire.
>   163.30   the Silkebjorg tyrondynamon machine [*tyros*, Gk "cheese"]

SILURIA.   Area on Eng-Welsh border once inhabited by the Silures, a Brit tribe. The Silurian geological period followed the Ordovician (see *Ordovices*).
>   51.29   haul us back to the craogs and bryns of the Silurian Ordovices

SIMPSON'S HOSPITAL   (16/27).   Balinteer Rd, Dundrum. It was founded in 1781 on the W side of Gt Brunswick St for "poor, decayed, blind, and gouty men."
>   43.07   Simpson's on the Rocks
>   211.24   symposium's syrup for decayed and blind and gouty Gough

SIMPSON'S-ON-THE-STRAND.   London restaurant, 100 Strand, the tourist's dream of Olde England.
>   43.07   Simpson's on the Rocks

SING SING.   Famous pris, 30 mi N of NYC, in Ossining (name of town changed from *SS*, 1901), NY.
>   485.28   he hung! Tsing tsing!
>   601.18   Botany Bay [prison colony]...singsing music

SIRIUS.   Star in constellation Canis Major; aka Canicula, the Dog Star. The brightest star in the sky. *Seirios*, Gk "glowing." It was the subject of many Babylonian, Egyptian (*Sotis*, 512.07), Gk, and Roman myths. For the Egyptians, its rising marked the beginning of their new year, called by the Romans *annus canarius*, the canicular year.
>   194.14   by the tremours of Thundery and Ulerin's dogstar
>   426.24   the sirious pointstand of Charley's Wain
>   512.07   Such is zodisfaction
>   512.36   solarly...the canicular year
>   513.01   Siriusly and selenely sure [Selene, Gk personification of the moon]
>   ?573.30   the depravities...of Canicula, the deceased wife of Mauritius

SIR PATRICK DUN'S HOSPITAL   (17/33).   Grand Canal St. Founded 1792; present bldg, 1808.
>   40.35   Sir Patrick Dun's

SITRIC ROAD   (14/34).   St, just N of Arbour Hill, parallel to Olaf Rd, *not* btwn Olaf Rd and Ivar St. Sitric was the legendary founder of Waterford.
>   12.32   Olaf's...Ivor's...and Sitric's place's between them

SKEPHUBBLE.   Tnld, par of Finglas, bar of Nethercross, N Co Dub; in Fingal. P W Joyce explains the name as "place of assembly" – rather the opposite of "skidoo."
>   503.16   skidoo and skephumble

SKERRIES.   Fishing vill and coast resort 18 mi N of Dub; its anc name was Holmpatrick – also the name of St Patrick's Isl, just off the coast. *Skjaer*, Nor "rock."
>   ?31.31   roadside tree the lady Holmpatrick planted
>   89.19   Lindendelly, coke or skilllies

316.12   bowing both ways with the bents and skerries

SKIBBEREEN.   Town, SW Co Cork. Its newspaper, the *Skibbereen Eagle*, warned the Czar of Russia that its eye was on him (*U* 137/139). JJ called *S* "the looniest town in Ireland" (*Letters* III, 428).

210.19   Val from Skibereen
302.13   Skibbering's eagles
315.34   Skibbereen has common inn

SKIDOO.   Tnld, par of Swords, bar of Nethercross, N Co Dub; in Fingal.
503.16   skidoo and skephumble

SKINNER'S ALLEY   (14/33).   Now Newmarket St, btwn Newmarket and the Coombe. The site of St Luke's (CI) is just E. Noted only for the "Aldermen of Skinner's Alley," a convivial soc claiming descent from the Dub Corporators who met in this obscure st when deposed by James II. Not to be confused with Skinner Row, the med st of the curriers, now (since 1833) Christchurch Pl.

43.03   oblate father from Skinner's Alley
532.32   Skinner's circusalley

SKIVINI, COURT OF.   NPN. When London became a municipality or "commune" in 1191 AD, it was governed by a mayor and 12 échevins or "skivini" who formed the "Court of Skivini."

536.31   Recorder at Thing of all Things, or court of Skivinis

SLADE SCHOOL.   Independent sch of art in Oxford, Eng.
165.36   slade off...plase to be seated and smile

SLANE.   Vill, Co Meath, on Boyne R, btwn Drogheda and Navan. The scene of many battles, from the 1st Viking attack in 948 to the Battle of the Boyne in 1690. There was a coll in *S* from 1512-1723. St Patrick lit his Paschal fire on *S* Hill, N of vill, on Easter Eve.

JJ's 1st draft of 274.29 reads "preparatory of Slane..." On this slight evidence, refs to Clane which might be conflated with *S* are included below.

?212.25   Throw us your hudson soap for the honour of Clane!
274.29   Dagobert is in Clane's clean hometown prepping up his prepueratory
509.36   pantoloogions...first perpersonal puetry...Cleaned
609.34   cabrattlefield of slaine

SLIEVE BLOOM.   Mt range, Cos Offaly and Laois. The Nore R flows along the S and SE borders in an easterly direction, then turns SE away from the range; it "takes leave of Bloom" 2 mi SW of Mountrath, Co Laois.

203.10   not where the Nore takes lieve of Bloem

SLIEVE LEAGUE.   Mt, Co Donegal. *Sliabh Liag*, Ir "mt of stones."
?273.05   peace!² Live, league of lex, nex and the mores!

SLIEVE MISH.   (1) Mt, Co Antrim, where St Patrick tended swine as a boy slave of Milchu (see *Census*). Aka Slemish. *Sliabh Mis*, Ir "mt of Mis."   (2) Mts, Co Kerry, base of Dingle Penin.

131.01   Mount of Mish, Mell of Moy
241.16   A mish, holy balm of seinsed myrries, he is as good as a mountain...
            Master Milchku
290.18   to mount miss (the wooeds of Fogloot!)
478.34   The woods of fogloot! O mis padredges!

SLIEVENAMOND.   Mt, Co Tipperary. The ref is to Charles Kickham's poem, "She lived beside the Anner,/At the foot of Slievenamond."
    503.31   Annar. At the ford of Slievenamond

SLIEVE SNACHT (SNAGHT).   2 mts in Co Donegal: one in Derryveagh Mts W of Letterkenny, the other NE of Buncrana. *Sliabh-sneachta*, Ir "snow mt."
    ?233.33   a skarp snakk
    502.04   By snaachtha clocka...hilly-and-even zimalayars

SLIGO.   Co, Connacht prov, NW Ire. *S* Town was the home of Yeats, and he is buried nearby. Baronies: Carbury, Coolavin, Corran, Leyny, Tireragh, Tirerrill.
    141.02   Sligo's sleek but Galway's grace
    577.35   blump for slogo slee!
    595.16   sly goings

SLUTSEND (15/37).   Aka West Farm. Tnld, par of Glasnevin, bar of Coolock, N Co Dub; in Fingal. Roughly the part of Prospect Cem, Glasnevin, S of Finglas Rd.
    503.14   Slutsend with Stockins

SLYNE, W, AND CO (15/33).   Draper's shop at 71 Grafton St, around the turn of the cent.
    548.27   the peak of Pim's and Slyne's and Sparrow's

SLYNE HEAD.   Promontory, SW of Clifden, Co Galway; the W-most part of mainland Ire N of the Shannon. "Slynagollow" is not an actual place-name. O Hehir explains it as *Ceann Léime na Gaillimhe*, ie, Leap (Slyne) Head of Galway.
    580.34   Slynagollow

SMETHWICK.   W suburb of Birmingham, Eng.
    481.21   Smithwick, Rhonnda, Kaledon [Eng, Wales, Scot]

SMOCK ALLEY THEATRE (15/34).   Built 1662 in Orange St, later Smock Alley, now site of ch of SS Michael and John (1815), Exchange St. Despite temporary interruptions for repair (1671-91) and rebuilding (1735), it was the principal theater in Ire for over a cent, until it closed in 1788.
    60.32   S.S. Smack and Olley's
    105.27   *From Abbeygate to Crowalley...Smocks*
    147.32   up Smock Alley

SMYRNA.   Now called Izmir, city and port on Meles R and Aegean Sea, W Turk. In anc times it was first Aeolian, then Ionian; both peoples claimed it as the birthplace of Homer, known as "son of the Meles."
    129.23   pigeonheim to this homer, Smerrnion
    481.21   humeplace...Smithwick

SNAEFELL, MT.   (1) Highest (2034 ft) peak on Isle of Man.   (2) Snaefellsjökull: mt and glacier, NW of Reykjavik, Iceland. Snaefellsness, in W Iceland, figures in the Eyrbyggla Saga.
    552.35   And wholehail, snaeffell, dreardrizzle or sleetshowers of blessing

SNOWDON, MT.   Mt, N Wales, the highest (3560 ft) in Wales.
    205.21   the snee that snowdon his hoaring hair

SNOWTON CASTLE.   Already in ruins by the early 19th cent, it stands in Co Meath just across the Delvin R from the cas at Naul (qv). The other names in the foxhunt route are all tnlds, but there is no *S* or Snowtown Tnld.

622.34   Heathtown, Harbourstown, Snowtown

SNUGBOROUGH.   (1) *S* Ho, off Vernon Ave in Clontarf area; in Fingal. I don't know whether it was yellow.   (2) Tnld, par of Castleknock, bar of Castleknock, N Co Dub; in Fingal.   (3) Tnld, par of Balgriffan, bar of Coolock, N Co Dub; in Fingal.   (4) *S* Ho, Rathfarnham; *S* Ho, Donnybrook, just W of Simmonscourt Ho; *S* Ho near Arklow, Co Wicklow; *S* Br, near Donard, Co Wicklow.
    503.14   Yellowhouse of Snugsborough
    565.36   it's snugger to burrow abed

SOCIETY FOR THE PROPAGATION OF CHRISTIAN KNOWLEDGE (S.P.C.K.). Brit missionary organization.
    ?23.04   spch spck
    80.20   Allhighest sprack for krischnians...propagana fidies

SOCIETY ISLANDS.   Polynesian isl group, Pacific O; named by James Cook, whose 1769 expedition was sponsored by the Royal Soc. Fr protectorate after 1843. Divided into Leeward Isles, incl Bora Bora, and Windward Isles, incl Tahiti. Coconuts are indigenous, monkey nuts aren't. "Drink the monkey" means to drink spirits from a coconut shell.
    337.29   hopes your hahititahiti licks the mankey nuts
    416.34   the Boraborayellers, blohablasting tegolhuts [+ the "Bora," Adriatic wind like the mistral]
    602.02–.05   Milenesia...leeward...windward

SODOM.   See *Cities of the Plain.*

SOFIA.   City, cap of Bulgaria. Tcherna Djamia (Russ, *Chernya Dyamya*), the "Black Mosque" of *S*, at different times has served as a pris and a ch.
    534.28   Strangler of soffiacated green parrots!
    537.24   Blanchette Brewster from Cherna Djamja, Blawlawnd-via-Brigstow

SOHO.   The cosmopolitan dist of cen London, allegedly named from the hunting cry once heard in *S* fields, where hares were coursed.
    36.30   every living sohole
    ?426.04   Rock me julie but I will soho!
    ?478.30   I am sohohold!

SOLFERINO.   Vill, SE Lombardy, N It. Site of indecisive battle 24 June 1859 btwn Fr and Sardinians under Napoleon III and Austrians under Emperor Francis Joseph.
    9.25   solphereens in action

SORRENTO (26/26).   *S* Rd runs SE from the cen of Dalkey (qv) to Vico Rd (qv), at *S* Pt, orig called "Land's End" (qv). The Clifton Sch, Dalkey, where JJ taught for 4 months in 1904, was on *S* Rd.
    246.24   Educande of Sorrento...Vico's road
    497.14   Vico, Mespil Rock and Sorrento

SOUTH AMERICA.   In *FW*, *SA* is the almost forgotten continent; the Amazon is one of the handmaidens of Anna Liffey, and there are scattered refs to Buenos Aires, Rio de Janeiro, the Andes, Putumayo (because of Roger Casement), and Tierra del Fuego (qqv), but the refs are fewer than to any other continent, and there seems to be no systematic attempt to incorporate its countries, cities, or geographical features.
    117.25   he dined off sooth american
    171.35   a short cut to Caer Fere, Soak Amerigas
    387.02   Suid African cattleraiders...tiara dullfuoco

SOUTH CIRCULAR ROAD (SCR).   Orig intended to mark the S boundary of Dub, like the NCR to the N, it runs from Island Br on the W through Kilmainham and Dolphin's Barn to Heytesbury St. The E section, along the Grand Canal to Ringsend, is no longer called SCR.

    256.32   N.C.R. and S.C.R.
    295.31   our twain of doubling bicirculars
    310.07   circumcentric megacycles
    321.13   east circular route
    547.33   ringstresse
    553.30   my nordsoud circulums

SOUTH CITY MARKET (15/33).   The block bounded by S Gt George's St, Exchequer St, Drury St, and Fade St. The Market was opened in 1881, almost entirely destroyed by fire, 27 Aug 1892.

    306.16   the Great Fire at the South City Markets

SOUTHEND-ON-SEA.   Resort town, N shore of Thamesmouth, Essex, Eng.

    291.26   Sexsex home, Somehow-at-Sea

SOUTHERN CROSS.   Constellation of the S hemisphere, aka Crux or Crux Australis. Like other constellations invisible from N latitudes, it was not named until the 17th cent.

    471.12   blessing hes sthers with the sign of the southern cross

SOUTHWARK.   The area on S bank of the Thames, London, across from the City. Also a st and cath.

    578.30   Norwood's Southwalk

SPAIN.   State, form kingdom, SW Eur, sharing with Port the Iberian Penin. Under Roman administration (before Augustus), S was divided into 2 provs, Citherior ("hither") S in the N (158.11) and Ulterior ("further") S in the S. The population of N cen S was called "Celtiberian" by anc writers; they were noted as the most warlike people in S, frequently rebelling against their Roman masters.

    50.20   the queen of Iar-Spain
    78.25   From both Celtiberian camps
    92.01   had broken exthro Castilian
    144.13   Soso do todas. Such is Spanish
    158.11   citherior spiane
    180.11   sponiard's digger
    213.34   a family in Spain
    233.35   baskly as your cheesechalk cow cudd spanich [echoes "Il parle français comme une vache espagnole"]
    263.13   Hispano-Cathayan-Euxine
    263.13   Castillian-Emeratic-Hebridian
    263.14   Espanol-Cymric-Helleniky
    346.03   *the spinach ruddocks...Hebeneros*
    348.30   *sunny Espionia*
    388.19   the Frankish floot...from Hedalgoland
    420.14   his pon...sabby
    447.27   greenest island off the black coats of Spaign
    463.35   prisonpotstill of spanish breans
    464.27   cock and the bullfight
    473.20   sombrer opacities...are sphanished
    477.26   highly lucid spanishing gold

?498.19   his pani's annagolorum
539.14   stolemines...in the sooth of Spainien
548.08   spunish furiosos
553.36   Hispain's King's trompateers
596.13   spawnish oel [øl, Nor "beer"]

SPARROW AND CO (15/33).   Ladies' and Gentlemen's Outfitters, 16 S Gt George's St.
548.27   the peak of Pim's and Slyne's and Sparrow's

SPECKLED CHURCH.   The identity of the speckled ch where the sexton Fox Goodman tolls the bells which reverberate throughout *FW* has been the occasion for inconclusive controversy. What is certain is that it is a trans of Ir *Cill Breac*, that the latter is indistinguishable in pron from *Coill Breac*, "speckled wood," and that many placenames with the syllable "kil," "kill," "kyle," etc, cannot certainly be derived from either a multi-colored woods or a mottled ch.
    The Chapelizod ch looks "speckled" to some, not to others. It is unlikely that Fox Goodman's bells are in Falkirk, Scot, a town whose names in Lat, Gael, and Eng have all meant "speckled church"; in Kylebrack, form a cas, now a sch in Co Galway; or in Kilbrack, Co Armagh. In Dub, however, the leading candidate is Kilbarrack (qv), though no bells sound in the ruins of its 13th-cent ch.
35.32   in the speckled church
?315.28   that mone met the Kidballacks...suttonly
327.24   when Kilbarrack bell pings saksalaisance
403.21   from out the belfry of the cute old speckled church

SPICE ISLANDS.   The Moluccas, an isl group in E Indonesia; from the 16th cent a source of spices, esp nutmeg, mace, and cloves.
    Acc to Grose, "Spice Island" was 18th-cent slang for privy or fundament.
263.F2   come bask to the isle we love in spice
456.20   the spirits of the spice isles, curry and cinnamon, chutney and cloves

SPITSBERGEN.   Arctic archipelago 360 mi N of Nor. Chief isls W *S*, North East Land, Edge I, Barents I. Discovered by Wm Barents, 1596; became officially part of Nor 1925.
312.25   it was wohl yeas sputsbargain

SPORTING TIMES.   The weekly "chronicle of racing, literature, art, and the drama," known as "The Pink 'un," publ in London 1865-1931; new series from 1946.
128.12   pinkun's pellets for all the Pale
185.09   these our sporting times...the pink one

SPREAD EAGLE (14/33).   An 18th-cent corset shop in the Coombe (Peter's *Sketches*, 89). Prob not included in the allusion are the 17th-cent *SE* tav in Winetavern St, or the *SE* in Bread St, Cheapside, London, where John Milton was born. The arms of Connacht include an eagle with wings spread (482.15).
106.22   *If my Spreadeagles Wasn't so Tight I'd Loosen my Cursits*
?482.15   fix up your spreadeagle and pull your weight!

SPY.   Belg town near Namur. In 1886 2 nearly perfect skeletons, with Mousterian (see *Moustier, Le*) artifacts, were found in the nearby Betche aux Roches cave. The paleolithic "man of Spy" ranked with "Neanderthal [qv] man" as a find.
    The 11th *EB* article which mentions *S* ("Ethnology") argues that there is only one human species and rejects the view that different langs imply different races:

"There are some fifty irreducible stock languages in the United States and Canada, yet...he would be a reckless theorist who held that there were therefore fifty human species."

    10.31   If you can spot fifty I spy four more

STAMFORD BRIDGE.   Vill, E Riding, Yorks, Eng; site of battle in 1066 in which Harold II defeated his brother and Harold Haardraade of Nor just before the Battle of Hastings.

    9.16   weet, tweet and stampforth foremost

STANDARD, THE.   Weekly journal publ in Dub, "An Irish Organ of Catholic Opinion"; since 1966 *The Catholic Standard.*

    439.36   Perousse instate your *Weekly Standerd*, our verile organ

STANDFAST DICK.   The name of a large rock or reef in the shallow Liffey long known as an obstacle to sailors. The city builders found the continuation of this outcrop S of the Liffey a welcome foundation for their work, and gave it its affectionate nickname. The City Hall and the Castle stand above *SD.*

    210.28   a reiz every morning for Standfast Dick

STAR AND GARTER.   The insignia of the Order of the Garter, it is also a common pub name. At various times it has been the name of a Dun Laoghaire coffeehouse (*ca* 1750), a hotel in D'Olier St (*ca* 1870), and a "free-and-easy" in Amiens St (*ca* 1900).

    211.01   a starr and girton for Draper and Deane
    266.02   The store and charter, Treetown Castle under Lynne
    471.09   their star and gartergazer

STATIONERS HALL (16/33).   In the 18th cent, it was on the N side of Cork Hill (15/34). In JJ's time, it was Her Majesty's Stationery Office, 6 Merrion St, Upr.

    106.12   *Entered as the Lastest Pigtarial and My Pooridiocal at Stitchioner's Hall*

STAUNTON.   There are at least 5 towns or vills in Eng named *S*: in Glocs, Worcs, Notts, and 2 in Herefordshire.

    ?534.35   Instaunton!

STEEVENS' HOSPITAL (13/34).   At *S* Lane and St John's Rd. Often called "Madame Steevens'." Dr Richard Steevens died in 1701, the day after bequeathing his estate to his sister Griselda for her lifetime, then to build a hosp. She turned over the estate to trustees to build the hosp at once, keeping 150 pounds a year and an apartment in the hosp.

    40.34   Madam Gristle

STELLA MARIS CHURCH (RC) (18/32).   The "Star of the Sea," in Sandymount.
    569.10   S. Mary Stillamaries
    601.26   S. Santamonta's

STEPHEN'S GREEN.   See *St Stephen's Green.*

STEPNEY.   E London dist and dock area. The first of "Dr Barnardo's Homes," "for the reclamation of waif children," was founded in 1871 in *S* Causeway which remained the hqs of the inst until it was razed in 1970. See *Barnardo.*

    578.36   Stepney's shipchild...waif of his bosun

STEYNE (LONG STONE) (16/34).   A pillar erected by the 1st Norse invaders not far from their landing place on the S bank of the Liffey, on the site later occupied by Crampton's Mon (qv) in Townsend St.

?56.14	O'dan stod tillsteyne at meisies
73.34	skatterlings of a stone...haught
75.14	broadsteyne 'bove citie
84.31	so many miles from bank and Dublin stone
247.04	from Elmstree to Stene
305.29	For auld lang salvy steyne
420.12	their ecotaph (let it stayne!)
505.21	But that steyne of law indead
518.10	headlong stone of kismet
539.03	the longstone erectheion of our allfirst manhere [menhir]

STOCKENS.   Tnld, par of Finglas, bar of Nethercross, N Co Dub; in Fingal.
503.15   Slutsend with Stockins

STOCK EXCHANGE (15/34).   In Anglesea St, also the cen for stockbrokers' offices, since the 19th cent.
106.18   *Egged Him on to the Stork Exchange...Customs*

STOCKHOLM.   Seaport city, cap of Swed. It is separated from the Baltic by a wilderness of isls collectively called the *skärgård* (skerries). The main quay for ocean-going ships in the Staden, or old city, is called the Skeppsbro.
Sköka, Swed "whore"; *holm*, Swed "island."
Astrid of Swed married Prince Leopold of Belg in 1926, and was Queen from 1934 until her shocking death in Switz in 1935 in the wreck of an automobile driven by her husband.
Skokholm Isl, off Milford Haven, Wales, is prob not referred to at 279.F27, despite the fact that on its ocean side is Wildgoose Race.
279.F27   that dog of a dag in Skokholme as I sat astrid
533.35   Holmstock unsteaden. Livpoomark
535.15   scargore on that skeepsbrow

STONEHENGE.   The famous group of standing stones on Salisbury Plain, Eng. Acc to an anc legend, they were magically transported from Ire by Merlin.
5.31   carhacks, stonengens...merlinburrow
69.15   A stonehinged gate

STONEYBATTER (14/34).   Rd, NW Dub, a section of the main rd to Navan. Its name combines Eng and Ir: *bóthar*, Ir "road." It has been conjectured that it was orig the route of Slighe Cualann, the anc rd from Tara through Dub to SE Ire: hence the orig "rocky road to Dub."
42.27	Stane [with other rds]
73.30	down coombe and on eolithostroton [*lithostroton*, Gk "stone pavement"]
242.23	stoney badder
291.11	the O'Hollerins of Staneybatter
467.15	stomebathred
553.29	stony battered

STORMONT.   On the S outskirts of Belfast, the site of the Parl of N Ire (since 1921), usually called "Stormont," and of *S* Cas, hqs of N Ire govt depts.
28.22   Angry scenes at Stormount

STOURBRIDGE.   Town, W of Birmingham, Worcs, Eng; known for fire-clay and fire-brick works.

184.12   a stourbridge clay kitchenette

STOW ON THE WOLD.   Town in Glocs, Eng.
503.21   This stow on the wolds, is it Woful Dane Bottom?

STRAIGHT ST.   In *Acts* 9:11, the Lord says to Ananias, "Arise, and go to the
street which is called Straight," (to restore Saul's sight). "The Street which is called
Straight" is the motto of C T M'Cready's *Dublin Street Names*. The actual st still
runs E to W to the gate of Damascus, and is now called *Derb-el-Mistakim*.
110.33   Kevin...trouved up on a strate that was called strete
491.09   our straat that is called corkscrewed
512.15   the stricker the strait
?576.20   straxstraightcuts

STRAND, THE.   London st, once fashionable, now commercial, from Charing Cross
to Fleet St. For the limerick quoted at 534.22–.31, see *Belgravia*.
534.27   He walked by North Strand with his Thom's towel in hand

STRANGFORD.   *S* Lough, an almost landlocked inlet of the sea in E Co Down;
and a town on the W side of its entrance. Plantation of this area by Scottish immi-
grants took place under James I after 1605 and by ex-soldiers under Cromwell in the
1650's.
577.33   the strangfort planters are prodesting

STRATHCLYDE.   Kingdom ("Clyde Valley"), SW Scot. It was plundered by (among
others) Ivar the Boneless, the Viking (d 873).
387.09   boneless...Strathlyffe

STRAWBERRY BEDS (8–9/35).   The area, actually known for its strawberries,
along the N bank of the Liffey btwn Chapelizod and Woodlands. The Wren's Nest
(qv) is at the W end.
20.25   strubbely beds
41.25   fraiseberry beds
?207.10   strawbirry reds
265.08   fraisey beds...the wren his nest
559.06   strawberry bedspread
604.17   Strubry Bess

STROMBOLI.   Active volcanic isl in the Liparian or Aeolian group N of Sicily.
128.18   fumes inwards like a strombolist
494.17   he'll quivvy her with his strombolo

STRUMON.   In Macpherson's *Temora*, Book III, the seat of the family of Gaul (one
of Fingal's commanders), near Selma (qv). The name is explained as meaning "stream
of the hill."
203.24   singimari saffron strumans of hair

STUTTGART.   City, W Ger. It does not have a univ, but Hegel was born and educated there.
150.11   Dr Gedankje of Stoutgirth

STYX.   In Gk myth, the underworld riv, flowing 7 times around the world of the
dead. Identified with waterfall near Nouacris in Arcadia, locally called *Mavro Neró*
("Black Water"). The gods swore oaths by the *S*; anc Gks regarded the Mavro Neró
as poisonous, also swore oaths by it. It was believed that anyone breaking the oath
would lie in a trance for a year, then be ostracized for 9 years.

206.04   She swore on croststyx nyne

SUFFOLK.   Eng co, in East Anglia. The "wey" is an anc measure of weight, varying widely. Acc to the OED, the wey of *S* cheese was 256 lbs.

283.14   weys in Nuffolk till tods of Yorek

SUFFOLK ST (15/33).   Off N end of Grafton St. At *S* St, just opp the present site of St Andrew's, was the site of the little hill of the Dan Thing Mote (qv).

215.25   Northmen's thing made southfolk's place
242.24   his Thing went the wholyway retup Suffrogate Strate

SUGARLOAF.   2 mts S of Bray, Co Wicklow; Great *S* and Little *S* are respectively W and E of the Bray-Wicklow rd. There was a 19th-cent *S* tav in Bray but none so far as I know in Dub.

208.07   a sugarloaf hat with a gaudyquiviry peak
243.28   ondulate her shookerloft hat from Alpoleary
?521.13   at the Raven and Sugarloaf...Jones's lame

SUIR RIVER.   The main riv of S cen Ire, it rises close to the source of the Nore R, flows S the length of Tipperary, and turns E past Waterford to Waterford Harb.

203.09   Are you sarthin suir?
319.06   it's a suirsite's stircus
387.30   suir knows
446.25   through suirland and noreland

SUKHUM-KALEH (SUKHUMI).   Seaport city, E coast of Black Sea, USSR. Form Turk, then Russ from 1829 but occupied by Turks in 1854, 1877.

296.F3   Thargam [Armenian, "interpreter"]...Suksumkale!

SUMMERHILL (16/35).   St, and the adjoining dist, NE Dub, which continues Parnell St to Ballybough Rd at the Royal Canal. There is also a *S* Rd in Dun Laoghaire.

12.28   the bergagambols of Summerhill
265.F2   expression still used in the Summerhill district

SUN, THE (14/33).   (1) 18th-cent tav in Thomas St, near Castle St.   (2) 17th-cent tav in Nicholas St.   (3) *S* Ale House, Dame St, 18th cent.

63.24   the Sun

SUNDA ISLANDS.   See *Malaysia*.

SUNKEN ROAD.   The "Hohle Gasse," a famous rd near Kussnacht on Lake Lucerne, Switz, where Wm Tell lay in wait for the tyrant Gessler. The rd ends at a chapel which is a pilgrimage site.

?371.03   swinglyswanglers [?Zwingli], sunkentrunk
478.14   sunkin rut

SUSQUEHANNA RIVER.   Major riv of NE US, emptying into Chesapeake Bay.

212.06   Selina Susquehanna Stakelum
594.30   she, hou the Sassqueehenna

SUTOR ST (LANE) (15/33).   Near Christchurch Cath, mentioned as early as 1190 AD as Vicus Sutorum, the "street of the shoemakers." Later known as Behind St (qv).

?326.27   my rere admirable peadar poulsen...to the secondnamed sutor

SUTTON (25/39).   The narrow isthmus joining Howth to the mainland.

3.05   scraggy isthmus
17.11   by the neck I am sutton on

?22.34   three shuttoned castles
315.29   he suttonly remembered
371.30   From Dancingtree till Suttonstone
?533.30   Let Michael relay Sutton
587.23   our sutton down
623.10   hoothoothoo, ithmuthisthy

SVEA.   Pre-Christian E Scand kingdom, whose cap was Uppsala. Svealand is today a region of cen Swed, comprising 6 cos.
607.20   We have caught oneselves, Sveasmeas, in somes incontigruity

SWABIA.   Ger, *Schwaben*. A med duchy, it is now a dist of Bavaria. "Schwaber" is Sw Ger for "German man."
70.04   swobbing
181.05   Swabspays
485.24   The swaaber!

SWAN, THE.   Inn in the play by Charles Selby, "The Boots at the Swan" (1842). Jacob Earwig, the boots, is comically deaf. For much of the play he impersonates a policeman.
63.35   for the boots about the swan, Maurice Behan
145.23   a policeman...or even that beggar of a boots at the Post

SWANEE (SUWANEE) RIVER.   An inconspicuous stream flowing from S Ga, US, to the Gulf of Mex, it was immortalized by Stephen Foster in "Old Folks at Home" for no better reason than its euphonious name.
289.02   weights downupon the Swanny
581.06   the swanee her ainsell

SWAN WATER, THE (17/32).   A small stream, now subterranean, a S bank trib of the Liffey W of the Dodder R before the embankment of the Liffey. As one of Anna Liffey's Dub handmaidens, it perhaps deserves the otherwise conjectural (except for 248.23) identifications below.
248.23   Sweet swanwater!
289.02   weights downupon the Swanny
450.05   minnowahaw, flashing down the swansway
548.33   swanchen's

SWEDEN.   Kingdom, NW Eur, S and E Scand penin; Ger, *Schweden*; Fr, *Suede*; Swed, *Sverige*. The orig Swedes (*Svear*) came from Svea (qv) or Svealand in cen *S*. In hist times, the Goths came from the cen Vistula basin, but acc to their own legends (much disputed by scholars) they came orig from "Scandze," mod Skåne, or S *S* (197.09), possibly by way of the isl of Gotland in the Baltic Sea.
The Nobel prizes for physics, chemistry, medicine, literature, and peace have been awarded by the Swed Academy since Alfred Nobel's bequest in 1896 (211.03, 306.04, 536.12). Mann, Yeats, and Shaw all received the prize for literature (211.01 –.02); JJ didn't.
The legendary King Ericus, known as "Windy Cap" (Olaus Magnus), could control the direction of the wind by turning his magic cap (220.25). Jenny Lind was the "Swedish nightingale" (360.02). A variety of large turnip is known in Eng as "swedes" (82.03, ?141.12).
82.03   tipperuhry Swede
?137.07   Swed Albiony
?141.12   tobaggon and sweeds

197.09	Urgothland, Tvistown on the Kattekat?
211.03	two mangolds noble to sweeden their bitters
220.25	Laxdalesaga...King Ericus of Schweden...magical helmet
306.04	his Noblett's surprize
360.02	sweetishsad lightandgayle
387.19	Fair Margrate waited Swede Villem
517.05	pigheaded Swede
536.12	Guestermed with the nobelities
?557.28	washleather sweeds
590.20	for true a sweetish mand
?603.17	be pursueded
607.20	Sveasmeas

SWILLY, LOUGH.   The estuary of the Swilly R, Co Donegal.
    211.36   whatever you like to swilly to swash

SWINFORD (SWINEFORD).   Town, Co Mayo. *Béal Átha na Muice*, Ir "Ford-Mouth of the Pig." There are Swinfords in Berks, Leics, and Worcs, Eng.
    ?296.F3   If you sink I can, swimford

SWITZERLAND.   Federal rep in cen Eur; Lat, *Helvetia*; Ger, *der Schweiz*; Fr, *Suisse*. *FW* displays little interest in *S* as a unique Eur country; but see *Zurich*.
    ?4.21   Helviticus committed deuteronomy
    93.06   Switz bobbyguard's [see *Vatican*]
    ?113.12   schwrites
    129.34   Suiss family Collesons
    176.35   a bedtick from Schwitzer's
    183.30   Swiss condensed bilk
    454.03   swisstart
    464.29   Father Freeshots Feilbogen in his rockery garden with the costard
                [*Freischütz*, Ger "marksman"; *Pfeil und Bogen*, Ger "bow and arrow"; costard, an apple; Wm Tell, QED]
    488.30   swiltersland

SWITZER'S   (15/33).   Long-established dept store on Grafton St.
    176.35   he collapsed carefully under a bedtick from Schwitzer's

SWORDS.   Town, N Co Dub, W of Malahide. The Ir name, *Sórd Cholaim Chille*, "St Columcille's Sword," indicates its foundation in the 6th cent as a monastery by St Columba; it was later (by the 13th cent) a country res of the Archbishops of Dub.
    ?90.10   Mickmichael's soords
    116.15   down swords the sea merged the oldowth guns
    266.F2   the Rev. B. B. Brophy of Swords

SYBIL HEAD.   Promontory at W end of Dingle Penin, Co Kerry. *Shibbeal*, Ir "Isabel," angl "Sybil."
    399.04   *from Sybil surfriding*
    501.13   priority call! Sybil!
    501.14   Sybil Head this end!

SYCAMORE ST   (15/34).   Orig *S* Alley, since 1869 *S* St; runs N from Dame St to Essex St, W of Eustace St. Site of Dub GPO 1709-1755, "Sycamore Tree" pub *ca* 1733, Dan Lowry's Star Music Hall and Theatre of Varieties, late 19th cent. Many refs to sycamores, usually associated with the Four Old Men, are not included here.
    ?24.31   under your sycamore by the keld water

95.21   firstnighting down Sycomore Lane
281.20   Sickamoor's so woful sally

SYDNEY.   City and cap, NSW, Australia, orig settled by Brit penal officials from
Botany Bay (qv). The *Bulletin* is a daily newspaper. The ballad about Mrs Porter and
her daughter was reported to T S Eliot from *S* ("The Wasteland," Notes).
For Sydney, NS, see *Nova Scotia*; see also *Sydney Parade Ave* (Dub).
60.27   Sydney Parade Ballotin
489.31   S. H. Devitt...tearly belaboured by Sydney and Alibany [for Michael
Davitt, see *Census*]
?553.31   syddenly parading
595.33   Thus faraclacks the friarbird. Listening, Syd!

SYDNEY PARADE AVENUE   (19/31).   Res st in Sandymount, SE Dub. In JJ's
"A Painful Case," Mrs Sinico is killed by a train at *SP* Sta.
60.27   Eastrailian poorusers of the Sydney Parade Ballotin
553.31   westlandmore...syddenly parading

SZÉKESFEHÉRVÁR.   Town, Hung, cap of co of Fejér; Ger, *Stuhlweissenburg*.
Form place of coronation and burial of Hung kings, but here only as cen of vineyard
country producing, among others, Feherbor wine.
171.26   winevat...magyansty...she has a feherbour

T

TAILORS' HALL   (15/33).   Est early 15th cent; the present bldg was built 1706
in Back Lane, opp St Audoen's Arch. *TH* was one of the largest public rooms in
Dub, site of many early 18th-cent balls, auctions, concerts; the tailors were notorious for riotous dinners on June 24.
?106.12   *Stitchioner's Hall*
510.14   Come to the ballay at the Tailors' Hall

T'AI SHAN.   Mt, Shantung prov, China; for 4 millennia it has been a sacred mt and
a pilgrimage site, with pilgrims climbing the rd to the temples on top.
131.35   confusianist...chinchin...like a footsey kungoloo around Taishantyland

TALAVERA DE LA REINA.   Town, cen Sp, 65 mi SW of Madrid. Site of one of
Wellington's great victories against the Fr, commanded by King Joseph Bonaparte,
27-28 July 1809.
9.36   Willingdone...Dalaveras fimmieras!...pettiest of the lipoleums

TALBOT ST   (16/34).   Continues Earl St E to Amiens St. Patrick Claffey's pawnshop, 28-29 *T* St, was next to the cor of Mabbot St.
447.13   Henry, Moore, Earl and Talbot Streets
?516.27   to the corner of Turbot Street, perplexing about a paumpshop

TALIESIN.   Vill in Cardiganshire (now N Dyfed) named after 6th cent Welsh bard.
The Book of Taliessin, early 14th cent, is one of the most important manuscripts of
early Welsh literature. JJ prob didn't know of Frank Lloyd Wright's houses, *T* East
and *T* West.
151.22   toes are always in retaliessian out throuth his overpast boots

TALLAGHT   (9/27).   Town, SW of Dub; *Taimhleacht*, Ir "plague-grave." Acc to legend, the Parthalonians, one of the peoples to invade Ire, all died of plague and were buried in a mass-grave at *T*. The Red Cow (qv) inn was S of *T*, Green Hills (qv) is to the N.

83.19	the Ruadh Cow at Tallaght
194.35	by Tallaght's green hills
334.33	it's Hey Tallaght Hoe on the king's highway
478.12	vallums of tartallaght
?479.24	plague-burrow

TAMIL.   People and lang of S Ind. "Mulligatawny," "cheroot," and "pariah" are *T* words.

?110.11	madh vaal of tares...its tamelised tay
498.17	paunchjab and dogril and pammel
?598.19	Ind...Panpan...Tamal without tares

TANKARDSTOWN.   Tnld, par and bar of Ratoath, Co Meath. There are 12 other tnlds named *T* in Ire.

97.04–.08	Tankardstown...louping the loup, to Tankardstown again

TARA.   Low hill 6 mi SE of Navan, Co Meath. The legendary royal seat of anc Ire, actually an important religious cen connected with worship of Maeb (Queen Mab, Maeve), seat of priest-kings who were High Kings of Meath (qv) and also heads of Uí Néill federation: the most powerful kings in Ire (380.21). The Feis Temrach was the religious festival at *T*, last held in 560 AD; by 728 AD *T* was politically insignificant, and the triumph of Christianity further contributed to its decline. But *T* is still one of the most famous places in Ire, commemorated by T Moore's poem, "The Harp That Once Through Tara's Halls." Macpherson may have changed the name to Temora (qv) in his Ossianic cycle, although the actual scene of his poem is in Co Antrim. Finally, the Stone of Destiny, Lía Fail (qv) once stood at *T*. *Teamhar*, "elevated place with a wide view"; it could be trans "Prospect Hill" (?476.11, 541.02).

Inevitably, *T* reminds *FW* of the tar-water which Berkeley praised as a panacea, and which was a trademark of James Clarence Mangan.

7.34	the fort...tarabom, tarabom
9.21	Tarra's widdars!
?10.16	madrashattaras
27.09	tarandtan plaidboy
131.09	Tiara of scones
151.20	Mortadarthella taradition
173.21	tarabooming
227.35	Tartaran...tarrascone
228.34	Cernilius slomtime prepositus of Toumaria
247.28	Tarara boom decay
267.F6	All abunk for Tararat!
319.25	swill of the Tarra water
320.03	tarrapoulling
326.14	Tera truly ternatrine
329.35	rain of Tarar
343.33	haftara having afterhis brokeforths
359.03	taratoryism, the orenore
365.17	kuschkars tarafs
375.24	the Tara Tribune
380.21	the Taharan dynasty

381.25	but, arrah
411.22	the fullsoot of a tarabred
?476.11	the watchers of Prospect
491.26	O Tara's thrush
?513.12	Taranta boontoday!
520.02	a tarrable Turk
535.08	this Nova Tara
541.02	your hill prospect
552.29	ollguns tararulled
?613.05	Taawhaar? Sants and sogs

TARANTO.   It prov, and its cap city, SE It. Named for the city are the tarantula spider, the dancing madness or "tarantism" of the 15th-17th cents, pop believed to be caused by the bite of the tarantula, and the tarantella dance, once believed to cure ·tarantism.
    513.12   Dawncing...Taranta boontoday!

TARASCON.   Town, Bouches-du-Rhône Dept, SE Fr. The allusion is to Alphonse Daudet's *Tartarin de Tarascon.*
    227.35   a Tartaran tastarin...tarrascone

TARDENOIS.   Town, Aisne Dept, NE Fr. The Tardenoisean culture of the Mesolithic period is named after the town.
    154.09   tardeynois

TARTARUS.   In early Gk myth (Homer) the underworld pris, far below Hades, where the impious were confined; later it became synonymous with Hades or with its anteregion (Virgil).
    ?531.34   Terreterry's Hole to Stutterers' Corner

TASMANIA.   Australian state and isl off SE tip of Australian continent. Orig called Van Dieman's Land; a convict settlement was est there in 1804 by Col David Collins, from King's Co, Ire.
    56.21   our Traveller...from van Demon's Land
    225.26   Van Diemen's coral pearl
    416.30   he had the Tossmania

TATTU.   A name given both to the town of Busiris and the town of Mendes in anc Egypt. In the *Book of the Dead*, Osiris is sometimes called "Lord of Tattu."
    486.14   Now I, the lord of Tuttu

TAVERN, THE.   Earwicker's public house (338.04) is no doubt everywhere, or everywhere where pints are drawn and songs are sung (as "the tavern" of 368.24 is that of Omar Khayyam's *Rubaiyat*, too), but its local habitation is in Chapelizod. Most often and most clearly it is called the "Mullingar," but there are also refs to it as the "Bristol." To this day the Mullingar House stands in Chapelizod at the point where the rd from Dub forks, turning left to the br over the Liffey, and angling right up the hill toward the Knockmaroon gate of Phoenix Park. Across the br on the S bank of the Liffey is the Bridge Inn, its name carved in stone on its facade; and "bristol" is OE for "bridge."
    Since HCE regularly splits into Shem and Shaun, who are among other things the banks of the Liffey, I think we can't do better than to suppose that the *T* is another of *FW*'s theatrical roles, performed on occasion by both of Chapelizod's tavs. Also, because the colors red and white are so often associated with the Shem-Shaun contrast, it may not be irrelevant that the Mullingar House is white stucco, while the

Bridge Inn is red brick.

In *FW* III.4, however, there are hints (565.34, 580.25) that Earwicker's establishment is sometimes at Lucan (qv), perhaps the latter's Hydropathic Hotel. If so, a little light may be cast on the otherwise inexplicable conflation of Chapelizod and Lucan throughout *FW*.

111.17	with fondest to the twoinns
113.18	Add dapple inn
262.26	Inn inn! Inn inn!
311.16	drinking...dubble in it
330.30	Knock knock...The Twwinns
338.04	A public plouse
?510.17	the whole stock company of the old house of the Leaking Barrel
523.26	Doddercan Easehouse
534.29	out of my double inns
565.34	Lucalised...stop at his inn
580.25	his hydrocomic establishment
?620.15	the twinngling of an aye

MULLINGAR HOUSE (10/34).   Named for Mullingar, the town in Co Westmeath where Milly Bloom was a photographer's asst, and where the women were "beef to the heel." *An Muileann Cearr*, Ir "left-handed mill"; the *MH* is on the left bank of the Liffey, facing the rd which leads across the br. It occupies the site of the Phoenix House (see *Chapelizod*), which appears in Le Fanu's *The House By The Churchyard* as "the jolly old inn just beyond the turnpike at the sweep of the road, leading over the buttressed bridge by the mill...first to welcome the excursionist from Dublin."

64.09	the Mullingcan Inn
138.19	the Mullingar Inn
265.08	the phoenix, his pyre
286.L3	*The boss's bess bass is the browd of Mullingar*
?321.33	that mulligar scrub
345.34	*the Mullingaria*
370.27	the porlarbaar of the marringaar
371.34	those Mullinguard minstrelsers
380.05	Mocked Majesty in the Malincurred Mansion

BRIDGE INN (10/34).   At the SE cor of the br over the Liffey; *bristol*, OE "bridge." In JJ's "A Painful Case," Mr Duffy drinks hot punch there and thinks about the dead Mrs Sinico. Most refs are conflated with "Bristol" or "Borstal" (qqv).

21.34	the bar of his bristolry
133.29	was schenkt publicly to brigstoll
?353.34	*birstol boys artheynes*
392.31	the Bristolhut
405.27	maltsight, in a porterhouse...the once queen of Bristol and Balrothery
421.13	Lost all License...Ereweaker, with your Bloody Big Bristol
512.05	father of Izod...brustall to the bear
539.21	platzed mine residenze...and ran and operated my brixtol selection here
?624.33	you were bragged up by Brostal

TEACH MIODHCHUARTA.   The great banqueting hall at Royal Tara (qv). The name means "house of the circulation of mead."

558.35	House of the cederbalm of mead

TEDDINGTON.   Town in Middlesex, Eng, on Thames R btwn Richmond and Kingston-upon-Thames; so named because the Thames is tidal just to that point. JJ might have learned this from Kipling's "The River's Tale": "At Tide-end-town, which is Teddington." In the refs, the main allusion is to Dub, town of the tidal Liffey. See *Island Bridge*.

    ?202.09   from Fonte-in-Monte to Tidingtown...Tidingtown tilhavet
    ?547.17   tiding down, as portreeve should

TEFFIA.   The anc name for terr comprising about the W half of Co Westmeath and a bit of Co Longford; Ir, *Teathbha*. It lies W of the plain of Bregia (qv).

    604.04   vinebranch of Heremonheber on Bregia's plane where Teffia lies

TEHERAN (TEHRAN).   Cap city and prov of Iran, N Iran.

    380.21   Taharan dynasty
    538.02   Marryonn Teheresiann

TELFORD AND TELFORD.   Organ builders, form at 109 Stephen's Green, W.

    552.26   the oragel of the lauds to tellforth's glory

TELTOWN.   Vill, Co Meath, 4 mi SE of Kells (Ceanannus Mor). Site of anc Tailteann, a royal res of Ire, and of Aonach Tailteann ("Tailteann Games"), pre-Christian Aug fair and games of the Uí Néill confederation, orig in honor of Queen Tailte, foster-mother of the Dedannan king Lugh of the Long Hand; games revived after 8 cents by the Ir Free State. Acc to a note prepared by JJ for Gorman's biography, JJ was invited by Yeats to participate in the bardic side of the revived Games, but refused.

    83.23   gamy queen Tailte
    386.27   going to the tailturn horseshow
    550.25   my telltale sports at evenbread

TEMORA.   Macpherson's epic, in 8 books, of Fingal, Ossian, and heroes of the Kingdom of Morven (qv). *Tigh-mhor-Righ*, "House of the Great King," is now Connor, S of Kells, Co Antrim, acc to Campbell's notes to *Ossian*. Another theory identifies *T* with Tara (qv).

    87.08   Yetstoslay and Temorah
    ?104.12   Hesterdays...to Morra
    ?141.35   for Tomorrha's big pickneck
    228.34   Toumaria
    593.13   Securest jubilends albas Temoram

TEMPLE.   (1) Built by the Knights Templar in the 12th cent, the site in the Strand, London, is now occupied by the Inner *T* and Middle *T*, 2 of the Inns of Court. *T* Bar, although located across the st from the Middle *T*, had nothing to do with the law; it marked the jurisdiction of the City of London, and a sovereign could not pass unless ceremonially admitted by the Lord Mayor. Removed 1878 as a traffic obstruction.   (2) *T* Bar in Dub (15/34) is the middle section of the st running W from Westmoreland St to Parliament St, just 1 block S of Wellington and Aston Quays; named after the *T* family, who lived here in the early 18th cent.

    391.12   divorced...innasense interdict, in the middle of the temple
    607.30   Solsking the Frist...will...show up above Tumplen Bar

TEMPLE OF ARTEMIS (DIANA) AT EPHESUS.   One of the 7 Wonders of the Anc World (qv), in Ephesus near mod vill of Aga Soluk, W Asia Min, near coast of Aegean Sea.

261.11   delighted in her dianaphous
553.12   templeogues

TEMPLEOGUE   (13/28).   Dist, SW Dub, W of Rathfarnham.
553.12   templeogues

TEPLITZ (TEPLICE).   Spa and city, Bohemia, W Czech. Its saline-alkaline springs
were favored for gout and rheumatism, also effects of gunshot wounds, hence sobri-
quet of "the warriors' bath." The Treaty of *T*, 1813, created a triple alliance of Austria, Russ, and Pruss against Napoleon.
333.36   toplots talks from morrienbaths

TERENURE   (14/30).   Dist, S Dub, btwn Harold's Cross and Rathfarnham. Form
called Roundtown.
142.13   Ager Arountown [*ager*, Lat "field"]
497.11   Rountown and Rush
539.33   my tenenure of office

TEXAS.   State, US. "Texas" is term for part of a Mississippi R steamboat, as in
"Texas hall" (opp captain's cabin). JJ could have learned this from *Huckleberry Finn*.
26.15   that there texas is tow linen
274.F3   Mr Potter of Texas

THAMES RIVER.   London's Liffey. Ger, *Themse*. The upr *T* (as at Oxford) is still
called the Isis.
199.01   in that mormon's thames
214.31   Icis on us!
327.09   trent of the thimes
?357.32   emblushing thems elves [*elv*, Nor "river"]
486.24   a stillstream of isisglass [*glas*, Ir "stream"]

THEATRE ROYAL   (16/34).   Before 1759, the *TR* of Dub was the Smock Alley
Theatre (qv), then the Crow St Theatre (qv); but the allusion is chiefly to the *TR* in
Hawkins St, opened 18 Jan 1821 by Henry Harris and completely destroyed by fire
9 Feb 1880, before the matinee of the Christmas pantomime, *Ali Baba*.
455.26   Royal Revolver...real globoes...regally fire...chrisman's pandemon
587.08   Theoatre Regal's drolleries puntomine

THEBES.   Anc city in Upper Egypt, now site of Luxor and Karnak; cen of Egyptian civilization until it declined after 10th cent BC. Of the many versions of the
Egyptian *Book of the Dead*, J S Atherton says, JJ prob used the Theban recension
(*Letters* I, 281).
134.35   Theban recensors...*Bug of the Deaf*
410.36   throth as the thieves' rescension

THÉLÈME, ABBEY OF.   In Rabelais's *Works* (I, 52 et seq) it was built by Gargan-
tua to be the opp of ordinary monasteries. On the S bank of the Loire, it was hex-
agonal, with 6 towers: Arctic on the N, then clockwise, Calaer, Anatole (E), Mesem-
brine (S), Hesperia (W), and Criere.
494.13   Arctura, Anatolia, Hesper and Mesembria weep in their mansions
?541.15   I matt them, pepst to papst, barthelemew

THERMOPYLAE.   Coastal plain in E Gr, btwn Mt Oeta and S shore of Gulf of
Lamnia, 9 mi SE of Lamnia. Scene of many battles, esp the stand made by the Gks
and their allies against the Persians in 480 BC.
9.25   this is their mobbily

THING MOTE   (15/34).   The assembly place, usually on a mound, est by the Vikings wherever they settled. In Dub, the *TM* was on a low hill S of the present Dame
St, at the intersection of Church Lane and Suffolk St. The hill of the *TM* was called
the Howe, Haugh, or "Howe over the Stein" (Steyne, qv), from *haugr*, Old Dan "hill,
sepulchral mound." In 1682 the mound was leveled and the material used to raise
the level of Nassau St. See *Hoggen Green*, *Hog Hill*.

18.12	Howe?...viceking's graab
18.16	thonthorstrok, thing mud
26.23	Howe of the shipmen, steep wall!
53.06	tales of the tingmount
58.01	His Thing Mod...madthing
74.02	skatterlings of a stone...haught crested elmer
76.14	this, liever, is the thinghowe ["slieve," angl Ir "mountain"]
?81.12	It was hard by the howe's there
215.24	Northmen's thing made southfolk's place
242.23	his Thing went the wholyway retup Suffrogate Strate
?289.14	Ellishly Haught's...doombody
331.19	diublin's owld mounden...Vikens...haughs and shaws
?346.26	Thingman placeyear howed
370.08	any old howe
386.20	darkumound numbur wan, beside that ancient Dame street
?454.04	Haugh! Haugh!
536.31	Thing of all Things
?553.23	Finmark's Howe [context is Phoenix Park]

THINGVELLIR.   Anc seat of the Althing, the Icelandic Nat Parl, since 930 AD.

328.27	all Thingavalley knows
460.32	I'll wait on thee till Thingavalla

THOLSEL   (15/33).   The Dub City Hall at Skinner's Row (now Christchurch Pl)
and E cor of Nicholas St, erected early 14th cent. Parl met there 1641-48. In 1611
the Dub Corp ordered the "making of a substantial platform, covered with lead,
over the Tholsell" (Gilbert, I, 163). The new bldg of 1683 was demolished *ca* 1809.

539.22	operated my brixtol selection here at thollstall
?541.23	did I thole till lead's plumbate

THOMAS ST   (14/33).   One of Dub's most anc sts, in the Liberties W of Christchurch Cath, it runs along the low ridge S of the Liffey which was the Dub end of
the Esker Rd (qv).

?53.31	a starchboxsitting in the pit of his St Tomach's
543.17	Thomars Sraid

THOUSAND ISLANDS.   A group of about 1500 isls in US and Can areas of the St
Lawrence R, E of Kingston, Ontario.

604.25	Habitant and the onebut thousand insels

THREADNEEDLE ST.   London site of the Bank of Eng, which of course is the
"Old Lady of Threadneedle St."

551.33	pass through twelve Threadneedles...camels' walk

THREE CASTLES.   The Dub coat of arms (qv) is 3 castles, flaming. But it is a not
uncommon Ir place-name. Threecastles in Co Wicklow, 3 mi NE of Blessington, was
on the border of the Pale (qv). Its 1 ruined cas is alleged to be the survivor of 3. In
Co Kilkenny, 3½ mi SE of Freckford, is *TC* Demesne, Ch, and Br. *TC* Head is just N

of Mizen Head (qv), W Co Cork. See also *Tredcastles*.

    18.06   tr'c'stle
    22.34   three shuttoned castles
    128.17   shot two queans and shook three caskles
    266.03   Treetown Castle under Lynne
    551.31   tricastellated

THREE JOLLY PIGEONS.   Country inn in Lissoy, Co Longford, identified with
the inn of the same name in Goldsmith's "The Deserted Village."

    480.03   Crouch low, you pigeons three

THREE PATRONS, CHURCH OF THE (RC)   (15/30).   In Rathgar, S Dub.

    601.23   S. Ruadagara's

THREE ROCK MOUNTAIN.   9 mi S of Dub, W of Dundrum-Enniskerry Rd. S
Joyce describes an outing there (when JJ was in Univ Coll) with Skeffington and
the Sheehys.

    227.20   to anger arbour, treerack monatan, scroucely out of scout of ocean
    372.28   Free rogue Mountone till Dew Mild Well...lyncheon partyng
    ?424.34   With his threestar monothong

THULE.   Anc name for the extreme N limit of the world, an isl 6 days sail N of
Brit. Conjectured to be the Shetlands, or part of coast of Nor. Virgil's *Georgics* I,
30, is the source of the phrase "Ultima Thule."

    134.01   either eldorado or ultimate thole
    235.19   praise send Larix U' Thule
    321.08   outback's dead heart, Glasthule Bourne

THURN AND TAXIS.   Form Ger state; the counts of *T* and *T* had a monopoly as
Ger Imp postmasters from 16th into the 19th cent.

    5.32   streetfleets, tournintaxes
    554.01   poster shays and turnintaxis

TIB AND TOM   (15/34).   A cluster of bldgs on Hoggen Green (qv) in the 15th
cent near Hoggen Butt where the citizens of Dub practiced archery (Gilbert III, 3).
For the elusive Tom and Tim, see *Census*.

    88.35   Tem...time...You butt he could anytom
    ?139.10   Timb to the pearly morn and Tomb to the mourning night

TIBERIAS.   Town on W shore of the Sea of Galilee, or Lake *T* (where Jesus divided the loaves and fishes and walked on water; *John* 6). Founded in 2nd decade of
1st cent AD and named after the emperor Tiberius, it became the chief cen of rab-
binic scholarship, where the Jerusalem Talmud was edited. The Massorite scholars in
T introduced the "points" for vowels in Heb script.

    115.11   Tiberias...gerontophils
    119.16   tiberiously ambiembellishing the initials majuscule
    123.30   Tiberiast duplex...signs of punctuation
    ?424.09   Tiberia...arestocrank

TIERRA DEL FUEGO.   Archipelago off S tip of S Amer; also name of main isl.

    387.03   Suid Aferican cattleraiders...all over like a tiara dullfuoco

TIKNOCK   (16/25).   Tnld, rd, and crossrds, S of Ballinteer on rd from Dundrum
to Three Rock Mt. The prostitute Honor Bright (211.33) was found shot to death at
T Crossroads in 1925. There is no *T* Cas, but the name comes from some sort of edi-

fice: *Teach-cnoc*, Ir "house of the hill."

   ?530.33   Kitty the Beads, the Mandame of Tipknock Castle!

TIMBUKTU (TOMBOUCTOU).   Town in Mali, W Afr; near Niger R, it was a cross-rds of caravan routes, known as the "port of Sudan in the Sahara." A Tuareg city for most of its hist, it was cap of the Songhoi emp in the 15th and 16th cents.

   288.23   his perry humdrum dumb and numb nostrums that he larned in Hymbuktu

TIMES, THE.   London's great morning newspaper, founded 1 Jan 1788; known in the 19th cent as "The Thunderer." It was in *The Times*'s series "Parnellism and Crime" (243.09) that Pigott's forgeries, later exposed by his misspelling of "hesitancy," were published; but although Pigott and the fatal word recur frequently in *FW*, *The Times* gets off scot-free despite its sustained opposition to Ir nationalism and Home Rule.

   199.01   he'd check their debths in that mormon's thames

TIMOR.   Isl, Malaysia, largest of the Lesser Sunda Isls. "Orangutang" is a Malay word meaning "man of the woods"; its habitat is Borneo and Sumatra, not *T*.

   342.35   *for tasing the tiomor of malaise after the pognency of orangultonia*

TIMOR SEA.   The arm of the Indian O btwn the NW coast of Australia and the Sunda isl chain from Java to *T* Isl.

   231.10   for Shing-Yung-Thing in Shina from Yoruyume across the Timor Sea

TINGSOMINGENTING.   Dan, "a thing like no thing," "a mere nothing." In *FW*, the home of the Gracehoper. The Ondt's home also amounts to nothing: see *Nixnix-undnix*.

   183.06   this was a stinksome inkenstink
   231.02   tingtumtingling
   253.08   ants...sauterelles...no thing making newthing
   343.09   Think some ingain think
   414.34   his cottage, which was cald fourmillierly Tingsomingenting
   415.25   What a bagateller it is!
   416.27   Tingsomingenting
   417.26   thingsumanything

TINTAGEL (TREVENA).   Vill and cas, N coast of Cornwall, ruins still visible. In literary legend, it was the birthplace of King Arthur and the stronghold of King Mark. But *FW* associates it mainly with the Cornish lang.

    By an unusual franchise, *T* became a "rotten borough" in the 18th cent; in 1784, the vicar of *T*, as the only qualified elector, returned 2 members of the House of Commons. In 1832, before the Reform Act transferred their votes, there were 10 resident qualified voters (594.04).

   232.21   in the languish of Tintangle
   287.F4   Basqueesh, Finnican, Hungulash and Old Teangtaggle
   419.15   like treacling tumtim with its tingtingtaggle...Corneywall
   594.04   Arcthuris...Kilt by kelt...We elect for thee, Tirtangel

TIPPECANOE RIVER.   Trib of Wabash R in Indiana, US. At the junction of the 2 rivs, Gen Wm Henry Harrison defeated Indians under Tecumseh in 1811. "*T*" became Harrison's nickname when he campaigned for the presidency of the US.

   65.32   tiptoptippy canoodle

TIPPERARY.   Co, Munster prov, subject of song, "It's a Long Way to Tipperary."

Baronies: Clanwilliam, Eliogarty, E and W Iffa and Offa, Ikerrin, Upr and Lwr Kilnamanagh, Middlethird, Upr and Lwr Ormond, Owney and Arra, Slievardagh.

9.30	a trip trippy trip so airy. For their heart's right there
82.03	fighting like purple top and tipperuhry Swede
110.36	Tipperaw raw raw rerraw
131.05	as the streets were paved with cold he felt his topperairy
?202.22	Tez thelon langlo, walking weary!
?262.L4	*Tailwaggers Terrierpuppy Raffle*
406.21	typureely jam
584.31	Tubbernacul in tipherairy
595.28	deep deep deeps of Deepereras

TÍR FA THUINN.   Ir, "Land Beneath Wave"; the Gaelic Atlantis (qv), which appears in many tales, eg, the *Voyage of Maildun* and *The Pursuit of the Gilla Dacker*. Its location is indeterminate: sometimes it is in the Atlantic, sometimes under Lough Neagh (qv), sometimes entered down a deep well or spring.

248.08	Arise, Land-under-Wave!

TÍR NA MBAN.   In the 10th-cent text of *The Voyage of Bran*, Bran and his followers stay so long on the enchanted isl of Tír na mBan, the Land of Women, where a cent is like a year, that when they return to land the 1st man to step on shore collapses into a pile of ashes. If the Prankquean spends "forty years" there between visits to Howth, she is absent from Howth for 21 weeks.

Inch Cailliach, "Island of Women," in Loch Lomond, Scot, is so named because it once held a nunnery.

21.27	the prankquean went for her forty years' walk in Tourlemonde
22.08	all the lilipath ways to Woeman's Land
22.14	the prankquean went for her forty years' walk in Turnlemeem
496.08	a minx from the Isle of Woman [*mynchen*, Ger "nun"]

TÍR NA NOG.   The "Land of Youth," where no one ages, another of the enchanted Otherworld Atlantic isls in Ir legends. Ossian spent 300 years there, returned to Ire on his white horse, and aged as soon as his feet touched the ground.

91.25	this world or the other world or any either world, of Tyre-nan-Og
134.22	brought us giant ivy from the land of younkers
479.02	my grandmother's place, Tear-nan-Ogre, my little grey home in the west

"TITANIC."   The 1912 disaster of the White Star liner "Titanic" appears in *FW* by way of the pop song, "It's Your Last Trip, Titanic, Fare Thee Well."

There was a White Star Canadian liner "Megantic" (379.31), built in 1908. It escaped disaster.

242.21	It's his last lap, Gigantic, fare him weal
379.31	It's our last fight, Megantic, fear you will
480.21	It's his lost chance, Emania. Ware him well

TIVOLI.   Town, 16 mi NE of Rome, site of Villa d'Este, and remains of anc temples and villas, esp Hadrian's Villa (once Temple of Vesta). Named for it are the *T* Gardens, Copenhagen, and the former *T* Music Hall, Burgh Quay (16/34), form the Lyric Theatre of Varieties.

?355.30	atween his showdows fellah, Misto Teewiley Spillitshops

TOBERBUNNY.   Vill, near Cloughran, Co Dub. *Tobar-bainne*, "Milk Well."

?430.36	tubberbunnies

TOBOLSK.   City in Tyumen Region of Siberia, USSR, where Irtysh and Tobol rivs join; trad a cen for political exiles.
    162.15   as sattin as there's a tub in Tobolosk

TOC H.   Talbot House, London, a WW I soldiers' recreation cen which became a Christian social service cen. Familiarly called "Toc H," the Army code for its initials.
    ?131.04   T.C.H.
    443.24   the usual XYZ type, R.C. Toc H, nothing but claret

TOKYO.   Cap city of Japan. Called *Yedo* until 1868, when it replaced Kyoto as imp cap, with name changed to Tokyo, "eastern capital."
    ?534.02   Kyow! Tak
    535.09   yeddonot need light oar

TOLKA.   (1) The little riv of N Dub, flowing through Glasnevin and Drumcondra to Dub Bay, through the former sloblands (201.18) of Fairview. The many residences of the Joyce family in N Dub were always within a few blocks of the *T*. The Delville (qv) estate (503.17) was on the banks of the *T* in Glasnevin.   (2) *T* tnld (503.17) is in the par of Finglas.   (3) *T* Br (130.21) carries Finglas Rd over the riv.
    16.06   You tolkatiff scowegian?
    52.09   Tolkaheim
    ?117.19   talkatalka tell Tibbs has eve
    ?125.04   Tulko MacHooley
    130.21   atolk [bridge]
    201.18   *slobs della Tolka*
    315.31   talka...clown toff
    ?317.07   tolk sealer's solder
    332.10   tolk of
    503.17   you're a delville of a tolkar!
    528.13   I lie with warm lisp on the Tolka
    ?541.18   all her tolkies shraking
    599.09   if tungs may tolkan

TOMAR'S WOOD.   At the Battle of Clontarf (qv), the aged Brian Boru followed the battle from *TW*, somewhere to the W of Clontarf. *Tomar*, Ir "Thor."
    68.31   sunkenness in Tomar's Wood
    ?543.17   Thorstan's, *recte* Thomars Sraid

TOMMEN-Y-MUR.   Near Festiniog, Wales; site of Roman camp on the Roman rd running generally parallel to the shore of Cardigan Bay.
    ?106.08   *Inglo-Andean Medoleys from Tommany Moohr*

TOMSK.   Adm dist (oblast), W Siberia, USSR, and its cap city. The *T* Regt defended Sevastopol in the Crimean War.
    509.05   retouching friend Tomsky, the enemy...rooshian

TONDUFF.   Mt, Co Wicklow, W of Bray.
    522.28   Do you think we are tonedeafs in our noses...bray

TONNERRE.   Town, Yonne Dept, in N Burgundy, N cen Fr. Not associated with any hist battle.
    ?9.23   Tonnerre! (Bullsear! Play!)

TON-THENA.   The name of a star in Macpherson's *Temora* and *Cathlin of Clutha*; it guided Larthon to Ire. Macpherson explains the name as meaning "fire of the wave."

602.30   beam of the wave his polar bearing, steerner among stars, trust
           touthena

TOOLEY ST.   In Southwark, London. The 3 tailors of *T* St addressed to the House
of Commons a petition beginning "We, the people of England." The name is a corruption of "St Olaf."
    53.29   Eagle Cock Hostel on Lorenzo Tooley street
   529.15   in the name of the three tailors on Tooley Street

TOPHET.   A location in the vall of Ben Hinnon near Jerusalem; once the site of
human sacrifice, it later became a place for the disposition of refuse, and its name a
synonym for Gehenna. 2 *Kings* 23:10; *Isa* 30:33; *Jer* 7:31–32.
   108.26   Siam, Hell or Tophet
   513.10   of Delphin's Bourne or...of Tophat?

TORA RIVER.   Riv in Macpherson's poem *Carric-Thura*.
   603.34   Tyro a tora

TORRES VEDRAS.   Town, W Port, noted for 28-mile stretch of fortifications begun in 1809 and extending to the Tagus R, from which Wellington hindered the Fr
march against Lisbon in 1810.
    9.21   Tarra's widdars

TORY ISLAND.   Isl, 7 mi off N coast of Co Donegal; anc haunt of pirates, esp
"Balor of the Baleful Eye," who had one eye whose glance could kill. The isl was
noted for its various clays, used for heat-resistant pottery. There are no rats on *T*
Isl; they were driven out by St Columcille. Mainlanders still use earth from the isl
against infestation of rats (24.31).
   The islanders trad elected a "king" (87.26).
   The term "tory" was first used in Ire as a name for dispossessed landowners who
had become outlaws. In the 17th cent it was applied to supporters of Roman Catholicism, later became (at first pejoratively) the Brit political term it is today.
  ?20.23   every busy eerie whig's a bit of a torytale to tell
   24.31   where the Tory's clay will scare the varmints
  ?42.28   northern tory
   87.26   kings of mud and tory
 105.26   *The Tortor of Tory Island*
 143.12   the course of his tory
 175.25   *Till the four Shores of deff Tory Island*
?359.26   Goes Tory by Eeric Whigs

TÖSS.   Sw riv and vall, E of Zurich; forms Lake Pfäffikon and flows into Rhine R.
 ?379.12   Aerian's Wall and the Fall of Toss

TOULON.   City and port, Var Dept, SE Fr; base of Fr Medit fleet.
 531.18   my new toulong touloosies

TOULOUSE.   (1) City, Haute-Garonne Dept, S Fr. Wellington's victory over Fr at
T in Apr 1814 was the last battle of the Penin War (9.26).   (2) The Rue de *T* in
Paris is an unimportant st off the Blvd Sérurier in the 19th Arr.
   9.26   Arthiz too loose
 531.18   my new toulong touloosies
 577.30   rue to lose and ca canny

TOURNAY (TOURNAI).   City, 45 mi SW of Brussels, Belg, on Schelde R. Much besieged in Netherlands wars 16th-18th cents; in WW I held by Germans 1914-18, severely damaged.

> 87.08   Tournay, Yetstoslay and Temorah

TOURS DE BEURRE.   The "Butter Towers" of the late middle ages in Rouen and other cities are supposed to have been built with money raised by dispensations from fasting. The ref in context seems to be to the smoke rising from a chimney of the Vatican (qv).

"Quintus Centimachus" was the Lat name for Conn of the Hundred Battles (see *Census*). Porphyry, the 3rd-cent commentator on Plotinus, wrote a treatise on abstinence (from animal foods).

> 100.17   Quintus Centimachus' porphyroid buttertower

TOWER OF LONDON.   On Tower Hill, City of London, N bank of Thames R below London Br. The White Tower is the Norman keep; among the towers on the walls are the Byward, the Beauchamp, the Bell, the Wardrobe, and the Bloody. The present ticket-office and refreshment room are on the site of the former Lion Tower. The Develin Tower is on the outer walls. The 2 little princes were murdered in the Bloody Tower in 1483. The Tower Royal (a corruption of "La Tour Riole"), destroyed in the Great Fire, was a 12th-cent palace in Cannon St, once the st of the Fr vintners, who called it La Riole (ie, Bordeaux).

> 77.19   the heptarchy of his towerettes, the beauchamp, byward, bull and
>   lion, the white, the wardrobe and bloodied
> 566.20   The two princes of the tower royal, daulphin and deevlin

TRAFALGAR.   Cape, SW Spain, NW of Strait of Gibraltar. Site of Nelson's decisive victory over Fr and Sp fleet, and of his death, 21 Oct 1805. The Nelson pillar in London is in *T* Sq, but Nelson's Pillar (qv) in O'Connell St, Dub, also commemorated *T*.

> 422.30   as Nelson his trifulgurayous pillar

TRALEE.   Town and port, Co Kerry, on *T* Bay; song, "The Rose of Tralee."

> 405.20   fourale to the lees of Traroe

TRANQUILLA CONVENT (RC)   (15/31).   In Rathmines Rd, Upr, Rathmines.

> 569.14   Tranquilla

TRANSITION.   Literary journal founded in Paris by Eugene and Maria Jolas in 1927. As "Work in Progress," *FW* was publ serially from the first issue, and continued sporadically through 1938.

> 100.01   Transocean atalaclamoured him

TREBIZOND.   City, Turk, on SE coast of Black Sea. Orig a Gk colony, Trapegus, of Sinope; from 1204 to 1461 AD it controlled the S Black Sea and was noted for its luxury. Princesses of its royal family were sought as wives by both Christian and Mohammedan princes.

> 165.22   hatboxes which composed Rhomba, lady Trabezond

TREDCASTLES.   None of the following is more than a suggestion: (1) Trecastle is a vill in Wales, where ogham stones were found.   (2) The Tedcastle Line operated shipping btwn Dub and Liverpool.   (3) Tedcastle and Co have long been coal merchants, form in Gt Brunswick St, now in D'Olier and Westmoreland Sts, and elsewhere.

No name resembling "*T*" is associated with Clondalkin (qv); the local cas is Drimnagh Cas. See *Three Castles*.

> 414.04   Mr van Howten of Tredcastles, Clowntalkin

TRENT.   City, NE It, Austrian until 1919. The Council of *T*, 1545-1563, est the principles of the Counter-Reformation, and ended all possibility of reconciliation btwn Protestantism and Roman Catholicism. It delegated to the Pope, however, the preparation of a new catechism, breviary, and missal.

531.03   sunctioned for his salmenbog by the Councillors-om-Trent [*salmebog*, Dan "hymnbook"]

TRENT RIVER.   Riv, cen Eng; W of Hull joins Ouse R to become Humber R.

200.34   Tell me the trent of it

327.09   as hard as the trent of the thimes

TRÈVES.   The Fr name of Trier, city in W Ger on the Moselle R. The cath contains as a relic the "Holy Coat of Trèves," alleged to be the seamless robe of Jesus. It has been exhibited since 1512, now only every 25 years, and in exhibition years the cath and city become a pilgrimage site attracting hundreds of thousands of pilgrims.

Despite *FW*'s spelling, neither the It town of Trevi in Perugia nor the famous Trevi fountain in Rome seem included in the allusion.

192.12   pledge a crown of Thorne's to pawn a coat off Trevi's

TRIESTE.   Seaport at head of Adriatic Sea on Gulf of *T* btwn NE It and NW Yugo on NW side of Istrian penin. JJ lived in *T* from 1905 to 1915 and again in 1919-20, working as an Eng teacher at the Berlitz Sch. *T* was once nicknamed *la città immediata* (228.22). The main thoroughfare of *T* is the Via di Corso, but the possible allusions to it at 84.27, 89.11, and 447.07 are all very questionable.

228.22   regain that absendee tarry easty, his città immediata

?234.03   tristiest cabaleer on

?279.F24   Bina de Bisse and Trestrine von Terrefin

301.16   And trieste, ah trieste ate I my liver!

TRINIDAD.   Isl, W Indies, in Atlantic O off NE coast of Venezuela. Also name of several towns and of an isl near Buenos Aires, Argentina.

492.30   to his trinidads pinslers

TRINITY CHURCH.   Former Chapel Royal in The Castle, now "Church of the Most Holy Trinity." The allusions are however to the music-hall song, "At Trinity Church I Met My Doom."

103.01   *At Island Bridge she met her tide*

240.10   Trinitatis kink had mudded his dome

326.04   A Trinity judge will crux your boom

498.19   at Kennedy's kiln she kned her dough

548.12   in trinity huts they met my dame

624.15   On limpidy marge I've made me hoom

TRINITY COLLEGE, DUBLIN (TCD)   (16/34).   Founded in 1592, on royal warrant from Elizabeth I. Its extensive grounds front on College Green, looking down Dame St (388.36, 548.12). It is known for its medical sch (424.11). Botany Bay (543.04, 601.17) is the pop name for the res court N of the main quad, Parliament Sq, an impossibly long six from the TCD cricket pitch (543.04). There is also a Trinity House, which controls shipping, in London (548.12).

112.30   Toga Girilis, (teasy dear) [TCD]

135.12   he has trinity left behind him

?180.09   green, cheese and tangerine trinity plumes

215.26   Latin me that, my trinity scholard

240.20	play for tirnitys
257.12	a fellows of Trinity
315.01	A butcheler artsed out of Cullege Trainity
?327.08	tramity trimming and funnity fare
386.22	prostituent behind the Trinity College
388.36	collegians green...poor scholars...all the old trinitarian senate
389.04	in the four trinity colleges
424.11	leave your libber to TCD
467.30	quadra sent him and Trinity too...cantab...oxon
?492.30	his trinidads pinslers at their orpentings
543.04	I sent my boundary to Botany Bay
548.12	in trinity huts they met my dame
601.17	they coroll in caroll round Botany Bay

TRIPOLI.   (1) Region in N Afr, now Libya, and its cap city. In 18th cent, one of the Barbary States.   (2) City and seaport, Lebanon. Orig a Phoenician federation of "three cities," Sidon, Tyre, and Aradus.   (3) The N part of Pimlico (st) in Dub was form called *T*.

8.15	the triplewon hat of Lipoleum
?533.02	when served with heliotrope ayelips

TRISTAN DA CUNHA.   Group of 3 small volcanic isls in S Atlantic and name of largest; the others are Inaccessible and Nightingale. Discovered by Port admiral Tristas de Cunha in 1506. An American named Lambert declared himself sovereign of the "Islands of Refreshment" but drowned in 1812 (191.05−.08). Occupied by Brit as dependencies of the Cape Colony, 1816. The population of *T da C* is given as 105 in *Bartholomew's Handy Reference Atlas of the World*, 10th ed (which JJ used).

159.32	on Tristan da Cunha, isle of manoverboard, where he'll make Number 106 and be near Inaccessible
?191.05−.08	drowner...liege...refreshment

TRITONVILLE ROAD   (18/32).   In SE Dub, near Ringsend. Before they moved to their present boathouses at Island Br, the Dub rowing clubs were on Thorncastle Rd, Ringsend, only a few blocks from *T* Rd.

203.13	Neptune sculled and Tritonville rowed
585.02	Neptune's Centinel and Tritonville Lightowler

TROUTBECK.   Riv, and vill, near Windermere, Cumbria, Eng. Both refs are to Anna Livia.

76.26	an old knoll and a troutbeck
578.21	her troutbeck quiverlipe, ninyananya

TROY.   Anc Troia, Ilion, or Ilium; city in the Troas, NW Asia Min, S of Dardanelles, mod Hissarlik (86.29, 254.30). Troad is the land of *T*, the NW promontory of Asia Min. *Troia*, It "sow," slang "whore" (86.29, 448.11).

11.36	Gricks may rise and Troysirs fall
55.03	Ilyam, Ilyum!
62.11	Emerald-illuim
86.29	pedigree pig...sty...*Qui Sta Troia*...hiss or lick
225.04	to go to troy and harff a freak
254.30	he whose hut is a hissarlik
381.31	like a Trojan
389.24	his troad of thirstuns
448.11	sow muckloved d'lin, the Troia of towns

538.07   ochtroyed to resolde...roohms...cartage
567.34   bikeygels and troykakyls
?581.20   orseriders in an idinhole...illian...willyum

TRULOCK, HARRISS, AND RICHARDSON, LTD   (16/33).   Gunsmiths, at 9
Dawson St around the turn of the cent. The brothers Trulock were also gunsmiths,
at 13 Parliament St.
    340.07   *his trulock may ever make a game*

TUAM.   Town, N Co Galway, on the Nanny R; site of great 6th-cent monastic sch,
and one of the Four Sees of Ire (qv) (283.L1); still the seat of an Archbishop (RC).
    113.02   postmantuam glasseries
    141.02   Mayo I make, Tuam I take
    211.10   for Nancy Shannon a Tuami brooch
    283.L1   *cashellum tuum*
    482.09   chuam and coughan!...Maho
    589.07   mayom and tuam

TUILERIES GARDENS.   Famous Paris gardens, btwn the Louvre and the Place de
la Concorde. Laid out in the 17th cent, the gardens were named (*tuile*, Fr "tile")
from the fire-clay formerly taken from the site.
    ?348.22   our miladies in their toileries
    552.14   tect my tileries

TULLAMORE.   Co town of Co Offaly. *An Tulach Mór*, Ir "The Big Hill."
    577.14   Urloughmoor...awfully

TULLOW.   Town, Co Carlow. Its anc name was *Tulach O bhFeidhlimadh*, "O'Feli-
my's Hill," now the tnld and par of Tullowphelim.
    ?324.10   Thallasee or Tullafilmagh

TULLYMONGAN.   Name of 2 tnlds near Cavan, Co Cavan, in anc terr of Breffny
(qv); orig the name of a hill above Cavan Town, now Gallows Hill. Called Tulach
Mongáin, "Hill of Mongan," by the Four Masters. Mongan was the 7th-cent reincar-
nation of Finn MacCool.
    99.26   a place of inauguration on the hill of Tullymongan
    332.05   −tullaghmongan− [in C-word]

TUMBARUMBA.   Town, NSW, Australia, in the mts a few mi N of Victoria border,
halfway btwn Sydney and Melbourne.
    596.11   from Tumbarumba mountain

TUNIS.   Cap city of Tunisia and largest N Afr city outside of Egypt.
    533.16   our fourposter tunies chantreying

TURKEY.   Rep, SE Eur (*T*-in-Eur) and SW Asia (*T*-in-Asia), including Asia Min.
The sultanate of the weakened Ottoman Emp (qv), further ravaged by WW I, was ef-
fectively replaced by a nationalist congress in 1919, with the Rep of *T* proclaimed in
1923. Of the many Turk tribes, the most important was the Osmanli (descendants of
the tribe of Osman), who gave their name to the people and lang now called Turkish.
    17.14   beuraly forsstand a weird from sturk to finnic
    34.01   stambuling...in leaky sneakers with his tarrk record
    43.08   Turkey Coffee
    98.10   in Asia Major, where as Turk of the theater
    113.26   talk straight turkey [*parlare turco*, It "to talk unintelligibly"]

144.14	I haven't fell so turkish
155.05	Tugurios-in-Newrobe or Tukurias-in-Ashies...constantinently
181.22	not even the Turk
215.21	turkiss indienne
235.06	Osman glory
235.08	turquewashed...Xanthos [qv; the riv of Troy]
235.17	Turkish hazels, Greek firs
248.20	Turkey's delighter
266.F1	I believe in Dublin and the Sultan of Turkey
281.F2	Translout that gaswind into turfish
284.27	ottomantic turquo-indaco
294.19	raucking his flavourite turvku
346.07	*Learn the Nunsturk*
347.36	*smolking his fulvurite turfkish*
348.21	thurkmen three
350.22	my billyfell of duckish delights
366.19	assault of turk ["a sod of turf"]
442.33	the muezzin of the turkest night
464.29	turkey in julep [Turkey-in-Europe]
483.08	**He would preach** to the two turkies
520.02	like a tarrable Turk
530.36	tuckish armenities
542.28	I turnkeyed most insultantly
581.10	a quareold bite of a tark
?586.30	turkling
594.34	a turnkeyed trot to Seapoint
?616.11	three Sulvans of Dulkey

TURKISH BATHS.   (1) 4-15 Lincoln Pl; Millar and Jury, props (16/33). Bloom's "mosque of the baths," with its minarets and exotic facade.   (2) Stephen's Green *TB*, 127 Stephen's Green, W (15/33). Fred Barrett's Bazaar was one door away at No 129.

597.14	sourdsite...the Moskiosk Djinpalast with its twin adjacencies, the bathouse and the bazaar

TURNAGAIN LANE   (15/34).   The old name (before 1797) of King's Inns St, off Parnell St.

248.33	2 Turnagain Lane

TURNPIKE.   The Dub turnpike system was introduced in the reign of George II. An 1821 map shows 10 Dub turnpikes, almost all located on the NCR and SCR at the crossing of main rds. The turnpike in Chapelizod was just E of the Phoenix Tav (where the Mullingar House now stands) at the curve of the Dub rd to the br. It is described on the 1st page of Le Fanu's *House by the Churchyard*. The Dub-Mullingar rd was a turnpike rd until 1853.

3.22	their upturnpikepointandplace is at the knock out in the park
31.01	Humphrey or Harold...jingling his turnpike keys
31.27	a turnpiker who is by turns a pikebailer
44.06	by the old tollgate, Saint Annona's Street and Church
132.32	our family furbear, our tribal tarnpike
293.13	the Turnpike under the Great Ulm
371.35	Mullinguard minstrelsers...par tunepiped road
570.04	It will give piketurns on the tummlipplads

Tollgates:

?4.08   Killykillkilly: a toll, a toll
?7.05   telling a toll
?52.25   Kang the Toll
?266.05   its toll but a till
?334.07   Mr 'Gladstone Browne' in the toll hut

TUSCANY.   Region, W It, incl Florence. It has long been known as the area in which the best It is spoken, except for pron, and the allusions pun on the definition of good It: "Lingua toscana in bocca romana" ("a Tuscan tongue in a Roman mouth").

89.24   A maundarin tongue in a pounderin jowl
518.25   Limba romena in Bucclis tucsada

TUSKAR LIGHTHOUSE.   On *T* Rock, off Carnsore Point, Co Wexford. Toscar (no connection) was one of Fingal's companions in Macpherson's *Ossian.*

25.26   the millioncandled eye of Tuskar sweeps the Moylean Main
245.01   from tusker toils...Lights...arcglow's seafire

TWELVE BENS.   Mts in Connemara, Co Galway, aka Twelve Pins.

6.01   workingstacks at twelvepins a dozen
?551.33   pass through twelve Threadneedles

TWO WORLDS.   The journal in which the Amer Samuel Roth reprinted fragments of *FW*, then known as *Work in Progress*, in 1925-26. In 1927, Roth pirated a number of chaps in a sep journal, *Two Worlds Monthly*, leading to hot protests and a lawsuit by JJ.

422.16   his unique hornbook...blundering all over the two worlds
530.02   two worlds taking off...shamshemshowman
619.11   we've lived in two worlds

TYBURN.   Once the London gallows for public hangings, near the present Marble Arch. Executions were transferred to Newgate after 1783, and were carried out publicly until 1868. The last man hanged in front of Newgate was the Fenian Michael Barrett, 26 May 1868.

504.24   Tyburn fenians snoring
540.15   Here Tyeburn throttled, massed murmars march

TYRE.   Now a seaport town, S Lebanon, it was in antiquity the cen of Phoenician civilization and sea power; noted for silk and Tyrian purple.

?51.14   haardly creditable edventyres
?91.25   Tyre-nan-Og
249.08   canopy of Tyrian awning
394.16   ships...as tyred as they were
395.06   foreretyred schoonmasters
?537.16   discontinue entyrely all practices

TYRONE.   Co, Ulster prov. *Tir-Eoghain*, Ir "land of Eoghan (Owen)" (ancestor of the O'Neills). See *Castle Tirowen.*

Baronies: Clogher; Upr, Lwr, and Mid Dungannon; E and W Omagh; Upr and Lwr Strabane.

?49.07   enlisted in Tyrone's horse

TYRRHENIAN SEA.   The Medit btwn Italy on the E and Corsica and Sardinia on the W.

330.09   there were no more Tyrrhanees

U

UGANDA.   Country, E Afr, N of L Victoria; exports ivory, among other products.
    428.10   [427.22 Tuskland...oliphants]...tarry among us...yougander
    545.09   decoration from Uganda chief in locked ivory casket

UISNEACH (USHNAGH).   Hill, 10 mi SW of Mullingar, Co Westmeath; trad regarded as the geographical cen of Ire. Called *Umbilicus Hiberniae* by Giraldus Cam-
brensis. The Stone of the Divisions (*Aill na Míreann*), now known as Cat Stone,
stands on SW of summit. In anc times, the Hill of *U* was the site of the May Day
Bealtaine Festival, a fire ceremony.
    ?49.04   the (Zassnoch!) ardree's shilling
    476.06   the knoll Asnoch
    499.23   this altknoll

UKRAINE.   Now a constituent rep of USSR in SW part, on N shore of Black Sea.
Ukrainians are the "Little Russians," and the indefinite area including Ruthenia (qv)
and E Pol is known as *Malorossiya*, Russ "Little Russia."
    338.22   Sling Stranaslang, how Malorazzias spikes her

ULEMA.   In Islam, those learned in theology and the laws founded on the Koran.
Also, in Moslem nations, a judicial council composed of such scholars and religious
chiefs.
    54.08   ulemamen

UL-ERIN.   In Macpherson's *Temora*, the star which guided sailors to the coast of
Ulster.
    194.14   Ulerin's dogstar

ULM.   City, W Ger, on Danube R; scene of battle 17 Oct 1805, in which Napoleon
defeated Austrians.
    ?293.14   Turnpike under the Great Ulm

ULSTER.   N prov of Ire; its cos are Antrim, Armagh, Derry, Down, Fermanagh,
and Tyrone; Cavan, Donegal and Monaghan. The former 6 (529.07) have constituted
N Ire since the partition consequent on the 1921 Treaty. The arms of *U* are a red
right hand (*lamh dearg*) on a white shield (the arms of the O'Neills). Among the Four
it is the prov of Matthew Gregory, and it represents North. The name is from anc
Uladh or Ulidia, Ir "tomb," pron "ulla"; its cap was Emania (*Emain Macha*), qv. At
times during its hist, it was as small as the present cos of Antrim and Down; strictly,
"Ulidians" were the inhabitants of that area, and "Ultonians" of the larger prov.
    In the Ir office of arms of heraldry, Ulster was King of Arms (498.11), with Cork
and Dub as Heralds and Athlone as Poursuivant. The long overcoat known as an "ulster" was originally made of Belfast frieze.
    For indirect allusions to *U* as one of the 4 provs, see *Provinces*.
    ?23.03   his rude hand to his eacy hitch
    40.21   Hosty...an illstarred beachbusker
    78.27   New South Ireland and Vetera Uladh
    85.11   auxter...redhand
    96.16   used her, mused her...

99.30	his dexter handcoup wresterected...bloody proper
?122.08	wrasted redhandedly from our hallowed rubric prayer
180.13	Cardinal Lindundarri
225.05	ulstramarines
229.17	Leimuncononnulstria
270.L4	*Ulstria, Monastir...*
283.L1	*Non plus ulstra*
316.02	their ulstravoliance
339.02	Ullahbluh! [*Ulaidh abu*, Ir "up Ulster!"]
343.01	*the pognency of orangultonia*
385.13	the Queen's Ultonian colleges
389.05	Ulcer, Moonster...
398.33	*bowels of the bank of Ulster*
‧451.13	the Ulster Rifles
467.29	Illstarred punster
482.29	You're up-in-Leal-Ulster
498.11	Ulster Kong and Munster's Herald
514.02	Normand, Desmond...
520.34	the rubricated annuals of saint ulstar
521.25	illconditioned ulcers
521.30	hulstler
522.04	Northern Ire! Love that red hand!
529.07	the six disqualifications
529.27	R.U.C's liaison officer [Royal Ulster Constabulary]
529.27	with their trench ulcers open
534.20	fallse roude axehand
546.33	Chief North Paw

ULVERTON RD (26/27).   In Dalkey, the main Dalkey-Dun Laoghaire rd; there are also *U* Pl, *U* Terr, and *U* Cottage. By coincidence, *ulve toner* is Dan for "wolf tones."

?318.33	wooving nihilnulls from Memoland and wolving the ulvertones of the voice

UMBALLA (AMBALA).   City and dist, Punjab state, Ind. Form a military hqs of Brit Ind.

?34.01	Dumbaling

UNDERGROUND.   The underground rlwys of London are called either "the Underground" or "the Tube," although strictly the former refers to the older lines which run in covered cuts, and the latter to the newer lines, which run in bored tunnels. The Bakerloo line connects Baker St and Waterloo Stas. See *Long Acre.*

41.20	our tubenny habenny metro
128.09	was an overgrind to the underground
348.31	*in thatthack of the bustle Bakerloo,* (11.32)
481.15	with his lavast flow and his rambling undergroands

UNT.   City and lake in the Egyptian *Book of the Dead.*

338.17	Conscribe him tillusk, unt

UNTERWELT.   Ger, "Underworld."

78.10	Gehinnon...Unterwealth...sheol

UPPERCROSS.   Bar of S Co Dub; its area stretches roughly from part of Rathfarn-

ham on the E to Clondalkin on the W, and from the Liffey S to the Wicklow border.
It includes part of Chapelizod.

    78.11   our Uppercrust Sideria of Utilitarios

    262.03   This bridge is upper. Cross.

URAL MOUNTAINS.   Mt range, USSR; *ca* 1640 mi long, from the great bend of
the *U* Riv in the S to Kara Bay in Siberia. The Urals are regarded as the boundary
btwn Eur and Asia. Russ, *Kamen* ("stone") or *Poyas* ("girdle").

Ural-Altaic is the family of langs including Turkish, Finno-Ugrian, Mongolian, and
Manchu.

    162.12   reading into the Persic-Uraliens hostery...Coucousien

    344.26   carcasses...pfierce tsmell of his aurals

    353.24   *Parsuralia...ivanmorinthorrorumble*

    494.16   The Ural Mount he's on the move

URANIA WINESHOP.   Frank Budgen talked "all one evening" with JJ in the *U*
wineshop (location unspecified) about conveying, in daylight language, the significance of dreams (*James Joyce and the Making of Ulysses*, 240).

JJ sometimes called his favorite Sw white wine, Fendant de Sion, "the archduch-
ess's urine."

    ?171.28   Fanny Urinia

URANUS.   Planet, 7th in distance from the sun; discovered only in 1781. Its 5 satellites are Ariel, Umbriel, Titania, Oberon, and Miranda (discovered 1948).

Ouranos, Gk "Heaven"; in myth the husband of Gaea, or Earth, and the father of
Chronos or Saturn, Time, who treated him badly. Urania is the Gk muse of astrology.
There is a Zurich obs (also a br) named Urania.

    ?171.28   Fanny Urinia

    185.31   the United Stars of Ourania

    494.29   giant sun...surabanded...I might have being his seventh

    504.24   Orania epples playing hopptociel

    583.16   known through all Urania soon

URSA MAJOR.   The most prominent constellation of the N hemisphere has been
known as the Bear (Gk, *Arctos*; Lat, *Ursa*) since the time of Homer. Other names
have been the Plough, the Dipper, the Wagon, and Charles's Wain. The 2 stars at the
end opp the handle (342.35) point to the Pole Star (the "Sailor's Only," 267.L2).
The constellation consists of 12 or more stars, 7 visible to the naked eye.

The Plough and the Stars was the flag of James Connolly's Ir Citizen Army, and
gave its name to Sean O'Casey's play.

    134.15   his number in arithmosophy is the stars of the plough

    267.L2   *The Big Bear bit the Sailor's Only*

    339.18   *his waggonhorchers, his bulgeglarying stargapers*

    342.35   *takes the dipperend direction...Sagittarius...Draco*

    426.25   the sirious pointstand of Charley's Wain

    461.01   water on the wagon for me being turned a star

    ?512.05   the bear...Megalomagellan

    581.14   the bluefunkfires of the dipper

    604.17   Sideral...gallaxion...waggonwobblers

URUVELA.   Buddha spent 6 ascetic years in the jungle of *U*, on the N-most spur
of the Vindhya mts, during his quest for enlightenment.

    61.36   The seventh city, Urovivla, his citadear of refuge

USHER'S ISLAND, USHER'S QUAY (14/34).   2 contiguous quays, S side of Liffey, btwn Victoria Quay and Merchant's Quay.
>   ?52.16   the now to ushere mythical habiliments
>   206.35   ushered round prunella isles

UTAH.   W US state; settled by Mormons (Latter Day Saints). In the context of primitive Mutt and Jute, the allusion may be to the tribe of *U* or Ute Indians.
>   ?16.10   Jute. – Yutah!

UTGARD (UTGAARD).   In Norse myth, the realm of giants, where Utgard-Loki had his cas.
>   424.20   –udgaard–lokki– [in C-word]

V

VACCINE OR COW POCK INSTITUTION (15/34).   Opened 1804 to give free inoculations against smallpox, it was at 62, later 45, Upr Sackville (now O'Connell) St. By the late 19th cent it became the Vaccine Dept of the Local Govt Board.
>   541.27   I corocured off the unoculated

VALECLUSA.   House in the vall of the Dargle R, Co Wicklow, near Glencree.
>   203.26   By that Vale Vowclose's lucydlac
>   528.22   Cluse her, voil her

VALHALLA.   In Scand myth, the hall in Gladsheim (Odin's home) destined for the reception of dead heroes. *FW* associates it particularly with Phoenix Park (qv), esp the Hollow and the Hole in the Wall.
>   5.30   wallhall's
>   69.07   wallhole did exist...garthen of Odin
>   91.30   heroes in Warhorror
>   156.25   Vale Hollow
>   156.32   Veiled Horror
>   258.02   gttrdmmrng. Hlls vlls
>   348.10   boomaringing in waulholler
>   379.12   volleyholleydoodlem
>   499.08   Woh Hillill! Woe Hallall!
>   541.22   Walhalloo, Walhalloo, Walhalloo
>   552.16   Sweatenburgs Welhell
>   553.22   the hallaw vall
>   565.02   Holl Hollow...guttergloomering
>   ?569.25   jollygame fellhellows
>   609.18   Wallhall

VANCOUVER FORESTERS.   It sounds like a military unit, but I have not identified it.
    The Anc Order of Foresters was founded in the 19th cent as a "Friendly Society." The Ir Nat Foresters (*U* 321/327, 535/547) marched in Dub parades, in green uniforms.
>   88.27   two childspies...three wicked Vuncouverers Forests bent down

VANHOMRIGH'S HOUSE (16/34).   Bartholomew Vanhomrigh (see *Census*) lived in Celbridge (qv) when Swift visited his daughter Esther there. Earlier the Vanhom-righs lived in cen Dub, on the S bank of the Liffey in the vicinity of the present George's Quay. The *Ballast Office Journal* for 20 Feb 1707-08 records the opinion that the channel of the Liffey should be dredged and banked "from Mr. Mercer's (formerly Vanhomrigh's) house directly with Green Patch, a little without Ringsend point" (Haliday, 235). *FW* moves Vanhomrigh's house across the riv to Mabbot's Mill (qv).

174.26   from Mr Vanhomrigh's house at 81 bis Mabbot's Mall as far as
          Green Patch
406.30   the sign of Mesthress Vanhungrig

VARIAN AND CO   (16/34).   Brush manufacturers, long at 91-92 Talbot St.
211.19   good varians muck for Kate the Cleaner
221.12   KATE (Miss Rachel Lea Varian...)
380.01   Variants' Katey...Variants' Katey
451.17   Like Varian's balaying all behind me

VARNA.   Bulgarian seaport, resort, and once important fortress, on the Black Sea. Occupied in 1828 by Russ, it was taken in 1854 by the Brit and Fr, who used it as a base for the invasion of Crimea.
339.11   his varnashed roscians

VARTRY RIVER.   Rising at the base of Mt Douce in Co Wicklow, it flows S to Roundwood, where it is dammed to form the reservoir which, since 1868, has been the main S Dub water supply. From the reservoir the much-diminished *V* traverses the Devil's Glen and ends at the sea inlet of Broad Lough, near the town of Wicklow. St Patrick landed in Ire at the mouth of the *V*, then called Inverdea.
126.21   catholick wartrey...prodestung boyne
205.26   Nannywater to Vartryville
290.19   vartryproof name, Multalusi (would it wash?)

VATICAN.   On Mons Vaticanus, Rome, prob after *vaticinium*, Lat "prophecy." It adjoins St Peter's Cath (220.34; Peter = "rock"). Contains, among other art galleries, the Pinacoteca, and the Borgia apartments, commissioned by Alexander VI. In the Sistine Chapel (157.08, 430.31) the ceiling, Michelangelo's masterpiece, looks down on awed visitors. *V* gardens, orig laid out in 16th cent, include fountains but no waterfalls (It, *cascata*). The dist around the *V* is the Borgo, also called the Leonine City, after Leo IV, who fortified it in the 9th cent. The Swiss Guard (93.06) are the Pope's own troops.

The Curia (157.26; Lat, "court") Romana comprises the administrative and judi-cial insts of the RC Church. Popes are elected by a "Conclave" or electoral assembly of cardinals; each day the smoke of burning voting papers from a *V* chimney signals to waiting crowds that there is no election yet (100.15, 157.26). The news of an election is announced from a balcony by the Cardinal Deacon (157.27).

93.06   Switz bobbyguard's curial but courtlike
100.15   infallible spike of smoke's jutstiff
139.34   not Vatandcan, vintner
?142.19   unify their voxes in a vote of vaticination
152.23-.27 [the Mookse] vacticanated his ears...borgeously letout gardens...
           cascadas, pintacostecas, horthoducts and currycombs
152.28   Ludstown
155.06   My building space in lyonine city
157.08   Nuvoletta...of sisteen shimmers, was looking down on them

157.26	with intrepifide fate and bungless curiasity...conclaved...coordinal dickens...their damprauch of papyrs and buchstubs
210.27	vaticanned viper catcher's visa for Patsy Presbys
220.34	The Rockery, Poopinheavin
243.31	papal legate from the Vatucum
309.21	vaticum cleaners
339.35	*popsoused into the monkst of the vatercan*
430.31	he looked a young chapplie of sixtine

VAUCLUSE.   Dept, SE Fr; named after Petrarch's fountain of Vaucluse (Valclusa), which gives rise to the Sorgues R.

203.26	By that Vale Vowclose's lucydlac
212.14	Fountainoy Laura
528.22	Cluse her, voil her

VAUXHALL.   Dist in Lambeth, S London. The *V* Gardens, laid out as a place of public entertainment, were immensely pop from the 18th cent into the 19th cent; closed 1859. *V* Br (580.01) crosses the Thames W of Lambeth Br.

Named after the London resort, Dub's *V* Gardens were est in 1793 at Blackrock, near the present People's Park (21/29). They went out of favor early in the 19th cent.

58.33	One of our coming Vauxhall ontheboards...waistend
?439.17	The valiantine vaux of Venerable Val Vousdem
550.35	duncingk the bloodanoobs in her vauxhalls
?580.01	ponted vodavalls for the zollgebordened

VEGA.   Brightest star in constellation Lyra. The annual meteor shower called the Lyrids radiate from a point near *V*.

518.13	heavenly militia...meatierities forces vegateareans

VENICE.   Seaport, NE It, on 118 isls in the Lagoon of *V*; often called the "Queen of the Adriatic," and scene of Shakespeare's *Merchant of Venice* (105.01, 435.02). The main thoroughfare of *V* is the Canale Grande, bridged by the Rialto (qv) and Accademia brs. The patron saint is St Mark, with his lion. The Bridge of Sighs (136.24) connects the ducal palace with the state prisons, over the Rio del Palazzo.

105.01	*Myrtles of Venice*
113.21	any Genoaman against any Venis
136.24	doffing the gibbous off him to every breach of all size
221.32	Phenecian blends
?232.11	call her venicey names! call her a stell!
435.02	*Smirching of Venus*
551.23	canal grand

VENUS.   The 2nd planet from the sun. At different points in its orbit it is the evening star and morning star, and as such was known to the ancients as Hesperus and Phosphorus, respectively. For the goddess of love, see *Census*.

In gambling slang, the best cast at dice (3 sixes) was once known as "Venus," the worst (3 aces) as "Canis" (299.L1).

245.23	Hesperons!
267.22	Vetus may be occluded behind the mou
?299.L1	*Canine Venus sublimated to Aulidic Aphrodite*
312.08	evenstarde and risingsoon
415.05	two spurts of fussfor...retrophoebia
?475.15	melanite phosphor
494.13	Arctura, Anatolia, Hesper and Mesembria [N, S, E, W]

538.23   were they moon at aube [Fr "dawn"] with hespermun
583.13   Bossford and phospherine...Urania...planets

VERDUN.   City, Meuse Dept, Fr; site of major WW I battle, but the allusion is to the *verdun*, or "*épée de Verdun*," a type of long sword once made here.
4.04   Verdons catapelting...Assiegates

VERGEMOUNT HALL (17/31).   Short st, off Clonskeagh Rd in SE Dub.
354.17   *after Meetinghouse Lanigan has embaraced Vergemout Hall*

VERONA.   City, NE It, scene of Shakespeare's *Two Gentlemen of Verona.*
569.31   two genitalmen of Veruno

VESUVIUS, MT.   Volcano, E side of Bay of Naples, It; its eruption of 24 Aug 79 AD buried both Pompeii and Herculaneum.
570.05   viceuvious pyrolyphics

VIA MALA.   The spectacular stretch of rd in the Grisons, Switz, on the highway up the ravine of the Hinterrhein toward the Splügen and San Bernardino Passes.
577.23   via mala, hyber pass, heckhisway per alptrack

VICAR ST (14/33).   Btwn Thomas St and Engine Alley, in the Liberties. 1st Draft of 84.18: "Vicar Street watch house." There is no police sta in Vicar St.
84.18   at the nearest watchhouse in Vicar Lane

VICO ROAD (26/25).   The shore rd from Dalkey to Killiney, along Dub Bay, SE of Dub. It intersects Sorrento (qv) Rd. *Vicus*, Lat (It, *vico*) "lane, alley."
?3.02   vicus of recirculation
98.19   closed his vicious circle
?134.16   moves in vicous cicles
246.25   Sorrento, they newknow knowwell their Vico's road
260.15   Old Vico Roundpoint [*rondpoint*, Fr "circus"]
452.21   The Vico road goes round and round
497.13   Vico, Mespil Rock and Sorrento
?614.27   wholemole millwheeling vicociclometer

VICTORIA NYANZA.   Lake (*nyanza*) Victoria, in cen Afr, the source (through the Albert Nyanza, qv) of the White Nile, long-sought and bitterly disputed by explorers and geographers in the 19th cent. John Speke was the 1st European to see Lake *V*, in 1858, and the 1st to discover its Nile outlet, in 1862.
23.20   soorcelossness...Undy gentian festyknees, Livia Noanswa?
89.27   *Unde gentium fe...?* No ah
105.14   *Victrolia Nuancee*
202.20   found the Nihil...Untie the gemman's fistiknots, Qvic and Nuancee!
558.28   Victa Nyanza
598.06   Nil. Victorias neanzas
600.12   Viggynette Neeinsee

VICTORIA PALACE HOTEL.   6 rue Blaise Desgoffe, Montparnasse, Paris. JJ and his family lived there from mid-Aug 1923 to Oct 1924. *Letters* I, 207: "In spite of the atmosphere of this 'Norweegickan' hotel I am [well] ."
Hugh Staples has suggested that the "VPH" motif in *FW* derives from a monogrammed blanket in this chilly hotel, or perhaps from the hotel laundry mark. The initials are echoed at 286.L1, 359.01, 440.02, and 596.06.
?99.13   bloody antichill cloak, its tailor's...tab reading V.P.H.

?284.F4   V for wadlock, P for shift, H for Lona the Konkubine

VIENNA.   City, NE Austria, on Danube R (qv); Ger, *Wien*; Fr, *Vienne*. The Graben
(545.34) is a main thoroughfare and shopping st (*Grab*, Ger "grave"; *Graben*, Ger
"trench"). Stock im Eisen (536.14) is an anc tree stump on the Graben, said to be
the surviving remnant of the holy grove around which anc *V* (Vindominia) grew. The
Prater (551.15) is the great park of *V*, btwn the Danube and the Danube Canal. Ring-
strasse (547.33) is the blvd which encircles the cen city, on the site of the fortifications dismantled in 1857. Schottenhof (538.32) is a block in the old town, orig the
abbey of the "Scoti" or Ir Benedictines.

    209.34   Vivi vienne, little Annchen!
    348.23   Vjeras Vjenaskayas [*Venskaya*, Russ "Viennese"]
    536.14   with stock of eisen all his prop
    538.32   upann Congan's shootsmen in Schottenhof
    545.34   in my graben fields sew sowage I gathered em
  ?546.31   the wiening courses of this world
    547.33   to ringstresse I thumbed her with iern of Erin
    551.15   to rodies and prater brothers; Chau, Camerade!

VILNA.   Now cap of Lith SSR, *V* was a Pol-Lith city until it became part of Russ
in 1795; from 1920 until 1939 it was Pol. Ger, *Wilna*; Pol, *Wilno*.
    339.33   *Lubliner...failing wilnaynilnay*

VIMEIRO.   Vill, W Port, 32 mi NW of Lisbon; site of victory of Wellington over
the Fr, 21 Aug 1808.
    9.36   Dalaveras fimmieras!

VINLAND (WINELAND).   Name given by the Norse seafarers *ca* 1000 AD to the
area of N Amer they discovered. It has been variously located from Labrador to New
Jersey, but most prob was Nova Scotia. See *Markland*.
    213.35   Markland's Vineland
    469.11   It's Winland for moyne

VIRGINIA WATER.   (1) Artificial lake S of Windsor Great Park, Berks and Surrey,
Eng.   (2) Lough Ramor at Virginia, Co Cavan. The Sale R flows in, the Blackwater
R flows out.
    365.09   cerpaintime...first virginial water

VIRGO.   Anc constellation; and also the 6th sign of the zodiac.
    26.13   Your feet are in the cloister of Virgo

VISITATION, CHURCH OF THE (RC)   (17/36).   On Fairview Strand, Fairview.
    601.25   S. Bellavistura's

VITERBO.   City, 55 mi NW of Rome, It. In 1271 Guy de Montfort murdered Henry, son of Richard of Cornwall, on the steps of the cath altar during worship. At *V*,
Pope Adrian IV (whose bull "Laudabiliter" gave Ire to Henry II) forced the emperor
Frederick I to acknowledge his vassalage by holding the Pope's stirrup. *V* became a
papal res in the 13th cent. In the mid-16th cent the "circle of *V*" around Cardinal
Reginald Pole was denounced to the Inquisition for heresy. In mod times *V* was part
of the Papal States until the unification of Italy in 1890.
    157.01   they viterberated each other

VOLGA RIVER.   The great riv of Russ in Eur, 2325 mi long. The "Volga Boat
Song" is an art-song version of the song of the *V* boatmen.
    211.13   volgar fractions

329.17   Roscranna's bolgaboyo...Holyryssia
352.17   *the volkar boastsung*

VOLTA CINEMA.   JJ pioneered cinema in Ire by opening (20 Dec 1909) and managing the *VC* at 45 Mary St; but the enterprise failed to prosper, and was soon ended by the owners. It is very questionable whether any of the following refs are specific allusions to the *V*.
?40.05   what with moltapuke on voltapuke
?284.09   may be involted into the zeroic couplet
?285.18−.21   volts...volts [11 times]
?403.16   She would kidds to my voult of my palace
?549.16   through all Livania's volted ampire

VOULZIE RIVER.   Trib of the Seine R, Seine-et-Marne Dept, Fr; subject of the poem, "Voulzie," by Hegesippe Moreau: "Is the Voulzie a great river with islands of fame?/No, but with a murmur as sweet as her name/a tiny running stream, with difficulty seen..."
578.16   So voulzievalsshie?

W

WABASH RIVER.   Riv, Indiana and Ill, US. Song: "On the Banks of the Wabash."
202.22   Such a loon waybashwards to row!
210.01   in her culdee sacco of wabbash
615.26   on the brinks of the wobblish

WAGRAM.   Vill, Austria, 12 mi NE of Vienna. Napoleon defeated the Austrian army there on 5-6 July 1809. Ave *W* in Paris ends at the Place de l'Étoile.
10.29   The wagrant wind's...Lumproar...de baccle

WALENSEE.   Lake, Switz, E of Zurich, mostly in Canton of St Gall. The "port" (*Haven*) might be lakeside towns of Walenstadt, Wessen, Murg, or Quarten. "Was wollen Sie haben?" (What will you have?) is standard bartender's greeting.
321.12   Wazwollenzee Haven

WALES.   Principality of UK forming the wide penin on the W of the isl of Brit. Lat, *Cambria*; Welsh, *Cymry*. Victor Pritchard (1579-1664) wrote *Canwyll y Cymry*, "Welshman's Candle." The mts of *W* can be seen from Ire on clear days, eg, from Black Linn, the highest point of Howth (447.16). The leek is the well-known symbol for *W* (56.36).
33.26   Welsh fusiliers
56.36   leeklickers' land
58.25   saxonlottie...cockaleak...Coldstream [Eng, Wales, Scot]
85.36   cymtrymanx bespokes
242.33   Englandwales
263.14   Espanol-Cymric-Helleniky
322.08   welsher
327.21   beyant the bayondes in Combria...Wiltsh muntons
329.32   Cymylaya Mountains
390.13   Tarpey, the Welshman

390.15	the four of the Welsh waves [see *Four Waves of Erin*]
412.34	Welsfusel mascoteers
447.16	first glimpse of Wales
464.06	Canwyll y Cymry, the marmade's flamme
480.12	welsher perfyddye
491.32	welshtbreton
?503.34	the reignladen history of Wilds
559.28	Welshrabbit teint [ie, yellow color]
590.13	Wu Welsher
618.34	Nollwelshian

WALKER ST.   In some versions of the ballad "Finnegan's Wake," "Tim Finnegan lived in Walker St..." This may be in Boston or NYC; in any case, there is no *W* St in Dub.
    245.22   waltzers of. Stright!

WALLACE COLLECTION.   The great art collection of Sir Richard Wallace (1818-1890) was bequeathed to the Brit nation by his widow, and is housed in Hertford House, Manchester Sq, London. Wallace inherited Ir estates and was a gov of the Nat Gallery of Ire.
    153.30   his everyway addedto wallat's collectium

WALLOP FIELDS.   Near the vills of Nether *W*, Middle *W*, and Over *W*, 5 mi NW of Stockbridge, Hants, Eng. Said to be the site of one of the last battles btwn Vortigern [see *Mercia*] and the Saxons.
    87.19   ever since wallops before the Mise of Lewes
    196.16   Wallop it well with your battle

WALSALL.   Industrial town, NW of Birmingham, Eng; home of *W* football team.
    378.19   Brystal Palace agus the Walsall!

WAPPING.   (1) Dock area, N bank of Thames R, London, just E of the Tower. *W* Old Stairs (533.17) is just E of entrance to *W* Basin.   (2) New *W* St in Dub, btwn North Wall Quay and Sheriff St (17/34).
    347.11   weeping stillstumms [*Wappenstillstand*, Ger "truce"]
    347.13   wapping stiltstunts
    ?510.25   that wapping breakfast
    533.17   Castrucci Sinior and De Mellos, those whapping oldsteirs

WARDMOTE.   The "Grand Court of Wardmote" is held annually at the Guildhall by the Lord Mayor of the City of London to receive election returns. Generally any meeting or inquest by the liverymen of a ward.
    132.24   mareschalled his wardmotes and delimited the main

WARD UNION STAGHOUNDS.   Famous hunt, Co Meath, formed in the 19th cent by union of the Dubber and Hillyhood Hunts. Its kennels are at vill of Ashbourne, 7 mi SW of Naul.
    622.25   the Wald Unicorns Master, Bugley Captain, from the Naul...the Stag

WARSAW.   Cap city of Pol; Ger, *Warschau*. The principal st is Marszalkowska.
    541.23   Under law's marshall and warschouw

WASH, THE.   Bay, E Eng, on North Sea. *FW* may generalize the name (373.05) to apply to Galway Bay, which is roughly the same shape and size.
    156.28   The Pills, the Nasal Wash (Yardly's), the Army Man Cut

211.36   to swilly to swash
373.05   Moherboher to the Washte

WASHINGTON, DC.   Cap city of the US. In the early 19th cent, Pierre L'Enfant laid out the city on what was once a swamp.
545.35   in black pitts of the pestered Lenfant he is dummed

WATERFORD.   Co, and its co town, Munster prov. Henry II arrived in Ire in 1171 AD at *W* Harb (?71.22) and James II quitted Ire from there after the Battle of the Boyne. A fortified Norse city and later Anglo-Norman, *W* Town was long Royalist, and in the 15th cent won the royal commendation "Urbs Intacta" for refusing to espouse the pretender, Lambert Simnel.
     Ballybricken (86.24) Green in *W* City was once a suburb where lived the pigjobbers who purchased the pigs for *W*'s bacon factories (John Garvin).
     Baronies: Coshmore and Coshbride, Decies within Drum, Decies without Drum, Gaultiere, Glenahiry, Kilculliheen, Middle Third, Upper Third.
     31.20   protosyndic of Waterford
     71.22   *You're Welcome to Waterfood*
     86.24   Irish muck [pig]...the ballybricken he could get no good of
     245.08   wextward warnerforth's hookercrookers
     ?483.30   ayr, plage and watford
     549.18   Wexterford's hook and crook lights
     595.12   waterfowls

WATERHOUSE AND CO (15/34).   Silversmiths, jewellers, and watchmakers, S side of Dame St. Projecting at right angles over the sidewalk, Waterhouse's clock spelled out its name (clockwise, naturally) from "W" at "3."
     88.01   Waterhose's Meddle Europeic Time
     ?177.28   *Wine, Woman and Waterclocks*
     213.16   senne eye or erewone last saw Waterhouse's clogh
     ?548.24   silvered waterroses

WATERLOO.   Vill, cen Belg, 12 mi S of Brussels. The Battle of *W* took place at nearby La Belle Alliance, 18 June 1815, where the Brit under Wellington and Prussians under Blücher decisively defeated Napoleon and ended his power. There is a London st game called "Battle of Waterloo" (176.10, with other games). The *W* Mus, at Mont St Jean, was est by Sgt Major Cotton of the 7th Hussars, who served under Wellington. Cotton publ a guide to the battlefield, *A Voice from Waterloo*. The mus was no longer in existence when JJ visited the battlefield in 1926, but may have been known to him through the description in Hugo's *Les Miserables. FW* 7.30–8.05 appears to be a précis of Chap LXX of *Les Miserables*, which mentions the Mus of *W*.

I.   Waterloo Place-Names

LA BELLE ALLIANCE.   Vill on the battlefield of *W*, S of Mont St Jean. The battle and battlefield of *W* are most commonly called on the continent "La Belle Alliance." Wellington and Blücher met there as the battle drew to a close. Associated with Iseult la Belle (246.20, 372.01). JJ sent a postcard to Larbaud, 22 Sept 1926, which shows *La BA*, and commented, "On the barn of the café is an...ad. for *Auld Reekie* tobacco!"
     There was a hackney setdown in Glasthule, Dun Laoghaire, called *La BA*, around the turn of the cent.
     7.33   this belles' alliance beyind Ill Sixty
     137.36   La Belle spun to her Grand Mount

144.12   first with me as his belle alliance
351.30   belle the troth on her alliance

HOUGOMONT and LA HAYE SAINT.   *H* is a chateau on W end of the battlefield, held by the Brit against repeated attacks throughout the battle. Attacks on *H*
and on *La HS*, a farm complex in the cen of the battlefield, were Napoleon's opening
moves, preparatory to the main attack against Wellington. The Fr finally took *La HS*
at great cost.

8.03   charmful waterloose country and the two quitewhite villagettes

MONT ST JEAN.   Vill S of the vill of *W* and just N of the battlefield.

8.29   Grand Mons Injun
?113.19   Mons held by tentpegs...whatholoosed
137.36   La Belle spun to her Grand Mount
274.02   man that broke the ranks on Monte Sinjon
359.34   Mount Saint John's, Jinnyland

QUATRE BRAS.   Vill S of the battlefield, where Wellington repelled the Fr under Ney on 16 June 1815, 2 days before the main battle, but then withdrew toward *W*.

8.19   his quarterbrass woodyshoes [The "Orange Toast" to Wm III credits
         him with redeeming his loyal Ir subjects from, among other things,
         "brass money and wooden shoes"; Wellington's Dutch-Belg troops
         were engaged at *QB*]

SUNKEN ROAD OF OHAIN.   Running along the E-W ridge which Wellington defended against repeated Fr assaults, it concealed his troops from the Fr to the great cost
of the latter.

?608.24   ohahnthenth...royalirish uppershoes

II.   Waterloo References:

8.02   Wallinstone national museum...waterloose country
?46.33   the general lost her maidenloo
71.09   lacies in loo water
73.05   to Mockerloo out of that
93.07   firewaterloover
105.30   *Inn the Gleam of Waherlow*
113.20   Mons held by tentpegs...whatholoosed
176.10   *Battle of Waterloo*
202.17   waterlows year
246.27   their baffle of Whatalose
312.30   the Wallisey wanderlook
314.09   —waultopoofooloo— [in C-word]
324.18   wodhalooing
343.16   *awstooloo*
354.23   wanderloot
359.34   waldalure, Mount Saint John's, Jinnyland
376.08   the Clontarf voterloost
428.20   waterloogged Erin's king
541.22   Walhalloo...mourn in plein! [V. Hugo: "Waterloo, Waterloo, morne
         plaine!"]
618.22   Wanterlond Road

WATERWORKS.   As early as 1245 AD water was conveyed by conduit from the
Dodder R at Templeogue to opp the Tholsel (qv). In the 17th cent, wooden water-
pipes of elm (542.06) were used in Dub; they survived into the early 19th cent. The
Dodder was the only source of Dub water supply until 1775, when reservoirs were

constructed at the N extremity of Blessington St, S of Phibsborough (15/35), and at Portobello (15/32). In 1868 the Vartry water works replaced the old Canal reservoirs with a huge storage reservoir at Roundwood (qv), Co Wicklow. See *Richmond Basin*.

    67.09   the gasbag where the warderworks

WATFORD.   Town, Herts; NW London suburb.

    483.30   ayr, plage and watford

WATLING ST.   (1) Roman rd in Brit extending from London to Wroxeter, near Shrewsbury. Held by some to have been the rd from Dover through London to Chester, *W* St was one of the 4 "Royal Roads" in Eng, and in late 9th cent was the boundary btwn Eng and Dan territory. Acc to Little, the name is a corruption of Gwyddelinsam, "The Road of the Irish." (2) *W* St (14/34) in Dub lies on the E side of Guinness's Brewery, btwn Thomas St and Barrack Br. In *FW* it is Luke Tarpey's res (24.20).

    24.20   Waddlings Raid
    42.26   *via* Watling, Ernin, Icknild and Stane
    134.20   the hard cash earned in Watling Street
    328.03   her wattling way for cubblin

WEALD.   The generic term for a wooded area, it is also the proper name of the tract, formerly wooded, of parts of Sussex, Kent, and Surrey, btwn the N and S Downs, Eng.

    "Weald and wold" (wood and hill) is a phrase for the world in general, in Victorian poetry.

    366.34   Whisht who wooed in Weald, bays of Bawshaw binding
    ?564.24   athwart the weald [allusion mainly to Phoenix Park]

WEAVERS' ALMSHOUSE (14/33).   *Recte* Townsend St Asylum, founded by weavers from the Liberties; it was in the cen of the Coombe (qv).

    43.18   weaver's almshouse

WEDMORE.   Vill, Soms, Eng. The "Peace of Wedmore" restricted the Danes to NE Eng, after Alfred defeated Guthrun at Edington in Wiltshire.

    391.27   peaces pea to Wedmore

WEDNESBURY.   Market town, Staffs, Eng. It was the site of a battle btwn Saxons and Britons, 592 AD.

    62.28   after the show at Wednesbury

WEIR'S PUB (16/34).   James Weir and Co, wine and spirit merchants, 6-7 Burgh Quay, around the turn of the cent.

    140.02   not Corry's not Weir's

WELLINGTON.   City, New Zealand (qv), on North Isl.

    ?335.17   Wullingthund...Wellingthund

WELLINGTON BRIDGE (15/34).   Officially Liffey Br, a single-arched metal footbridge, connecting Liffey St on the N with *W* Quay and Crampton Quay on the S. Also called Cast Iron Br, Metal Br, and Ha'penny Br (the toll until 1919; no toll since then). Built 1816.

    11.21   keys and woodpiles of haypennies...brooches
    ?203.07   a landleaper, wellingtonorseher
    286.11   Wellington's Iron Bridge

WELLINGTON MONUMENT (13/34).   The 205-ft granite obelisk (*recte W* Testimonial) erected in 1817 in Phoenix Park S of the E end of the Main Rd. The Dub Corp refused permission to erect it in St Stephen's Green, where the stat of George II was then located, so it was erected on the site of the old Salute Battery (25.16). Visible from many parts of Dub, it has been pop called the "overgrown milestone." The sides display the names of the Iron Duke's victorious battles, and there are bronze bas-reliefs at the base. A monumental equestrian statue planned for the N side was never added.

6.31	overgrown babeling
8.35	Willingdone mormorial tallowscoop
9.34	Willingdone...marmorial tallowscoop
?13.28	polepost
25.15	our supershillelagh...manument...battery block
36.18	*duc de Fer's* overgrown milestone
36.24	willing to...upon the monument
?44.04	our maypole once more where he rose of old
47.07	Wellinton's monument
53.15	the monolith rising stark
54.28	as straight as that neighbouring monument's fabrication
?69.06	Where Gyant Blyant fronts Peannlueamoore [see *Glasnevin: O'Connell Monument*]
88.24	Holy Saint Eiffel, the very phoenix!
?126.12	Wellingtonia Sequoia
254.14	his moanolothe inturned
322.33	millestones of Ovlergroamlius [Oliver Cromwell]
?335.33	Arthurduke...where obelisk rises when odalisks fall
504.32	overthrown milestones
539.01	our mostmonolith
539.03	longstone erectheion
567.02	Wellington memorial
570.36	everthrown your sillarsalt
581.24	his monomyth
595.22	vellumtomes muniment, Arans Duhkha
?610.04	Who his dickhuns now rearrexes from undernearth the memorialorum?

WELLINGTON MUSEUM.   At Hyde Park Cor, London, the res of the Duke of *W*, purchased as a gift to him in 1820. Known as Apsley House, the mus was not formally renamed *WM* until 1952.

8.01	Wallinstone national museum
8.10	Willingdone Museyroom

WELLINGTON QUAY (15/34).   On S side of Liffey; before the 19th cent it was Custom House Quay, the site of the Old Custom House.

?203.07	lie with a landleaper, wellingtonorseher

WELLINGTON ROAD (17/32).   Res st, SE Dub, btwn Clyde Rd and Pembroke Rd; just NW of Herbert Park. *W* Park was, around 1900, a terr at the E end of Adelaide Rd.

85.10	one of our umphrohibited semitary thrufahrts...to walk, Wellington Park road

WEST END.   The fashionable W dist of cen London, incl Westminster, Belgravia, and Brompton on the S, Hyde Park and Mayfair in the center, and Bayswater and

Marylebone on the N.

    58.35   waistend pewty parlour
    292.06   *Spice and Westend Woman*
    320.17   [.07 civille row] wastended shootmaker
    336.29   peckadillies at his wristsends meetings
    541.33   fluted up from the westinders

WESTEREAVE.   The name of 2 tnlds in the bar of Nethercross, N Co Dub, one in the par of Finglas, the other in the par of Killeek; both in Fingal.

    503.14   Westreeve-Astagob

WEST INDIES.   See *India, West Indies.*

WESTMEATH.   Co, Leinster prov; separated from Co Meath in 1543. Baronies: Brawny, Clonlonan, Corkaree, Delvin, **Farbill,** Fartullagh, Fore, W Kilkenny, Moyashel and Maghera-Dernon, Moycashel, Moygoish, Rathconrath.

    129.01   wurstmeats for chumps and cowcarlows
    595.17   larksmathes...homdsmeethes...quailsmeathes

WESTMINSTER.   Bor of cen London, N bank of Thames R. *W* Abbey is now the repository of the Lia Fáil (qv), aka the Stone of Scone.

    131.10   scones...Liam Fail...Westmunster
    ?454.09   occurred to westminstrel Jaunathaun

WESTMORELAND LOCK HOSPITAL (16/34).   Cor of Townsend and Luke Sts. Opened 1792 for treatment of venereal disease in Donnybrook Rd, later exchanged premises with Hosp for Incurables (qv); limited to women patients about 1820. Usually called "the Lock." Honor Bright was a Dub prostitute murdered in Wicklow.

    211.33   all lock and no stable for Honorbright Merreytrickx
    423.25   till that hag of the coombe rapes the pad off his lock
    542.29   rotundaties...over raped lutetias in the lock

WESTMORELAND ST (15/34).   Main thoroughfare, leading to College Green from Lwr Sackville (now O'Connell) St and O'Connell Br.

    514.24   Sackville-Lawry and Morland-West
    553.30   my eastmoreland and westlandmore

WEST POINT.   US Military Academy, on Hudson R, 50 mi N of NYC. Cadets are called "West Pointers."

    ?92.07   Wet Pinter's
    162.17   I dannoy the fact of wanton to weste point

WEXFORD.   Co, and co town, Leinster prov. Known to Ptolemy as Menapia, the Ir name of *W* Town is Loch Garman (Carman); it was prob the locus of the Carman Games, or Fair (see *Carman*). The mod festival of music and the arts held annually in the fall (?531.15) has no known connection with Toulouse-Lautrec. The 1st Anglo-Normans landed in Ire near *W* (see *Baginbun*). Song: "The Boys of Wexford" (about the 1798 insurgents).

    Baronies: N and S Ballaghkeen, Bantry, Bargy, Forth, Gorey, Scarawalsh, Shelburne, E and W Shelmaliere.

    133.28   the boys of wetford hail him babu
    245.08   wextward warnerforth's hookercrookers
    531.15   me lautterick's pitcher by Wexford-Atelier
    549.18   Wexterford's hook and crook lights
    595.12   wagsfools

WHEEL OF FORTUNE   (15/33).   Public house on W side of Stephen's Green, late
17th cent (Gilbert, I, 190). The "Wheel of Fortune" is a card in the Tarot pack.
    ?235.21   parise send Larix U' Thule...seeds was sent by Fortune
    405.24   porterhouse...Saint Lawzenge of Toole's, the Wheel of Fortune

WHITBY.   Town, Riding, Yorks, at mouth of Esk R. A fishing and shipbuilding
town, its manufactures don't include hats. At the Synod of *W* in 659 AD, to settle
differences btwn the Ir and Eng churches, a main issue was the Ir tonsure (Ir clergy
shaved the front half of the head instead of the crown); the other was the computa-
tion of the date of Easter.
    587.11   his Whitby hat, lopping off the froth

WHITEHEAD.   Seaside resort in Co Antrim, N side of Belfast Lough.
    535.22   Is that yu, Whitehed?
    535.26   old Whitehowth...poor whiteoath
    ?536.14   haute white toff's hoyt

WHITE HORSE.   *FW* conflates a number of "white horse" allusions; most are not
topographical, but I list them together here as a way of sorting them out.
    (1) The *WH* of Wanstead is a figure almost 400 ft long cut into the side of a chalk
hill near Uffington, Berks, Eng; by trad it orig celebrated Alfred's victory over the
Danes (?106.01, 132.12, 600.28).   (2) The white horse was the emblem of the
House of Hanover. Under George I and George II, many Brit inns changed their signs
from "Royal Oak" (etc) to "*WH*" (388.16, 510.30).   (3) "*WH*" was not a pop name
in Dub, but Gilbert (*History* I, 157) notes an early 17th-cent inn of that name in
Winetavern St (?510.30).   (4) Wellington's favorite horse, Copenhagen, was a chest-
nut, but Napoleon's (at Waterloo), Marengo, was white (8.17,21; 388.16).   (5) Wm
III was usually pictured riding a white horse (75.15, 135.22).   (6) "O'Donohue's
White Horses" is an Ir phrase for waves on a windy day. Acc to legend, O'Donohue
appears every 7th year on Mayday, on the lakes of Killarney (106.01, 347.01).
    (7) The play *The White Horse of the Peppers* is by Samuel Lover (see *Census*) (214.15).
        8.17   same white harse, the Cokenhape...[.21] big wide harse
        75.15   kingbilly whitehorsed in a Finglas mill
        84.27   a whit the whorse for her whacking
        106.01   *Of all the Wide Torsos in all the Wild Glen, O'Donogh, White Donogh*
        132.12   a whitehorse hill
        135.22   his little white horse decks...our doors
        137.06   heer lays his bequiet hearse, deep
        214.15   the ghostwhite horse of the Peppers
        347.01   a white horsday
        388.16   Lapoleon...on his whuite hourse of Hunover
        510.30   This was his innwhite horse. Sip?
        600.28   so boulder...show that...the white alfred

WHITELEY'S DEPARTMENT STORE.   The London dept store of William Whiteley, Ltd, in Queensway, Bayswater; founded 1863 in Westbourne Grove, it was the
1st of the great London stores.
    127.12   to the shoolbred he acts whiteley

WHITE SHIP, THE.   The ship carrying Henry I's son Wm from Normandy to Eng,
which sank (25 Nov 1120), drowning Wm and precipitating a contest for the crown.
    387.25   off the whate shape...drowning...drowned

WHITWORTH BRIDGE   (14/34).   Now Father Mathew Br, just above the Four

Courts, it connects Church St and Bridge St, on the site of the original Ford of the Hurdles (see *Dublin: Baile Átha Cliath*). King John's Br, erected on this site 1210, fell and was rebuilt, 1385. Present br built 1818. The pop name "Old Bridge" survived through the 19th cent.

13.14	old butte new
63.14	hir newbridge is her old
?84.27	a whit the whorse
?234.09	breiches...goldenest
263.05	a father theobalder brake
?322.11	poor old bridge's masthard
443.28	Father Mathew's bridge pin
?521.05	Essexelcy...the Golden Bridge's truth

WICKLOW.   Co, and co town, Leinster prov. *W* has been called "The Garden of Erin (or Ire)." There are 3 lighthouses on *W* Head, the E-most coastal area of the co. Baronies: Arklow; N and S Ballinacor; Newcastle; Rathdown; Shillelagh; Upr and Lwr Talbotstown.

W Town, a harb town, was orig a settlement of the Vikings, who maintained a navigational beacon fire there and called the town Wykingloe (*loe*, Old Dan "blaze").

29.23	a wicklowpattern waxenwench
62.19	ere-in-garden
175.03	the pleb was born a Quicklow
199.17	staynish beacons on toasc
203.01	county Wickenlow, garden of Erin
277.16	as shower as there's a wet enclouded in Westwicklow
290.24	Arklow Vikloe
375.33	In this tear Vikloe
549.18	Wykinloeflare
595.16	waglugs
626.18	the hillydroops of Vikloefells

WIGAN.   Manufacturing and former coal-mining town in Lancashire, Eng. At the turn of the cent most of the coal burned in Dub came via Liverpool from the *W* area.

551.03	she chauffed her fuesies at my Wigan's jewels

WILLIAM III, STATUE OF   (15/34).   The equestrian stat erected in College Green 1 July 1701 was long a symbol of the Prot Ascendancy, a point of contention btwn the Orange faction, for whom it was a rallying point, and Ir nationalists. Before it was finally blown up in 1929, and removed, it was frequently covered with tar and grease, defaced, or partially blown up. Generations of Dubliners commented on the fact that the stat faced the Castle, turning its back on TCD.

75.15	a kingbilly whitehorsed
135.12	hestens [*hesten*, Dan "horse"] towards dames troth...like the prince of Orange and Nassau...trinity left behind him
322.33	the statutes of the Kongbullies

WILLIAMS AND WOODS, LTD   (15/34).   Manufacturing confectioners and preserve makers, 204-206 Gt Britain (now Parnell) St. It advertised its preserves as "Purity Jams."

27.17	Williamswoodsmenufactors...on every jamb

WILLIAMSTOWN   (21/29).   Form name of res area, S of the intersection of Merrion and Ailesbury Rds, and just N of Blackrock; a rlwy sta and form tram stop.

8.01   Wallinstone national museum ["Williamstown national museum" in
1st Draft]

?600.30   his showplace at Leeambye [*Liam-by*, Ir and Nor "William-town"]

615.20   between Williamstown and the Mairrion Ailesbury [ie, the Rock Rd
tramline, going N]

WINDERMERE.   Longest lake in the Lake Dist, NW Eng; and town on its E shore.
The "Lake Poets" were Wordsworth, who lived in Grasmere, just N of *W*, and Coleridge
and Southey, who lived in Keswick, still farther N.

212.36   *Die Windermere Dichter* [*Dichter*, Ger "poets"]

WINDSOR.   Town, S of Eton, Berks, Eng. *W* Palace, the royal cas founded by Wm
the Conqueror, is still a royal res. Shakespeare: "The Merry Wives of *W.*"

227.02   The many wiles of Winsure

341.23   *winsor places*

551.01   windtor palast

WINDSOR AVENUE   (17/36).   Runs N off Fairview Strand. The Joyce family
lived at No 29 from 1896 to 1899; the landlord was the Rev Mr Hugh Love. *U*
242/245: "29 Windsor Ave. Love is the name?...The reverend Mr. Love."

420.24   Noon sick parson. 92 Windsewer. Ave.

WINDSOR PLACE   (16/33).   Short st off Pembroke St, Lwr.

341.23   *winsor places*

WINDWARD ISLANDS.   Group of isls, incl Barbados, in the W Indies, form a
Brit colony. The name indicates that they are the most exposed of the Lesser Antilles to the NE trade winds.

351.08   a wheeze we has in our waynward islands, wee engrish

?524.19   hereckons himself disjunctively with his windwarrd eye [*ey*, Old
Dan "island"]

WINDY ARBOUR   (17/29).   Dist, SE Dub, N of Dundrum. Site of Cen Mental
Hosp.

588.32   the behanshrub near windy arbour

WINETAVERN ST   (15/34).   Short st from Christchurch Cath to the Liffey
at Richmond Br.

536.21   Oscarshal's winetavern

WINNINGS.   Tnld, par of Naul, bar of Balrothery W, N Co Dub; in Fingal.

503.15   Winning's Folly Merryfalls

WINTER GARDEN PALACE   (15/33).   19th-cent tav and dance hall, at the
cor of Stephen's Green and Cuffe St. It was one of JJ's favorite haunts when he
was a student at Univ Coll down the st.

551.01   in our windtor palast it vampared for elenders

WITWATERSRAND.   Ridge of rocky hills in Transvaal, S Afr; pop known as
"The Rand." Site of major goldfields. Johannesburg is about in the cen of the *W*;
Roodesport is a mining cen W of Johannesburg. The Roodebergen Mts are in the
former Orange Free State. *Rand*, Dut, Eng, "border, edge."

?113.08   the rereres on the outerrand

250.24   If you cross this rood as you roamed the rand

WOLIN (WOLLIN).   Isl off NW coast of Pol, form in Pomerania, Ger. The town of *W* is near site of Viking fortress of Jomsborg (qv). The anc Wendish trading town of Julin has been identified as *W*.

    309.16   ruad duchy of Wollinstown...[310.03] Jomsborg, Selverbergen
    321.12   Wazwollenzee Haven

WOLVERHAMPTON.   Town and bor in Staffs, Eng, 12 mi NW of Birmingham. Henry H Fowler, Viscount *W* (1908), was chancellor of the duchy of Lancaster 1905-1908.

    442.09   Knickerbocker, the lanky sire of Wolverhampton

WONDERLAND.   Lewis Carroll made it a place, and gave it a landscape and inhabitants. For everything else, see the chap on Carroll in J S Atherton's *The Books at the Wake*.

    270.20   Though Wonderlawn's lost us for ever. Alis...broke the glass!
    276.F7   A liss in hunterland
    374.03   old Dadgerson's dodges...wonderland's wanderlad'll
    528.18   through alluring glass or alas in jumboland
  ?576.21   to goal whither, wonderlust
    618.22   on Wanterlond Road...alce

WOODEN MAN (15/34).   A large oaken figure which stood on the S side of Essex St, near Eustace St, from the late 17th cent through the 18th cent. Aka *The Upright Man*, with sexual overtones, by Dublin wits. The figure dwindled because of the practice of breaking off splinters from it for kindling. The 18th-cent printer George Faulkner, who had a wooden leg, was called the "Wooden Man in Essex St," after the figure.

  ?135.27   upright one, vehicule of arcanisation
  ?261.23   Ainsoph,[3] this upright one
  ?518.24   he was heavily upright man
    535.04   Sexsex...before his hostel of the Wodin Man

WOODHENGE.   Prehistoric circle 1½ mi NE of Amesbury, Wilts, Eng; near Stonehenge. First discovered from the air.

    596.13   the Diggins, Woodenhenge, as to hang out at

WOOD QUAY (15/34).   On the S side of the Liffey, E of Winetavern St.

    11.21   keys and woodpiles
  ?200.02   robe the wood

WOOLSACK.   The red bag of wool which is the official seat of the Lord Chancellor as Speaker of the Brit House of Lords. Its symbolism goes back to the reign of Edward III.

    493.20   Ota...bumpsed her dumpsydiddle down in her woolsark

WOOLWICH.   Bor in SE London; contains the Royal Arsenal, Royal Artillery Barracks, Royal Military Academy, and other military institutions.

    347.09   Milesia [militia] asundurst Sirdarthar Woolwichleagues

WOOVIL DOON BOTHAM.   The name is a motif in *FW*, but still a mystery. Matthew Hodgart (*AWN* No 18 [1963], p 3) adduces as possibilities Wardfell, now S Barrule, Isle of Man; Dean's Bottom near Dartford, Kent, Eng; and others. There is also a Water Dean Bottom on Salisbury Plain, Wilts, Eng. One might add that St Patrick was born near Dumbarton, on the Clyde R, S Scot.

    93.18   the dears at Bottome...dun
    340.09   Warful doon's bothem
    369.12   Woovil Doon Botham
    503.21   Woful Dane Bottom

594.12   warful dune's battam

WORMWOOD GATE (14/34).   Orig built as part of the Dub walls before 1280 AD, it was near the present cor of St Augustine St and Cook St; the name was a corruption of Ormond Gate, itself a corruption of Gormond's Gate. The context of the ref is London, not Dub, however. See *Wormwood Scrubs.*
     ?579.33   cripples gait...warmwooed woman scrubbs

WORMWOOD SCRUBS.   In NW London, btwn Hammersmith and Willesden. Known particularly for *WS* Prison.
     579.33   warmwooed woman scrubbs

WREN'S NEST (8/35).   Tav (still there) at the W end of the Strawberry Beds on the N bank of the Liffey W of Chapelizod.
     265.10   fraisey beds...the wren his nest is niedelig

WYNN'S HOTEL (15/34).   At 35-37 Lwr Abbey St since the 19th cent, although for some years around the turn of the cent it was known as Telford's Hotel.
     137.05   watch our for him in Wynn's Hotel
     440.09   *Percy Wynns*...S. J. Finn's
     609.15   inplayn unglish Wynn's Hotel

X

XANADU.   The allusion to the city of Coleridge's "Kubla Khan" is uncertain, and so are allusions to the sacred river Alph (see *Alpheus*); it is curious, esp given the riv's name, that *FW* knows so little of the poem which Coleridge dreamed.
     ?277.18   And Sein annews

XANTHOS.   Riv, SW Asia Min (mod Turk), flows SW and S to Medit. Aka Scamander; mod Koca. In the *Iliad*, *X* is the riv and plain of Troy: "the great deep-eddying river who is called Xanthos by the gods, but by mortals Skamandros" (*Iliad* XX, 74).
     214.30   Holy Scamander
     235.09   turquewashed...Xanthos! Xanthos! Xanthos!

Y

YALE UNIVERSITY.   In New Haven, Conn, US; *Y* Coll from 1716 to 1887. Yale men do not like to be called "old boys."
     346.07   *How Old Yales boys is making rebolutions for the cunning New Yirls*

YANGTSZE RIVER.   Great riv of cen China, flowing from Tibet to the China Sea, and its basin; aka Chiang Kiang, "long river." In its upr reaches, aka Kinsha Kiang ("River of Golden Sand"), farther down as the Pai-shui Kiang, and in Szechuan as the Min Kiang (from its trib, the Min).
     213.36   takes number nine in yangsee's hats
     299.25   a yangsheepslang with the tsifengtse

YARE RIVER.   Riv, Norfolk, Eng; flows into N Sea at Yarmouth (aka Gt Yarmouth), a major herring fishing port.

    200.16   Yare only teasing!

    331.29   the mounth of the yare

YELLOW FORD.   On the Blackwater R, 2 mi N of Armagh; site of Battle of the *YF*, 1598, in which the Eng army under Sir Henry Bagenal was routed by Hugh O'Neill, Earl of Tyrone, beginning a general rebellion.

"Yellow Wat and the Fox" is the air of T Moore's "Oh Doubt Me Not."

    89.12   how yellowatty on the forx was altered

YELLOW HOUSE.   (1) Public house in the country, S of Rathfarnham; it was well-known from the 18th cent into the 20th. The Colums (*Our Friend JJ*, 53) describe an expedition to the *YH* by JJ and his father.   (2) In cen Dub, the "Yellow House in the Tenters" was in the Liberties; destroyed 1918.

Neither of these is in Fingal (qv) as the context of 503.14 requires.

    ?360.30   greendy grassies yellowhorse

    ?503.14   Yellowhouse of Snugsborough

YELLOWSTONE PARK.   Nat park, in Wyoming, crossing borders of Montana and Idaho, US. The 1st (1872) and largest US Nat Park. Noted esp for its geysers and roadside bears.

    430.06   the first human yellowstone landmark (the bear...)

YEMEN.   Country on Arab penin, on E shore of Red Sea. Known to ancients as Arabia Felix. The name means "right side" — as anc geographers viewed it from Alexandria.

    ?536.28   Well, yeamen, I have bared my whole past...on both sides

YGGDRASIL.   The "world-tree" of Norse myth, an evergreen ash tree whose roots, trunk, and branches bind together hell, earth, and heaven. Its 3 roots (505.04) go down into the realm of death, the realm of the giants, and Asgard (qv), the realm of the gods. Beneath it the 3 Norns live by the Spring of Fate. "Ygg" is one of the names of Odin.

    88.23   Yggdrasselmann? Holy Saint Eiffel

    332.02   a big treeskooner

    503.07   an evernasty ashtray

    503.30   An overlisting eshtree?

    504.35   missado eggdrazzles

    505.04   over her triliteral roots

YOKOHAMA.   City and seaport, Japan, 18 mi S of Tokyo. When Japan was opened to foreigners by the Japan-US Treaty of 1859, *Y* was designated as the trading port. *FW* seems to regard this fact as analogous to the scheme to make Galway (qv) a great transatlantic port ("Atlantic City," 482.09).

    482.11   the weslarias round your yokohahat

YONKERS.   A sep city just N of the Bronx, NYC, it is part of metropolitan NY. The orig grant of land in 1646 to Adrian van der Donck came to be called "De Jonkheer's Land," or estate of the young lord, as Van der Donck was known to his tenants.

    ?134.22   brought us giant ivy from the land of younkers

YORK.   City, Yorks, N Eng. Called by the Romans Eboracum (442.08); the famous 9th Legion was stationed there. In 921, the Dan King of Dub became also the ruler of *Y*. The archdiocese of *Y* is 2nd only to Canterbury in the hierarchy of the Ch of Eng. St Peter's Cath is usually called the Minster, or *Y* Minster.

In the Wars of the Roses, the Anglo-Irish replicated the controversy, with the Butlers (Ormond) supporting *Y*, and the rest of Ire, led by the Geraldines, supporting Lancaster. The badge of Richard III was not the White Rose, but a boar (71.12).

Todwick and Todmorden are towns in Yorkshire, but the allusion at 283.15 is to the "tod," an anc measure of weight, esp of wool, usually of 28 pounds. In cricket, a "yorker" is a bowled ball which bounces at the batsman's feet (567.36, 583.36).

71.12	*York's Porker*
95.02	old Minace and Minster York
190.19	taken the scales off boilers like any boskop of Yorek
283.14	weys in Nuffolk till tods of Yorek
374.06	Torkenwhite Radlumps, Lencs.
442.08	the Baas of Eboracum
461.09	the dusess of yore cycled round the Finest Park
465.32	Be Yorick and Lankystare
485.12	Rose Lankester and Blanche Yorke
491.19	*arkbashap af Yarak*
534.02	anew York gustoms
567.36	behowl ne yerking at lawncastrum
569.18	Cantaberra and Neweryork
576.22	as different as York from Leeds
583.36	rising bounder's yorkers

YOUGHAL.   Coastal town and bay, SE Co Cork. *Eochaill*, Ir "yew wood." The Eng name is pron "yawl." Mizen Head (qv) and *Y* are the W and E boundaries of the S coast of Co Cork.

    582.26   paved her way from Maizenhead to Youghal

YS (IS).   Legendary Breton city, which became a lost underwater city, like that of Atlantis or Lough Neagh (qqv), when the king's scapegrace daughter opened sluice-gates in the wall protecting it from the sea.

393.30	knockneeghs...(ys! ys!)
?570.12	where yestoday Ys Morganas war
601.05	the citye of Is is issuant (atlanst!)

YUGOSLAVIA (JUGOSLAVIA).   Rep, SE Eur, formed 1918, name adopted 1931. The Skupshtina was the Yugo parl.

137.33	freedom of new yoke for the minds of jugoslaves
343.15	*scoopchina's desperate noy's totalage*

YVERDON.   Town, Canton of Vaud, Switz, S end of Lake Neuchâtel; a resort, with sulphur baths.

    ?559.13   Flagpatch quilt. Yverdown design

Y.W.C.A.   The Young Women's Christian Association, founded 1855 in Eng, adopted its present name in 1877 and has branches all over the world. In many cities it provides residences, club rooms, and educational programs in its own bldgs. The Danish YWCA is "Kristelig Forening for Unge Kvinder."

141.18	X.W.C.A. on Z.W.C.U., Doorsteps, Limited
267.L3	*Forening Unge Kristlike Kvinne*
391.02	1132 or 1169 or 1768 Y.W.C.A.

Z

ZANZIBAR.   Former sultanate, Brit protectorate, now part of Tanzania, E Afr; *Z* is an isl in Indian O off NE coast of Tanganyika.

    182.09   zinnzabar!

ZEALAND (SEALAND, SJAELLAND).   Largest of the isls of Den; contains Copenhagen.

    111.01   puteters out of Now Sealand
    171.02   Rosbif of Old Zealand
    257.36   Sealand snorres

ZINGARI CRICKET CLUB.   A London club (*zingari*, It "gypsies") whose touring side's annual visit to Dub during the Horse Show week in August was the occasion for a gala ball at the Lodge in Phoenix Park.

    112.07   the Zingari shoolerim

ZION, MT.   Hill in NE part of Jerusalem (qv); its name came to stand for both Jerusalem and the people of Israel. Pop called the "Temple Mount," but incorrectly since the Temple of Solomon was on nearby Mt Moriah. Also site of the alleged tomb of David.

    192.35   your crazy elegies around Templetombmount joyntstone...–jesusalem
    470.16   onmountof Sighing!
    571.12   Yes, sad one of Ziod?

ZUIDER ZEE ("SOUTHERN SEA").   N Sea inlet on N coast of Neth; since 1932 closed by a dike and renamed the IJsselmeer. The area of the former *ZZ* btwn the dike and the outer (Frisian) isls is now the Wadden Zee.

    538.25   Haddem [?Edam]...any suistersees or heiresses

ZURICH.   City, cap of *Z* canton, Switz, at NW end of Lake *Z*, where the Limmat R (qv) issues from it; the Sihl (qv), a trib of the Limmat, is *Z*'s other riv. The city is embraced on the N by the Zurichberg and on the S by the Uetliberg. Orig a Celtic settlement, it became the Roman town Turicum (228.22). Its patron saints are Felix, Regula, and Exuperantius; the 1st two (340.13–.15, 610.08–.10) introduced Christianity in the 3rd cent; they represent *Z*'s virtues, Prosperity and Order (*Letters* I, 336). The Sw Reformation began in *Z* with Zwingli in 1518.

    JJ first came to *Z* for a week in Oct 1904, on his way with Nora from Paris to Trieste; they lived in *Z* from June 1915 to Oct 1919 and visited it frequently, a month at a time, in the 1930's. Escaping from wartime Fr, they returned to *Z* in Dec 1940, and JJ died there on 15 Jan 1941 and is buried in Fluntern Cem. Among JJ's favorite *Z* resorts were the concert hall, the Tonhalle (165.09), and the Pfauen ("Peacock") restaurant (205.29). The main shopping st and promenade is the Bahnhofstrasse (556.25); JJ's poem of that name is in *Pomes Penyeach*. The old town of *Z* is the Niederdorf (541.25). Dolder (266.18) is a res section and hotel, on the Zurichberg. Milchbuck (596.01) is a *Z* quarter and site of a semi-annual fair (*Bock, Messe*, Ger "goat," "fair"). The main *Z* postoffice is the Sihlpost (75.04, 200.22). Manessestrasse (?505.24) is named for burgomaster Rüdige von Manesse, who collected the first codex of minnesinger manuscripts.

Z's sedately riotous festival is Sechseläuten, held in Apr, when an effigy of the Bögg, a snowman representing Winter, is ceremonially burned in the Bellevueplatz as the bells ring out for 6 PM (32.02, 58.24, 213.18, 268.02, 327.24, 339.22, 441.33, 492.14, 508.29, 528.17, 536.11, 568.13, 600.24, 610.14). For this together with other possible echoes of Z places see Fritz Senn, "Some Zurich Allusions in *FW*," *The Analyst* XIX (1960).

?14.04	brogues, so rich in sweat
70.08	he might the same zurichschicken [*zurückschicken*, Ger "send back"]
75.04	sigilposted what in our brievingbust
165.09	management of the tonehall
200.22	the sillypost
205.29	turgos the turrible, (Evropeahahn cheic house...)
228.22	catch the Paname-Turricum [ie, the Paris-Zurich train]
?266.18	doldorboys and doll
340.13	*regulect all the straggles for wife...relix of old decency*
?505.24	Dr Melamanessy
541.25	praharfeast upon acorpolous and fastbroke down in Neederthorpe
556.25	long the grassgross bumpinstrass
596.01	at milchgoat fairmesse
610.08−.14	our ervics fenicitas...his rugular lips...Skulkasloot!

APPENDIX

The following place-names have not been included in the Alphabetical Gazetteer because all the allusions are only to products or organizations rather than to the places.

Arras, France (tapestry)
53.02,   568.36

Beaune, France (wine)
58.15,   372.07

Cayenne, French Guiana (pepper)
120.14,   351.10

Champagne, France (wine)
138.31,   162.08,   407.31,   462.09,   539.32

Chartreuse, France (liqueur)
451.24

Clydesdale, Scotland (horse)
553.35

Coldstream, Scotland (Guards)
58.25

Cologne, Germany (eau de)
204.33,   624.24

Delft, Netherlands (pottery)
304.26,   403.11

Demerera, Guyana (brown sugar)
334.05

Eton, England (collar)
292.29

Gordon, Scotland (Highlanders)
392.34

Hackney, England (coach; named not for town but for hiring out of hackney horses)
39.05,   284.F3,   529.19

Havana, Cuba (cigars)
38.30,   53.26,   417.12

Hesse, Germany (Hessian boots)
97.13,   459.07

Inverness, Scotland (cape)
35.10

Jalapa, Mexico (purgative drug)
550.15

Jerez, Spain (sherry)
58.15,   97.16,   256.12,   357.19,   625.01

Jodhpur, India (boots)
329.02

Kersey, England (cloth)
322.17

Landau, Germany (carriage)
353.27,   568.06

Latakia, Syria (tobacco)
450.11

Leyden, Netherlands (jar)
585.16

Limousin, France (vehicle)
376.03

Madapolam, India (cloth)
396.09

Nanking, China (cloth)
321.34

Paisley, Scotland (fabric)
497.30

Pilsen, Czechoslovakia (beer)
37.32,   313.14,   492.18

Sedan, France (chair, but not named for city)
469.35,   492.20,   554.03

Shantung, China (silk fabric)
240.30

Tabasco, Mexico (sauce)
230.06,   329.01

Tattersall's, London (plaid)
516.06

Tilbury, England (carriage, but probably not named for the town)
554.02

Tokay, Hungary (wine)
172.24

Waterbury, Connecticut, US (watches)
35.28,   290.06